C0-AZS-452

Community Corrections

Community Corrections

Marilyn D. McShane
California State University—San Bernardino

Wesley Krause
San Bernardino County Adult Probation

MACMILLAN PUBLISHING COMPANY
NEW YORK
Maxwell Macmillan Canada
TORONTO

Editor: Christine Cardone
Production Supervisor: Andrew Roney
Production Manager: Nicholas Sklitsis
Cover illustration: © Westlight Stock Photography

This book was set in Aster and Helvetica by V&M Graphics
and was printed and bound by R.R. Donnelley & Sons Company
The cover was printed by Phoenix Color Corp.

Copyright © 1993 by Macmillan Publishing Company,
a division of Macmillan, Inc.

PRINTED IN THE UNITED STATES OF AMERICA

All rights reserved. No part of this book may be reproduced or
transmitted in any form or by any means, electronic or mechanical,
including photocopying, recording, or any information storage and
retrieval system, without permission in writing from the Publisher.

Macmillan Publishing Company
866 Third Avenue, New York, New York 10022

Macmillan Publishing Company is part of
the Maxwell Communication Group of Companies.

Maxwell Macmillan Canada, Inc.
1200 Eglinton Avenue East
Suite 200
Don Mills, Ontario M3C 3N1

Library of Congress Cataloging-in-Publication Data
McShane, Marilyn D., 1956–
    Community corrections / Marilyn D. McShane, Wesley Krause.
        p.   cm.
    Includes bibliographical references (p.) and indexes.
    ISBN 0-02-379765-7 (paper)
    1. Community-based corrections—United States. I. Krause,
Wesley. II. Title.
HV9304.M37 1993
364.6′8—dc20   92-24
                                                      CIP

Printing: 2 3 4 5 6 7   Year: 3 4 5 6 7 8 9

To my husband and colleague
Frank "Trey" Williams
For all his patience and support

M.D.M.

To my sons Aaron and Brian

W.K.

Preface

Today the myriad programs that fall under the wide umbrella of community corrections may seem confusing and unorganized. Each state, federal, and local jurisdiction has a unique approach to community corrections. The names of programs and their structural frameworks are as individual as the historical, social, and political events that shaped them. However, there are several key factors that make their analysis more meaningful. These include the program goals, the legal context of their operation, the administering agent, and the type of client serviced. These key concepts provide the framework for the journey of this text.

Often when the technical names and titles are put aside it is apparent that most programs have more in common than they do in contrast. Probation and parole are more similar than different and a meaningful exploration of them will bear this out. Likewise, probation and parole officers have characteristically similar roles. The theme of this work is to highlight those similarities through the common bond of community corrections.

Because of the varied approaches to community corrections across the country, the chapters of this text focus on general similarities and differences of programs and not on their technical names and structures. In the past, probation and parole represented the entire range of community corrections programs. In textbooks, they were often presented as two dichotomous entities. Students concentrated on memorizing the differences between them.

Today, some community corrections programs do not even use the terms probation and parole. In other areas, these two traditionally different services may be located in the same government agency. Probation, parole, and their descendant operations now borrow from the same continuum of program components, namely, intensive supervision, restitution, electronic monitoring, and community service. In addition, these individual program components may serve as independent sanctions and as the means for diversion from the official criminal justice system.

ORGANIZATION

The text is divided into four sections. The first section consists of an overview of community corrections systems. Chapter 1 presents the philosophy and design of community corrections programs. Community-based punishments are contrasted with incarceration in terms of the goals, costs, and perceived benefits of each. Chapter 2 describes the full range of sentencing options available to the court. This section focuses on discretion and the process of decision making, particularly the role of the pre-sentence investigation. Chapter 3 describes the different structures of community corrections systems throughout the country.

The second section of the book deals with the actual community corrections programs available for adult offenders. Chapter 4 covers probation, its history, and current uses. Chapter 5 explains electronic monitoring and house arrest. Chapter 6 describes intensive supervision. Chapter 7 covers financial punishments and community service, which includes programs that administer restitution and fines. Chapter 8 discusses the decision to grant parole and Chapter 9 describes the readjustment of previously incarcerated offenders in the community after release.

The third section of the book focuses on the juvenile offender. Chapter 10 introduces the concept of diversion, the tradition of formal intervention, and the use of community corrections programs with juveniles today, which includes many of the same approaches used with adults, such as restitution, intensive supervision, and probation. However, more attention is paid to prevention in the juvenile population than in adults. Chapter 11 covers the history and current regulation of status offenders, including the runaway and the truant. Chapter 12 explores specific programming that has been historically significant as well as contemporary strategies for servicing juveniles in the community.

The fourth and final section deals with a number of people and process issues. Chapter 13 covers the official response to violations of community corrections contracts. Also included in this section is an overview of the legal challenges that have been raised against the required conditions of supervision. Chapter 14 explains the role of the community supervision officer. This chapter provides an in-depth look at probation and parole officers and the changing demands of the work environment. The material presented here is particularly useful for those criminal justice students who are considering a career in community corrections.

Chapter 15 highlights a variety of special needs populations under community supervision. These include the elderly, AIDS patients, the handicapped, the mentally ill, and the mentally retarded offenders as well as the many specific crime category offenders such as arsonists, shoplifters, and sex offenders. Today a large percentage of the supervised population of offenders falls into some special need category or some particular type of treatment group.

One of the largest groups of special needs offenders are those with histories of substance abuse. Chapter 16 explores the range of treatment approaches to drug and alcohol abuse and the types of programs that have been developed in these areas.

The final chapter, Chapter 17, is devoted to exploring research issues in community corrections. The most useful designs for research studies are covered as well as the ethical issues involved in conducting research. The purpose of evaluating programs and the most appropriate methods for doing so are also explained. The application of research results to program evaluation and policy formation is often neglected in other texts. Although each chapter of this work addresses the research that has been conducted to date, this last chapter synthesizes the role of research in community corrections programming.

SPECIAL FEATURES

Each chapter begins with a short statement of purpose and a list of learning objectives. A general summary concludes each chapter and key terms introduced are highlighted. Practice in forming decisions and opinions about these topics as well as listening to others respond to them is valuable in building professional character. The ability to formulate opinions about the various moral and ethical issues involved in corrections should be considered part of the student's basic education. Discussion questions are provided to help stimulate thought about some of the moral and ethical dilemmas that underlie programming of this nature.

A wide range of perspectives, from historical to political, sociological, economic, and legal, are considered. Each sentencing alternative is accompanied by the classic and most current research findings on the subject. References are provided so that these studies can be obtained from the library and explored more fully.

ACKNOWLEDGMENTS

The authors gratefully acknowledge the guidance and assistance of many professional friends and colleagues. These include the reviews and suggestions of Robert Bing III, University of Missouri, St. Louis;

J. Randy Farrar, Federal District Court of Appeals, Tyler, Texas; Mary Parker, University of Arkansas, Little Rock; Dale Sechrest and Frank P. Williams, California State University, San Bernardino; and Joseph Vaughn, Central Missouri State University, Warrensburg, Missouri. We would also like to personally thank our editor, Christine Cardone, and her staff for all their help and encouragement.

For contributions of information and materials we thank Joyce Frevert, Gary Paytas, Betsy Platt, Gerald Boatman, P. Joseph Lenz, Dr. Paul Boccumini and Wilmer Lusk of the San Bernardino County Probation Department. Also, we thank Sue Pautler, Federal Probation Officer, Lizbeth Benner-Wick, Parole Agent, California Department of Corrections, and James Peters, Supervisor, Nevada Parole and Probation.

Finally, we would like to express our gratitude to the following reviewers who provided valuable advice and assistance: Stan Stojkovic, University of Wisconsin–Milwaukee; Ellen F. Van Valkenburgh, Jamestown Community College; Anna V. Wilson, Eastern Kentucky University; Mary L. Parker, University of Arkansas–Little Rock; William E. Osterhoff, Auburn University–Montgomery; Robert L. Bing III, University of Texas–Arlington; J. Steven Smith, Ball State University; and Michael T. Petrik, Nassau Community College.

Contents

PART II.
Adult Community Corrections Programs   85

CHAPTER 4.
Incarceration Alternatives   87

CHAPTER 11.
Programming Experiments for Juvenile Offenders   **303**

PART IV.

The People and the Process

CHAPTER 12.

Legal Issues in Community Corrections

CHAPTER 13.

The Community Supervision Professional

CHAPTER 14.

Managing the Client with Special Needs 401

I

The Theory and Structure of Community Sentences

1

An Overview of Community Corrections

As redemptive measures, our probation and parole laws have added vital wheels to our machinery of justice. They have gone far toward enabling us to deal with the individual as an individual and not as mere human grist, to be fed into an unthinking machine, and have thus made possible more ample provision for his reformation.[1]

— William G. Hale

OBJECTIVES

After you have finished this chapter, you should be able to do the following:

1. Describe some of the reform movements that have taken place in corrections both within and outside of penal institutions.
2. Explain the role of rehabilitation in community corrections.
3. Give examples of the types of informal justice programs that have been developed over the past twenty years.
4. Describe the role that schools, churches, volunteer groups, the media, and private citizens may play in community corrections programs.

PURPOSE

This chapter explores the philosophy behind the use of punishment. Historically, as the values and attitudes of society change, so do its goals. Over time, there have been many shifts in the methods and justifications for punishment. Some of the rationales include retribution, deterrence, incapacitation, and rehabilitation. We try to clarify the differences between the terms *punishment* and *corrections* as well as those between *indeterminate sentencing* and *determinate sentencing*. This chapter introduces a wide range of community corrections programs that have been developed to meet the changing needs of our criminal justice system. One example of a strategy used off and on throughout history is informal community justice such as mediation and victim–offender reconciliation. Because informal strategies circumvent the official criminal justice process, they are often referred to as *diversion programs*. The remainder of the chapter distinguishes between these informal methods and formal alternative sentences.

INTRODUCTION

Eighteen-year-old Matthew Tole pled guilty to rendering criminal assistance to a hate crime: burning a cross on the lawn of a black family. The judge deliberately looked for a punishment that might make a lasting impression on the young man who allegedly followed along in a group's malicious crime. He ordered Tole to read *The Diary of Anne Frank* and to submit a book report to the court. The judge hoped to sensitize the Seattle youth to the injustices of racist persecution through his reading the grim Holocaust tale.[2]

The case of Matthew Tole illustrates the way in which the courts attempt to design sentences to fit offenders. Because Tole was young, the judge felt he might learn from the sentence and change his behavior. Because the youth was not a leader of the criminal activity, the judge believed that a jail or prison term might have been unnecessarily harsh. Because Tole was a first offender, the judge might have sensed that some type of punishment within the community that would emphasize the youth's community responsibilities might be an effective deterrent to future crime.

The judge's selection of a community corrections sentence for Matthew illustrates a growing trend in the courts today. The popularity of community sentences reflects their ability to serve the needs of the community, the offender, and the criminal justice system.

DEFINING COMMUNITY CORRECTIONS

The term *community corrections* describes sentences that provide alternatives to the incarceration of offenders in state prisons. These sentences often include participation in programs that are located in the same areas in which offenders work and live. Community corrections sentences are designed to consider both the safety of the local residents as well as the treatment needs of the offender.

A community corrections sentence recognizes that some offenses do not require the intervention of the state for punishment. Traditional state sanctions, such as imprisonment, may not be necessary for less serious offenses. For example, almost 2 million Americans are arrested every year for drunk driving. Ninety percent of those arrested are also convicted.[3] The community must have practical and affordable punishments to address this population.

Sanctions developed within the community are alternatives to sentences that remove the offender from his or her family, job, and neighborhood. The underlying theme of community corrections is that justice is an active process. The offender must participate in this process. Supporters of community corrections recognize that many offenders can still be valuable and contributing members of society despite having a criminal conviction.

The study of community corrections involves many academic orientations and perspectives. The way corrections programs are developed and operated cannot be understood outside the context of a variety of sociopolitical influences. Trends in government, economics, history, and social movements all affect the type of correctional policies that are formulated and implemented. Periods of conservative restraint may be followed by experiments in liberal reform. Criticisms of experimental reform projects may in turn lead to the adoption of more conservative control measures. Thus, changing cycles of strategy dominate community corrections.

Legislators, citizen action groups, researchers, and criminal justice system personnel may all have different views on what is necessary to make corrections effective. Yet for any program to be successful they all must work together.

To assess the quality, efficiency, and effectiveness of present community corrections systems, we must first decide what it is we believe such a system should accomplish. Our ideas and expectations about the goals of punishment are the cornerstone of our investigation into the value of our current system. By critically analyzing the operation and results of contemporary corrections, we can visualize ways to improve the system.

PUNISHMENT AND CORRECTIONS

One important distinction that must be made before beginning a discussion of the philosophy of community corrections is the difference between punishment and corrections. Although the terms are often used interchangeably, they have two distinct meanings. A *punishment* is a formal reaction to a crime or wrongdoing. Punishment is the cost that a society attaches to an offender as a consequence of his or her committing a crime. A punishment may serve no purpose other than to provide balance, *retribution*, or "an eye for an eye." Retribution is similar to the notion of revenge in that a punishment is given because the offender "deserves it."

Many people believe that incarceration or imprisonment is a punishment that serious offenders deserve. They believe that offenders have forfeited their right to live free in society by violating its laws. Long ago, offending persons were often banished from their villages or countries. We now use prison as a type of symbolic banishment.

Corrections is a belief in some kind of positive behavior change which is the result of treatment within the system. Corrections is a process more than a response. The success of corrections depends on whether a convicted person learns a lesson or is rehabilitated during the sentence. In contrast, punishment does not need to result in some outcome that can be evaluated. Punishment simply occurs as a result of some act defined as wrong. It is rarely subjected to evaluation.

Retribution, or revenge, is perhaps the earliest goal of punishment known. However, from about the beginning of the eighteenth century, thinkers of the classical period of criminology (roughly 1760 to the 1820s) considered revenge to be nonutilitarian. They reasoned, for example, that no further good would come from killing a person who had killed someone else. Scholars such as Cesare Beccaria argued that deterrence was the only legitimate basis for punishment. In 1764 Beccaria wrote about punishment, "The purpose can only be to prevent the criminal from inflicting new injuries on its citizens and to deter others from similar acts [p. 42]. . . . For a punishment to be just it should consist of only such graduations of intensity as suffice to deter men from committing crimes [pp. 47–48]."[4]

Deterrence implies that the threat of punishment or an actual past punishment will stop a person from engaging in future crime. This concept is known as *specific deterrence* because each individual person must actually be punished for the possibility of further punishment to affect his or her future behavior.

General deterrence, on the other hand, suggests that people can be deterred indirectly by the punishment of others. By simply seeing or reading about someone else being punished, we will restrict our behavior. For example, seeing a person pulled over to the side of the highway by a police officer may deter passersby from speeding.

According to Martin Wright, the success of deterrence is based on either enforcement or punishment.[5] Deterrence by enforcement suggests that the certainty of getting caught or the probability of being detected must be strong before a person is actually swayed from criminal behavior. Deterrence by punishment means that the severity of the prospective punishment is strong enough to deter someone from ever committing that crime. For some people spending a night in jail may be a strong enough deterrent, whereas for others the possibility of a life in prison may be the only deterrent.

The reform movement that culminated in the classical period of criminology was successful in adding deterrence to the existing retributive motives for punishment. Consequently, it was believed that sanctions needed to be only so severe as to outweigh the benefits of the crime to the criminal. These sentiments continued throughout the 1700s. Many people felt as Charlton Lewis did when he commented, "The entire abandonment of retribution as a motive is the first condition of a civilized criminal jurisprudence."[6]

Just how civilized jurisprudence was during the eighteenth century is debatable, particularly when one views the implementation of deterrence-related punishment. Some of the deterrence mechanisms included branding letters associated with crimes on the offender, graduated fines as well as graduated whippings, and shaming in the pillory and stocks. These punishments seemed to accomplish both goals popular at

Public spectacles of punishment were meant not only to deter the offender from committing new crimes but to teach others a lesson as well. *(Brown Brothers)*

this time. First, they attempted to make the punishment proportionate to the crime. Strokes with the lash and hours in the pillory were adjusted accordingly. The harshness of the penalty would just slightly outweigh the benefits of the crime. Second, it was hoped that the public humiliation of the punishment and its lesson would deter others from committing similar offenses.

Another punishment used during the 1700s was for offenders to perform "degrading" work in the public streets. Consequently, the convicted were often exposed to fights, sympathetic crowds, and the availability of prohibited items. One historical account explains how prisoners in Philadelphia cleaned the streets while weighted down with a heavy ball and chain.

> After they had swept around them as far as the ball and chain would permit, the manacled prisoners would pick up the balls and carry them to a fresh spot. The more malicious of them would often throw down the balls in such a manner as to injure passers-by. Most of the convicts were professional thieves, and adroit street robberies were frequently perpetrated by them.[7]

Humanitarian groups, such as the Philadelphia Society for Alleviating the Miseries of Public Prisons, intervened. The Philadelphia society was made up of many prominent citizens from a variety of religious backgrounds, including a number of Quakers. One of the founders of the society, Dr. Benjamin Rush, was a surgeon and one of the signers of the Declaration of Independence.[8] The group sought to have laws passed that would put the offender into what they believed was a more private, protective, and reforming environment—solitary confinement. The group pressed for the establishment of prisons that would accomplish this goal. The fortress-like prisons would keep prisoners off the streets away from ridicule and negative influences.[9] The society's efforts were rewarded when in 1790 the law imposing "continued hard labour publicly and disgracefully imposed" was repealed.

As prisons and jails sprang up all over the country during the early 1800s, they boasted a more humane alternative to the cruel nature of physical beatings and public ridicule. It was not long, however, before the penitentiaries developed their own negative reputations. Only a short time after opening, most facilities were overcrowded. Official visitors gave them disparaging reviews as places of sickness, violence, and despair. As several historical analyses have implied, a search for sentencing alternatives was part of a second wave of reform in the first three decades of the twentieth century. The direction of this movement may not have been so much a demonstration of faith in community corrections as a revolt against traditional warehouselike prisons and solitary incarceration.

Correctional reform movements in the early 1900s took two paths. The first was within the prison setting itself, and the second was a movement away from prisons into the community.

REFORM WITHIN THE INSTITUTION

In a few prisons across the country, progressive leaders sought to create communities within their populations. One such reformer was Thomas Mott Osborne, who anonymously spent a week as an inmate in New York's Auburn prison to gain insight into its problems. Osborne was certain that such a repressive environment caused deviance and brutality. He sought to create an environment at the New York State Penitentiary, Ossining (Sing Sing) when he became warden in 1914.[10] Osborne's plan was to prepare inmates for return to society by giving them responsibility for their own conduct while incarcerated, which was accomplished through a board of elected inmate delegates. As Rothman explains:

> The Mutual Welfare League was to be the major governing body of the prison. Inmates would elect a Board of Delegates, who in turn would elect an Executive Board. This Board would constitute the prison's rule-making and enforcement body, subject to review by the Delegates. Its members would supervise the inmates in the shops and in the yard. It would orga-

nize various fund-raising events, and use the proceeds to provide movies and more recreation facilities. It would also select a judiciary board to hear cases of infractions and levy penalties.[11]

Osborne's model of a prison community was later attempted by Howard Gill in the early 1930s at the Norfolk Prison Colony in Massachusetts. There, prisoners were assigned to the new prison concept of "dormitories" that would be therapeutic as well as social. Inmates were classified "upon the basis of their attitude and cooperation in carrying out their individual programs, and the extent to which they can be relied upon to take active part in the community program.[12]

Success in the prison community was an indication of the prisoner's progress, or rehabilitation. Release from prison was often contingent on the prisoner's ability to manifest positive behaviors while institutionalized. For that reason, offenders were often given an *indeterminate*, or open-ended, *sentence*. Release was earned through a demonstration of good behavior and citizenship skills. Convicted felons facing an indeterminate term of prison usually served somewhere within the wide range of years allowed by law. Examples of an indeterminate sentence were 5 to 15 years or 15 years to life. Prison officials could then decide, based on an inmate's conduct, when he or she was ready to be released.

The prison community model worked well with the indeterminate sentence because corrections officials had continuous opportunities to view and record each inmate's adjustment. Completion of assigned tasks and successful interactions with staff and other inmates were signs of progress toward release. However, it was also possible for incorrigible inmates who did not show progress to be kept in prison indefinitely.

Although the prison community model did not survive in later large penitentiaries that were crowded with hardened criminal populations, it was a design with a future. Its use would later be instrumental in establishing community-based residential facilities with smaller populations of less serious offenders. This model is used extensively today to build responsibility, self-esteem, and citizenship skills.

COMMUNITY CORRECTIONS

The second path of reform was an increasing use of community resources in correcting local felons. In even the earliest operations of American courts, the community played an important role in sentencing. When institutions were not available, the mentally ill, the degenerate, and drunkards were relegated to the custody and supervision of relatives and volunteers in the area. In the first part of the 1800s, probationlike sentences were an informal practice used at the discretion of the judge. As states adopted formal community alternatives to incarceration, a broad range of treatments and services became available.

THE COMMUNITY AND THE PROMISE OF REHABILITATION

The era of enthusiasm for progressive criminal justice system reforms was best exemplified in the rise of rehabilitation. In 1901 Henry Boies, member of the Board of Public Charities and of the Committee on Lunacy of the State of Pennsylvania, explained the relationship between punishment and rehabilitation:

> Punishment cannot be abandoned as the main deterrent agency of the law because some persist in criminality in defiance of punishment. No laws, either of God, nature, or man, are universally obeyed. It is to be expected that only the great sane and sound majority of mankind will obey and observe law and respond to rational motives. The abnormal and obdurate class demands of science special additional treatment. The response to this demand is reformation, the cure of the abnormal and diseased condition which prevents obedience to law.[13]

Rehabilitation, then, realized that punishment alone would not deter all offenders, perhaps only the rational. Something else, some type of change would have to make a person stop committing crimes. The belief that mental illnesses and inherited criminal tendencies accounted for much crime also pointed to a need for intervention. Rehabilitation as a justification for punishment or corrections meant making the punishment fit the criminal. Individualized punishment as well as treatment would be developed according to the physical and mental abilities of each offender.

The people involved in the reform of punishment were the same people confronting the many social, moral, and economic problems of the early 1900s. They rejected the depersonalization that big business and industry were bringing to the country and to the community. Among social service workers of this period, there was great faith in the spirit of the individual and in rehabilitation. During this period, it was believed that rehabilitation would not occur within prison. Instead, community alternatives seemed the proper environment in which treatment should take place.

One of the basic measures of rehabilitation is conformity. Does the offender adhere to the goals and processes of an orderly society? When inside a correctional institution, conformity is linked to the ability to keep out of disciplinary trouble and to join in self-help programs such as Alcoholics Anonymous and drug treatment. Within the prison, officials also look for the ability of the inmate to adapt to work and daily life routines as a sign of rehabilitation. Outside of prison, conformity means the ability to maintain steady employment and to take care of one's financial responsibilities. It also means the ability to abide by all the rules and laws of society. Conformity is indicated by one's attitude toward authority figures such as police, probation officers, and employers.

The term *rehabilitation* implies that the offender has the background and capabilities of a productive citizen. First, however, he or she must be reeducated or redirected toward the value of such a way of life. Many experts prefer to use the term *habilitation*. Habilitation focuses on the fact that many offenders grew up in criminogenic environments without ever acquiring moral sensibilities or the necessary schooling or vocational background to maintain an independent and crime-free lifestyle. For this group, habilitation more accurately describes the need to be exposed for the first time to a wide range of basic life skills.

Over the past 30 years there has been tremendous skepticism about the ability of corrections to alter either the behavior of the individual or the crime rate in general. Many experimental treatments were tried, particularly with delinquents and drug offenders. It was not long before these programs came under the scrutiny of persons concerned about the money spent and the amount of crime that still seemed to plague the nation. Although individual programs appeared to have some success, no treatment seemed particularly effective across groups of offenders or under a variety of circumstances. Still, no one attempted a comprehensive analysis of the issue until the 1970s.

In 1974 a controversial expression of concern about rehabilitation came from a group of researchers in New York. Douglas Lipton, Robert Martinson, and Judith Wilks studied the results of more than 200 treatment-oriented programs for offenders.[14] Their report, since renamed "Nothing Works," chronicled the contradictory findings of methods that appeared to work in one setting and then not in another similar situation. Fearing that the report would not be approved for publication because of its negative findings, Robert Martinson published a preliminary version in the journal *The Public Interest*.[15] It is this version with which most people are familiar. It came to be commonly called the Martinson report. The researchers concluded, "With few and isolated exceptions, the rehabilitative efforts . . . have had no appreciable effect on recidivism."

At this point, debate arose over just how the success of programs should be measured. The Martinson report was criticized as oversimplistic and too pessimistic.[16] As Palmer explained, 48 percent of the 82 studies originally examined by Martinson and his colleagues had positive or partially positive findings.[17] Palmer pointed out that Lipton, Martinson, and Wilks evaluated a wide range of programs with a variety of success levels. However, the report counted as failures any program that had more recidivism in the experimental treatment group than in the regular treatment or no-treatment group. Rather than condemn all efforts that were not 100 percent successful, Palmer said we should be asking, "What methods work best for which types of offenders, and under what conditions or in what types of settings." Palmer's philosophy is that some things work for some people.

Although the accuracy of the methodology of the Lipton, Martinson, and Wilks study was dubious at best, its weaknesses did nothing to abate the severe crisis in confidence it inspired. Some experts go so far as to blame the Martinson report for the decline in rehabilitation efforts and treatment innovations. Others believe that a broader conservative and punitive-oriented social movement away from investments in treatment was taking place even without the influence of the Martinson report.

What is agreed upon, however, is that social scientists were slow to counter the Martinson report and challenge its methodology. Years later, examinations of the data show that many of the treatment programs investigated were having what would be considered by today's standards to be fair to reasonable success rates. In fact, in a 1977 report Martinson and Wilks argued that parole supervision appeared to be more effective in reducing recidivism than was simply discharging offenders from prison at the end of their sentences. After analyzing a substantial number of data sets, the authors concluded that "in 74 of 80 comparisons the mean of the recidivism rates for parole is lower than for 'max out'," a term for those that have discharged their sentences at release.[18] Despite this apparent change of heart by two previous critics of rehabilitation, skepticism about the ability of treatment programs to rehabilitate offenders, particularly those who had been incarcerated, plagued corrections from the late 1970s through the 1980s.

Two somewhat conservatively optimistic positions on rehabilitation have evolved in the 1980s and 1990s. One is the *differential intervention* position, and the other is the *basic treatment-amenability* position. As explained by Palmer, the differential intervention view is that some programs have probably been successful with certain types of offenders within subgroups of those persons receiving treatment. The quest would be to match the proper treatment to each offender either by offense type or by some group of personal traits that seem to respond to one treatment over another. For example, first-time offenders may do better in drug treatment programs than those offenders with previous convictions, or alcohol abusers may do better in group therapy than drug abusers do.

The differential intervention position holds that research has not been comprehensive enough to demonstrate prior program successes and that programs have not been designed with the proper evaluation components included that would make such study feasible. There is also some feeling that if programs had been designed better or with more intensive treatments, they may have been successful.[19]

The second view on rehabilitation, basic treatment–amenability, postulates that it is the general disposition of the offender that determines his or her potential success. In this view there are only two types of offenders: those who will respond to treatment and those who will not. Palmer explains that the basic treatment–amenability position claims that "(1) certain offenders (e.g., the 'bright, verbal, and anxious') will respond to many treatment approaches, presumably under most conditions or settings and (2) most remaining offenders will respond to few if any approaches, again, regardless of conditions or settings."[20] The latter part of this philosophy conveys pessimism about the ability of any program to reach most offenders.

Amidst the controversy over rehabilitation, several trends have appeared. One is the use of determinate sentencing, and the other is a return to a retributive motive for punishment.

Determinate sentencing means that a person receives and serves a full set sentence, not a range of possible years. Instead of receiving 5 to 15, a person is sentenced to exactly 8 years in prison, no more, no less. Under determinate sentencing, there is no parole or early release for good behavior. Prison officials do not have any power or discretion to shorten the amount of time an offender serves. Perhaps a lack of faith in the ability of corrections professionals to rehabilitate or to determine when someone is rehabilitated has led to this focus on serving only set terms. Determinate sentencing can also be seen as a way to prevent prisons from holding offenders for extended periods in the conviction that each offender can be "saved." This practice can be seen not only as expensive but, according to current theory, as futile.

A second trend emerging from the controversy over rehabilitation is that there has been a resurgence in the popularity of retribution. Experts as well as the general community have expressed doubt about the usefulness of the other philosophical rationales for punishment. Writers such as Fogel and von Hirsh have chronicled the resurgence of retribution in the form of "just deserts".[21]

The term *just deserts* was originally used by the eighteenth-century German philosopher Kant to reflect the moral necessity of punishment. More than revenge, just deserts reflects both the debt the offender owes to society and the obligation society holds to punish the offender.[22] The concept of just deserts was expanded into a justice model by David Fogel. This model is explicit in terms of the purpose of punishment, particularly incarceration. As Fogel explains, "The prison is responsible for executing the sentence, not for rehabilitating the convict."[23]

Because retribution, or just deserts, as a basis for punishment does not necessarily involve corrections or rehabilitation, some people may question whether community corrections should entertain the goal of rehabilitation. The search for the proper justification for punishment and the direct implications punishment has for programming have created a lack of consensus over current needs. In Colorado a survey of the general public found that most people believed that *incapacitation* was the most important purpose of sentencing and that rehabilitation was only a secondary motive.[24]

Perhaps because of the philosophical void created by the controversy over punishment and corrections models, criminal justice professionals have been able to resort to a number of superficial crime-reducing strategies. Without a consensus about the goals of the criminal justice system, these new strategies have been introduced without any serious challenge or opposition. During the past few years, officials in law enforcement have adopted these new measures to counter the public's view that the crime problem is overwhelming the system. One of these new strategies is asset forfeiture.

ASSET FORFEITURE: RETRIBUTION, DETERRENCE, OR PROFIT-MAKING SCHEME?

Asset forfeiture, or the confiscation of property linked to crime, has become a popular high-profile trend. One of the more controversial questions of this process is how closely the property must be connected to the illegal activity in order to be considered subject to seizure.

Asset forfeiture is most commonly associated with drug offenses. According to McAnany and Histed, asset forfeiture may serve as a sentence following a conviction, or it may be a "specialized civil sanction directed against the property itself" regardless of who the owner is and how disassociated that owner may be from the offense.[25] In fact, forfeiture laws have been expanded to allow authorities to seize possessions without even charging the owner with a crime.

Regardless of how it is used, asset forfeiture seeks to deter people from engaging in a criminal enterprise. It also introduces the ulterior goal of bringing money and goods resulting from crime directly into the control of the law enforcement agency.

One rationale used by law enforcement to justify asset forfeiture programs is that they really need the boats, cars, houses, and firearms they confiscate to fight the war on crime. From 1986 to 1991, the Federal Justice Department collected more than $1.5 billion in its forfeiture fund. Items seized in 1990 alone represented $460 million in cash and property. The Justice Department estimated that 1991 forfeitures would exceed $500 million.[26] Officials also reported that over $500 million of the fund had been used in prison construction.[27]

Not all asset forfeitures are related to drug crime. In Portland, Oregon, a new law has enabled officials to seize the cars of persons arrested for drunk driving on a suspended license and of those soliciting prostitutes. Although 13 vehicles, including an 11-ton delivery truck, were seized in the first few months, many persons are skeptical about the benefits of the program. Officers admit that most of the vehicles were worth less than $1000. At this rate, it is doubtful that the value of the vehicles seized will exceed the administrative expense of operating the program.[28]

The American Civil Liberties Union (ACLU) has been especially critical of asset forfeiture programs. To ACLU lawyers, the process violates the due process clause of the constitution by confiscating property before a conviction. Explained one ACLU representative, "We don't think there's anything wrong with impounding a car if someone is drunk and keeping it for a short period of time, but certainly not until after a conviction should there be a forfeiture."[29]

Statistics have demonstrated the lack of protection for the innocent in forfeiture proceedings. In a 10-month period the *Pittsburgh Press* documented 510 forfeiture cases involving innocent people—or people possessing a very small amount of drugs. The constitutional question here is that if the law allows only a $1000 fine for possession of a small amount of a drug, is it proper for authorities to seize and keep a $10,000 car?

Forfeiture laws have the potential for discriminating against the poor. With less access to banking services, the poor are more likely to be carrying cash for significant purchases such as cars and furniture. However, the possession of a large amount of cash is also grounds for police suspicion of drug trafficking. Thus, these persons and their money are more likely to be subject to seizure and forfeiture.

Take for example a case reported by the Associated Press concerning a gardening contractor from Nashville, Tennessee:

> The gardening contractor bundled up $9,600 from last year's profits in February and headed for Houston to buy flowers and shrubs. He makes

Controversial asset forfeiture policies allow for the seizure of millions of dollars in cash and property, often without an arrest or conviction. *(© Pat Benic, UPI/Bettmann News Photos)*

the trip twice a year. As he waited at an airport gate, two police officers who searched him seized his money. They believed he was buying or selling drugs, the newspaper reported. The police let Jones go, gave him a receipt and kept his money. No evidence of wrongdoing was produced and no charges were filed. The money was never returned.[30]

A similar case occurred in Louisiana when Johnny Sotello gathered up $23,000 and drove to an auction. Sotello was stopped by police, and the cash and his truck were seized because the sheriff's deputies speculated that they could have been used to buy and carry drugs. Although he was never charged with a crime, it took two years before he was able to get back his truck. Only half of the money was ever returned.[31]

Obviously, to be an effective and fair punishment, asset forfeiture must be applied in a conscientious manner that is not inconsistent with due process. Otherwise, incidents of abuse could damage the reputation of this sanction to the point at which the public will not tolerate its use. It is possible that if this measure were carefully used in the future, it could become a meaningful community-based sanction.

THE NATURE OF COMMUNITY CORRECTIONS

Normally, community-based programs are located within the neighborhoods of the people they service. There are three basic types of community-based criminal justice programs: (1) pretrial release programs, (2) informal justice programs, and (3) community corrections programs. Of these, only the last two are "corrections" oriented.

Pretrial Release Programs

Pretrial release programs refer to mechanisms that allow a suspect to be free from confinement while awaiting trial. In some discussions, these programs are combined with community corrections programs because in their designs they involve balancing the needs of the defendant and the community.

Persons who are arrested and then released pending trial are often subjected to the same assessment processes as those already convicted of a crime. These processes may include determining individual needs as well as potential risks to the community. In addition, both pretrial release and community corrections involve attempts to minimize the negative effects of incarceration. The reason for minimizing the potential harm of confinement is different, however. In pretrial release, the focus is on the fact that the suspect is still considered legally innocent. Therefore, punitive restrictions, such as being placed in jail, should be used only when the suspect represents some kind of potential harm to the community.

The programs used for pretrial release involve a number of different kinds of contracts. To obtain financially secured bail, one must post all or a percentage of a dollar amount in order to be released. When no collateral is required, persons are released on their own personal recognizance. This means that they have promised to return for trial.

In an analysis of 47,000 felony cases filed against persons in 75 counties across the United States, the Bureau of Justice Statistics found that two-thirds of the defendants were granted pretrial release. Almost 50 percent of those released were processed within twenty-four hours. Subsequently, 66 percent of the pretrial release defendants were convicted of the initial felony, and 79 percent of those persons not granted release were eventually convicted. Surprising statistics from the study included the findings that about 18 percent of those released were arrested for a new felony while awaiting trial. Of these cases, almost two-thirds were again granted pretrial release.[32]

The time during which a defendant is released prior to trial is designed to allow him or her to prepare adequately for court. Preparations may involve extensive contact with an attorney. Because the nature of pretrial release programs is significantly different from that of community corrections programs, these programs are not considered in the discussions that follow.

Informal Justice Programs

As a result of differing preferences for the treatment of those who commit crimes, two systems for processing offenders have evolved. The first is the formal, or official, processing system, and the second is an informal network for diverting offenders away from the courts. Only recently, however, have we begun to refer to the latter process as *diversion*.

Diversion

Today, the term *diversion program* is used to describe an organized effort to use alternatives to the traditional processing of offenders in the criminal justice system. Almost all the standard diversion programs take place in the community. These alternatives may be undertaken any time after the discovery of the initial criminal act and prior to adjudication. Formal prosecution is halted or suspended in favor of processing the defendant by noncriminal disposition.[33]

A person may be diverted from the criminal justice system by police, probation, or the courts. That is, the person may be diverted at a number of different steps in the criminalizing process—before arrest, before charges are filed, or before trial. The key is that the formal process stops before an adult is convicted, or a juvenile is adjudicated, or an affirmative finding of delinquency is made.

Although diversion may be exercised with adults as well as youngsters, it is most often done with the latter. Clearly, most arrests involving juveniles are resolved in methods that divert them from the courts. However, there is great variation among the juvenile diversion policies of the states. As a study by Teilman and Landry has pointed out, police referral patterns in one state resulted in only 20 percent of the arrested juveniles going through the courts, whereas in another state as many as 75 percent of those arrested went through formal court processing.[34] The difference may be explained by the number of alternative community resources available, such as juvenile or social service agencies. Also, overcrowding in existing programs administered by the court may motivate some jurisdictions to allow diversion. Thus, officials often make choices about who would be the best candidates for diversion.

Diversion is more likely to be practiced with misdemeanants and less serious juvenile offenders than with felony offenders and adults. Furthermore, diversion may be limited to specific offenses and conditions. For example, in California adult diversion is limited to two categories of offenses: possession of small quantities of drugs and spouse abuse. Diversion in this state occurs after a filing of a complaint by the prosecutor.[35] Upon acceptance of a defendant for a diversion program, criminal proceedings are suspended. When the defendant completes the diversion program, the case is dismissed. The advantage of diversion for the defendant is that there is no record of criminal conviction. In contrast, probation officers in California have broad discretion in diverting cases from the juvenile court. Only a few serious felony cases are restricted from diversion, and even these are eligible with approval of the prosecuting attorney.

Jurisdictions may also vary on the "pureness" of their form of diversion. Some programs may represent total and final separation from the formal process. Others may be preliminary attempts to divert a defendant from the courts. In many cases, these preliminary diversions can be withdrawn should alternatives fail. As a result, the person can be brought back into the formal system for processing. The use of a back-up formal system to diversion has led some critics to charge that it really was not true diversion in the first place.

Dispute Resolution and Mediation

Some informal justice, or diversion, programs focus on dispute resolution and include arbitration, conciliation, and mediation. According to Wright mediation is defined as follows:

> Negotiation between persons or groups in conflict, including victims and offenders, with the assistance of mediators who facilitate the process but do not impose a solution. The aim may be to express feelings, resolve a dispute, or agree on reparation. The term usually refers to face-to-face negotiation, but the mediators may act as go-betweens for those unwilling to meet. This method is often called "shuttle diplomacy," conciliation or indirect mediation.[36]

The goals of dispute resolution have been expressed by Vorenberg as the following:

1. Involving the community in the reduction of community tensions.
2. Relieving the courts of the burden of minor cases and allowing more attention to serious cases.
3. Improving the process for handling disputes by exploring underlying problems without strict court rules and time limitations.
4. Increasing access to justice brought about by prompt hearings, elimination of legal costs and by the availability of convenient locations and evening and weekend hours.[37]

Support for the informal justice movement is related to popular involvement in the criminal justice system. Citizens have voiced preference for a more informal legal system. A more informal system would allow citizens to play active roles in the justice process. This would mean decentralized, democratically structured "courts." These courts, or tribunals, would be independent of political influence or organization.[38]

Dispute resolution centers received support from the government during the late 1960s when diversion of juveniles from the criminal justice system was popular. The movement toward informal dispute resolution continued over the next twenty years. By 1980 there were more than 100 dispute resolution centers operating in the United States. In addition, the American Bar Association sponsors a committee on dispute resolution.[39]

According to Sally Merry, most informal justice programs in this country focus on a noncoercive process.[40] Victims and offenders volunteer to participate. In such a process, the mediator has no real enforcement power. On the other hand, some jurisdictions enact legislation that gives hearing officers the power to impose settlements. This is more likely to be the case where lower, municipal courts are overburdened and time and money are limited.

There are basically three ways in which informal justice programs may be structured. One way is when the court system itself develops a project. An example of a court-sponsored effort is the night prosecutor program in Columbus, Ohio, where informal hearings take place during evenings and weekends in the prosecutor's office. The cases are heard by student volunteers from law schools who help parties to come to some kind of solution without the intervention of the court.[41] Second, informal justice programs may be coordinated with the court system but run by a separate agency that may be a nonprofit organization or private foundation. The third kind of program is designed and operated by community residents themselves. Citizens may form rotating committees to hear and settle disputes in their neighborhoods.

Victim–offender reconciliation is the term used to describe a process by which offenders and victims are brought together face to face to discuss the effects of a crime and its resolution. According to Dittenhoffer and Ericson, reconciliation is a negotiation process that focuses on the

Bringing together victims and offenders in the dispute resolution process involves a great deal of mediator skill. *(© Maureen Fennelli/Comstock)*

harm done and how the offender might make amends.[42] It is explained that victim–offender reconciliation can provide restitution to victims, lessen the trauma and anger of the victim, and provide a punishment that avoids the expense of incarceration. It is also believed to be important to demonstrate the actual amount of harm done by a crime, a process that it is hoped will facilitate the offender's acceptance of responsibility and accountability for his or her actions. The process of reconciliation is one of humanizing the participants, who are often depersonalized in the formal criminal justice system.

One of the criticisms of informal justice systems is that so far they have been dedicated to the more trivial and inconsequential kinds of cases. Neighborhood disputes over noise, fences, and pets are not uncommon. Preoccupation with disputes of this nature tend to detract from the ability of informal mechanisms to reach their potential as alternate legal systems. Another criticism of current informal justice programs is that they focus primarily on the legal harms and wrongs and sometimes neglect broader issues and other parties involved, such as witnesses and neighbors. It has been argued that to be philosophically consistent, community justice programs should address the needs of all persons affected by disputes.

In 1991 Mark Umbreit and Laurie Smith published a research study of more than 375 misdemeanor and felony cases referred for mediation. [43] Fifty percent of the cases resulted in face-to-face mediation, and 9 percent used indirect mediation. Almost all the mediated cases resulted in restitution agreements. Some victims received monetary payments, some personal services, and some simply apologies from the offender. Both offenders and victims reported being satisfied with the mediation process. In some cases, the victims wanted answers from the offender, most victims wanted to explain how the crime had disrupted their lives, and some even wanted to help in the rehabilitation process. The young offenders who participated in the study made such admissions as, "it was hard meeting him face to face," "it was kind of scary and nerve-racking," "I felt kind of stupid and guilty because he was real sad, but it felt better after I had a chance to apologize."[44]

Community Corrections Programs

Many *community corrections programs* are alternative sentences or formal alternatives to the use of incarceration. Some people argue that the term *alternative sentence* puts unnecessary emphasis on the idea that the sentence is an alternative to prison, which in reality is not always the case. Some community corrections programs are designed to provide services *following* periods of incarceration. Additionally, in many instances, community sentences are more appropriate for many less serious offenses. Misdemeanors and other lesser felonies, particularly those that do not involve any personal threats or violence, may well be served by participation in community justice programs. For these crimes prison would not even be considered. In a survey of Colorado residents, citizens responded that community sentences were appropriate for first- and second-time property offenders, for treating offenders with substance abuse problems, and even for some first-time violent offenders.[45] Over the years a variety of programs have been developed to meet such sentencing needs.

Some community corrections programs may be residential, but most are nonresidential. The major reason community programs are so much less expensive than incarceration is that the offender lives at home. Programs that involve moving to treatment or residential areas outside the client's normal surroundings may represent alternatives to prison, but they are not really community-based programs.

With all the media coverage of correctional options today, it is sometimes difficult to identify community-based programs simply by their titles. Traditionally, community programs are characterized by low-level security measures and are controlled by local governments. It is important to note that not all programs located in the community are necessarily community based. The state or other private agencies may be operating programs locally. Some people also erroneously assume that if a program is operated by anyone other than the state or federal government, it is community based. Many privately run programs operate under state contract and remain fairly isolated from the community despite their location in urban and rural neighborhoods. Finally, just because a corrections program is structured with minimal control and supervision, it is not necessarily community based.[46] The state may often operate minimum security camps and centers in a variety of community settings. These programs should not be confused with community corrections.

SUMMARY

The development of the current American corrections model has been a progressive evolution. Its formation, however, has not been without recurring themes and philosophic ironies. Generally, the concept of corrections can be viewed as a more efficient and humane practice than punishment alone.

The prison was originally developed as a more civilized alternative to the gallows and other public punishments. As one historian explains, there was no exceptional faith in this movement; it just seemed like a more efficient and humane improvement.[47] Many characteristics of the prison communities founded by reformers such as Thomas Osborne and Howard Gill in the early 1900s occur in community corrections centers and halfway houses today.

Community corrections programs evolved as an alternative to the penitentiary in the growing belief that many offenders returned from incarceration worse off than when they left and that many offenses did not require such a harsh sanction. Community corrections was also viewed as an efficient and humane improvement.

Over the past few decades, retribution, or punishment for punishment's sake, has resurged in popularity. Its appeal may be viewed partly as a consequence of a lack of confidence in rehabilitation. Sentencing strategies have changed from more indeterminate to more determinate. The intrusive nature of many therapeutic treatments and the frustration of trying to "fix" those who do not want to be "fixed" has limited efforts at rehabilitation. It has also led critics to claim that punishment with no strings attached is more efficient and humane.

The debate continues over the proper moral justification for sanctions, but programs that mix both punishment and corrections continue. Out of economic necessity and faith, judges sort offenders into categories for sentencing. In one group will be those that must be incarcerated. In the other group will be those that may be treated in the community. Community corrections implies that program responsibilities are in the hands of political subdivisions at lower levels than the state. Programs are usually administered by counties and municipalities. Community corrections also means that the offender is less segregated from society than in more traditional punitive settings.[48]

Lately there has been more pressure for jurisdictions to clarify their approaches to community corrections, to make programs specific, and to evaluate their operation critically. Those jurisdictions that receive funding have promised to accommodate greater numbers of offenders in a more effective manner. Effectiveness appears to be measured by community safety, crime prevention, and the integration of offenders into the ranks of productive citizens.

As of 1990, twelve states had redefined their commitment to community corrections through specific legislation.[49] The passage of corrections acts symbolizes the current movement of both state and local government toward alternatives to prison and jail. Although the intent of such legislation may be to reduce overcrowding and the associated expenses, it also signals a willingness to explore and adopt new ideas and to experiment with the latest techniques. There is always hope that the creative formula that will prove successful will be found.

KEY TERMS

punishment	determinate sentence
retribution	just deserts
corrections	incapacitation
specific deterrence	asset forfeiture
general deterrence	pretrial release programs
indeterminate sentence	informal justice programs
rehabilitation	diversion programs
habilitation	victim–offender reconciliation
differential intervention position	community corrections programs
basic treatment-amenability position	alternative sentence

DISCUSSION QUESTIONS

1. What should be the goal of punishment? How can we determine if our goals have been achieved?
2. What is the purpose behind informal justice programs? How would you design such a program for your neighborhood?
3. Identify the ways in which different civic groups or leaders in your community are or could be involved in community corrections.
4. What are the problems faced in trying to get various citizen groups, such as schools, churches, and businesses, to work together in a community corrections project? How would you overcome these difficulties so these groups could work together toward a community corrections goal?

END NOTES

1. Hale, William G. (1918). Crime: modern methods of prevention, redemption and protection. *Journal of the American Institute of Criminal Law and Criminology* 9 (August): 244.

2. *San Bernardino Sun* (1991). Cross-burning teen ordered to read 'Anne Frank.' June 30: A5.

3. Jacobs, James (1989). *Drunk driving*. Chicago: Univ. of Chicago Press.

4. Beccaria, Cesare (1764). *On crimes and punishments*. Translated by Henry Paolucci. Indianapolis: Bobbs-Merrrill, reprinted 1963.

5. Wright, Martin (1991). *Justice for victims and offenders*. Philadelphia: Open Univ. Press.

6. Lewis, Charlton (1899). The intermediate sentence. *Yale Law Journal* 9: 18–19.

7. Scharf, J. T., and T. Wescott (1884). *A history of Philadelphia, 1609–1884*, vol. I, p. 144. Philadelphia: L. H. Everts.

8. Barnes, Harry, and Negley Teeters (1943). *New horizons in criminology*. New York: Prentice-Hall.

9. Takagi, Paul (1975). The Walnut Street jail: A penal reform to centralize the powers of the state. *Federal Probation* 39(4):18–25.

10. Rothman, David (1980). *Conscience and convenience*. Boston: Little, Brown.

11. Ibid., p. 120.

12. Ibid., p. 395.

13. Boies, Henry (1901). *The science of penology*. New York: Putnam, Knickerbocker Press, p. 116.

14. Lipton, Douglas, Robert Martinson, and Judith Wilks (1975). *The effectiveness of correctional treatment: A survey of treatment evaluation studies*. New York: Praeger.

15. Martinson, Robert (1974). What works?—Questions and answers about prison reform. *Public Interest* 35(2):22–54.

16. Roberg, Roy, and Vincent Webb (1981). *Critical issues in corrections*. St. Paul: West Publishing.

17. Palmer, Ted (1975). Martinson revisited. *Journal of Research in Crime and Delinquency* 35:133–152.

18. Martinson, Robert, and Judith Wilks (1977). *Criminal Justice Newsletter*, vol. 18(15): 7.

19. Sechrest, Lee, Susan White, and Elizabeth Brown (1979). *The rehabilitation of criminal offenders: Problems and prospects*. Washington, DC: National Academy of Sciences.

20. Palmer, Ted (1983). The effectiveness issue today. *Federal Probation* 47(2):3–10.

21. Von Hirsch, Andrew (1976). *Doing justice*. New York: Hill & Wang.

22. Hawkins, Richard, and Geoffrey Alpert (1989). *American prison systems*. Englewood Cliffs, NJ: Prentice Hall.

23. Fogel, David (1975). *. . . We are the living proof . . .* Cincinnati: Anderson.

24. Mande, Mary, and Kim English (1989). *Executive summary*. Research Unit, Colorado Division of Criminal Justice, Denver.

25. McAnany, Patrick, and Cliff Histed (1990). Assets forfeiture: Empirical notes from the press. Paper presented at the annual meeting of the American Society of Criminology, Baltimore.

26. *San Bernardino Sun* (1991). Seizure law ensnares innocent, paper says. August 11: A4.

27. Thornburgh, Dick (1991). U.S. attorney general cited in the American Correctional Association's "Justice Department Forfeitures Turn Drug Profits into Prison Funding." *On the Line* 14(3):2.

28. Hale, Sally C. (1990). Portland seizes cars in crackdown on prostitution, drunk driving. *San Bernardino Sun*. January 7: A5.

29. Ibid.

30. *San Bernardino Sun* (1991). Supra note 25, p. A4.

31. Ibid.

32. Bureau of Justice Statistics (1991). *Pretrial release of felony defendants, 1988*. Washington, DC (February).

33. Rovner-Pieczenik, R. (1974). Pretrial intervention strategies: An evaluation of policy-related research and policymaker perceptions. Washington, DC: National Pretrial Intervention Service Center, American Bar Association, Commission on Correctional Facilities.

34. Teilman, Katherine, and Pierre Landry (1981). Gender bias in juvenile justice. *Journal of Research in Crime and Delinquency* 18:47–80.

35. State of California Welfare and Institutions Code, Section 653.5, 653.7, and 654. From *West's California Juvenile Laws and Court Rules* (1991). St. Paul: West Publishing, pp. 93–96.

36. Wright, Martin (1991). Supra note 5, p. xi.

37. Vorenberg, E. W. (1983). American Bar Association special committee on alternative means of dispute resolution. In *The juvenile justice standards handbook*, ed. Alaire Rieffel. Chicago: American Bar Association.

38. Henry, Stuart (1985). Community justice, capitalist society, and human agency: The dialectics of collective law in the cooperative. *Law and Society Review* 19(2):303–319.

39. Twain, David, and Laura Maiello (1988). Juvenile conference committees: An evaluation of the administration of justice at the neighborhood level. *Journal of Criminal Justice*, 16(16):451–461.

40. Merry, Sally (1982). Defining 'Success' in the neighborhood justice movement. In *Neighborhood justice: Assessment of an emerging idea*, ed. R. Tomasic and M. Feeley. White Plains, NY: Longman.

41. Wahrhaftig, Paul (1981). Dispute resolution retrospective. *Crime and Delinquency* 27(1):99–108.

42. Dittenhoffer, Tony, and Richard Ericson (1983). The victim offender reconciliation program: A message to correctional reformers. *Univ. of Toronto Law Journal* 33(3): 315–347.

43. Umbreit, Mark, and Laurie Smith (1991). Minnesota mediation center produces positive results. *Corrections Today* 53(5):192.

44. Ibid.

45. Mande and English, *Executive summary*.

46. Coates, Robert (1974). Community-based corrections: Concept, impact, dangers. In *Juvenile correctional reform in Massachusetts*. Washington, DC: National Institute for Juvenile Justice and Delinquency Prevention Office of Juvenile Justice and Delinquency Prevention.

47. Rothman, David (1971). *The discovery of the asylum*. Boston: Little, Brown, p. 62.

48. McSparron, James (1980). Community correction and diversion. *Crime & Delinquency* 26(2):226–247.

49. Bloom, Barabara (1990). Community corrections: Expanding community-based alternatives. Report to Assembly Public Safety Committee. Petaluma, CA: Barbara Bloom and Associates.

2

Sentencing Options

The only thing we can say with certainty is that we still know comparatively little about how to deal effectively with offenders.[1]
— Norman Carlson, Director, Federal Bureau of Prisons

PURPOSE

This chapter describes the options that a judge has when sentencing felony offenders. The discussion also covers the role of discretion in the decision-making process. Two recent trends, laws imposing mandatory sentences and the use of sentencing guidelines, both reduce the amount of discretion available to judges.

The various types and levels of sentences are defined and differentiated. Combined sentences and the use of private consultants as sentence planners are relatively new practices in the courts. This chapter compares the costs of the various sentencing options. Although most reports compare the intermediate sanctions to the cost of incarceration, it is also possible to compare the various community options to one another.

The key instrument that assists the judge in making sentencing decisions is the presentence investigation. Several controversial issues surround the use of the presentence report, including the probation officer's role in compiling the presentence report and the officer's liability for errors included in the document. The chapter also discusses the confidentiality issues surrounding the preparation of this document.

Finally, we look at the advantages of community corrections programming. It appears that intermediate sanctions satisfy the public demand for punishment and accountability. However, opinion polls and surveys that legislators rely on in gauging public sentiment do not always reflect the full scope of people's perceptions about the appropriateness of these community alternatives to prison.

OBJECTIVES

After you have completed this chapter, you should be able to do the following:

1. Identify some of the advantages of community corrections and those persons most likely to benefit from these programs.
2. Discuss the sentencing options that the judge has and the factors that may be considered when the judge is deciding the appropriateness of each for a defendant.
3. Explain how the various sentencing options compare in terms of cost.
4. Describe the information contained in the presentence investigation report. What efforts, if any, are undertaken to ensure its confidentiality?

INTRODUCTION

The judge studied the 29-year-old defendant's long record of petty offenses and wondered what to do. This time, Russell Hackler had stolen two six-packs of beer from a small grocery. Although an expensive prison term did not seem warranted in this case, the judge was certainly in the mood to make an impression on the repeat offender. In granting four years of probation, the judge ordered Hackler to report to the court every weekday before work and to attend Alcoholics Anonymous meetings three times a week. The judge also required the defendant to wear a T-shirt that read "I'm on Felony Probation" on the back and "My record and two six-packs equal four years" on the front.

The sentence given by the judge in this case is an example of the way the courts are trying creative new ways to fit punishments to offenders. Part of the reason for these efforts is frustration with the failures of traditional approaches to corrections. Another part is the faith that something that has not yet been attempted may make a difference.

Not everyone would agree with the appropriateness of the judge's decision in the Hackler case. According to Andrew von Hirsch, some penal-

A controversial t-shirt and sentence were given to Russel Hackler by a California judge. (© Fred Mertz/PEOPLE Weekly © 1990)

ties offend the dignity of civilized people and should not be part of a humane system.[2] He explains, "An example is compulsory self-accusation, e.g. making convicted drunken drivers carry bumper stickers indicating their drinking habits. There is no way a person can, with dignity, go about in public with a sign admitting himself or herself to be a moral pariah."[3]

Sentences that invite public ridicule or shame may also be unconstitutional. In People v. Johnson, an Illinois appeals court struck down such a probation agreement. The court held that forcing Ms. Johnson to publish a picture of herself being booked, along with an apology, in the local paper was too punitive. The judges held that such a requirement was more drastic than the conditions authorized by the state for probation. They added that such negative publicity could have harmful psychological effects that would be "inconsistent with rehabilitation."

Although the philosophy of such sentences remains controversial, the outcomes are more concrete. In this case, Russell Hackler pled guilty to charges of second degree burglary and petty theft within three months of his infamous sentence on the first charge. This time he received four years and eight months of prison time. At the hearing, the defendant still proclaimed that the T-shirt punishment was a good idea, but he argued that because the police were "out to get him," it just didn't have a chance to work.

The idea of tailoring punishments to specific offenders is not new. Individualized punishments were a hallmark of Positive Criminology in the early 1900s. The turn of the century brought scientific advances to our understanding of behavior. The variety of biological, physiological, genetic, psychological, and sociological factors viewed as responsible for human actions highlighted the necessity for individual explanations of crime. With each different set of circumstances came specific problems and needs. The most effective sentences were seen as those tailoring punishment to fit each individual offender.

Today, however, attempts to devise and implement individual strategies for crime intervention are costly and time-consuming. Too many cases and too little time have rendered individualized planning unrealistic.

Traditionally, employees of the court have attempted to make professional assessments of individual offenders and the proper sentencing recommendations. Judges, prosecutors, defense attorneys, and probation office investigators have assembled data on each case along with the advice of psychologists, social workers, and educators. Even after a person is convicted and sentenced to a period of incarceration, parole boards and other corrections officials must make determinations about an offender's early release to parole. As Figure 2–1 indicates, almost 75 percent of all convicted offenders are being supervised in the community. However, the evaluation and assessment processes which courts

Figure 2.1

At year end 1989, an estimated 4.1 million adults—about 1 in every 46—were under the care or custody of a corrections agency. (*Source: Probation and Parole 1989*, BJS Bulletin [November 1990], NCJ-125833)

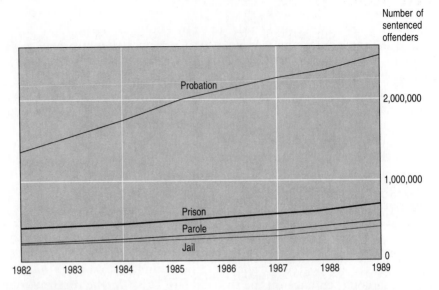

All correctional populations are increasing

From yearend 1980 to yearend 1989, the number of adults in the U.S. —
• on probation grew by 126%
• on parole grew by 107%
• in jails and prisons grew by 114%.

Most offenders are supervised in the community

About 75% of all convicted offenders are being supervised in the community — not in prisons or jails.

The number of adults on probation and parole has reached a new high

At yearend 1989 —
• 2,520,479 adults in the United States were on probation
• 456,797 were on parole.

During 1989 —
• the number of adults on probation grew by nearly 6%
• the number on parole grew by 12%.

Probation and parole populations grew in every region during 1989

The number of prison parolees supervised in the community rose —
17% in Southern States
14% in Western States
10% in Midwestern States
6% in Northeastern States
5% in the Federal system.

The probation population increased in every region. The highest increase was in the West (9.4%), the lowest in the Northeast (1.2%).

In 1989, the greatest numbers of adult probationers were in —
Texas with 291,156
California with 285,018
Florida with 192,495
New York with 128,707
Georgia with 125,441.

and professionals use in determining such sentences and releases have been criticized as unscientific and inconsistent. In fact, the courts are often accused of using biased and subjective judgments in making sentencing recommendations and decisions.

THE ROLE OF DISCRETION

The most important and often least understood aspect of the corrections professional's job is the use of discretion. In the processing of criminal cases through the justice system, *discretion* refers to the power to decide how a case is handled. Although a person's job may involve independent decision making, the discretion used is often subject to supervisory review.

In the criminal justice system, professionals are given a great deal of discretionary authority in carrying out their duties. The decision of the police to stop and question someone, the prosecutor's determination to proceed with charges, and the judge's finding on the appropriate sentence are all discretionary.

The use of discretion implies that the conclusions reached are influenced not only by rules, policies, and laws but by personal and experiential factors as well. One goal of our system is that discretion is not abused. All the actors in the criminal justice system strive for controlled and fair decisions based on the evidence at hand. One way to control discretion is to have supervisors or higher levels of authority review the decisions made at various stages of the justice process.

Each day corrections professionals make decisions based on either the most scientific evidence or simple instinct that change the lives of offenders and the society in which they live. Community corrections officers may take part in decision making in almost all phases of criminal proceedings concerning their clients—from arrest and pre-trial confinement to sentencing and supervision. Van Dine calls one kind of decision *"in/out decisions."*[4] Such decisions determine whether the offender goes to prison or jail or remains in the community. The decisions include whether to recommend a term in prison or jail, whether to release a person from prison or jail, and whether to revoke an offender's status as probationer or parolee and send him or her to prison.

A list of the kinds of discretionary decisions made either entirely or partly by probation and parole officers appears in Box 2–1.

STUDIES OF DISCRETION IN SENTENCING

In analyzing the variations that occur in sentencing, Thomson and Zingraff determined that disparity could be accounted for by a number of factors, including (1) variations in the social and political environment of each jurisdiction, (2) variations that could be attributed to a particular judge, (3) variations that arose from differing victim-defendant relationships, and (4) the point in the process at which decisions were made.[5] With regard to jurisdiction, there is some indication that

BOX 2–1

Decisions in Which Probation and Parole Officers May be Involved

1. Power to influence whether their clients receive bail or pre-trial release
2. Power to influence the nature of charges brought against their clients by the prosecutor's office
3. Power to influence the sentencing disposition of the criminal cases of those under their supervision
4. Authority to effect client's arrest with or without a warrant
5. Authority to issue warrants on clients
6. Authority to search and seize evidence without a warrant
7. Power to detain clients in custody
8. Power to determine (specify or "file") charges in instances of probation or parole violation
9. Power to effect commitment of offenders to institutions through initiation of revocation and other procedures
10. Power to effect modification or termination of probation or parole obligations

Source: Adapted from Herbert Roll (1980). "Discretionary Decision Making in Probation Agencies." *Improving Management in Criminal Justice.* Alvin Cohn and Benjamin Ward (Eds). Beverly Hills, CA: Sage: 53–72.

lower courts and urban courts may produce more discrimination, that is, sentencing differences that cannot be accounted for by the defendant's prior history or the seriousness of the offense itself. It is also possible that when victims and defendants are of differing racial and economic backgrounds, the sentences will be more harsh. Thomson and Zingraff indicate that discriminatory decision making in the early phases of processing, such as arrest or charging, may make later decisions appear more rational and legitimate.

The use of offense severity, the number of pending cases, or prior convictions to explain varying sentences appears to be reasonable and defensible. These variables are considered "legal" because they relate directly to decision making. A criminal history or a violent offense appears to warrant, or justify, the use of more serious sanctions, but "extra-legal" variables, such as race, sex, and economic background, do not.

Despite our theoretical commitment to unbiased sentencing, the criminal justice system is often not consistent or fair. Many studies have pointed out that employed, wealthy, or upper-class and educated defendants receive less severe sanctions in the court than do defendants without these characteristics.[6] In studies by Chiricos, Jackson, and Waldo;

Wolfgang and Riedel; Pope; Hagan; Gibson; Myers; and LaFree; sentences were found to be directly related to the race of the offender or the victim.[7]

Examining the probation sentences given to males and females, Williams did not find any difference in the length of terms each received.[8] Yet in another study, Daly and Lind speculated that judicial concern for the welfare of dependent children has led to more lenient sentences for mothers with young children than for males as economic providers.[9] In still another study that specifically looked at single-parent males, Bernstein, Cardascia, and Ross found that these men also received an advantage at the dispositional stage.[10]

In 1983 after studying data from three states, Petersilia determined that minorities were given harsher sentences at conviction. She explained that after controlling for the defendants' age, offense, and priors, "the average sentences in California are 6.5 months longer for Hispanics and almost 1.5 months longer for Blacks than for Whites; in Michigan, average sentences are more than 7 months longer for Blacks than Whites; in Texas, average sentences are more than 3.5 months longer for Blacks and 2 months longer for Hispanics than for Whites."[11] However, seven years later, Petersilia concluded that changes in sentencing practices in California had virtually eliminated racial bias.[12] Crediting the state's Determinate Sentencing Act for imposing strict guidelines on sentencing, she likened the new process to computer scoring.

THE SHIFT TOWARD DETERMINATE SENTENCING STRATEGIES

Like California, many states have developed determinate sentencing strategies such as sentencing guidelines. When implemented, the guidelines give the judges specific parameters within which a sentence must fall. These guidelines are developed on the basis of offense seriousness and criminal history. For each type of offender and offense, the range of the possible sentence is very narrow. For example, for a first offender convicted of automobile theft, the punishment may be one year of probation. For an aggravated robbery, a first offender must serve between 23 and 25 months in prison. The judge is not allowed to deviate outside this two-month range. When judges do decide that a different sentence is appropriate, they must supply written justification for going outside of the statutory guidelines. An example of the sentencing guidelines used by Minnesota is given in Table 2–1.

Although sentencing guidelines are one form of more determinate sentencing, there are also other strategies that may include abolishing parole or other early-release mechanisms. Corrections officials do not have the authority to release prisoners before the full completion of

Table 2–1   Minnesota Sentencing Guidelines Grid

Severity Levels of Conviction Offense		Criminal History (# of Prior Offenses) (Presumptive Sentence Lengths in Months)						
		0	1	2	3	4	5	6 or more
Unauthorized use of motor vehicle Possession of marijuana	I	12[a]	12[a]	12[a]	15	18	21 24 23–25	
Theft-related crimes ($150–$2500) Sale of marijuana	II	12[a]	12[a]	14	17	20	23	27 25–29
Theft crimes ($150–$2500)	III	12[a]	13	16	19	22 21–23	27 25–29	32 30–34
Burglary-Felony intent Receiving stolen goods ($150-$2500)	IV	12[a]	15	18	21	25 24–26	32 30–34	41 37–45
Simple robbery	V	18	23	27	30 29–31	38 36–40	46 43–49	54 50–58
Assault, 2nd degree	VI	21	26	30	34 33–35	44 42–46	54 50–58	65 60–70
Aggravated robbery	VII	24 23–25	32 30–34	41 38–44	49 42–53	65 60–70	81 75–87	97 90–104
Assault, 1st degree Criminal sexual conduct, 1st degree	VIII	43 41–45	54 50–58	65 60–70	76 71–81	95 89–101	113 106–120	132 124–140
Murder, 3rd degree	IX	97 94–100	119 116–122	127 124–130	149 143–155	176 168–184	205 192–215	230 218–242
Murder, 2nd degree	X	116 111–121	140 133–147	162 153–171	203 192–214	243 231–255	284 270–298	324 309–339

Italicized numbers within the grid denote the range within which a judge may sentence without the sentence being deemed a departure.

First-degree murder is excluded from the guidelines by law and continues to have a mandatory life sentence.

Cells below heavy line receive a presumptive prison sentence.

Cells above heavy line receive a presumptive nonprison sentence.

The numbers in these cells refer to duration of confinement if probation is evoked.

[a]One year and one day.

Source: Sandra Shane-DuBow, Alice P. Brown, and Eric Olsen, *Sentencing Reform in the United States: History, Content, and Effect*, U.S. Department of Justice, Washington, DC, p. 165, 1985.

their sentences. The effect is that judges cannot transfer to prison experts the responsibility of determining when the offender is ready to return to society. Some people feel that this is unfortunate because the courts and corrections could work together to ensure that releases are used appropriately. Judges would often like to see an offender incarcerated or under supervision only until the offender receives treatment or completes some kind of therapy.

In many jurisdictions discretion has also been taken away from judges by laws that dictate specific punishments for certain crimes from which the judge cannot deviate. These *mandatory sentences* may require a person to serve time in prison for a certain offense or for a second or third conviction of that crime. By law, a person cannot be placed on probation regardless of how appropriate a judge may feel a community supervision sentence would be.

Mandatory sentences also refer to laws that require that a person serve a certain amount of time in prison or jail. A mandatory sentence may be five years in prison, or in some cases, life in prison. Thus, a finding of guilt in this instance means that the punishment stipulated by law is automatic.

Many judges feel that the courts and not the Congress are better qualified to determine the most appropriate punishments for crimes. In a few cases, judges and juries have refused to find defendants guilty if they do not believe the mandatory punishment is appropriate, even if the evidence of guilt is overwhelming. One federal judge was so upset by what he thought were harsh mandatory sentences for first-time offenders that he quit his job in protest.[13] This kind of revolt indicates that those who dispense justice do not want to be controlled by statutes. Judges often feel constrained by mandatory sentences, particularly when a case is atypical or when there are extenuating circumstances.

OTHER SENTENCING TRENDS

In attempts to be more efficient, economical, and fair, new sentencing strategies have been developed and tested. One new approach is the use of private consultants to arrange appropriate sentencing plans. For a fee, these experts spend time developing penalties that mix the proper balance of punishment, prevention, and rehabilitation into a sentence. The consultants make the employment and community service arrangements that are best suited to the clients' needs and abilities.

Several of these private sentence-arranging services are being used. In one case, the organizer of a marijuana-smuggling ring was directed to open and operate an AIDS hospice. In another case, a consultant developed a six-point sentencing plan for a Vietnam veteran who was stealing farm equipment to support his drug habit. His probation

Table 2–2

		Emphasis on the Community	
		Low	High
		---	---
Emphasis on	High	rehabilitation	reintegration
the Offender	Low	restraint	reform

sentence included outpatient psychiatric care, repayment of the theft losses, periodic drug testing, and 300 hours of community service with the fire department.[14] Judges find many of the sentences to be creative and effective, particularly in the cases of low-risk offenders. However, such a consulting service is usually available only to defendants who can afford the initial or up-front expense of several hundred to several thousand dollars per case. In some states, grants have paid for sentence-preparation services; in yet other cases, offenders themselves pay the sentencing consultant by making monthly installments during their prison terms.

As professionals in the criminal justice system differ from one another in sentencing philosophies in general, they also hold a variety of opinions on the goals of sentencing in each individual case. One such difference occurs when there are two possibly conflicting priorities: those of the community and those of the offender. As O'Leary and Duffee explain, correctional policies are formed on the basis of these different priorities.[15] As Table 2–2 demonstrates, a high level of emphasis on the offender and the community would result in programs that facilitate reintegration, whereas those that concentrate on the offender and not the community are simply oriented toward rehabilitation.

According to Vince Fallin, to gain the support of the public, the legislature, and the courts, a community corrections program must achieve the following:

- Be perceived as reasonably safe.
- Meet the public desire for punishment by including elements like control, nonpaid labor, and victim restitution.
- Promote rehabilitation possibilities through treatment and employment skills.[16]

LEVELS OF SANCTIONS

As one might suspect, the sentencing options that a judge considers are more complex than simply whether or not to incarcerate. Typically, the judge has several alternatives to incarceration that he or she may assess individually or in some combination. Some of the punishments may seem minor, such as paying a fine or spending the night in jail. An offender may also be required to pay for the damages caused by vandalism or an accident resulting from criminal negligence. The punishments attached to misdemeanor crimes or minor felonies are usually of a short term and may incorporate a one-time payment.

Probation is a sanction that may be used for both felonies and misdemeanors. A term of probation is given in months or years, and the offender must report on a regular basis to a supervising agent. During the period of supervision, the offender must live within the guidelines of the probation contract or face harsher penalties.

Serious felonies often result in punishments referred to as *intermediate sanctions*. This term is used because the offender is not going to prison or is not at risk of a death penalty but does face much stiffer penalties than simply fines or traditional probation.

A variety of punishments fall within the range of intermediate sanctions. Most are served within the community in periods of less than ten years. One of the confusing aspects of community sentencing is that an offender may be given several different sentence requirements at once or may be required to serve several kinds of sentences, one after another, before a commitment is fulfilled. The sanctions may include fines, restitution, and terms of probation and community service.

Intensive supervision probation, a much stricter form of probation, is another intermediate sanction. Because intensive supervision involves more surveillance and control, it is often called a "prison without walls." Persons on intensive supervision may be restricted to their homes or apartments, or they may be monitored by electronic equipment. Intermediate sanctions such as intensive supervision, home confinement, and electronic monitoring, may also be used as more punitive measures for offenders who have been unsuccessful on less restrictive forms of probation.

Some intermediate sanctions may include periods in jail or prison, followed by a term of probation supervision. This practice is often referred to as *combined sentences*. In some states the exact amount of jail time that may accompany a probation term may be specified by law. For example, Texas allows up to 15 days of jail time to be added to probation terms. This practice may be appropriate for cases in which the offense itself was serious enough to require incarceration but mitigating circumstances also tempered the kind and length of such confinement.

Let us consider the case of Andy Rollins. Rollins pled guilty to two counts of the Lewd Act Upon A Child for fondling both his 12-year-old stepdaughter and her 14-year-old friend on several different occasions. The crimes were considered serious because of the nature of the offense, the trauma to the victims, and the violation of a position of trust that occurred. In mitigation, it was offered that the defendant voluntarily surrendered to police, pled guilty, and has been active in both group and individual counseling ever since. The defendant had no prior record of criminal conduct, used no threats or violence toward the girls, is legally blind, and was a victim of child molestation as a youngster. The stepdaughter has expressed concern that Rollins not go to jail. She also hopes that the family will soon be reunited. Although the mother is not ready for Rollins to return home, she is worried that the system is not responding to her daughter's need to see her stepfather or to resolve her guilt over his likely incarceration.

After considering all the relevant factors in Rollins's case, the probation office recommended that judgment be withheld and that Rollins serve five years of probation. The probation term would include one year in jail and the payment of various court fees.

Terms of jail and probation may also be combined with the use of group homes for treatment or restitution. For example, under the restitution center program in Texas, a typical stay is three months to one year. Following release from the center, the offender is placed on intensive supervision for a short period before being transferred to a regular probation schedule.

The federal government also uses combined sentences. In Florida, a federal magistrate sentenced a Fort Lauderdale man to three months in prison followed by three years of probation for shouting racial slurs and threats against a neighbor. The term of probation also included 100 hours of community service. The judge settled on the combined sentence because the defendant showed sincere remorse for his actions and apologized to the victim.[17]

THE PRESENTENCE INVESTIGATION

The *presentence investigation* (PSI) is a critical tool in the judge's decision process about sentencing. The document that results from the investigation gives up-to-date information about many aspects of the offender that are important in determining the most appropriate sentence. In most jurisdictions, it is the responsibility of the probation department to prepare the presentence investigation and presentence report.

In a criminal case, the PSI is usually conducted after the conviction of a defendant and before sentencing. Because juveniles are neither "convicted" nor "sentenced" in legal terminology, their reports are often called *predisposition reports* (PDRs). The purpose of either report is to assist the court in making rational decisions about the disposition of a case, such as whether to grant probation. The report may also be used to determine the appropriate length of a sentence and to help plan the services that an offender will need, such as drug treatment or mental health counseling, while under the supervision of the criminal justice system.

The information gathered in the presentence investigation or the predisposition report may be used as a data base from which to conduct research on offenders and the criminal justice system. If the same kind of information is gathered in all jurisdictions, then research can compare outcomes in a number of places or examine differences among them. Thus, some researchers have called for uniformity or standardization of these reports. Standardization would require that in addition to collecting data on the same variables (such as age, race, and marital status), the measurements be grouped or described in the same way (such as the same six age groupings or the same seven choices of racial groups).

The PSIs or PDRs come in various sizes. Some contain as many as 300 items. Generally, the document contains information on the following:

- The current offense. The defendant's version of the events, including attitudes toward the crime and any victims, the official or police report of the crime, an offense description, the plea, and the findings of the court.
- Any prior criminal record of the defendant (juvenile and adult), either misdemeanor or felony. The data may also include previous arrests.
- Personal history. Personal data, family data, data on parents, siblings, education, employment, physical and mental health, military service, financial assets and liabilities.
- Evaluation of the defendant, problems, needs, services that could help, test results or results of observations by clinical professionals.
- Recommendations. Alternatives to incarceration, plans for treatment, determinations as to whether the defendant is violent and poses a risk to the community, whether probation would be appropriate.

In many jurisdictions the content of the PSI has been shaped by legislation calling for special assessments and records. Where victim compensation and restitution programs have been instituted, information relative to each case is taken in the form of a victim impact statement. This statement, which becomes a part of the PSI, includes estimates of damage or injury caused by the crime.[18]

In making recommendations about the disposition of a felony case, probation officers must use all the resources available to ensure that their recommendations are fair and defensible. To do so, professionals must be careful that their findings be based on supportable facts and concrete evidence. Because the investigators are susceptible to emotional prejudices in certain circumstances or when dealing with particular offenders, it is important that they remain aware of their feelings and how these feelings could influence their reporting.

Frazier, Bock, and Henrella studied the content of presentence investigations in Florida and found that officers preparing the reports treated the cases of males and females in substantively different ways.[19] It was concluded that the crimes of males were more likely to be discussed by officers in terms of prior record, offense seriousness, and employment history. The crimes of females were more likely to be presented in terms of psychological variables such as state of mind and mental health. The authors suggest that the courts are influenced by traditional gender roles when making sentencing decisions.

Because of the large number of reports needed and the number of hours involved in compiling each report, departments have had to devise strategies to accomplish the increased volume of work. The various strategies include using specifically designated officers or paraprofessional staff to do nothing but prepare reports, using shorter report forms in the cases of less serious crimes or first offenders, and contracting with private companies to prepare the reports. The strategy most commonly used is the shortform approach, but as Clear and Burrell report, the same amount of investigation usually goes into each report.[20] The time savings realized is usually only a small amount of clerical time and some judicial reading time as a result of reducing the report from about ten to two pages.

The use of private companies to prepare PSIs is not without controversy. Although the delegation of criminal justice services to private businesses is becoming more common in our system, many people argue that ethically, private enterprises do not belong in the sentencing decision process. Others doubt that the private corporation can produce reports that are better or less expensive than the government can. However, it can be argued that the temporary use of such a service in periods of demand could prevent having to hire extra staff that are not continually needed.

Confidentiality and the Contents of the PSI

Case law has determined that a judge has a great deal of discretion as to the sources of information used in the sentence selection process. Traditionally, the sentencing phase of a trial is not considered to be as vulnerable to prejudicial information as is the guilt and innocence phase. During a trial, the rules for the evidence that can be admitted are very strict. Many characteristics of a person's past or personal life are legally irrelevant to the central fact of the case—did the person commit the crime or not? For that reason, information such as employment history, drug use, or determinations that a person is an unfit parent are not normally admitted at trial. It is understood, however, that when the appropriate sentence is being decided, more in-depth information is needed. Thus, the presentence investigation contains many facts and observations that may be only minimally related to the case. In fact, *hearsay*, a source of information not ordinarily allowed in criminal trials, may be included in the PSI. Allowing hearsay means that second-hand information about a person, or testimony from a person not immediately available for confrontation or confirmation, may be included in the report. For this reason, the defense has a great deal of vested interest in the contents of the report.

Jurisdictions vary in whether or not prior arrests that did not result in charges or prior charges that did not result in convictions should be allowed in the report. In many courts, it is safe to assume that if the information is relevant to the case at hand, it will be considered.

There is also great variation among the states over the confidentiality of the information in the PSI and who may have access to it. As part of a growing trend toward disclosure, many courts allow a defendant to see the PSI. In other courts, disclosure may be limited to the defendant's lawyer. As of this time, the Supreme Court has not called it a violation of constitutional rights for a court to refuse to disclose the content of a PSI. The only exception has been a capital punishment case in which the failure to disclose was seen as a violation of the defendant's rights (*Gardner* v. *Florida*). In some states (e.g., Montana, New York, and Florida), disclosure of the information in a PSI is required by law. In others (e.g., Louisiana and Pennsylvania), the law requires only limited disclosure, which generally means that only negative or derogatory information must be disclosed. Still other states (e.g., Maryland, Oklahoma, and Georgia) leave disclosure decisions to the courts.

Some courts allow the defense to cross-examine the author of the PSI or permit experts to contradict the findings in the document. As one would expect, the more damaging the information in the presentence report, the more likely it is that the defense will be given a chance to refute the findings.

Liability and the Preparation of the PSI

It is continually stressed to probation officers preparing reports that they are legally liable for the information contained in them. In one lawsuit, the preparers of an inaccurate PSI were found liable for failure to show the report to the plaintiff prior to sentencing. However, the court is likely to look at the kind of errors before placing any blame on the officer. Liability may be limited to proving that an officer acted maliciously or deliberately in falsifying information in a PSI.

In a recent case, a federal appeals court held that probation officers are "absolutely immune" from liability for errors in the PSI. Because the preparation of the report is considered a critical element in the judicial function of sentencing, officers may be granted the same immunity given to judges. This *judicial immunity* privilege extends to those occasions when officers' activities are "integrally related to the judicial process." That is, the officer is acting at the request of the court when he submits the investigation and recommendations of the PSI.

Immunity may also cover instances when the officer is exercising "discretion comparable to that exercised by a judge."[21] Over the years, courts have acknowledged that the possibilities of lawsuits would "seriously erode the officer's ability to carry out his independent fact finding function and would as a result impair the sentencing judge's ability to carry out his judicial duties" (*Turner* v. *Barry*).

OTHER RELEVANT SENTENCING VARIABLES

The judge may consider other variables at sentencing in addition to the facts presented in the PSI and the resources available for corrections programs. One is the effect that the conviction may have on the career and lifestyle of the offender. Although this is a controversial aspect of sentencing, favoring those who have "the most to lose," it is a reality that many judges cannot help but consider. A lawyer is disbarred and can never practice her profession again. A priest is defrocked and can no longer follow his life's calling. A famous athlete is prohibited from ever participating in competition by a national sports association. A politician can never hold public office again. Long after sentences are served, the effects of these convictions weigh heavily in the form of wasted careers. To what extent is loss of a professional career a punishment in itself? Should a judge consider the social and economic suffering of a destroyed reputation as a sanction that has been levied?

THE GOAL OF ALTERNATIVE SENTENCES

The goal of alternative sentences such as intermediate sanctions is often advertised as the provision of options that fill a needed gap between probation and prison. Many criminologists boast that such measures produce more proportionality, or balance, in sentencing. This proportionality, or balancing of interests, is illustrated in the case of Robert Moody.

Robert Moody seemed to be more a victim than an offender. He had witnessed his father sexually abusing his sisters and constantly beating his mother and forcing her into prostitution. Robert's brother was condemned to a mental institution because his father had sliced open his head with a screwdriver. After years of being physically and verbally abused by this man, Robert shot him. After killing his father, the boy rode to the police station on his bicycle and confessed. Although there was little question of the 18-year-old's guilt, the judge was perplexed about the proper sentence for this voluntary manslaughter conviction.

In open court, the judge suggested that the letters he was receiving on this case should contain more practical guidance and solutions. Believing that the judge was looking for advice, newspapers published his plight and the public responded with their views on the case. More than 700 letters appeared on the judge's desk. The judge admitted that he was impressed by the results and not insensitive to the wishes of the majority. He placed young Robert on five years of probation, two years of which were to be spent in missionary work.

The case of Robert Moody demonstrates the influences that many factors have on the sentencing process. The severity of a typically serious charge like manslaughter is mitigated by a number of factors important not only to the court but to the community as well. Every day the courts consider thousands of cases for sanctioning within the community although most are less controversial than the one just described.

Critics of the present community corrections movement complain that important ulterior motives also lie behind the popularity of intermediate sanctions.[22] These include cost, convenience, and the extraction of certain monetary benefits to the criminal justice system as well as to the community. It is important to recognize these supplementary goals in order to avoid policy conflicts in the implementation of these sanctions further down the line.

CONSIDERING THE COST OF PUNISHMENTS

Although judges would be reluctant to say officially that sentencing decisions take into consideration the cost of the various alternatives, it is more realistic to admit that they do. With limited resources and a full range of sentencing options at varying costs, judges must develop criteria for prioritizing the use of the more expensive sanctions such as incarceration.

Recent reports indicate that the United States now has the highest incarceration rate in the world. For every 100,000 people in this country, there are 426 in prison and jail. The two countries that once had incarceration rates comparable to those of the United States are South Africa and Russia. These two countries now have rates much lower than the United States—333 and 268 per 100,000, respectively. In particular, black males in this country are four times more likely to be incarcerated than in South Africa.[23]

One government report shows that this country spends 3.2 percent of its total budget on criminal and civil justice. About 1 percent of the justice funds are spent on corrections.[24] In addition, a far greater proportion of the corrections monies is spent on institutions than on probation and parole.

In Georgia, officials admit that they were forced to consider community corrections alternatives because of a lack of prison space and the courts' response to overcrowding. In a 15-year period, the state encountered major litigation over prison conditions, which cost them over $60 million. To meet court-ordered standards, their largest state prison was reduced from 3300 beds to 1400.[25] Such a reduction in capacity means that alternative sentences must be readily available.

Recent estimates in jurisdictions in several states have been compiled in an attempt to determine the comparative costs per day of the most common sentencing options. As could be predicted, there are significant cost differences among the sentencing options as well as among states on each option. The 1988–1989 *Report of the Kentucky Corrections Cabinet* listed the cost of state prison per prisoner at $34 per day and the cost of probation/parole supervision at $2.83, whereas one county in Texas listed those same costs as $42 and $0.67, respectively.[26] The *Corrections Yearbook* published by the Criminal Justice Institute in 1985 estimated that the cost of supervising probationers for a year ranged from $156 in Connecticut to $1500 under the federal system. The average cost for the year was $584.[27] On the other hand, the average cost of incarcerating a person in prison for a year is somewhere around $14,000 per year. Incarceration is an expensive proposition in states with large offender populations, such as Florida, Texas, and California. In California the state spends an estimated $360 million a year to imprison its offenders.[28] States with large offender populations also save the most by maximizing their use of less costly community corrections programs.

In prisons as well as in community corrections, the cost of running programs for special populations with distinct needs is even higher. One alternative community treatment program for juveniles that emphasizes intensive education and supervision asserts that it can successfully service juveniles at $4500 each. Still, the cost of incarcerating the same youth in a detention facility would be $28,000.[29]

ADVANTAGES OF COMMUNITY SENTENCING

There are many reasons why community sentencing is an attractive option for low-risk offenders. First, the law is enforced, which serves the purpose of providing an adequate punishment and, it is hoped, a deterrent to all potential offenders. Second, community sentences provide avenues of rehabilitation for the offender that give access to a number of educational, vocational, and treatment programs. By avoiding incarceration, the offender is able to minimize the negative effects of extended terms in prisons and jails. The family of the offender is able to remain

One of the advantages of community corrections programs is the accomplishment of worthwhile projects that instill pride in participants and area residents. (© *Mark Altman/The Image Works*)

close to their loved one, who is able to continue to provide support for them. This support translates into tax savings for the community in that it will not have to provide the family with costly social services and welfare.

Finally, there are many economic arguments for the use of community corrections programs. One is that such programs are a much less expensive alternative than incarceration. Although community sentences may be less costly than prison terms, it is important to remember that they are still not the least expensive response to crime. Diversion out of the criminal justice system into other community treatment programs is less expensive than supervision. To do nothing at all would theoretically be even less expensive, although perhaps unwise.

Depending on the offender, citizens may find that community corrections programs offer adequate protection against the continued criminal conduct of persons under supervision. Correctional personnel believe that they can adequately monitor and control offenders they recommend to remain in the community. Thus, different levels of supervision have been devised to offer surveillance at a level proportionate to the amount of risk the offender represents.

Specific community corrections programs can be designed around the special needs of offenders. In one program that is a cooperative effort between a private foundation and a county community corrections division, many services are offered. The format is a variety of "flexible non-residential services at one centrally located community-based center for adult offenders and their families".[30] Included are theft groups, women offenders' programs, property offenders' groups, a women's domestic abuse program, a men's domestic abuse program, parenting programs for men and women, a program for children and adolescents from violent homes, a custody and visitation dispute program, a support group for women leaving prostitution, an employment program, a traffic offender's program, and a financial management program.

IRONIES OF COMMUNITY CORRECTIONS

Many people mistakenly automatically categorize sentences of imprisonment as tough and "just deserts" and sentences of community supervision as lenient. In reality, a typical community sentence today is likely to incorporate a number of harsh penalties that may be stacked together. A person may be ordered not only to house arrest, drug treatment, and restitution but also to pay court costs, fines, and service fees. A 1984 study by Gottfredson and Taylor found that Maryland legislators believed the public wanted tougher state-controlled criminal sanctions.[31] However, a survey of the citizens of the same area found that most of them favored community strategies such as parole and rehabilitation centers. Although policymakers estimated that 63 percent of the public would favor abolishing parole, in actuality only 29 percent did. Furthermore, state policymakers believed that only 39 percent of the public would favor more community rehabilitation centers, yet 73 percent of those surveyed did. The point of the study was that many legislators act on what they think the public wants, which may not be what the public wants at all.

In a related study years later, Bennett found that most people favored community-based sanctions for offenders over prison as long as they felt the programs were strict and well managed.[32] In this survey respondents were given the choice of prison or probation for each of 25 crimes. An average of 63 percent of persons questioned felt that prison was the best option for each of these crimes. However, after reading about a variety of community supervision programs, such as restitution, intensive supervision, and drug treatment, only 27 percent of the readers still chose to send the offender to prison.

In a closer examination of these results, Bennett excluded the least serious crimes that were more likely to be considered good options for community supervision. He was then left with twelve of the original 25 crimes. For these more serious offenses, the survey respondents initially believed that 77 percent should go to prison. In the subsequent questioning following the introduction of the variety of strict community sanctions, only 41 percent still opted to send offenders to prison.

Bennett theorized that what the public wants most is accountability, not just incarceration. However, community corrections programs must provide strict supervision of offenders who will be held accountable to the public not only for their crimes but for their future behavior.

Media evaluations of certain sensational crimes or sentencing events does much to confuse our image of how the public really wants to respond to crime. Judging from media coverage, the public's punishment orientation would seem particularly punitive. Community supervision sentences are often stereotyped as "getting off easy" while incarceration is often equated with "justice." This is troubling to some scholars who fear that the public is desensitized to the punitiveness of many of the community sanctions. As von Hirsch explains, "These sanctions often involve substantial deprivations: intensive supervision and home detention curtail an offender's freedom of movement, a community-service program exacts enforced labor, a day-fine may inflict substantial economic losses."[33] Von Hirsch even questions whether or not some of the community corrections sentences have gotten out of proportion to the seriousness of the crimes committed.

The intentions of those who formulate and support community corrections legislation are not always realized in the end product. In 1983 church and corrections workers in Missouri submitted a plan for the *Missouri Community Corrections Act*, 1983, that would place control of community corrections in a new and separate organizational structure apart from state adult corrections and probation and parole services. However, the vision of these community volunteers was not evidenced in the formulation of this new organization. To their disappointment, the new programs were placed under the existing structure of Probation and Parole. Thus, the initial proponents were denied what they believed would be a new opportunity to address offender needs in a different way.[34]

Another of the troubling results of community corrections has been that many offenders fail to complete their sentences. As a result of these failures, many offenders ultimately end up in jails and prisons. The irony is that one of the original goals of such programming was to reduce overcrowding in the jails and prisons. Thus, as Cochran explains, community corrections is placed "in the 'catch 22' situation of being seen as a primary cause and a primary solution to prison crowding."[35]

The actual number of offenders who fail on community supervision is likely to increase as the numbers assigned increases. Although most books and articles on community corrections point out its value as a solution to crowded prisons and jails, it has only recently been viewed as an overcrowded system itself. However, as Rosenfeld and Kempf discovered, many jurisdictions have more crowding in community corrections programs than in their institutions.[36] All across the country the average number of supervision cases assigned to each officer has increased dramatically. In Los Angeles, half of the clients are supervised by officers carrying more than 1000 offenders on their caseload.[37]

Today there is a great need for coordination of sentencing priorities and resources within the criminal justice system to address the problem of overload. Funding, staffing, and program planning must be organized effectively so that the most popular sentencing strategies can continue to operate without jeopardizing their goals. Proposals for the most efficient way to provide community corrections services is the focus of the chapters ahead.

SUMMARY

The criminal justice process contains many opportunities for authorities to use discretion. Police may decide whether to arrest suspects, prosecutors may decide whether to press charges, and judges may determine whether a convicted person should be sent to prison. In deciding whether to release an offender into the community, a judge relies on both factual information and personal beliefs about each case. The primary source of information about a case is the presentence investigation.

The presentence investigation, usually completed by probation officers, contains factual information and the personal assessments of the preparer. The report also includes the impressions of other persons interviewed about the case, including victims, the offender's family, and psychological professionals. The goal of fair sentencing is not to eliminate personal impressions but to have objective and unbiased means for forming them.

Today, however, judges are given less discretion in sentencing than ever before. The use of mandatory sentences, sentencing guidelines, and determinate sentences all limit the amount of control both the judge and corrections officials have over the disposition of cases. When legislators put into law "automatic" restrictions on sentences, they reduce the courts' ability to tailor sentences to the convicted individual. In addition, the criminal justice system may not rely on the offender's future behavior (in prison or on supervision) to determine the outcome of a sentence (parole or successful completion of probation). Some people believe that this makes the process more mechanical and perhaps unfair, but others see it as more structured and thus more fair.

The decision to release criminals into the community to serve their sentences is not without its legal, political, social, and economic consequences. Today, the offender in the community corrections system has less education, fewer skills, and fewer family and peer support systems than ever before. The most critical needs facing this client group are employment and substance abuse treatment.[38]

Professionals working in community corrections have fewer resources and larger caseloads than ever before. The public and other government agencies are critical of the performance of the criminal justice system. Many people expect more and more out of the system even though it receives a diminishing proportion of resources. The community is also critical of offenders placed under community supervision. Like the system, offenders also contend with fewer resources and more personal problems. It is up to the community, the criminal justice system, and those it services to work out new strategies and new solutions for achieving their shared goals.

CASES

Gardner v. Florida, 430 U.S. 349, 1977.
People v. Johnson, 44 Crl. 2015 (Ill. App. Ct. 1988).
Turner v. Barry, 856 F. 2d 1539 (DC Cir. 1988).

KEY TERMS

discretion
in/out decision
mandatory sentence
intermediate sanctions
combined sentences

presentence investigation
predisposition report
hearsay
judicial immunity
Missouri Community Corrections Act

DISCUSSION QUESTIONS

1. What role, if any, should cost play in determining the kinds of sentences given to offenders? How much weight should a judge give to public opinion about certain cases?
2. How is discretion used in the sentencing process, and how can it be controlled?
3. Are some community corrections punishments personally degrading and therefore unethical?
4. How could the presentence investigation be improved? What information would you look for in sentencing that is not currently included?

END NOTES

1. Carlson, Norman (1974). *Corrections Digest* 5(9) (May 1): 1.
2. Von Hirsch, Andrew (1990). The ethics of community-based sanctions. *Crime and Delinquency* 36(1):162–173.
3. Ibid, p. 168.
4. Van Dine, Steven (1990). The in/out decision. In *Prison utilization study: Risk assessment techniques and Florida's inmates*, vol. 1. Tallahassee: Division of Economic and Demographic Research of the Joint Legislative Management Committee.

5. Thomson, Randall, and Matthew Zingraff (1981). Detecting sentencing disparity: Some problems and evidence. *American Journal of Sociology* 86(4):869–880.

6. Chambliss, William J. (1969). *Crime and the legal process*. New York: McGraw-Hill. Chambliss, William J., and Robert B. Seidman (1971). *Law, order and power*. Reading, MA: Addison-Wesley.

7. Chiricos, Theodore, Phillip D. Jackson, and Gordon Waldo (1972). Inequality in the imposition of a criminal label. *Social Problems* 19 (Spring):553–572; Wolfgang, Marvin, and Marc Riedel (1973). Race, judicial discretion, and the death penalty. *Annals* 407 (May): 119–133; Pope, Carl E. (1975). Sentencing of California felony offenders. Analytic Report #6. Albany, NY: Criminal Justice Research Center; Hagan, John (1977). Criminal justice in rural and urban communities: A study of the bureaucratization of justice. *Social Forces* 55 (March): 597–612; Gibson, J. L. (1978). Race as a determinant of criminal sentences: A methodological critique and a case study. *Law and Society Review* 12 (Spring): 455–477; Myers, M. A. (1979). Offended parties and official reactions: Victims and the sentencing of criminal defendants. *Sociological Quarterly* 20 (Autumn): 529–540; La Free, Gary D. (1980). Variables affecting guilty pleas and convictions in rape cases: Toward a social theory of rape processing. *Social Forces* 58 (March): 833–850.

8. Williams, Frank P. (1979). Chivalry in King Arthur's court: An examination of sex and processing in the criminal justice system. Paper presented at the annual meeting of the Academy of Criminal Justice Science, New Orleans, LA.

9. Daly, Kathleen, and Meda Chesney-Lind (1989). Rethinking judicial paternalism: Gender, work-family relations, and sentencing. *Gender and Society* 3(1):9–36.

10. Bernstein, I., J. Cardascia, and C. Ross (1979). Defendant's sex and criminal court decision. In R. Alvarez and K. G. Lutterman and Assoc. (eds), *Discrimination in organizations*, pp. 329–354. San Francisco: Jossey-Bass.

11. Petersilia, Joan (1983). *Racial disparities in the criminal justice system*. Prepared for the National Institute of Corrections by the Rand Corporation. Santa Monica, CA: Rand, p. 93.

12. *San Bernardino Sun* (1990). Study: Racial bias not factor in prison terms. February 16:A10.

13. Asseo, Laurie (1991). Judges balk at federal sentencing. *San Bernardino Sun*, July 13:A3.

14. Gest, Ted (1989). Personalized penalties. *U.S. News and World Report*, November 20, p. 75.

15. O'Leary, Vincent, and David Duffee (1971). Correctional policy—A classification of goals designed for change. *Crime and Delinquency* 17(4):380.

16. Fallin, Vince (1989). Gaining support for sentencing options. *Corrections Today* 51(6):66, p. 68.

17. *San Bernardino Sun* (1991). Racial slurs, threats net prison term. July 7:A6.

18. Lawrence, Richard, and Shelva Johnson (1990). Effects of the Minnesota Sentencing Guidelines on probation agents. *Journal of Crime and Justice* 13:77–104.

19. Frazier, Charles, Wilbur Bock, and John Henretta (1983). The role of probation officers in determining gender differences in sentencing severity. *Sociological Quarterly* 24(2):305–318.

20. Clear, Todd, Val Clear, and William Burrell (1989). *Offender assessment and evaluation: The presentence investigation report*. Cincinnati: Anderson Publishing.

21. Crane, Richard (1988). Legal issues. *Corrections Compendium* 13(4):2.

22. Corbett, Ronald, and Gary Marx (1990). No soul in the new machine: Technofallacies in the electronic monitoring movement. Paper presented at the annual meeting of the American Society of Criminology, Baltimore, Maryland.

23. American Correctional Association (1991). New study reports U.S. has highest incarceration rate in the world. *On the Line* 14(2):1.

24. Bureau of Justice Statistics (1990). *Justice expenditure and employment, 1988*. Washington, DC: U.S. Department of Justice.

25. Fallin, Vince (1989). Supra note 16, p. 68.

26. Kentucky Corrections Cabinet (1990). *Kentucky corrections cabinet facts and figures 1988–1989*. Frankfort, KY.

27. Camp, George, and Camille Camp (1985). *Corrections yearbook*. The Criminal Justice Institute, South Salem, NY.

28. *San Bernardino Sun* (1991). California's parole problem is a crime. October 11:A3.

29. Project New Pride (1985). *Project new pride*. Washington, DC: U.S. Government Printing Office.

30. Kolman, Anita, and Claudia Wasserman (1991). Theft groups for women: A cry for help. *Federal Probation* 55(1):48–54.

31. Gottfredson, Stephen, and Robert Taylor (1984). Public policy and prison population: Measuring opinions about reform. *Judicature* 68(4–5):190–201.

32. Bennett, Lawrence (1991). The public wants accountability. *Corrections Today* 53(4):92, 94–95.

33. Von Hirsch, Andrew (1990). Supra note 2, p. 163.

34. Gilsinan, James (1986). Creating a reform environment: A case study in community corrections and coalition building. *Criminal Justice Policy Review* 1: 329–343.

35. Cochran, Donald (1989). Corrections' 'Catch 22.' *Corrections Today* 51(6):16–18.

36. Rosenfeld, Richard, and Kimberly Kempf (1991). The scope and purpose of corrections: Exploring alternative responses to crowding. *Crime and Delinquency* 37(4): 481–505.

37. Laboton, Stephen (1990). Glutted probation system puts communities in peril. *New York Times*, June 19, A16.

38. Cochran, Donald (1989). Supra note 35.

3

Organization and Function of Community Corrections

1. Explain the use of standards in community corrections programming.

2. Describe the use of subsidy programs in funding community corrections activities.

3. Define the interstate compact and explain how it is used today.

4. Discuss the agencies that may be responsible for community corrections programs in any jurisdiction. Be prepared to diagram an example of an organizational chart that describes the relationship between the office in charge of all correctional programs and its subordinate activities.

PURPOSE

This chapter examines the structure and organization of community corrections programs in the United States today. There are different levels of involvement for the community, from total planning and control to little or no interaction, when programs are dominated by the state. One area of exploration is the role that schools, churches, and volunteer groups play in community corrections programming. More formal roles are assigned to the legislature, the courts, and the executive offices of government. The functions of these government branches are described in detail.

The chapter presents models that illustrate the distribution of authority in corrections systems across the country. Each model is analyzed for strengths and weaknesses. The text focuses on the coordination that takes place between the various government and private agencies that deal with community corrections populations. One of the interesting by-products of the relationship between interested agencies and community corrections programs is the development of local, state, and national standards. The role of standards in shaping the quality and delivery of services in community corrections is discussed. The chapter concludes with an overview of subsidy programs and the use of interstate compacts. Each of these topics can be seen as a way in which related agencies network. The networking process allows each agency to accomplish goals with maximum efficiency and effectiveness.

INTRODUCTION

The organization of community corrections systems across the country reflect great diversity and individuality. In any state, community corrections programs are likely to reflect that area's political and economic history as well as its correctional philosophy.

There are different levels on which the community can be involved in its corrections programs. In order of involvement from high to low, Duffee and McGarrell call the levels *community-run, community-placed,* and *community-based* programs.[1]

In *community-run systems*, local citizens have almost complete control over programming goals and operations. Residents may work on committees that establish policies for programs, and they may allocate funding according to their perceptions of the most worthwhile activities. In community-run systems, programs reflect the philosophy of local citizens, their safety concerns, and their faith in rehabilitation. Crime is a shared experience for which each community member feels responsible. Consequently, community corrections programs reflect the norms and values of the people who live there. One of the drawbacks of community-run systems is that they rely on cooperative interaction between community agents and leaders. Local politics, past experiences, and competition among programs located close to one another may put a tremendous strain on daily operations. Community-run systems also rely almost totally on local funding, which is less stable and more subject to fluctuation than state- or federally-funded efforts.

Community-placed systems are almost totally funded and operated by the state or by the federal government. Although supervision takes place on a local basis, policy formulation and resource allocation come from a nonlocal authority. The authority, whether state or federal, acts as a central headquarters in charge of community corrections programs. In this role, the authority delegates responsibilities to workers in regional offices who are in charge of carrying out programs. The regional offices are charged with enforcing uniform standards of supervision. One of the drawbacks of community-placed programs is that they sometimes appear to operate independently of the needs and desires of the local community. In some instances, they even seem insensitive to their environment. Much public relations work creating ties between the community and the programs is necessary for community-placed systems to be effective. Citizens need to feel that they have some say in the kind of community corrections programs that take place around them instead of feeling invaded by them.

Community-based corrections is a blend of the two models just described. The state or other extra-local sources provide much of the funding resources and the technical expertise for the operation of programs. The community retains a significant amount of power to design and implement program goals. According to Duffee and McGarrell, community-based activities allow the community to receive the benefits of new ideas and strategies from the outside while still retaining the control of and commitment to their programs.

WHO IS INVOLVED IN COMMUNITY CORRECTIONS?

Theoretically, it is possible to assume that many and various community members are responsible for and active in a community corrections program, including the following:

Residents

By participating as a voter, each citizen can contribute support for community corrections projects. Ballot measures that criminalize conduct, increase sanctions for existing crimes, dictate forms of punishment, or request funding for corrections programs are subject to voter approval. Citizens who feel strongly about any measure should contact friends and neighbors for support. They should also correspond with their legislators and volunteer in organizations that they feel are worthwhile. Individual volunteers can participate directly in the activities of a program or help raise money and obtain material donations for services. Community corrections programs will be only as strong as residents allow them and help them to be.

Volunteer Groups

As with each community resident, volunteer groups can participate in fund-raising activities for community corrections programs. Such fund-raising projects may pay for special trips, equipment, or training. Community volunteers may also spend time visiting with troubled youths or collecting the furniture and clothing items that clients need.

Volunteers provide a valuable service to community corrections agencies by augmenting the efforts of full-time staff. There are volunteer programs in both residential and field service programs. In residential programs, volunteers may offer support on special occasions, such as holiday celebrations, or they may simply support day-to-day routine activities. Volunteers may develop supportive relationships with offenders during residential treatment that may be continued later in the community. Volunteers often have access to community resources and can assist offenders in finding work, constructive recreation, and vocational or educational programs.

In youth programs, the relationships formed with volunteers fill a role similar to those in a "Big Brother" or "Big Sister" program. Volunteer groups come in all ages from Girl Scouts and Boy Scouts to college fraternities and sororities to lodges and their auxiliaries. Agencies should actively solicit volunteer groups to assist them in special projects or in everyday activities.

Civic Organizations and Leaders

The support of respected civil leaders does much to enhance the image of any community correctional agency. Many citizens look to their civic leaders for opinions on the value of programs. Most important, by keeping informed on programs in the area, civic leaders can dispel rumors and myths about the activities of the programs.

In many cases, civic leaders are persons who head well-known civic organizations and clubs that may be involved in literacy programs or fund-raising for drug treatment centers. Victims' groups may work with sentencing officials to arrive at equitable restitution settlements. Community leaders may help to coordinate projects that use offenders to perform community service. Civic organizations may use their reputation to influence legislative actions that have an impact on community corrections programs.

Local Law Enforcement Agents

It is a common policy for community corrections providers to coordinate their work with that of local law enforcement agents regarding the status of their clients. Police and sheriffs' deputies act as additional monitors when persons under supervision are out on the streets. In some jurisdictions, local law enforcement agents make arrests when persons under supervision violate the conditions of their contract. Local law enforcement agents are also contacted when prisoners are given furloughs or work releases in the community. Likewise, local law enforcement agents are notified when persons under the supervision of other jurisdictions are visiting in or moving to a new area.

In the past, communication between community corrections providers and local law enforcement agents has not always been clear or consistent. There is a continual need to build better working relationships between these two groups. Because the law enforcement agents' jobs are geared toward community protection and control of offenders, they must stay informed of the whereabouts of persons under supervision. While on patrol, an officer will often see clients in places where they should not be and at times when they are not allowed to be out. Thus, these officers may report to the community corrections staff, which enhances the program's ability to provide surveillance.

Churches

The church has always been an influential force in the lives of its members. The charitable and humanistic mission of the church has

Volunteers from churches and other civic organizations provide supportive relationships to residents of community treatment centers. (*Courtesy of House of Mercy, Des Moines, IA*)

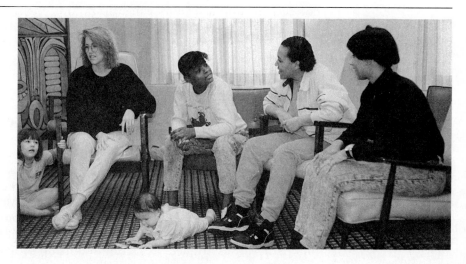

made it an important mediator between the offender and the community. Many developers of community corrections programs have sought the assistance and the backing of local churches. This support base has always been instrumental in alleviating the doubts of many area residents about the programs. However, there is considerable need for outreach work to build better relationships with the wide range of religious leaders. Some organizers have found that churches are reluctant to identify crime and drug abuse as being within the range of their responsibilities. Others report that the clergy are often too overburdened to offer help outside their own membership or are skeptical about working with persons outside their particular faith.[2]

One approach to getting the church involved in community corrections has been the formation of a spiritual concerns committee, a group that is usually composed of several religious leaders from a given area. These leaders meet to offer assistance to community corrections agencies and to determine the religious needs of the clientele under the supervision of corrections. Many juvenile facilities have areas set aside in which religious services can be conducted for youth in custody. In addition, counseling services can be offered to youth through the religion of their choice. The services offered to families by the various religious groups can rebuild family ties. The church may offer support to parents who are attempting to cope with delinquent children. It can also assist a spouse or others living in the home in dealing with the drug dependency or other crime-related behaviors of adult family members.

A spiritual concerns committee can also serve as a link to the community for the correctional agency. As committee members learn about the role of community corrections, they can inform their congregations. This learning process can help to build a constituency of support for the agency. The exchange between community religious leaders and corrections administrators can help both of them to better understand the problems that contribute to crime in the community. Furthermore, it can provide a forum for the development of new programs that can effectively address these problems.

Colleges and Universities

Perhaps the most important role for higher education in community corrections is assistance in program and offender research. Working together, schools of higher education and community agencies can design research agendas to solve emergency problems as well as to evaluate policies and operations. The school staff can join the corrections staff in analyzing data related to clients and programs. More effective polices and procedures can often result from these cooperative research efforts.

The university and college may be an important source of volunteer and paid staff assistance. Research internship programs developed over the past ten years give students college credit for hands-on experiences in community corrections agencies. Internships may last for a semester or for an entire year. Besides providing valuable learning and working experiences, the use of student interns is an important manpower resource for the agencies. In Michigan social science juniors and seniors work twenty hours each week in a high-risk program for youthful offenders. The interns monitor compliance with individualized treatment plans by making home, work, and school visits, informing staff of all important case updates, and assisting in group recreational activities. In addition, candidates for doctorates in psychology provide diagnostic testing for family and group therapy in this program.[3]

Colleges and universities also provide a place for corrections practitioners to continue their formal education. Staff members and administrators can gain the necessary credentials and graduate degrees related to their particular fields.

Businesses and Corporations

Community businesses may sponsor vocational training and apprenticeship programs that train offenders and eventually even hire them. Through various legislative incentive programs, corporations in the past, have received tax credits for hiring workers who are traditionally difficult to place in employment. Offenders who participate in supervised community corrections programs may be assisted in finding jobs not only to support themselves but to ensure that they are able to pay the financial obligations that arise from a conviction. A defendant may owe restitution, fines, court costs, and supervision fees. Local businesses may supply personnel officers to assist in job placement and to provide information about job openings. Social service agencies often compile lists of job openings for clients to look through. However, an effective referral service matches the best applicants with the most appropriate job openings in the community.

The Media

Community corrections leaders should not overlook the importance of the media in helping to publicize the beneficial aspects of any program. An important role for the media is their assistance in building a positive community image for local corrections programs. Reporting on the accomplishments of clients under supervision and minimizing the negative does much to enhance good relations between the programs and the public. Although fair and balanced reporting of the news is certainly a worthwhile goal, the media should not engage in sensational headlining or careless speculation about the risk of community corrections programs. Community corrections officials should make continuous efforts to keep the media informed of the successes of their clients, including restitution and fines paid, community service carried out, and graduation from educational, vocational, and treatment programs.

Landlords

One of the most important needs of offenders under community supervision is adequate housing. An organization of community landlords can ensure that decent, affordable housing is available to them. This organization can encourage their members not to engage in practices that discriminate against offenders who are trying to establish permanent housing. When an offender is under supervision, his or her financial obligations are strictly monitored and enforced. Therefore, these clients are good risks as tenants.

WORKING TOGETHER FOR COMMUNITY CORRECTIONS' GOALS

In Kentucky an entire community was involved in developing an alternative supervision strategy for juveniles. Approximately one-half of all juveniles currently under state supervision there are involved in day treatment programs that eliminate the need for incarceration by providing a broad range of alternative services. The juveniles attend day treatment school programs managed by the department of social services and go home at night. The program includes social workers and teachers in an instructional and counseling format that focuses on vocational education and job placement. The interesting feature of this program is the variety of community resources that are used. Judges screen referrals, the schools supply support services and even help offenders of school age integrate back into the regular school system in some cases, and community leaders serve on advisory committees and help to arrange job placements for the youths. The program also encourages their parents to volunteer in the program.[4]

In our society today, we view community corrections programs and policies as an extension of the will of the people. We believe that what society wants in the way of corrections resources is translated into actions by the government. The responsibility for administering proper punishments is placed in the hands of the legislative, executive, and judicial branches of government, which have separate responsibilities yet also serve as checks and balances against one another. No one branch has dominant authority over such a function as community corrections. Instead, each is monitored by the other two to ensure that programs are lawful, meaningful, and effective.

The Role of the Legislature

The legislature directs the development of community corrections in many ways. First, senators and representatives in each state as well as in the federal government enact and revise a penal code. The passage of bills related to the code dictates which offenders receive what kinds of sentences for each kind of crime. Through acts voted on by members of the legislature, certain kinds of offenders, such as violent or habitual criminals, may be denied access to parole and probation. The legislature also establishes sentences of minimum length.

The legislature must approve the funding for community corrections activity. Elected representatives may respond to a proposed budget by increasing or decreasing the amounts targeted for various corrections activities. They may also specify the ways in which they believe funds should be used. For example, during 1985 the Colorado legislature noted the ineffectiveness of state parole officers with caseloads of more than 200 clients. Consequently, they voted the funds needed for the creation of ten new parole officer positions.[5] The legislature can also establish commissions and boards to oversee certain correctional procedures or to develop standards for operating programs.

The Role of the Chief Executive

The chief executive of the state or federal government may influence community corrections in several important ways. When entering office, chief executives, such as the United States president, a state governor, or a city mayor, set priorities for the kinds of corrections programs to be developed in their jurisdictions. Next, the executives appoint or approve the nomination of persons who serve on corrections boards. Chief executives also appoint the directors of departments of corrections, juvenile institutions, and community services.

A primary task for the chief executive is the responsibility for constructing budgets. The initial appropriation of funds, later voted on by the legislature, determine what monies each corrections program receives.

The Role of the Courts

The courts play a direct role in the use and evaluation of community corrections programs. The courts may prefer certain programs and order offenders into them. Judges favor programs that they believe will best suit the needs of a particular defendant or group of defendants. The court may make regular referrals to some programs whereas other programs may find themselves with few clients. The courts may also pass judgment on the constitutionality of policies and procedures used in carrying out correctional programs. Appeals courts review the appropriateness of sentences issued by the lower courts. The appeals courts may determine that some of the requirements of probation and parole are unconstitutional. Such conditions then become void and unenforceable.

One of the often proposed advantages of community corrections is that it enhances the networking among related criminal justice agencies in a jurisdiction. Police, sheriffs, and probation, parole, and court personnel should work together to develop programs that protect the community and fulfill corrections goals as well. Once programs are developed and implemented, it is necessary for a variety of agencies to oversee their operations. The public or private organizational structure that contains each agency dictates the distribution of power, authority, and resources. The also determine how to maintain accountability.

ORGANIZATION AND STRUCTURE OF COMMUNITY CORRECTIONS PROGRAMS

There are as many kinds of organizational structures in community corrections programs as there are states, and, depending on the region and its resources, within one state there are many varieties of community corrections programs. A way to avoid confusion about who is responsible for what programs is first to determine who has custody or supervision of the convicted person.

Except for federal crimes, felony offenders are tried and sentenced within the jurisdiction of a state or county court. Each jurisdiction, however, has its own history and value system that is influenced by its rural or urban nature and by the views of the people who live there. Thus, it is possible that sentencing philosophies and strategies may vary within a state governed by one penal code or set of statutes.

For felony cases, each county (or parish in Louisiana) or state court has control over the offender for sentencing. After sentencing, the county must relinquish control of all offenders ordered to serve time in

Table 3–1 Providers of Probation/Parole/Aftercare Services (as of June 30, 1990)

	Number Board Members*	Adult Paroling Authorities	Adult Parole Services	Adult Probation Services	Juvenile Parole/Aftercare Services	Juvenile Probation Services
AL	3	Bd of Pardons & Paroles	Bd of Pardons & Paroles	Bd of Pardons & Paroles	Co Courts	Dept Youth Svcs ($ only) & Co Cts
AK	5(PT)	Bd of Parole	Dept of Corrections	Dept of Corrections	No parole/aftercare	DHSS/Div Family & Youth Svcs
AZ	7	Bd of Pardons & Paroles	DOC/Cmty Svcs Div	State Courts	DJC/Parole Admin	State Courts
AR	7 (PT)[1]	Bd of Parole & Cmty Rehab	DOC/Div of Pardons & Paroles	Adult Prob Commission	DCFS/Courts	DCFS/Courts
CA	9	Bd of Prison Terms**	DOC/Parole & Cmty Svcs Div	Co Depts	DYA/Parole Svcs Branch	Co Depts
CO	7	Bd of Parole	DOC/Div of Cmty Svcs	Judicial Districts	DOI/Div of Youth Svcs	Judicial Districts
CT	11 (PT)[2]	Bd of Parole	DOC/Div of Parole**	Office of Adult Prob	Dept Children & Youth Svcs	Superior Court/Family Div
DE	5 (PT)[2]	Bd of Parole	DOC/Div of Cmty Corr	DOC/Div of Cmty Corr	DSCYF/Div Youth Rehab**	DSCYF/Div Youth Rehab**
DC	4	Bd of Parole	Bd of Parole	DC Superior Ct/Social Svcs Div	DHS/Youth Svcs Admin	DC SUperior Ct/Social Svcs Div
FL	7	Prob & Parole Cmsn	DOC/Prob & Parole Svcs	DOC/Prob Div	DHRS/Children, Youth & Fam Svcs	DHRS/Children Youth & Fam Svcs
GA	5	Bd of Pardons & Parole	Bd of Pardons & Parole	Bd of Pardons & Parole	DHR/Div of Youth Svcs & Co Courts	DHR/Div Youth Svcs & Co Courts
HI	3(PT)[3]	Paroling Authority	Paroling Authority/Field Svcs	State Judiciary/Prob Ofc	DPS/Youth Corr Facility/Cmty Svcs Sect	State Judiciary/Family Courts
ID	5 (PT)	Cmsn for Pardons & Parole	DOC/Div Field & Cmty Svcs	DOC/Div Cmty Corr Svcs	Dept Health & Welfare	Dept. Health & Welfare and Co Cts
IL	13	Prisoner Review Bd	DOC/Cmty Svcs Div**	Judicial Circuits	DOC/Juv Field Svcs**	Judicial Circuits
IN	5	Parole Bd	DOC/Parole Svcs Section	Judicial/County Courts	DOC/Parole Svcs Section	Judicial/County Courts
IA	5(PT)[2]	Bd of Parole	DOC/Div Cmty Corr Svcs	DOC/Div Cmty Corr Svcs	DHS/Bur Adult, Children & Family Svcs	Judicial Districts
KS	5	Parole Bd	DOC/Parole Svcs**	Judicial Districts	DSRS/Youth Svcs	Judicial Districts
KY	7	Parole Bd	CC/Dept Cmty Svcs & Facilities	CC/Dept Cmty Svcs & Facilities	CHR/Div of Family Svcs	CHR/Div of Family Svcs
LA	5	Bd of Parole	DPSC/Div of Prob & Parole	DPSC/Div of Prob & Parole	DPSC/Div of Youth Svcs	DPSC/Div of Youth Svcs
ME	5(PT)	Parole Bd[3]	DOC/Div of Prob & Parole	DOC/Div of Prob & Parole	DOC/Div of Prob & Parole	DOC/Div of Prob & Parole
MD	7	Parole Commission	DPSCS/Div of Parole & Prob	DPSCS/Div of Parole & Prob	Dept of Juv Svcs	Dept of Juv Svcs
MA	7	Parole Bd	Parole Bd	Office of Cmsnr of Prob/Courts	DYS/Bur of Cmty Svcs	Office of Cmsnr of Prob/Courts
MI	7	Parole Bd	DOC/Bur of Field Svcs	DOC/Bur Field Svcs & Dist Cts	DSS/Ofc Children & Yth Svcs/Co Cts	DSS/Ofc Children & Yth Svcs/Co Cts
MN	4(PT)[4]	DOC/Office Adult Release**	DOC/Prob Par Supv Rel/ Co Cts or CCA	DOC/Prob Par Supv Rel/ Co Cts or CCA	DOC/Prob Par Supv Rel/ Co Cts or CCA	DOC/Prob Par Supv Rel/ Co Cts or CCA
MS	5(PT)	Parole Bd	DOC/Cmty Svcs Div	DOC/Cmty Svcs Div	DHS/OYS/Cmty Svcs Div	DHS/OYS/Cmty Svcs Div
MO	5	Bd of Prob & Parole	DOC/Bd of Prob & Parole	DOC/Bd of Prob & Parole	DSS/Div Youth Svcs & Jud Circuits	Judicial Circuits
MT	3(PT)	Bd of Pardons	DVCD/Cmty Corr Bureau	DVCD/Cmty Corr Bureau	Dept. Family Svcs	Judicial Districts
NE	5	Bd of Parole**	DCS/Adult Parole Admin**	Neb Prob Admin	DCS/Juv Parole Admin**	Neb Prob Admin
NV	5	BD of Parole Cmsnrs	Dept of Parole & Prob.	Dept of Parole & Prob.	DHR/YSD/Youth Parole Bureau	District Courts
NH	5 (PT)	Bd of Parole	DOC/Div of Field Svcs**	DOC/Div Field Svcs** & Dist Cts	DHHS/DCYS/Bur of Children	DHHS/DCYS/Bur of Children
NJ	9	Parole Bd**	Bureau of Parole**	The Judiciary/Prob Div	Bureau of Parole**	The Judiciary/Prob Div
NM	4	Adult Parole Bd	CD/Prob & Parole Div	Div of Prob & Corr Alt/Co Courts	YA/Cmty Svcs Div/JPB	YA/Cmty Svcs Div
NY	19	Bd of Parole	Div of Parole	Div Prob & Corr Alt/Co Courts	Div for Youth/Div of Parole	Div Prob & Corr Alt/Co Courts
NC	5	Parole Commission	DOC/Div Adult Prob & Parole	DOC/Div Adult Prob & Parole	Admin Office of Courts/Juv Svcs Div	Admin Office of Courts/Juv Svcs Div
ND	3(PT)	Parole Bd	DCR/Div of Parole & Prob	DCR/Div of Parole & Prob	DCR/Div of Juv Svcs	DCR/Div of Juv Svcs/Supr Cts

Table 3–1 *(continued)*

	Number Board Members*	Adult Paroling Authorities	Adult Parole Services	Adult Probation Services	Juvenile Parole/Aftercare Services	Juvenile Probation Services
OH	9[5]	DRC/Div of Parole & Cmty Svcs & Parole Bd	DRC/Div of Parole & Cmty Svcs	DRC/Div of Parole & Cmty Svcs & Co Courts	Dept of Youth Svcs	Co courts
OK	5 (PT)	Pardon & Parole Bd	DOC/Div of Prob & Parole	DOC/Div of Prob & Parole	DHS/Div of Children & Yth Svcs	DHS/Div of Child & Yth Svcs, Co (3)
OR	5	Bd of Parole & Post Prison Supv	DOC/Cmty Svcs Br/Co Cts	DOC/Cmty Svcs Br/Co Cts	DHR/CSD/Ofc Juv Corr Svcs	Co Courts
PA	5	Bd of Prob & Parole** & Co Cts[6]	Bd of Prob & Parole** & Co Cts	Bd of Prob & Parole** & Co Cts	Co Courts (Prob & Aftercare)	Co Courts (Prob & Aftercare)
RI	6 (PT)	Parole Bd	DOC/Div of Field Svcs	DOC/Div of Field Svcs	DCTF/Div of Juv Corr Svcs	DCTF/Div of Juv Corr Svcs
SC	7 (PT)	Bd Prob, Parole & Pardon Svcs	Dept Prob. Parole & Pardon Svcs**	Dept Prob. Parole & Pardon Svcs**	Dept Youth Svcs/Cmty Div	Dept Youth Svcs/Cmty Div
SD	3 (PT)	Bd of Pardons & Paroles	Unfied Judicial Sys/Ct Svcs Dept	Unified Judicial Sys/Ct Svcs Dept	Unfied Judicial Sys/Ct Svcs Dept	Unified Judicial Sys/Ct Svcs Dept
TN	7	Bd of Paroles	BPParoles/Par Svcs	DOC/Div of Prob**	DYD/Prob Div**	DYD/Prob Div**
TX	18	Bd of Pardons & Paroles	TDCJ/PPD/Parole Supv	Cmty Justice Assis Div/Dist Cts	TYC/Cmty Svcs Div/Ofc Par Supv	Co Depts
UT	5	Bd of Pardons	DOC/Field Operations Div	DOC/Field Operations Div	DHS/Div of Youth Corr	Juv Courts
VT	5 (PT)	Bd of Parole	AHS/Dept of Corrections	AHS/Dept of Corrections	AHS/DSRS[7]	DSRS/Div of Social Svcs
VA	5	Parole Bd	DOC/Div of Adult Cmty Corr	DOC/Div of Adult Cmty Corr	Dept Youth & Fam Svcs	Dept Youth & Fam Svcs
WA	5	Indeterminate Sent Review Bd	Div of Corrections	DOC/Div Cmty Svcs & Co Cts	DSHS/Div of Juv Rehab	Co Courts
WV	3	Bd of Prob & Parole[8]	DOC/Div Prob & Parole	DOC & Judicial Circuits	DOC (Compact) and DHHR	DOC (Compact), DHHR & Jud Circuits
WI	4	Parole Commission	DOC/Div Prob & Parole	DOC/Div Prob & Par	DHHS/Div Yth Svcs/Co Soc Svcs Depts	Co Social Svcs Depts
WY	5 (PT)	Bd of Parole	Dept of Prob & Parole	Dept of Prob & Parole	Dept of Prob & Parole	Dept of Prob & Parole
US	9	Parole Commission**	Admin Ofc of US Courts	Admin Ofc of US Courts/Div of Prob		

*All members serve full-time unless coded "PT."

**Accredited by Commission on Accreditation for Corrections

1. AR — 3 full-time, 4 part-time.

2. Chairman serves full-time; members part-time.

3. ME — Parole Board hears pre-1976 cases of parole. Flat sentences with no parole under criminal code effective 5/1/76.

4. MN — Executive Officer & two Deputy Executive Officers (CCA Cmty Corr Act)

5. OH — Plus 11 hearing officers

6. PA — The Board of Probation and Parole administers adult services when sentence is over 2 yrs; county courts when sentence is 2 yrs or less.

7. VT — No functional juvenile parole system. Children in custody go into placement and eventually return to community under supervision of caseworker.

8. WV — Under state statute, parole is considered probation.

The following states have one or more independent county, municipal or city departments: CO, GA, IN, KS, KY, LA, MO, NE, NY, OK, TN, WY. All Boards are independent except MD, MI, MN, OH, TX, WI.

Source: American Correctional Association (1991). *Directory: Juvenile & Adult Correctional Departments, Institutions, Agencies & Paroling Authorities.* Laurel, MD: ACA.

the state prison system. Once a prisoner is given over to the custody of the state, the state maintains control until the term of the sentence is completed, which is why parole and other programs that supervise populations released from prison are usually operated by the state.

The responsibility for carrying out sentences that do not involve incarceration in prison remains in the jurisdiction of the courts that impose punishment. If a person serves a sentence in jail, he or she never leaves the custody of the local (county or city) jurisdiction. Persons sentenced to probation generally remain in local jurisdiction unless probation is revoked and the offender is sent to state prison.

A breakdown of the way in which each state's corrections system is organized is given in Table 3–1. The table explains who is responsible for making decisions about prison releases (column 2), who is in charge of adult parole programs (column 3), and who is in charge of adult probation (column 4). The agencies responsible for juvenile probation and parole services are listed in columns 5 and 6.

Table 3–1 shows the many different combinations of agencies used in corrections services in any state. The best way to describe the division of authority in programming is to illustrate it in an organizational flowchart, as shown in Figure 3–1.

In Figure 3–1 we see that all community corrections programs are under the authority of the state department of corrections. In states using this structure, the community corrections function is highly centralized in that the authority lies in a central office or agency. This is the model followed by Maine and Virginia, although in Maine determinate sentencing has been instituted and the only discretionary parole decisions being made are on convictions handed down before 1976. When all programs are administered by the state, there may be a parole and/or probation agency or a community corrections division of the state department of corrections. In this model the state is divided into districts or regions that administer both probation and parole services.

The flowchart in Figure 3–2 shows that the state department of corrections is in charge of adult prisons, parole, and probation. However, some other state or local agency is responsible for juveniles. This is the case in North Carolina where the administrative office of the courts is responsible for juveniles. In Oklahoma the division of children and youth services provides all juvenile services. Other states following this

Figure 3–1

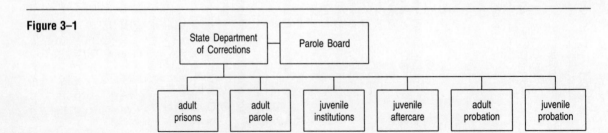

Figure 3–2

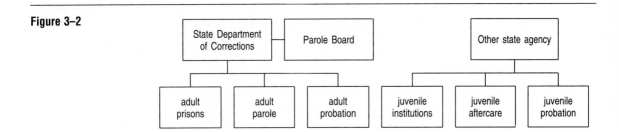

model are Georgia and Florida. By examining Table 3–1, you can see which agencies in each state are responsible for juvenile aftercare and probation.

Another possible organizational structure gives the state department of corrections authority over both juvenile and adult parole, but the probation function for both adults and juveniles falls to the county. This is the arrangement found in Hawaii and in Indiana. It is illustrated by Figure 3–3.

The most diversified structures are those in which a different authority administers each of the functions: adult parole, adult probation, juvenile parole, and juvenile probation. This model is a *decentralized system*. Connecticut uses such a structure. The Department of Corrections, Division of Parole is in charge of adult parole. Separately, the Office of Adult Probation handles its own population. Juvenile aftercare is provided by the Department of Children and Youth Services. Juvenile probation is run by the Family Division of the Superior Court. All are state agencies, but four separate agencies are represented in their community corrections structure.

Another way to analyze the organizational differences in the arrangements of correctional functions is to analyze each population served across the states to determine if any general patterns exist.

Adult Parole

For the most part, adult parole systems are programs in which offenders have been released from state prisons. A state parole system is usually under the authority of a parole board or parole commission. Parole programs are generally operated by the state department of corrections.

Figure 3–3

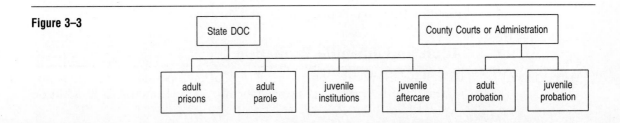

In some states, there may be a separate parole or field division within the department of corrections to handle the parole function, as is the case in Tennessee, Utah, and Illinois. In some states, the department of corrections has two separate divisions, one for probation and one for parole services, as in Louisiana, Missouri, and Florida.

The Parole Board or Parole Commission

The parole board or parole commission is a group of elected or appointed officials who are paid staff members or who are volunteers on a part-time or full-time basis. Currently, about one-half of the states that use parole boards have full-time members. The board's responsibility is to review all cases eligible by statute for release and to determine which warrant an affirmative response.

In approximately 41 states, the governor appoints the members of the parole board.[6] Such appointments may be subject to legislative approval. Because parole releases involve some degree of prediction risk, politicians are usually careful to appoint persons particularly knowledgeable in the criminal justice area. Appointees may also be persons who are well respected in the community.

In one controversial South Carolina appointment, the governor selected a wealthy businessman whose teenage daughter had been raped and murdered by a stranger. Although the grieving father alleged that he could review potential cases fairly, critics believed that he was not an emotionally appropriate participant. On the other hand the governor can campaign for reelection on the assertion that he or she has served the needs of victims in the parole process.

Juvenile Parole

Juvenile parole programs may also be operated by the state department of corrections, as is the case in Virginia, Wisconsin, Arizona, and Maine. In Texas and California, a state youth commission or youth authority operates both institutions and parole services for this population. In other states, juvenile parole, aftercare programs, and probation services may be operated by state agencies such as the division of human services, the department of social services, or the department of health and rehabilitative services, as in Mississippi, New Hampshire, and Florida. In still other states, juvenile parole services may be funded through the local county or municipal government. This is how aftercare is structured in Alabama, Pennsylvania, and Arizona.

Adult and Juvenile Probation

The state currently conducts all probation operations in thirty two states, whereas twelve states have locally operated systems. In addition, six states have some kind of combined state and local authority as the basis of their programming. Probation services for both adults and juveniles are organized in a number of formats. Clear and Cole describe the possible assignments of responsibility in Table 3–2.[7]

As Table 3–2 shows, the governor or state executive may be responsible for some programs, and state or local courts may be responsible for others. Local executive authority includes county administrators or county supervisors. In some areas, the local executive may vest the authority to operate a probation department in a chief probation officer, who would then be responsible for adult or both adult and juvenile operations in that county.

According to Hurst and McHardy, there has been a trend toward the movement of juvenile corrections programs away from the control of the state department of corrections.[8] In most cases, programs such as juvenile probation have been shifted to state departments of youth services or children and youth services. Currently, when juvenile probation is run by the state, it may be in the department of corrections, a department of youth services, or a department of social services. Otherwise, juvenile probation is run locally. For example, probation services for juveniles in California, Indiana, and Texas are provided by each county, either through the courts or through a separate county probation department.

In California adult probation is administered by county probation departments. In other states (e.g., Colorado and Kansas), adult probation services are placed under the supervision of a county or district court. Refer again to the organizational structures outlined in Table 3–1 (page 62–63).

As the table shows, in states such as Idaho the state may fund and operate probation and other community corrections programs. However, these programs are organized into areas or districts that respect the jurisdictional boundaries of the sentencing courts.

Table 3–2 Probation Assignments

Adult Probation	Juvenile Probation
State executive	State executive
State executive	Local judiciary
State judiciary	State judiciary
Local judiciary	Local judiciary
Local executive	Local executive
Local executive	Local judiciary
State executive	State judiciary
Local executive	State judiciary

Figure 3–4   FLOW-CHART OF FEDERAL JUSTICE SYSTEM

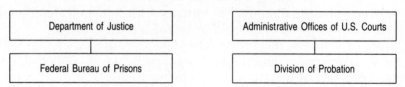

Federal offenders remain under the jurisdiction of the federal system, which is self-contained and provides all its own probation, parole, and prison programs. The federal government even has its own police service—the marshal's office. The marshal's office is responsible for the housing and movement of federal prisoners outside of institutions. Figure 3–4 is a flowchart of federal correctional services which shows that the Department of Justice is responsible for administering the Federal Bureau of Prisons. However, parole decisions are made by the United States Parole Commission. Federal probation falls under the jurisdiction of the administrative office of the U.S. courts. Probation officers in the federal system are appointed by the federal judiciary.[9]

NEW TRENDS IN THE ORGANIZATION OF COMMUNITY CORRECTIONS AGENCIES

Over the past twenty years several new trends in programming have challenged existing organizational and operational policies of community corrections agencies. The first trend is that traditional parole systems have been abolished in several states. As mentioned earlier, the parole board in Maine functions only to hear the cases of prisoners who were incarcerated prior to 1976. Everyone who went to prison after that time is serving an exact, or "flat," or "determinate," sentence that does not allow for parole. The philosophy of *determinate sentences* is that "what you see is what you get." Therefore, it takes five full years to discharge a five-year sentence completely. Previously, a person on a five-year sentence might serve three years before making parole. The remaining two years of the sentence would then be spent in the community on parole supervision.

Advocates of determinate sentencing believe that this system prevents sentence "inflation." Inflation occurs when judges give longer prison terms to ensure that the offender does not get out early. In Maine, those sentenced after 1976 will be coming out of prison with their entire prison term served.

Not everyone approves of determinate sentencing. Many people believe that the term of parole helps offenders to readjust to the community under controlled conditions. This control period may result in more successful reintegration, they feel. In fact, some research indicates that those who complete their terms on parole have lower recidivism rates than those who are discharged directly from prison.[10]

In other states where parole has been abolished, a person may be sentenced first to serve a specified amount of time in prison and then a separate, subsequent term of probation. In West Virginia, parole is considered like probation. This service is provided by the state's division of corrections, as is probation.

An interesting arrangement of the prison/community supervision combination is called *shock probation*. Shock probation occurs when the local jurisdiction sentences an offender for a term of years in prison but then takes him or her out of prison after only a short time. The release from prison must occur within a limited period after sentencing. This practice hinges on the legal power of the court to extend its jurisdiction for a certain number of days into a state prison term. It is only during this extended period that a judge may alter the original sentence. This limited period is usually anywhere from 90 to 180 days. After the time limit has passed, the prisoner is considered under the control of the state. Therefore, only the state can release the prisoner after the jurisdictional authority has transferred.

If the county decides to grant a term of shock probation, it retrieves the offender from the state prison, suspends the prison term, and places the person on probation. The difference between shock probation and other types of mixed prison and probation sentences is that theoretically in the practice of shock probation the offender does not know ahead of time that the prison term may be changed to probation. It is hoped that the experience of actually being in prison will shock him or her into good behavior during probation.

Newly incarcerated Texas prisoners must meet certain criteria (first prison sentence, nonviolent crimes) to apply or petition for shock probation. The request is sent from the prison to the county where the person was convicted. In a follow-up study of the Texas program, it was found that many offenders had anticipated being released early. Probation officers estimated that 65 percent of the felony shock probationers expected their early release.[11] Some offenders may have even made plea bargain arrangements for shock probation. When probationers themselves were surveyed, 44 percent had prior knowledge of their impending release.[12]

Another difference between shock probation and other forms of mixed sentences is the length of time a person has been incarcerated. Under shock probation, the terms of prison served are usually shorter than those when normal prison and probation sentences are combined. Table 3–3 gives a breakdown of the types of shock probation currently used.

Table 3–3 Characteristics of Shock Incarceration Programs, 1988

State	Year Program Began	Number of Programs	Number of Participants	Average Number of Days Served	Placement Authority	Voluntary Entry	Voluntary Dropout	Located in Larger Prison	Release Supervision
Alabama	1988	1	53	90	Judge	–	yes	yes	regular
Arizona	1988	1	35	120	Judge	no	no	yes	varies
Florida	1987	1	66	101	Judge	no	no	yes	moderate
Georgia	1983	2	200	90	Judge	yes	no	yes	varies
Louisiana	1987	1	51	120	Corrections Dept./Judge	yes	yes	yes	intensive
Michigan	1988	1	120	90	Judge	yes	no	no	intensive
Mississippi	1985	1	197	180	Judge	no	yes	yes	regular
New York	1987	2	445	180	Corrections Dept.	yes	yes	no	intensive
Oklahoma	1984	1	150	120	Corrections Dept.	no	no	yes	varies
South Carolina	1987	2	85	90	Judge	yes	yes	yes	varies
Texas	1989	1	200 (capacity)	–	Corrections Dept./Judge	no	no	yes	varies

Source: Doris Layton Mackenzie and Deanna Bellew Ballow (June 1989). *Shock Incarceration Programs in State Correctional Jurisdictions—An Update*, Report #214, Washington, DC: National Institute of Justice.

COMMUNITY SUPERVISION IN RURAL AREAS

Although the community supervision functions of rural areas are often the same as those in larger urban and metropolitan areas, the resources are not. In some counties in Minnesota, there is one agent who supervises all juveniles on probation and all adults on both probation and parole, as well as all adult misdemeanants, some of whom are 100 miles from medical and other major treatment referrals. As one officer explained:

> There are pluses and minuses to being the only agent in the county. I've had to deal with some people all the way through the system from juvenile through adult supervised release. On occasion, I probably would be more effective holding family counseling sessions, since I have several members from the same family on probation.[13]

Rural supervision has many personal advantages for its officers. As one officer explained, "People want to know you more than just on a professional basis. This is reflected in the number of birth announcements and wedding and graduation invitations you receive."[14] However, being part of a very small staff also means calls late at night and on the weekends when the sheriff's department needs assistance. Officers may spend many hours transporting offenders from place to place.

It can be speculated that rural jurisdictions sentence many borderline cases to state correctional facilities simply because there are not enough

Because rural areas have fewer social service resources than larger urban areas, community corrections professionals find themselves performing a wide variety of supportive roles. (*Courtesy of House of Mercy, Des Moines, IA*)

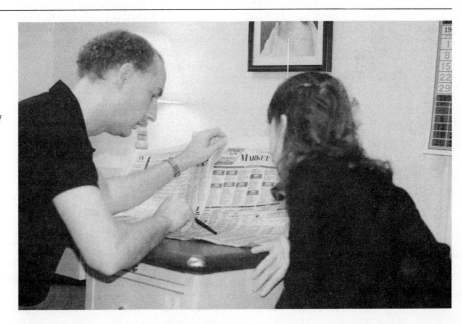

intermediate-level services in the area. As a result of a lack of alternatives, offenders are subject to more restrictive punishments than their urban counterparts are.

SUBSIDY PROGRAMS

Obviously, it would be cheaper for local governments simply to ship all offenders to the state for their entire terms of punishment. However, it is also obvious that the state could not afford such a policy. As a result, some balance must be achieved between the economic abilities of both local and state governments to deal with law breakers. Several strategies have been devised to share the expense and responsibility for corrections. Some states provide economic incentives to their local governments to process and treat their own offenders within the communities. These incentives are most often referred to as *subsidies*.

Subsidies may be awarded to local corrections agencies in several forms. One form is *grants* that are applied for by a local government. The various local agencies may compete for a limited amount of state funding available through grants. An example of a grant program is a fund for supervision and treatment programs set up in Indiana. During 1988, $3.5 million was set aside in grants to 25 counties. Programs funded by the grants included community service and restitution, house arrest, victim–offender reconciliation, and work-release.[15]

A second form of subsidy is an *award* given to an agency that is based on the agency's implementing programs that comply with state standards. With this method, all qualified agencies may receive awards without having to compete against one another. In New York probation funding is tied to compliance with specific state standards that include space and design guidelines for probation offices, requirements for staff development, rules for case record management, and supervision guidelines for monitoring probationers and for revoking violators.[16]

A third form of subsidy is a *reimbursement* for a certain percentage of the local cost of community corrections programs. Some subsidies may be paid as a set fee per day for each offender that the city or county chooses to service in the community.

A fourth form of payment is a *calculated sum* of funds from the state that is based on some kind of demographic formula, such as a certain level of reduction in prison commitments. This form of subsidy serves as an incentive for local officials to establish and maintain community corrections services because the more offenders diverted from the state, the more funds the county receives.

It is important to realize at this point that although the subsidy brings financial support to community corrections programs, the programs still require a significant amount of local funding to initiate and maintain. A lack of the necessary "seed money" has often discouraged some jurisdictions from participating in incentive programs. On the other hand, some experts argue against offering communities money to do what they should already be doing anyway.

Local governments are currently experiencing great fiscal distress. Many of them complain that they are unable to offer proper financial support for their programming needs. Some people wonder if, by offering subsidies, the states are avoiding their responsibilities by coercing local authorities into assuming the task of monitoring offenders. For example, in Minnesota the state deducts $25 per day from the money a county is eligible to receive for every day a felon spends in state custody on a sentence of five years or less.[17] Thus, general assumptions are being made about the risk of offenders serving short sentences. Assumptions that such offenders are probably of low risk and should have been kept in the community translate into financial penalties to the county. This may seem to work to the disadvantage of any jurisdiction experiencing an increase in nonviolent crime. Knowing that the state will exact a penalty for sending burglars and car thieves to prison for short sentences will almost force the courts to lengthen sentences beyond what they consider appropriate. If a county believes it cannot service all the offenders eligible for community service, authorities may even be inclined to prosecute fewer cases.

Over the years a number of subsidy programs have been established through community corrections acts passed in various states. One of the first was in California in the mid-1960s. In this program, communities were paid $4000 for every offender diverted from the state system. According to Bloom, "A 1977 evaluation found that between 1966 and 1975, state commitments had been reduced by 35,000 and counties had earned subsidies totalling more than $145 million. Additionally, Probation Subsidy accounted for a taxpayer savings of about $10 million annually."[18] However, the value of the California subsidy program did not appear to hold up over time. As one report concluded, ". . . the monies received by counties have not only not increased but have shrunk by inflation. By 1975, the purchasing power of the $4000 state payment to counties was worth only $2230, a drop of nearly 50 percent."[19]

In Minnesota under the Community Corrections Act of 1973, counties may receive subsidy payments for providing local correctional services. To be eligible for funds a county's plan for programs must be approved by the commissioner of corrections. Today, 28 of the state's counties, representing approximately 60 percent of the total population, receive subsidy funding. Minnesota's appropriation for the act in 1988 was $13.3 million.[20]

In Kansas a community corrections act was implemented in 1980.[21] It provided funds for counties that developed and improved probation programs that resulted in reduced commitments to state prisons. The Kansas programs targeted nonviolent first- and second-time felony offenders. Michigan also passed a community corrections act in 1980;

however, no actual funding was committed to it until several years later.[22] It is doubtful that effective large-scale programs can be implemented without some financial assistance from the state.

One of the underlying assumptions of the community corrections acts of the 1960s, 1970s, and 1980s was that public safety would not be jeopardized by such programs. This assumption is difficult to demonstrate given that the goals of the programs were to offer the county financial incentives to keep in the community offenders who had previously been sent to prison. One of the more controversial aspects of this dilemma is how to determine if public safety has been jeopardized. If the level of crime committed by offenders decreases or simply remains the same, is that sufficient evidence that public safety has not been jeopardized?

To properly control the growing number of offenders monitored in the community because of subsidies, departments were likely to classify those who would have otherwise gone to prison as of higher risk. Thus, caseloads began to be distinguished by high and low levels of supervision. Offenders who would have ordinarily remained in the community were often of low risk and received minimal supervision. Those who were newly diverted to the state became the high-risk and maximum supervision cases. This kind of resource distribution may have even led to minimum supervision caseloads receiving less attention than they had previously. Thus, it is possible that neither group was receiving the level of supervision they had theoretically warranted. According to one report, the Minnesota Community Corrections Act was criticized because increases in local costs of supporting the programs were not balanced by improvements in community safety.[23]

STANDARDS FOR THE OPERATION OF COMMUNITY CORRECTIONS PROGRAMS

One of the consequences of state subsidy funding of community corrections programs has been increased state intervention in the operation and evaluation of local activities. By controlling funds, the state has been able to order communities to adhere to certain minimum standards in the design and function of corrections programs. Regardless of the nature of the funds, any monies from state or federal sources used in community corrections are likely to be tied to some kind of performance contract. One way that communities have met these expectations is to develop and implement written standards governing everything from room furnishings to counseling credentials. The standards developed are thought to reflect the minimum requirements regarded as necessary for the health and safety of all involved with the program as well as of the greater community. It is also hoped that by following professionally recognized standards the rehabilitation potential of any program will be maximized.

There are basically three levels from which standards may be generated: local, state, and national. Whereas local standards may be developed within a single agency, state and national standards are usually the result of a committee or commission of recognized experts in the field. An example of a national board for setting standards is the National Advisory Committee on Criminal Justice Standards and Goals. More specifically, in corrections the American Correctional Association (ACA) has developed a set of standards recommended for agency adoption across the country. The ACA represents professionals from all areas of corrections, including probation and parole. The American Bar Association has also developed several sets of standards that advise on the regulation of juvenile programs and case processing as well as dispute resolution programs.

Within a state, probation and parole authorities often operate under a specific set of guidelines for community corrections that are separate from institutional standards. The goals of such guidelines probably include influencing legislation, defining the purpose and philosophy of probation and parole within that state, establishing uniformity of operations of community corrections departments among the various counties, and protecting the profession and individual departments against external attacks. Box 3–1 shows a sample community plan.

Separate standards have often been developed to govern adult and juvenile programming. Topic areas for standards include health care, education programs, training for staff, classification of offenders, legal responsibilities in treatment, and policies for dealing with violent behavior.

Without official standards, many experts argue, officials have little guidance about the quality of their program or staff. Following all or most of the standards recommended by a national or state authority may lead to the program's receiving *accreditation*. Being granted accreditation may in turn lead to additional or continued funding from various sources. Accreditation may also serve as a legal defense when policies are challenged in court. If your agency is following procedures developed by experts who are recognized throughout the country or state, it can be a legal advantage. It would be hard to argue that you are not carrying out your duties properly. However, the existence of professionally mandated standards also makes it difficult for an administrator to claim a lack of knowledge about such a policy or criteria. The development of professional guidelines places more responsibilities on agency leaders to adhere to certain minimum levels of performance despite any difficulty in doing so.

Most corrections officials view the adoption of standards through the accreditation process as an effective management tool. Also, because the use of standards and accreditation is generally favored by the legislature, it is often possible to receive additional financial support to achieve compliance with current professional guidelines.

BOX 3–1

A Sample Community Corrections Plan

Objectives of the Plan

- To provide the courts an extensive presentence assessment for nonviolent, nonhabitual offenders who can be retained in the community with a structured sentence.
- To reduce by 60% the number of nonviolent, nonhabitual offenders committed to state youth centers or prisons.
- To provide more sentencing alternatives for the judges.
- To extract restitution from 70% of the offenders sentenced to community corrections through direct payment to victims for their losses or through court-ordered community service when no victim has been identified or when monetary restitution is not feasible.
- To reduce the costs of crime by avoiding the expense of institutional confinement, and by requiring offenders to repay victims for their losses and to pay court costs.

Target Population

- Adult nonviolent felons who:
    - —are first or second time felony offenders, and
    - —have no prior history of convictions for violent felonies, and
    - —have no history of serious psychological disorders that would render them a danger to the community, and
    - —would be likely candidates for state prison commitment in the absence of a structured community corrections sentence.
- Juvenile nonviolent felons or misdemeanants who have characteristics similar to those youths who in the past have been committed to state youth centers.

Programs in the Plan

- Intensive Supervision Program for Adults and Juveniles:
    - —Evaluation team to identify prison- or youth center-bound offenders and prepare alternative sentence plans for the courts.
    - —Intensive supervision involving 16–20 contacts per month between target offender and case manager as a local substitute for the supervision and structure of institutional confinement.
    - —Restitution or community service plan arranged for each offender and monitored by case manager.
    - —Employment services including job-readiness training, vocational training, and job search assistance.
    - —Educational services to assist offenders to acquire basic skills, achieve functional literacy, or obtain a high school diploma.
    - —Counseling for individual, family, or substance abuse problems.
    - —Case manager assistance to help offenders develop suitable living arrangements, realistic household budgets, and time management plans.

BOX 3–1   (*continued*)

- Child Abuse and Neglect Intervention Services:
    —Central clearinghouse to coordinate and track referrals to agencies of all child abuse and neglect cases.
    —In-home services where counselors work with families on parenting skills, anger control, and household management.
    —Crisis intervention for children and families.

Source: Reprinted with permission of the American Correctional Association from *Community Corrections Act*: Technical Assistance Manual. Copyright 1983.

California passed legislation that allowed for the development of two levels of punishment for driving while intoxicated (DWI). Because research had not shown that any one approach to drunk driving was more effective than another, the state did not feel as though it could mandate only one kind of program. Therefore, it allowed counties to develop the programs they believed best. Local authorities could establish their own standards and choose their own providers for their first-time DWI offender programs. Many chose to use an educational program format that has been accredited by the state department of motor vehicles. Programs for second-time DWI offenders, on the other hand, must follow standards set by the state department of alcohol and drug programs. Although program providers may still be selected on the local level, they must be approved by the state.[24]

The use of standards and the accreditation process is an example of how a community corrections agency is affected by outside organizations and policies. Another example of an outside organization that provides a means of networking for correctional programs is the use of the interstate compact.

INTERSTATE COMPACTS

In 1983 after numerous threats, Charles Thurman beat and stabbed his wife until she was close to death. The case was not extraordinary in that the defendant received a 14-year prison sentence but in that his wife was awarded almost $2 million in a lawsuit against police in Torrington, Connecticut, for their alleged failure to protect her against her husband. This case established the constitutional right of a victim of domestic violence to police protection and also led to the passage of a law requiring such crimes to be prosecuted with or without the victim's pressing charges. Seven years later, Thurman was released from prison despite the protests of his ex-wife. The judge approved Thurman's request to serve out the rest of his sentence in Kentucky where his father lived. The catch was that Kentucky had to approve of such a transfer. If they did, Connecticut would have to arrange his transportation because of Thurman's being released directly to Kentucky and not in Connecticut.

Although requests for interstate transfer of probationers and parolees is not unusual, it is not every day that the requester is the subject of a TV movie as Thurman was. It is understandable that no state is anxious to take in the problem offenders of another state, but the courtesy of such exchanges is a critical element of the relationship between the states. It is the hope of any state approached in the way Kentucky was that they will be able to quietly absorb such transferees with little public attention or protest. Then, when faced with a similar situation, they will be able to expect the same kind of favor from another state. This cooperative relationship between the states is a vital part of the interstate agreement called "the Compact."

The Interstate Compact for Adult Offenders was established in 1937 and was originally signed by 25 member states. Today, this agreement, or contract, has been joined by all 50 states. The states agree to entertain requests for courtesy supervision of probationers and parolees from other states. In exchange, when needed, a state may also request out-of-state supervision for its offenders. The state that sends the offender retains legal control or jurisdiction over the prisoner, and it receives periodic progress reports from the supervising state. An officer or office to receive and process all requests is usually designated. In some states, a single office relays all requests, whereas in others juveniles and adults may be handled separately, or probation and parole requests may be handled by two different state agencies. This requires that corrections officials in the county requested must be contacted to see if such supervision would be feasible. More than 200,000 probationers and parolees

Under the Interstate Compact for Adult Offenders, persons may request to serve their probation or parole term in another state. (*Courtesy of the Georgia Department of Corrections*)

BOX 3–2

Reply to Interstate Compact Request

June 19, 1967

James C. Kellog, Chief Probation Officer
Santa Barbara Probation Department
Coastal Area Office
7568 Lansing Blvd
Santa Barbara, California

Dear Mr. Kellogg,

I am in receipt of your request for verification of local residence of the above-named minor. In accordance with your request, I paid a visit to the home, and looked over the situation.

Copperwood Road winds across a gentle knoll known locally as "Smelter Hill," which, in the event of a clear day, offers an excellent view of the Wool Rock Manufacturing Co. and the Fuel & Iron Steel Mill. The neighborhood is occupied primarily by families of somewhat modest means. The rocky unpaved streets and simple dwellings are what one would expect to find in some of the less affluent areas of border towns. The residents of the area are markedly free from any morbid compulsivity toward order and cleanliness. The neighborhood can be considered a liberal one inasmuch as a "Support Your Local Police" movement is not likely to originate there.

When this officer first drove up to the home, he was greeted by a group of pre-school-age children who cursed him roundly. The yard is uncluttered by grass or shrubbery. Instead, it is richly decorated with paper, cans, tires, and other native artifacts. The home itself is constructed of genuine adobe, given an even more authentic appearance by weathering which has reduced the outer walls to little more than sand. No paint spoils the natural finish. The bathroom facilities are located a convenient 30 yards downwind. The interior of the home is far cleaner than one might expect and, although the furnishings probably were purchased at Goodwill, they are in a passable state of repair. The home is somewhat free of noxious odors.

The family is well-known to us. A brief perusal of our files indicates that most of the children have been referred to our office on numerous occasions. The most common offenses shown for them (the minor's uncles and aunts) are larceny, shoplifting, assault and battery, burglary, disturbing the peace, and malicious mischief. Other offenses that they have committed with less frequency included escape from the state boys' school, assault with a deadly weapon, rape, robbery, and attempted murder.

The family unit presently consists of the minor's grandparents, one of his aunts and three of his uncles. The father and one of the uncles are the only family members who are employed. One of the uncles is unemployable due to an only partially successful prefrontal lobotomy he performed on himself with a .22 rifle four years ago. All things considered, this seems to be the type of placement that will be quite effective in transforming the minor's pre-delinquent behavior.

Unfortunately, we will not be able to accept supervision of this very interesting case. It is the policy of our office to accept referrals from out of state agencies *only* when they are referred through the proper channel, i.e., the Interstate Compact on Juveniles.

BOX 3–2 (*Continued*)

Further, this office does not appreciate requests for home evaluations and/or courtesy super-vision which are received weeks after the individual has actually been placed in our community. It has long been office policy that, unless there are extremely extenuating circumstances, this de-partment will not make home evaluations or provide courtesy supervision "after the fact." It is our position that this type of situation creates unnecessary hardship and confusion for the re-ceiving agency, as well as resulting in many highly unsatisfactory placements for the minors we are supposed to be helping and that the situation will certainly not be improved by allowing this practice to continue unchecked. Perhaps if some of the courts and their related agencies become aware that their requests will not be honored unless they discharge their function properly, some changes may occur. The Interstate Compact on Juveniles is not now the strongest instrument in operation, and its weakest link is the area of probation and the courts. It is certainly not being strengthened by bypassing it to make a "dump-the-child-in-the-community-and-then-ask" type of referral.

I sincerely regret our inability to help you in this matter. Please be assured of our utmost co-operation in all properly referred matters.

Very truly yours,
G.H. Hayes, Chief Probation Officer
Pueblo County, Colorado

relocate in another state each year. Because many requests are not ap-proved, the actual volume of cases handled is much higher. Over the past few years, many states (e.g., Arizona and Colorado) have computer-ized their systems for processing requests so that information is readily available and easily transmitted. In addition, more staff members have been trained in the processing of interstate compact requests so that they may be expedited. If the case will not constitute an unrealistic bur-den to the department, a state will usually comply. However, as shown in a letter from a Colorado probation officer (see Box 3–2), some requests are problematic. Although this actual case was processed in 1967, the sentiments about following correct procedure are still appreci-ated today.

Advantages of the Interstate Compact

The greatest advantage in the use of the interstate compact is that it can serve to reunite families. Most research studies on offender recidivism seem to indicate that family support is an important insulator against further criminal activity. With the emotional and financial help of loved ones, persons under supervision may be more successful at employment and community integration, which are also related to low recidivism rates. Some states seek to maximize the success probability of interstate transfers by accepting only those who have a legitimate need to relocate to their state for employment or to be with their families.

One of the administrative and economic advantages of the compact is that if an offender commits a violation of supervision, he or she may be returned to the state of original jurisdiction without extradition. This is an important cost saving because extradition procedures can take considerable time and manpower to accomplish.

Disadvantages of the Interstate Compact

One of the potential problems in the use of the interstate compact is that some states may be asked to receive disproportionately more offenders than they send out. In 1987, for example, 1,342 Mississippi offenders were being supervised in other states while that state was supervising only 916 out-of-state clients.[25] The same problem occurred in Arizona where 982 offenders had been accepted for local supervision and more than 1,100 had been accepted for out-of-state caseloads. The statistics kept on out-of-state transfers often demonstrate distinct patterns. For example, Texas and California send most of their cases to each other, whereas Michigan, Massachusetts, and Maine receive most of their cases from Florida. Otherwise, most transfer relationships are between neighboring states such as Georgia and Alabama, and Missouri and Kansas.

SUMMARY

There are many different approaches to the organization and structure of community corrections systems. Historical, political, and economic influences shape the lines of authority controlling community corrections functions. In most cases, community corrections responsibilities lie either with a state agency or a county court, and sometimes these responsibilities may be divided between separate agencies for juveniles and for adults. As a rule, states with large offender populations are also more likely to have more layers of administration and bureaucracy than are states with fewer persons to be serviced.

Community corrections systems must depend on a variety of related governmental agencies within which its mission and goals are inextricably woven. These complex organizations of networking agencies must also be flexible as resources and populations change.

The use of shock probation, subsidy funding, and the interstate compact are examples of programs that rely on the interrelationship between the state and local corrections agencies and between states. The mutual interests and needs of these agencies also allow for the development of standards for operating and evaluating community corrections programs.

KEY TERMS

community-run programs   grant
community-placed programs   award
community-based programs   reimbursement
decentralized systems   calculated sum
determinate sentence   accreditation
shock probation   Interstate Compact
subsidy

DISCUSSION QUESTIONS

1. Describe the structural model that is followed by your state for the organization of its community corrections system.
2. Discuss the legal and ethical dilemmas posed by the use of the Interstate Compact for transferring the supervision of probation and parole clients? Do the benefits seem to outweigh the problems?
3. Is the payment of community corrections subsidies a viable funding strategy from the state's perspective? Why or why not?
4. What are the potential problems related to the use of statewide and even national standards for the operation of community corrections programs?

END NOTES

1. Duffee, David, and Edmund McGarrell (1990). Community corrections: A community field approach. Cincinatti: Anderson, pp. 30–32.
2. Bennett, Susan (1990). "Community organizing and implementation of the community response to drug abuse program." Paper presented at the annual meeting of the American Society of Criminology, Baltimore.
3. Sharp, Ray, and Eugene Moore (1988). The early offender project: A community-based program for high risk youth. *Juvenile and Family Court Journal* 39(1): 13–20.
4. Bowling, Linda (1987). Day treatment for juveniles: A boon in bluegrass country. *Corrections Today* 49(3): 104–106.
5. Colorado Department of Corrections (1987). *Annual report, FY 1985–86.* Colorado Springs, CO.
6. Smith, William, Edward Rhine, and Ronald Jackson (1989). Parole practices in the United States. *Corrections Today* 51(6): 22–24.
7. Clear, Todd, and George Cole (1990). *American corrections*, 2nd ed. Pacific Grove, CA: Brooks Solidus Cole.
8. Hurst, Hunter, and Louis McHardy (1991). Juvenile justice and the blind lady." *Federal Probation*, 55(2): 63–68.
9. Clear and Cole, *American corrections*.
10. Martinson, Robert, and Judith Wilkes (July 18, 1977). *Criminal Justice Newsletter* 8(15):7.

11. Vito, Gennaro (1984). Developments in shock probation. *Federal Probation* 48(2): 22–27.

12. Texas Department of Corrections (1982). Division of Data Services, Huntsville, Texas, p. 6.

13. Arola, Terryl (1991). Minnesota corrections: Perspectives from probation and parole officers. *Corrections Today* 53(2): 228–230.

14. Zahnow, Stacy (1991). Minnesota corrections: Perspectives from probation and parole officers. *Corrections Today* 53(2): 228–230.

15. Indiana Department of Corrections. *Annual report fiscal year 1987–88.* Indianapolis.

16. McSparron, James (1980). Community correction and diversion. *Crime and Delinquency* 26(2):226–247.

17. Ibid.

18. Bloom, Barbara (1990). Community corrections: Expanding community-based alternatives. Report to Assembly Public Safety Committee. Petaluma, CA: Barbara Bloom and Associates, p. 1.

19. Center on Administration of Criminal Justice (1977). *An evaluation of the California probation subsidy program: A summary.* Davis, CA; Univ. of California, p. 16.

20. Minnesota Department of Corrections (1990). *1987–88 Biennial report.* St. Paul, MN.

21. Kansas Department of Corrections (1990). *Annual report on community corrections.* Topeka, KN.

22. Musheno, Michael, Dennis Palumbo, Steven Moody, and James Levine (1989). Community corrections as an organizational innovation: What works and why. *Journal of Research in Crime and Delinquency* 26(2): 136–167.

23. Stratham, J. (1981). *Minnesota community corrections act evaluation.* St. Paul, MN: Department of Corrections Crime Control Planning Board.

24. California Department of Alcohol and Drug Programs (1982). *Task force report AB 541, first offender program.* Sacramento: Report to the Legislature, State of California.

25. Mississippi Department of Corrections (1988). *Annual report FY 1987.* Jackson, MS.

Adult Community Corrections Programs

CHAPTER 4

Incarceration Alternatives

There is but one sound argument in favor of probation, outside of the economic one frequently advanced, and that is that, rightly administered, it substitutes intelligence and humanity for ignorance and brutality in the treatment of offenders.[1]

— *Sheldon Glueck, Criminologist, 1933*

PURPOSE

This chapter presents an overview of alternative sentences currently used with adult offenders. One of the more popular methods for determining appropriate correctional programming, the case classification method, is discussed in detail. The various models for predicting probation and parole performance, including risk assessment, are highlighted. The chapter emphasizes the moral, ethical, and scientific difficulties in trying to use standardized formulas to predict human behavior. Focusing on the most commonly used sanction, probation, the chapter includes a history of probation in the United States. A more in-depth discussion of probation follows, including the various forms used today. Examples are given of the most common contract terms used in supervision agreements. The chapter concludes with a close examination of current probation programs that highlights the cost of the various programs, the problems that arise, and the difference between the performance of men and women clients.

OBJECTIVES

After you have finished this chapter, you should be able to do the following:

1. Describe research findings on the success of alternative sentences.

2. Outline the important historic events in the development of contemporary probation programs.

3. Discuss the various levels of supervision that may be imposed on offenders with community sentences.

4. Explain how the different kinds of alternative sentences compare to the cost of incarceration.

INTRODUCTION

The auditorium was hot and crowded. The music blared, and hundreds of fans pressed against the barricades that separated them from the stage. The star, Vanilla Ice, invited the frenzied youths into the aisles closer to the front. The brass rails snapped, the fire codes were violated, and Vanilla Ice was placed on four months of probation. The chart-topping rapper was also required to pay $500 for the ordinance violations. However, the fine will be suspended if the performer successfully completes his probation.

Every year thousands of people, even some celebrities, are placed on probation. The popularity of probation is linked to several beliefs about its benefits. First, it is anticipated that punishment in the community will spare an offender the negative and debilitating effects of prison. Second, it is commonly accepted that community sentences are less expensive to operate than prisons and jails. Third, the offender is punished locally and allowed to repay the damages directly to the community in a variety of sentencing options.

Many experts feel that by working and receiving treatment in the community an offender has more potential for meaningful rehabilitation or for the mastery of basic social and vocational skills. For famous figures like Vanilla Ice, authorities claim that their influence over others in potentially dangerous circumstances cannot be ignored or trivialized. It is hoped that the negative publicity of an arrest will lead to future caution that may prevent a tragedy.

ALTERNATIVE SENTENCES: PROBATION

As discussed earlier, a judge has several options in sentencing a convicted offender. The first decision is whether the convicted person should be incarcerated or allowed to serve out a sentence on community supervision. The decision to allow the offender to remain in the community is based on the perceived risk that the person represents to the community. Also considered is the likelihood that a community supervision program will properly address his or her needs. In addition, the judge weighs public sentiment about the seriousness of the crime committed and the usefulness of incarceration for each particular offender.

Once the judge has decided that community supervision is appropriate, there are several program options to evaluate. The availability of programs and resources that match the needs of each client is also a critical factor. In designing a community supervision plan, the court balances the concerns of the community with the needs of the offender. A sentence may include punitive measures designed to deter future crime, or it may include rehabilitative and treatment aspects designed to encourage law-abiding behavior. Some of the options available include restitution, community service, fines, electronic monitoring, probation, and intensive supervision. Each of these sentencing options may be selected alone or in combination with other requirements. Chapters 4 through 7 describe these program options in detail.

One of the first documented cases of community supervision being granted on a regular basis was in Boston, Massachusetts, in the 1840s. A shoemaker named *John Augustus* would bail out drunks. In his own home, he would care for them and assist them in finding work. It is recorded that over the years he bailed out and supervised more than 2000 persons. His dedication to this practice earned him the nickname of *"Father of Probation."*

Perhaps the most significant aspect of John Augustus' work is that many of the procedures he used in working with offenders in the early nineteenth century are used in *probation* today. Reports of Augustus' interaction with the court show that he conducted careful screening and investigation of potential cases. His techniques of supervision included helping offenders find housing, education, and work. He also developed a system of making progress reports to the court. In fact, those reports show that of his first 1100 cases, only one forfeited bond.[2]

Throughout the remainder of the nineteenth century, defendants were released on their own recognizance on an informal basis in their state courts. Others like John Augustus volunteered to supervise clients who were mostly petty thieves, down-and-outs, the uneducated, and the unskilled. The first paid probation officer to serve the court was authorized by law in Massachusetts in 1878.[3]

In jurisdictions where probation was used, judges treated community supervision terms like suspended sentences. However, it was not long before prosecutors began raising questions about the constitutionality of such a practice. Some prosecutors felt that the court had an obligation to impose a sentence on persons found guilty and that to suspend the sentence was to subvert the law. Proponents of the new suspended terms argued that the practice was like the court using its authority to grant a judicial reprieve.

This issue was initially brought before the court in 1894 when a district attorney appealed a suspended sentence that had resulted in probation. The prosecutor's appeal is known as *People ex rel Forsyth* v. *Court of Sessions*. Although the court decided in favor of the practice of probation, many states quickly passed legislation making the practice official by statute. Such state legislation ensured the legitimate basis of probation against future legal attacks. In New York such legislation was enacted in 1901. This state statute directed judges to appoint a person to act as a probation officer. The act suggested that officers might be selected from "among private citizens, male or female, from clerks of the district attorney's office in the county where the court making the appointment was held. In addition, any police officer, constable, or peace officer could also be appointed as a probation officer."[4]

This period of dramatic changes in penal laws and social policies from approximately 1900 to 1930 is known as the progressive era in criminal justice. As Dean-Myrda and Cullen explain, progressive reformers of this time held three major beliefs that made the movement away from incarceration toward community corrections seem logical.[5] The first belief was that treatment was more important than punishment. The second belief was that individualized treatment approaches were best. Sentences of indeterminate length would allow an offender to be on a rehabilitation program designed specifically for that person. In addition, this reform program would progress at the offender's own pace. Third, the progressives believed that the state would use its authority to do good. These reformers trusted that the state would always act with the best interests of the offender in mind. They also believed that the state would not abuse its discretion.

As a result of this progressive spirit, states across the country enacted legislation to formalize a probation system. By 1900 seven states had probation statutes. By 1915 the number of states with similar programs had grown to 33. Although all states had some form of juvenile probation by 1927, adult probation was not a regular service in every state until 1956.[6]

Federal Probation

The adoption of a formal system of probation occurred much later for the federal courts than for the states, probably because the federal courts processed far fewer offenders. They were not burdened by as large a convicted population as were the states. There were fewer federal laws and thus fewer federal violations that one could conceivably commit. The slow development of the federal corrections system is evidenced by the fact that the government boarded its prisoners in local jails and did not even build a federal prison until 1895—almost seventy years after states began constructing prisons.

Like the states, then, federal judges began slowly and informally to seek appropriate sentences for a wide range of offenders. Many of the convicted appeared to be good candidates for community supervision. Practices like probation were used by the federal courts until challenged in 1916 when the U.S. attorney general asked the courts to vacate the judgment on a case in which a suspended sentence had been imposed. In this decision, often called the *Killits Decision*, the Supreme Court agreed with the government's attorney. The judges held that it was not within the power of the federal courts to suspend a sentence.

Although the decision in *Killits* formally stopped the practice of federal probation, it was continued informally by judges who devised alternative methods for giving conditions similar to probation. For example, some judges would continue cases for several months while the defendants had an opportunity to pay back victims, find jobs, or become sober.

   The benefits of probation for the federal courts were not lost on the National Probation Association and other penal reformers of this time. Soon their campaign to renew probation legally was revived. Finally, in 1925 Congress passed the Federal Probation Act. Although the message of the act was significant, Congress appropriated very little money with which to establish a probation system. Each judge was limited to only one probation officer who was placed under the Civil Service. There was enough money to hire only eight probation officers, so most of the other 130 judges relied on volunteers. In the early stages of federal probation, as many as 40,000 people were supervised by volunteers. Probation still lacked the support of the attorney general who referred to the program as "part of a wave of maudlin rot of misplaced sympathy for criminals that is going over the country."[7]

The Development of a Professional Probation Staff

As probation caseloads grew, it became obvious that volunteer staff alone could not meet the needs of the courts. In New York, officers from Catholic, Protestant, and Jewish societies served as probation officers.[8] Wealthy private citizens were encouraged to donate funds to pay the salaries of workers in the probation movement. In addition, police were reassigned to function as probation officers while continuing to draw their pay as municipal employees. As Lindner and Savarese explain, "The most striking characteristic of these early probation officers was, without any doubt, their tremendous dissimilarity to each other. Their selection as a probation officer was often an accident of history wholly dependent upon the legislation within a particular jurisdiction. There was great variation among officers in terms of their educational and vocational preparation."[9]

Early Criticisms of Probation

According to some social historians, the development of probation programs was neither uniform nor smooth. As Rothman notes, probation spread with no real thought.[10] It was implemented in a superficial, routine, and almost careless manner. It was an urban rather than a rural phenomenon. The popularity of probation in the cities was tied to its utility in plea bargaining during the 1920s and 1930s. A review of who received probation during this period appears to indicate that many serious charges were "bargained down" to make the burden of prosecutors and the courts easier.

The Controversy Over Success

By far the greatest criticisms of the practice of probation are related to the expectation of rehabilitation. The development of probation programs throughout the 1960s and 1970s had a strong rehabilitative emphasis. The media are quick to expose every probationer or parolee who engages in further criminal activity. In addition, critics point to the seemingly increasing crime, drug use, and aggregate recidivism rates as evidence that rehabilitation has failed.

There is little disagreement that the most pressing needs that probationers have are financial aid, housing, employment, and obtaining educational and vocational credentials.[11] It has also been shown that there is a direct correlation between receiving services addressing these needs and being successful on probation.[12] However, there is a desperate lack of these services. The few resources that are available to meet these needs are often poorly coordinated with probation agencies. As the General Accounting Office found "of the 250 cases identified as needing vocational training, 37 percent were referred to other agencies and 8 percent of the cases were handled by the probation officers. The other 55 percent either were not referred or sought services on their own. Of those in need, only 19 percent completed a (vocational) program. . . ."[13]

The Goals of Probation

With both funding and space for incarceration being limited, some criminologists feel that probation is a necessary strategy for relief. Others argue that offenders selected as suitable for probation are not the same as those who would normally go to prison and that probation would be misused as a mechanism for relieving otherwise crowded institutions.

In a recent survey conducted by Thomas Ellsworth, more than 700 probation professionals were questioned about the goals of probation. Given a number of rehabilitation and enforcement goals to choose from, respondents selected a balance of each as the most important for probation. Ellsworth believes that his findings demonstrate the existence of dual goals in probation. This is especially significant because much of the current literature seems to focus on the enforcement and control aspects of supervision. As Ellsworth explains:

> These findings give rise to the perception that while much of the rhetoric about community protection is operationalized in terms of statutory change, increased commitment rates to correctional facilities, and the use of new, innovative protective practices such as home detention, electronic monitors, and intensive supervision, much more of the rhetoric about community protection is simply that, rhetoric. Much about probation has changed over the last 10 years, but there appears to be a core element which has resisted change and continues to focus its energies in the direction of rehabilitation.[14]

Today, probation strategies appear to be focused on two levels. One is to grant probation only to low-risk, non-violent offenders, and the second is to exercise a greater degree of control over probationers with increased surveillance, intensive supervision, and technological advances in monitoring.

The Legal Basis of Probation

The power of the courts to suspend sentences and place defendants on probation comes from statutes. It is not a power vested naturally in the courts. The Supreme Court has held that probation should not be considered a form of "prison without walls" but, rather, a period of conditional liberty that is protected by due process.

By definition, *probation* is the suspension, or setting aside, of a sentence. Suspension results in the preservation of the individual's freedom in the community under professional supervision. The period of supervision imposes specific behavioral conditions on the offender in the form of an agreement, or contract. The contract includes provisions for the revocation of the community supervision for serious breaches of those conditions.

There are several points at which a probation sentence may begin. Although probation is always ordered at the time of sentencing, the date it begins may be delayed if the offender is initially incarcerated. When probation is granted in lieu of a prison or jail sentence, it usually begins right away. Otherwise, probation begins following the completion of a prison or jail sentence. Although people view *shock probation* as a mechanism that allows early release from prison, others see it as a probation sentence that starts out with a deterrent message about the realities of prison should the offender violate probation.

Typical Probation Contracts

Before an offender begins a term of probation, all the restrictions and conditions of this sentence are carefully discussed. Each probationer signs a contract that is an agreement to abide by whatever conditions are designated as necessary. There have been a few occasions on which offenders have found the conditions too restrictive and have opted to spend shorter periods in prison or jail instead.

The kinds of conditions imposed by the probation contract may be divided into two groups: those that attempt to *control* and those that attempt to *reform* the offender. Control conditions dictate the things that the offender may not do, where he or she may or may not go, and schedules of reporting. Reform conditions outline expectations for participation in education and counseling programs, family support, and a drug-and-alcohol-free lifestyle. Typical conditions that are imposed include the following:

- Violate no law.
- Report to the probation officer in person as directed.

- Cooperate with the probation officer in all rehabilitation plans.
- Do not leave the state without written permission from your probation officer.
- Keep your probation officer informed of your residence at all times.
- Seek and maintain gainful employment.
- Be at home at 10 P.M. Sunday through Thursday nights of the week and no later than 12 P.M. on Saturday and Sunday.
- Do not possess or have under your control any dangerous or deadly weapons.
- Submit to a search of your person or residence or property under your control at the direction of the probation office.
- Do not use or possess any controlled substance without a medication prescription and even then only after a written notice is given to the probation office by a physician.
- Submit to alcohol or controlled substance tests at the direction of the probation officer. Each test is subject to a $7.50 fee, which will be collected by the probation officer.
- Do not possess any drug paraphernalia, hypodermic needles, syringes, or any device used for sniffing or ingesting a controlled substance. Do not possess any chemical or lab equipment that could be used for the manufacture or sale of any type of controlled substance.
- Refrain from using alcoholic beverages or frequenting places where such beverages are the chief item of sale.
- Do not associate with convicted felons, users or sellers of controlled substances, the victim, or any codefendant.
- Carry a copy of the terms and conditions of probation on your person at all times and offer them to any peace officer, whether requested or not, upon contact with said peace officer.
- Maintain a complete list/inventory of your possessions and give a copy to your probation officer.
- Pay restitution.
- Pay court costs.

In addition, special conditions may be tailored to address specific characteristics of the offender or offense.

For sex offenses/prostitution:

- Have no association or contact with children under eighteen.
- Do not possess or have under your control any pornographic material.
- Do not solicit or accept rides.
- Do not occupy a hotel or motel room unless it is registered in your own name.
- Do not approach motorists or pedestrians not previously known to you and engage in conversation in a public place.

For business or credit offenses:

- Do not possess or use a credit card.
- Do not maintain a checking account or complete or endorse any checks unless they are made payable to yourself, and do not have any blank checks in your possession without permission of the probation officer.
- Submit a monthly record of income and expenditures to the probation office.

For drug-related crimes:

- Submit to AIDS testing.
- Do not sell or donate blood or plasma.
- Do not possess any portable or car telephone or any paging device.

For Auto theft, DWI, or other traffic-related crimes:

- Do not drive or possess keys to any automobile, truck, or motorcycle or other motor vehicle unless it is legally registered to you except in the course of employment and then only with written permission of the registered owner.
- Do not operate a motor vehicle unless properly licensed by the state department of motor vehicles.
- Surrender your driver's license to the court.

For Confessed or Suspected Gang Members:

- Do not wear clothing (badge, bandanna, button, cap, hat, scarf, or emblem) associated with gangs or make any gang hand signs.
- You shall not be present in any gang gathering area.
- Do not appear at any court building, including the lobby, hallway, courtroom or parking lot, unless you are a party, defendant, or subpoenaed witness in a court proceeding.
- You shall not be on any school campus or within one block radius of any school campus unless you are enrolled or with prior administrative permission from school authorities.

Overall, a probation contract should explain clearly which services the agency will provide and those that must be obtained through other resources. Service delivery often breaks down when clients are forced to seek out programming on their own without referrals. When clients feel abandoned, they are likely to become discouraged and fail.

The Use of Probation Today

Probation may be given for a wide variety of offenses. In California a mother was placed on three years of probation for failing to ensure that her two children attended school. Authorities alleged that the first- and third-grade children had been absent 38 days in the past two years. The children had also been tardy a number of times and had not been enrolled for three months during one period.[15] In Florida a 25-year-old woman convicted of delivering cocaine to her newborn baby through the umbilical cord when taking the drug herself received a 14-year probation term. An electrician in Indiana took money from two elderly couples and never completed the wiring on their homes. He received a five-year probation term.

A wide range of offenders—from those convicted of relatively minor to more serious crimes—are eligible for consideration for probation. The length of the sentences may vary as well as the conditions that may be imposed. In a sense, each probation contract is custom-tailored to meet the circumstances of the case at hand. One of the most important ways to make decisions about the kind of supervision that is appropriate is the use of a classification instrument. Such instruments are discussed on pages 97–103.

A Nationwide Report on Probation

The results of a federally funded study of 12,000 probationers sentenced in 1986 gives us a good look at the current trends in community corrections. The probation sentences examined came from 32 countries nationwide. The report was written by Mark Cunniff and Mary Shilton

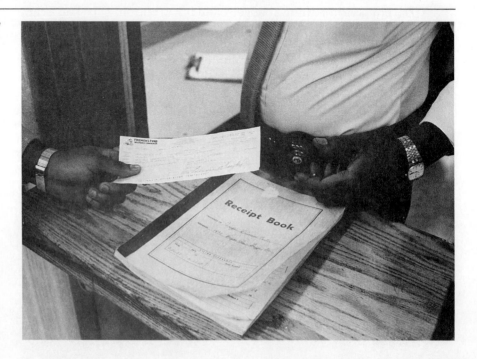

Most offenders have to pay some type of financial assessment as part of their community supervision contract. (*Courtesy of the Georgia Department of Corrections.*)

and published in 1991.[16] One part of the report focuses on the kinds of sanctions imposed on probationers.

Most probationers (85 percent) had to pay some kind of financial assessment as part of their contract. The assessments were most commonly in the form of court fees, supervision fees, and restitution. About half of all probationers in this study paid court fees, 32 percent paid supervision fees, and 29 percent paid restitution. The less frequent use of restitution does not imply that it is not a popular sanction, only that many offenders have committed crimes for which restitution, by definition, is not applicable. Such offenses include possession of weapons, prostitution, and possession and sale of narcotics.

Also explained in the study was that half of those offenders sentenced to probation were also required to serve some time in jail. The use of combined sentences indicates that probation is not simply an alternative to incarceration but part of a sentencing strategy that may also rely on incarceration. Community service was required of 12 percent of those studied, and drug testing was mandatory for about one-third. Drug and alcohol treatment was instituted in the plans of 41 percent of the offenders, and 12 percent were ordered into mental health counseling. A tendency for contracts to require offenders to obtain at least a GED high school equivalency has been noted in the past decade.

The Development of Classification Systems

In 1973 the Wisconsin Bureau of Probation requested thirty-seven new positions to reduce the high ratio of clients to officers. In the state's 1973 budget, the positions were granted, but the legislature also mandated that the bureau implement a workload inventory system and specialized caseloads. This resulted in the Case Classification/Staff Development Project, which received federal funding under the Law Enforcement Assistance Administration. The system was implemented in 1975 and was composed of four elements:

1. An offender risk assessment scale.
2. An offender needs assessment scale.
3. A workload budgeting and deployment system.
4. A management information system.[17]

The Wisconsin model was viewed by the National Institute of Corrections (NIC) as a well-researched and adaptable system. In 1981 the Wisconsin system was adopted as a model probation system by the NIC. The model uses predictive classification assignments to differentiate between offender groups as to the likelihood of recidivism. Such predictions are of great value to the probation administrator faced with limited resources and a desire to concentrate those resources in the most efficient and effective manner. As a result, offender classification has gained widespread acceptance among probation departments. The vast majority of agencies have some form of formal, "paper drive" classification system.[18] In California, for example, most county probation departments have adopted a classification system for their adult caseloads and are moving toward an adoption of classification for juvenile caseloads.

Case Classification

When someone is sentenced to probation, the agency begins an assessment process that develops an individualized supervision plan. This process is often referred to as *case classification*. The two primary goals of case classification are identifying client needs and assigning each person to the appropriate level of supervision. Assignment to a particular level of supervision, such as intensive supervision or minimum supervision, is generally determined by the probation department following the grant of probation. However, in more serious cases, the sentencing judge may request a higher level of supervision.

Case classification occurs as the result of an assessment of a client's risk to the community or his or her needs for services. Assessment has historically been the result of the intuitive judgment of the probation officer. Formal instruments of risk assessment and classification have been designed to eliminate the subjective nature of judgments that officers often made about the predicted behavior of their clients. Preconceived ideas about certain offenders often cause an officer to focus on aspects of the client's life as indicators of risk. For example, some officers see the use of drugs and alcohol as a primary cause of delinquent behavior. These officers are likely to classify drug or alcohol users as having a high-risk status and to minimize the problems of other offenders who are equally involved in crime but who do not use drugs or alcohol.

The use of drugs or alcohol is only one variable that contributes to an offender's probability of success, and it must be weighed appropriately with other variables. For this purpose, actuarial scales (risk instruments) have been constructed. When applied accurately, these scales do a much better job of predicting which offenders are likely to fail and which are likely to succeed. Classifying offenders into caseloads of high, medium, and low supervision by means of these instruments is far superior to officer judgment. The scales consider many variables and are weighted such that the predictive ability of each variable is considered in correct proportion to all others.

In the past decade, most departments have developed their own standardized risk-assessment scales that consist of two sets of variables. One set (risk predictors) is statistically linked to the probability that the client will reoffend. The second set (need variables) consists of measures of social deficiencies that indicate the level and nature of intervention services.

BOX 4–1

A Typical Needs Assessment Scoresheet*

Academic/vocational skills   Score ____
- (−1) high school or above skill level
- (0) adequate skills for everyday
- (+2) low skills - minor adjustment problems
- (+4) minimal skills - major adjustment problems

Employment   ____
- (−1) satisfactory employment, 1 year +
- (0) secure employment, student, retired, homemaker
- (+3) unsatisfactory employment but has adequate skills
- (+6) unemployed, unemployable, no skills

Financial Management   ____
- (−1) good credit, long-term self-sufficiency
- (0) no current difficulties
- (+3) situational or minor difficulties
- (+5) severe difficulties/bad checks, credit

Marital/Family Relations   ____
- (−1) strong relationships and support
- (0) relatively stable relationships
- (+3) some disorganization but could improve
- (+5) major disorganization and stress

Companions   ____
- (−1) good support and influence
- (0) no adverse relationships
- (+2) associations w/occasional negative results
- (+4) associations almost all negative

Emotional Stability   ____
- (−2) exceptionally well adjusted, responsible
- (0) no symptoms of emotional instability
- (+4) symptoms limit but do not prohibit functioning
- (+7) symptoms prohibit adequate function (anger or retreat)

Alcohol Usage   Score ____
- (0) no interference with functioning
- (+3) occasional abuse, some function disruption
- (+6) frequent abuse, disruption, needs treatment

Other Drug Use   ____
- (0) no interference with functioning
- (+3) occasional abuse, some function disruption
- (+5) frequent abuse, disruption, needs treatment

Mental Ability   ____
- (0) able to function independently
- (+3) some need for aid, potential for adjustment may be mildly retarded
- (+6) severe deficiencies, limits to independent functioning

Health   ____
- (0) sound physical health, seldom ill
- (+1) handicap or illness interferes with functioning on a regular basis
- (+2) serious handicap or chronic illness

Sexual Behavior   ____
- (0) no apparent dysfunction
- (+3) real or perceived situational or minor problems
- (+5) real or perceived chronic or severe problems

Overall Assessment of Needs   ____
- (−1) Well adjusted
- (0) No needs
- (+3) Moderate needs
- (+5) High needs

TOTAL SCORE   ____

*Sample constructed from a review of ten risk assessment instruments used nationwide.

The information obtained in the assessment process is used to direct offenders into the most appropriate programming. Assessments can be treatment oriented in that they indicate those deficiencies in medical, psychological, emotional, and life skills with which the offender may need assistance. A client may be directed toward drug treatment or educational programs that are based on the assessment of needs. An example of a survey of needs assessment is given in Box 4–1. The other method of classification involves assigning clients to various levels of supervision according to their perceived degree of risk. However, classification in this area is hardly an exact science. For example, if we understood exactly what it is that makes people obey the rules of society and if one factor could explain law-abiding behavior in everyone, then we could simply test each probation candidate for the level of this factor. Those persons who scored highest on measures of this factor would be considered the best risks for community supervision.

As it is, we have only selected a pool of variables that we think best predicts success under community supervision. Higher levels of supervision, including more restrictions, are usually imposed on those offenders who scored highest on the scales for risk assessment. The level of risk is usually derived by using a point scale that measures traits such as age at sentencing, number of prior felony convictions, drug abuse history, employment history, and the number of address changes in the year before sentencing. The assignment to caseloads of maximum or minimum supervision is usually done by determining a number of points that distinguish high- from low-risk offenders. Someone with a score of 25 on a 30-point scale may be assigned to a small, intensively supervised group. Another offender with a score only a point or two lower may be assigned to a caseload with much less contact with the supervisor. An example of a risk assessment scale is given in Box 4–2.

In Texas, risk assessments are mandated by law to allow the state to evaluate whether community programs are servicing the populations for which they were designed. The state's interest in such evaluation is tied to the annual grant payments made to community corrections facilities. The results of these evaluations demonstrate whether the community agencies are serving the appropriate risk categories of offenders. Some high-risk offenders may be a threat to the safety of the community and may be assigned to more secure correctional environments.[19]

The risk assessment instrument used in Texas is alleged to be very accurate in predicting outcomes on probation. According to Longmire and Schauer, those probationers identified as posing minimum risks are much less likely to fail on supervision than those assigned as medium or maximum.[20] In addition, probationers at the medium level are more successful than risk cases at the maximum level. Much the same format is used in Illinois. The instrument employed there measures only factors that have been shown to be predictive of probation outcome. A study of the Illinois classification process found that high-risk cases were nearly

BOX 4–2

A Typical Risk Assessment Scoresheet*

Area	Score
Attitude	___

- (0) Motivated to change, receptive to help
- (1) somewhat motivated but dependent
- (2) rationalize behavior, unwilling to change

Age at first adjudication of guilt ___
- (0) 24 or older
- (1) 20–23
- (2) 19 or younger

Number of prior terms adult or juvenile probation/parole ___
- (0) none
- (1) one or more

Number of prior adult or juvenile revocations ___
- (0) none
- (1) one or more

Number of prior felony adjudications of guilt or juvenile commitments ___
- (0) none
- (1) one
- (2) two or more

Adult or juvenile adjudication for ___
- (0) none
- (1) burglary, theft, auto theft, robbery
- (2) worthless checks or forgery
- (3) both of the above

Area	Score
Adult or juvenile adjudications for assaultive offense within the last five years	___

- (0) no
- (1) yes

Number of address changes in last 12 months ___
- (0) none
- (1) one
- (2) two or more

Percentage of time employed last 12 months ___
- (0) 60% or more
- (1) 40–59%
- (2) Under 40%
- (0) not applicable

Alcohol Usage problems ___
- (0) no interference with functioning
- (1) occasional abuse, some disruptive
- (2) frequent serious abuse, needs treatment

Other drug use problems ___
- (0) no interference with functioning
- (1) occasional abuse, some disruptive
- (2) frequent serious abuse, needs treatment

TOTAL SCORE   ___

*Sample constructed from a review of ten risk assessment instruments used nationwide.

three times as likely to have major adjustment problems than did lower-risk cases.[21]

The National Institute of Corrections (NIC) has developed a model to demonstrate how the risk/needs classification process attempts to direct cases to levels of supervision. Risk/needs classification is used primarily to determine the *quantity* of supervision a client will receive. After that, case management classification (CMC) determines the *quality* of services a client needs. The CMC consists of a 45-minute interview that follows a specific set of questions. The scoring of this questionnaire suggests to the officer the kind of services the agency should deliver to the probationer.

The CMC process designates four kinds of offenders: *selective intervention* (SI), *casework control* (CC), *environmental structuring* (ES), and *limit setting* (LS). Probationers on selective intervention require the least agency intervention. Their crimes are frequently precipitated by situational circumstances. Their social abilities are good. Their family and other support structures are also adequate, as are their educational and employment skills. In contrast, individuals on casework control require substantial agency services and support from various community resources. Drug-dependent personalities are found in this group. Their crimes may be directly linked to their social problems, and successful rehabilitation requires effective treatment and control of these problems.

Cases on environmental structuring suffer from significant social inadequacies. They may be of low intelligence or may have very poor social skills. They are frequently illiterate and have few employable skills. They require substantial services to ameliorate their problems and allow them to function in society. The limit setting category includes those individuals who are strongly oriented toward a criminal lifestyle. These clients are manipulative and committed to crime as a way of life. The appropriate response to this group of offenders involves limited social services but a high level of surveillance and enforcement of the conditions of probation.

Because of limited resources, many probation departments that have adopted the NIC model only apply the CMC to those cases that score as maximum on the risk/needs assessment. After classification, these high-risk cases are assigned to intensive supervision probation (ISP). Under these programs, caseloads are kept small so that officers can provide the maximum level of surveillance and service. Cases classified as regular or minimum on the risk/need assessment may be assigned to limited supervision (LTD). Contact with such probationers is minimal because the caseloads may run from a few hundred to more then a thousand individuals. Microcomputers have recently been employed in these LTD caseloads to assist officers in keeping track of such things as fine payments, counseling contracts, and other court directives. The computers also provide reminder reports to officers to assist them in following up on court dates and other events that could easily be lost in the paperwork shuffle of such large numbers of cases.

Information about cases at all levels of supervision is fed into a management information system (MIS), which provides important data to all levels of the departments. These data are used to guide operations. The information fed into the MIS is compared to a *workload standard*. Workload standards are measures of the average time required to complete various tasks relating to a case. For example, a presentence investigation for the court may require 12 hours to complete. If an officer has 120 hours of actual time available each month (after subtracting vacation, sick leave, and administrative duties), he or she can complete 10 investigations a month. Similarly, each maximum supervision case may require 8 hours of officer time a month to provide the high levels of contact and service established for these cases. An ISP officer could then provide this level of service to only 15 clients.

The management information system processes data about the number and nature of cases in the department and compares this information to the already established workload standard. The resulting analysis tells department management the number of cases that can be served at the various levels of supervision, given the staff resources available. This information allows the department administration to manipulate assignment of staff for the most effective deployment of resources. It is then hoped that the department will be able to focus the resources on their priority functions. The information developed in the MIS also facilitates long-term planning and provides a database for the evaluation of departmental programs. The NIC model is displayed in Figure 4–1.

Controversies over Classification Models

Not everyone is pleased with the development of models that create formulas for work production and case classification. The idea of standardized amounts of time for the completion of tasks is in direct contrast to the belief that each case is individualized and each treatment plan unique. Some agencies are still small enough for staff to believe that they should have input into work division and resource allocation. There is often resentment of computer-generated solutions to problems of staffing and caseload management.

In addition, many officers see classification as an infringement on their "professional" discretion. In particular, officers with many years of experience believe in their own powers of judgment and instincts about a client. Consequently, there is a mistrust of the use of standardized classification instruments. In some cases, the standardized assessment tools were created by academics and researchers who are viewed by some practitioners as being out of touch with the real world. Consequently, many officers do not trust these instruments and prefer their own intuition concerning an offender's level of risk.

Caseload Sizes

The varying levels of intensity of probation supervision are characterized not only by the perceived level of risk in each case but also by the frequency of contact between the probation officer and the client. The level of intensity is reflected in the size of the caseload for which each probation officer is responsible.[22] The typical classification of caseload sizes are: ideal, intensive, normal, and minimum.

Figure 4.1

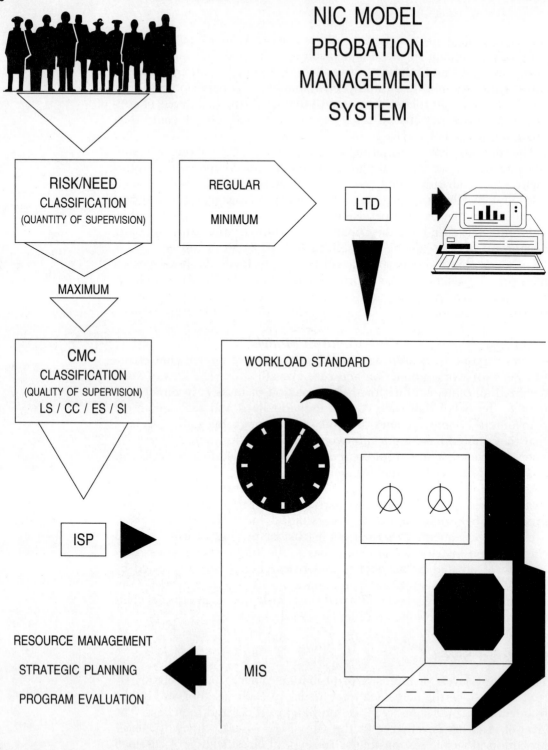

NIC MODEL PROBATION MANAGEMENT SYSTEM

RISK/NEED CLASSIFICATION (QUANTITY OF SUPERVISION)

REGULAR

MINIMUM

LTD

MAXIMUM

CMC CLASSIFICATION (QUALITY OF SUPERVISION) LS / CC / ES / SI

ISP

WORKLOAD STANDARD

RESOURCE MANAGEMENT

STRATEGIC PLANNING

PROGRAM EVALUATION

MIS

With an ideal caseload, the officer is able to provide maximum services to each client. Time and resources are sufficient to give each probationer the attention and assistance required. For the purpose of comparison, we will say that this ideal number is 50 clients.

An *intensive supervision* caseload requires officers to spend almost twice as much time with each offender as is spent with a normal caseload. Instead of two visits a month, for example, the client may be required to make four visits, and phone contacts may be required daily instead of weekly. Therefore, the caseload for this kind of client is approximately half of the ideal load, or 25 probationers.

A *normal* caseload more accurately reflects the status quo in probation today. Realistically, an officer has more clients than can be given adequate attention. Supervision checks are more likely to be periodic spot checks, and contacts are most likely made by phone. A normal caseload is twice that of an ideal load, so it averages about 100 clients. In fact, in 1989 the average probation caseload was 107 clients.[23]

Under extreme circumstances, such as sentencing overloads and understaffing, agencies may develop *minimum* caseloads of clients who have been proven to be trustworthy over a period and whose contacts have been reduced to monthly or bimonthly visits or even to phone calls or postcards. Many of these clients are finishing their terms of supervision

Community corrections workers complain that when caseload sizes get too high they are forced to spend less time counseling with and checking up on their clients. (*Courtesy of the Georgia Department of Corrections.*)

or have been assessed at the lowest risk levels possible. Under these circumstances, an officer may carry as many as 250 minimum supervision clients.

These caseload levels—normal, ideal, intensive, and minimum—were compared for client success in a study in San Francisco in the late 1960s. It was determined that probationers in minimum caseloads performed as well as those in normal caseloads, and that under intensive supervision, violations were not reduced. In fact, persons under intensive supervision had increased levels of noncriminal contract violations, such as failing to pay supervision fees and violating curfew. Researchers on the San Francisco project concluded that the level of supervision had little effect on the success of probation.[24]

The theory behind reduced caseloads is that officers will be able to spend more time checking up on and counseling offenders. However, there is some indication that reduced caseloads are more likely to result in officers' spending more time on their reports and paperwork than on anything else. It has been suggested that the officer role must be specifically redesigned to include more direct supervision time if that is to be the purpose of the caseload reductions.[25]

Size of the Probation Population

The number of offenders placed on probation in the United States grows every year. Probation is currently the most commonly used correctional disposition in this country. Roughly 80 percent of all persons convicted of misdemeanors and 60 percent of those convicted of felonies are sentenced to probation.[26] It is somewhat of a misnomer to refer to probation as an alternative to imprisonment because most of the offenders eligible for probation are convicted of less serious charges than are generally considered appropriate for incarceration.

In a study of 32 countries across the nation by Cunniff and Shilton, it was found that the percentage of felony sentences resulting in probation ranged from a high of 75 percent in Hennepin County, Minnesota, to a low of 30 percent in New York County.[27] Figures from a 1988 Bureau of Justice Statistics report show a record 2,356,483 probationers in this country, an increase of 4.9 percent over the previous year.[28] Of course, the rate of growth in probation is not the same across the nation. Percentage increases in probation populations can be misleading because states with small numbers of probationers will appear to have larger percentage increases when even a small number are added. Also, not every jurisdiction within a state is increasing its use of probation. In Houston, Texas, for example, the proportion of convictions that resulted in probation dropped from 36 percent in 1985 to 25 percent in 1988. In this part of Texas, there has been a dramatic decrease in the likelihood of drug offenders receiving probation.[29]

One of the best ways to compare the growth in probation populations among states is by using the ratio per 100,000 adults. Examining these figures, we find that the South has the highest probation figures—1,487 probationers per 100,000 adult residents. According to the Bureau of Justice Statistics, which accumulates these data, the ratio in the South in 1989 surpassed that for the Midwest by 358 persons, the Northeast by 355, and the West by 309.[30] The bureau also reported that the District of Columbia had the highest individual rate of persons on probation—2,587 per 100,000 adult residents. Georgia, Texas, Maryland, and Massachusetts also had more than 2,000 persons on probation for every 100,000 adult residents. At the end of 1988, Texas reported the largest number of persons on probation—nearly 289,000. Federal probationers accounted for 2.6 percent of the national caseload. During 1988 there were more than 1.4 million admissions to probation supervision. Of the reporting jurisdictions, Florida reported the largest number of entries (204,000). Entries to federal probation were 1.8 percent of the nation's admissions.

Profile of Probationers

The majority of probationers are white males. Fewer than half of probationers have a high school degree. Although women still comprise a small minority of those on probation, their offenses show a striking parallel to those of the male probation population. A recent study of female offenders on probation caseloads in Massachusetts revealed that, although the majority of women had been convicted of drug and property offenses, 16 percent were on probation for offenses involving violence. Roughly one-third of the women had been convicted of crimes against property—comparable to the offenses of male probationers. Females, however, were more likely than their male counterparts to be on probation for drug-related offenses—37 percent as compared to 23 percent. Female offenders also tended to be somewhat older than males on probation and made their first criminal court appearance later in life. Women also tended to have fewer prior convictions. As with male probationers, the female population tended to have serious problems with alcohol and drug abuse. However, females were more likely to be involved with drugs rather than with alcohol.[31]

Age and offense history are considered by practitioners to be indicators of the probability that a person will reoffend. Therefore, these variables are crucial in determining the amount of supervision and services that a probationer receives. Because female offenders are more often older and have fewer prior convictions, they tend to receive fewer probation services and a lower level of supervision. At the same time, female probationers tend to have high levels of service needs. Sixty-two percent of those examined in the Massachusetts study were drug and alcohol abusers.[32] Other needs of the female offender are likely to include education and employment training, child care, assistance in finding suitable housing, and counseling in family relations.

Cost of Probation

State and local governments operate more than 2,000 probation agencies nationwide.[33] According to probation expert Joan Petersilia, funding for probation services has not kept pace with the growing number of clients.[34] She explains that for every dollar spent in criminal justice, a quarter goes to corrections and only three cents of that quarter go to probation. Even though most criminal justice agencies nationwide have received increased budgets over the past ten years, probation is the only operation that has experienced financial cutbacks.

The Corrections Yearbook of 1985 reported that the cost of keeping a probationer on supervision for one year in the United States ranged from $156 in Connecticut to $1,500 in the federal system.[35] Most of the 44 states that reported costs averaged about $584 a year. As McDonald explains, it is difficult to evaluate the meaning of these figures because we really do not know what factors were taken into consideration in determining costs in each state.[36] That is, because there is no standard formula for determining the cost per probationer per year, it is difficult to compare one state's figures with another's. One system may actually compute the cost per offender per day on the basis of services rendered and salary of staff, whereas another jurisdiction may simply divide the total operating budget by the number of clients serviced.

Research on the Effectiveness of Probation

A study by Petersilia, Turner, Kahan, and Peterson tracked a group of felony probationers in Los Angeles over a 40-month period.[37] The researchers determined that 65 percent of the group were rearrested and 34 percent of that group received a term in jail or prison. Seventy-five percent of those rearrested were charged with burglary, robbery, or other violent crimes. The study concluded that most felony probationers were a significant threat to the community. It was also found that attempts to predict those who would be rearrested were only about 70 percent accurate. Therefore, it would not be easy to single out those most likely to reoffend while on probation.

The study by Petersilia identified four factors related to recidivism while on probation:

- *The kind of conviction*: property offenders had the highest recidivism rate, violent offenders were second highest, and drug offenders were third highest.

- *The number of prior juvenile and adult convictions*: the higher the number of priors, the more likely the probationer was to recidivate.
- *Income at arrest*: regardless of the amount of money a probationer is earning, any income at all is associated with lower rates of recidivism.
- *Household composition*: if a person is living with a spouse or children, he or she is more likely to be successful on probation.

In a study with somewhat different findings, Roundtree, Edwards, and Parker determined that the variables related to success on probation were the highest grade of school completed, prior criminal record, the age at first arrest, the number of prior arrests, whether the offense committed was a felony or misdemeanor, and the length of the probation sentence.[38] These researchers claimed that race, sex, age at which a person dropped out of school, age of the commission of the present offense, marital status, employment at the time of the offense, and the kind of offense were *not* related to success or failure on probation (see Table 4–1).

Several studies have been conducted that attempt to compare groups placed on probation alone with groups of probationers who receive some additional treatment or service. The purpose is to try to determine what enhancements might make probation more effective. Any condition that significantly improves the probability of success may then be required when appropriate. A number of strategies, such as polygraph monitoring and psychotherapy, have been attempted and examined.

Since the development of polygraph technology, judges have been attracted to the possibility of using or threatening to use polygraph tests on probationers or probation applicants. One judge believed that having potential probationers admit to all prior offenses, including those for which they had never been suspected, was a good way to start probation

Table 4–1 Variables Related to Success or Failure on Probation.

Factors Related to Failure	Factors Not Related to Failure
School grade completed	Race
Number prior arrests	Sex
Offender classification	Age of leaving school
Prior criminal record	Type of offense
Age at first arrest	Marital status
Length of probation term	Employed at time of offense
	Age at time of present offense

Source: Roundtree, Edwards, and Parker (1984).

off on a clean slate. In a study of offenders placed on probation and a comparable group on probation with polygraph monitoring, Abrams and Ogard found that those who were subject to polygraph monitoring had significantly lower rates of recidivism.[39]

In a study of sex offenders, one group was placed on intensive supervision probation and a comparable group on probation with group psychotherapy. The researchers found no significant differences in the recidivism rates of the two groups of sex offenders.[40] Because the rates of recidivism in both groups was fairly low (7.2 percent and 13.6 percent respectively), one could hypothesize that both intervention methods, intensive supervision and group psychotherapy, were fairly successful.

The Pitfalls of Probation: A Warning

In 1933 noted criminologist Sheldon Glueck outlined the pitfalls of probation as follows:

1. The danger of overselling or promising more than could be expected or delivered.
2. The danger of overemphasizing laws or "systems" rather than clients and qualified personnel.
3. The danger of operating without the intimate cooperation of existing social institutions or agencies.[41]

These potential problems are still relevant today. In fact, probation's weaknesses have been recently listed by Timothy Fitzharris. They include probation's unclear mission; overstated, unspecified, and unmeasurable objectives; a lack of strategic planning and effective management techniques; and a history of inadequate funding. Some of the suggestions for improvement by Fitzharris entail strong national leadership, an active clearinghouse of research and training resources, the development of formal and informal communication networks with the community, and a more aggressive approach to technical assistance and technology transfer.[42]

SUMMARY

Probation is one of the most common sentencing outcomes. Various punishments, such as fines, community service, and restitution, may be attached to a probation contract. And a number of restrictions, such as electronic monitoring, drug testing, and curfews, may be included in the term of probation. Probation supervision may be assigned in varying stages of intensity, and the requirements may be modified over time with good or bad behavior.

Probation sentences are often referred to as "middle range" sentencing options. By leaving the offender within the community, the sentence encourages the work ethic and personal responsibility while still inflicting a measure of punishment in the form of restrictions and accountability. Although the goal of probation is to serve justice by providing punishment and rehabilitation opportunities, it also provides protection for the community. Protection is usually achieved first by carefully screening the offenders considered for community supervision and then by closely monitoring them during the period of the sentence. The restrictive conditions imposed on the offender allow the supervising officer to exercise control over the offender and may also serve to promote habilitation and rehabilitation. The court may also order the probationer to attend treatments such as drug and alcohol counseling, family therapy, and/or educational and vocational programs.

A system of classification for probation cases has been adopted by community corrections agencies in an effort to provide greater efficiency and effectiveness in management. With the fast pace of growth in the client population occurring at a time when funding was leveled or reduced, managers were faced with difficult decisions. By distributing cases equally into large unmanageable caseloads, only minimal services could be provided to clients. An alternative was to select certain cases for high levels of service while providing minimal service to all others. Recognizing that some clients pose a greater threat to the community than others, this seemed a rational choice. However, the difficulty has always been selecting those clients that are of high risk.

Community corrections managers must skillfully blend the technology of case management with a humanistic understanding of the needs of both staff and clients. A scientific prediction of human behavior in any given instance is still only an educated guess. The "best way" to assign cases, determine risk, and evaluate client needs is an illusive concept that practitioners struggle with daily. Careful research can assist us in making our decisions more informed, more fair, and perhaps more effective.

CASES

People *ex rel Forsyth* v. *Court of Sessions*, 141 N.Y. 288, 36 N.E. 386 (1894).
Ex parte United States (Killits), 242 U.S. 27, 37 S.Ct. 72, 61 L.Ed. 129 (1916).

KEY TERMS

John Augustus
probation
shock probation

risk assessment
needs assessment
case classification

Case Management Classification
selective intervention
casework control
environmental structuring
limit setting
management information system

workload standard
ideal caseload
intensive supervision caseload
normal caseload
minimum caseload

DISCUSSION QUESTIONS

1. Examine the list of typical probation conditions. Which are control conditions and which are reform? Which would seem to have a greater likelihood of being violated?
2. As a probation officer, what methods would you use to detect violations of probation conditions? How could you assist the probationer in avoiding violations?
3. What factors would you use in a risk assessment scale? What variables would distinguish a high-risk case from a low-risk case?
4. Look at the needs assessment scoresheet in Table 4–1. What factors are given the most weight and why?

END NOTES

1. Glueck, Sheldon (1933). *Probation and criminal justice*. New York: Macmillan.
2. Allen, Harry, and Clifford Simonsen (1989). *Corrections in America*. New York: Macmillan, p. 193.
3. Clare, Paul, and John Kramer (1976). *Introduction to American corrections*. Boston: Holbrook Press, p. 74.
4. Lindner, Charles, and Margaret Savarese (1984). The evolution of probation. *Federal Probation* 48(1): 3–10.
5. Dean-Myrda, Mark, and Francis Cullen (1985). The panacea pendulum: An account of community as a response to crime, in *Probation, Parole and Community Corrections: A Reader*, ed. Lawrence Travis, pp. 9–29. Prospect Heights, IL: Waveland Press.
6. Allen and Simonsen, *Corrections in America*, p. 194.
7. Goldfarb, Ronald, and Linda Singer (1973). *After conviction*. New York: Simon & Schuster, p. 197.
8. Lindner and Savarese (1984). Supra note 4, p. 4.
9. Ibid., p. 5.
10. Rothman, David (1980). *Conscience and convenience: The asylum and its alternatives in progressive America*. Boston: Little, Brown.
11. Cromwell, Paul, George Killinger, Hazel Kerper, and C.D. Walker (1985). *Probation and parole in the criminal justice system*. St. Paul, MN: West Publishing.
12. Killinger, George, and Cromwell, Paul (1978). *Corrections in the community: Alternatives to imprisonment*. St. Paul, MN: West Publishing.
13. General Accounting Office (1976). *State and county probation systems in crisis*. Washington, DC: U.S. Government Printing Office, p. 4.

14. Ellsworth, Thomas (1990). Identifying the actual and preferred goals of adult probation. *Federal Probation* 54(2): 10–15.

15. Monteagudo, Luis (1990). Fontana mom prosecuted for children's absenteeism. *San Bernardino Sun,* 25 October: B1.

16. Cunniff, Mark, and Mary Shilton (1900). *A sentencing postscript II: Felony probationers under supervision in the community.* Washington, DC: Bureau of Justice Statistics, U.S. Department of Justice.

17. Baird, Christopher (1979). *Classification in probation and parole: A model systems approach.* Denver, CO: National Institute of Corrections.

18. Clear, Todd, and Kenneth Gallagher (1985). Classification devices in probation and parole supervision: An assessment of current methods. *Crime and Delinquency* 31: 424.

19. Komala, Merly, Val Shepperd, and Michele Moczygemba (1990). *The felony offender risk assessment study: Progress report.* Austin, TX: Community Justice Assistance Division, Texas Department of Criminal Justice, p. iv.

20. Longmire, Dennis, and Edward Schauer (1987). *The case classification system in Texas: Is it working?* Austin, TX: Texas Adult Probation Commission and Sam Houston State Univ.

21. Baird, Christopher, and Richard Prestine (1988). *Revalidation of the Illinois risk assessment system.* Madison, WI: National Council on Crime and Delinquency.

22. Lohman, John, A. Wahl, and R. M. Carter (1967). *The San Francisco Project, Research report No. 11: The intensive supervision caseload.* Berkeley, CA: Univ. of California School of Criminology.

23. Camp, George, and Camille Camp (1990). *The corrections yearbook: Probation and parole.* South Salem, NY: Criminal Justice Institute, p. 14.

24. Robison, J. O., Wilkins, R. M. Carter, and A. Walil (1969). The San Francisco Project: A study of federal probation and parole: Final report. Unpublished paper, San Francisco Project.

25. Glaser, Daniel (1983). Supervising offenders outside of prison, in *Crime and Public Policy,* ed. James Q. Wilson, pp. 207–227. San Francisco: Institute for Contemporary Studies.

26. Petersilia, Joan (1988). Probation reform, in *Controversial Issues in Crime and Justice,* ed. J. Scott, p. 168. Newbury Park, CA: Sage.

27. Cunniff and Shilton (1990). Supra note 17.

28. Bureau of Justice Statistics (1989). *Probation and parole 1988.* Washington, DC: U.S. Department of Justice, p. 1.

29. Golden, James, Kimberly Tester, and Margaret Farnworth (1990). Court responses to felony DWI and drug offenses in Harris County Texas, 1978 to 1988. Paper presented at the annual meeting of the American Society of Criminology, Baltimore, MD.

30. Bureau of Justice Statistics (1989). Supra note 28, p. 1.

31. Archibald, Matthew (1989). Women and crime: New perspectives. *APPA Perspectives* Summer: 29–30.

32. Ibid., pp. 29–30.

33. Bureau of Justice Statistics (1988). *Report to the nation on crime and justice.* Washington, DC: U.S. Department of Justice.

34. Petersilia, Joan (1988). Supra note 27, p. 169.

35. Camp and Camp (1985). *Corrections Yearbook,* pp. 74–75.

36. McDonald, Douglas (1989). The cost of corrections: In search of the bottom line. *Research in Corrections* 2(1): 1–25.

37. Petersilia, Joan, Susan Turner, James Kahan, and Joyce Peterson (1985). *Granting felons probation: Public risks and alternatives.* Santa Monica, CA: The Rand Corporation.

38. Roundtree, George, Dan Edwards, and Jack Parker (1984). A study of the personal characteristics of probationers as related to recidivism. *Journal of Offender Counseling, Services and Rehabilitation* 8: 53–61.

39. Abrams, S., and E. Ogard (1986). Polygraph surveillance of probationers. *Polygraph* 15(3): 174–182.

40. Romero, Joseph, and Linda Williams (1983). Group psychotherapy and intensive probation supervision with sex offenders: A comparative study. *Federal Probation* 47(4): 36–42.

41. Glueck, Sheldon (1933). Supra note 1, p. 9.

42. Fitzharris, Timothy (1984). The federal role in probation reform. In *Probation and Justice*, ed. Patrick McAnany, Douglas Thomson, and David Fogel, pp. 387–409. Cambridge, MA: Oelgeschlager, Gunn & Hain, Publishers.

House Arrest and Electronic Monitoring

I believe the collective we of which I am a member must remember who we are and who we deal with, and not be swept up by space-age technology, wartime "jingoism" and the unfounded promise of expedience and low cost at the expense of the social costs that prevail.[1]
— Gary Graham, Division Director, Adult Program Services
Administrative Office of Supreme Court of Arizona

PURPOSE

This chapter details the use of house arrest and the role that electronic monitoring (EM) plays as an alternative to institutional confinement. While not everyone on house arrest is electronically monitored, we consider all of those on monitoring systems to be on some form of house arrest. The legal and sociological issues concerning this type of programming are discussed. This includes how house arrest and electronic monitoring programs affect the offender, their families and society in general. The text explains the increase in the use of house arrest and electronic monitoring as well as variations in programs across the country. Finally, the chapter details the methods used to evaluate or measure the success of these programs.

OBJECTIVES

When you have completed this chapter, you should be able to do the following:

1. Understand the use of house arrest and electronic surveillance in various jurisdictions.

2. Be able to explain the constitutional issues surrounding the use of electronic monitoring.

3. Be prepared to discuss some of the advantages and disadvantages of using electronic monitoring in conjunction with house arrest.

4. Be able to outline the results of follow-up studies on the successes and failures of some of the electronic monitoring programs in current use.

INTRODUCTION

The use of *house arrest,* or *home confinement,* is not new. The concept has long been associated with the suppression of political enemies and radical thinkers. Galileo was confined to his home for making public his belief that the earth revolved around the sun, an idea contradictory to dominant religious thought at the time.[2] Other famous house arrestees include Czar Nicholas II of Russia and his family, Winnie Mandela in South Africa, Lech Walesa in Poland, and more recently Soviet President Mikhail Gorbachev during a short-lived Communist coup.

In the United States, the physical structure and orientation toward control of military bases make house arrest "or confinement to quarters" a practical and easily monitored procedure.[3] Under house arrest, a person has limited access to the outside world and a highly regimented schedule. It is easy to see why the military use of such a restriction is popular and effective. However, for the rest of modern society, home confinement on a large scale is unrealistic mainly because of the manpower and tools necessary to ensure the restraint of offenders.

LEVELS OF HOME CONFINEMENT

The level of home confinement varies depending on the goals of the program. There are three basic levels of home confinement that range from the least restrictive to the most restrictive. *Curfew* is the lowest level and is used in some intensive programs of probation supervision and work release. When given a curfew, the client is required to be at home after a certain hour. The curfew time may vary between weekday evenings and weekend evenings. Although curfews have been imposed on offenders as a condition of probation and parole for many years, electronic monitoring appears to be a way to improve on the enforceability of this sanction. Juveniles are more likely to receive curfew orders than adults are.

Home detention is a more restrictive level of confinement. This sanction allows the client to be away from home during certain blocks of time on a regular schedule—for example, hours for work, education, job training, counseling, and so on. For instance, participants may be expected to be at work from 8:00 A.M. until 5:00 P.M. on weekdays. They may also be scheduled to be away from 7:00 P.M. until 9:00 P.M. on Thursday evenings for a group counseling session. Regulations may also allow persons on monitoring to attend religious services on Saturdays or Sundays from 9:00 A.M. until 12:00 P.M.

The third level of confinement, *home incarceration,* is the most restrictive. This kind of house arrest requires the client to be at home at all times except for very specific and limited activities.[4] Those exempted activities may include medical or psychological treatment or visits to the probation department. A person may initially be placed on home incarceration and over time, graduate to less restrictive forms like home detention and curfew.

Joan Petersilia of the Rand Corporation estimates the number of people sentenced to house arrest in 1985 at 10,000.[5] One research report estimates that approximately 20 percent of those on house arrest are being electronically monitored.[6] Approximately two-thirds of all offenders placed on house arrest with monitoring devices are required to pay a fee for program participation.[7] They may also have to pay fines, make restitution, and perform community service.

FLORIDA'S HOUSE ARREST PROGRAM

Florida initiated a house arrest program from the enabling legislation of the Correctional Reform Act of 1983. The state's house arrest program was originally designed as a response to overcrowded prisons and jails, targeting offenders who would otherwise be incarcerated. Interestingly, however, a study by the National Council on Crime and Delinquency later reported that only about 53 percent of offenders in the program would have gone to prison had the program not existed.

As of June 1989, the house arrest program, known as Community Control, had an enrollment of more than 9,000 offenders called "controlees," of whom 340 were also being electronically monitored.[8]

Since its inception, the Florida Community Control Program has serviced approximately 48,000 felons.[9] Offenders are supervised by community control officers who work nights and weekends to monitor compliance. Participants are allowed to leave their homes only for court-approved employment, rehabilitation, or community service activities. In addition, persons in the program must provide free labor for public service projects and pay supervision fees ranging from $50 to $80 a month.[10]

Although Florida has the most active house arrest program in the country, many other states have developed similar activities. In some jurisdictions, house arrest programs for juveniles have been in operation longer than those for adults. In some places, such as Kenton County, Kentucky, house arrest is used only in conjunction with electronic monitoring.

THE USE OF ELECTRONIC MONITORING

Although the use of *electronic surveillance* was initiated, in the mid-1960s, it was not developed into a marketable product until almost fifteen years later.[11] When adequate telemetry technology was finally introduced, it renewed interest in home confinement. This idea was of particular concern to Judge Jack Love in New Mexico, who was searching for alternatives to incarceration. His state had recently experienced a brutal and bloody riot in the state penitentiary, and the judge believed that less serious offenders should not be exposed to such violence. Allegedly, the judge had been impressed by a comic strip in which Spiderman was tracked by a wrist transmitter. An engineer recruited by the judge is said to have designed the first *electronic monitoring* device, which was worn around the ankle.[12] In 1983 Judge Love pronounced the first sentence of electronically monitored home confinement.[13]

Electronic monitoring systems were designed to allow continuous surveillance of the offender through computer signals transmitted from the offender's home to the control station. Because electronic monitoring is now the basic tool used to ensure compliance with house arrest orders, the terms are often confused. It is important, therefore, to distinguish home confinement, or house arrest, as the broader program and the alternative to incarceration. Although not all house arrest programs employ electronic monitoring, most electronic monitoring is used for some kind of home confinement. Electronic surveillance is merely one means of monitoring the client's adherence to the terms of the home confinement sentence.

There is a variety of electronically monitored home confinement programs throughout the country. Programs differ in the kinds of offenders eligible to participate, the length of the terms spent on such a restriction, and the conditions imposed on participants. Electronic monitoring programs also vary in the kind of electronic equipment used, the agency that monitors the offenders, the cost for both the client and the agency, and the maximum number of participants in each area's program. A majority of the offenders in home confinement programs are required to work during the day and are restricted to their homes at night and on the weekends. While they are at home, the electronic devices ensure that they do not leave.

ELECTRONIC MONITORING EQUIPMENT

There are basically two types of electronic monitoring systems: *continuously signaling devices* and *programmed contact devices*. About 54 percent of the programs use a continuously signaling device that requires the offender to wear a transmitter that sends a radio signal to a receiver attached to the phone that communicates with a control computer at the central agency.[14] The receiver monitors the offender's transmitter unit, which is worn on the wrist or ankle. The offender's transmitter unit broadcasts an encoded signal to the receiver at regular intervals over a range of about 200 feet. Basically, the receiver tells the control computer if there have been any interruptions in its monitoring of the offender's transmitter. The control computer logs in all disruptions in communication between the transmitter and the receiver. Control computers are programmed with the offender's schedule so that it reports only absences or breaks in communication during unauthorized periods of time.

In the early generation of monitoring devices manufacturers experimented with a neck transmitter. This equipment had to be welded together, however, and it was too bulky to be considered practical. Although the neck transmitter was criticized as appearing to be too punitive, some authorities feel that the excess weight and size served as a good reminder to the offender of being monitored.

The psychological impact of the equipment on the wearer is an interesting aspect of monitoring that has not been well developed in research studies. Evaluators of one juvenile electronic monitoring program found that the youths used the bracelet as proof that they could not participate in delinquent activity regardless of peer pressure to do so. The bracelet made the youth's fears of being sent to the state school "believable to the other juveniles and they did not continue tempting the youth to go with them."[15]

The ankle transmitter is perhaps the equipment most preferred because it is less noticeable. One researcher for the Texas Youth Commission claimed that he wore the anklet transmitter as an experiment and it was several days before his wife even noticed it.[16] However, female offenders claim that the device is too conspicuous when they wear dresses. The

Probation officer explains the operation of the electronic monitoring device to his client as it is attached to the ankle. (© F. Paolini/Sygma)

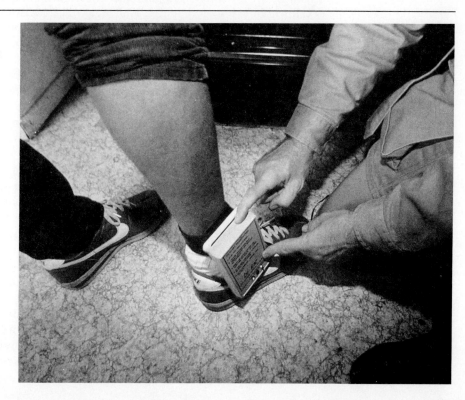

transmitters weigh approximately 6 ounces and are matchbox size. If the device is in any way tampered with, an alarm goes off on the receiving unit, which then signals the control computer.

In programmed contact systems, the control computer calls the offender at random intervals or at designated times and reports on the contacts. Computer print-outs generated at the central office record any abnormal activity, such as failures of telephone lines or electricity, tampering, or absences of the offender.

There are several kinds of programmed contact systems, each of which requires that a phone call be responded to by some action of the wearer. Some systems use voice verification that requires the offender to respond to several questions. Others are visual verification, an electronically transmitted snapshot of the person answering the phone. Still other systems require the respondent to insert a wrist device into a verifier box. The use of a verifier is described as follows:

> The inmate has 10 seconds to get to the telephone, state his name and the time into the receiver. Then he inserts the wrist transmitter into a slot on the verifier. The transmitter sends an electronic tone back to the computer, verifying that the correct monitor has responded to the phone call. . . If the wrist monitor doesn't activate the verifier or if the inmate doesn't answer the phone, the computer calls his home back within two minutes. If the second call goes unanswered, the computer makes a third call within two more minutes. If there is still no answer after three tries, the computer activates a pager worn by a sheriff's deputy who then drives to the inmate's home to check up on him.[17]

One advantage of this system is that the verifier can detect if the wearer is impaired. Appearance, voice, or difficulty inserting the wristlet (which may be an indicator of intoxication) can be signs of impairment. A disadvantage is that wearers will be disturbed at night by having to respond to the call. About 37 percent of all programs currently in operation use programmed contact devices.[18]

A third approach to electronic monitoring is to combine both a continuously signaling device and a programmed contact device in a hybrid system that has the advantages of each. Approximately 9 percent of programs have now adopted this kind of equipment.[19] As Schmidt explains, the hybrid model normally works like a continuously signalling device.[20] When the control computer is alerted to an unauthorized absence, however, it converts to a programmed contact device and calls the offender for a verification. If the offender fails to respond to the verification request, a violation note is made.

Proponents of electronic monitoring admit that the devices are not without error in identifying violations. Thunderstorms, failures or fluctuations in electronic power, and certain kinds of rooms (high levels of metal) or body positions (fetal) may trigger false reports. FM radio stations and cordless telephones can also interfere with the transmitter signal. Certain telephone features like call waiting and call forwarding can be used to trick the system. Therefore, officers often review phone bills to ensure that these services have not been installed.[21]

In one electronic monitoring program, operators reported that field monitoring units shorted out, water leaked into the battery (particularly in Florida), and some of the batteries corroded. In addition, spurious tamper signals resulted in officers responding to a number of false alarm calls.[22]

Joseph Vaughn, an electronic monitoring researcher, notes that the equipment is still fairly new and that reports on its durability are not available yet.[23] He speculates that wearing the devices on some parts of the body may result in more stress on the equipment than if worn elsewhere. This problem was noted in one program where the transmitter straps stretched, split, or became limber. In some cases, the bands stretched from 8.5 to 9.25 inches, allowing parolees to slip them off.[24]

Follow-up interviews with officers involved in an electronic monitoring program revealed that they were quite unprepared for the actual amount of time equipment problems would require. Although there was an awareness of the potential difficulties, officials found that telephone line compatibility, blocked signal transmissions, blotched computer output, software glitches, and general transmitter malfunctioning took up more time than anticipated.[25]

Over the past few years electronic monitoring technology has improved so much that the number of equipment problems has been significantly reduced. According to Schmidt, the transmitters "have been made smaller and their signals unique to one receiver/dialer so that if two offenders are in one location the signals can be distinguished. The computer programs now allow an offender's schedule to include leaving and returning several times in the same day, thus providing supervision staff with a clearer picture of the offender's activities."[26] Some systems are advertised as having the capability to transmit breath analysis on the spot for clients with histories of alcohol abuse.

According to some researchers, the rapidity of improvements and changes in electronic monitoring equipment has made it difficult to assess the quality of the products. As soon as equipment is thoroughly evaluated, the industry is able to claim that the materials are outdated and that the new equipment does not contain the earlier problems, thus necessitating a whole new round of evaluation studies. As one group of researchers noted:

> The evaluations of the present generation of equipment now being prepared by the National Institute of Justice will also be outdated by the time they are completed. Consequently, the manufacturers of electronic monitoring equipment are insulated from the results of technical reviews of their product as long as they continue to innovate.[27]

THE ELECTRONICALLY MONITORED POPULATION

A 1987 survey conducted by the National Institute of Justice found that twenty-one states had electronic monitoring programs with more than 800 offenders enrolled. By 1988 there were 2,300 offenders in 33 states in similar programs.[28] A year later, the number of people on electronically monitored home confinement was estimated at 7,200. The number of people estimated to be on electronic monitoring on any given day between 1986 and 1989 is shown in Figure 5–1. Estimates for 1991 place the daily number of offenders on electronic monitoring at somewhere between 12,000 and 14,000 people.[29]

As of this writing, all but three states have programs.[30] The number of offenders being supervised by electronic equipment is expected to double in 1992. This is a large population when you consider that the first assignment to electronic monitoring was not made until 1983.

Electronically monitored home confinement programs are not distributed evenly within the United States. In 1990 Michigan reported that in that state alone there were more than 2,000 offenders on electronic monitoring.[31] Together, Florida and Michigan account for almost 50 percent of all offenders on electronic monitoring.[32] However, California, Texas, Illinois, and North Carolina have also reported significant increases in the number of these programs.

Figure 5.1

Estimated daily monitored population in the United States, 1986–1989.

(*Source:* U.S. Department of Justice, National Institute of Justice, *Electronic Monitoring and Correctional Policy* by C. M. Friel, J. B. Vaughn, R. del Carmen; and *The Use of Electronic Monitoring by Criminal Justice Agencies*, 1988 by Annesley K. Schmidt; and the present 1989 survey.)

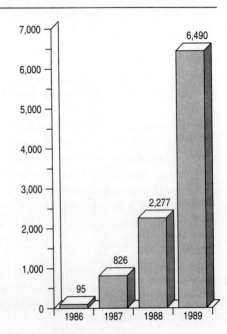

Table 5–1 Offense Categories of Individuals in Federal, State, and Local Electronic Monitoring Programs, 1987–1989

Offense Category	1987 (Percentage)	1988 (Percentage)	1989 (Percentage)
Against the person	5.6	9.7	11.8
Drugs	13.5	15.3	22.0
Fraud	3.3	3.8	2.3
Major traffic	33.4	25.6	18.9
Property	18.2	20.1	31.7
Sex	2.8	4.0	1.4[a]
Weapons	1.2	1.3	2.2
Multiple offenses	10.2	6.1	0.9[b]
Other	11.8	14.2	8.9
Total Offenders	823	2,274	1,320 (sample)

[a]Neither of the jurisdictions best known for the monitoring of sex offenders was included in the sample—this decline is likely an accident of sampling rather than a significant trend.

[b]The decline in "multiple offenses" is probably an artifact caused by form design. The 1989 form offered respondents an opportunity to precode responses and only limited space for multiple offenses.

Source: Renzema, Mark, and Skelton, David: *The Use of Electronic Monitoring by Criminal Justice Agencies*, 1989, Sec 3, p. 4. National Institute of Justice. Bureau of Prisons, Office of Research and Evaluation, Washington DC.

In 1990 the typical participant in an electronic monitoring program was a male, under thirty years of age, although the range in age was from 10 to 79 years.[33] In the past few years, there has been more use of house arrest with juveniles under the age of seventeen.

One-third of all offenders selected for home confinement are convicted of major traffic violations, particularly drunk driving. According to one study, however, electronic monitoring is now being used with perpetrators of the more serious offenses.[34] In Los Angeles a judge sentenced a prostitute with the AIDS virus to electronically monitored home confinement. Table 5–1 gives a breakdown of the offense categories for a sample of persons assigned to electronically monitored supervision that was drawn from all over the country.

In 1987, 75 percent of the offenders being electronically monitored were probationers. By 1989, the proportion of probationers was only 25 percent.[35] This means that electronic monitoring is being used for a greater variety of alternatives, including parole, juvenile diversion, and pre-trial release. Although half of the programs are operated by state and local correctional agencies such as probation and parole offices, 23 percent are contracted to a private monitoring service and the rest are operated by public agencies such as police, sheriffs, and the courts.

In conjunction with the U.S. Parole Commission and the Federal Probation System, the Federal Bureau of Prisons has developed its own electronic monitoring program. Under this new project, home confinement substitutes for the use of a halfway house for selected offenders being released from federal prison. Candidates selected for this early release program are technically on parole although they are supervised by the probation system. Participants are allowed to leave their homes only with advance approval and only for the purposes of employment or job search, essential shopping, medical treatment, or religious observances. A reward system is built into this program to enable successful clients to earn limited amounts of curfew leave for "constructive leisure time activities." These respites from house arrest can also be withdrawn as a sanction for violations of minor rules.[36]

The federal government claims that its house arrest program allows more offenders to be released from prison than if every offender had to wait for halfway house opportunities. However, authorities also admit that the house arrest method does not offer the full range of transitional services that would be provided in a residential center for community corrections. It may be theoretically possible, then, to distinguish between the levels of need in offender groups and to assign them to programs accordingly. In the initial operation of this federal electronically monitored program of house arrest, those offenders who were perceived as needing more assistance in readjusting to the community were placed, instead, in halfway houses.

The federal sentencing guidelines specifically reject home incarceration as an alternative to prison. The federal view is that house arrest and electronic monitoring should be approved only for offenders assigned to probation or some other form of conditional release. Thus, for federal officials, these programs are not an alternative to incarceration but an alternative method of community supervision.

Table 5–2   Types of Participant Restrictions in Three EM Programs[a]

Jurisdiction	Offenders Targeted	Offenders Excluded
Washtenaw Cty, MI	Felony offenders	Escape or assault history Narcotics dealers
Palm Beach Cty, FL	Selected work release	Sex offenders or those with crimes against persons
Kenton County, KY	Misdemeanants	Alcohol dependents

[a]Data compiled from separate reports from each of the jurisdictions.

Table 5–2 demonstrates some of the populations targeted for or excluded from electronic monitoring (EM) programs. Ironically, many programs do not accept drug and alcohol offenders, whereas others (e.g., Genessee County, Michigan) target that group out of their intensive supervision population.[37]

CHARACTERISTICS OF THE ELECTRONIC MONITORING SENTENCE

Most electronic monitoring programs are designed for relatively short durations (from a few weeks to six months). In a study of electronic monitoring programs throughout the country, it was determined that the average term was 79 days.[38] Under unusual circumstances, however, monitoring periods of as long as three years have been used. Such was the case of Charles Rothenberg, who spent almost seven years in prison for setting his son on fire in a failed murder and suicide attempt. When paroled, Rothenberg was required to stay away from his son, remain in his parole jurisdiction, have weekly psychiatric counseling sessions, be accompanied by a parole officer 24 hours a day, and wear an electronic surveillance bracelet for the three-year term. The extreme conditions in this case were a result of the pressure of public protest over his release.

As mentioned earlier, most programs of house arrest combined with electronic monitoring require the offender to contribute to the cost of supervision and equipment. Payments are deducted from the client's earnings. In some cases, rates are scaled according to income level, but in other jurisdictions the fees are the same for everyone. Table 5–3 demonstrates the range of fees assessed for participation in electronically monitored home confinement programs.

Under most state sentencing structures, only a judge may impose the requirement that an offender be electronically monitored at home. This issue was raised in *Carson* v. *State* when officials in Florida attempted to revoke a community control sentence because the defendant failed to

Table 5–3　Rates Paid by Offenders on EM in Five Jurisdictions Nationwide[a]

Jurisdiction	Offenders' Daily Pay
Orange County, CA	– $ 2.
St. Louis County, MO	– $ 4.
N. Humboldt Jud. Dist, CA	– $ 7.
Palm Beach County, FL	– $ 9.
Jefferson County, MO	– $ 10.

[a]Data compiled from separate reports from each of the jurisdictions.

wear an electronic monitoring device. Ruling in favor of the defendant, the court held that because the judge had not imposed the condition of wearing the devise, the state could not claim that the condition had been violated. Florida law at that time did not grant community officers the authority to impose electronic monitoring on those under their supervision.

CONSTITUTIONAL ISSUES IN THE USE OF ELECTRONIC SURVEILLANCE

When the constitutionality of electronic surveillance is questioned, the court must consider a number of issues. Some concerns relate to the expectations and standards of our society and some to the status of the convicted. The court looks first to prevailing social attitudes when deciding whether a punishment is equitable and humane. Over time, social values change, and court decisions attempt to conform with current norms. In attempts to mirror the values of society, judges will prohibit those practices that "shock the conscience of society." However, the court also realizes that the rights and freedoms a person expects to be afforded are limited or diminished if he or she is convicted. It is up to the courts, then, to determine how to restrict the convicted, what rights are to be limited, in what ways these rights can be limited, and which rights are fundamental and cannot be relinquished.

It is obvious that our society has grown more tolerant and complacent about the technological invasion of our privacy. We hardly notice that our persons and possessions are x-rayed in airports and banks, that store dressing rooms film our every move, that many business and entertainment facilities monitor us through two-way mirrors, and that our financial records are open to all who process our credit purchases. Because of society's ambivalence toward personal scrutiny in the guise of security or social control, it would seem difficult for offenders to challenge electronic monitoring as being unduly harsh or restrictive.

One of the basic questions that must be settled before any legal analysis of EM programs can be attempted is, "What is electronic monitoring?" Many criminal justice professionals as well as legal scholars do not agree on the nature and limits of this punishment.

In a 1990 Pennsylvania appeals case, *Commonwealth* v. *Kriston*, the justices found that electronic surveillance was not the same as imprisonment. An offender who was revoked from probation and incarcerated could not receive credit toward the discharge of his prison sentence for the time he had spent on house arrest. A majority of the judges believed that credit could be obtained only from serving in an institution. However, one judge, Judge Popovich, contradicted in a fiery dissent that "home confinement, enhanced by the imposition of stringent restraints on an offender's liberty, satisfies the definition of 'imprisonment'." He remarked that, "Once upon a time, a man's home was his castle, but now, through the advent of electronic home confinement, prison authorities have the technology to transform a man's home into his dungeon."[39]

Other legal issues that arise over this alternative sentence can be categorized under the following headings:

1. The Right to Privacy (First and Fourth Amendments). Although a convicted person is considered by the courts to have a limited expectation of privacy when confined, the home has traditionally been the area where citizens have enjoyed the greatest freedom from interference. Because a person enters into an agreement, such as a probation or parole contract, with the court before being monitored, the terms set and the ability of the officer to enforce these terms is accepted as reasonable. In a sense, the client has volunteered. Also, electronic devices are not considered unreasonable invasions of privacy because they are used to enforce curfew and travel restrictions, both of which serve legitimate (defensible) goals. "Theoretically, the officer could watch each probationer to ensure that he is complying with those restrictions. The courts have refused to hold that scientific enhancement raises any constitutional issues which visual surveillance would not also raise."[40]

2. The Right to be Protected Against Self-Incrimination (Fifth Amendment). Fifth Amendment claims would allege that persons being supervised were in essence providing testimony that could be used against them. It is the person's own actions that trigger the equipment that signals a violation report. In a way, electronic monitoring is "self or participatory monitoring."[41] It is unlikely, however, that such a Fifth Amendment argument would amount to a constitutional violation because the evidence would be used only to revoke probation or parole and would not result in a new conviction. Del Carmen and Vaughn add that electronic devices "do not per se violate the right against self-incrimination because what that right protects is merely the right against testimonial, not physical self-incrimination."[42]

3. The Right to be Protected from Illegal Search and Seizure (Fourth Amendment). Issues of search and seizure may be raised when a supervising authority uses information gained through electronic surveillance as evidence in a revocation proceeding. The defendant may claim that the evidence was obtained illegally in that no search warrant was procured in the process or in that no probable cause existed for the search. However, previous court decisions have said that probationers may be subject to warrantless searches by probation officers. In addition, the person being monitored has agreed to the conditions of home confinement, including random accountability checks.

   If the courts determine that electronic monitoring is like a search, it would probably still be permissible because current policy usually provides the parole and probation officer with the power to conduct searches. Now that electronic monitoring units are also incorporating drug and alcohol tests into their feedback, the issues of search and seizure may become more important and legally controversial.

4. The Right to Equal Protection Under the Law (Fourteenth Amendment). Claims alleging a violation of the equal protection clause would assert that the criteria for participation in the electronically monitored home confinement program discriminate against certain protected classes of people, namely, the poor. Many electronic monitoring programs require that the offender have a suitable place to live and a telephone and be able to pay fees for the use of the equipment. These requirements may cause young and indigent offenders to challenge the prerequisites as being unconstitutional. To establish unconstitutionality, the offender may have to show that other similarly situated offenders, who have money and a place of their own, receive less restrictive punishments, such as home confinement. The incarcerated poor would then attempt to establish that, except for a lack of funds, he or she would be eligible for an electronic monitoring program.

   Advances in technology may help to remedy this potential discriminatory impact because future services will not be limited to those who have phones. As Schmidt explains, one manufacturer now "produces equipment that allows an officer to drive near the offender's house and tune in to the frequency of the monitor, thus determining if the offender is home without the officer leaving his car or the offender knowing when the check is being made."[43]

5. The Right to be Free from Cruel and Unusual Punishment (Eighth Amendment). The way that Eighth Amendment violations are usually raised in cases of alternative sentences is that some condition imposed by the court is claimed to be unduly harsh or excessive. The severity is usually measured in comparison to the crime or to the sentences given to others who have committed a similar crime. As Del Carmen and Vaughn explain:

> The use of an anklet device does not appear to violate the cruel and unusual punishment standard used by the courts in corrections cases. Its effects are not oppressive, nor does it subject the user to humiliation or degradation. Compared to incarceration, it is certainly less restrictive and much more humane.[44]

It is important, however, that electronic monitoring should not interfere with other rehabilitation efforts in which the offender may be involved.

ADVANTAGES OF ELECTRONICALLY MONITORED HOME CONFINEMENT

The restriction of one's liberty and freedom to move about is an essential element of any punishment. Limitations on movement and social activity serve to remind offenders of their diminished status, which is a consequence of crime. We can say that home confinement serves as retribution, a possible goal of punishment. If the experience of restriction is unpleasant enough, it may serve as a deterrent to future crime. As one offender explained, being limited to a range of 150 feet was frustrating.

With house arrest, the restrictions imposed are designed to incapacitate the offender, thus protecting society. Studies of those who violate community sentences have demonstrated that certain times of the day and week are more likely to provide opportunities to engage in crime or prohibited activities. Thus, the schedules of electronic monitoring target those times and theoretically incapacitate the offender during those high-risk times, namely, weekends and nights. The conditions are also similar to curfews that remove the offender from high-risk environments as well.

Because home confinement can be used in conjunction with other punishments, such as fines and restitution, it is essential that those offenders being supervised be able to work. In addition, by attending therapy and self-improvement groups, the client can take advantage of the rehabilitation potential of such sentences. Proponents of electronically monitored home confinement argue that this kind of sentence serves a number of punitive yet reparative purposes. It addresses the needs of society but allows for the rehabilitation of the offender and reintegration back into society.

Another advantage of electronic monitoring programs is their potential for preserving relationships within the offender's family. Criminal justice literature often refers to offenders' families as hidden victims in the system because they lose touch with significant others who are often providers and caretakers. By being at home, offenders can continue to work and contribute to the support of the family and to maintain relationships with spouses and children. Otherwise, family ties, particularly to younger children, are often irrevocably broken during incarceration.

Not all family members are optimistic about the deterrent capacity of electronic monitoring, however. In one jurisdiction, a young man was continually violating EM on Sunday mornings despite his claims that he had not gone anywhere. On investigation, authorities found that his mother chained him to the front porch outside the house each time she left for church. The woman proclaimed that she did not trust the youngster alone in her house while she was gone.

Surveying offenders who had completed sentences of electronic monitoring, Rubin found that some of them tried to keep their relatives from finding out about the house arrest sentence.[45] One participant explained that he seemed to lose the respect of his children by being confined to the house and separated from outside activities.

One California judge, curious to experience electronic monitoring, put himself on the device for seven days. He admitted that after only one day the electronic ankle bracelet made him feel "claustrophobic" and that he wanted to "kick it off." The judge's wife also complained when he was unable to run normal errands. Despite his attempts to comply with the requirements of his confinement, the judge recorded two violations for leaving the premises.[46]

One of the biggest selling points of this alternative sentence is that it will alleviate crowding of prisons and jails, and save money. According to Petersilia, electronically monitored house arrests costs about $5,000 a year per person, not including costs assessed to the offender.[47] This figure is often compared to the average cost of incarcerating someone, which is about $35,000 a year. In another comparison, Goss estimated that the average cost of personnel and equipment for a day of monitoring is about $9, whereas for incarceration it is about $35 a day.[48]

It is clear that electronic monitoring is a cost savings only if the program is used to divert offenders who would have otherwise gone to prison or jail. Although this supervision may cost less than incarceration, it is not necessarily less expensive than other forms of supervision or less expensive than no supervision whatsoever. For example, in Michigan judges were introduced to the concept of electronic monitoring through its use as an enhancement to community supervision for those offenders who had already been selected for probation. The judges were not ready to substitute the electronic system as punishment for felons targeted for prison.[49] The program developers in Michigan hoped to win the confidence of the judges in the technology so that eventually more serious offenders would be considered candidates for electronic monitoring. Until such time, the use of the monitoring devices will not relieve the system from overcrowding.

One potential cost-saving use of electronic monitoring would be on home confinements those offenders who would for medical reasons require expensive care during incarceration: inmates who need special treatment, special medications and services, or special accommodations. Pregnant inmates, AIDS patients, quadraplegics, cancer patients, and the seriously disabled elderly are some of the cases that constitute significant expenditures of financial and manpower resources for jails and prisons. As of this writing, the estimated cost of caring for AIDS patients in prison ranges up to $600,000 per inmate.[50] In addition, small increases in the number of elderly and handicapped mean the allocation of entire clinics to meet demands for health care within corrections departments.

Table 5–4   Cost of Electronic Monitoring

1 Software package (In-House Arrest Program)	$ 3,500
1 PC computer w/disk drv, printer & screen	$ 4,000
1 PC communications panel (for WATS link)	$ 6,000
45 receiver/dialer/transmits ($795 ea)	$ 35,000
Total cost	$ 49,275
Payback as of January 1, 1986:	
Daily charge per offender	$ 9.00
Total offender days to date	4765

Source: Palm Beach County, Florida Sheriff's Department (1987).

Part of the cost savings of electronic monitoring is having the offender pay for the expenses involved in community supervision. However, using this rationale, *any* community program that assesses fees or daily service charges would bring in money. Still, it appears easier to calculate costs for electronic monitoring systems because they rely heavily on equipment rather than on human services, which are less concrete (see Table 5–4 for a typical cost breakdown).[51]

CRITICISMS OF ELECTRONICALLY MONITORED HOME CONFINEMENT

In addition to the legal problems already mentioned, critics of electronic monitoring and house arrest voice technical and ethical concerns. Seventy-four percent of the probation officers and prosecutors surveyed in Memphis, Tennessee, believed that offenders would learn how to "outsmart" the monitoring equipment and that this kind of sentence would permit them to commit new crimes.[52] Ironically, in this study, one-third of the prosecutors and probation officers responding were uncertain if electronic monitoring posed any ethical or legal problems.

Still others criticize electronically monitored home confinement as dehumanizing, taking out the personal relationship between officers and their clients and replacing it with a machine. One probation program director admits that he is fearful

That the prospect of implants, electronic lobotomies, and automatons might become an unfortunate reality. I submit that increasing modern technology can lead to a decreasing human technology. . . . Imagine the worst scenarios of the laser probation officer, bracelets, anklets and implants. I fear the potential of a nighttime electronic call when the computer cannot recognize the suicidal threats of a client, while human interaction could conceivably prevent a potential human tragedy.[53]

These fears may be realistic. One probation officer has already advocated the use of a transmitter implanted beneath the skin as a more effective alternative to the ankle device.[54] Plans have also been suggested for using tracking mechanisms within the monitors so that the exact location of the offender can be determined from the unit's transmitter. This would greatly enhance the surveillance aspect of the service and perhaps serve as a deterrent to violations.

There is no doubt that the use of electronic monitoring devices has changed the role of the supervising officer. Because rehabilitation seems to be deemphasized in favor of control functions, Corbett states that the profession of probation officers has become deskilled or deprofessionalized.[55] The monitoring functions, he argues, are clerical in nature, and the advanced college degrees of the "counseling" officer are no longer necessary. Petersilia reported that officers using these mechanisms reported that they had little time to counsel or rehabilitate offenders.[56] Some writers suspect that the change from a social service orientation to more of a police function will alter the type of personality attracted to this field.[57] Corbett likened the Orwellian "Big Brother" functions to a RoboPO similar to the science fiction robot police officers of the movies.[58]

On the other hand, it has been suggested that increases in technology can be counteracted with increases in human interaction. Realistically, the telephone check has been a part of supervision for years. The computer is only a more modern tool for detecting violations; it cannot inspire alternatives. As Erwin explains, "It takes an officer with excellent communication skills and human touch to maintain a meaningful and strong role as a motivator and counselor over the static of the equipment."[59] A survey of parolees in an electronically monitored house arrest program found that half believed the program to be more punitive than being placed in a halfway house.[60]

The advantages of electronic surveillance may vary with the kind of supervision under which the offender is placed. After using electronic monitoring for 18 months, probation officers in an intensive supervision program in Georgia did not feel it had contributed any additional advantage over the supervisory techniques they were already using.

One of the problems in Georgia's experience was that the monitoring was actually done by an out-of-state private vendor that supplied violation notifications to the state. The company's equipment was operated by a variety of technicians who were not able to adjust to the individual cases of each probationer and to the officers' preference for handling them. As Erwin explains, "While the probation officers gave specific curfew times and notification instructions for each case being monitored, there were several incidents in which the officer did not receive notification of violations with the immediacy that was desired.[61] In addition, the officers administered alcohol tests during visits using their own Alcosensor; they viewed their own test as being more reliable than the results received on the electronic breath-tests.

Overall, the ISP staff in Georgia believed that the electronic service was poorly duplicating the monitoring that they themselves were providing with intensive supervision. The officers did admit, however, that a central monitor at a residential facility operated on a 24-hour basis by their own agency might be an effective enhancement to surveillance.[62]

Although the use of electronic monitoring seems to ensure that offenders are where they are supposed to be, it does not guarantee the quality of the time spent at home. Unless the clients are actually being monitored for alcohol or drug use, they may continue in a pattern of substance abuse at home.

Also, despite orders not to associate with other felons, peers who are negative influences may still visit persons under house arrest. Explained one judge who declined to place a convicted drug dealer on electronic monitoring, "Home detention would not stop the defendant from selling drugs."[63] In fact, in Chicago a convicted car thief confined to his apartment and wearing an electronic ankle bracelet was charged with luring a man inside for a drug deal and shooting him. The suspect had served time in prison before being accepted into the early-release, home confinement program. Commented one advocate of monitoring, "We should bear in mind that the program did what it was intended to do: keep the man at home."[64]

While house arrest and electronic monitoring allow offenders to remain close to their families, their restrictions may impose hardships on everyone living there. (© *Joan Tedeschi/Comstock*)

In some cases, members of the offender's family may engage in behaviors that conflict with the goals of the program. There is no guarantee that relations with spouses and children will not deteriorate or suffer increased conflict during the period of home confinement or electronic monitoring. Many families may resent the intrusion of the electronic equipment and their reduced access to phone service during the sentence.

Examining 93 probationers and parolees on electronically monitored home confinement, Holman found that offenders who characterized their family environment as poor were less likely to be successful in the program than those who rated their family situation as good.[65] Holman's research also indicated that offenders suffering from depression were more likely to fail in the program than those who scored in the normal range on psychological indexes.

A legal issue that centers on the agency rather than the offender is the potential liability associated with the agency's failure to respond to violations. The courts have held that probation and parole agencies have an obligation to supervise their clients and to respond appropriately to violations of the conditions imposed on the offender. Failure to meet this obligation may place the public at risk. A new offense committed by a probationer or parolee could result in litigation against the agency responsible for supervision.

A high incidence of violations is a common characteristic of electronic monitoring programs. Some violations are only equipment failures, but many are early efforts by the clients to "test" the reliability of the equipment and the program staff. Other violations are more serious infractions of the conditions of release. All require some decision and action by the program staff.

To make the process of handling violations easier, it is important to explain clearly to the offender all aspects of the equipment and its use. When offenders attend special training sessions on the equipment or sign statements that they understand how the equipment works, then it is easier to distinguish legitimate errors from intentional acts. Being sure that each client is familiar with the operation of the equipment can eliminate the defense of "I didn't know" when initial violations are registered.

One point that critics of many of the alternative sentences raise is the possibility that this technology will encourage judges to put on home confinement offenders who might otherwise have received less serious punishments or diversion from the formal criminal justice process altogether. The effect of bringing offenders within the formal system of punishment when they might ordinarily have avoided it is called *net widening.*

In the study of community corrections, net widening is seen as an effect that stigmatizes more people as "criminals" and requires more resources in manpower and money to supervise. The people who fall into the net are those who might have had their sentences suspended, or the charges dismissed, or informal treatment agreements may have been developed for them had it not been for the option of an official program option like home confinement. Consequently, they receive a more serious sentence simply because it may be available. There is the possibility, however, that a shortage of equipment can result in a prison sentence for someone who might otherwise have been diverted from prison.

Milton Avol is a good example of someone given an electronically monitored sentence who might have otherwise received a fine. Avol, a Beverly Hills neurosurgeon, was sentenced to serve 30 days of home confinement for health and safety code violations in the Los Angeles apartment building he let deteriorate. The judgment contains popular and ironic justice because the "slumlord" was forced to dwell in his own neglected tenements.[66]

Net widening has important implications for several aspects of electronic monitoring. If the program's goals are to reduce institutional populations and save limited resources, the failure of the programs to target the correct population will result in increases in commitments and increased costs. It may happen that offenders who would have been placed on regular probation are now given the more expensive electronic equipment with a resulting higher cost of surveillance. In addition, as the monitoring equipment becomes more sophisticated, the possibility of detecting violations increases, and offenders who were once considered not serious enough for prison may be revoked and incarcerated. Parolees placed on electronic monitoring may also be returned to prison at a higher rate than those without such supervision.

The effect of making more groups eligible for prison because more are likely to fail at electronic monitoring may actually increase prison overcrowding. This is an ironic consequence given that electronic monitoring was originally envisioned as a way of reducing prison populations.

Net widening also raises constitutional concerns. One assumption of the cases supporting the use of electronic monitoring is that it is less intrusive of an offender's civil rights than are traditional forms of incarceration. However, if it could be demonstrated that electronic monitoring is being applied to those who would not have been incarcerated for their offense, the intrusion becomes less defensible. When intrusions go beyond an expected or acceptable level, then the punishment may seem more severe than other alternatives to incarceration. A person who receives a more severe sentence than others with similar records may challenge such a sanction under the Equal Protection Clause of the Fourteenth Amendment.

Net shrinkage refers to the possibility that electronic monitoring may be used for offenders who should have gone to jail or prison. If electronic monitoring is used as a substitution for prison simply because there are not enough beds in prison, then it may not be serving the purpose for which it was developed. Although there is an obvious cost benefit in using less restrictive means for serving sentences first—i.e., before resorting to incarceration—many citizens may believe that such an intermediate sanction undermines the safety of the general public.

For electronic monitoring to result in neither net widening nor net shrinking, we must assume that there is a specific offender population whose needs meet the specific criteria the program was designed to address. To protect against the overinclusive or underinclusive use of electronic monitoring, Walker suggests the establishment of quotas.[67] Having a fixed percentage of cases assigned to electronically monitored home confinement might ensure that it serve as an appropriate punishment and is not manipulated by political or economical events.

MEASURING THE SUCCESS OF ELECTRONIC MONITORING

Despite the tremendous popularity of electronically monitored home confinement programs in the late 1980s, skeptics await proof that the programs will make good on their promises. Most of the information available on electronic monitoring programs consists only of reports on the number of successful completions. For example, the North Carolina Department of Corrections cites an 83 percent rate of successful completions in the 2½ years of use before 1990. However, this figure does not give us any insight into the quality of the supervision experience, and it does not give any follow-up information on the ability of those who have completed the program to remain crime free.[68]

Few scientifically conducted experimental studies have been undertaken on electronic monitoring programs. Most reports are simply reviews of cases that all take place under similar circumstances. It is difficult, then, to determine if electronic monitoring really works or whether other aspects of the supervision are responsible for the apparently high success rates. There may be influences from the family, community, treatment, or corrections agency resources that contribute to a client's positive behavior while under supervision. A useful study would be one that compared groups of similar offenders under several variations of supervision programs, some of which use different levels of electronic monitoring. Evaluations would also have to be made of everything from community security and cost effectiveness to reduced recidivism and significant behavioral changes.

Interpreting reports of program outcomes can be difficult unless all aspects of the reporting methodology are understood. As Rogers and Jolin remind us, program directors can "significantly influence their success figures by changing entrance requirements, by increasing or decreasing surveillance, and by altering their tolerance for technical violations of program conditions."[69] One Ohio sheriff, for example, admits that their program uses only model prisoners to avoid the embarrassment or controversy of failures.[70]

In a study by Baumer, Maxfield, and Mendelsohn clients in both adult and juvenile offender groups were subjected to electronic monitoring.[71] The researchers found that almost half of each group admitted to at least one unauthorized absence during the supervision period. Both groups had four persons abscond. The primary reason given for the failure of adults in the electronic monitoring program was technical violations of their supervision agreements (13 percent of the participants). In the group of 78 adults, only one was arrested for a new crime during the monitoring period, and the offense was minor. However, 17 juveniles, or 22 percent of that group, were arrested within the 90-day period of monitoring, and the offenses were much more serious. Of particular interest in the juvenile program was that only 17 percent of the electronic telephone checks resulted in a positive contact.

Despite the low level of response to the computer monitor, the four absconders, and the 17 persons who were arrested for serious charges, officials still claimed a success rate of 98.6 percent in this program. The success rate was calculated on the basis of the total number of participants who remained *after* subtracting those who had absconded. Some experts may argue that the success rate should be calculated on the basis of the original total, which included those who fled. This calculation would give a success rate of 93.5 percent. Many people would also like to know how 17 juveniles could be arrested on serious charges and still be considered successful program participants.[72]

Other current data gathered on monitoring programs have raised the possibility of a relationship between the length of house arrest and successful completion of the program. As Table 5–5 shows, the longer the clients spent on house arrest and monitoring, the lower the failure rate was.

Despite the fact that many professionals in the criminal justice system support home confinement and electronic monitoring as an alternative to incarceration, there has not been much empirical research to support its success. Although program completion rates may be high, these programs are usually of a short term, and evaluators look to see how long

Table 5–5   Length of Program and Failure Rates of Four EM Programs

Location	Length of Program (max.)	Failure Rate
Palm Beach Cty, FL	120 days	5.5%
San Diego, CA	90 days	7.5%
Clackamas Cty, OR	average 33 days	9.0%
Kenton Cty, KY	average 30 days	13.0%

graduates of electronic monitoring are able to remain arrest-free once the period of surveillance is over. For example, Clackamas County reported that only 9 percent failed to complete the requirements of their program. However, 18 to 30 months after the completion date 43 percent of those who had been electronically monitored had been rearrested.[73] Although researchers claim that offenders on other programs were rearrested at a higher rate (47 percent), these figures lead one to question the goals of the program itself.

In a recent national study, Renzema and Skelton speculated that age may be related to the successful completion of electronic monitoring terms.[74] Their research found that the success rate was 69 percent for clients 12 to 24 years of age, 77 percent for those between the ages of 25 and 31, and 80 percent for those older.

One of the major selling points of these programs has been the comparatively lower cost of electronic monitoring compared to confinement. Yet a number of programs have encountered unanticipated costs in actually operating this service—for example, extra telephone lines, special interconnections, underestimated long-distance charges, and supplies.[75]

THE MARKETING OF ELECTRONIC MONITORING TECHNOLOGY

The business of designing, producing, and operating electronic monitoring programs is a growing enterprise. According to one count, there are at least fourteen major manufacturers of the equipment. Reports indicate that the market leader, BI Inc., enjoys an $11 million annual revenue.[76] Each year these vendors flock to corrections conferences and meetings of parole and probation associations with an enticing display of new products. Some of the advertisements of these manufacturers are included here (see pages 139–141).

THE FUTURE OF ELECTRONICALLY MONITORED HOME CONFINEMENT

The use of electronically monitored home confinement has been fairly limited until recently. However, it is argued that the developing technology will have a great impact on the nature of future surveillance operations. One of the major influences of the technological revolution is that the price per unit to operate such systems is expected to decrease.[77]

The price may become very attractive, but it will still be necessary to sell criminal justice officials on the benefits of such a system. One western county reported that although they had equipment for 70 parolees,

INTOXIMETERS
BREATH ALCOHOL TESTING EQUIPMENT

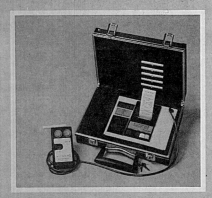

- Three digit display
- Easy to use, one step operation
- Will run up to 3000 tests before it needs rebuilding
- Bright digital readout, can be read under all lighting conditions
- 95% or better correlation with blood
- Can be used at all temperatures between 0°F-100°F
- No special storage required
- Portable, weighs just 6 oz.
- Safe, sanitary to use, no direct contact with body fluids
- Full range of results from 0 - 0.40% blood alcohol
- Cost per test is the lowest available today
- Operates on a standard 9v Alkaline battery
- Fail-safe low battery indicator
- Automatic Zeroing
- Over 30,000 in use, worldwide
- U.S. Department of Transportation approved

Used with an ALCO-SENSOR III, this programmed printer gives an automatic print-out of time, date and test results. Has automatic zeroing. Easy pushbutton operation with up to 5 program choices. Operates on a rechargeable battery, with a low battery indicator.

ALCO-SENSOR (Light Display)
A pocket sized breath alcohol tester which light displays results as Pass, Warn or Fail.

ALCO-SENSOR
A pocket sized breath alcohol tester which light displays results to two decimals (0.00%)

CLIP AND MAIL
☐ Please contact me for a demonstration
☐ Please send literature

ON:
☐ ALCO SENSOR ☐ RBT III

Intoximeters Inc.
1901 LOCUST ST., ST. LOUIS, MO 63103
(314) 241-1158   (314) 241-7757

NAME: TWO INITIALS AND LAST NAME

TITLE

COMPANY NAME

ADDRESS

CITY   STATE   ZIP CODE

PHONE
(AREA CODE)

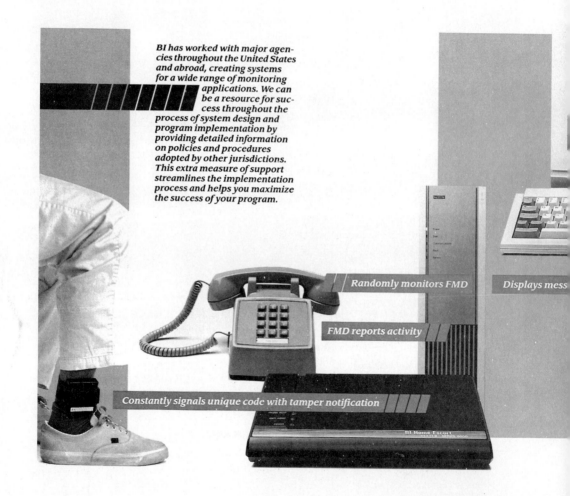

BI has worked with major agencies throughout the United States and abroad, creating systems for a wide range of monitoring applications. We can be a resource for success throughout the process of system design and program implementation by providing detailed information on policies and procedures adopted by other jurisdictions. This extra measure of support streamlines the implementation process and helps you maximize the success of your program.

Randomly monitors FMD

Displays mess

FMD reports activity

Constantly signals unique code with tamper notification

Optional display at remote site

Prints alarms and reports

141

they enrolled only 35. Pressures from their administrators to increase the number enrolled only frustrated the officers because, despite the officers' recommendations, judges were not sentencing offenders to the program.[78] It appears that judges must be convinced of the value of a program before they use it with any regularity.

One of the problems consistently identified by evaluators of house arrest programs is that offenders are usually returned to an environment that was conducive to their original offense. It is feared that the negative influences and habits developed there will sabotage the offender's ability to rehabilitate and that the technology only enhances our ability to detect such failure. One solution to this problem has been addressed by a California program that provides offenders with *foster,* or *surrogate homes* in which to serve their monitored period of house arrest. As explained by Williams, Shichor, and Wiggenhorn, who are advocates of surrogate homes:

> The surrogate homes were selected to match, as far as possible, the individual needs of the offenders. In addition, the areas in which the homes are located were purposefully located outside of the offender's previous environment. Homes were located either through word-of-mouth or through advertisements placed in local newspapers. Owners were paid $16.00 daily for room and board and almost universally provided other services such as transportation, employment leads, and guidance to the parolee.[79]

Preliminary reports from the surrogate home project show positive results. The surrogate family provided good role models and an impartial accounting for the parolees' whereabouts that helped to offset any inconsistencies of the electronic equipment. Besides the advantage of increased surveillance and accountability, the program was able to reduce the amount of contact parolees had with their previous associates. A full evaluation of the program remains to be done, however.

For the most part, electronic monitoring has been applied to low-risk cases—that is, to offenders whom officials considered to be "safe" risks for release to the community—which is reflective of program officials' desires for successful outcomes as well as the conservative political climate in which these programs have developed.[80] The public and the political bodies that fund programs have been hesitant to embrace alternatives to incarceration for more serious offenders. Increasing pressure from the costs of incarceration may eventually change this attitude.

SUMMARY

According to some critics, electronic monitoring did not become popular until prison overcrowding forced virtually every criminal justice agency to pursue alternatives to incarceration.[81] Home confinement and electronic monitoring are currently used as alternative sentences by a number of supervising agencies, including probation and parole agencies. It is important to keep in mind, however, that electronically monitored clients are only a very small portion of those offenders serving community sentences.

Although it is obvious that electronic monitoring serves legitimate correctional goals, each case must be free from the implication that its use is arbitrarily or frivolously to harass. No one person in a community should be singled out for this treatment where no ongoing program with set criteria for its use exists. Legally, the use of electronic monitoring must meet some specific need related to the offender and the offense.

Supporters of home confinement and electronic monitoring cannot guarantee that offenders will not engage in criminal activity while at home or that they will not violate conditions of their probation. Still, the technology of supervision has improved to the point at which many aspects of offenders' lives can be strictly controlled while maintaining an "intermediate" sanction.

Many critics bemoan the technological dehumanization and desocialization of social services like probation and parole and the violative image of "Big Brother." Others argue that it is not the technology per se that is offensive but the way in which it is used that is intrusive. Von Hirsch points out that throughout history secret police in many countries have invaded the lives of the citizens without any gadgetry whatsoever:

> Intrusion depends not on technology but on the extent to which the practice affects the dignity and privacy of those intruded upon. Frequent, unannounced home visits may be more disturbing than an electronic telephone monitor that verifies the offender's presence in the home but cannot see into it.[82]

One final concern is the inherent conflict in the simultaneous goals of surveillance and rehabilitation. Over the years, the role of probation and parole officers has continually evolved with correctional philosophy and technology. Therefore, if the client population changes as the result of this new technology—that is, if more serious offenders are maintained in the community rather than incarcerated—the role of the probation or parole officer is destined to change again. However, if the net is not widened and society benefits from a reduction in the use of jails and prisons, if offenders and their families are positively affected by the community sentence, and if the contributions made by these offenders and the money saved by a reduced need for jail and prison beds is realized, then the seemingly contradictory goals of surveillance and rehabilitation are both achieved. These are big ifs. It is important that evaluations of electronic monitoring programs carefully consider all these implications and effects. Unfortunately, many new programs have been initiated without the benefit of a good tracking and evaluation system to analyze results. There should be some agreement among professionals on what constitutes successful completion of a house arrest or electronic monitoring sentence.

One concern of criminal justice experts is that the application of this and other crime-fighting technology is as likely to be governed by political imperatives as by analytical assessment. The encroachment of high-tech surveillance into the lives of all of us is a potential problem, as a perhaps prophetic musical group (ironically named The Police) described in a song, "I'll Be Watching You." Criminologist Gary Marx explains that the lyrics of this hit song accurately reflect our latest technological capabilities:

every breath you take	(breath analyzer)
every move you make	(motion detector)
every bond you break	(polygraph)
every step you take	(electronic anklet)
every single day	(continuous monitoring)
every word you say	(bugs, wiretaps, mikes)
every night you stay	(light amplifier)
every vow you break	(voice stress analysis)
every smile you fake	(brain wave analysis)
every claim you stake	(computer matching)
I'll be watching you	(video surveillance)[83]

CASES

Carson v. *State* (531 So.2d 1069, 1988).

Commonwealth v. *Kriston* (568 A.2d 1306, 1309, 1990).

KEY TERMS

house arrest or home confinement	continuously signaling device
curfew	programmed contact devices
home detention	net widening
home incarceration	net shrinkage
electronic monitoring or electronic surveillance	surrogate (foster) homes

DISCUSSION QUESTIONS

1. Which groups of offenders would you select and which would you purposefully exclude from your house arrest or electronic surveillance program? Explain your choices.
2. Examine the advertisements for electronic monitoring systems. What are the emphasized features and why?
3. When or under what conditions does the use of electronically monitored surveillance become intrusive or violative of one's constitutional rights?
4. What is an optimum length of time one should serve under electronic monitoring? Is there a point after which it may become counterproductive? Why?

END NOTES

1. Graham, Gary (1988). High-tech monitoring—Are we losing the human element? *Corrections Today* 50(7):92.
2. Corbett, Ronald, and Ellsworth Fersch (1985). Home as prison: The use of house arrest. *Federal Probation* March: 133–137.
3. Goss, Mike (1989). Electronic monitoring: The missing link for successful house arrest. *Corrections Today* 51(4):106.
4. Hofer, P.J., and B. S. Meierhofer (1987). *Home confinement*. Washington DC: Federal Judicial Center.
5. Petersilia, Joan (1986). Exploring the option of house arrest. *Federal Probation* June:50–55.
6. Byrne, James, Linda Kelly, and Susan Guarino-Ghezzi (1988). Understanding the limits of technology: An examination of the use of electronic monitoring in the criminal justice system. *Perspectives* Spring:30–37.
7. Renzema, Marc, and David Skelton (1990). Trends in the use of electronic monitoring: 1989. *Journal of Offender Monitoring* 3(3):14.
8. Papy, Joseph, and Richard Nimer (1991). Electronic monitoring in Florida. *Federal Probation* 55(1):31–33.
9. Florida Department of Corrections (1989). *Annual report*. Tallahassee, FL.
10. Ball, Richard, C. Ron Huff, and J. Robert Lilly (1988). *House arrest and correctional policy*. Beverly Hills: Sage, p. 91; Papy, Joseph and Richard Nimer (1991); supra note 8.
11. Schwitzgebel, R. K. (1967). Electronic innovation in behavioral sciences: A call to responsibility. *American Psychologist* 22:364–370.
12. Ball, Richard, C. Ron Huff, and J. Robert Lilly (1988). Supra note 10.
13. Goss, Mike (1990). Serving time behind the front door: Electronic monitoring programs provide prison alternatives. *Corrections Today* 52(4):80.
14. Renzema, Marc, and David Skelton (1990). Supra note 7, p. 14.
15. Charles, Michael (1989). Research note: Juveniles on electronic monitoring. *Journal of Contemporary Criminal Justice* 5(3):165–172.
16. Jeffords, Charles, (1991). Chief of Research, Texas Youth Commission. Personal communication, 15 March.

17. *Richmond Times-Dispatch* (December 16, 1989). Reprinted with permission as "Virginia County Tries Home Incarceration Program." *Corrections Today* 52(1):100.

18. Renzema, Marc, and David Skelton (1990). Supra note 7, p. 14.

19. Ibid.

20. Schmidt, Annesley (1989a). Electronic monitoring. *Journal of Contemporary Criminal Justice* 5(3):133–140.

21. Schmidt, Annesley (1991). Electronic monitors—Realistically, what can be expected? *Federal Probation* 55(2):47–53.

22. Klein-Saffran, Jody Beck, and James Beck (1990). Expanding electronic monitoring: Practices and policy implications. Paper presented at the annual meeting of the American Society of Criminology, Baltimore.

23. Vaughn, Joseph (1987). Planning for change: The use of electronic monitoring as a correctional alternative, in *Intermediate Punishments: Intensive Supervision, Home Confinement, and Electronic Surveillance*, ed. B. McCarthy, pp. 153–168. Monsey, NY: Criminal Justice Press.

24. Klein-Saffran, Jody Beck, and James Beck (1990). Supra note 22, p. 8.

25. Broderick, K., and Charles Hanna (1990). Field officers: The impact of role-taking in an intensive supervision program. Paper presented at the annual meeting of the Academy of Criminal Justice Sciences, March, Denver, CO.

26. Schmidt, A. (1989). Supra note 20, p. 135.

27. Byrne, James, Linda Kelly, and Susan Guarino-Ghezzi (1988). Supra note 6, p. 32.

28. Schmidt, Annesley (1989b). *Electronic monitoring of offenders increases*. Washington, DC: National Institute of Justice, p. 1.

29. Renzema, Marc (1991). As cited in Annesley Schmidt, Electronic Monitors-Realistically, What can be Expected? *Federal Probation*. 55(2):47–53.

30. Renzema, Marc, and David Skelton (1990). Supra note 7, p. 14.

31. Putnam, Jim (1990). Electronic monitoring: From innovation to acceptance in five years. *Corrections Today* 52(6):96.

32. Schmidt, A. (1989b). Supra note 28, p. 2.

33. Renzema, Marc, and David Skelton (1990). Supra note 7, p. 16.

34. Ibid.

35. Ibid.

36. Klein-Saffran, Jody Beck, and James Beck (1990). Supra note 22.

37. Putnam, Jim (1990). Supra note 31, p. 96.

38. Renzema, Marc, and David Skelton (1990). Supra note 7, p. 16.

39.

40. Del Carmen, R., and Joseph Vaughn (1986). Legal issues in the use of electronic surveillance in probation. *Federal Probation* June:65.

41. Corbett, Ronald, and Gary T. Marx (1990). No soul in the new machine: Technofallacies in the electronic monitoring movement. Paper presented at the annual meeting of the American Society of Criminology, Baltimore.

42. Del Carmen, R., and Joseph Vaughn (1986). Supra note 40, p. 66.

43. Schmidt, A. (1989a). Supra note 20, p. 135.

44. Del Carmen, R., and J. Vaughn (1986). Supra note 40, p. 66.

45. Rubin, Barry (1990). Offender attitudes toward home arrest. *Journal of Offender Monitoring* 3(3):10–11.

46. Abrahamson, Alan (1991). Home unpleasant during house arrest, judge learns. *Corrections Today* 53(4):76.

47. Petersilia, Joan (1987). House arrest is worthy innovation—If it's not just for the well-off. *Perspectives* Fall:8.

48. Goss, Mike (1990). Supra note 13, p. 80.

49. Putnam, Jim (1990). Supra note 31, p. 96.

50. Hammett, Theodore (1986). *AIDS in prisons and jails: Issues and options*. Washington, DC: U.S. Department of Justice.

51. Palm Beach County Sheriff's Department (1987). Palm Beach County's in-house arrest work release program, in *Intermediate Punishments: Intensive Supervision, Home Confinement and Electronic Surveillance*, ed. B. McCarthy, pp. 181–187. Monsey, NY: Willow Tree Press.

52. Johnson, Byron, Linda Haugen, Jerry Maness, and Paul Ross (1989). Attitudes toward electronic monitoring of offenders: A study of probation officers and prosecutors. *Journal of Contemporary Criminal Justice* 5(3):153–164.

53. Graham, Gary (1988). High-tech monitoring—Are we losing the human element? *Corrections Today* 50(7):92.

54. Criminal Justice Newsletter. (1983). 14(7):4.

55. Corbett, Jr., Ronald (1989). Electronic monitoring—Forcing a redefinition of probation officers' duties. *Corrections Today* 51(6):74.

56. Petersilia, Joan (1986). Exploring the option of house arrest. *Federal Probation* June: 50–55.

57. Moran, T. K., and Charles Lindler (1985). Probation and the high-technology revolution: Is a reconceptualization of the traditional probation officer role model inevitable? *Criminal Justice Review* 10(1):25–32.

58. Corbett, Jr., Ronald (1989). Supra note 55.

59. Erwin, Billie (1990). Old and new tools for the modern probation officer. *Crime and Delinquency* 36(1):61–74.

60. Klein-Saffran, Jody Beck, and James Beck (1990). Supra note 22.

61. Erwin, Billie (1990). Supra note 59, p. 68.

62. Ibid., pp. 67–68.

63. Peck, K. (1988). High-tech house arrest. *The Progressive* July:26–28.

64. Mahoney, Michael (1990). Comments made as the director of the John Howard Association to Dirk Johnson for publication in "Convict in home custody accused of killing." *The New York Times*. Reprinted in *San Bernardino Sun*, 2 December.

65. Holman, John (1990). Factors related to mental health status of offenders sanctioned with electronic monitoring home confinement. Paper presented at the annual meeting of the Academy of Criminal Justice Sciences, Denver, CO.

66. Petersilia, Joan (1987). Supra note 47, p. 8.

67. Walker, James (1990). Sharing the credit, sharing the blame: Managing political risks in electronically monitored house arrest. *Federal Probation* 54(2):19.

68. North Carolina Department of Corrections (1990). *Update* 3(1):March, April.

69. Rogers, R., and Annette Jolin (1989). Electronic monitoring: A review of the empirical literature. *Journal of Contemporary Criminal Justice* 5(3):142.

70. Walker, James (1990). Supra note 66, p. 16.

71. Baumer, Terry, Michael Maxfield, and Robert Mendelsohn (1990). A comparative analysis of three electronically monitored home detention programs. Paper presented at the annual meeting of the American Society of Criminology, Baltimore.

72. Ibid.

73. Rogers, R., and Annette Jolin (1989). Supra note 69.

74. Renzema and Skelton (1990). Supra note 7, p. 17.

75. Schmidt, Annesley (1989b). Supra note 28, p. 4.

76. *Wall Street Journal* (1990). Home monitoring of criminals is poised to break loose, industry analysts say. 3 December: B–8C.

77. Corbett, Ronald, and Gary T. Marx (1990). Supra note 41, p. 4.

78. Broderick, K., and Charles Hanna (1990). Supra note 25.

79. Williams, Frank, David Shichor, and Allan Wiggenhorn (1989). Fine tuning social control: Electronic monitoring and surrogate homes for drug using parolees—A research note. *Journal of Contemporary Criminal Justice* 5(3):177.

80. Charles, M. (1989). The development of a juvenile electronic monitoring program. *Federal Probation* 53(2):3–12.

81. Clear, Todd (1988). A critical assessment of electronical monitoring in corrections. *Policy Studies Review* 7(3):671–681.

82. Von Hirsch, Andrew (1990). The ethics of community-based sanctions. *Crime and Delinquency* 36(1):165.

83. Marx, Gary (1985). I'll be watching you. *Dissent* Winter:26–34.

6

Intensive Supervision

OBJECTIVES

On completing this chapter, you should be able to do the following:

1. Identify the kinds of clients who are likely to be recommended for intensive supervision.

2. Explain the typical conditions of an intensive supervision contract.

3. Describe the New Jersey and Georgia models for intensive supervision.

4. Discuss the results of research on the effect of intensive supervision programs.

We cannot afford to be soft on crime. On the other hand, we cannot afford to exclusively rely on punishment which will ultimately bankrupt us.[1]

— Attorney General William Guste, Louisiana, in a request to state lawmakers to support intensive supervision.

PURPOSE

This chapter explores the concept of intensive supervision. It begins with a discussion of how and why intensive supervision was developed and the ways in which it is used today. The chapter discusses both intensive supervision of probation and intensive supervision of parole. It also describes special programs of intensive supervision for juveniles.

The differences between regular and intensive supervision are carefully distinguished. Intensive supervision is perhaps the most controversial kind of community supervision in terms of success. This chapter covers the extensive research and debate that have developed on this topic. The text also describes some of the more popular program designs for intensive supervision found in the United States today.

INTRODUCTION

Imagine that someone calls your boss every day to make sure you arrived at work on time. This same person calls your apartment every night to ensure that you are in by 9:00 P.M. The person asks questions about your friends, scrutinizes your paycheck stubs, and calls members of your family to inquire as to your whereabouts and behavior. At any moment, your apartment may be visited by agents of the system, or you may be called on to give a urine sample. You owe 30 percent of what is left of your paycheck after taxes to a variety of county court services. Welcome to intensive supervision.

Intensive supervision is a concept that has been adopted for both probation and parole programs. It is more commonly used in probation, however, and the emphasis of this chapter reflects this tendency. According to a recent government report, intensive supervision is the most common form of intermediate sanction used today. The report also states that intensive supervision probation has been in existence longer than any of the other forms of modified probation.[2] As one writer explained, intensive supervision may actually represent what local communities want probation to be.[3] Regular, less intensive probation programs are realistically what most jurisdictions can afford, however.

All intensive supervision programs (ISP) have similar goals. They are designed to protect the community while providing supervision, surveillance, and services. Offenders normally selected for ISP include juveniles, low-risk offenders who would otherwise go to prison, and high-risk probationers who might fail with less supervision. Also targeted for ISP are high-needs groups that may include offenders with medical problems and those seeking treatment for drug and alcohol abuse that may not be provided in jail or prison.

CHARACTERISTICS OF INTENSIVE SUPERVISION PROGRAMS

In many ways there is great similarity between intensive supervision programs all across the country. Intensive supervision programs are typically characterized by any of the following elements:

- Small caseloads
- More frequent contacts between officer and client
- Periodic performance reviews
- More restrictions on offenders and more use of curfew and house arrest
- More use of drug and alcohol testing
- More use of teams of officers
- More frequent use of revocation

Small Caseloads

The average caseload size for an intensive supervision officer is about 25 clients in contrast to regular probation caseloads that may carry anywhere from 75 to 125 clients. One national survey cited the average number of ISP clients per caseload at 22. The average number for regular probation caseloads was 120.[4]

More Frequent Contacts Between the Officer and Client

Officers supervising a client caseload tend to have two types of contacts. One type is directly between the officer and the client. In monitoring the whereabouts and activities of each client, the officer may employ any one of three methods of contact: face to face visits, telephone contact, or correspondence through the mail. In most cases, correspondence through the mail or postcard contacts are reserved for clients who have been successful throughout their term of supervision and are nearing completion of their sentence.

The second type of contact is called a *collateral contact*. A collateral contact is made when an officer checks with family, friends, or employers of clients to verify that the specified conditions are being followed. Collateral contacts are commonly made by personal visits or by telephone.

Intensive supervision contracts may initially require clients to report daily to their probation officers. (*Courtesy of the Georgia Department of Corrections*)

The number of required face-to-face or telephone contacts as well as collateral contacts are greater for ISP clients than for those on regular probation. In Wisconsin, for example, offenders subject to the high risk offender/intensive supervision procedures receive twice the amount of supervisory attention as do regular probationers and parolees.[5] Contacts are usually arranged at high-risk times, such as in the evening and on weekends, because it is important to design a contact schedule that does not interfere with work. It is not uncommon to have the most contacts scheduled during the first six months of intensive supervision. With good behavior, the number of contacts may be reduced in the later stages of the term. In Illinois, ISP contracts often call for five to seven contacts a week between officers and their clients.[6]

Periodic Performance Reviews

At regular intervals during the intensive supervision program, offenders are evaluated by probation staff to assess compliance and progress. In Colorado, for example, ISP clients are reviewed every three months. The status of those who have been successful may be downgraded to fewer contacts, or the clients may be transferred to a regular probation caseload. The contracts of offenders who have incurred violations may be modified to increase surveillance and restrictions. The community sentences of some may be revoked and prison terms imposed.

More Restrictions on Offenders and More Use of Curfew and House Arrest

It is not uncommon for intensive supervision programs to use house arrest, electronic monitoring, and curfews. Some curfews may be as early as 7:00 P.M. When electronic monitoring is used, it is intended to increase surveillance and to substitute for personal contacts. In addition, offenders on intensive supervision may also be required to make restitution, perform community service, and pay supervision fees.

More Use of Drug and Alcohol Testing

In some intensive supervision probation programs, offenders do not know from day to day if they will be called for drug testing. In one program, clients are required to phone a drug hotline six days a week and listen for their coded number on a prerecorded message. If their number is given, then they must report for a drug test. The frequency with which these tests are prescribed is determined by the staff's perceptions of each offender's drug problem, and the court ordered testing requirements.[7]

More Use of Teams of Officers

In a team-structured unit, officers are paired with a surveillance-oriented technician. The surveillance function includes home and work checks or monitoring with electronic tracking devices. Caseload size is often readjusted if a program operates with teams. For example, in

Table 6–1 Comparison of Failure Rates for Intensive Supervision and Regular Probation

	Percentage on ISP	Percentage on Regular Probation
Misdemeanor arrests[a]	51	35
Misdemeanor conviction[a]	40	23
Felony arrest	37	31
Felony conviction[a]	28	22
Technical violation	41	38

[a]Statistically significant differences.

Source: Latessa, Edward (1987). The incarceration diversion unit of the Lucas County Adult Probation Dept. Report number 7. Department of Criminal Justice. Univ. of Cincinnati: Cincinnati, OH.

Illinois members of a two-officer team carry a caseload of 25, whereas three-member teams assume a caseload of 40 with all officers supervising each case.[8] In Los Angeles, probation officers work closely with area police who are familiar with the client caseload. Sharing information about client restrictions and activities helps enhance the surveillance capability of each office.[9]

More Frequent Use of Revocation

Because ISPs represent the strictest form of community supervision, there is often no recourse but revocation for offenders who violate it. For most offenders, an ISP is the last resort before incarceration. In addition, the intensive surveillance measures imposed under ISPs often lead to increased detection and risk of revocation. Some experts argue that because intensive supervision candidates are of higher risk than are regular probationers, it is not surprising that they are more likely to commit offenses that lead to revocation. Table 6–1 demonstrates this tendency in recidivism rates for intensive and regular probationers in Lucas County, Ohio.[10]

DEVELOPMENT OF INTENSIVE SUPERVISION PROGRAMS

Intensive supervision was initially used as an experimental form of parole in California in the 1950s.[11] In the 1960s other community corrections programs in New Jersey, Kentucky, and California began to use aspects of intensive supervision. Initially, the focus of these efforts was to improve the effectiveness of probation and parole. Higher success rates were linked to the use of "just the right" ratio of clients to supervisors. This search for the magic number resulted in reducing the caseloads of the individual officers and increasing the number of contacts they made with each client.[12] In addition, early forms of intensive supervision probation and parole emphasized rehabilitation. Research compared the outcomes of clients on the smaller intensive caseloads with clients on the traditional, larger caseloads.

Many probation departments developed ISPs in the 1970s and 1980s under the provisions of state community corrections acts. These legislative acts provided state funds in the form of subsidy payments to counties that developed programs to divert prison-bound offenders into community services. Because many of the offenders selected for this new program were of higher risk than would normally be assigned to probation, intensive supervision programs were a popular way to meet the requirements.[13] However, a study of the kind of clients sentenced to ISPs in Bexar County, Texas, found that more serious offenders were

Table 6–2   Selected Intermediate Sanction Programs, by State and Type of Program[a]

State	House Arrest	Intensive Supervision[b]	Electronic Monitors[c]	Shock
Alabama	X	X	X	X
Alaska		X		
Arizona	X	X	X	X
Arkansas		X		
California		X	X	
Colorado		X	X	
Connecticut		X	X	
District of Columbia		X	X	
Delaware	X	X	X	
Florida	X		X	
Georgia	X	X	X	X
Hawaii	X	X	X	
Idaho		X		
Illinois		X	X	
Indiana	X		X	X
Iowa		X	X	
Kansas	X	X	X	X
Kentucky	X	X	X	
Louisiana	X	X		X
Maine		X		
Maryland		X	X	
Massachusetts		X		
Michigan	X	X	X	X

Table 6–2   *(continued)*

State	House Arrest	Intensive Supervision[b]	Electronic Monitors[c]	Shock
Minnesota	X		X	
Mississippi	X	X	X	X
Missouri	X	X	X	
Montana		X	X	
Nebraska		X	X	
Nevada	X		X	
New Hampshire	X	X	X	
New Jersey		X		
New Mexico	X	X	X	
New York	X	X	X	X
North Carolina	X	X	X	
North Dakota				
Ohio		X	X	
Oklahoma	X		X	
Oregon	X	X	X	
Pennsylvania		X		
Rhode Island				
South Carolina	X	X	X	X
South Dakota	X	X		
Tennessee		X	X	
Texas	X	X	X	X
Utah		X	X	
Vermont	X	X	X	
Virginia		X		
Washington		X		
West Virginia	X	X	X	
Wisconsin	X	X	X	
Wyoming		X	X	X
Total	**27**	**44**	**37**	**13**

[a]Data are based on a GAO phone survey of correctional agencies conducted during spring and summer of 1989. Although data are categorized by state, this does not imply a statewide program. Many of the programs listed are limited to a small number of jurisdictions or a few clients. Some programs were pilot programs that have since been discontinued. Data on the alternative sanctions, such as fines, restitution and community service, are not reported because they are used so rarely as stand-alone programs for felony offenders.

[b]Intensive supervision refers to any form of ISP program, whether probation or parole or both.

[c]Electronic monitoring refers to any type of electronic monitoring component, regardless of whether employed as an adjunct of ISP or house arrest or, rarely, as a stand-alone program.

Source: *Intermediate Sanctions: Their Impact on Prison Crowding, Costs, and Recidivism Are Still Unclear.* Washington, D.C.: Government Accounting Office, September 1990.

not the ones being placed in ISP. Instead, researchers found that younger, white, female offenders were more likely to be under ISPs. This group was also more likely to be single, poorly educated, and to have a sporadic work history.[14] Although members of this group may have actually been persons diverted from prison, there is some doubt whether prison would have been the most appropriate sentence for these less serious offenders.

Contemporary ISP programs emphasize their ability to divert offenders from the more crowded and expensive prisons, a change in focus that appears to have resulted in major differences in the way ISPs are now operated. Three basic differences distinguish the ISP programs of today from the original programs. First, according to Jeffrey Senese, programs are more control oriented, emphasizing surveillance.[15] Second, programs are more likely to include retributive, or punitive, facets such as paying restitution and serving short terms in jail. Third, supervision contracts often include the payment of fees by the offender for services or per diem charges to cover the expense of the program. This practice reflects current budget constraints and attempts to have offenders defray the costs of running supervising agencies.

There are many different forms of intensive supervision in jurisdictions all across the country, most of them used by probation departments. In fact, a Bureau of Justice Statistics survey reported that 41 percent of probation agencies have some type of specialized unit providing intensive supervision service.[16] A few ISPs, such as that of New Hampshire, are found in parole agencies (see Table 6–2).

The particular function and design of an ISP depends on the philosophy of the sentencing jurisdiction that controls it. Jeffrey Senese cites three distinct philosophies or models for the design of

Table 6–3   Models for Intensive Supervision Program Design

Model	Emphasizes	Tools Used
Justice	Aspects of punishment	Threats, coercion increased officer/client contacts
Balanced punishments	Both punishment and treatment, needs reintegration	Rewards and close monitoring with promotions for good behavior to less supervision
Treatment	Development of client skills and self-discipline	Treatment goals, restitution as a character builder

Compiled from Jeffrey D. Senese (1990). "Intensive Supervision Probation and Public Opinion: Who Cares One Way or the Other?" Paper presented at the Annual Meeting of the American Society of Criminology; Baltimore.

an ISP (see Table 6–3).[17] He calls the first one the justice model, the philosophy of which emphasizes the punitive aspects of supervision and the use of threats and coercion to gain compliance. These programs include increased contacts between officers and clients and the use of community service and restitution as punishments. The second model balances the offenders' treatment needs with their punishment while keeping in mind the potential risk of each participant to the community. The balancing process maintains the dual goals of reintegrating the offender into the community while also focusing on successful completion rates. Finally, the third model is treatment and rehabilitation oriented. The author suggests, however, that treatment today is likely to include control and retribution as instrumental in the development of the client's self-discipline.

DEVELOPING A MODEL OF INTENSIVE SUPERVISION PROGRAMS

The two most widely recognized forms of ISP are based on the models developed in Georgia and New Jersey, each of which is now described in detail.

The New Jersey Model

In New Jersey, ISPs are a clear mixture of punishment and treatment components. The programs also directly address the need to divert offenders from the more expensive and less rehabilitation-oriented sentence of prison. The unique feature of the New Jersey model is that participants are drawn from the state prison population.

New Jersey inmates selected for the ISP will have served some time in prison or jail before they become eligible for this intensively supervised release. It is hoped that the time spent incarcerated will serve as a lesson to offenders on what prison is really like. The goal is for offenders to learn how harsh a prison sentence is so that they will then be deterred from future criminal conduct. Theoretically, the shock of incarceration will motivate the offender to succeed on probation to avoid being incarcerated again.

In New Jersey, inmates apply for release from prison into the ISP. Applicants are carefully screened and selected after they have been incarcerated for a minimum of 60 days.[18]

While on ISP, New Jersey probationers average 27 contacts a month with their supervising officer. Even those ISP participants who are in the advanced or later stages of supervision receive more frequent contacts with their officer than offenders on regular probation.[19] Random drug testing for substance abusers may occur as often as three times each month. Offenders in the New Jersey ISP average 16 hours a month of community service, and 97 percent maintain employment. The high employment rate is perhaps mitigated by the fact that the state maintains a very low unemployment rate overall. In one interim evaluation of the first 14 months of the New Jersey program, it was determined that the 226 clients had paid more than $100,000 in taxes and more than $50,000 in fines, restitution, and victim compensation. In addition, 86 percent of the clients had completed their community service obligations.[20]

In one evaluation, New Jersey reported that most offenders who failed the program did so within the first 180 days of supervision. Approximately 40 percent of those on ISP were returned to prison within one year of admission to the program. Three-quarters of that group had violated their agreements by testing positive for illegal drugs.[21] According to one report, none of those who had new convictions had committed violent offenses. However, because the program selects only nonviolent offenders for participation, this finding is somewhat insignificant.

Overall, New Jersey's ISP claims to average a 4 percent postcompletion recidivism rate. Although it is not explained why, one report of the New Jersey ISP indicates that program participants earned an average income that was twice that of regular probationers.[22] It may be that initial findings from New Jersey's ISP reflects the careful screening that goes into the selection process. Of the original 18,000 applicants for the program, only 226 were selected. Thus, small samples from large populations may represent hand-picked groups with a higher success potential than groups receiving other sentences.

The average cost per ISP participant per day in New Jersey in 1988 was $16.56, which is about $6,000 a year, in contrast to the average $22,000 a year for each prison inmate.

The Georgia Model

The Georgia model differs from that of New Jersey in that it is more of a diversionary measure. Participants are selected for this program in lieu of spending any time at all in prison. Offenders may be referred to the program directly as a first sentence, or referral may be a more restrictive sentence that results from violating regular probation. A typical breakdown of ISP participants in Georgia shows about 42 percent each of property and substance offenders and only a small percentage of violent offenders.

Georgia's format has been referred to as "surveillance-oriented probation" because of the division of supervision duties between probation officers and surveillance officers. Probation officers have the traditional responsibilities of helping the client adjust in the community and attend treatment. Surveillance officers do check-ups only. Supervision teams are made up of two surveillance officers and a probation officer.

According to the Georgia Department of Corrections, the intensive supervision program is

. . . Divided into two tracks—standard and home confinement. Each track is comprised of three phases of supervision with each reflective of decreasing restrictions and program requirements. Probationers usually spend six to twelve months under ISP and, upon successful completion of the program, are transferred to regular probation supervision.[23]

The terms of ISP in Georgia are strict. Clients must contact their supervisors anywhere from once a day to once a week, depending on the phase of the program they are in. Clients are required to work or enroll in school as full-time students. Each probationer must complete 132 hours of community service and submit to random drug and alcohol tests. In addition to participating in treatment and counseling programs, clients must observe curfews, pay fees and court costs, and request permission before they travel.[24]

Between 1982 and 1985 Georgia boasted an 84 percent success rate in its intensive supervision programs. The low overall recidivism rates include the finding that only 5 percent of the unsuccessful cases committed new offenses. Most participants maintained employment and paid restitution as well as service fees averaging $25 a month.[25] It was also determined that drug offenders did better under ISP than under regular supervision.[26] The frequent weekend and evening contacts as well as urinalysis monitoring were credited with the success of this group.

According to figures from Georgia in 1983, the ISP cost approximately $15.69 per person per day to operate. Participants paid probation fees that the state claimed allowed the programs to be self-supportive.

The state also claimed to have reduced prison rates by 10 percent as a direct result of intensive supervision. However, other reports indicated that more than 30 percent of the ISP clients scored as a minimum risk on the classification instrument which may simply mean that persons who did not really need intensive supervision were using this more expensive form of supervision.[27] It may also mean that the program was targeting many offenders who would not have gone to prison anyway. If so, then the potential diversion capability of the program was reduced.

A Model for Juvenile Intensive Supervision Programs

In Detroit, Michigan, as in many other urban areas, juveniles selected for intensive supervision are serious, but mostly nonviolent, offenders facing their first state commitment. When juveniles are committed to the state, they are in most cases removed from the home and sent to large institutions. The intensive supervision programs that are called in-home or home-based programming were developed as alternatives to the cost of maintaining large juvenile institutions. The new juvenile ISPs are operated either by the court or by private agencies.

In a two-year follow-up study of the Michigan ISPs, officials calculated that juveniles in home-based programming had no higher rates of recidivism than did a comparable group of youths committed to the state. Rates of recidivism include both official police reports and self-reports, or admissions, of delinquent activity by the juveniles themselves. Although the ISP seemed to pose no greater risk to the community than the tougher sentence of commitment, the ISP cost one-third less to operate.[28]

In 1991 the National Council on Crime and Delinquency (NCCD) proposed a model for an intensive supervision program for juveniles that was based on the juvenile's progression through the five phases of the program. The phases are as follows:

1. Short-term residential placement or incarceration.
2. Day treatment with education and other special-services programming on site.
3. Outreach and tracking with the officer's meeting frequently with the client and family, teachers, significant others; aggressive case management.
4. Transition to regular supervision.
5. Release from supervision.[29]

Examining Other Intensive Supervision Programs

One popular strategy for the format of intensive supervision is the use of program phases that allow for promotions to progressively less restrictive levels of monitoring. The ISP in Contra Costa County, California, is an example of such a design. Participants move through three distinct phases.

Phase 1: 60 days with a minimum of weekly probation officer contacts, 12 drug tests, employment verification and job counseling referrals as necessary.

Phase 2: 180 days (if successful at phase 1) with a minimum of two face-to-face contacts a month and two drug tests a month, or continued use of a telephone call-in system, surveillance checks, employment verification, and referral for treatment and counseling as necessary.

Phase 3: remainder of term (if successful at phase 2) with a minimum level of supervision, one face-to-face contact a month, surveillance checks, drug tests, and employment verification when appropriate.

The Kansas Adult Intensive Supervision Program is similar to the one in Contra Costa County except that it is operated in four phases, which

Table 6–4   Adult ISP Minimum Standards in Kansas

	Phase 1	Phase 2	Phase 3	Phase 4
Contacts				
Face to face	3/wk	2/wk then 1/wk	1/wk then 2/month	1/month

are described in Table 6–4. Each individual judicial district in Kansas runs its own program, but the districts are held to standards developed by a committee of state department of corrections personnel, community corrections directors, and parole supervisors.

Another strategy for intensive supervision is *intensive restitution*. In 1988 the Alabama Department of Corrections began a program of supervised intensive restitution for parolees. Intensive restitution is operated as are other intensive supervision programs except that there is an emphasis on making restitution payments, performing community service, and paying supervision fees. Offenders participating in this program are supervised by officers who may carry caseloads of anywhere from 5 to 24 program participants. Results of the program are shown in Table 6–5. Statistics from the various districts show success rates of anywhere from 71 to 93 percent. It is interesting that the district with the highest offender-to-staff ratio had the lowest success rate. Officials have always believed that lower client-to-supervisor ratios would improve success; however, program results have not always confirmed this belief.

In summary, the format of ISPs may be designed according to the kind of person selected for participation. The various types of offenders chosen may be a reflection of where the applicants are being drawn from. New Jersey diverts its ISP population directly from prison, for example, but other states are less certain that offenders selected for their ISPs would actually be bound for prison otherwise. Many participants are simply high-risk probationers who may have succeeded under a less restrictive form of supervision.

To ensure that ISP clients are really being diverted from prison, Texas judges must sign a statement that each person sentenced to ISP would have otherwise gone to prison. In Texas, persons come to ISP from probation revocation, from shock probation, or from a direct sentence. To receive a direct sentence, the person must have one of the following:

- One or more prior commitments to prison or jail.
- One or more convictions.
- A chronic unemployment problem.
- A documented problem with alcohol dependency.

Table 6–5 Results of the Alabama DOC ISP Program.

District	Number of Offenders	Number of Staff	Money Received	Success Rate
Atmore	24	1	$6,000 restitution $11,000 supervision fees	71%
Birmingham	50	2	$30,700 restitution $25,000 supervision fees	92%
Decatur	100	4	$45,200 restitution $42,000 supervision fees	92%
East Thomas	125	5	$39,300 restitution $63,300 supervision fees	*
Elba	20	3	$12,000 restitution $20,000 supervision fees	80%
Hamilton	15	3	1970 hrs community service $38,300 restitution $27,000 supervision fees	*
Camden	15	1	$1,600 restitution $4,700 supervisory fees	90%
Montgomery	25	3	$32,500 restitution $34,300 supervisory fees	93%

*Success rate unreported

Source: Alabama DOC–Annual report 1988

- Limited mental capacity.
- A serious current offense.

Reports show that about 12 percent of the clients are cases of shock probation, 34 percent result from revocation hearings, and 54 percent are directly sentenced to ISP from the court.[30]

RESULTS OF INTENSIVE SUPERVISION PROGRAMS

There has been some concern that intensive supervision programs continue to operate without ever being formally evaluated.[31] Periodic evaluations determine which aspects of the programs are working, which should be revised, and which should be abandoned altogether. Because there is great variation in the programs available and the offenders involved, program evaluations are needed to distinguish the most promising features.

A 1983 report on the use of ISP in Texas found that about 50 to 60 percent of the participants were clearly diverted from prison. Results of the ISP cases analyzed, however, found that after 15 months 27 percent had their probation revoked and 23 percent absconded. The report concluded that despite the unsuccessful cases, the program had been able to reduce 445 of the ISP clients from intensive supervision at a rate of approximately $5 a day to regular supervision at a cost of about $0.50 a day. Program administrators boasted that this sentencing option averted the need to construct 3,000 additional prison beds—a cost saving to the state of $8.3 million.[32]

Kentucky reported that its ISP program maintained a 77 percent success rate.[33] Positive resolutions were defined as successful completion of the supervision, a reduction in the level of supervision, or being maintained on the program without any serious violations of conditions. Kentucky has even developed an additional step between ISP and regular probation that is called the Advanced Supervision Program in which officers carry loads of 50 clients and also supervise those who show signs of failing on regular probation as well as those who have been successful in the ISP and are moving toward regular probation.

Not all reports from ISPs have been positive. Case records from five counties in New York were audited in 1987, and serious deficiencies were found. It was determined that only 67 percent of the required personal contacts were being made and that only 44 percent of the required home visits took place. In addition, only 47 percent of the court-ordered conditions were fully complied with and in another 26 percent of the cases there was no evidence of any compliance. In 25 of the 66 cases analyzed in depth, the probationers had been arrested. In seven of those cases, however, the court had not even been informed of the arrest.[34]

One of the problems of intensive supervision is that the most intensive part may be the officer's paperwork and running around to verify information and attend hearings. In one report it was determined that between 38 and 69 percent of the time officers put in on cases was taken up by travel, waiting (particularly for court hearings), and completing paperwork.[35]

RESEARCH FINDINGS ON INTENSIVE SUPERVISION PROGRAMS

Research studies conducted on ISPs find that many of them start off more optimistic about their capabilities than may be realistic. One program, for example, intended to test clients for drugs six times a month. In reality, however, they were able to conduct only three tests in that period. Resorting to fewer tests than originally planned may reduce the credibility of this part of the program with the clients and among the staff.

Intensive supervision programs that conduct more drug and alcohol testing may have highter rates of technical violations. (*Courtesy of the Georgia Department of Corrections*)

Previous studies on the ISPs reflect average recidivism rates of about 10 percent for new arrests and 20 percent for technical violations of the probation contract. Some researchers argue that positive results, such as low recidivism rates, may be related to the offenders selected for participation rather than an effect of a program itself.[36] Programs that hand-pick offenders who have greater potentials for success may fare better than those that target drug offenders or some other high-risk population. When subjects from a generally eligible pool were randomly assigned to either regular probation or ISP, the results were somewhat different. In a study designed to use random assignment, Petersilia and Turner found that 30 percent of the ISP group had a technical violation and about 20 percent had a new arrest. These authors cautioned that their findings were perhaps affected by the fact that the subjects were all drawn from California where ISPs are used for high-risk populations.[37]

One of the basic findings of research on intensive supervision programs is that these programs place more emphasis on surveillance and control than do other forms of community corrections. The longer programs have been in operation, it seems, the more preoccupied administrators become with control.[38] Also, according to Byrne, surveillance aspects of supervision continue to expand whereas treatment services seem to remain at a constant level.[39]

Effects of Caseload Size and Number of Contacts

Because the cornerstone of ISPs is the reduced size of caseloads and the increased number of client/officer contacts, it is not surprising that most ISP research has focused on these variables. The best known of these studies, the San Francisco Project, found that the smaller caseload appeared to produce higher rates of technical contract violations. Otherwise, the smaller caseload did not seem to be significantly more effective than were the larger caseloads. However, one of the important limitations of this study was that it was conducted within the federal probation system. Many people would argue that this population of offenders is significantly different from that of any state jurisdiction.

Although caseload size did not appear to be more positively associated with program success in adult federal offenders, it has been viewed as being significant with juvenile offender populations. As Lipton, Martinson, and Wilkes observed, "A clear finding is that intensive supervision is associated with reduction in recidivism among males and females under 18 years of age. This conclusion is based on five studies in which youthful subjects were randomly assigned to various forms of intensive supervision and to supervision for varying periods of time up to a maximum of 26 months."[40]

There is also speculation that the amount of overall ISP activity within a jurisdiction may affect the levels of success of not only the intensively monitored caseloads but other levels as well. In one jurisdiction there were so many ISPs that the number of offenders on regular supervision fell to a level that caused that group to resemble an ISP caseload. Although this situation could cause regular probationers to have the potential to receive more services, there is no guarantee that clients on regular probation will benefit.

An agency emphasis on intensive supervision programming may result in reduced services for clients at other levels of supervision. Under any form of supervision, there is never a guarantee that a smaller caseload will result in more contacts. There is also no guarantee that the time spent in each contact will increase or that the quality of the contact will improve.

In a study of juveniles in probation and aftercare programs in Maryland, researchers determined that the high-risk cases were no more likely to be seen by their counselors than were low-risk youths. In fact, delinquents who were placed out of the home appeared more likely to receive counselor attention than those who remained living at home. The authors of this study called it "ironic" because "once youth are returned home from an institutional or community residential placement (precisely when they are most at risk for failure), they are less likely to have contact with a field services juvenile counselor than they did while in placement.[41]

One problem that has been noted in the research on numbers of contacts at differing levels of supervision is that what evaluators may be measuring is simply a difference in enthusiasm for accurately reporting contacts. Officers with smaller caseloads may find it easier to track and tabulate their contacts than do overworked employees with larger caseloads.[42] Officers with large caseloads may make all the required contacts, but their paperwork may fall behind and not accurately reflect their activities.

Other research findings on intensive supervision have been more positive. A comparative study of high-risk offenders in Wisconsin showed that the group in the ISP had fewer returns to prison on new convictions (5 percent) than a matched group of offenders on regular supervision (29 percent). Although both groups had assaultive criminal histories, the ISP clients had a lower incidence of convictions for violent offenses (3 percent) than did the group on regular supervision (12 percent). In this study it did not appear that the higher levels of contact between the ISP participants and their supervisors contributed to greater rates of detection of misconduct. However, the cost of the ISP was two to three times more expensive to administer than was regular probation.[43]

Overall, there appear to be three factors associated with successful intensive supervision programs. One is that the programs have therapeutic integrity, which means that the programs are able to focus consistently on the most important conditions and goals. One way to achieve integrity is to minimize additional requirements such as fines, restitution, drug treatment, and community service that may overwhelm the offender and result in less motivation. Even though judges and the public may favor an array of punitive and rehabilitative measures, there is a point at which additional mandates become self-defeating. Goals should be given priority and only the most important one or two addressed. The second factor associated with success is that the program demands be reasonable, which would require that judges and probation officers consider the individual circumstances and abilities of each offender when setting conditions. It has been demonstrated that the more controling and demanding a contract is, the more violations occur. Persons subjected to particularly long periods of intensive supervision may be at a higher risk of failure. The third desirable program characteristic is that offense-specific treatments be available. As Whitfield explains, "Special programmes for sex offenders, drug abuse, auto-crime, etc. seem to have more credibility, a sharper focus and greater effect.[44]

SUMMARY

According to Clear, Flynn, and Shapiro, the pressure to develop intensive supervision programs across the country has been "so widespread that no administrator can call his organization's panoply of probation methods complete without it."[45] However, there are three justifications for the development of intensive supervision programs.

One such justification is tied to the overcrowding of prison and juvenile institutions. This approach views intensive supervision as a necessary alternative to an overtaxed system of incarceration, and the underlying assumption is that intensive supervision can provide a cheaper but equally effective control measure for prison-bound offenders who are considered to be too great a risk for regular probation.

Another justification is that intensive supervision is a remedy for the failures and shortcomings of regular probation. It implies that there are some inherent weaknesses in traditional probation arrangements that make a more comprehensive and directed style of supervision necessary.

The third justification argues that there is a separate and distinct population that can be served only by intensive supervision. The persons selected for intensive supervision are neither candidates for regular probation nor incarceration. It stresses that intensive supervision is viable in and of itself and not as a result of the failures of other sentences. It is not a result of pressures for more control or less expense.

As Clear et al. explain, the results of the first wave of intensive supervision programs have not been dramatically successful.[46] There is also some suggestion in the literature that if the surveillance aspect of ISPs begins to dominate the programming, then recidivism rates will be higher. It is assumed that the more someone is watched, the more likely it is that they will be detected violating their contract. An increase in revocations would consequently drive up the same incarceration rates that ISPs were designed to reduce. The irony in the development of surveillance programming is that it may "exacerbate rather than alleviate the (prison) crowding problem."[47]

Joan Petersilia has outlined the organizational conditions that must be present for an ISP to be successfully implemented:

- The project must have clearly articulated goals that reflect the needs and desires of the community.

- The project must have a receptive environment in both the "parent" organization and the larger criminal justice system.

- The organization must have secure administrators, low staff turnover, and plentiful resources.

- The organization's leader and the project director must be committed to the objectives and values of the program.

- The staff's practitioners must make the project their own without being coerced into it. They must participate in its development and have incentives to maintain its integrity during the change process.[48]

More specifically than the directives outlined by Petersilia, it is important that the methods for selecting candidates for intensive supervision follow some set agency policy. The criteria for such decision making should be based on research findings and should consider a broad range of social, political, and economic factors. The assessment of risks and needs should not be based on the individual discretion or intuition of any one person or office.

DISCUSSION QUESTIONS

1. What are the strengths and weaknesses of current intensive supervision programs?
2. Why does it seem logical that intensive supervision programs would be more successful while it is also apparent that they have higher rates of violation?
3. Historically, what have been the motivations behind the development of intensive supervision programs? How might "ulterior motives" for its use affect program outcomes?
4. If you were to design an intensive supervision program, what characteristics or policies would you select to guarantee that the supervision is "intensive"?

KEY TERMS

intensive supervision   intensive restitution
collateral contacts   surveillance-oriented probation

END NOTES

1. Guste, William (1986). Quoted by Capitol News Bureau in "Prison Alternative Eyed." *Baton Rouge Morning Advocate*. 12 March:C.
2. United States General Accounting Office (1990). *Intermediate sanctions: Their impacts on prison crowding, costs, and recidivism are still unclear*. Washington, DC: U.S. General Accounting Office, p.30.
3. Schuman, Alan (1989). The cost of correctional services: Exploring a poorly charted terrain. *Research in Corrections* 2(1):27–34.
4. Byrne, James, Arthur Lurigio, and Christopher Baird (1989). The effectiveness of the new intensive supervision programs. *Research in Corrections* 2(2):1–48.
5. Wisconsin Department of Health and Social Services (1989). *Reducing criminal risk: An evaluation of the high risk offender intensive supervision project*. Madison, WI: Office of Policy and Budget.
6. Thomson, Douglas (1990). How plea bargaining shapes intensive probation supervision policy goals. *Crime and Delinquency* 36(1):146–61.
7. Petersilia, Joan, and Susan Turner (1990). Comparing intensive and regular supervision for high risk probationers: Early results from an experiment in California. *Crime and Delinquency* 36(1):87–111.

8. Thomson, Douglas (1990). Supra note 6, p.148.

9. Nidorf, Barry (1989). Community corrections: Turning the crowding crisis into opportunities. *Corrections Today* 51(6):82, 84.

10. Latessa, Edward (1987). The incarceration diversion unit of the Lucas County Adult Probation Department: Report number 7. Cincinnati, OH: Department of Criminal Justice, Univ. of Cincinnati.

11. Senese, Jeffrey (1990). Intensive supervision probation and public opinion: Who cares one way or the other? Paper presented at the annual meeting of the American Criminological Society, Baltimore.

12. Carter, Robert, and L. Wilkins (1984). Caseloads: Some conceptual models, in *Probation, Parole and Community Corrections,* ed. Robert Carter and Leslie Wilkins. New York: Wiley.

13. Jones, Peter (1990). Expanding the use of noncustodial sentencing options: An evaluation of the Kansas Community Corrections Act. *The Howard Journal* 29(2):117.

14. Williams, Frank, Charles Friel, Chuck Fields, and William Wilkenson (1982). *Assessing diversionary impact: An evaluation of the intensive supervision program of the Bexar County Adult Probation Department.* Huntsville, TX: Sam Houston State Univ.

15. Senese, Jeffrey (1990). Supra note 11, p. 3.

16. Bureau of Justice Statistics (1989). *Probation and parole—1988.* Washington, DC: U.S. Department of Justice.

17. Clear, Todd, Suzanne Flynn, and Carol Shapiro (1987). Intensive supervision in probation, in *Intermediate Punishments: Intensive Supervision, Home Confinement and Electronic Surveillance,* ed. Belinda McCarthy. Monsey, NY: Criminal Justice Press.

18. Pearson, Frank, and Alice Harper (1990). Contingent intermediate sentences: New Jersey's intensive supervision program. *Crime and Delinquency* 36(1):75–86.

19. Pearson, Frank, and Alice Harper (1990). Supra note 18, p.77.

20. Pearson, Frank (1985). New Jersey's intensive supervision program: A progress report. *Crime and Delinquency* 31(3):393–410.

21. Pearson, Frank (1987). *Research on New Jersey's intensive supervision program* (final report). Washington DC: National Institute of Justice, U.S. Department of Justice.

22. Pearson and Harper, Contingent intermediate sentences, p. 83.

23. Georgia Department of Corrections (1988). *Probation's role in a balanced approach to corrections.* Atlanta: Division of Probation, p.12.

24. Ibid.

25. Erwin, Billie, and Lawrence Bennett (1987). New Dimensions in probation: Georgia's experience with intensive probation supervision (IPS). *Research in Brief.* Washington, DC: National Institute of Justice, U.S. Department of Justice.

26. Bureau of Justice Assistance (1988). *Intensive supervision probation and parole (ISP).* Washington, DC: U.S. Department of Justice, p.19.

27. Whitfield, Richard (1990). Probation—Does more mean better? *International Journal of Offender Therapy and Comparative Criminology* 34(3):vii–xii.

28. Barton, William, and Jeffrey Butts (1990). Viable options: Intensive supervision programs for juvenile delinquents. *Crime and Delinquency* 36(2):238–256.

29. Krisberg, Barry, Deborah Neuenfeldt, and Audrey Bakke (1991). Juvenile intensive supervision programs: The state of the art. *NCCD Focus,* February.

30. Bureau of Justice Assistance (1988). Supra note 26, p.19.

31. Immarigeon, Russ (1985). *Probation at the crossroads: Innovative programs in Massachusetts.* Boston: Massachusetts Council for Public Justice.

32. Vara, Richard (1983). Study says strict supervision plan for probationers working. *The Houston Post.* 6 March:6D.

33. Kentucky Department of Corrections (1990). *Kentucky Corrections Cabinet Facts and Figures, 1988–89.* Planning and Evaluation Branch Kentucky Corrections Cabinet. Frankfort, KY.

34. New York State (1988). *Intensive supervision program: Report 87–S–10.* Albany: Office of the Comptroller.

35. Altschuler, David (1991). The supervision of juvenile offenders in Maryland: Policy and practice implications of the Department of Juvenile Services workload study. Baltimore: Johns Hopkins Univ., Institute for Policy Studies, p.3.

36. Petersilia, Joan, and Susan Turner (1990). Supra note 7 p.89.

37. Ibid.

38. Byrne, James, Linda Kelly, and Susan Guarino-Ghezzi (1988). Understanding the limits of technology: An examination of the use of electronic monitoring in the criminal justice system. *Perspectives.* Spring:30–36.

39. Byrne, James (1990). The future of intensive probation supervision and the new intermediate sanctions. *Crime and Delinquency.* 36(1):6–41.

40. Lipton, Douglas, Robert Martinson, and Judith Wilkes (1975). *The effectiveness of correctional treatment: A survey of treatment evaluation studies.* New York: Praeger, p.70.

41. Altschuler, David (1991). Supra note 35, p.2.

42. Banks, J., A.L. Porter, R.L. Rardin, T.R. Siler, and V. Unger (1977). Evaluation of intensive special probation. *Summary, Phase 1 Evaluation of Intensive Special Probation Projects, Law Enforcement Assistance Administration.* Washington, DC: U.S. Government Printing Office, U.S. Department of Justice, pp.34–432 (p. 254).

43. Wisconsin Department of Health and Social Services (1989). *Reducing Criminal Risk: An evaluation of the high risk offender intensive supervision project.* Madison: Office of Policy and Budget.

44. Whitfield, Richard (1990). Supra note 27, p. xi.

45. Clear, Todd, Suzanne Flynn, and Carol Shapiro (1987). Supra note 17, p.31.

46. Ibid.

47. Byrne, James, Arthur Lurigio, and Christopher Baird (1989). Supra note 4, p.38.

48. Petersilia, Joan (1989). Implementing randomized experiments: Lessons from BJA's intensive supervision project. Preliminary Report. Santa Monica, CA: The RAND Corporation, p.8.

7

Community Service and Economic Sanctions

PURPOSE

This chapter examines several community corrections options in greater detail than in earlier chapters. The use of community service is explored, as well as economic sanctions. The most popular economic sanctions today are asset forfeitures, court costs, supervision fees, restitution, and fines. The material covered includes who usually receives economic sanctions, the structure of the various service and payment programs, and what the research has found regarding the outcomes of these options. The text also discusses the case law that has influenced the management of these alternative sentences.

OBJECTIVES

On completion of this chapter, you should be able to do the following:

1. Explain the purpose of restitution centers. Describe the typical daily routine inside a restitution center.

2. Discuss some of the explanations that have been given for the success of restitution programs for juveniles.

3. Describe the difference between fines, restitution, and forfeiture of assets.

4. List some of the possible steps that courts could take to ensure higher collection rates from fines.

5. Distinguish between the day-fine system and the fixed-sum system for setting fines.

INTRODUCTION

A 39-year-old dentist in California is convicted of running a drug lab. He claims he needed the money to pay off his dental school loans. Having no previous criminal history, he is sentenced to provide dental service to the poor along with a fine and a term of probation. Three young males are arrested for spray painting graffiti on the side of a building. For the next five weekends, they will clean gang graffiti off those same buildings under the supervision of juvenile authorities. Sixteen men and women are arrested throughout the operation of a New Year's Eve sobriety roadblock for driving under the influence of alcohol. Their combined fines total more than $5000. The people described here are part of a trend of community service and economic sanctions that pervades popular justice.

ECONOMIC SANCTIONS

Much of society's concern about crime is the financial toll it takes on all communities. Direct costs include medical care for injuries, loss of productivity from workers who have been victimized by crime, damage to property, the cost of employing more police, and lower property values in high-crime areas. Some costs, such as the fear or pain and suffering that victims of crime experience, are hard to measure. Consumers pay higher costs for goods to offset what businesses lose in thefts.

The Bureau of Justice Statistics estimates that in 1985 crimes of violence, theft, burglary, larceny, and motor vehicle theft cost victims $13 billion. Drunk driving accidents represented another $13 billion loss. Banks claim to have lost over $70 million in automated teller machine fraud. Only about one-quarter of court-ordered child support payments are made.[1] Federal income tax evasion was projected to cost close to $82 billion.[2]

The legal system, including police, courts, and corrections, also operates at great expense. The entire process—from investigating a crime to punishing a convicted offender—involves many expenses that range from salaries and paperwork to facilities and equipment. In 1985 the operation of state and federal criminal justice agencies cost more than $45 billion.[3] Attempts are often made to recoup a portion of these funds by having offenders make payments to the courts or to victims as part of their punishment.

Historically, prisoners have often been required to work to defray the costs of their confinement. Inmates toiling in the fields for pennies a day was a symbol of the debt they owed society and the costs paid back to the state for "room and board." Since the late 1960s, community corrections programs have also instituted a number of plans to collect funds from the offender to defray the cost of crime and of "corrections."

Community supervision agencies have established three major categories of payments. Offenders may receive multiple economic sanctions out of any or all three of these categories. The first category is *service fees*. Fees may be assessed for the use of a public defender, for costs associated with the preparation of a presentence investigation, and for drug testing or assessments of drug and alcohol abuse. After sentencing, fees may be collected from the offender and paid toward treatment programs or community supervision. From 1980 to 1986, the number of states charging probation fees grew from 9 to 24.[4]

The second category of payments is a group of *special assessments* that may be levied to support a number of general funds for criminal justice. Payments to these general funds may be unrelated to a person's offense and may be charged across the board to all convicted persons. Crime-stoppers fees, criminal justice planning fees, and funds for victim compensation are all examples of special assessments.[5]

Service fees and special assessments are the monetary sanctions experiencing the greatest growth in sentencing today, but they may also be legally controversial. The Michigan Supreme Court ruled that some criminal justice functions are expenses that the public alone must bear. The judges reasoned that offenders can only be expected to pay for those services directly related to apprehension, adjudication, and correctional supervision (*People* v. *Fisher*).

The third kind of payment that may be collected from offenders is a broad category that includes court costs, fines, and restitution. *Court costs* are set fees that go toward the maintenance of criminal court and law enforcement services. *Fines* are monetary sanctions usually based on the severity of the crime. *Restitution* is a court-ordered payment to compensate the victim of a crime for loss or damage to property. Restitution has become popular because society recognizes that crime takes a great financial toll on victims, many of whom can least afford the losses.

The notion of requiring offenders to compensate victims for the harms suffered from crime can be found in the histories of ancient civilizations. Over time, as our conception of justice grew more legally sophisticated, we moved from the idea of the victims' settling matters with their transgressors to the idea that a crime was an act against the king (or later, the state). As government intervened between the victim and the offender, the purpose of punishment took on other priorities, including deterrence, retribution, and incapacitation. Victims who sought compensation for their losses were referred to civil courts.[6]

With the rise in victims' movements since the 1960s, restitution programs have been revived and revamped. In 1982 the federal government enacted the *Victim and Witness Protection Act*, which mandated the consideration of restitution as a punishment. Two years later, the *Victims of Crime Assistance Act* also enforced the need for restitution options.[7] That same year, the Federal Comprehensive Crime Control Act specifically called on the courts to incorporate alternatives such as restitution, fines, and community service, when sentencing offenders to probation.[8] Many people believe that the interest expressed by the federal government in these options set a trend. The passage of these federal acts signaled a movement that was soon mirrored in state legislation.[9]

In 1988 another bill, the *Federal Welfare Reform Act,* was passed to make enforcement of court-ordered payments easier. This legislation allows courts to garnish the wages of persons who fail to make child-support payments. The amount taken from the paychecks is standardized so that judges are not able to use their discretion in setting payment amounts.[10] Court-ordered payments such as child support are not considered criminal sanctions, but the interest and penalties that may accrue when they are not paid are.

Many important criminal justice organizations have also recognized the need for a wide range of options for community sentences. The American Bar Association, the U.S. National Advisory Commission on Criminal Justice Standards and Goals, and the U.S. Presidential Task Force on Victims of Crime have all endorsed the use of restitution.[11]

RESTITUTION

Theory Behind Restitution

Restitution programs are designed to make offenders accountable for their actions and responsible for the consequences. The image conveyed in sentencing is that a tie to society, either to an individual victim or to the whole community, has been broken and must be restored. One way to reunite the wrongdoer with the community is for the offender to make restitution. Under a sentence of restitution, monetary payments are made by the offender to either the particular victim or to a general fund that makes payments to victims for loss or injury incurred as a result of crime.

The existence of a general fund for restitution is important because many crimes do not have a specific victim and many victims suffer losses in crimes for which no one is ever apprehended or convicted. Thus, the general fund allows victims to be compensated when they might not be under other circumstances. Also, offenders who might otherwise serve jail time or other more restrictive sanctions are given the opportunity to make their punishment a social contribution.

The theoretical basis and operation of restitution programs is not without practical debate and moral controversy. The sentence of restitution may be viewed as a possible deterrent to future property crime because it will lower the possible profits from such offenses.[12] However, according to Gil Geis, offenders who are ordered to pay restitution are often making payments with money that should be going to the support of their families. As a consequence, it is possible that the family is collecting welfare or food stamps while the offender makes restitution payments. Geis also questions whether it is fair to allow some people to use their financial resources to pay off a punishment while others serve harsher and more restrictive punishments. Geis contends that "financial well-being has always polluted some aspects of the idea of equality in the criminal justice system."[13]

Who Makes Restitution?

Almost all restitution programs exclude certain kinds of offenders from eligibility, particularly chronic offenders or violent offenders or those with drug-related crimes. As far as the developers of restitution programs are concerned, serious crimes, such as assault, child abuse, and the sale of a controlled substance, are simply not adaptable to restitution. It is hard to imagine how one could restore or repair the circumstances that are altered by these crimes. For restitution to be meaningfully applied, programs may restrict participants to perpetrators of financial or property crimes.[14]

Even with restricted eligibility, restitution may not be appropriate if the offender does not acknowledge responsibility or remorse for the offense. Restitution is also not desirable when the victims are strongly opposed to the use of such an option.

Setting the Amount of Restitution

A critical issue in the use of restitution is setting the proper amount to be paid. By definition, restitution is for the amount of loss only. From past experience, we know that victims tend to overestimate the cost of the loss or damage and offenders tend to underestimate that figure.[15] In most cases, the amount of restitution attached to a criminal sentence can be established only by a judge.

When setting the amount of restitution, the court must consider the defendant's ability to pay (See *United States* v. *Mahoney, United States* v. *Atkinson*, and *United States* v. *Durham*). This entails an examination of the defendant's wages, family obligations, and other debts, as well as living expenses. A bank teller who has embezzled thousands of dollars and lost it all in gambling will not be able to pay back much on a $12,000 yearly salary.

Today, the courts are still rather uncertain as to what weight a person's current financial status should be given in reducing or augmenting a restitution order. As a Pennsylvania court explained in *Commonwealth* v. *Wood*, ". . . an order of restitution may properly require additional or alternative employment, a reduction of expenses, and even a temporary change in lifestyle in order to achieve that sense of responsibility which signals effective rehabilitation."[16]

To ensure that the court has at least considered all relevant information, the presentence investigation should contain as much financial data as possible.[17] Although legal experts disagree over the possibility of modifying sentences, it may be appropriate to amend the probation contract at a later date if the financial circumstances of the offender change dramatically.[18]

A report on probation contracts in 32 counties across the country found that higher financial assessments were taken from low-risk offenders than were taken from higher-risk offenders. The average assessment was $2172; however, the average total payment per probationer was only 45 percent of that figure, or $972. The authors of the study concluded that probation terms are set by time, year, or months of supervision, and not by money paid. Therefore, it is conceivable that community sentence periods are often completed before full payments are made. It has even been implied that financial assessments are purposefully set high just to see how much the offender will be able to pay off.[19]

In a study of offenders in the Chicago area, it was found that over a three-year period the average rate of restitution collection was only 34 percent of the total due.[20] In a follow-up study in the same area, offenders were notified by registered mail that their restitution was unpaid and would result in adverse action. This warning proved to be an effective method of collection enforcement. Researchers concluded that for every dollar spent on the notification campaign, there was a return of $38.75 in defaulted payments.[21]

Effectiveness of Restitution

Some corrections experts support the idea that restitution can be used alone as an effective sanction to less serious crimes. Others argue that it should be used only in conjunction with other penalties. One of the reasons people believe restitution should not be used alone is that, by itself, it may be insufficient punishment. This leads to some questions about just how serious should a punishment be before it is considered sufficient or effective.

In the late 1700s, writers of social criticism complained that the justice system was especially hard on the poorer classes and that punishments were too severe in relation to the actual harm caused by many crimes. Philosophers such as Cesare Beccaria (1738–1794) and Jeremy Bentham (1748–1832) hoped to reform the penal system so that punishments would be in proportion to the crimes that were committed. They also hoped that future punishments would resort less to death and physical torture.

According to these reform principles, to be effective a punishment should just slightly outweigh the benefit or rewards of the crime. Scholars of this period felt that the slightly greater punishment that came from being caught was the key to deterring crime. For example, the death penalty at this time was used for a wide variety of crimes ranging from what we might consider very minor to very serious. As Cesare Beccaria wrote in 1764, "Whoever sees the same death penalty, for instance, decreed for the killing of a pheasant and for the assassination of a man or for forgery of an important writing, will make no distinction between such crimes, thereby destroying the moral sentiments, which are the work of many centuries and of much blood."[22]

The notion of making a punishment only a few degrees greater than the crime is based on the belief that people are rational and will choose only "economical" pursuits. If a punishment consists of just restitution and if the restitution is for the amount of the loss only, then that sanction may be viewed as equal to the crime and not worse. Thus, some argue, it will not deter.

In a study by Galaway and Marsella, 67 percent of the victims, 80 percent of the police officers, and 100 percent of the probation officers said that restitution alone is not enough punishment.[23] Professionals in this field believe that restitution contracts need the framework of supervision (another sanction) for two reasons. First, many professionals feel that the restitution process needs to be guided by someone who ensures that the offender is identifying with the principles of reform and is aware of the possibilities for internal change.

The second reason for not using restitution alone is more technical. Some professionals believe that restitution should be treated as a condition required during a period of probation, thus putting restitution under the broader control of probation so that it could be more effectively enforced. If offenders fail to fulfill their restitution responsibilities, probation could be revoked. The possibility of revocation is a built-in mechanism for remedial action that restitution alone would not have.[24]

The popularity of restitution programs in this country has grown rapidly since the middle 1970s. Between 1977 and 1985 the number of juvenile restitution programs increased from 15 to over 400.[25] Today there are juvenile restitution programs in every state.[26]

Ensuring that offenders will pay their restitution in full and on time sometimes requires a high level of supervision. Such monitoring may not be accomplished under traditional probation programs where caseloads are heavy and contacts with offenders are irregular. In addition, many courts prefer a greater level of restriction and accountability than can be offered within the traditional community supervision framework. Thus, residential restitution centers have been developed to make recovery of the obligated funds a priority in the offender's life. These restitution centers often serve as an intermediate program between incarceration and community supervision. In many cases, the centers act as a short-term monitoring facility where offenders can demonstrate their ability to work and to make successive payments on their restitution sentences.

Restitution Centers

A *restitution center* is normally a secured facility within the community where the offender is sentenced to live until a restitution debt is paid in full. The goal of the experience is for the offender to complete a restitution sentence without committing any new offenses or violating the rules of the program. The focus is primarily on developing the work habits and skills needed to sustain employment.

Restitution centers are usually operated by the county or by a private operator contracted with by the county. The restitution center is staffed by both treatment personnel and security officers. The length of stay for a resident is usually anywhere from 6 months to 2 years. During the day, the offender goes to an outside job, returning each night to the highly structured program center.

The regimen of a typical restitution center is not easy. Schedules are rigid and demanding, and rules are strictly enforced. Frequent drug testing is conducted, and privileges must be earned. One Texas restitution center admits that 7 out of 10 prospective residents choose prison over their residential restitution program. At one of the 17 facilities currently in operation in the state, offenders punch a timeclock when they go to work each day, transported by the center's own van service. A job counselor helps them find employment, and businesses receive a tax credit for hiring these workers.

The use of an employment counselor or job placement specialist is important because many of the offenders do not have the abilities to find jobs on their own or the skills that employers are looking for. Program specialists often give potential employers the assurance that the workers will be closely monitored by the restitution center. Employment counselors can also explain special incentives, such as tax breaks, for employers who hire certain targeted employees, among whom may be summer youth employees, vocational rehabilitation referrals, and ex-offenders who are veterans. Another incentive program that employers may not be aware of is a federal bonding service provided by the U.S. Department of Labor.[27] The bonding service is particularly useful because offenders are often in high-risk categories that make them ineligible for the commercial bonding needed for many jobs.

On returning from the job to the restitution center at night, the offender must go through a high-level security check that includes metal detectors. Residents may be promoted up to five levels of increasing privileges if they do well and meet the criteria for each promotion. Promotion decisions are made by a staff vote. Residents may participate in programming such as the GED and training for education and life skills as well Alcoholics Anonymous and Bible study. The probation department is the primary overseer of this facility, which is tightly controlled by alarms and video cameras. Residents are locked in their rooms at night, and only the top levels of residents are allowed outside. When residents are promoted to level five, they may use their own vehicles.

According to one report, Texas Restitution Centers diverted 3000 offenders from the state's prison system in the years from 1983 to 1988. Between 1984 and 1988, approximately 61 percent of the residents successfully completed their terms. It is estimated that a restitution center operates at approximately $30 per resident per day compared to incarceration at $37.50 per inmate per day. However, the restitution center has the financial advantage of collecting room and board from its working clients. From 1984 to 1988, the residents paid $4.5 million toward their care at the centers, an additional $386,440 in probation fees and $931,000 toward their dependents' support. Seventy-five percent of those who came to the center were unemployed, but only 25 percent were unemployed at the time of their discharge.[28]

Reported Success and Failure of Restitution Programs

Even though restitution provides direct financial support to victims, policy analysts are not convinced that restitution serves as a meaningful punishment. However, the value of the punishment can be demonstrated by showing that offenders who complete restitution are less likely to commit further crimes. Studies that have evaluated restitution programs have usually focused on either the ability of the offender to complete payments or the impact of the program on future rates of recidivism. Both have been considered as indicators of success. Evaluations have also been done on both juvenile and adult restitution programs as well as private and public programs.

Findings on Adult Programs. Studies of adult restitution programs to date present mixed results. Harlow and Nelson described a Quincy, Massachusetts, program called "Earn-It" in which offenders ordered to pay restitution were referred to 50 to 60 participating community employers.[29] Offenders were carefully matched with employers, and employers retained the right to reject any candidates about whom they were uneasy. The authors explained that approximately 80 percent of restitution orders were paid and that the program was able to divert one-quarter to one-third of the caseload from traditional supervision programs such as probation.

Another report came from 10 cities in Ohio, Indiana, and Illinois that used a restitution program called "Prisoner and Community Together." Program operators claimed that 98 percent of the restitution orders were completed.[30] In a study of adult parolees, Heinz, Galaway, and Hudson reported that those who completed restitution had fewer post-release convictions than did a similar group of offenders who did not have restitution orders.[31]

Findings on Juvenile Restitution Programs. As with the adult programs, research and reports on juvenile restitution programs display mixed results. Some programs claim success rates as high as 98 percent, and others go as low as 57 percent.[32] In a federal study evaluating juvenile restitution programs, researchers concluded that offenders paid 75 percent of the dollar amounts ordered by juvenile courts. More than 85 percent of the juveniles successfully completed their restitution requirements. At least 90 percent of the restitution funds were collected from youngsters who paid the money themselves; the remaining 10 percent was supplied by parents or other sources.[33]

In a juvenile restitution program in Orange County, California, officials claimed that 68.6 percent of the total amount of damage and loss of the crime was recovered and that 100 percent of the contracts were completed.[34] The benefit of this program may have been that the juvenile participants were diverted from the official criminal justice process by volunteering for this program. Successful completion held the added incentive of avoiding a criminal record.

In a study of four juvenile restitution programs across the country, it was found that youths in three out of four of the programs had lower rates of recidivism over a three-year follow-up period than did juveniles who were in nonrestitution alternative programs. In Boise, Idaho, Washington, DC, and Clayton County, Georgia, offense rates for youths who participated in the program decreased significantly. In Oklahoma County, however, none of the treatment types used (probation, restitution, or restitution and probation combined) appeared to have any effect on subsequent crime rates.[35]

A study by Schneider, Griffith, and Schneider found that juveniles sentenced to restitution as their only punishment were less likely to recidivate than those who received restitution in addition to other punishments.[36] Critics are quick to point out that perhaps only the "best" kids are selected for participation in restitution programs, thus prejudicing the results in favor of success. There appears to be some support for the idea that restitution may be more effective with "better," less criminal youngsters. A study on successful completion of restitution in Kalamazoo County, Michigan, found that juveniles with prior offense histories were less likely to complete their restitution contracts than were those with no previous offenses.[37]

One of the reasons restitution may be successful in preventing crime or delinquency is that it interferes with or suppresses other activities in the lives of its participants. For example, the time spent working to pay the restitution may be time away from negative activities or influences. It may be that the experience itself is not as convincingly positive as it is a diversion from other negative pastimes.

An experience in restitution is a practical resolution that is not overly idealistic or moralistic. It may be easy for even immature offenders to understand the logic of restoring something lost or taken. This rationale may also be easier to comprehend than other sanctions because it concentrates on the real victim and not on the offender.

One of the benefits of restitution is that is a very specific punishment with a definite beginning and end. When offenders have finished paying off the debt, they have the opportunity to feel the satisfaction of having completed a goal. The justifications for this punishment may be more readily understood than being locked up for the "good of society." To an offender who has no conception of who "society" really is, incarceration may appear to be of no real benefit or purpose.

One link to successful restitution programs may be the level of maturity of the offender. Studying the maturity levels of probationers as well as their attitudes toward their sentences, Van Voorhis found that those who perceived their sentence as lenient were more likely to fail at restitution.[38] Offenders who demonstrated higher levels of maturity and who emphasized the reparative aspects of their sentences were more likely to succeed. Offenders of low maturity who just wanted to get their sentences over with quickly also seemed to do well on restitution. Those offenders who believed that restitution was "a good deal," that they were getting away lightly, were more likely to fail.

Anne Schneider studied the results of six restitution projects and speculated that youths who experienced a sense of citizenship as well as remorse for previous crimes were less likely to recidivate.[39] She hypothesized that youth who were not incarcerated had a more positive self-image and were more likely to see themselves as potential law-abiding citizens.

According to Shichor and Binder the advantages of a restitution program are as follows:

> (a) Restitution is related to damage done and therefore it would be viewed as fair by the juvenile; (b) restitution obligations are specific, thus allowing a sense of accomplishment; (c) the juvenile is actively involved in the treatment program; (d) completion of restitution provides a socially appropriate way of expressing guilt and regret (e) completion of obligations should elicit a positive response from others which in turn might increase the self-respect of offenders.[40]

Restitution and the Victim

One of the reasons restitution has been popular is that it provides a measure of compensation to the victim. It is viewed as a means of giving the victim the "experience of justice"[41] and of reintegrating the interests of the victim into the justice system.[42] Ironically, some of the harshest criticisms of restitution concern the treatment of victims in the process. As Zehr and Umbreit argue, many programs are administered in a haphazard manner, are poorly organized, and are inconsistent.[43] It appears that both courts and program operators use much discretion in designing and implementing restitution sentences, which may lead to disparity in the treatment of offenders and victims. The authors explain:

> Real victim concerns are rarely taken seriously in either the structuring or operation of restitution programs and actual restitution to victims usually takes second place to goals such as punishment and rehabilitation. Victims may be consulted to help determine financial losses, but rarely are allowed to participate further.[44]

There is debate over whether the further participation of victim in the restitution process has a positive effect on the offender. Several authors contend that the meeting of victims and offenders in a face-to-face situation is perhaps one of the components leading to success in privately operated programs.[45]

For the victim, restitution is a merging of civil and criminal court remedies.[46] That is, the civil court suit, or tort, that victims may use to extract payment also serves a punitive function that it is hoped will be rehabilitative. The following example is illustrative. The parents of an 18-year-old girl killed in a drunk-driving accident sue the defendant for $1.5 million. Instead of the $1.5 million judgment, the judge orders the defendant to write a check for $1 to the parents every week for 18 years. Although this amounts to only $936, the judge is convinced that the experience will be emotionally painful enough to serve as a punishment. As a judgment, this sentence serves a more retributive function than is normally seen in civil court.

Although this type of punishment may seem to fit the offender, it may fail to consider the needs of the parents. In a similar case, the judge refused to impose such a penalty, claiming that the parents did not need to be reminded of their loss every week with a check. Rather, the judge held, they needed to get on with their lives. With such a small judgment as $1 per week, the parents can hardly convert the award to some positive tribute to their deceased child, such as a scholarship or a victims' program. To the dismay of victim advocates, one court made it very clear what the goal of restitution was. "As one of the eight specific statutory options available to a Connecticut court imposing a sentence of probation, restitution is intended to promote the rehabilitation of the offender, not compensate the victim" (In re Pellegrino).

COMMUNITY SERVICE SENTENCES

The Origin of Community Service Sentences

Community service has been hailed as the fastest-growing industry in the criminal justice system.[47] According to McDonald, community service sentences were formally instituted in this country by judges in Alameda County, California, in the late 1960s.[48] These sanctions were initially given to indigent women convicted of violating traffic and parking laws.

> Too poor to pay a fine, these women were likely to be sentenced to jail. But putting them behind bars imposed a hardship on their families. By imposing community service orders, the court broadened their store of available penalties, extracted punishment from the offenders, lightened the suffering visited upon their innocent families, avoided the cost to the public of imprisonment, and produced valuable services to the community

at large. As Alameda County's judges gained experience with the new sentencing option, they broadened the program to include male offenders, juveniles, and persons convicted of crimes more serious than traffic or parking violations.[49]

England uses community service sentences more than any other country, but programs can also be found in Canada, Australia, Denmark, Germany, France, the Netherlands, Norway, and Portugal.[50]

Defining the Scope of Community Service

Although some professionals consider community service to be a kind of restitution, it has a specific focus. It is a "court order that an offender perform a specified number of hours of uncompensated work or service within a given time period for a nonprofit community organization or tax-supported agency."[51] Some jurisdictions may also refer to this sentence as *volunteer service,* or *reparation.*

As in restitution, terms of community service may be reserved for the nonviolent, less serious, and predominantly first-time offenders. The requirements of community service may be imposed in addition to restitution or in the case of a victimless crime. Offenders assigned to this punishment may work at libraries, parks, animal shelters, on litter pick-up details, and in various community centers such as shelters for the homeless. Persons responsible for the selection of community service sites should ensure that the work does not directly support a particular political or religious cause.

In Texas, for example, the law is very clear about the conditions under which a probationer may perform community service. The amount of work is restricted to between 40 and 1000 hours, during which the defendant may not work more than 8 hours a week. In addition, the court makes an effort to place offenders in work that is consistent with their skills and employment history.[52]

The amount of community service to be performed may be set according to a formula that equates service time to its alternative, usually jail time. For example, 8 hours of community service may be required

Used by permission of Johnny Hart and NAS, Inc.

for every day that would have been spent in jail for the same offense. If certain amounts of damage or loss had occurred, the offender may be required to perform enough hours of labor at a hypothetically set ratio of pay to equal the cost of the repairs or replacement of the damaged articles.[53] The difference between community service and restitution in these cases is that the person is not really paid and no money actually changes hands.

Issues in the Administration of Community Service Sentences

One of the drawbacks of the large-scale use of community service is the availability of persons to supervise it. Many community service programs are scheduled for weekends when regular business or agency operators are unavailable to direct such work activity. In Rhode Island, for example, everyone convicted of DWI is required to perform community service. Because of the difficulty in placing all 5000 offenders per year, judges are more inclined to impose the minimum sentences of ten hours of service.[54] Even with such a reduction in sentences, the state needs the participation of approximately 250 job sites. As an alternative, many corrections programs have grouped offenders into work crews that are supervised by staff members on community projects such as building a structure or cleaning up an area.

In the federal probation system, offenders are likely to be referred to an umbrella social service agency that has access to a variety of programs. This agency acts as a clearinghouse for placements. The specific agency could be a local United Way office; in some areas a board of community representatives may select assignments.[55]

To ensure that each offender receives the proper community service placement, Georgia hired a community service coordinator in each of its 45 judicial circuits. Coordinators are responsible for developing and maintaining community service programs in their areas. These coordinators have developed relationships with more than 1500 agencies that use the services of the probationers in a variety of fields from marine biology to maintenance. In some areas, structured work details, including construction crews, operate on 40-hour-per-week schedules or on weekend details. The state estimates that the community service workers together provide over 1 million hours of work a year.[56]

Following a sensational trial that ended in a conviction for slapping a police officer, the famous Hungarian actress Zsa Zsa Gabor was sentenced to perform 120 hours of community service in a shelter for homeless women. The community service was in addition to three days in jail and a $13,000 fine. Although Gabor alleged that she gave beauty tips to the women, donated turkeys at Thanksgiving, and made fund-raising appearances, the court did not find her efforts to be in the true spirit of the sentence. Consequently, the judge ordered her to perform 60 more hours, despite the shelter's claim that she had completed her sentence.[57] It could be that the judge felt that Gabor's fund-raising work took her outside of the shelter work itself. The judge may also have viewed Zsa Zsa's donation of turkeys as an attempt to buy her way out of service.

Zsa Zsa Gabor is not the only celebrity to have been handed a community service sentence. Ex–presidential aide and Marine officer Oliver North was sentenced to 1200 hours of service in a Washington, DC, youth group for his part in a government cover-up scandal. White House aide Michael Deaver received a sentence of 1500 hours of providing drug and alcohol counseling in a shelter clinic. The skipper of the Exxon oil carrier that spilled off the coast of Alaska was sentenced to 1000 hours of scrubbing the beaches affected by that spill. Baseball legend Pete Rose was ordered to perform 1000 hours of community service assisting physical education teachers at five inner-city public schools after first serving a five-month prison term for tax violations. The former baseball manager hoped to complete the community service requirement by working 40 hours a week for 25 weeks.

The "famous" offenders just described join 200,000 to 500,000 other "ordinary" people across the country who perform community service.[58] Critics of these celebrity sentences argue, however, that notables often exploit these experiences to enhance their public profiles and bolster their images.

Former Cincinnati Reds manager Peter Rose was ordered to perform community service as part of his sentence for a federal income tax conviction. (© *Mark Lyons, A/P Wide World Photos*)

BOX 7–1

A Case of Creative Restitution

A former U.S. Marine convicted of vandalizing the California Vietnam Veterans Memorial was ordered Tuesday to spend a year's worth of weekends scrubbing the Capital Park monument. Recalling the soldiers who lost their lives in the war—including his son's best childhood friend—an emotional Municipal Court Judge R.G. Vonasek sentenced Stanley Eugene De La Cruz to clean the memorial four hours each weekend for a total of 208 hours.

"If somebody asks you what you're doing and why you're doing that, tell them you did something bad to the memorial and you're paying for it," the judge told Da La Cruz. A jury convicted the 33-year-old landscaper of a misdemeanor vandalism charge in May for breaking a 6-inch piece off a life-sized M–16 bronze rifle on the monument in February. . . . "I didn't think it was going to be this bad," De La Cruz said after the sentencing, "I thought they were just going to give me a fine." He was ordered to pay court costs and attend an alcohol rehabilitation program. A county probation report said De La Cruz had been drinking with friends at the time of the incident. De La Cruz had contended all along that breaking the rifle was an accident. He said the gun barrel broke off when he grabbed it to pull himself to his feet from a kneeling position . . . the probation report recommended jail time for De La Cruz, but Vonasek instead imposed the cleaning chores, a sentence proposed by a disabled Vietnam veteran and a member of the commission that erected the memorial.

Source: Ken Chavez, Sacramento Bee, June 20, 1990. Reprinted with permission.

In Texas the owner of a flea market that used a lion act as a promotion was found criminally responsible when a young girl was mauled. In addition to a $5000 fine, the owner was ordered to make six radio and television announcements for a child abuse awareness program. The media spots cost the Houston businessman $25,000 to produce and air.[59] Ironically, the public service announcements were done in the same format as the commercials for his furniture store.

As in the case of the Exxon skipper, judges often attempt to tailor their community service sentences to fit the crime. The judge may design a community service sentence that is more of a psychological lesson to the offender than a service to the community.

Psychological Effects of Community Service

Placing a person into a community service environment that may cause serious emotional reactions is a controversial ethical issue. Such placements may not be productive for either the offender or the agency. For example, in some jurisdictions DWI offenders are made to scrub the floors in emergency rooms because it is believed they will benefit from the sight of blood and gore that accidents cause. In one case, a young man in Virginia was convicted of manslaughter when his drunk-driving accident caused the death of his date. As punishment, the judge required him to spend a year talking to groups about the evils of drunk driving. A Sacramento, California, man convicted of vandalizing a Vietnam memorial was sentenced to scrub that monument for four hours every weekend for a year.

Given potential emotionally charged settings, it may be important to assess the ability of the offender to handle the psychological stress of a particular punishment. Some of the punishments sets offenders up for public condemnation and the continual affirmation of guilt. Because many offenders are immature and do not handle stress well, if at all, the "teach them a lesson" approach may cause more problems than it addresses. Counseling and monitoring offenders, particularly young offenders, during community service may prevent the experience from causing permanent emotional damage.

Liabilities in Community Service Programs

There is currently no existing case law to define areas or circumstances of liability for workers who are performing community service. We do know, however, that government agencies and private programs that place clients in community work programs face certain responsibilities for the conduct of those clients.

Two basic areas of liability must be considered with operating community service programs. The first is injury that may befall the worker while performing the community service. Accidents may include a tree

Many probation programs are concerned about their legal liability for workers on community service and have had to purchase special insurance. (*Courtesy of Georgia Department of Corrections*)

limb falling on a client who is helping to clear out a wooded park or someone who falls down stairs while cleaning in a hospital. Currently, there is no national standard for protecting public or private sector programs for such accidents. Many community service programs pay into workers' compensation insurance and carry an insurance policy for personal liability protection. Workman's compensation covers clients who are injured while performing work under court order and provides for the client in the event that the illness or injury prevents the client from continuing regular paid employment.

The second area of liability is for third parties (e.g., organizational staff or private citizens) who may be harmed by the client in some way. An example of an injury to a third party would be a jogger assaulted by a person on community supervision who is picking up trash on the side of the road. The organization in which the offender was placed may be held responsible if the client was improperly trained or supervised. The placing agency, such as a probation department or a court, may be held responsible if it failed to inform the public service organization of any risk involved in the client's placement.

In a northern California county, a client was placed in a school by a private agency to perform community service. After the client attempted to molest a school child, it was discovered that the client had a prior history of sex offenses against children. Both the private agency and the probation department were named in a lawsuit. The probation department was named because it had not provided the private agency with information about the prior record. Had the court directly referred the defendant to the private community service agency, the public agency would not have been involved in the litigation because courts are immune from such liability. However, when an administrative agency such as a probation department is involved, the public agency may be sued. If the defendant in the litigation can show negligence on the part of the agency and damages resulting from the client's behavior, it is likely that the public entity will be held liable.[60]

The Benefits of Community Service

According to the director of a community service option program in Texas, 34 percent of the offenders who successfully complete their sentences continue to provide volunteer work at their previous assignments.[61] Many Texas offenders sentenced to restitution centers are also required to perform community service. Figures for 1984 to 1988 show that the residents of one restitution center completed nearly half a million hours of community service over the five years, or close to 100,000 hours a year. If this work had been done at minimum wage, it would have translated into a $1.6 million cost saving to the community.[62]

The state of Washington has been imposing community service sentences on at least one-third of all felony offenders. The state operates a community service program called "Community Services Work." The industry program sponsored by the Department of Corrections has supervised 7000 worker from 1984 when the program began until 1988 when they reported on their progress. Offenders had been sentenced to perform 1.2 million hours of community service at 768 job sites throughout the state. Participants in the program kept their regular jobs, supported their families, and paid their crime-related debts. Millions of dollars were recovered in restitution, victim compensation, fines, and court costs.[63]

As one criminal justice professional explains, the community service sentence offers something for everyone. "For liberals, the community service order offers a program that avoids prisonization, provides for treatment, and incorporates an individualized sanction. For conservatives, the community service order offers a program that reduces operating costs of prisons, makes fines and probation 'stiffer' sentencing options and provides reparation to the community-at-large."[64]

FINES

Fines are one of the oldest and most widely used punishments in the American justice system. The use of fines may predate the laws contained in the Code of Hammurabi at approximately 1750 B.C.[65]

Fines may serve as a sole punishment for misdemeanors or as part of a combination sentence in more serious cases. In West Germany, judges were encouraged to give more fines and reduce the number of offenders sent to prison for sentences of less than six months. As a result, the number of inmates imprisoned on sentences of less than six months dropped from 113,000 a year to 11,000. The judges did not simply decrease the number of prison terms handed down but instead gave more sentences of fines. The number of offenders who received only fines during that period increased 17 percent.[66]

As when ordering restitution, judges should be cognizant of each offender's financial resources. In one national study, only 64 percent of those judges questioned said they had "information about the offender's employment status in most or all cases, only 41 percent said they had information on the offender's income, and only 25 percent had information on the offender's assets in most or all cases.[67]

A survey in Harris County, Texas, found that 29 percent of felony probationers had been assessed fines that averaged $708 per probationer.[68] According to one critic, the rate of fines has not kept pace of the years with the rise in inflation. As evidence, he points out that DWI fines in New York have hardly increased since they were passed in 1910. New York law in 1910 had a maximum fine of $500 for a misdemeanor DWI, and the figure today is still the same. If you compare the two fines in constant dollars, you would have to admit that the fines have actually decreased over the past 82 years.[69]

Setting Fines

Two basic arrangements are currently used in courts for determining the value of a fine. The traditional method is a *fixed-sum fine*, or a value set according to the offense committed. Thus, specific offenses have "going rates," and the same dollar amount is set for each offender fined, regardless of his or her economic status or ability to pay. This method has obvious advantages for affluent offenders and may disadvantage the poor.[70] According to Judith Greene of the Vera Institute of Justice, the "traditional practice of setting fine amounts at the 'lowest common denominator' tends to restrict the use of fines to the least serious categories of offenses."[71] Because the fines are kept low in fairness to the poor, judges are reluctant to use them as a sanction for crimes more serious than misdemeanor crimes.

Under a fixed-sum system, the maximum range of fines is set by law. The fines are scaled only according to the seriousness of the crime. In some jurisdictions, all misdemeanors may involve the same fee, as may all felonies.

A second method of setting the value of fines is the *day-fine system*. Setting fines under the day-fine system involves a two-step process, which is described by Greene as follows:

> First the court sentences the offender to a certain number of day-fine units (e.g., 15, 60, 120 units) according to the gravity of the offense, but without regard to his or her means. Then the value of each unit is set at a share of the offender's daily income (hence the name 'day-fine'), and the total fine amount is determined by simple multiplication. The percentage share of income used in valuing the day-fine units varies across the different countries which use this system, as do methods of accounting for the offender's family responsibilities or capital wealth, but the basic idea assures routine imposition of equitable fine sentences, the punitive impact of which is in proportion to the crime.[72]

A grid for calculating the amount of a day-fine unit is shown in Table 7–1.

Court Decisions on the Use of Fines

Several important legal decisions have directed the process of assessing and managing fines. The U.S. Supreme Court has consistently ruled that when the possible punishments for an offense do not include incarceration, then the punishment for not paying a fine on that offense cannot be imprisonment. In *Williams* v. *Illinois* the defendant was given a prison sentence and a fine. The fine was due the day the prison term ended. A statute in that state allowed a separate term of imprisonment to begin immediately for the failure to pay that fine. The U.S. Supreme Court deemed that such a statute resulted in discrimination against the poor. Concurring in this opinion, Justice Harlan eloquently chastised the state as follows:

Table 7-1 Dollar Value of One Day-Fine Unit by Net Daily Income and Number of Dependents

Net Daily Income ($)	Number of Dependents (Including Self)							
	1	2	3	4	5	6	7	8
3	1.28	1.05	.83	.68	.53	.45	.37	.30
4	1.70	1.40	1.10	.90	.70	.60	.50	.40
5	2.13	1.75	1.38	1.13	.88	.75	.62	.50
6	2.55	2.10	1.65	1.35	1.05	.90	.75	.60
7	2.98	2.45	1.93	1.58	1.23	1.05	.87	.70
8	3.40	2.80	2.20	1.80	1.40	1.20	1.00	.80
9	3.83	3.15	2.48	2.03	1.58	1.35	1.12	.90
10	4.25	3.50	2.75	2.25	1.75	1.50	1.25	1.00
11	4.68	3.85	3.03	2.47	1.93	1.65	1.37	1.10
12	5.10	4.20	3.30	2.70	2.10	1.80	1.50	1.20
13	5.53	4.55	3.58	2.93	2.28	1.95	1.62	1.30
14	7.85	4.90	3.85	3.15	2.45	2.10	1.75	1.40
15	8.42	5.25	4.13	3.38	2.63	2.25	1.87	1.50
16	8.98	5.60	4.40	3.60	2.80	2.40	2.00	1.60
17	9.54	5.95	4.68	3.83	2.98	2.55	2.12	1.70
18	10.10	6.30	4.95	4.05	3.15	2.70	2.25	1.80
19	10.66	8.78	5.23	4.28	3.33	2.85	2.37	1.90
20	11.22	9.24	5.50	4.50	3.50	3.00	2.50	2.00
46	25.81	21.25	16.70	13.66	10.63	9.11	7.59	4.60
47	26.37	21.71	17.06	13.96	10.86	9.31	7.75	4.70
48	26.93	22.18	17.42	14.26	11.09	9.50	7.92	6.34
49	27.49	22.64	17.79	14.55	11.32	9.70	8.08	6.47
50	28.05	23.10	18.15	14.85	11.55	9.90	8.25	6.60
51	28.61	23.56	18.51	15.15	11.78	10.10	8.41	6.73
52	29.17	24.02	18.88	15.44	12.01	10.30	8.58	6.86
53	29.73	24.49	19.24	15.74	12.24	10.49	8.74	7.00
54	30.29	24.95	19.60	16.04	12.47	10.69	8.91	7.13
55	30.86	25.41	19.97	16.34	12.71	10.89	9.07	7.26
96	53.86	44.35	34.85	28.51	22.18	19.01	15.84	12.67
97	54.42	44.81	35.21	28.81	22.41	19.21	16.00	12.80
98	54.98	45.28	35.57	29.11	22.64	19.40	16.17	12.94
99	55.54	45.74	35.94	29.40	22.87	19.60	16.33	13.07
100	56.10	46.20	36.30	29.70	23.10	19.80	16.50	13.20

Source: Sally Hillsman. 1990. "Fines and Day Fines," *Crime and Justice: A Review of Research* edited by Michael Tonry and Norval Morris. Vol. 12 (Chicago: University of Chicago Press). Reprinted with permission. University of Chicago Press.

While there can be no question that the State has a legitimate concern with punishing an individual who cannot pay the fine, there is serious question in my mind whether, having declared itself indifferent as between fine and jail, it can consistently with due process refrain from offering some alternative such as payment on the installment plan. There are two conceivable justifications for not doing so. The most obvious and likely justification for the present statute is administrative convenience. . . . The second conceivable justification is that the jail alternatives serves a penological purpose that cannot be served by collection of a fine over time. It is clear that having declared itself satisfied by a fine, the alternative of jail to a fine serves neither a rehabilitative nor a retributive interest. The question is, then, whether the requirement of a lump sum payment can be sustained as a rational legislative determination that deterrence is effective only when a fine is exacted at once after sentence and by lump sum, rather than over a term. This is a highly doubtful proposition, since, apart from the mere fact of conviction and the humiliation associated with it and the token of punishment evidenced by the forfeiture, . . . the deterrent effect of a fine is apt to derive more from its pinch on the purse than the time of payment. That the Illinois statute represents a considered judgment, evincing the belief that jail is a rational and necessary trade-off to punish the individual who possesses no accumulated assets seems most unlikely, since the substitute sentence provision, phrased in terms of a judgment collection statute, does not impose a discretionary jail term as an alternative sentence, but rather equates days in jail with a fixed sum. Thus, given that the only conceivable justification for this statute that would satisfy due process—that a lump-sum fine is a better deterrent than one payable over a period of time—is the one that is least likely to represent a considered legislative judgment, I would hold this statute invalid.

The opinion in *Williams* was supported by a similar case a year later—*Tate* v. *Short*. In this Texas case, Tate accumulated nine traffic offenses that totaled $425 in fines. By law, the only punishment attached to such traffic offenses was fines. When the indigent offender was unable to pay his fine, it was converted at $5 a day to 85 days in jail. The Supreme Court remarked that the state could not convert a fine-only policy into a jail term when indigent defendants did not have a means to pay. The Supreme Court did not say that you could not eventually use incarceration as an enforcement method if all else fails. However, the justices did assert that they expected the state first to attempt less drastic measures that would facilitate the offender's efforts to make payments.

Likewise, in 1983 in *Bearden* v. *Georgia* the Supreme Court elaborated on this policy. The justices held that probation should not be revoked simply because the defendant was not able to meet the fine and restitution requirements imposed as part of his release. In this case, Bearden had made initial payments but had been laid off from work and was unable to pay the next installment. Agencies were cautioned to make reasonable attempts at alternative solutions to payment problems before resorting to incarceration.

> Poverty does not insulate those who break the law from punishment. When probation is revoked for failure to pay a fine, I find nothing in the Constitution to prevent the trial court from revoking probation and imposing a term of imprisonment if revocation does not automatically result in the imposition of a long jail term and if the sentencing court makes a good-faith effort to impose a jail sentence that in terms of the State's sentencing objectives will be roughly equivalent to the fine and restitution that the defendant failed to pay. . . . The Court holds, however, that if a probationer cannot pay the fine for reasons not of his own fault, the sentencing court must at least consider alternative measures of punishment other than imprisonment, and may imprison the probationer only if the alternative measures are deemed inadequate to meet the State's interest in punishment and deterrence.[73]

Controversy Over the Role of Fines

Although retributive in nature, fines also serve to deter the offender from further criminal conduct. Theoretically, fines should be relatively easy to administer. Most fines can be regulated by existing court or corrections agencies. In addition, the collected fines are often used to help defray the expenses of running the criminal justice system. Some small towns have been known to derive almost all their revenue from fines. Reports indicate that each year more than $1 billion in fines is collected by the criminal courts.[74]

In the federal courts, fines are most commonly given to white-collar criminals and drug offenders (see Figures 7–1 and 7–2), a tendency that may reflect the courts' expectations that these offenders have the means to make payments. However, as Figure 7–2 demonstrates, some offenders (namely, the white-collar group) are more likely to pay their fines. Although white-collar offenders represent only 30 percent of the fines incurred, they represent 68 percent of the total collections. On the other hand, drug offenders represent 32 percent of the fines applied but only 7 percent of the debt actually collected. Failure to pay explains why the federal criminal debt balance is $968 million, whereas the amount collected is only $82 million, roughly 8.5 percent.

The appropriate use of fines is not without controversy. An appellate court in *People* v. *Baker* struck down a lower court order for a physician to pay $90,000 in costs and supervision fees. The reviewing court explained that current state law allowed limited fines only as part of probation and that fines should be used toward rehabilitation and not toward financing the machinery of the state. That appeals court was no doubt irritated by the sentencing judge's comments to the defendant, which were as follows:

Now, I am going to impose a very substantial fine against you, sir, and I guess you are going to wonder why it's so substantial. And first of all, I think that you are able to in some wise reimburse the county and the state for the costs of your prosecution. You have brought about all of this, and 99 percent of the time, defendants in the position that you are, Dr. Baker,

Figure 7.1

Most criminal debt reflects two types of offenses. (*Source*: Testimony by Lowell Dodge, Director U.S. General Accounting Office. *Administration of Justice Issues: Overview of Civil and Criminal Debt Collection Efforts*. Washington, D.C.: U.S. Department of Justice [July 31, 1990].)

White Collar Crime

30%   32% — Drugs

38%

Others

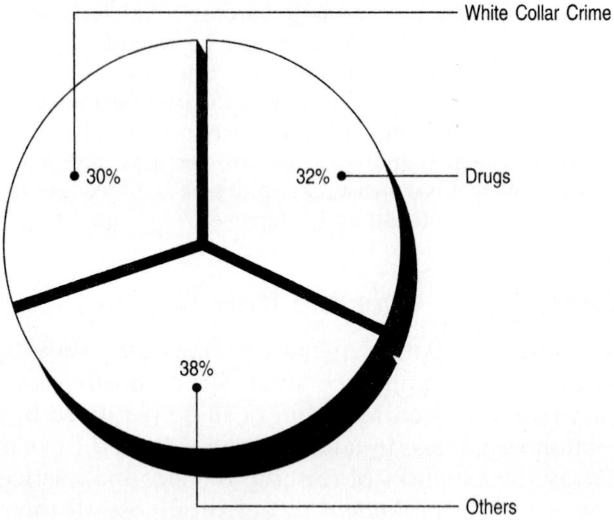

Criminal Debt Balance = $968 Million

September 1989

Figure 7.2

Most collections were for white collar crime. (*Source*: Testimony by Lowell Dodge, Director U.S. General Accounting Office. *Administration of Justice Issues: Overview of Civil and Criminal Debt Collection Efforts*. Washington, D.C.: U.S. Department of Justice [July 31, 1990].)

7% Drugs

25% — Other

68%   White Collar Crime

Criminal Debt Collections = $82 Million

September 1989

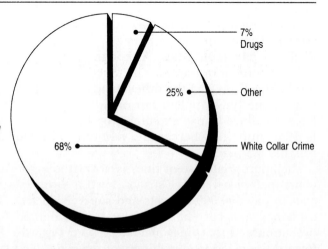

do not have the funds to reimburse the taxpayers for this, and I am going to order this very substantial amount so that you can reimburse the county and the state for the cost of your prosecution, and also in some wise to maybe pay something for your staying out of jail, because the Court seriously thought about imposing some time in jail as a condition of probation but I am not going to do that. I hope that you will learn your lesson and you will conduct yourself in a proper way from here on in. You are to pay a fine of $90,000.00, plus penalty assessment, to the probation officer within a period of 30 days.[75]

Current Administration of Fines

Across the country there is a tremendous variance in who is responsible for administering and collecting fines. These responsibilities may be spread out among judges, court clerks, prosecutors, probation officers, and parole officers.

Figure 7–3 shows the authority for collecting fines in the federal criminal court system. Federal agents, such as the Federal Bureau of Investigation and the Federal Drug Enforcement Agency, refer cases to the U.S. Attorney General's office. Those offenders given fines as part of a sentence will have a criminal debt record with the Federal Debt Collection Unit. The federal report also indicates that most debt is over one year old. Most collections take place from recent cases.

Figure 7.3

Prosecution and collection process for criminal fines. (*Source:* Testimony by Lowell Dodge, Director U.S. General Accounting Office. *Administration of Justice Issues: Overview of Civil and Criminal Debt Collection Efforts.* Washington, D.C.: U.S. Department of Justice [July 31, 1990].)

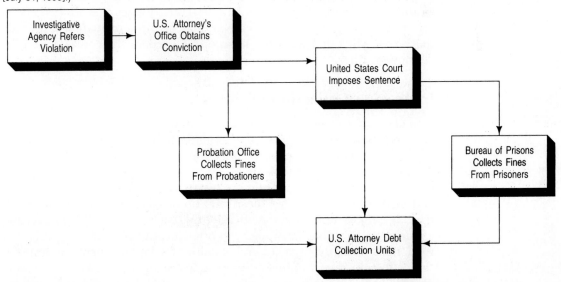

Although the effort to collect fines takes a considerable amount of time and personnel, critics say it is often one of the most poorly coordinated and administered functions of the justice system.[76] The diffusion of responsibility for fines is a major collection problem.

In most cases, there is no incentive for those collecting fines to do a thorough job because the collection office does not realize the profits. In many jurisdictions, funds collected from fines go to other state and local services, such as libraries, schools, and literacy programs.[77] Most agents also believe that their limited resources are needed for operations other than the collection of fines. Understandably, courts and law enforcement agents are not eager to expend their own resources collecting funds that will not be spent in their departments.

Contributing to the problem of collecting fines are the limited options available to coerce fines from offenders who do not promptly pay. One study found that drug offenders had the lowest success level in making fine payments.[78] A majority of judges surveyed in 1984 believed that offenders who fail to pay fines do not think anything will happen to them. Still, these judges admitted that their courts' own administrative methods were responsible for much of the nonpayment problem.[79] Many offices responsible for fine collection believe that there are insufficient methods and resources available to enforce fine collection.

Most jurisdictions do not relish the idea of revoking a person's probation or parole sentence even if the failure to pay a fine is intentional. First, a warrant must be issued, which places an additional burden on law enforcement to serve and make an arrest on a warrant. An offender is usually jailed subsequent to arrest, and court hearings must be held. In many cases, the administrative cost of following up on an unpaid fine may amount to more than the fine itself. As expensive and inefficient as this may seem, 68 percent of upper-court judges and 85 percent of lower-court judges surveyed in a National Institute of Justice study said that arrest warrants were the procedures used in their jurisdiction for delinquent fines.[80]

Improving Collection of Fines

It is clear that progressive and intermediate steps are needed to maximize payments without disproportionately increasing operational costs. Some methods used to ensure collection of fines use a positive strategy of encouragement and incentives for people to make their payments. Other collection strategies are more negative, relying on coercion, threats, and increased sanctions for those who do not pay. Still others are fairly neutral, simply reminding the offender that payments are due or overdue.

The suggestion has been made to offer incentives, such as percentage reductions for early payment and penalties for late payments, to improve the collection rate. Another idea includes using telemarketing firms to provide reminder-telephone calls to those who are late with payments.

Tacoma, Washington, reports having used telemarketing techniques and, in the first two years, collecting $375,000 at a cost of $26,000. The court adds that 20 percent of all cases assigned to the telemarketing company have been paid in full.[81]

Collection agencies may use even a wider range of methods to ensure that continued payments are received. In a Washington study, delinquent cases were randomly divided between three types of follow-up strategies. The collection agency had the most success, retrieving 20.6 percent of the potential funds from its assigned cases. The third-party billing service was able to account for 14.3 percent of its potential fines, and the court-generated late notice achieved only 5.7 percent.[82]

Another suggestion for collecting a fine is to have the courts accept credit-card payments. By accepting credit-card payments, the court would shift the collection responsibility to the bank issuing the card. Theoretically, officials believe that offenders may be more inclined to charge their debt promptly than if they waited to raise the cash for the payment.

Most experts recommend that courts or other collection authorities use some form of computerized notification system. The computer would keep track of each offender's payment schedule and print reminder postcards when payments are late. The computer would also alert officials when a reminder fails to bring in a delinquent payment. Some systems automatically make reminder phone calls, and others send out computer-generated postcards. Programs may also include second and third notices with increasingly severe warnings.

Research from England and West Germany indicates that simply notifying offenders of delinquent fines by mail has been very successful and inexpensive.[83] A Virginia report suggests taking or suspending an offender's drivers license for failure to pay fines. It also advocates a way to block renewal of the offender's motor vehicle registration if fines remain unpaid.[84]

Another positive approach is the use of *amnesty days*. To clear the books of outstanding debts, a county may offer people a chance to pay only their original fines by setting aside accrued penalty charges. Over time, the penalties may become so large that people are discouraged from settling the debt and default on payment. The county may issue warrants on these debts, but often this system becomes backlogged due to the lack of personnel to service the notices.

In one amnesty program, offenders made payments on tickets that were up to 10 years old. One woman was able to pay the original $300 she owed and not the $1400 tab that had accumulated. Another man paid a $645 ticket and avoided serving time in jail. [85]

Prevention may be the best strategy for avoiding delinquent fines. There are several keys to successful fine operations. First, fines should be specifically tailored to the ability of the offender to pay. Second, the time allotted for payment should be relatively short. Finally, the offender should sign a contract agreeing to the terms of payments.[86]

Success of Economic and Community Service Sanctions

Although there has been little research on the effectiveness of such sanctions as restitution, fines, and community service, there is no doubt about their popular appeal. Because these sentences appear to be cost effective yet punitive, the public favors their use. Despite the attractiveness of these punishments, the public should hold the justice system accountable to demonstrate that the punishments really work. Experts who criticize the increased use of fines and restitution claim that the collection of fees and information about the success of these sentences has not kept pace. Some officials argue that the accumulation of individual assessments has taken place without a comprehensive plan or realistic policy. The director of the National Institute of Corrections, Raymond Brown, wrote in 1988 as follows:

> The bulk of this growth in economic sanctions appears to be unplanned, resulting from a wide variety of motivations. New fees are created and imposed without any policy foundation for the total body of economic sanctions within a jurisdiction. While individually, the assessments appear appropriate, taken in total, the assessments levied on an individual offender may result in limited likelihood of collection. What may occur is a competition among agencies for what little monies are collected.[87]

As a result of haphazard growth in economic sanctions, contradictory practices have developed as well as inequities between agencies and cases. In some instances, offenders have been required to pay fees disproportionate to their crimes and to their ability to pay.[88] The National Institute of Corrections recommends that jurisdictions adopt formal guidelines and policies governing the use of economic sanctions. Such guidelines would be ethically fair and legally defensible.

Despite the cautions, there are some indications of the deterrent, or rehabilitative, value of economic sanctions. Glaser and Gordon reported that financial penalties were associated with lower recidivism rates.[89] Their study compared offenders with similar records who were given (1) probation alone, (2) probation with economic sanctions, or (3) terms of incarceration. The offenders who were assessed financial penalties were less likely to recidivate than either of the other two groups.

The results of a national study of a variety of systems of fee collection summarize what we know about recovering costs. According to Dale Parent, who conducted the study, several factors increase the likelihood of payment.[90] They include the use of program fees, such as for supervision and room and board, rather than service fees, such as for drug testing. These fees are set at modest levels and target the greater correctional population for payments, particularly misdemeanants. Parent also suggests that programs be given high priority by judges and correctional administrators and that from the beginning offenders who are unable to pay be screened out. Parent concludes that fee collection is most successful when (1) agency administrators have an incentive to collect fees, (2) procedures allow for swift and certain sanctions for non-payment, (3) nonprofessional staff assume most routine payment duties, and (4) the monitoring of the payment schedule is automated or computerized.

When Alternative Sentences Fail

An offender can fail to meet the requirements of the alternative sentences discussed in this chapter in several ways. One way is to fail to pay any of the restitutions or fines owed or to fail to perform the community service as directed. In such cases, the sentence may be revoked and the offender sent to prison or jail. In other instances, the court may extend the community service terms throughout the period an offender is on intensive supervision or on house arrest.

Modifying the sentences of violators may seem like an effective penalty, but it can have other effects on the community corrections system. The modifications may ultimately increase the number of staff needed to maintain the increased caseloads that will result from longer periods of supervision.

Finally, as a solution to nonpayment, fines may be increased or late charges assessed. The drawback to either of these penalties is the low probability that those who did not pay their original fines will now pay the greater fines.

SUMMARY

Community service and economic sanctions are the culmination of several trends in the criminal justice system, one of which is to make sentences more individualistic in the hope of having offenders complete them successfully. Punishments in these cases are tailored to the offense as well as to the perpetrator in an effort to match needs with abilities and potential. Another force shaping this movement is the attempt to make the punishment serve victims, society, and the justice system itself. One way this is accomplished is to have the offender pay for the loss or damage that occurred in the course of a crime. For example, in 1989 fines and restitution costs levied against doctors who filed fraudulent Medicare claims totaled $63 million nationwide.[91]

Economic sanctions are popular because they can be added to almost all punishments and they can be adjusted individually. Legislators supporting the use of economic sanctions can still appear to be tough on crime because the offender is being made to "pay," yet these alternatives may be used in place of already crowded prisons.[92]

Both restitution and community service seem to try to provide a moral lesson that will in some way reform the offender and encourage positive ties to the community. Restitution is often more appropriate for property offenders. The amount of money needed to complete restitution usually corresponds with the part of the loss that was uncollectable through other means.

According to Jacobs, there are several barriers to effective use of community service.[93] One is the problem of liability insurance to cover the persons performing the work. Another is locating useful work assignments on which participants will be adequately supervised.

Compared to the other common forms of alternative sentences, fines serve a more punitive purpose. Although fines are a means of retribution, they also serve to deter persons from reoffending. When one researcher compared recipients of fines to those receiving probation or community service, those with fines were more likely to say that the primary purpose of their sentence was deterrence than were the other two groups.[94]

CASES

Bearden v. *Georgia*, 461 U.S. 660, 103 S.Ct.2064, 76 L.Ed.2d 221 (1983).

Commonwealth v. *Wood*, 446 A.2d 948 (1982).

In re Pellegrino, 42 B.R. 129, (1984).

People v. *Fisher*, 237 Michigan 504.

People v. *Baker*, 37 CA App 3d, 108 (1974).

Tate v. *Short*, 401 U.S. 395, 91 S.Ct. 668, 28 L.Ed.2d 130 (1971).

United States v. *Mahoney*, 859 F.2d 47 (7th Cir. 1988).

United States v. *Atkinson*, 788 F.2d 900 (2nd Cir. 1986).

United States v. *Durham*, 755 F.2d 511 (6th Cir. 1985).

Williams v. *Illinois*, 399 U.S. 235, 90 S.Ct. 2018, 26 L.Ed.2d 586 (1970).

KEY TERMS

service fees
special assessments
court costs
fines
restitution
Victim and Witness Protection Act
Victims of Crime Assistance Act

Federal Welfare Reform Act
restitution center
community service
volunteer service or reparation
day fine
Federal Comprehensive Crime
  Control Act

DISCUSSION QUESTIONS

1. How should fines be assessed? Should a person who has more money pay a greater fine than someone who has very little money when both have committed the same crime? How much weight should be given to the ability to pay?
2. What is the proper role for victims in the restitution process? What should be the relationship between the victim and the offender?
3. What type of community service sentences could be developed in your area? What type of offenders would be sentenced to these programs, and why?
4. Develop a process for the collection of fines that would maximize potential revenues. Who would be in charge, and why?
5. Gregg Peterson embezzled $200,000 from the credit company where he worked and subsequently lost it gambling at the racetrack. Company officials have agreed to let him keep his $22,000-a-year job if he returns the funds. Peterson is divorced and has an eight-month-old baby. Work out a realistic repayment schedule, keeping in mind his living expenses.
6. How would you design a research project to determine the relative effectiveness of restitution, fines, and community service?

END NOTES

1. Wingert, Pat (1988). And what of deadbeat dads? *Newsweek*, 19 December, p. 66.
2. Bureau of Justice Statistics (1988). *Report to the nation on crime and justice*. Washington, DC: U.S. Department of Justice, p. 114.
3. Ibid.
4. Baird, Christopher (1986). *Fees for probation services*. Boulder, CO: National Institute of Corrections.
5. Mullaney, Fahy (1988). *Economic sanctions in community corrections*. Washington, DC: National Institute of Corrections, U.S. Department of Justice, p. viii.
6. McDonald, Douglas (1987). *Restitution and community service*. Washington, DC: National Institute of Justice, p. 1.
7. Hudson, Joe, and Burt Galaway (1989). Financial Restitution: Toward an evaluable program model. *Canadian Journal of Criminology* 31(1):1–18.
8. Carter, Robert, Jack Cocks, and Daniel Glaser (1987). Community service: A review of the basic issues. *Federal Probation* 51(1):4–10.
9. Ibid.
10. Wingert, Pat (1988). Supra note 1, p. 66.
11. Hudson, Joe, and Burt Galaway (1989). Supra note 7, p. 2.
12. Roy, Sudipta (1990). Offender-oriented restitution bills: Bringing total justice for victims: *Federal Probation* 54(3):30–36.
13. Geis, Gilbert (1990). Crime victims: Practices and prospects, in *Victims of Crime*, ed. Arthur Lurigio, Wesley Skogan, and Robert Davis, p. 263. Newbury Park, CA: Sage.

14. Courlander, Michael (1988). Restitution programs: Problems and solutions. *Corrections Today* 50(4):165–167.

15. Mayne, Carol, and Gordon Garrison (1979). *Restitution: An analysis of the use of restitution during 1977 in Provincial Court Charlottetown, Prince Edward Island and examination of the many aspects of restitution.* Charlottetown, PET: Probation and Family Court Services, Prince Edward Island Department of Justice.

16. *Commonwealth* v. *Wood* 446 A.2d 948 at 950. (See Cases, page 200.)

17. Adair, Jr., David (1989). Looking at the law. *Federal Probation* 53(1):85–88.

18. Ibid., p. 88.

19. Cunniff, Mark, and Mary Shilton (1990). *A sentencing postscript II: Felony probationers under supervision in the community.* Washington, DC: Bureau of Justice Statistics.

20. Lurigio, Arthur (1984). The relationship between offender characteristics and the fulfillment of financial restitution. Chicago: Cook county Adult Probation Department.

21. Lurigio, Arthur, and Robert Davis (1990). Does a threatening letter increase compliance with restitution orders?: A field experiment. *Crime and Delinquency* 36(4):537–548.

22. Beccaria, Cesare (1764). Reprinted. *On Crimes and Punishments.* Indianapolis: Bobbs-Merrill, p. 63.

23. Galaway, Burt, and W. Marsala (1976). An exploratory study of the perceived fairness of restitution as a sanction for juvenile offenders. Paper presented at the Second International Symposium on Victimology, Boston, MA.

24. Schneider, Peter, William Griffith, and Ann Schneider (1982). Juvenile restitution as a sole sanction or condition of probation: An empirical analysis. *Journal of Research in Crime and Delinquency* 19(1):47–65.

25. Hudson, Joe, and Burt Galaway (1989). Supra note 7.

26. U.S. Bureau of Justice Assistance (1988). *Restitution by juveniles.* Washington, DC: U.S. Bureau of Justice Assistance.

27. Courlander, Michael (1988). Supra note 14, p. 166.

28. Lawrence, Richard (1990). Restitution programs pay back the victim and society. *Corrections Today* 52(1): 96–98.

29. Harlow, Nora, and E.K. Nelson (1990). Probation's responses to fiscal constraints, in *Community Corrections*, ed. David Duffee and Edmond McGarrell, p. 177. Cincinnati: Anderson Publishing.

30. Ibid.

31. Heinz, J., B. Galaway, and J. Hudson (1976). Restitution or parole: A follow-up study of adult offenders. *Social Sciences Review* 50:148–156.

32. Schneider, Peter, William Griffith, and Anne Schneider (1982). Supra note 24.

33. Schneider, Anne, and Jean Warner (1989). *National trends in juvenile restitution programming.* Washington, DC: Office of Juvenile Justice and Delinquency Prevention. p. 9.

34. Shichor, David, and Arnold Binder (1982). Community restitution for juveniles: An approach and preliminary evaluation. *Criminal Justice Review* 7(2):46–50.

35. Schneider, Anne, and Jean Warner (1989). Supra note 33.

36. Schneider, Anne, W. Griffith, and A. Schneider (1998). Supra note 24.

37. Roy, Sudipta (1990). The impact of restitution program on juvenile offenders: A case study in Kalamazoo, Michigan. Paper presented at the annual meeting of the American Society of Criminology, Baltimore.

38. Van Voorhis, Patricia (1985). Restitution outcome and probationers' assessments of restitution: The effects of moral development. *Criminal Justice and Behavior* 12(3): 259–287.

39. Schneider, Anne (1990). *Deterrence and juvenile crime: Results from a national policy experiment.* New York: Springer-Verlag.

40. Shichor, David, and Arnold Binder (1982). Supra note 34, p. 47.

41. Zehr, Howard (1989). Justice: The restorative vision. Elkhart, IN: MCC United States, Office of Criminal Justice.

42. Galaway, Burt (1988). Restitution as innovation or unfilled promises? *Federal probation* 52(3):3–14.

43. Zehr, Howard, and Mark Umbreit (1982). Victim offender reconciliation: An incarceration substitute. *Federal Probation* 46(4):63–68.

44. Ibid., p. 65.

45. Galaway, Burt (1988), supra note 42; Coates, R., and Gehm, R. (1985). *Victim meets offender: An evaluation of victim offender reconciliation programs*. Michigan City, IN: PACT Institute of Justice.

46. Staples, William (1986). Restitution as a sanction in juvenile court. *Crime and Delinquency* 32(2):177–186.

47. Kaplan, David, and C. Bingham (1990). A new era of punishment. *Newsweek*, 14 May; 50–51.

48. McDonald, Douglas (1987). Supra note 6

49. Ibid., p. 1.

50. Hudson, Joe, and Burt Galaway (1990). Community Service: Towards program definition. *Federal Probation* 54(2):3.

51. Carter, Robert, J. Cocks, and D. Glasser (1987). Supra note 8, p. 4.

52. Del Carmen, R. (1989). *Probation law and practice in Texas*. Huntsville, TX: Criminal Justice Center, Sam Houston State Univ., p. 96.

53. Hudson, J. and B. Galaway (1990). Supra note 50, p. 6.

54. Jacobs, James (1989). *Drunk driving*. Chicago: Univ. of Chicago Press, p. 121.

55. Probation Division, Administrative Office of the United States Courts (1989). Implementing community service: The referral process. *Federal Probation* 53(1):3–9.

56. Georgia Department of Corrections (1988). *Probation's role in a balanced approach to corrections*. Atlanta: Georgia Department of Corrections. p. 10.

57. Kaplan, David, and C. Bingham (1990). Supra note 47.

58. Ibid.

59. Piller, Ruth (1988). Probated sentences take new meaning. *Houston Chronicle*. 16 March: B2.

60. Gainer, Mira. California League of Alternative Sentencing Programs. Personal communication, February 19, 1991.

61. Piller, Ruth (1988). Supra note 59.

62. Lawrence, Richard (1990). Supra note 28, p. 98.

63. Agencies of the State of Washington (1988). *Biannual report, 1985–1987*. Olympia, WA: Office of Financial Management, p. 24–25.

64. Bondi, Connie (1990). When policies conflict: Can retributive state policy goals be met effectively by rehabilitative alternative sentencing strategies? Paper presented at the annual meeting of the academy of Criminal Justice Sciences, Denver, CO, p. 5.

65. Hillsman, Sally, Barry Mahoney, George Cole, and Bernard Auchter (1987). *Fines as criminal sanctions*. Washington, DC: National Institute of Justice, p. 1.

66. Ibid., p. 3.

67. Cole, George (1989). Innovations in collecting and enforcing fines. *National Institute of Justice Research in Action*, No. 215, July/Aug:2–6.

68. Wheeler, Gerald, Amy Rudolph, and Rodney Hissong (1989). Economic sanctions in perspective: Do probationers' characteristics affect fee assessment, payment and outcome? *APPA Perspectives*, Summer:12–17.

69. Jacobs, James (1989), Supra note 54, p. 118.

70. Greene, Judith (1990). *The Staten Island day fine experiment.* New York: Vera Institute of Justice, p. 1.

71. Ibid.

72. Ibid.

73. Krantz, Sheldon (1988). *Corrections and prisoners' rights.* St. Paul: West Publishing.

74. Hillsman, S., B. Mahoney, G. Cole, and B. Auchter (1987). Supra note 65. p. 2.

75. 112 Cal Rptr 142.

76. Hillsman, Sally (1988). The growing challenge of fine administration to court managers. *The Justice System Journal* 13(1):5–16.

77. Cole, George (1989). Supra note 67, p. 3.

78. Gillespie, Robert (1989). Criminal fines: Do they pay? *Justice System Journal* 13(3):365–378.

79. Cole, George (1989). Supra note 67, p. 3.

80. Hillsman, S., B. Mahoney, G. Cole, and B. Auchter (1987). Supra note 65.

81. Cole, George (1989). Supra note 67, p. 5.

82. Wick, Karen (1988). Evaluating three notification strategies for collecting delinquent traffic fines. *Justice System Journal* 13(1):64–72.

83. Hillsman, S., B. Mahoney, G. Cole, and B. Auchter (1987). Supra note 65.

84. Virginia Department of Criminal Justice Services (1987). *Unpaid fines, court costs and restitution in district and circuit courts in the Commonwealth.* Richmond, VA: Virginia Department of Criminal Justice Services.

85. *San Bernardino Sun* (1991). Victorville offers amnesty to traffic violators, 16 July : B1.

86. Cole, George (1989). Supra note 67, p. 4.

87. Brown, Raymond (1988), in Mullaney, Fahy (1988). Supra note 5, p. v.

88. Mullaney, Fahy (1988). Supra note 5, p. 13.

89. Glaser, Daniel, and Margaret Gordon (1988). *Use and effectiveness of fines, jail, and probation.* Los Angeles: Univ. of Southern California, Social Science Research Institute.

90. Parent, Dale (1990). *Recovering correctional costs through offender fees.* Washington, DC: National Institute of Justice.

91. Lynch, Rene (1990). San Fernando Valley doctor accused of $1 million Medicare fraud. *San Bernardino Sun*, 4 September : B4.

92. Lawrence, Richard (1991). Reexamining community corrections models. *Crime and Delinquency* 37(4):449–464.

93. Jacobs, James (1989). Supra note 54, p. 121.

94. Thorvaldson, S. (1980). Toward the definition of the reparative aim, in *Victims, Offenders and Alternative Sanctions*, ed. J. Hudson and B. Galaway. Lexington, MA: Lexington Books.

8

Bridging Programs

OBJECTIVES

On completion of this chapter, you should be able to do the following:

1. Explain the differences between the various release mechanisms, such as furloughs, halfway houses, and parole.

2. Describe the function of the parole board.

3. Define tentative or presumptive parole dates and discuss the advantages and disadvantages of using them.

4. List some of the rights and privileges that a person may lose or have suspended as a result of a felony conviction.

5. Explain the findings of research on release outcomes and what we know now about recidivism.

PURPOSE

This chapter explores the various processes that release the incarcerated offender to the community. One of the most common release mechanisms is parole. Although state laws and the courts that sentence offenders determine who is eligible for releases such as parole, there is still some discretion involved in deciding when each eligible person will return to the community. The parole decision involves the work of parole agents and parole boards or commissions as well as the expectations of the public. The text describes the factors used to determine if someone is an appropriate candidate for release. Other discharge options involve furloughs, early release, and transitional living arrangements such as halfway houses and prerelease centers.

The remainder of the chapter discusses the factors related to the ex-offender's successful reintegration into society. Topics include the social, psychological, and legal barriers to participation in the full range of community activities. Many of the difficulties that an ex-offender faces are a direct consequence of a conviction. However, some of the problems the newly released inmate encounters are the product of biases and stereotypes within ourselves and within our communities. The chapter suggests educational, vocational, and counseling services that may assist the offender in adapting to his or her surroundings. Returning to work and the family are only two of the areas that reintegration programs emphasize.

INTRODUCTION

Whether inmates are released from prison early and are on supervision or whether they have completed their entire sentence, they face obstacles to reintegration with society. These barriers are social, economic, and even political in nature.

In many ways ex-offenders face the same obstacles to success as do nonoffenders who have similar personal characteristics. These traits include low income, limited skills and education, and a poor work history.

BRIDGING

Bridging is a term used to describe efforts to ease offenders' readjustment to the community after incarceration. When imprisoned, individuals go through many emotional and behavioral changes that alter their perception of who they are and how they fit into society. Incarceration means a lifestyle of emotional extremes that may foster fears and insecurities in inmates' minds. The strictly disciplined schedules and over-enforcement of even minor rules make lasting impressions on those who spend time behind bars. In addition to changing the way such persons see themselves, the experience of incarceration may negatively alter the way they relate to others.

Although it is difficult to adjust to life in prison, it is also difficult to adjust to community life after being incarcerated. As one newly released man explained, "You have to relearn how to talk with people. If somebody bumps into you, you don't have to hit him. Here you learn to say, 'excuse me.'"[1] Because this adjustment process is so important in preventing recidivism, various programs and services have been developed to aid in recovery. The goals of bridging programs are to speed the successful reintegration of the ex-offender into the community.

Although the term *reintegration* implies that offenders were integrated in their communities before incarceration, this may not be the case. For each person, there will have been varying degrees of involvement or integration within the greater community that can be visualized on a continuum from little or none to a fully integrated social life.

If ex-offenders are able to achieve the same level of integration that they previously experienced, we could accurately use the term reintegration. For most offenders, however, it would probably be more desirable to achieve a greater degree of involvement, or integration, than they previously knew. This would include taking on the responsibility of a regular job as well as performing community service and attending activities that may be required by release or parole contracts. It is part of the goal of bridging programs to help offenders achieve their desired level of community involvement.

low integration high integration

Figure 8.1
Degree of integration in society before incarceration.

There are many different forms of bridging programs. Some emphasize supervision and the monitoring of conditionally released offenders. These programs are characterized by having specified times for the clients to call in or stop by. Periodic drug and alcohol testing may be done, and the clients must often demonstrate proof of employment or attendance at treatment programs. Other bridging programs focus on treatment and rehabilitation. Counselors are referral agents who facilitate the clients' access to the services required by their treatment plans. These services can include educational, vocational, or mental health programs. A third kind of program emphasis addresses the basic survival needs of the clients, such as a place to live and regular meals.

It is possible to structure bridging programs to encompass two or three of the focuses just described. Many facilities have been designed on the theory that successful reintegration is tied to meeting all the needs of the offenders, in one place. The common-sense aspect of this coordinated treatment philosophy says that if ex-offenders have to run around to too many resources for assistance, they may become discouraged. As a result, many clients simply give up trying to abide by the rules of supervision, especially when it is difficult to find adequate transportation to and from appointments. Many offenders do not have their own cars and must rely on friends, relatives, and public transportation to get around.

Statistics show that more than 80 percent of those released from prison receive some kind of supervision in the community.[2] Consequently, many varied programs relate to community supervision. Programs range from services that prepare inmates for release while they are still incarcerated to those that help ex-offenders even after they have completed their sentences.

Furloughs

A furlough is a temporary release from incarceration that may last anywhere from a few hours to a few days. During a furlough, a prisoner may leave the facility unsupervised, but each person on furlough is given a specific deadline for return. In most instances, local law enforcement authorities receive notification of all furloughs within their jurisdiction. Concern about the smuggling of prohibited items back into prison from the outside following furloughs has led most departments to stripsearch everyone returning from furlough. Inmates may also be required to submit to drug and alcohol testing on return from any furlough.

Furlough programs were initiated during the 1960s as part of a rehabilitative effort to ease the offender's transition into the community. During furloughs, offenders become reacquainted with their families and look for jobs, housing, or schooling. Furloughs may serve as a management tool to reward inmates for good behavior, which is especially useful for exemplary inmates who have been incarcerated for many years. Such inmates may otherwise, by virtue of their sentence, never be released. Furloughs have also been used to temporarily relieve overcrowding when the prison or jail populations exceed court-ordered limits.

A survey by the editors of *Corrections Compendium* determined that all states, as well as the Federal Bureau of Prisons, use some form of furlough program. Approximately 53,000 inmates received a total of 200,000 furloughs by corrections institutions in 1987.[3] According to departmental officials, furloughs are an important morale factor among inmates and a good preparation for release.

A number of factors are considered in the decision to grant a furlough. The most commonly used variables are the inmate's security (or risk) classification, the amount of time already served, the proximity of the inmate's projected release date, the offense committed, and behavior the inmate has demonstrated while incarcerated. As of 1988, 36 states allowed furloughs for prisoners serving life sentences.[4] The guidelines for furloughs in South Carolina are given in Box 8–1.

Over the years the courts have entertained the notion that a prison administrator can be held liable for the decision to grant a furlough should the released prisoner commit a serious crime. In one of the more controversial cases, Massachusetts officials were charged with deliberate indifference following a murder committed by an inmate on furlough. The released prisoner had allegedly murdered the woman he had threatened to kill months before. In this case, *Estate of Gilmore* v. *Buckley*, the parents of Patricia Gilmore attempted to hold state hospital officials liable for the deadly actions of Bradford Prendergast. Although Prendergast had been denied parole, he was out on furlough when he murdered Gilmore.

The primary issue in the Gilmore case was not so much the furlough as it was that hospital officials failed to initiate civil commitment proceedings against Prendergast on the basis of his mental health problems. However, the court found that hospital officials did not act with deliberate indifference in releasing Prendergast from the state's criminal psychiatric facility. The state was able to demonstrate that their fur-

BOX 8–1

Supervised Furlough in South Carolina

South Carolina enacted a Supervised Furlough Program in 1981, and the General Assembly modified the program in 1983, 1986, and 1987. Following is a summary of the program as provided for in Section 24-13-710, S.C. Code of Laws.

The Department of Corrections and the Department of Probation, Parole, and Pardon Services have developed a cooperative agreement for the operation of the Supervised Furlough Program. The program permits carefully screened and selected inmates who have served the mandatory minimum sentence as required by law or have not committed any one of certain specified crimes* to be released on furlough prior to parole eligibility under the supervision of the Department of Probation, Parole and Pardon Services. These inmates have the privilege of residing in an approved residence and continuing treatment, training, or employment in the community until parole eligibility or expiration of sentence, whichever is earlier.

The statute further provides that to be eligible for the program, an inmate must: (1) maintain a clear disciplinary record for at least six months prior to consideration; (2) demonstrate to Department of Corrections officials a general desire to become a law-abiding member of society; (3) satisfy any other reasonable requirements imposed upon him by the Department; (4) have an identifiable need for and willingness to participate in authorized community-based programs and rehabilitative services; and (5) have been committed to the Department of Corrections with a total sentence of five years or less as the first or second adult commitment for a criminal offense for which the inmate received a sentence of one year or more.

The Department of Corrections has established certain criteria which must be met by an otherwise eligible individual: no outstanding holds, wanteds, or detainers; must not have been removed from participation in a community program within six months of eligibility for supervised furlough; must not be released directly from a psychiatric unit; must not have escaped or been returned from escape within six months of eligibility; must not currently be a participant in the Extended Work Release Program; must have a residence in South Carolina verified and approved by the Department; must not have a pending disciplinary action that qualifies as a major institutional rules infraction; must have served at least six months of his sentence and be within six months of release; and must have served six months free of a major disciplinary infraction prior to eligibility date.

When placed in the Supervised Furlough Program, an inmate comes under the supervision of agents of the Department of Probation, Parole, and Pardon Services who insure the inmate's compliance with the rules, regulations, and conditions of the program, as well as monitoring the inmate's employment and participation in prescribed and authorized rehabilitative programs.

*(Criminal sexual conduct in the third degree; or a lewd act upon a child under the age of fourteen; or a violent crime (i.e. murder, criminal sexual conduct in the first and second degree, assault and battery with intent to kill, kidnapping, voluntary manslaughter, armed robbery, drug trafficking, arson in the first degree, and burglary in the first and second degree).)

Source: SCDC Annual Report FY 1988–89.

lough program had had a success rate of just over 99 percent before this incident. The judgment further held that the failure to petition for commitment was too far removed from the murder to hold hospital officials responsible.

Despite the finding in *Gilmore*, fears of liability for damages or injuries caused by inmates on furloughs have decreased the system's willingness to allow more of the special releases. Concern about liability has also limited potential releases to only the lowest-risk offenders. To this date, however, the most damage to inmates' chances of getting a furlough did not result from a court decision but from a political campaign.

In the 1988 presidential race, candidate George Bush's most successful and emotional appeal to voters was through a television commercial that sensationalized a rape committed by convicted murderer, Willie Horton, while Horton was on furlough in the state of the opposing candidate. When Bush won the election, politicians across the country feared that their careers would be in jeopardy if a furlough resulted in tragedy in their state. Consequently, there was a political backlash in furlough programs as legislators rushed to insulate themselves from potential harm.

Ironically, revisions to the federal prison furlough program under President Reagan and then-Vice-President Bush actually increased offender eligibility through 1985. By the end of 1989, however, Bush as president succeeded in having new exclusions added. New limitations prevented serious drug offenders, drug distributors, and those with a record of violent personal crimes or weapons-related crimes from being given furloughs.[5] An example of the effects of this movement can be seen in the furlough statistics from Connecticut (Table 8–1). As the table shows, in 1988 the number of furloughs granted decreased by 13 percent from the previous year.[6] The number of furloughs continued to decrease the following year, dropping by almost 48 percent.

Table 8–1 Yearly Trends in Connecticut Furloughs

Fiscal Year	Number of Furloughs	Change from Previous Year	Percentage of Change from Previous Year
1984–1985	26,221	7,231	+38.1
1985–1986	31,855	5,634	+21.5
1986–1987	35,132	3,277	+10.3
1987–1988	30,522	−4,610	−13.1
1988–1989	16,016	−14,506	−47.5

Source: Annual Report for Connecticut Department of Correction (August 1989). Hartford, CT: Connecticut Department of Corrections.

Community Corrections Centers

Whereas a furlough is a temporary visit in the community, a community corrections center is a transitional facility that houses inmates waiting for release on parole. The difference between halfway houses and community corrections centers is that to be eligible for a halfway house, the offender will already have been released from prison and, in most jurisdictions, paroled to a halfway house. A community corrections center, on the other hand, is a staging area that offers intensive prerelease programming to offenders awaiting official release.

Parole

One of the oldest formal systems of early release in this country is *parole.* By definition, parole is a conditional release to the community of an offender who has been incarcerated. There is no constitutional right or guarantee of parole. Parole is a privilege granted by federal or state authorities. As the U.S. Supreme Court specified in *Greenholtz* v. *Nebraska:*

> There is no constitutional or inherent right of a convicted person to be conditionally released before the expiration of a valid sentence. The natural desire of an individual to be released is indistinguishable from the initial resistance to being confined. But the conviction, with all its procedural safeguards has extinguished that liberty right: Given a valid conviction, the criminal defendant has been constitutionally deprived of his liberty.

The executive branch of government controls the parole function for the state. Thus, inmates in state prisons or juveniles committed to state facilities must be paroled by an executive order. Only the chief executive of a state, that is, the governor, has the power to release an offender from a state institution earlier than the court has mandated in its sentence.

The specific conditions or terms allowing for release are enumerated in a written contract. Violations of that contract may result in the termination of community supervision and the parolee's return to prison or jail. As in probation, a professional officer monitors the conduct of those offenders who have been released into a supervision program.

As of January 1989, there were approximately 407,000 persons on parole in the United States, a figure that represented 11 percent of all offenders under the care or custody of the criminal justice system. It also represented 224 out of every 100,000 adult residents in this country.[7]

History of Parole and Other Release Programs

Parole was first used in the United States as a release mechanism from the Elmira Reformatory in New York around 1880. Elmira was a progressive institution for young offenders that was run by reformer

Zebulon Brockway. During his tenure at Elmira, Brockway initiated many popular corrections innovations. The reformatory offered educational and vocational programs as well as a carefully planned "mark," or reward and classification system that allowed inmates to earn their own release.[8] The system was based on three classifications. As Rothman explains, "The inmate entered at grade two and if he behaved himself well (fulfilling work and school assignments and committing no disciplinary infractions), he could earn up to nine marks a month, thus six months or fifty-four marks later, he could win promotion to grade one—the only grade from which he could be released."[9] Today, earning privileges in a "token economy" is a popular concept of behavior modification practiced in many juvenile institutional settings. In many instances, the potential for release is related to successive rewards and promotions.

Release on parole from Elmira required that the offender had maintained good conduct while incarcerated and had a suitable employment plan. After release, the ex-inmate reported regularly to a "guardian," or sponsor, for a six-month period. Interestingly enough, experts believed that supervision periods of longer than six months would be discouraging for the participants and thus counterproductive.

Early American parole systems were also designed to service women when they were discharged from prison. However, the idea of simply turning women out into the community on completion of their sentences was always more difficult for the patriarchal justice system.

New York's Elmira Reformatory opened in 1876 and boasted of new rehabilitation strategies. The institution's vocational and academic programs, including the promotion for early release, were soon copied in reformatories all over the country. (*UPI/Bettmann Archive*)

Many of the women were homeless, or officials viewed their homes as "scenes of temptation."[10] One solution was to send the women to group shelters almost like the present-day halfway house.

In Boston in 1864 a private group that had received a small amount of state funds opened the Temporary Asylum for Discharged Female Prisoners. Likewise, in Detroit in the late 1800s, women were sent to a "house of shelter" not far from the prison. The shelter emphasized religious values and domestic and academic improvement. As a reward for good behavior, the women were allowed to swing their arms freely when walking rather than clasping them tightly behind their backs. Other rewards included prettier uniforms and the opportunity to decorate one's room. When the release process terminated, the women were placed into "good" homes as domestic servants.[11]

By 1900 20 states offered parole and 44 states had instituted parole systems by 1922. Currently, all states operate some type of parole release.

The Parole Process

Parole Eligibility. Although parole is not *constitutionally* mandated, it is possible for a state to write a law that requires each inmate to be considered for parole upon eligibility. For example, in Nebraska the law specifically directs the state parole board to release all eligible inmates unless they fall into one of the disqualifying categories. In most states today, eligibility for participation in parole programs is usually set by statute. The legislature, then, controls the criteria that offenders must meet before they can apply for release on parole.

Eligibility for parole is a legal status. It is an objective determination that may be assessed by anyone who understands the criteria. The specific criteria vary from state to state. One of the most common criteria is the amount of time served. Depending on the state, offenders may have to serve anywhere from one-third to three-fourths of a sentence before being considered eligible for parole.

Another commonly used criterion for determining parole eligibility is the kind of offense a person has committed. By law, certain violent or repeat offenders are ineligible for parole. Many states have written statutes that expressly prohibit parole for persons convicted of murder, rape, armed robbery, or kidnapping. Other states allow the prohibition as an option that may be imposed by the judge. This exclusionary status, such as "life without parole" or "25 years without consideration for parole," is designated at sentencing.

The Role of a Parole Officer. Parole officers may work in several places within the parole system. Although the most commonly recognized role of parole officers is supervising released offenders in the community, their work also includes input into the initial parole release decision. In this capacity, parole officers work within institutions preparing case files on inmates who become eligible and apply for parole.

They may also be called *caseworkers* or *parole counselors*. The tasks performed in this job include answering inmates' questions about parole eligibility, preparing case files on the inmates being considered for early release, interviewing the inmates about their future plans, and preparing recommendations on each candidate for paroling authorities.

Parole Plans.   The release decision weighs heavily on the ability of an inmate to develop a comprehensive and realistic parole plan. A parole plan may be submitted in writing or may be described in an oral interview. Components of a good plan include a place to live, a job, transportation, assumption of family responsibilities, and appropriate uses of leisure time. A 1975 study by the American Correctional Association found that 38 out of 50 parole boards required an offender to have a detailed plan. The applicant had to have a job or "satisfactory other resources, which could include a place to stay where the person would be taken care of until he could find a job, a social security check, personal financial resources, a training slot," and so on before parole release would be granted.[12] The parole-granting process in Texas is shown in the flowchart of Figure 8.2. Notice the importance of the role the parole plan plays in this process.

Presumptive Parole Dates.   Generally speaking, parole dates are set by a parole board or parole commission following a review of the prisoner's file and in some cases a personal interview. However, a few states have instituted systems that automatically set up all eligible inmates for parole release as long as they meet certain specified criteria or guidelines. All offenders who are not excluded by law from parole (by having a violent offense history, for example) are considered for parole and may even be given an advance notice of that date. This advance notice is called a *presumptive parole date*. The word *presumptive* means that unless the offenders lose eligibility status (by misbehavior, e.g.), they can expect to be released on the date assigned.

One often-argued aspect of parole is whether or not inmates who will be eligible for parole should know their release dates in advance and, if so, how far in advance notification should be. Some experts believe that inmates should be given tentative or presumptive parole dates on entering prison to enhance prison discipline. Each inmate would then have an incentive to maintain a good record and to avoid trouble. The presumptive date would apply only if the inmate followed all directives, and the date could be extended if there were disciplinary problems.

The use of the presumptive parole date is often advocated by inmates and institutional staff because it allows for more realistic planning for release. Advance notice can be used positively by inmates as well as their families to prepare for the release. Education and job plans often take time to arrange; knowing a release date would facilitate these plans. Advocates of presumptive parole dates also suggest that this system serves as a genuine incentive in a prison where there are few incentives or rewards.

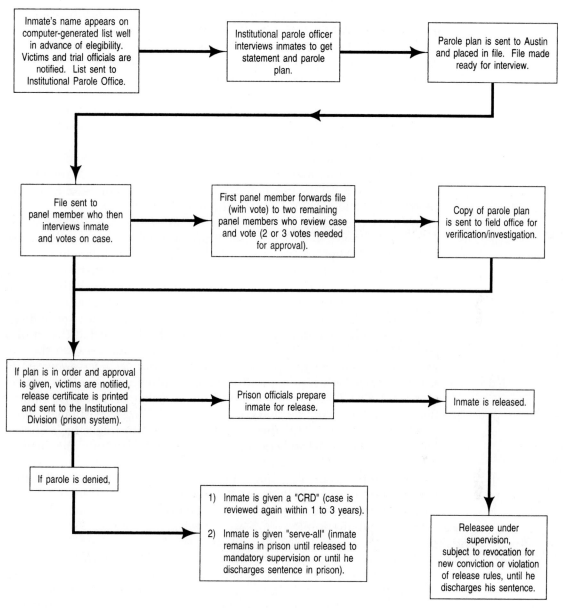

Figure 8.2

Parole procedures during 1990.

(*Source: Annual Report 1990,* Austin, TX: Texas Department of Criminal Justice.)

The Texas legislature passed a law giving the parole board the authority to assign tentative parole dates to incoming prisoners. The corrections system expects inmates to participate in education and counseling programs while incarcerated in order to be considered for release. Critics of the state statute argue that its function is primarily cosmetic because in each case the board uses its discretion in deciding whether to issue a tentative date. The board may also decide not to release an offender once that date arrives if it no longer appears appropriate to do so.[13]

Opponents of presumptive parole dates believe that for rehabilitation to occur the inmate's release date should be determined over time. They believe that parole is a privilege that must be earned with sincere and continuous effort. They hope that by not being given a release date in advance the inmate will strive to make progress in treatment programs, in work, and in social activities. These activities can provide inmates with personal enrichment as well as credit toward parole. Many professionals feel that not having a predetermined release date is an added incentive to participate in health and education programs and to avoid disciplinary problems.

In a 1982 study of this issue, new prison inmates were divided into two groups. One group received notice of the projected date of their release on parole and the other group did not. Researchers monitored those who were told their presumptive parole dates to see if this knowledge would adversely affect their time in prison. Results indicated that the group with notice of a parole date did not get into any more disciplinary trouble than did the control group who had no indication of a possible release date. The only difference in behavior between the two groups was that the group with presumptive parole dates appeared to enroll in fewer educational and vocational programs than the control group did. The authors of this study suggested that the lower enrollment figures did not mean that this group was less willing to participate in rehabilitation. In fact, they theorized that this group might have chosen fewer but more relevant courses compared to the group that had to apply for parole. The control group may have felt obligated to enroll in a variety of programs they did not even want just to impress authorities who granted paroles. This theory led the researchers to think that those who were trying to earn parole may have overreacted in their efforts to achieve rehabilitation.[14]

Parole versus Mandatory Supervision.   Early releases approved by a parole board are often called *discretionary releases* because they rely on the judgment of the individuals who review the case. When offenders are placed on parole, they remain under supervision until their sentences would have been completed had they remained in prison. An example is calculated in Box 8–2.

Trends across the country in 1989 seemed to show that fewer releases were being made by the discretionary authority of parole boards. One survey in 1989 indicated that after 1976, eleven states as well as the federal government had eliminated or restricted their parole boards' authority to grant discretionary releases.[15] According to statistics from 1977 and 1987, the number of parole board generated releases has

BOX 8–2

Example of Calculation of Time Served with a Parole Release

Sentence length: 12 years
State allows parole consideration after 50% served: 6 yrs
Date sentence began: 2–7–85
Parole eligible: 2–7–91
Parole granted: 8–18–91
Person remains on parole until: 2–7–97.

However, a person who has his or her parole revoked returns to prison on 12–3–94. This person will, most likely, lose credit for all the time served on parole. He or she will return to custody with credit only for the time served in prison from 2–7–85 until release on parole, 8–18–91 which is 6 years, 6 months and 11 days.

total sentence	11 years	11 months	30 days
minus time served	6 years	6 months	11 days
left to serve	5 years	5 months	19 days
date return prison	12–3–1994		
plus time left to serve	5 years	19 months	5 days
date end sentence	5–22–2000		

Unless this offender makes parole again, he or she will remain in custody from the date of return 12–3–94 until his or her accumulated prison time equals 12 years, which would be 5–22–2000.

---

declined from 72 percent of those exiting facilities to 41 percent.[16] Those inmates not given an early release by a parole board were, for the most part, released when their earned credit for good time added to the time served equaled the full length of the sentence. Some states call this practice *mandatory supervision.*

The number of offenders released on mandatory supervision has statistically increased steadily while discretionary releases have declined. The number of persons granted mandatory supervision releases grew from 6 percent of all releases in 1977 to 31 percent in 1987.[17] Offenders on mandatory release are treated the same as those who have received their parole from a discretionary authority. As with prisoners released by parole boards, those on mandatory supervision are under the control of the state until the original sentence or term of years has expired. An example of the calculation of an early release date based on the good-time credit earned is given in Box 8–3. If an inmate misbehaves before this release date, prison authorities can subtract good time, thus lengthening the inmate's stay.

BOX 8–3

Example of Calculation of an Early Release Date Based on Good-Time Credit

Today's date	5–31–92	
Date sentence begins	3–01–82	
Actual time served	2–30–10	or 10 yrs, 2 months, 30 days (or 123 months)

Good time earned   5 days per month = 123 × 5 = 615 days
615 days = approx. 20.5 months or 1 yr 8.5 months

Add the good time	1 yr	8 months	15 days
to the actual times served	10 yr	2 months	30 days
Total time =	11 yr	11 months	15 days

If this person was serving a 12 year sentence, he or she would have enough actual and good time earned to release in the next two weeks. This demonstrates how a 12 year sentence can be served in about 10 years and 3 months.

However, the offender will be on community supervision until a full 12 years has been served or:

3–1–82
+12 years
3–1–94

The Parole Hearing.   The parole board considers many different aspects of a case when deciding whether to grant parole. Traditionally, members of the board look at the offense committed as well as the offender's criminal history. In many instances, the presentence investigation provides information about a case. The board or commission may also consider prior dismissed charges if a defendant had been previously indicted, as well as hearsay evidence and even allegations of criminal activity for which the prisoner was never charged. A history of serious or repeated offenses makes it difficult to justify an application for early release.

The importance of a criminal history is that it offers the decision maker some insight into the seriousness of the violation that may occur should the parolee recidivate. For example, someone who has written bad checks in the past may not appear as risky as someone who has mugged people because of the nature of the possible future crime. Although past behavior is often unreliable in making predictions about future behavior, it remains one of the basic variables for determining risk.

Since 1923, parole authorities have used predictive instruments to gauge the success potential of a candidate.[18] Many of these instruments calculate the risk of the offender's recidivating by using standardized scores much like those used in the probation decision process. Parole authorities may use the risk scores as guidelines when making the parole release decision. As of 1989, approximately 19 states used some form of risk assessment in the parole decision-making process.[19] One of the most popular risk prediction devices is the Salient Factor Score.

The Salient Factor Score.   The Federal Parole Commission designed the *Salient Factor Score* instrument to indicate the likelihood that an offender will be successful on parole.[20] The instrument contains six items that a number of research studies have shown to be associated with recidivism. The higher an offender scores, the more likely he or she is to have a favorable supervision period and the lower is the probability of recidivism. The items used to calculate the Salient Factor Score appear in Box 8–4.

Offenders who score from 8 to 10 on this index are considered to be a very good risk, and those who score 6 to 7 to be a good risk. Those who score between 4 and 5 are a fair risk, and those who score below 4 are a poor risk. The Salient Factor Score is a popular method of risk assessment because it is easy to score. It is also easy for prisoners, prison staff, and persons outside the corrections system to understand.

The United States Parole Commission has conducted research on the ability of the Salient Factor Score to predict who will be successful on parole. Studies show that the Salient Factor Score may range anywhere from 50 to 90 percent accurate in predicting success during the first year of release.[21] As the years go by, even more of those initially predicted to be successful will recidivate. Another related method of risk assessment is to use the Salient Factor Score in a more complex matrix (see Figure 8.3) that allows for the weighing of the seriousness of the present offense. Thus, as the Salient Factor Score increases and as the offense becomes more serious, the level of risk on parole increases. As the score moves away from the less serious offenses and the low Salient Factor Scores (quadrant 1), the risk levels increase.

A third commonly used device for predicting risk allows paroling authorities to consider the behavior of the inmate while incarcerated. As demonstrated in Figure 8–4, this is a sequential, or elimination, model that begins with a pool of all persons eligible for parole. From this group, those who have had good disciplinary records while incarcerated remain in the selection process and those with serious disciplinary charges are screened out. Once those with good disciplinary records are identified, they are further broken down into those with serious and those with non-serious prior criminal histories. The process then eliminates those inmates with serious criminal histories. Finally, parolees are selected from the group that remains—well-behaved inmates without serious prior records.

BOX 8–4

Salient Factor Score Instrument

A. Prior Convictions/Adjudications (Adult or Juvenile)   —

> None = 3
> One = 2
> Two or three = 1
> Four or more = 0

B. Prior Commitments of More Than 30 Days (Adult or Juvenile)   —

> None = 2
> One or two = 1
> Three or more = 0

C. Age at Current Offense/Prior Commitments   —

> Age at commencement of the current offense:
> 26 years of age or older = 2*
> 20-25 years of age = 1*
> 19 years of age or younger = 0

D. Recent Commitment-Free Period (3 years)   —

> No prior commitment of more than 30 days (adult or juvenile), or released to
> the community from last such commitment at least three years prior to the
> commencement of the current offense = 1
> Otherwise = 0

E. Probation/Parole/Confinement/Escape Status of Violator at This Time   —

> Neither on probation, parole, confinement, or escape status at the time of
> the current offense; nor committed as a probation, parole, confinement or
> escape status violator this time = 1
> Otherwise = 0

F. Heroin/Opiate Dependence   —

> No history of heroin or opiate dependence = 1
> Otherwise = 0

Total Score   —

*Exception: if five or more prior commitments of more than thirty days (adult or juvenile), place
an × here __ and score this item = 0

Figure 8.3

Matrix for predicting parole success.

(*Source*: Donald Gottfredson, Colleen Cosgrove, Leslie Wilkins, Jane Wallerstein and Carol Rauh [1978]. *Classification for Parole Decision Policy.* Washington, DC: National Institute of Law Enforcement and Criminal Justice.)

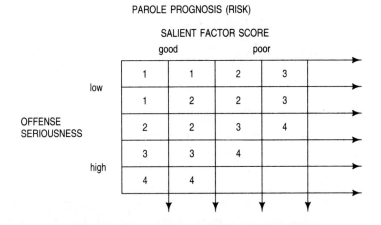

Issues in the Use of Risk Assessment.   The use of risk assessment devices is questionable because of the emphasis on the past activity of the offender as a basis for predicting future behavior. Some penologists argue that this practice is unfair. Others (e.g., Andrew Von Hirsch) contend that punishment should be based on what offenders deserve on the basis of their present crime and not what experts predict about their future behavior. This just-deserts model avoids the problem of moral responsibility for mistakes in prediction. The potential for error in the prediction of risk can be diagrammed as in Figure 8.5.

As Figure 8.5 illustrates, two kinds of possible errors may occur. One is to predict that someone will not commit another crime, when in fact they do. This *false negative* is perhaps the scenario that parole authorities fear most. When these cases occur, they often haunt authorities with bad publicity and even lawsuits. The costs include injury to the

Figure 8.4

Sequential or elimination model of risk assessment.

(*Source*: Donald Gottfredson, Colleen Cosgrove, Leslie Wilkins, Jane Wallerstein, and Carol Rauh [1978]. *Classification for Parole Decision Policy.* Washington DC: National Institute of Law Enforcement and Criminal Justice.)

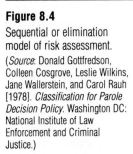
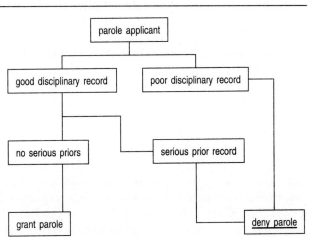

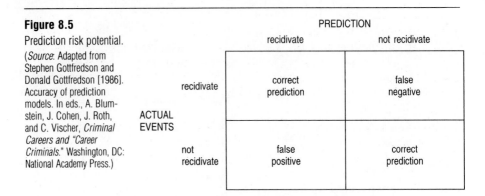

Figure 8.5

Prediction risk potential.

(*Source*: Adapted from Stephen Gottfredson and Donald Gottfredson [1986]. Accuracy of prediction models. In eds., A. Blumstein, J. Cohen, J. Roth, and C. Vischer, *Criminal Careers and "Career Criminals."* Washington, DC: National Academy Press.)

victim, crimes that appear to have been preventable, and a loss of credibility for the system.[22] For example, parole board members were impressed when award-winning author Norman Mailer advocated the release of a newly discovered writing talent, Jack Abbott. Just a short time after release, however, Abbott stabbed and killed a young waiter in a cafe for no apparent reason. The ability of the board or criminal experts to have predicted Abbott's behavior has been the subject of considerable controversy and a lawsuit filed by the victim's widow.

On the other hand, to predict that persons will fail on parole and then to deny them the opportunity for release when in actuality they would not have violated is also problematic. Such caution may result in the waste of expensive prison or jail space. In addition, these candidates are denied freedom and the opportunity to begin life again. Although this *false positive* outcome may not cause the agency the embarrassment of the false negative, it is a tragedy for the individual offender and his or her family and also results in a loss of credibility for the system.

Authorities in Colorado believed that the use of a device for risk prediction would eliminate much of the controversy and personal guilt associated with decision making. Officials in Colorado legislated the use of risk assessment guidelines in 1987.[23]

Other Release Considerations. Another variable considered in the release decision process is the demeanor and attitude of offenders at the hearings. Parole commissions and boards will often interview offenders to facilitate the assessment of each case. During the interviews, officials hear and consider the applicants' versions of the events leading to their crimes.

Another factor traditionally cited as important to parole boards is that offenders should show remorse or regret for having committed their crimes. The board also weighs offenders' chances for success on the outside, particularly in terms of employment, education, family, and avoiding further criminal involvement. The members of the board may make predictions about offenders' success on the basis of their instincts as to whether the offenders appear to have learned a lesson from their incarceration.

Some critics argue that personal evaluations of inmates' attitudes are most unreliable. It is suggested that more articulate offenders, who are better at portraying the attitudes that the board wants to hear, will succeed. Inmates who are less able to express themselves, but are perhaps no greater risk, will fare worse.

In addition to these primary considerations in making the parole decision, several other factors may be influential. One is how long it would be before an offender would be completing the entire sentence anyway. If an inmate has accumulated 5½ years of credit on a six-year sentence, then release would come soon even without parole. By granting this particular offender parole, however, the board could ensure a period of supervision to facilitate reintegration into the community. By being allowed a period of supervision, the offender can use a wide range of services, such as counseling, education, employment, and housing referrals. Many parole candidates appear to decision makers to be people who would do better under a transitional period of supervision when first released than if abruptly left on their own.

Citizen Input into the Parole Decision.   As part of the decision-making process, the parole board may receive input from interested citizens. The input of third party participants may be obtained on a formal or informal basis, depending on the structure of the process in a given jurisdiction. Anyone who wishes to support an inmate's parole request may submit letters of recommendation and reference, including job opportunities, offers of a place to live, or testimony about how the inmate has changed for the better during incarceration. Such letters or testimony are often provided by family members, community representatives, or officials of a church.

Persons who have been victimized by crime have a vested interest in the decision to release the offenders who have harmed them. More than one-third of the states have procedures for obtaining victim input into the parole hearing process.[24] In some jurisdictions, victims may protest an offender's parole application by writing to or appearing before the parole board. In other places, a protest is a formal document that can be filed only by a criminal justice official such as a sheriff, police chief, judge, or district attorney. Therefore, victims who wish to speak against someone's possible parole must do so through one of these officials in their community. In this way, criminal justice officials act as a screen to distinguish between legitimate complaints and frivolous vendettas.

There is always considerable media attention when a well-known offender is considered for parole. Murderers like Charles Manson and Sirhan Sirhan have come up for parole regularly in the many years that they have been incarcerated, each time the proceedings attract public scrutiny. An assistant prosecutor in the Charles Manson mass murder case has attended 42 hearings to protest the possible parole of Manson and members of his "family" of murderers. Explains the attorney, "They want to get out and rejoin society, but society doesn't want them. I feel a responsibility to society to make sure that these people don't get out."[25] The five were convicted in 1971 and received life sentences but have received parole hearings regularly since 1978.

In response to continued public disapproval of the release of violent offenders, California passed legislation extending the length of time between parole reviews for those serving life terms for multiple murders. Explaining that the yearly review of such infamous killers as Manson, his followers, and Sirhan Sirhan is unproductive and simply inflames the public, the governor signed a bill that changed the yearly review to every three years. A short time later, the governor signed another bill that set the period between reviews at five years.[26]

Critics of this legislation argue that the opportunities for the hearings are an incentive for good behavior that serves a positive purpose in prison. Inmates who look forward to hearings are easier to control in confined settings. Without the incentive for review, prison administrators fear that rehabilitation will be much more difficult to achieve.

An important fact to remember is that this new law cannot be applied to persons who committed their crimes before its enactment. To do so would be to violate the ex post facto clause of the Constitution.[27] Therefore, offenders such as Manson and Sirhan must be reviewed at the intervals of time prescribed by law at the time of their offenses.

Parole Denial. According to the Model Penal Code written by prominent members of the Bar Association, there are four primary justifications for denying parole. *First*, there is substantial risk that the offender will not conform to the conditions of parole. *Second*, the offender's release may depreciate the seriousness of the crime or promote disrespect for the law. Behind this concept is the assumption that certain offenses deserve a certain amount of time served; to consider someone for release any earlier is inappropriate. Although parole boards may often mitigate what they believe is a particularly harsh sentence by allowing parole, in cases of particularly heinous or ruthless crimes, they will not do so.

Third, parole may be denied if the person's release would have an adverse effect on institutional discipline. If inmates up for parole have been troublesome or disruptive in prison, they should not be rewarded. Thus, unruly inmates would not receive parole, regardless of the length of time already served or the fact that their crime was not particularly serious. The denial of parole for persons who misbehave in prison serves as an example and a strong message to other inmates.

Fourth, parole may be denied if the offender needs to continue in some type of correctional treatment program. Officials often believe that they should not disrupt valuable educational programs, vocational training, or substance abuse treatments by permitting early release. Parole authorities may view such treatment programs as essential components of the offender's later reintegration into society. Furthermore, parole decision makers often look for successful completion of these

BOX 8–5

Notice of Parole Panel Action

DEAR SIR:

After careful and thorough review of all the facts in your case, the most significant reasons for the decision to deny parole are circled below.

1. Parole not in the best interest of society and/or inmate at this time
2. Criminal behavior pattern
3. Nature and seriousness of the offense
4. Number of current offenses
5. Lengthy involvement with or habitual use of narcotics
6. Multi-offender
7. Lengthy criminal history
8. Prior probation revoked
9. Poor adjustment in institution
10. Parole violation on previous sentence, or this sentence
11. Serious violation of institutional rules and regulations
12. Repetition of similar offenses
13. Protests by community
14. Delinquent sex behavior history
15. Medical reasons
16. Inadequate parole plan
17. Use of weapon in current offense
18. Assaultive
19. Time served insufficient to assess parole suitability
20. Lengthy involvement with or habitual use of alcohol

After careful consideration of all the factors in your case, the panel recommends:
Participation in character development program, if available would increase parole prospects

1. Drug counselling
2. AA counselling
3. Enrollment in an education program
4. Vocational education

Consult with the institutional parole officer to develop a parole plan.

programs as an indication that the person is willing and equipped to change on the outside.

The factors that authorities consider to be legitimate reasons for denying parole are listed in the example of an adverse action notice in Box 8–5. The example gives the reasons cited for parole denial from a review of several state policies. Long and serious criminal histories are a major reason that parole is denied. Other factors include poor preparation for release and negative behavior while incarcerated.

In most states, inmates must receive written notification of the reasons they have been denied parole. About half of the states allow inmates to appeal a parole denial.[28]

The Parole Contract.   Requirements placed on offenders under a parole contract are much like those imposed on probationers. The terms of parole may require a person to work, make restitution and fine payments, pay supervision fees, complete community service, seek counseling and substance abuse treatment, and avoid certain places, people, and activities. Box 8–6 (see pages 228–229) reproduces a typical mandatory supervision or parole contract as used in Texas.

A survey by the American Bar Association found that the number of conditions in the typical parole contract ranged from four to over 20. The average number was approximately 13.[29]

Federal Parole.   Federal parole was essentially eliminated following the passage of the Sentencing Reform Act of 1984. According to this act, a sentencing court must select a sentence from the guidelines provided by federal statute. These statutes developed by the United States Sentencing Commission prescribe a certain conviction term for each crime that is based on offense behavior and offender characteristics. The process is explained as follows:

> An offense behavior category might consist, for example, of "bank robbery/committed with a gun/$2500 taken." An offender characteristic category might be "offender with one prior conviction not resulting in imprisonment." The Commission is required to prescribe guideline ranges that specify an appropriate sentence for each class of convicted persons determined by coordinating the offense behavior categories with the offender characteristic categories. Where the guidelines call for imprisonment, the range must be narrow: the maximum of the range cannot exceed the minimum by more than the greater of 25 percent or six months.[30]

The judge usually applies penalties for federal crimes that fall within the guidelines specified by law. If, however, circumstances are presented that necessitate a sentence outside the guidelines, the judge must prepare a justification for doing so. This style of sentencing is called *determinate sentencing*. Determinate sentencing replaced the existing indeterminate structure that allowed much more judicial discretion. The use of discretion resulted in more disparity between sentences and also resulted in persons with like crimes and histories sometimes getting very different punishments. Under *indeterminate sentencing*, the court would assign a range of years of imprisonment and allow the parole board to determine the exact amount of time a defendant would serve. Under determinate sentencing, the court sets a specific amount of time to be served that can be modified only by the granting of good-time credits and work credits. Credit for good behavior may reduce the sentence by only a set maximum amount. It is believed that this sentencing method not only reduces disparity between similar sentences but also prevents the seriousness of some sentences from being eroded.

Because parole was virtually eliminated by this change, a new form of monitoring was needed for those offenders given sentences that included a period of community supervision. The new supervision program is called *supervised release*. It differs from parole in that it is an extension of the initial sentence rather than an early release. Whereas an early release seems to cut a sentence short, supervised release is a period of controlled surveillance added on to the end of a completed sentence. This add-on is done at the time of the original sentence so that the offender is well aware of what to expect. Violation of the conditions of this supervised release may result in additional confinement. The period of confinement imposed as a result of a violation of the conditions of supervised release is generally shorter than would be imposed for a violation of probation.

The Number of Parolees.   As of January 1988, there were 362,192 people on parole supervision. About 95 percent of all persons on parole were from state commitments and only 5 percent were finishing federal sentences. Between 1987 and 1988, the total parole population increased about 11 percent. According to one source, parole was the fastest growing of the four correctional components in both 1986 and 1987.[31] The Bureau of Justice Statistics reported in 1988 that approximately 201 out of every 100,000 adult citizens were on parole.[32]

According to some authorities, the number of paroles has increased dramatically over the past six years. The number of cases involving high-risk and hard-to-manage felons has increased as well.[33] Some of the increase in paroles is simply attributed to the steadily growing number of incarcerated offenders. When prisons reach capacity and overcrowding occurs, then one may expect to see the number of paroles increase dramatically.

One way that states have dealt with prison and jail overcrowding is to design more early-release programs. One such method was facilitated through the use of emergency powers acts passed by the state legislatures to empower governors to authorize the corrections or parole board to release additional prisoners. Although the prisoners may all be eligible for parole in that they have already served the required time to be considered for parole, they would not otherwise be selected for release. Use of emergency powers acts to solve crowding problems has so far proven to be only a temporary and superficial solution. Some critics argue that the use of emergency powers acts takes away the true meaning of parole, which is earning release through good behavior.

BOX 8–6

Rules and Conditions of Mandatory Supervision as Provided by the Texas Board of Pardons and Paroles. Article 42.12

I acknowledge receipt of the rules and conditions of mandatory supervision and recognize that my release on mandatory supervision is conditional and I shall be deemed as if on parole. I agree to abide by the following terms and conditions:

1. Release and Reporting:
   a) I shall go directly to the destination approved by the Board of Pardons and Paroles.
   b) upon arrival, I shall report (as instructed) immediately to the Parole Officer or person whose name and address appear on my Certificate for Mandatory Supervision
   c) I shall submit a full and truthful report to my Parole Officer on forms provided for that purpose before the fifth (5th) day of each month or as instructed by my Parole Officer.
   d) I shall promptly and truthfully answer all inquiries directed to me and furnish all information requested of me by the Board of Pardons or Paroles or by my Parole Officer.
   e) If, at any time, it becomes necessary to communicate with my Parole Officer for any purpose and he is not available, I shall direct my communication to the Board of Pardons and Paroles (address and phone numbers attached).

2. Employment and Residence:
   a) I shall report to my place of employment; work diligently in a lawful occupation and support my dependents, if any, to the best of my ability.
   b) I shall secure the written permission of my Parole officer before changing my residence or place of employment, and will allow any representative of the Board of Pardons and Paroles to visit in my residence and place of employment at any reasonable time.

3. Travel: I shall secure the <u>written</u> permission of my Parole Officer before I leave the state to which I am released; and I will secure <u>written</u> permission from my Parole Officer to travel beyond the boundaries of the counties adjoining the county to which I am released.

4. Alcohol and Drugs:
   a) I shall not use alcoholic beverages or liquors to excess or in a manner injurious to my Mandatory Supervision release.
   b) I shall not go into, remain about, or frequent business establishments whose primary function is the sale or dispensing of alcoholic beverages or liquors for on-premises consumption.
   c) I shall not illegally possess, use, or traffic in any narcotic drugs, marijuana, or other controlled substances. I further agree to participate in chemical abuse treatment programs in accordance with instructions from my Parole Officer.
   d) I shall freely cooperate and voluntarily submit to medical and/or chemical tests and examinations for the purpose of determining whether or not I am using or am under the influence of alcohol, narcotic drugs, marijuana, or other controlled substances.

BOX 8–6   (*continued*)

5. Weapons: I shall not own, possess, use, sell nor have under my control any firearm, prohibited weapon or illegal weapon as defined in the Penal Code, nor shall I unlawfully carry any weapon nor use, attempt or threaten to use any tool, implement or object to cause or threaten to cause any bodily injury.

6. Associates:
   a) I shall avoid association with persons of criminal background unless specifically approved by my Parole Officer in <u>writing.</u>
   b) I shall not enter into any agreement to act as "informer" or special agent for any law-enforcement agency.

7. Legal Obligations: I shall obey all municipal, county, state and federal laws.

8. General Provisions:
   a) I shall consult with my Parole Officer before entering marriage.
   b) I agree to abide by any special conditions of Mandatory Supervision as stipulated in writing by the Board of Pardons and Paroles or my Parole Officer.
   c) I hearby agree to abide by all rules of Mandatory Supervision and all laws relating to the revocation of Mandatory Supervision including, but not limited to, appearance at any hearings or proceedings required by the jurisdiction in which I may be found.
   d) I shall pay, during the period of my supervision, any and all outstanding fines and court costs adjudged against me to the clerk of the court of conviction, and I agree to provide my supervising officer with documentation verifying the payment by me of said amounts.

I hearby certify that I fully understand and accept each of the above conditions under which I am being released and agree that I am bound to faithfully observe each of the same. I fully understand and agree that a violation of or refusal to comply with any of the conditions of Mandatory Supervision shall be sufficient cause for revocation of Mandatory Supervision and of an arrest upon a warrant issued by the Board of Pardons and approved by the Governor; and I further understand that when a warrant is issued by the Board of Pardons and Paroles or Governor charging a violation of Mandatory Supervision rules and conditions, the sentence time credit shall be suspended until a determination is made by the Board of Pardons and Paroles or the Governor in such case and such suspended time credit may be reinstated by the Board of Pardons and Paroles should such Mandatory Supervision be continued, as provided by law. I understand and agree that while under Mandatory Supervision I am in the legal custody of the Department of Corrections subject to orders of the Board of Pardons and Paroles and that I will receive credit on my sentence day for day (without commutation time): I further understand and do agree that in the event of revocation of this release on Mandatory Supervision, time spent on Mandatory Supervision will <u>not</u> be credited to my sentence.

signed and agreed

_____

It is important to remember that not everyone who is released from prison is released on parole. Many offenders complete their sentences before being released. Although these persons are not subject to supervision, they are often in need of services to facilitate their adjustment to community life. The next section explains some of the services and programs that may be used by those released from prison regardless of whether or not they are on supervision.

Halfway Houses

On Monday morning January 7, 1991, baseball great, Pete Rose, left federal prison after serving a five-month sentence for tax violations. His destination was Talbert House, a halfway house in Cincinnati, where he was to spend three months in a transitional program, performing community service. Rose, baseball's all-time hits leader, shared a room with two to three other newly released prisoners. Unlike the average ex-offender, however, Rose would make paid public appearances, sign autographs, and supervise the building of his new home in Boca Raton, Florida.[34]

Aside from an occasional celebrity felon, the average halfway house program manages to maintain a low profile in the community. *Halfway houses* are distinguished from other programs in that they serve as a residential facility for offenders who are being monitored or supervised on some form of early release. Some offenders serve portions of their probation term in a halfway house. Most persons assigned to halfway houses are on parole.

The length of time a person stays at a halfway house ranges anywhere from 8 to 16 weeks. The average term is about 90 days.[35] Across the United States there are at any one time, bedspaces in halfway houses for approximately 10,000 adults.[36] This means that between 30,000 and 40,000 persons a year could be served by these facilities. However, occupancy rates often fell well below this potential, some as low as 50 percent.[37]

A 1991 government report on the Federal Bureau of Prison (FBOP) concluded that the system's halfway houses were underutilized—with an average occupancy rate of 73 percent. The FBOP had contracts for over five thousand halfway house beds yet only assigned about 3675 released inmates to those spaces. One of the problems in filling allotted spaces in halfway houses appears to be administrative confusion over which inmates are considered suitable for placement according to FBOP policy. For example, some wardens consider restrictions against inmates with a "history of violence" or "any use of a weapon" as too vague to assist them in selecting the best candidates for referral. Exactly what constitutes an act of violence or a weapon is not specified nor is it clear if incidents that occurred very long ago are still relevant.

A breakdown of the original conviction offenses of persons placed in the federal halfway house system is given in Figure 8.6. While it may

Figure 8.6

Original offenses
of halfway house
residents.

(*Source: Prison alternatives: Crowded Federal Prisons Can Transfer More Inmates to Halfway Houses*, Washington, D.C.: U.S. General Accountng Office [Novermber 1991], p. 15.)

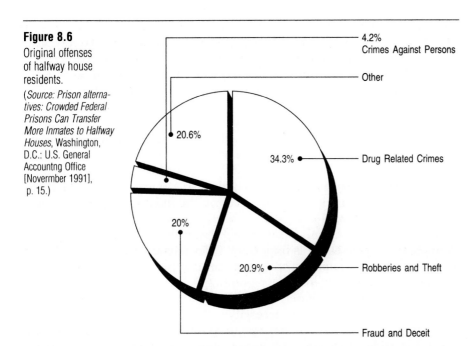

4.2%
Crimes Against Persons

Other

20.6%

34.3% — Drug Related Crimes

20%

20.9% — Robberies and Theft

Fraud and Deceit

Note: Crimes against persons include homicide, assault, and criminal sexual abuse.

seem unusual that persons with drug related crimes make up a significant portion of the halfway house clients, it is important to remember that this is perhaps the most common offense record found among federal prisoners.

Authors of the federal report determined that some wardens were more aggressive in making halfway house referrals and placements than others. The report also indicated that inmates should not be given the option of refusing the halfway house placement if it is deemed appropriate for them by prison officials. As data from the federal study revealed, 83 percent of the residents were able to find employment and the average length of stay was eighty-five days per resident. Finally, the researchers estimated that full use of available halfway house space could serve released inmates at a significant cost savings. While the average cost of incarcerating a prisoner in the federal system in 1990 was $49.20 per day, halfway houses operated during that period at $32.67 per resident per day.[38]

The rules that govern life in the halfway house are designed to be restrictive yet to offer the resident opportunities to exercise judgment and responsibility. Most residents work outside the home, but they are required to check in and out as they arrive and leave. Drug testing, individual and group counseling, regular chores, and recreational activities may all be a part of the halfway house program. In Pennsylvania, for example, community resources are an important source of programming and services. One Philadelphia facility relies on the Volunteers of America to provide an on-site drug abuse counselor. This facility also uses the Greater Philadelphia Community Center for Corrections as a source of vocational training programs. The trades that can be learned through this program include dry cleaning, restaurant practice, janitorial services, and electronics.[39]

In selecting clients for a halfway house program, administrators should try to service offenders who will be settling in the area once they are released from supervision. Unfortunately, participants are often drafted from the entire pool of eligible state parolees who are looking for space in any halfway house. Under these circumstances, it is often difficult for corrections experts to agree on the most appropriate criteria for selecting clients.

Some corrections administrators feel that it is the experience of living in the halfway house that is important. They particularly endorse the intermediate level of supervision found there. Other administrators stress the reintegration of ex-offenders into a specific neighborhood or community. However, the latter would make the matching of clients to future geographical homes a necessity.

It often happens that inmates awaiting release agree to go to halfway houses outside their area of geographical preference for fear that another opening may not come along. Pressure on facilities to remain operating at a higher capacity may supersede the selection of residents most likely to remain in that area.

There is great variation across the country in the placement of responsibility for operating halfway houses. These houses are run by a private corporation, a private but nonprofit organization, or by state or local government. A board of directors may control many privately run houses. Centers run by the government are most likely supervised by a parent agency such as the commissioner of corrections or the county department of human services. For example, in Minnesota halfway house, services are provided by a number of private nonprofit vendors except for a residential facility for American Indian offenders that is operated directly by the state department of corrections.[40]

There is also great variation in the kind of facility used for a halfway house. Some of them may actually be in large houses, whereas others use parts of apartment complexes or renovated hotels. Allen, Carlson, Parks, and Seiter reported that one kind of facility does not appear to be any more successful than another, but there will be considerable difficulty in making some structures appear "homelike."[41]

The Success of Halfway Houses

As in other areas of community corrections, it is often difficult to measure success in halfway houses. It is often problematic to conclude that specific programs or even individual aspects of programs have been influential in a client's successful transition into community life.

Halfway houses provide a stable and supportive environment in which to become adjusted to the community. Many provide job placement assistance as well as group, individual, and family counseling. (© *Ellis Herwig/Stock Boston*)

In a Montgomery County, Maryland, halfway house, newly released offenders stay an average of 120 days. The program requires residents to hold jobs and contribute 20 percent of their earnings to the center. About 20 percent fail the program and return to prison or jail. Another 3 percent abscond.[42]

Statistics on a community halfway house in Manchester, New Hampshire, reveals that of the 193 admitted to the program between 1986 and 1988, 125 were successfully paroled. Forty-five participants violated house rules and returned to prison, seven absconded, and 33 remained in the program. The residents made payments to the state of over $46,000 in support and restitution and $84,000 in room and board payments.[43]

Texas halfway houses claim to have fewer cases returned to prison compared to those who are released from prison on other arrangements. Even those residents who had higher risk scores seemed to do better in halfway houses than similar releases not in halfway houses. Although the halfway houses experienced cases of clients absconding and breaking the rules of the facility, their residents seemed to commit fewer assaultive offenses. In addition, releasees with a history of drug and alcohol abuse seemed to have more success in a halfway house placement than did those who did not go to such a program.[44]

In a study in Tennessee, two researchers looked for the characteristics of those offenders most likely to fail in a halfway house program. Data were collected over a six-year period on 75 residents of the facility. Those most likely to recidivate were those who had multiple prior prison incarcerations and a recent conviction for violent crime.[45] As the authors of the study explain:

> Residents who had been in prison two or more times are highly likely to recidivate during residence at the halfway house (approximately 90 percent), whereas those residents who were on probation and had no prison experience, as well as those with only one prison term, failed to complete the program only about 20 percent of the time.[46]

Liability for Offenders in Halfway Houses

In a lawsuit in 1991 a privately operated halfway house was found liable for the rape and murder committed by a resident. The decision in *Dudley* v. *Offender Aid and Restoration of Richmond, Inc.* alleged that the company "knew or should have known" that the inmate they were responsible for was dangerous. Documentary evidence supported that the defendant had a violent and dangerous history and that he was characterized as an "unacceptable parole risk."[47] It was also evident from records that the inmate warranted continuous and close supervision.

In their own defense, the halfway house attempted to argue that the victim was not a known or suspected target to whom they owed a duty to protect. However the court replied that "the victim, although not foreseeably at risk as an individual, was a member of a class consisting of those persons within a given area of danger—that is, the area foreseeably accessible to the felon during his hours at large as a result of the halfway house's negligent failure to control him."[48]

What is interesting about the *Dudley* case is that the court seemed to hold the private company to a higher standard of duty than it might a public agency. The justices added that "the interests of society are more appropriately balanced against the interests of private parties who, for hire, take charge of dangerous felons."[49]

The results of the *Dudley* case may frighten some prospective halfway house operators away from the business, resulting in fewer facilities and fewer opportunities for this valuable bridging experience. On the other hand, the results may be analyzed as a somewhat rare and extreme incident representing the "worst-case scenario." As legal expert Richard Crane explains:

> Here, the offender not only met none of the criteria for placement in this halfway house, but he was also convicted of this murder, and three unrelated, but strikingly similar crimes. In such cases, courts will go out of their way to find grounds on which to hold someone liable. Had the

inmate been properly placed at the facility and had this been a single act of violence, it's unlikely that the court would have held that the halfway house owed a duty to this otherwise unforeseeable victim.[50]

The court's decision may serve as a reminder to operators about the care that must be used in selecting clients. The justices also implied that operators must use appropriate control and surveillance of residents at all times.

Halfway Out, Now Halfway In

Traditionally, halfway houses were established to provide services and a place to live for offenders who had just been released from prison or jail. Today, however, a number of facilities have been established for parole violators. The new *halfway-in house* is an intermediate step in a potential return to incarceration. The house serves as a more restrictive setting in which the activities of the violating parolee may be supervised. The goal of these facilities is to offer more intensive monitoring of violators who have been unsuccessful in their own home setting. This measure avoids having to send parole violators back to already overcrowded prisons for what usually amounts to short periods. If a more economical supervision method than incarceration is adequate to control the behavior of the parolee, then costly prison terms and revocation proceedings can be avoided.

Day Reporting Centers

Day reporting centers were first used in this country in Massachusetts in 1986 as an early-release option for those incarcerated. According to one authority, offenders participating in this program live at home and report to the center each day, usually in the late afternoon or early evening. With the assistance of a case manager at the center, the clients fill out a 24-hour itinerary for the next day that includes where they will be at all times and how they will get from place to place.[51] In addition, offenders are required to call into the center twice a day to confirm their schedule. Drug and alcohol testing is also routinely conducted.

In Springfield, Massachusetts, a day reporting center that had served more than 100 clients over a 15-month period was evaluated in 1988. The center's clients were referred directly from the county jail, from the prerelease center operated by the jail, and from the Western Massachusetts Correctional Alcohol Center. The program required between 7 and 10 contacts per client per day. Results showed that only one of the clients was arrested for committing a new crime. Eighty-three percent of those with no prior incarcerations and 76 percent of those with previous incarcerations successfully completed the program.[52] Administrators felt confident in reporting that this program did not endanger public safety.

BARRIERS TO THE REINTEGRATION OF THE EX-OFFENDER

Many difficulties face offenders upon release from incarceration. One is that society imposes certain social penalties on them in addition to their sentence. The ex-offender may be required to relinquish certain citizenship privileges as a result of a felony conviction. The nature and extent of restrictions on citizenship privileges varies among jurisdictions and are set by statute. The restrictions are often referred to as the *collateral consequences* of a felony conviction.

Forfeiture of Citizenship Privileges

As of 1987, eleven states permanently denied convicted felons the right to vote, and twenty states would not return voting rights until an offender had completely discharged his or her parole.[53] Many states also restrict ex-offenders' access to public employment, public office, and jury service. In a majority of states, legislation forbids anyone convicted of a serious felony from owning a firearm.

Another consequence of a felony conviction is that the person may be required to register with authorities wherever he or she lives or moves. Persons convicted of sex or drug offenses, arson, or child molestation are most often targeted by registration laws. Information kept in registration files is often used by authorities in criminal investigations of new crimes. Consequently, ex-offenders may find themselves questioned whenever a new crime similar to their criminal history is committed in the area.

Stigma as a Social Reaction to Ex-offenders

Sociologists studying the effects of the sociolegal status of offenders use the term *stigma* to describe negative attitudes toward persons with a certain characteristic or trait. A criminal record is a stigma.

Society's intolerance for criminal or deviant behavior is reflected in biases that may be encountered when ex-offenders seek jobs, housing, or membership in social organizations. Through special regulations and restrictions, society may attempt to label ex-offenders as lesser citizens. Unless a person has a healthy self-image and self-confidence, the burden of the social stigma and the isolation that may result from it can lead to depression and bitterness. Our society places tremendous value on working and becoming successful. If barriers to employment, housing, and social activity exist for offenders, then failure to integrate or reintegrate may occur as soon as they fill out their first application.

Barriers to Employment

Ex-offenders face great obstacles in trying to obtain meaningful and well-paying jobs. Almost 80 percent of those sent to prison have few or no vocational skills.[54] Low levels of formal education, a poor or non-existent work history, and the absence of reliable transportation are just a few of the problems that face ex-offenders who are seeking jobs. In addition, a number of earlier studies have demonstrated that many employers remain strongly opposed to hiring someone who has served time in prison or jail.

In a classic 1962 study, Schwartz and Skolnick showed an applicant folder to four groups of potential employers.[55] Each group saw a different candidate for a job as an unskilled laborer. The four candidates varied only in the background characteristic of criminal record. The researchers had invented an assault charge for which the outcome varied among the applicants. One applicant had been convicted of assault, the second had been acquitted in an assault case, the third had also been acquitted in an assault case but had also enclosed a reference from a judge affirming the finding of innocence. The fourth candidate's folder mentioned no previous arrest. Only one employer in 25 expressed an interest in the candidate with a conviction. Only three employers would have hired the defendant who had been acquitted but did not have an explanation letter, whereas six employers considered the acquitted applicant who had the reference letter. Nine employers reacted positively to the applicant with no record of arrest. Schwartz and Skolnick concluded that contact with the legal system, even if it resulted in an acquittal, creates a negative image or stigma that works against being hired. A conviction record proved to be an even greater barrier to employment. As Schwartz and Skolnick remarked, the criminal record produced, "a durable if not permanent loss of status.[56]

Twenty years later, Homant and Kennedy conducted a similar study using simulated employee cases.[57] In this experiment, the employees each had a different social stigma: one was significantly overweight, a second was an ex-offender, and the third had a history of mental illness. Questions about their employability were asked of college undergraduates from a variety of disciplines. The researchers found that criminal justice students reacted more negatively toward the ex-offender and that business majors were noticeably more negative toward the overweight person. Students studying in the helping professions gave their lowest scores to the person with a history of mental illness. Homant and Kennedy implied that ex-offenders may suffer the same effects of social stigma that other negatively stereotyped groups do. This study may help us view the ex-offender label in some proportion, but it does not offer much optimism for employment prospects.

Research over the years has suggested that the quality and quantity of employment are the most consistent predictors of success on parole. A 1985 study in Illinois found that 65 percent of all recidivists were not employed at the time of their rearrest.[58] Research also indicates that full-time employment is better than part-time and that part-time is better than none. Because obtaining and keeping a job are so important to newly released offenders, employment service programs are needed. Employment service programs may be sponsored directly by the community corrections agency or provided by a contracted private or public service office. Although some prisons and jails try to provide some pre-release job services to offenders, these efforts are often very limited in scope and in the number of offenders served.

Services to Meet the Needs of Ex-offenders

Services that can be provided to the unemployed ex-offender are assessment, counseling, the development of job-seeking skills, and skills training.

Assessment

Many offenders have no idea what kinds of jobs they would be good at or what kinds of skills they have. Because so many offenders experienced failure at the elementary school level where reading and writing skills are emphasized, they feel that most of the "good" jobs are beyond their grasp. A number of assessment tests can be given prior to career counseling, including measurements of interests, aptitudes, and achievement.

Interest tests are more of an explorational device to help clients focus in on what kinds of jobs they might want. Many clients have unrealistic perceptions of what some occupations entail. Some job titles sound good, but the clients do not realize that the job tasks are concentrated in areas that they might find boring or that the jobs may require years of schooling. Some clients may insist on only one job or career and without prompting may not consider others.

Aptitude tests provide feedback to the clients on where their educational and vocational strengths and weaknesses lie. These tests measure potential abilities or undeveloped talents that people may not even realize they had. The tests are also important tools for confronting clients with more realistic ideas about career possibilities. Some aptitude tests focus on vocational skills, such as mechanical or dexterity skills. High scores in these areas often help elevate the self-esteem of clients who have done poorly in traditional academics all their lives. Educational aptitude tests predict future achievement in certain areas of study, such as foreign language or the law. Educational, or scholastic aptitude, tests are often required for admission to college programs.

Achievement tests measure knowledge that a person has already obtained. Math and English achievement tests help assessment specialists determine the grade level equivalent at which a client is functioning. Achievement scores may be needed before clients can be placed in certain vocational or GED classes to ensure that all participants can function at the appropriate level for the training or vocational classes offered. Clients who do not meet the minimum level required by the courses would have difficulty following the coursework and completing assignments.

Counseling

Another pre-employment service is counseling. Offenders often have problems dealing with their conviction records when on the job or looking for work. Others may have to deal with leaving children to go to work for the first time. Work relationships or integrating community supervision requirements with their job may be issues that offenders want to discuss in counseling. Effective group or individual counseling sessions may enhance an employee's adjustment to the job as well as readjustment to the community.

Developing Job-Seeking Skills

One of the most important needs ex-offenders have is help in developing job-seeking skills. Constructing a résumé or preparing for an interview can seem to be insurmountable tasks to the inexperienced or insecure client. The pressure on most clients to find work and make payment schedules simply adds to the tension of the employment process. The best assistance in this area is direct, hands-on practice. Mock applications can be filled out, and simulated interviews can be videotaped and played back for constructive review. Classes on résumé writing can be given, but the actual feedback and advice on design is critical.

Skills Training

Released offenders also need skills training. Although most incarcerated offenders need skills training, few ever receive any. This is unfortunate given that those who participate in job-training programs are less likely to recidivate.[59] To be successful, the training program must be relevant to the current job market. In this regard, prison vocational programs have always been subject to criticisms. Although the quality of training in many institutions has improved over the past decade, many industrial programs offer work, and not skills training. In addition, some of the training relates to skills that are not transferable to the outside job market, such as making license plates.

One possible solution to the employment needs of ex-offenders would be the development of programs that provide supported work training. Like sheltered workshops for the handicapped, these programs provide a low-pressure environment in which to learn technical skills and good employment habits. The idea of giving companies tax breaks for hiring those who are more difficult to employ is not new. Under the government's Comprehensive Employment Training Act in the 1970s, employ-ers were given tax incentives for hiring difficult-to-place workers. They were also given matching funds toward the specifically targeted employ-ees' salaries. In the past, inadequate funding and community support have been the two major obstacles to making these training programs successful.[60]

Finally, many ex-offenders simply need help in finding a job. Community supervisors or the referral agencies they coordinate with will often provide job-locating services. The local community employ-ment office can often place those ex-offenders seeking employment. Some self-help ex-offender programs operate their own job bank as do military veterans' groups.

An example of an ex-offender program that is run by the state depart-ment of corrections but administered autonomously by its own execu-tive director and staff is Project MORE (Model Offender Reintegration Experience) in New Haven, Connecticut. The program was designed to assist the newly released ex-offender with the problems of readjustment to the community. Reports from Project MORE show that the staff places 85 percent of their clients in jobs.[61]

Personal Development and Family Needs

Newly released ex-offenders face a number of concerns about their per-sonal and family future. As Quinn and Holman explain, prisoners often downplay the seriousness of their family problems while in the parole application process for fear it will jeopardize their chances for early re-lease.[62] Consequently, they often have few plans or solutions developed for coping with family difficulties.

An offender's release from incarceration is certainly a stressful event for a family, regardless of the amount of time served. In 16 states the court may terminate parental custody rights upon a felony conviction or imprisonment. In addition, a conviction may serve as grounds to demonstrate a parent's unfitness in adoption proceedings. In 28 states a felony conviction is grounds for divorce.[63]

Almost 80 percent of the women being released from jail in a 1982 study by Lewis had minor children.[64] Many of these women, however, had not been living with the children at the time of their arrest. Included in many releasees' plans are desires to be reunited with their families and to regain custody or visitation rights with children from whom they had become voluntarily or involuntarily separated. Still oth-ers are trying to reestablish relationships with spouses or loved ones, which may be difficult given the time and events that have transpired since their incarceration.

The range of offender services needed on release is wide. Aside from employment and family problems, many ex-offenders are anxious to receive some type of formal education, such as completing a GED or starting college. Others may require support services, such as medical treatment, welfare, childcare, and housing. In a study of females being released from jail, Lewis found in 1982 that almost half were addicted to drugs or alcohol and almost one-fifth had additional serious health problems.[65]

THE SUCCESS OF BRIDGING PROGRAMS

There is often considerable controversy over what constitutes success on parole. Some people simply want to see that an ex-offender has not committed any new offenses. Others look for a consistent work record and financial responsibility. Still others may equate success with positive interactions with family and neighbors as well as involvement in community activities. Traditionally, reports and research have dealt almost exclusively with recidivism as the major indicator of parole performance. Because of the almost exclusive dependence on rearrest as an evaluation measure, there has been little research on other indicators of parolee adjustment.

Earlier follow-up studies of parolees done before 1970 have suggested that most reconvictions occur within the first five years after release. Offenders who were younger at the time of their first conviction were considered more likely to recidivate. Property offenders were also more likely to recidivate, and men had higher reconviction rates than women.[66]

More recently, in a 1988 study of New Jersey parolees after three years, Corbo found that almost two-thirds (62 percent) of the parolees were rearrested within the study period.[67] In fact, those in this study who were rearrested averaged close to three arrests each. Forty-nine percent of the total group of parolees were reconvicted, with an average of two convictions each. Of the total, 22 percent were returned to prison within the three years. In addition, 6 percent were reincarcerated on technical violations of their conditions, and another 3 percent absconded. These findings are not unlike other research reports on the subject of parolee recidivism.

When examining recidivism by sex, few studies have found significant differences between the rearrest rates of males and females on parole.[68] In one that did, Eisenberg found that after one year, women had a lower recidivism rate than did men.[69] Studying recidivism rates at two federal coed facilities, Smykla found that one had a higher rate of male recidivism and the other had a higher rate of female recidivism.[70] Among the female population, women who were serving time for larceny, prostitution and auto theft were more likely to be rearrested and reconvicted than women convicted of other crimes.[71]

Age is a variable that continues to be related to success on parole. As said earlier, the younger the offender is when first arrested, the higher is the subsequent rate of recidivism. A Bureau of Justice report on parolees between the ages of 17 and 22 found that 69 percent were rearrested for a serious crime within six years of their release. What is also interesting about the findings of this study is that 10 percent of this sample of just under 4000 ex-offenders were responsible for a very high number of subsequent crimes: 36,000 new felonies or serious misdemeanors were committed, which included 6700 violent crimes and 19,000 property crimes. Also of interest was that 20 percent of the subsequent arrests occurred in states other than the state of parole. Although many of those arrested had completed their paroles and were free to move, many were not. Approximately 37 percent of the sample were still on parole. Overall, 53 percent of the total group were convicted of a new offense, and 49 percent were returned to prison.[72]

In a study of Massachusetts parolees, it was determined that the classification a person received when released was related to the outcome of supervision. Those classified as cases of minimum or moderate risk were less likely to recidivate than were persons assigned to higher-risk levels. Also related to recidivism or failure on parole were heroin use, having a history of prior parole revocations, and having prior convictions for serious offenses.[73]

Factors found to be related to successful completion of parole include having at least a twelfth-grade education, having a stable employment record prior to imprisonment, and having been raised within the natural family. In one study, program participation in prison was not related to lower recidivism rates, but Salient Factor Scores were considered a good predictor of success.[74]

Over the past few years, the emphasis on reducing criminal justice expenditures by instituting supervision fees has given us another possible indicator of parole performance. In Arizona, for example, parole supervision fees collected in 1990 amounted to $307,540.[75] The state considered this to be evidence of the program's success. Perhaps the ability to maintain employment and to make continued financial payments is a sign of positive integration in the community. This view could even be considered to be a broader definition of success than simply avoiding arrest. However, keeping a job and making payments is also no guarantee that a person is avoiding criminal behavior.

THE MEDIA AND EX-OFFENDERS

Each time a serious crime is committed by a parolee or an ex-offender, there is considerable media attention that generates public controversy over the release process. Most complaints center around the release decision and the amount of follow-up or supervision that the ex-offender receives. A 1990 newspaper story in California blamed the increase in bank robberies on addicts and "ex-cons." An FBI agent quoted in the article said that parolees have a hard time finding steady, legal employment.[76] Although the article seemed to make a specific finding about the robberies, it was rather trite. These bank robberies, in fact most crimes, were committed by people who had already committed crimes. Ex-offenders and parolees make up a large percentage of those who have committed crimes so it is not surprising that these groups account for a significant number of bank robberies.

The public's perception of the risk of ex-offenders and parolees in the community comes primarily from newspaper articles, television, and films that portray them as dangerous and destined to a life of crime. In 1990 the Home Box Office Network released a film based on the daily work of one parole officer and his high-risk caseload of 50 parolees. The film crew followed the officer for a year as he supervised his high-control caseload that included many dangerous sex offenders. Although the images portrayed in the movie may have made the officer's job seem exciting and may have glorified the action-oriented aspects of the work, it hardly represented the typical caseload or parolee.

Other negative parole publicity occurs when there is public outcry over the impending release of a particularly infamous prisoner. Such was the case of Lawrence Singleton, who was convicted of raping and severing the arms of his victim, a young girl hitchhiker. Although his eventual parole was mandated by law, it was erroneously reported as a discretionary release. The mistaken belief that the parole board had granted Singleton an early release infuriated the public, and massive protests were launched against his residence in several of the communities where he was designated to stay. The state department of corrections ended by housing him on state property directly outside a prison facility.

There are many lessons to be learned from this case. One is that despite their desire to provide "exciting" or "newsworthy" information to the public, the media often fail to learn or convey concepts of the criminal justice system accurately. As Curran explains, "Few reporters understand the difference between probation and parole, the dissimilarities between discretionary release and mandatory release, or the function of earned time or gained time and its effect in radically altering the sentence structure."[77]

The media are powerful influences in our assimilation of information and our formulation of opinions. It is clear, therefore, that agencies must work with both the media and the public to promote understanding of the system. Accurate information about how the parole system operates will promote trust and build better relations with the community. Positive relationships will be valuable assets, especially in times of crisis or when particularly vulnerable situations such as the Lawrence Singleton case arise.

A number of methods to enhance the community's relationship with parole agencies have been suggested. One idea is to produce a video on the mission and operation of parole for release to the media. Another suggestion is to invite selected media or community leaders to attend a session of the parole board. Parole administrators can meet regularly with members of the media, write editorial pieces for the local newspapers, and circulate throughout the community brochures on the positive aspects of parole.[78]

SUMMARY

Parole is one of the fastest-growing forms of community supervision today. Prison overcrowding has forced officials to increase the number of early releases from state facilities. Although it is not the most popular solution to the crowding problem, it is the one most commonly used.

The decision to grant parole means the beginning of the rebuilding of the family and social lives of the released prisoners. This decision means not only that the offenders have served their punishment but that they have the desire to return to the community as law-abiding citizens.

The decision making involved in parole release is far from scientific. Although factors that have been linked to recidivism by research are considered, personal discretion is also involved. Attempts to reduce possible personal bias in decision making have been made through the development of standardized assessment instruments. Risk-assessment tools like the Salient Factor Score are now part of parole consideration in every state. Still, liability for the actions of released offenders is a legal problem faced by parole boards and parole officers.

Persons may be released on parole directly into the community or through halfway houses and day reporting centers. A person will often complete a period in a halfway house or on intensive supervision before graduating to regular supervision. The period of parole depends on the amount of time remaining on the parolee's original sentence. Indeterminate sentences are more conducive to parole. However, some determinate sentences build in a period of community supervision following release.

Programs for ex-offenders should include access to education, medical services, job training, and family counseling. Unlike other high-needs groups, ex-offenders face the possibility that a felony conviction may create more of a barrier to meaningful employment than all their other problems. With much of parole success linked to steady employment, it is clear that programming services must focus there.

Important community resources for released offenders include schools, churches, low-cost medical clinics, employment agencies, and specific ex-offender support groups or services. Veterans' programs, legal clinics, and low-income housing assistance may also provide help. One popular concept has been clearinghouses that provide referrals to community services in the area. Ex-offenders can simply call or stop by the clearinghouse for information about jobs, education programs including financial aid, and self-help groups.

Successful reintegration means more than just changes in the attitudes and behaviors of the ex-offender. The family and the entire community must accept responsibility for helping the ex-offender to achieve rehabilitation goals. This help comes from the support of community corrections programs, the staff who work in them, and the persons who participate in them.

CASES

Atkins v. *Snow*, 48 CrL 1464 (11th Cir., 1991).

Dudley v. *Offender Aid and Restoration of Richmond, Inc.*, 487 CrL 1521 (VA S.Ct. 1991).

Estate of Gilmore v. *Buckley*, 608 F.Supp. 554, 1985.

Greenholtz v. *Inmates of the Nebraska Penal and Correctional Complex*, 442 U.S. 1 (1979).

KEY TERMS

bridging programs
reintegration
furlough
parole
Zebulon Brockway
caseworkers or parole counselors
presumptive parole dates
discretionary release
Salient Factor Score

mandatory supervision
false positives/false negatives
supervised release
halfway house
day reporting centers
collateral consequences
stigma
MORE

DISCUSSION QUESTIONS

1. What weight should be given to victims' protests over offenders' paroles?
2. Read through the terms and conditions of the example parole contract. Do all seem reasonable? Which terms might cause the offenders to commit the most violations?
3. Should those who make furlough or parole decisions or those who supervise offenders be liable for their conduct? If so, how and under what conditions should liability be assessed?

4. What are the benefits of parole to society? What are the benefits to the offender being released? How should the two be balanced in operation?

5. What specific programs for offenders should be developed to assist in the reintegration process?

6. To what extent should members of the community be involved in the reintegration process? In what ways might citizens participate in this process?

7. What are the motives of the media in regard to reporting crimes that involve ex-offenders? Are the roles of the media and community corrections too different to allow for a mutually beneficial relationship?

8. Look through your community for social service resources that might be used by ex-offenders in your area. Are there enough? If so, how do you know?

9. Is reintegration a realistic goal for offenders? Why or why not?

END NOTES

1. Media General News Service (1990). Reprinted as "Maryland halfway house balances community fears and inmates' needs." *Corrections Today* 52(2):218.

2. Bureau of Justice Statistics (1989). *Probation and parole 1988.* Washington, DC: U.S. Department of Justice.

3. Marlett, Marj (1988). *Corrections compendium.* Quoted in *On The Line*, Newsletter, "Furloughs receive increased attention." College Park, MD: American Correctional Association.

4. Ibid.

5. Malcolm, Andrew (1989). Bush administration guidelines make prison furloughs tougher. *New York Times,* reprinted in *San Bernardino Sun,* 27 August: A6.

6. Connecticut Department of Corrections (1989). *Annual report.* Hartford, CT: State Department of Corrections.

7. Bureau of Justice Statistics (1989). Supra note 2, p. 3.

8. Pisciotta, A. (1989). Eugenics, social control and the state: Progressive penology at the Indiana Reformatory, 1897–1923. Paper presented at the annual meeting of the American Academy of Criminal Justice Sciences, Washington, DC.

9. Rothman, David (1980). *Conscience and convenience.* Boston: Little, Brown, p. 34.

10. Powers, E. (1959). Halfway houses: An historical perspective. *American Journal of Corrections* 21(4):20.

11. Rafter, Nicole H. (1985). *Partial justice: Women in state prisons 1800–1935.* Boston: Northeastern Univ. Press.

12. Parker, William (1975). *Parole: Origins, development, current practices and statutes.* College Park, MD: American Correctional Association, Parole Corrections Project Resource Document No.1, p. 217.

13. Marble, Guy (1990). From an editorial comment in "Letters to the Editor." *The Echo, Texas Prison News* 61(10):2.

14. Stone-Meierhoefer, Barbara, and Peter Hoffman (1982). The effects of presumptive parole dates on institutional behavior: A preliminary assessment. *Journal of Criminal Justice* 10(4):283–298.

15. Smith, William, Edward Rhine, and Ronald Jackson (1989). Parole practices in the United States. *Corrections Today* 51(6):22, p. 24.

16. Rhine, Edward, William Smith, Ronald Jackson, and Lloyd Rupp (1989). Parole—issues and prospects for the 1990s. *Corrections Today* 51(7):78.

17. Smith, William, Edward Rhine, and Ronald Jackson (1989). Supra note 15.

18. Eaglin, James, and Patricia Lombard (1981). Statistical risk prediction as an aid to probation caseload classification. *Federal Probation* 45(3):25–32.

19. Smith, William, Edward Rhine, and Ronald Jackson (1989). Supra note 15, p. 24.

20. United States Sentencing Commission (1990). *Guidelines manual*. Washington, DC: U.S. Government Printing Office.

21. Hoffman, Peter, and Barbara Stone-Meierhoefer (1977). *Post release arrest experiences of federal prisoners—A six year follow-up*. Washington, DC: U.S. Parole Commission.

22. Clear, Todd, Val Clear, and William Burrell (1989). *Offender assessment and evaluation: The presentence investigation report*. Cincinnati: Anderson Publishing, p. 16.

23. Enright, Ray (1988). Colorado parole: Exacting an imperfect science. *Corrections Today* 50(3):46.

24. Smith, William, Edward Rhine, and Ronald Jackson (1989). Supra note 15.

25. Webber, Dawn (1991). Prosecutor works to keep Manson "Family" in prison. *San Bernardino Sun,* 28 January: A3.

26. *San Bernardino Sun* (1990). Stretch out time on parole hearings, 31 August: A15.

27. Smith, William, Edward Rhine, and Ronald Jackson (1989). Supra note 15.

28. Ibid., p. 28.

29. American Bar Association (1973). *National Survey on Parole*. Washington, DC: ABA Criminal Justice Section.

30. United States Sentencing Commission: 1990:1.1 (28 U.S.C. SS 994 (b) (2)).

31. Smith, W., E. Rhine, and R. Jackson (1989). Supra note 15, p. 24.

32. Bureau of Justice Statistics (1988). *Probation and parole 1987*. Washington, DC: U.S. Department of Justice.

33. Rhine, et al. (1989). Supra note 15, p. 78.

34. Erardi, John (1991). *USA Today,* 7 January:1C.

35. Walsh, Charles, and Scott Beck (1990). Predictors of recidivism among halfway house residents. *American Journal of Criminal Justice* 15(1):137–156.

36. Allen, Harry, Eric Carlson, Evalyn Parks, and Richard Seiter (1978). *Halfway houses*. Washington, DC: National Institute of Law Enforcement and Criminal Justice.

37. Thalheimer, D. J. (1975). *Cost analysis of correctional standards: Halfway houses*. Washington, DC: American Bar Association.

38. *Prison alternatives: Crowded federal prison can transfer more inmates to halfway houses* (1991). Washington DC: U.S. General Accounting Office, GAO/GGD–95–5, November.

39. Pennsylvania Department of Corrections (1990). *1987–88 Annual report*. Camp Hill, PA: Penn. Dept. of Corrections, p. 22.

40. Minnesota Department of Corrections (1990). *1987–88 Biennial report*. St. Paul: Minnesota Department of Corrections, p. 15.

41. Allen, Harry, Eric Carlson, Evalyn Parks, and Richard Seiter (1978). Supra note 36, p. 13.

42. Media General News Service (1990). Supra note 1, p. 218.

43. New Hampshire Department of Corrections (1988). 1986–1988 Biennial report. Concord: New Hampshire Department of Corrections, p. 65.

44. Eisenberg, Michael (1985). *Release outcome series: Halfway house research*. Austin: Texas Board of Pardons and Paroles.

45. Walsh, Charles and Scott Beck (1990). Supra note 35, p. 154.

46. Ibid.

47. Crane, Richard (1991). Legal issues. *Corrections Compendium* April:2–3.

48. Ibid., p. 3.

49. Ibid.

50. Ibid., p. 235.

51. Larivee, John (1990). Day reporting centers: Making their way from the U.K. to the U.S. *Corrections Today* 52(6):84.

52. McDevitt, Jack (1988). *Evaluation of the Hampton County day reporting center.* Boston, MA: Crime and Justice Foundation.

53. Burton, Velmer, Francis Cullen, and Lawrence Travis (1987). Collateral consequences of a felony conviction: A national study of state statutes. *Federal Probation* 51(3):52–60.

54. Tomlinson, Thomas, and Gregory Smith (1990). Developing vocational rehabilitation networks in rural communities. Paper presented at the annual meeting of the Academy of Criminal Justice Sciences, Denver, CO.

55. Schwartz, R., and Skolnick, J. (1962). Two studies of legal stigma. *Social Problems* 10:133–138.

56. Ibid., p. 135.

57. Homant, R., and D. Kennedy (1982). Attitudes toward ex-offenders: A comparison of social stigmas. *Journal of Criminal Justice* 10(5):383–391.

58. Illinois Criminal Justice Information Authority (1985). *Research bulletin: Repeat offenders in Illinois.* Chicago: ICJIA.

59. Currie, Elliot (1983). Fighting crime, in *Criminal Justice 83/84—Annual Editions*, ed. John Sullivan and Joseph Victor, 102. Guilford, CT: Duskin Publishing Group.

60. Richey, Charles (1977). Judge Richey's unique perspective, *Crime and Criminals—Opposing Viewpoints*, ed. D. Bender and G. McCuen. St. Paul, MN: Greenhaven Press.

61. Caso, Frank (1990). Warren Kimbro of Project MORE: Rehabilitation starts from the individual. *Crisis* 98(4):34–36.

62. Quinn, James, and John Holman (1990). Intrafamilial control among felons under community supervision: An examination of the significant others of electronically monitored offenders. Paper presented at the annual meeting of the Academy of Criminal Justice Sciences, Denver, CO.

63. Burton, Velmer, Francis Cullen, and Lawrence Travis, III (1987). Supra note 52.

64. Lewis, Diane (1982). Female ex-offenders and community programs: Barriers to service. *Crime and Delinquency* 28(1):40–51.

65. Ibid., p. 42.

66. Hood, Roger, and Richard Sparks (1970). *Key issues in criminology.* New York: McGraw-Hill.

67. Corbo, Cynthia (1988). Release outcome in New Jersey 1982 release cohort: A 36-month follow-up study. Newark, NJ: New Jersey Criminal Disposition Commission.

68. Hoffman, P. B. (1982). Females, recidivism, and salient factor score. *Criminal Justice and Behavior* 9(1):121–125.

69. Eisenberg, Michael (1985). *Factors associated with recidivism.* Austin: Texas Board of Pardons and Paroles.

70. Smykla, J. O. (1979). Do coed prisons work? *Prison Journal* 59(1):61–72.

71. Van Horne, B. A. (1979). *A study of selected variables, including the MMPI, as predictors of adult female recidivism.* Dissertation Abstracts International, January.

72. Beck, Allen, and Bernard Shipley (1987). *Recidivism of young parolees.* Washington, DC: Bureau of Justice Statistics.

73. Zwetchkenbaum-Segal, Rebecca (1984). *Case preparation aid follow-up study: Major findings.* Boston, MA: Planning, Research and Program Development Units, Massachusetts Parole Board.

74. Eisenberg, Michael (1985). Supra note 68.

75. Arizona Department of Corrections (1991). *1990 Annual report.* Phoenix: Arizona Department of Corrections.

76. Rodriguez, James (1990). Bank robbery rash blamed on addicts, ex-cons. *San Bernardino Sun,* 13 December: B1.

77. Curran, John (1989). A priority for parole: Agencies must reach out to the media and the community. *Corrections Today* 51(1):30, 34.

78. Ibid., p. 32.

III

Juvenile Community Corrections Programs

The Juvenile and Alternative Sentences

The faddist nature of diversion has produced a proliferation of diversion units and programs without generating a close look at whether the juvenile subject to all this attention is receiving a better deal.
— Donald Cressey and Robert McDermott[1]

PURPOSE

The chapter begins with a discussion of the philosophy of juvenile justice. Today, we see two major options as reactions to delinquency. One is the traditional formal processing of youths through the criminal justice system, and the other is diverting youthful offenders to alternative community programming. This chapter explores the advantages and disadvantages of each of these two possible paths. In describing the formal court process, the text covers the historical, social, and economic factors that influenced the development of the juvenile justice system. The major philosophical and legal differences between adult and juvenile corrections policies are highlighted. A number of treatment strategies that have been tried with juveniles over the years are explored. Emphasis is placed on the way in which particular treatment goals have come and gone in cycles of popularity, only to reappear in slightly altered forms years later.

OBJECTIVES

At the conclusion of this chapter, you should be able to do the following:

1. Describe the concept of *parens patriae* and the way this doctrine has influenced the process of juvenile justice.

2. Describe what is meant by a *balanced approach* to juvenile justice.

3. Discuss the legal differences between the criminal justice processing of adults and of juveniles.

4. Explain the concept of diversion and how it is used with juveniles today.

INTRODUCTION

No one is certain what was going through the minds of the two youths, 15 and 16 years old, when they set fire to the hair of their disabled class-mate who suffered from cerebral palsy. The judge sentenced them to one year of probation that would include 100 hours of community service working with handicapped people. It was hoped that perhaps the young people would learn a lesson about the seriousness of their actions. Maybe they would develop a sensitivity toward the plight and needs of the handicapped. They were also ordered to have no further contact with the victim.[2]

The term *juvenile* is from the Latin word for "young." The word *delinquent* is also from Latin, and it means "to fail." Today, the phrase juvenile delinquent is used to define a legal status. Delinquents are usually those who are brought before the courts because their conduct has come to the attention of law enforcement officials. Delinquency is a much broader term than is crime. Not all delinquent behavior is criminal, but all criminal behavior committed by young people is also delinquent. When a young person's behavior violates social regulations, although not a specific law, that behavior is called a *status offense*. Status offenses include drinking, skipping school, and running away from home. The term *status offense* is used because the behavior is prohibited by virtue of the person's status as a child. If the same acts were committed by an adult, they would not be punishable.

The term *juvenile delinquent* also has sociological and psychological implications. Delinquency is associated in many people's minds with kids who come from low-income areas, broken homes, or dysfunctional families. Delinquents are also predicted to do poorly in traditional academic settings and to have few opportunities in the competitive job market.

American society has always tried to control delinquency. Over the years, however, experts have argued whether or not certain delinquent acts by children should be the subject of a formal social response. Those who agree that there should be a response still disagree whether the youths should be punished or treated, removed from the home or kept with the family but under supervision. A number of strategies have been developed that address specific "acting-out" behaviors, such as truancy, experimenting with drugs, and participating in gangs. Options that avoid incarceration have almost always been preferred, however. For example, in Tennessee in 1985, 90 percent of all adjudications for serious crimes by juveniles resulted in probation, warnings, or counseling. Only 6 percent resulted in commitment to a state juvenile institution.[3]

THE CONCEPT OF JUVENILE DIVERSION

The concept of *diversion* suggests that the less contact one has with the formal justice system, the better. At one time, this strategy was referred to as *radical nonintervention*. Supporters of this idea, such as Edwin Lemert and Edwin Schur, proposed that less was better than more, and none at all was best. Explained Schur, "Traditional delinquency policy has proscribed youthful behavior well beyond what is required to maintain a smooth-running society or to protect others from youthful depredations."[4]

The primary advantage of diversion is that it allows a youngster to avoid the label of juvenile delinquent. When applications are made later in life for jobs or other reasons, the person can avoid the stigma of having been adjudicated a delinquent. Diversion also seeks to minimize the contact a juvenile has with the system, particularly the negative effects of detention.

Aside from the sociopsychological advantages of diversion, it is also a cost-saving measure. In San Bernardino County, California, for example, 11,478 juveniles were arrested in 1987. However, less than one-fifth of these cases appeared before the juvenile court.[5] The majority were diverted from the formal juvenile court process. The cost savings to the system were enormous. Furthermore, the disposition of cases occurs much more expeditiously when diversion is used. Whereas a disposition in juvenile court may require eight weeks or longer, a diversion disposition by a probation officer can occur in a few days. Many people may argue that going through the formal adjudication can serve as a powerful deterrent to future crime, but others may counter that the swiftness of disposition has a more significant impact on the wayward youth.

Probation officers also have broad discretion in the kinds of dispositions available under diversion programs. They may require a minor to pay restitution, provide a community service, or seek and complete a counseling program. Furthermore, they may require a minor to submit to supervision by a probation officer for a limited period. Only detention in a secure facility and removal from the physical custody of the parents are beyond the scope of diversion.

Over the past decade Florida has shown a commitment to intensifying diversion efforts. Funding for intervention and diversion programs increased 182 percent between 1978 and 1987, and commitment to alternative programs increased 267 percent. Funding for traditional institutional training schools increased only 11 percent.[6]

DISADVANTAGES OF DIVERSION

One of the major criticisms of diversionary programs is that, regardless of the name, diversion is often as much of a formal response to crime as any other method. The fear is that youths who may have had charges dismissed in the past are now being dragged into the net of diversionary programming. As Bullington, Sprowls, Katkin, and Phillips explained, "Increasing the number of programs for juvenile offenders is incompatible with the idea of diversion from the system. New programs, however we label them, are certainly a part of the overall system for responding to delinquency, and sending youngsters to those programs cannot fairly be characterized as keeping them out of the system."[7] To other critics this possibility carries some heavy legal concerns as well. Diane Gottheil argued, "Not only does diversion keep people in the system, but it also does so in the absence of due process."[8]

The public has also been somewhat cautious in accepting diversion as proper disposition in juvenile matters. With a growing public perception that juveniles are responsible for a great deal of serious crime, some people view diversion as coddling the offender. Diversion may seem to be too easy on young offenders. It puts them out of the reach of the more serious consequences or punishments, such as detention.

For probation departments and court systems that are overloaded and underfunded, diversion is the first line of defense in keeping the system afloat. Diverting offenders at the entry point reduces the overall workload of the juvenile justice system. This is one positive aspect of diversion. However, when carried to extremes by seriously overburdened courts, diversion may result in the setting aside of cases that need formal adjudication. Judges may fear that they may be blamed in the future for not taking stricter action on a diverted juvenile who later commits a serious crime.[9]

Budget cuts may reduce the effectiveness of diversion by limiting the number of staff available for alternative programs and practices. Financial stress may mean the reassignment of diversion staff to the work of the formal justice system. Cases may be summarily closed without appropriate sanctions rather than reviewed for possible placement in diversion programs. A lack of funds may also result in inadequate follow-up and evaluation of cases.

JUVENILE DIVERSION PROGRAMS

There have been a number of approaches to diversionary programming for juveniles, some dating back to the early 1900s. For a long time, first-time offenders were given the option of joining the military service to avoid further adjudication. Today, delinquents who have committed anything but minor offenses are not considered eligible for military service. In addition, delinquents without the necessary education skills or anyone with a history of drug abuse are screened out in the application process.

Several examples of diversionary programs are discussed in this section. Some, such as drug treatment and wilderness programs, focus on a particular therapeutic intervention technique to solve the youths' personal problems. Others, such as dispute resolution and youth account-ability boards, are designed to formulate punishments that can be de-signed and implemented by informal community networks.

Drug treatment constitutes a large proportion of juvenile diversion programming. If the court believes that drug abuse was the basis of the youngster's criminal activity and that the juvenile is amenable to treat-ment, such a diversion strategy may be used. The youth may be sent to a public or private treatment facility knowing that if he or she does not successfully complete the program, then more formal legal sanctions will be applied.

Another current format for diversion programs is the *wilderness expe-rience*—programs that try to build self-esteem, self-confidence, team-work, and problem-solving skills in participants. Many developers of such programs hope to confront the problems within each child that may have led to acting out and delinquency.

Dispute resolution, or mediation, is another form of diversion pro-gramming. Community volunteers work with youngsters accused of committing crimes and bring the youths together with the complaining parties or victims of crime. Vandalism and property theft are common crimes for which dispute resolution is effective. The victims and the cost of the crime are more easily determined for these offenses, and punish-ments can be adjusted accordingly. In joint sessions, the negotiators try to work out a resolution of the incident that will be acceptable to all parties involved. The most common agreements reached in dispute reso-lution are informal probation, restitution, and community service.[10]

In the early 1980s, Idaho authorized a diversion program that used *community volunteers* to review minor law violations committed by juveniles. The idea was not new. Similar programs had been developed at least as early as 1945. The concept involved the formation of a Youth Accountability Board composed of 14 community members. The board met weekly to review cases referred by the county prosecutor's office. These cases were minor offenses committed by juveniles who had no prior record of delinquent acts. In lieu of a formal court proceeding, the minors and their parents would agree to have the Youth Accountability Board review the offense and impose a disposition. The options avail-able to the board included community service and restitution.

Perhaps the most important aspect of this program is not the diver-sion of youth from the formal justice system but the involvement of community members in handling problems within their own neighbor-hoods. Through their participation, community members become aware of the everyday occurrences of minor crime. Participants on the board see the "criminals" who commit these crimes for the ordinary youth that they really are. Through dialogue, the board arrives at appropriate options for the resolution of cases, a process that provides a bridge between the community and the criminal justice system. It allows the community to become responsible for solutions to minor crimes rather than deferring them to an overburdened justice system to correct all the problems.[11]

HISTORY OF FORMAL INTERVENTION WITH JUVENILES

What we know about the discipline of children in ancient times can only be hypothesized from the art, diaries, letters, ancient writings, and stories passed down through history. Under Mosaic law, roughly 900 years B.C., children could be stoned to death for cursing a parent or being stubborn or rebellious.[12] A child who struck a parent could be killed by strangulation.[13]

Up until the fourteenth century, little attention was paid to children. They were treated similarly to adults and were subject to the same punishments, such as death and slavery. Throughout the Middle Ages, they were not safeguarded from the harsh realities of life. Young children were often used for the sexual gratification of adults.[14] During the 1300s, children were portrayed as delightfully innocent and playfully simple. From about the 1400s on, meeting the needs of children became important, including curtailing their freedom, providing them more protection, and gradually institutionalizing education programs, especially for boys.

Parental responsibility for the well-being of children became a concern around the sixteenth and seventeenth centuries. Children were viewed as vulnerable, and childhood was recognized as an important stage of life. Fueling this movement was the philosophical revolution of the Renaissance period and the Protestant Reformation. People saw themselves as more civilized and enlightened. They wrote guides for parenting and began to teach the moral education of the child. At this time, religion dictated perceptions in human nature. Like everyone else, children were seen as inherently wicked but salvageable with proper discipline. The disciplinary regime included physical punishments and education on modesty and obedience.

Early American Traditions Concerning Juveniles

In the early colonies, guardians such as parents had limitless power over their children. Children were considered possessions with no legal right to protection. In Connecticut, for example, a 1642 law prohibited children from displaying "any stubborn or rebellious carriage against their parents or governors."[15] In Massachusetts in 1646, the death penalty could be assessed for young people over 16 years of age who cursed or struck their parents (except in self-defense). However, according to most laws, children under seven were considered legally incapable of formulating intent. They could not be held criminally responsible for their actions.

Not all authorities of this time approved of such harsh penalties for youngsters, even for serious crimes. Faust and Brantingham explained that laws were often not enforced against children because there were no separate or different penalties available.[16] Authorities did not want to subject the children to the adult punishments. This failure to enforce laws was referred to as *nullification*. The tendency to nullify laws in the cases of children was a good sign that a separate system for juveniles would be necessary to control their behavior in an appropriate fashion.

When the Industrial Revolution began in the late 1700s, a middle class emerged from the working class. A less extended and more nuclear family developed that was influenced by the church and the community. The community seemed to go from homogeneous to heterogeneous. Mandatory public education was viewed as a way to restore uniformity to the melting pot society. Compulsory school attendance laws were first passed in 1852 in Massachusetts. By 1918, every state had such legislation.[17]

By the early nineteenth century, the country was engulfed in changes that would alter family and work relationships forever. The Industrial Revolution replaced craftsmen with machines. Competition for jobs displaced children who had previously been employed in the factories. Consequently, children stayed at home longer and remained in school later than ever before. The fabric of neighborhoods and cities was changing also. Immigrants crowded into the tenements of fast-growing cities where poverty and disease were rampant. Authorities responded to the increasing "problem populations" by building jails and penitentiaries for criminals. They also built poorhouses and workhouses for the drunk and lazy, and almshouses for the widowed, orphaned, infirm, and down-and-out. Asylums were established for the insane. The institutionalization movement spread to include the development of Houses of Refuge in the 1800s specifically for youngsters.

The Houses of Refuge were designed to moderate the negative influences of a rapidly industrializing society and to safeguard children from the corruption of the urban setting. In this controlled environment, vagrant, abandoned, neglected, and delinquent children would be given a "proper" upbringing, separate from the unhealthy atmosphere of adult institutions. The Houses of Refuge held a vast array of juvenile offenders. They ranged from the petty criminal to the willfully disobedient who was turned over to authorities by distraught parents. Part of the philosophy of the Houses of Refuge of the 1800s included the belief that parents, friends, and relatives should not visit the residents. In fact, the closer the relatives were to the children, the less likely they would be permitted to visit.

It was thought that under the proper discipline children could be reformed and that the effects of the improper and disordered backgrounds they had come from could be compensated for. The remedy was to be uniforms, corporal punishment, a code of silence, and the removal of the influence of the "dregs of society."

There were usually two ways in which children came under the supervision of the state. The most common was if the children were orphaned, abandoned, or given up by their parents as unruly and ungovernable. The second way in which children might find themselves as wards of the state was on the rare occasions when the state interceded in the best interests of the children and stripped the parents of parental rights. The state considered itself a benevolent father-like figure that would always choose what was best for the children.

One of the results of progressive reforms was the establishment of a separate court system for juveniles. It was believed that only with separate facilities, with a philosophical orientation toward helping or "saving" the child, could individual treatment take place. In 1899 the first juvenile court was established in Chicago, Illinois. By 1919 all but three states had passed juvenile court acts that allowed this new court jurisdiction over dependent, neglected, and delinquent youths.[18]

Parens Patriae

The state's acquired authority to make decisions about the care and treatment of children came from a legal doctrine or philosophy called *parens patriae*. Literally, this concept meant that the state was the ultimate parent. In a sense, the state had only delegated this authority to the natural parents, and it could be withdrawn if the parents proved unworthy of the responsibility. When parents were negligent or "unfit," the state interceded and assumed control of the children. As Goddard explains, "The state takes the place of the parents and should exercise all the care and interest of a wise and fond parent. It is not a matter of punishing and turning loose. It is a matter of bringing up the child until the child needs no further care."[19]

Because the state would be making all decisions with the needs of the children in mind, juvenile courts were not viewed as an adversarial relationship as were the adult courts. The juvenile court system was designed to be a family court. Its methods were informal, and each decision was to be individually tailored to the youth involved.

Likewise, institutions were seen as substitutes for family care. Under the care of a "fatherly" institution, children would be educated, taught discipline and the value of hard work, and given a proper religious upbringing.

Negative Influence of the Neighborhoods

Although not everyone agreed on the benefits of institutionalization for children, there was consensus on the negative influence of the streets. There was great concern, especially among the middle and upper classes, that delinquents, particularly immigrant children, would not adapt to the culture of American society. It was feared that they would grow to be a threat to all dearly held values.

Reformatories believed in teaching youngsters the discipline of hard work. These youths were being prepared for the time when they reached the age of release from state custody. (*Brown Brothers*)

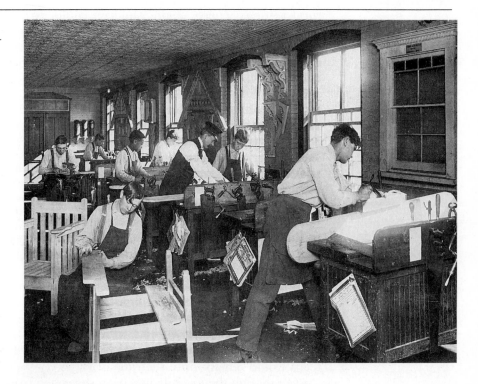

Reformers such as the Children's Aid Society, The Society for the Prevention of Cruelty to Children, and the Society for the Reformation of Delinquents, did not appreciate the warehousing of children in institutions. They championed the shipment of trainloads of state wards, many of them orphans, to the West and Midwest where youngsters were placed under the care of families of farmers who were happy to have the extra help. It was felt that hard work on the farms would teach the children the proper values and work ethic they would need to succeed in life. Between 1854 and 1929, more than 150,000 children were given a set of new clothes and a Bible and shipped to these foster homes. Unfortunately, few of the children were actually adopted by the families who took them in. Historians agree, however, that the children of the orphan trains were probably better off than abandoned children who were left to fend for themselves in the urban streets.[20]

Courts and the Treatment of Delinquency

Before the mid-1900s, criticisms of juvenile institutions had spurred reforms that led to the building of smaller facilities based on a "cottage" model. The smaller units allowed more separation by age, race, sex, and dangerousness. These units held mostly nonserious offenders and were designed like schools. Many of these smaller institutions were located in rural settings where, again, children could experience the benefits of hard labor in farming. It was evident that the juvenile authorities perceived treatment goals to serve both individual needs as well as the benefit of the greater society. This perception is demonstrated in the case of Scott described in 1921:

> Committed for setting fires. Two physicians certified that boy was insane but the judge did not feel satisfied to send him to an insane hospital. It is true that there is insanity in the family. Boy had convulsions until he was five years old, said to have been of epileptic nature. Always a good boy at home and in school. Examination at Bureau showed an intelligence level of eleven years with no sign of insanity and scarcely a trace even of psychopathy. Physical examination showed infected tonsils. These we removed. He was kept for observation four months. His behavior in the cottage was splendid all this time. When he spoke of the fires he said he did not know why he did it but was sure he would never do such a thing again. He will never be brilliant but with the right treatment he will be useful. He ought never to marry unless he is sterilized but that will of course be hard to control.[21]

In large urban areas where young offender populations were growing, the state introduced the reformatory as a progressive improvement in institutions. The reformatory, or "reform school," was often used as a temporary placement for unruly or incorrigible teens. Many of these teens would remain until their majority.

Even though the juvenile had been separated from the adult in a wide variety of industrial school, detention center, and boarding home environments, there was no guarantee that the children were safe from each other. Experts soon discovered that the youths preyed on each other and that the younger and weaker were victims of physical and sexual violence, extortion, and exploitation. Critics complained that many youngsters left these institutions much worse than when they entered. As Reckless and Smith explained, "There is transmission of experience and habits from the more to the less sophisticated children. . . . Strict disciplinary measures produce antisocial and antagonistic attitudes in some children . . . and young children suffer more from fear, humiliation, and separations from parents."[22]

It was the anti-institutional reformists of the early 1900s who first developed probation and parole. Juvenile probation followed closely behind the development of the juvenile courts. Within five years of the establishment of the juvenile court in Cook County, Illinois, five states passed legislation authorizing juvenile probation officers. A 1918 survey of the 321 juvenile courts across the country found that each offered probation programs.[23] Almost without exception, the juvenile courts served as the appointing and supervising entity for juvenile probation services.[24] This relationship firmly established the inherent power of the courts to develop philosophy, establish policy, and direct the programs of the juvenile probation department.

At this same time, a great deal of time and money were spent on trying to unravel the causes and cures of delinquency and juvenile gangs. Poverty, broken or disorganized families, the culture conflict that arose over immigrants adjusting to the American way of life, and the industrial era were all seen as negative influences. In 1932 a young University of Minnesota graduate studied young males who had become vagrants. He found that about 65 percent came from broken homes. One or both parents had died in 51 percent of the cases. Twenty-five percent reported divorces and separations within the family and frequent beatings while at home.[25] Children were responding to the disorder around them in the city with alienation and antisocial behaviors. As Rothman explained:

> Desperate need could cause children to steal; the demands and routine of factory work could prompt a girl to search for easier ways to make a living. Unsatisfied economic ambitions could often lead immigrant parents to exploit their children—and the pressure to bring home money might tempt them into crime. Also, mothers were often so busy working that they were unable to supervise their children; and illness and industrial accidents caused frequent deaths among parents, forcing homeless children to take up a life in crime.[26]

Many social, economic, and technological changes in the period of World War II influenced public attitudes about the role of children and the appropriate treatment of delinquency. In 1938 the Fair Labor Standards Act was passed, which abolished child labor. During the war, however, many states relaxed their child labor laws, and the rise in employed youths climbed dramatically.[27] Developmental psychology also played a role in changing society's values relating to the raising of children. In 1946, Dr. Benjamin Spock, a rising star in the newly developed field of the "psychology of parenting," published *The Common Sense Book of Baby and Child Care*.[28] This work became a bible for millions of women across the country who sought advice on the health and psychological well-being of their children.

Change also came from within the justice system. In the 1960s the juvenile courts came under substantial criticism from higher courts and even from the United States Supreme Court. In a series of cases on the treatment of juveniles, the nation's highest court issued indictments of the juvenile system. In *Kent* v. *United States*, one justice wrote: There " . . . may be grounds of concern that the child receives the worst of both worlds; that he gets neither the protections accorded to adults nor the solicitous care and regenerative treatment postulated for children."

The juvenile courts were reformed over the next few years to give their wards more protection. However, many critics were not satisfied with the corrections options that existed. Institutions were often exposed in scandalous reports of harsh treatment, neglect, and a lack of rehabilitation programs. During the 1970s, there was a second significant cycle of anti-institutionalization. Through the 1974 Juvenile Justice and Delinquency Prevention Act, federal funds were withdrawn from public training schools in an effort to encourage communities to develop their own correctional alternatives. Forty-four states complied with this initiative and received financial incentives for initiating community care programs for their own delinquents.[29] The act also targeted the removal of status offenders from institutions and challenged the states to divert these youths from the criminal justice system altogether. Massachusetts responded by permanently closing the majority of its juvenile institutions. A number of social experiments followed, generally emphasizing community treatment and noninstitutional programs for delinquent youth.

LEGAL DIFFERENCES BETWEEN ADULTS AND JUVENILES TODAY

Even while the doctrine of *parens patriae* still lingered in the courts, the due process model of justice revolutionized the treatment of juveniles in the criminal justice system. The legal process for youths became less informal and paternalistic and more like the adult court. Because juveniles can be incarcerated and deprived of their freedom, the courts want to be sure that they are protected against punishment without due process.

Through a series of court decisions, juveniles gained more safeguards within the justice system. These safeguards are the same due process rights as those awarded some years earlier to adults in criminal trials. Included are the right to notification of charges and notification of the right to an attorney, the right to be free from self-incrimination, the right to confront witnesses at the hearing, the right to call witnesses to testify on the accused's behalf, and the requirement that a juvenile be found guilty beyond a reasonable doubt.

On the other hand, there are still several rights that adults enjoy that juveniles are *not* guaranteed. Juveniles currently do not have the right to the following:

- A trial by jury.
- A grand jury indictment.
- Bail set at a reasonable amount.
- A public hearing.

Juveniles in the criminal justice system today still benefit from a few of the privileges of a separate and informal court. Some of the privileges juveniles have retained that adults do not have include the following:

1. Provisions limiting the public's right to access to law enforcement and juvenile court records.
2. Provisions against the photographing and fingerprinting of juveniles.

3. Permanent record sealing in some cases when majority is reached.
4. Adjudication as a juvenile that does not necessarily equal a conviction (for the purposes of reporting criminal activity in past).
5. A record of juvenile proceedings that does not prohibit a young person from later obtaining civil service jobs.

One intent of these five provisions is to shield youths from the immediate stigmatizing effects of a criminal label. The provisions also consider that youngsters will conform as they get older and will want to participate within society without being permanently scarred by mistakes of the past. As the court explained in *Wescott* v. *Yuba City*, "The purpose of the juvenile court law is to protectively rehabilitate juveniles and the maintenance of the confidentiality of juvenile court records is a necessary corollary of that purpose."

As explained earlier, the juveniles courts have moved steadily toward a more adultlike model. In the eyes of some legal theorists, there is a disadvantage to the movement of the juvenile court away from an informal system. Although many procedural protections have been introduced over the years, children have lost some of the individualized treatment that came from the juvenile court. In addition, juveniles today also are more likely to be sent to adult courts for trial if the offenses with which they are charged are serious and if state statutes permit. When the juvenile court waives its right to jurisdiction over youth, then they are subject to the full range of adult penalties.

Many experts see the juvenile court reforms as a protection against arbitrary rulings and abuses of power. Still others view the movement toward an adultlike system as a sign that the public has lost patience with juvenile crime and is seeking harsher punishments. One survey indicated that people did not view a juvenile's age as a mitigating factor in the commission of a capital murder. Only 22 percent of the respondents believed that the fact that a defendant was only 15 years old would cause them to reconsider their assessment of a death penalty.[30]

At the same time, however, another survey showed that the public prefers to see juveniles, even more serious repeat offenders, sentenced for specialized treatment rather than incarcerated in state institutions. Citizens questioned in a study commissioned by the National Council on Crime and Delinquency favored educational, vocational, and drug treatment programs for youthful offenders. The study also revealed that there was much about youth crime and the juvenile justice system that the public did not understand.[31]

In addition to the public's lack of understanding of juvenile justice policy, there are often debates, confusion, and frustration among professionals within the system. The philosophical pendulum has swung away from liberal to conservative policies several times in recent decades. Nowhere in the entire criminal justice system is the conflict between treatment or helping and punishment or control so apparent as in the handling of juveniles.

PROFILE OF JUVENILE DELINQUENTS TODAY

There are two major sources of information about the amount and type of delinquent activity today. One is official police reports, and the other is from the information that is self-reported by young people in surveys. Not long ago, a Bureau of Justice Statistics report claimed that property crime arrests peak at age 16 and that violent crime arrests peak at age 18. It was also determined that juveniles are responsible for about 17 percent of all arrests for serious crimes (homicide, rape, assault, and robbery). They are also responsible for over 30 percent of arrests for all other FBI Uniform Crime Report Index offenses.[32]

A more recent self-report study of more than 1000 high school students in a northeast city found that much of the delinquent behavior reported by these youngsters never came to the attention of police. Although self-reports showed that males committed 1.7 offenses to every one committed by females, the arrest ratio was 3.88 males arrested for every female arrested.[33] Ninety-two percent of the males and 78 percent of the females admitted to engaging in at least one technically illegal behavior in the previous year. The offenses listed by males were more likely to be fighting and property damage, whereas the females admitted to more substance abuse.

According to Bergsmann, the typical delinquent female comes from a single-parent family and is a high school dropout.[34] She may also have been a victim of either physical abuse or exploitation. Over half are black or Hispanic, live in urban ghettos, and have experienced placement in foster care. Most of them lack adequate work and social skills and have a history of substance abuse. Emotionally, the female delinquent often suffers from low self-esteem. Many are depressed and as one report showed, have tried suicide.[35]

JUVENILE PROBATION

Although almost every state had a working juvenile probation system by 1930, the actual goals and techniques for administering programs took much longer to evolve. In many jurisdictions, the juvenile and adult probation offices remained separated. The options, services, and procedures for violations that developed were significantly different between the two age groups. Many experimental programs were conducted with juvenile populations that were never applied to adults. Unlike adults, juveniles were more likely to be living at home and attending school. Each of these environments provided information and cues to the needs and problems in a juvenile's life. Over the years, a number of treatment strategies developed in probation, including alternative education and living facilities.

It was not long, however, before these experimental programs came under attack. Concerns were voiced by the general public, politicians, and professionals. What followed during the late 1970s and 1980s was a growing preference for a "get-tough" policy in juvenile justice. Media reports of drug abuse, youth violence, and gang warfare spurred strong reactions to what seemed to be liberal policies from the 1960s and 1970s. Among the policy reactions was a movement to transfer delinquent youth to the jurisdiction of the adult criminal courts where sentences could be longer and harsher. Other reactions included a lowering of the age for adult criminal court jurisdiction and mandatory sentencing, which allowed the use of lengthy sentences to state correctional facilities.[36]

In the 1990s, both academics and practitioners have recognized the need to control the swing of the juvenile justice pendulum. Policymakers have attempted to fashion a rational approach that would satisfy both the liberal and conservative viewpoints. In 1990 the American Probation and Parole Association took the position that juvenile justice should seek a "balanced approach." The balanced approach recognizes that in the history of juvenile justice, neither the helping-treatment-rehabilitation orientation nor the control-surveillance-punishment orientation has been individually successful. When one side has dominated juvenile justice policy, there have been concessions to the other. The constant swing from one dominant philosophy to another has resulted in "philosophical schizophrenia plaguing juvenile probation and the entire juvenile justice system."[37] Excessive swings in philosophy are counterproductive both for the profession and for the youth it serves.

The balanced approach seeks the essence of both liberal and conservative programs. It then tries to blend these philosophies into working principles that complement rather than conflict with each other. The balanced approach synthesizes four key principles: (1) accountability, (2) community protection, (3) competency development, and (4) individualization. The authors of the balanced approach suggest a mission statement for juvenile probation such as: "The purpose of juvenile probation is to protect the community from delinquency, to impose accountability for offenses committed and to equip juvenile offenders with the required competencies to live productively and responsibly in the community."[38]

Programs commensurate with the goal of community protection include supervision options such as house arrest, substance abuse testing, electronic monitoring, and intensive supervision. As with adults, juveniles may be ordered to comply with a number of conditions on release into community programs like probation. Also like adult probation, the terms of juvenile probation may vary in the degree of intensity, with some youngsters reporting more frequently than others. Curfews and mandatory school attendance may also be imposed on some probationers.

Accountability has traditionally included punishment, or revenge, which has received little support in juvenile justice. However, new programs involving reparative sanctions such as restitution and community service hold promise as a form of accountability. These programs fit well into existing philosophies of juvenile justice. Programs for competency development now replace the traditional concept of rehabilitation. Competencies can stress academic, vocational, social, or other daily living skills. Programs that substitute learning models for traditional "medical model" approaches try to rectify the social deprivations found in the environment of many delinquent youth. These programs emphasize survival skills.

The final principle, individualized assessment, has its roots in the theory that each youth has a special set of background and social influences, talents, deficiencies, and problem behaviors that must be examined on an individual basis. Assessment may involve looking at a child from three perspectives: the law, treatment, and risk (see Box 9–1). First, a case may be classified into various legal categories, including delinquent, status offender, and dependent (neglected or abused). Diagnostic assessments follow this differentiation process to determine appropriate forms of treatment. Treatments may include specialized programs such as drug and alcohol counseling and group or family therapy. A juvenile may have to be sent to a certain facility or geographic location to receive a particular treatment. Finally, a variety of caseload assignments may be made on the basis of the level of risk the youth represents. The level of risk determines the supervision level the youth is assigned to in the community.

In Minnesota, the balanced approach has meant combining aspects of both the justice and the treatment model. Table 9–1 shows how the integrative approach tries to maximize the positive and minimize the negative aspects of both traditional approaches. As the superintendent of the Minnesota correctional facility explained, "A strict justice model sets up an adversary relationship between residents and staff. . . . It provides little opportunity for human relationships, and scant hope that self-improvement is possible."[39] He also added that, "an indeterminate treatment model places too much authority in the hands of treatment staff." Residents may lose hope if they perceive that they will never be able to please those responsible for releasing them.

A good way to understand the change from the medical model, or rehabilitative emphasis, programs of the 1960s and 1970s to a balanced approach is to compare the two kinds of programs. The first is called Project New Pride, which began in Denver, Colorado, in 1973. It is a good example of a treatment-oriented program based on the medical model. Program goals are increased school achievement, remediation of learning disabilities, employment, and improved social functioning. The format is a holistic approach using a comprehensive, integrated, and individualized system of services. The service components include intensive supervision, diagnostic assessment, alternative education, school reintegration, job preparation, and job placement.[40] Over the years,

BOX 9–1

Individualized Assessment from Three Perspectives

1. LEGAL CLASSIFICATION

>   Dependent
>   Status offender
>   Neglected or abused child
>   Chronic delinquent

2. TREATMENT PRESCRIPTION

>   Drug or alcohol treatment
>   Self-esteem, adventure experiences
>   Family counseling
>   Group interaction skills

3. RISK ASSESSMENT

>   Violent offender
>   History of supervision infractions
>   Repeat property crimes
>   Gang or drug involvements

recidivism rates are reported to have been lower than 20 percent. Almost half of the participants have returned to high school or have completed GEDs. Three-fourths successfully held full-time jobs.[41]

The second program, the Regional Youth Education Facility, is an example of a balanced approach program. It was established in California in 1984 by the legislature as a sentencing alternative for 16- and 17-year-old juveniles. All these minors were awaiting out-of-home placement in juvenile halls. This program was designed for youth who were approaching the point at which their delinquent conduct was serious enough to result in a commitment to the state's most secure facility. The Regional Youth Education Facility was designed to provide these youngsters with effective adult and community survival skills and to instill in them responsibility and accountability for their behavior. The program specifications called for a short-term (6 month) intensive educational experience, including such program elements as competency-based education services, testing and treatment for visual and perceptual problems, individualized remedial educational plans for those with diagnosed learning disabilities, electronic and computer

Table 9–1 Philosophical Approaches to Punishment and Treatment for Juveniles

	Treatment Model	Justice Model	Balanced/Justice Treatment Model
Philosophy	Parens patriae	Criminal law	Integration
Sanctions	Sanctions fit the offender	Sanctions fit the crime	Sanctions fit both offender and crime
Determinateness	Indeterminate consequences	Determinate consequences	Determinate consequences but treatment flexibility
Releases	Release when rehabilitated	Release when time is served	Release guidelines Specific release review Release date given but may go home early if goals are met

Source: Gerald O'Rourke, 1989. "Minnesota combines justice and treatment for juveniles to create best of both worlds." Corrections Today 51(4):100, 102.

education, physical education, vocational training, work experience, victim awareness education, and restitution. Additionally, following release from the residential program, there would be follow-up intensive probation supervision for six months. The 40 minors entering the program were assigned to level one of a five-level system. At the first level, the minor remained in secure custody within the institution. With progress in the program, each juvenile would earn the second level of programming and would be allowed some activities in the community under the direct supervision of the staff. Subsequent levels allowed the minor increasing freedom and responsibility without direct staff supervision. At each level, the youth had to complete assignments. This was followed by evaluations by staff and a review for promotion to the next higher level.

An evaluation of the program found that the youth from the Education Facility had a significantly lower level of recidivism than comparable youth who completed traditional programs. Educational gains were significant, with an average reading increase from grade level 7.8 to 9.7. Accountability was shown by payment of restitution to victims. Twenty youths entering the program in 1987 paid a total of $5942 in restitution. The victim awareness program conducted pre- and post-tests of the juveniles' attitudes. Researchers found a significant improvement in the participants' sensitivity and awareness of the suffering of victims. Another indicator of accountability was community service. In a 22-month period, the youths gave over 9000 hours of community service. They also contributed 148 pints of blood to the local blood bank.

Personality testing at the beginning and end of the program suggested increases in emotional stability, extroversion, and leadership. The tests also showed that the juveniles demonstrated less depression, self-blame, and resentment. Job placement was another important aspect of the program. It was noteworthy that half of the youth had obtained permanent, well-paying jobs by the time they completed the program.[42]

Both Project New Pride and the Regional Youth Education Facility used individualized assessment and treatment, alternative education, and job preparation and placement. Both claimed to be successful in altering the behavior of participants and preventing further criminal activity. However, the Regional Youth Education Facility stressed the currently popular goal of accountability by making the victim's perspective, restitution, and community service part of the program goals. The Education Facility also built accountability into its program structure by offering five promotional levels of responsibilities and rewards.

Predicting Success in Juvenile Probation

In predicting success with juvenile probationers, officers most often look for cooperation. They also look for low levels of hostility and anger and for positive social values that link the juvenile to the community. Some of the behaviors that may lead to revocation of parole include misbehavior at home, violation of curfews, and unexcused absences from school. Other indicators include a failure to cooperate during probation meetings and hostile and disruptive behavior at school. A study by a Michigan task force concluded that two major factors placed youth at the highest risk of recidivism: (1) adjudication for a nonstatus offense at 13 years of age or younger, and (2) two or more police contacts prior to the offense leading to adjudication.[43]

Martin is about to fail at probation. He has been on formal probation for about 90 days. In that time he has managed to alienate his whole family. His parents have had Martin in counseling and have returned him to a private Christian school. Both of these efforts appear to have failed in changing his behavior. Martin continually steals from family members for no clear reason. Continued formal probation would offer little prospect that Martin would change his behavior. In placement, he would be exposed to new consequences and limits for his negative behavior. It is hoped that individual and family counseling will have an impact on him. In addition, he would receive 24-hour supervision, and his chances to misbehave would be minimized.

Unfortunately, many communities like Martin's do not have the resources to provide alternatives that fall between probation and placement. An intermediate step that offers more restriction than probation, yet is less drastic than placement, is *intensive supervision*.

Intensive Supervision Probation for Juveniles

As with high-risk adults, high-risk juvenile offenders are more likely to be put on intensive supervision probation. Also found on intensive supervision are young offenders who would otherwise have gone to prison. Theoretically, intensive supervision programs seek not only to establish rehabilitative strategies but to maximize limited resources in preventing further crime. It is hoped that intensive supervision will also reduce incarcerated populations. At present, it is estimated that about one-third of all juvenile courts use some form of intensive supervision.[44]

A description of one Ohio juvenile intensive supervision probation program found that youths started their sentences with five days in a detention facility, followed by two weeks of house arrest. Each youth then had 10 additional days of having to seek permission from the counselor before going anywhere. During the final period of intensive supervision, the youth reported daily, obeyed strict curfews, and attended school, counseling, and drug treatment sessions. The youth also had to submit to periodic urinalysis tests. Trained family advocates were sometimes assigned to a juvenile's case to provide in-home family services. Violations of supervision conditions were addressed by additional time in detention or on house arrest. Researchers for the project reported that after one year, 60 percent of the juveniles serviced had committed no new crimes. Although these youths were not as successful as others under less restrictive forms of supervision, they performed better than was projected for this high-risk population.[45] It was also found that commitments to state institutions during this period were significantly reduced.

Three different ISP programs were developed in Detroit to reduce the number of commitments to state institutions. In these programs, caseworkers monitored an average of eight clients each and conducted 12 contacts for each probationer per month. Some of the contacts were by phone, others were at the juveniles' homes or at the probation office. The supervisors facilitated their clients' participation in counseling and other social services, including employment and recreational youth groups. Researchers compared the juveniles who had been through these Detroit programs to juveniles with similar criminal records who had been committed to state institutions. In a two-year follow-up study, they found that the two groups had similar rates of recidivism. The findings showed that the intensive supervision program was no less effective than incarceration in deterring future criminal activity. The researchers were left asking "How much is really accomplished by incarcerating young offenders in expensive facilities for a few months each if their prospects for long-term improvement are apparently no better than those of youths on probation?"[46] Given that intensive supervision is far less expensive than incarceration, the Detroit programs seemed to be a viable alternative to institutionalization.

Juvenile Restitution Programs

A 1985 survey of juvenile courts reported that about 65 percent of the larger jurisdictions and 33 percent of the smaller jurisdictions had formal restitution programs for juveniles.[47] To some theorists, the growth in popularity of restitution is seen as a shift in punishment philosophy from treatment to accountability. At face value, restitution may appear contradictory to the goals of treatment. However, many experts see accountability as a therapeutic step in behavioristic treatment strategies.

Juvenile restitution programs suffer from some design problems that are less common with adult participants. For one thing, many juveniles do not have transportation to take them to potential work sites. With wages that are usually much lower than those of adults, the juvenile may have even less to give toward restitution after public transportation costs are deducted. Limits on transportation decrease the geographical area in which juveniles may seek work. In addition, juveniles attending school have far less time available for work than does the average adult.[48]

OTHER SANCTIONS FOR DELINQUENTS

Citing exasperation with the seemingly insignificant effects of current sanctions, many states have invented new penalties in an effort to impress young offenders. As an example of the new creative measures, some states have enacted laws that revoke the driver's license of young offenders for certain drug or alcohol violations. These "Use and Lose" statutes are designed to serve both as a punishment and a deterrent by withdrawing a privilege that is precious to most young people, the freedom of driving. This sanction may be imposed for drug- and alcohol-related crimes even if driving is not specifically involved in the offense. For those offenders too young to drive, many states have included a clause that allows for the postponement of the issuance of a driver's license for one year to anyone convicted of these offenses.

With more serious adjudications, court and social service authorities may seek out home placements for juveniles. Placement may mean foster care, group homes, camps, or a larger institutional treatment program. Placement of juveniles outside the parents' homes is a severe sanction as

Delinquency prevention programs rely on publicity and positive peer influence to deter young people from crime, gangs, and drugs. (© *Amy Zuckerman/Impact Visuals*)

well as an expensive alternative and is most appropriately used when resources in the community are not likely to be effective in bringing about a positive change in behavior. To be sure that only juveniles who have exhausted other alternatives go into placement, some jurisdictions have adopted a classification screening process that requires that a risk/need classification be completed before the dispositional phase of the juvenile court hearing. If the classification score is low, a reviewing official or committee may require probation officials to seek alternatives to placement. Assignment to specific placement may also be made by classification. California, for example, has adopted a comprehensive classification instrument designed to ensure that minors are placed in facilities that are best suited to their needs. In turn, the facilities are periodically evaluated to see that the promised services are delivered.

DELINQUENCY PREVENTION

One of the areas in which communities find criminal justice intervention most worthwhile is delinquency prevention. Efforts range from the development of specific delinquency prevention programs to changes in laws and school policies to combat drugs, gangs, and dropping out of school.

A strategy that has gained popularity in recent years is holding parents financially accountable for the delinquent acts of juveniles. According to Geis and Binder, all states but New Hampshire have enacted laws that allow victims to collect compensation directly from parents for the intentionally delinquent acts of their children. In a variation of this process, district attorneys have also taken advantage of laws that allow them to press criminal charges against parents whose children are involved in delinquent activity. In California, the Street Terrorism Enforcement and Prevention Act permits the arrest of parents whose children become suspects in a crime and the parent had knowingly failed to control or supervise the child.[49]

Authorities can also charge parents with a variety of "contributing to the delinquency of a minor" crimes. Although many of these parental responsibility laws have been on the books for years, they have only recently been revived and used. The purpose of these two types of legislation, officials explain, is that parents will be forced to be more active in controlling their children if criminal and financial liability are attached. Thus, it is hoped that such possible punishments will act as deterrents to future delinquent activity.

SUMMARY

The American criminal justice system has changed dramatically throughout its history. In recognition of social and political changes, the rights of the poor, women, and minority groups have evolved to the standards previously available only to white, male property owners. The development and maintenance of a separate judicial and correctional component for juveniles has been less influenced by its adult counterpart. Historically, the juvenile justice system has remained independent of precedents in the adult arena. This distinction was illustrated in the 1971 case *Ames* v. *City of Hermosa Beach* when the court held that laws which "forbid discrimination upon basis of color, race, religion or national origin do not forbid treating juveniles and minors differently from adults in appropriate circumstances."

It is also important to understand that ideas about the "best" way to deal with delinquency have continuously changed over the years. Even so, a few basic strategies seem to be recycled periodically. The concept of taking a child away from the influences of a "bad" neighborhood, diverting the child from the official processing of the criminal justice system, and the popularity of institutions all resurface again and again.

From the viewpoint of reducing future delinquency, labeling theorists might argue that diversion reduces recidivism by limiting the immersion of the offender in the justice system, thus also limiting the reinforcement of the delinquent label. The disposition is handled at the police station or in a probation office. In most cases, no prosecutor, defense attorney, judge, or other artifacts of a formal proceeding are involved. Youths who are not diverted from the system are processed through the courts and adjudicated.

Historically, one of the differences between adult and juvenile court processing has been the authority to intervene in the lives of youths when there is little official or legal need to do so. Juveniles have hearings rather than trials, but the judge determines the sanctions to be arranged. As in adult courts, reports are prepared by the probation department with investigating officers' suggestions for treatment or placement of the juveniles.

Today, there is a greater tendency for people to view serious crimes committed by youths under 18 as "adult" offenses that should carry "adult" punishments rather than as delinquency. Community corrections options for juveniles, as for adults, are more likely to be recommended and approved of by the general public if the offenses that led to conviction are minor.

The basic difference in the community sentencing of adults and juveniles is the options available to the judge. One of the major decisions that the judge makes is whether to place children outside of the home in some type of residential facility. The popularity of incarcerating juveniles in institutions has risen and fallen in cycles over the years. Serious offenders may be committed to the custody of the state and placed in juvenile institutions or detention centers, but the majority are placed in local community treatment programs. Some of these programs are residential, whereas others do not require the juveniles to live in. However, the judge may still order youngsters to foster care or group homes in lieu of their returning to the family. From this temporary home setting, the juveniles attend treatment on a regular basis, meet with a probation officer, and are periodically evaluated by the court. One of the goals of the treatment program is usually the eventual return of the juveniles to their families.

CASES

Fare v. *Michael C.*, 442 U.S. 707, 99 S.Ct. 2560, 61 L.Ed.2d 197 (1979).

Kent v. *United States*, 383 U.S. 541, 86 S.Ct. 1045, 16 L.Ed.2d 84 (1966).

Wescott v. *Yuba City*, 104 Cal App. 3d 103, 163 Cal Rptr 385.

Ames v. *City of Hermosa Beach*, 16 Cal.App.3d 146, 93 Cal.Rptr 786.

KEY TERMS

status offense

juvenile delinquency

diversion

radical nonintervention

wilderness experience

dispute resolution or mediation

nullification

parens patriae

balanced approach

DISCUSSION QUESTIONS

1. Is delinquency normal? What types of delinquent conduct should be officially responded to by the criminal justice system?
2. What is the value, if any, of the concept of *parens patriae*? Should juveniles be treated differently from adults in the criminal justice system? If so, to what degree?
3. Explain the social and economic benefits of diversion. In your opinion, when should it be used?
4. Discuss the effects of the 1974 Juvenile Justice and Delinquency Prevention Act. Should the government dictate juvenile justice policy to the states by manipulating funding?
5. Should parents be held criminally or financially liable for the delinquent acts of their children? Under what circumstances?
6. On the basis of the profile of the typical female juvenile offender, what type of programming would you develop to service this population?

END NOTES

1. Cressey, D., and Robert McDermott (1973). *Diversion from the juvenile justice system.* Ann Arbor: National Assessment of Juvenile Corrections, Univ. of Michigan, pp. 59–60.
2. *San Bernardino Sun* (1991). Teens who tried to set hair ablaze sentenced, 27 March: B4.
3. Champion, Dean (1989). Teenage felons and waiver hearings: Some recent trends, 1980–1988. *Crime and Delinquency* 35(4):577–585.
4. Schur, Edwin (1973). *Radical non-intervention: Rethinking the delinquency problem.* Englewood Cliffs, NJ: Prentice Hall, p. 154.
5. San Bernardino County Probation (1988). *1988 Report.* San Bernardino, CA: San Bernardino County Probation Office, p. 50.
6. Springer, Merle (1988). Youth service privatization. *Corrections Today* 50(6):88.
7. Bullington, Bruce, James Sprowls, Daniel Katkin, and Mark Phillips (1978). "A critique of diversionary juvenile justice. *Crime and Delinquency* 24(1):59–71.
8. Gottheil, Diane (1979). Pretrial diversion: A response to the critics. *Crime and Delinquency* 25(1):65–75.
9. DeAngelo, Andrew (1988). Diversion programs in the juvenile justice system: An alternative method of treatment for juvenile offenders. *Juvenile and Family Court Journal* 39(1):21–27.
10. Whitehead, John, and Steven Lab (1990). *Juvenile justice.* Cincinnati: Anderson Publishing, p. 315.

11. State of Idaho, Department of Health and Welfare. No author or date on the materials, which were obtained from Yvonne Lopour, a former member of the board in Payette County, Idaho.

12. Exodus: 21:18–21; Leviticus: 20:9.

13. Exodus 21:15.

14. Kratcoski, Peter, and Lucille Kratcoski (1990). *Juvenile delinquency*. Englewood Cliffs, NJ: Prentice Hall.

15. Bremner, Robert, ed. (1970). *Children and youth in America*. Cambridge, MA: Harvard Univ. Press, p. 37.

16. Faust, Frederick, and Paul Brantingham (1979). Models of juvenile justice—Introduction and overview, in *Juvenile Justice Philosophy, 2nd ed.*, ed. Frederick Faust and Paul Brantingham, pp. 1–36. St. Paul, MN: West Publishing.

17. Lipshutz, Mark (1977). Runaways in history. *Crime and Delinquency* 23(3):321–332.

18. Reckless, Walter, and Mapheus Smith (1932). Juvenile delinquency. New York: McGraw-Hill, p. 233.

19. Goddard, Henry (1921). *Juvenile delinquency*. New York: Dodd, Mead, p. 96.

20. Taylor, Mark (1990). Woman tracks past of orphan train kids. *The Arizona Republic*, 25 December: C2.

21. Goddard, Henry (1921). Supra note 19, p. 84.

22. Reckless, W., and M. Smith (1932). Supra note 18, p. 242.

23. Ibid., p. 244.

24. Hurst, Hunter 1990. Juvenile probation in retrospect. *APPA Perspectives* Winter:16–19.

25. Minehan, Thomas (1934). *Boy and girl tramps of America*. New York: Farrar & Rinehart, pp. 247–253.

26. Rothman, David (1980). *Conscience and convenience*. Boston: Little, Brown, pp. 51–52.

27. Lipshutz, Mark (1977). Supra note 17, p. 330.

28. Spock, Benjamin (1946). *The common sense book of baby and child care*. New York: Hawthorn Dutton.

29. Waegel, William (1989). *Delinquency and juvenile control*. Englewood Cliffs, NJ: Prentice Hall.

30. McShane, M., and F. Williams, III (1989). Data from a 1987 crime poll. Huntsville, TX: Sam Houston State Univ.

31. Steinhart, David (1988). *California opinion poll: Public attitudes on youth crime*. San Francisco: National Council on Crime and Delinquency, p. 1.

32. Rossum, Ralph, Benedict Koller, and Christopher Manfredi (1986). *Juvenile justice reform code: A model for the states*. Claremont, CA: McKenna College, Rose Institute of State and Local Government.

33. Feyerherm, William (1981). Measuring gender differences in delinquency: Self-report vs. police contact, in *Comparing Female and Male Offenders*, ed. M. Warren, pp. 46–54. Beverly Hills, CA: Sage.

34. Bergsmann, Ilene (1989). The forgotten few: Juvenile female offenders. *Federal Probation* 53(1):73–78.

35. Crawford, J. (1988). *Tabulation of a nationwide survey of female inmates*. Phoenix, AZ: Research Advisory Services.

36. Armstrong, Troy, Dennis Maloney, and Dennis Romig (1990). The balanced approach in juvenile probation: Principles, issues and application. *APPA Perspectives* Winter:8–13.

37. Armstrong, Troy, Dennis Maloney, and Dennis Romig (1990). Supra note 35, p. 9.

38. Ibid., p. 10.

39. O'Rourke, Gerald (1989). Minnesota combines justice and treatment for juveniles to create best of both worlds. *Corrections Today* 51(4):100.

40. U.S. Juvenile Justice and Delinquency Prevention Office (1981). *Replication of Project New Pride* (by New Pride, Inc.). Washington, DC: U.S. Government Printing Office.

41. McCarthy, Belinda, and Bernard McCarthy (1984). *Community based corrections*. Monterey, CA: Brooks/Cole.

42. Skonovd, Norman (1989). *Regional youth education facility.* Sacramento: State of California, Department of Youth Authority.

43. Sharp, Ray, and Eugene Moore (1988). The early offender project: A community-based program for high risk youth. *Juvenile & Family Court Journal* 39(1):13–20.

44. Armstrong, Troy (1988). National survey of juvenile intensive supervision (Part 1). *Criminal Justice Abstracts* (June):342–348.

45. Wiebush, Richard (1990). Programmatic variations in intensive supervision for juveniles: The Ohio experience. *APPA Perspectives* Winter:26–35.

46. Barton, William, and Jeffrey Butts (1990). Viable options: Intensive supervision programs for juvenile delinquents. *Crime and Delinquency* 36(2):238–256.

47. Schneider, Anne, and Jean Warner (1989). *National trends in juvenile restitution programming.* Washington, DC: Office of Juvenile Justice and Delinquency Prevention, p. 2.

48. Courlander, Michael (1988). Restitution programs, problems and solutions. *Corrections Today* 50(4):165.

49. Geis, Gilbert, and Arnold Binder (1990). Sins of their children: Parental responsibility for juvenile delinquency. Paper presented at the annual meeting of the Academy of Criminal Justice Sciences, Denver, CO.

Changing Perspectives on the Status Offender

The juvenile justice system is a paradox. In the name of benevolent intervention and rehabilitation, it has operationalized a sentencing and parole procedure that discriminates against females, the young, and the least serious offenders.

— Gerald Wheeler[1]

OBJECTIVES

On completion of this chapter, you should be able to do the following:

1. Explain the historical differences in the treatment of male and female status offenders.

2. Discuss the significance of the Juvenile Justice and Delinquency Prevention Act of 1974.

3. Describe current trends in the treatment of the status offender.

4. Discuss the apparent link between delinquency, running away, and child abuse.

PURPOSE

This chapter explains the creation and enforcement of legislation governing status offenses in this country. The text describes the treatment of status offenders from a labeling perspective. Therefore, a discussion of the sociological effects of criminal processing includes the concepts of stigma and sexism. Existing research on the effects of labeling is also discussed. The impact these studies have had on the movement away from the formal processing of status offenders is described. The deinstitutionalization of status offenders is presented as a critical step in this movement. Finally, the chapter discusses current community programs that try to address the population of juvenile status offenders. The philosophy of intervention is examined from a critical perspective.

INTRODUCTION

As mentioned in the previous chapter, a status offense is an act that would not be considered illegal for an adult but is conduct for which a child may be charged and adjudicated in juvenile court. The state uses its legal interest in the child to take steps to prevent and deter future similar actions by the child.

Status offenses include running away from home, drinking, skipping school, sexually promiscuous behavior, associating with gangs, and loitering. It is also considered a status offense to be found in places where it is unlawful for a youngster to be, such as gambling halls and adult movies. Traditionally, status offenders were also those children who parents considered to be ungovernable, unruly, or unmanageable. Special categories of status offenders include Children In Need of Supervision (*CHINS*) and Persons (or Minors) In Need of Supervision (*PINS* and *MINS*). These children are under the jurisdiction of social service agencies and/or the courts.

HISTORICAL BACKGROUND ON STATUS OFFENDERS

The American juvenile court came into existence at the turn of the century. Its underlying philosophy was that the court would act *in loco parentis*, which translates as, "in the place of parents." This philosophy allowed the court to secure the welfare of wayward children.

In addition to having jurisdiction over juveniles who violated laws, the court also involved itself in the lives of children who were "unruly." These children had violated social norms by running away from home, being truant from school and staying out past curfew. All these behaviors showed that the child was "incorrigible." The status offender was considered an "incipient delinquent."[2] This status placed the youngster somewhere between being a dependent child who had no parent or guardian and one who was a criminally-oriented delinquent.

Intervention

The original purpose of intervention with status offenders was expressed in the firm belief that, if treated, the wayward behavior of the child would be reformed. It was also hoped that more serious pursuits in criminal conduct could be prevented. Case history after case history was published describing the developing misbehavior of a truant or runaway. These cases supposedly showed how the subject's behavior had gradually increased in immorality and illegality until he or she was robbing banks and shooting policemen. A theory evolved that if left untreated, predelinquent behavior would lead to delinquent behavior that would eventually become more serious criminal acts. This theory is referred to as the *escalation hypothesis*.[3]

The escalation hypothesis is based on a medical analogy to pathological growth or disease. Thus, status offenses were simply predelinquent behaviors that would be followed by more serious delinquent conduct. Court intervention and treatment were first aid to stop the spread of such a disease.

To date, there has been little evidence to support the escalation hypothesis. Researchers have more commonly found a variety of other patterns that better describe delinquency. According to Rankin and Wells, these include the following:

- *De-escalation*: where as youths grow older their involvement in any status, delinquent, or criminal activity decreases.
- *Persistence*: where youths participate in only one type of illegal behavior or status offense over the entire period of adolescence.
- *Offense heterogeneity*: where youths may commit both status offenses and delinquent acts but in random order so that the more serious conduct does not necessarily follow the status offenses. In fact, the most serious offenses may be committed first.[4]

A research study by Weis conducted in 1979 found support for the heterogeneity position. In his sample, most youngsters were "versatile," committing both status and delinquent crimes.[5]

Heterogeneous offense careers were also demonstrated in a study of Arizona youths. This two-year follow-up study of 4900 status offenders placed in a diversion program, did not find any evidence of criminal career progression or escalation.[6]

Perhaps the most famous examination of juvenile careers was a longitudinal study of delinquency conducted by Wolfgang, Figlio, and Sellin.[7] Almost 10,000 cases were included in the sample made up of boys born in 1945 who lived in Philadelphia. Only 35 percent of these youngsters had official contact with the police, and only 18 percent of this group could be considered chronic offenders. Interestingly enough, these chronic offenders did not gradually become involved in more serious crime. Instead, many began their delinquent careers with a relatively serious offense.

Theories of Delinquency and the Movement for Nonintervention

Crime and delinquency theories of the first half of the twentieth century were based primarily on assumptions about the nature and behavior of the lower classes. Theories of subculture and social disorganization focused on crime as a socioeconomic response to conflict between the classes. It was thought that lower and immigrant classes were unable to adjust to the social expectations of the middle and upper classes.

In the late 1950s and 1960s, however, new evidence came from researchers conducting self-report studies. For self-report data, researchers interviewed or surveyed large groups of youngsters, including delinquents, asking about their activities. These studies determined that middle- and upper-class teenagers were also engaged in a full range of delinquent activities that the current theories could not explain. The findings contrasted with official sources of crime statistics, which seemed to concentrate crime within the poorer and minority classes. To these researchers, the difference appeared to be in how the law was enforced. That is, teens from middle- and upper-income neighborhoods were more likely to avoid the attention of law enforcement authorities. Even if the middle-class youngsters were caught, they were more likely to escape the formal labeling process associated with the courts.

Theorists who studied crime from a *labeling* perspective believed that it was the reaction of society that perpetuated delinquent behavior. Although the initial offense, or *primary deviance*, might not be significant, the process of tagging the youngster as a "delinquent" was. This label forced the youth to internalize society's perception of him or her. Thus, those who were vulnerable to the negative feedback that resulted from the label of "delinquent" would struggle with their self-concept. Adopting the views of those around them would result in the young person's redefinition of himself as "no good" and "troublesome." Consequently, juveniles engaged in further delinquent activity as part of the process of becoming the person that everyone thought they were. This transformation was referred to as *secondary deviance* by labeling theorists.[8] Secondary deviance may mean that the subject begins to dress and talk like other "delinquents". He or she may also seek out and associate with others who have been similarly labeled.

In a labeling analysis of school "skippers," Crespo explained that truancy becomes a commitment that may lead to the person viewing himself or herself as unfit for school.

> The student becomes committed to skipping through the fun he has doing it; through the contrast it provides with his experiences in school; through the obligations and pleasures he shares with skipping friends; and through the several difficulties skipping generates for the possibility of catching up. . . . systematic skipping becomes a matter of identification rather than commitment as students become more and more identified with a version of themselves as marginal to school life. When the skipper finally views himself in the same terms as the school views him, he drops out.[9]

Stigma

Labeling theorists also referred to the delinquent label as a *stigma* that elicited negative reactions from the rest of society. It was clear that, on the basis of emotional and physical resources, children would vary in their ability to resist stigmatization or to avoid its negative impacts. The impacts included reduced social acceptability, barriers to economic and social opportunities, and diminished overall life chances.[10] As a result of the emphasis on stigma, it became clear that poor and minority youth were at greater risk. They were more likely to develop negative self-images and move toward a self-fulfilling prophecy of criminal futures. Involvement with the legal system was viewed as a stigma-producing event.

Theorists of the labeling perspective entreated policymakers to develop new and alternative processing strategies that were intended to help youngsters avoid becoming involved with the system for as many years as possible. This strategy of avoiding formal processing through the criminal justice system has been called *nonintervention*. An advocate of this idea, and author of the book *Radical NonIntervention*, Edwin Schur exhorted officials to let youngsters alone whenever possible.[11] However, as Gibbons and Krohn explained, this perspective does not really give authorities any clear sign of when and under what circumstances letting a child "alone" is called for.[12] Neither does it indicate when intervention may be necessary and wise.

Other Influences on the Reform of the Juvenile Justice System

During the late 1960s and early 1970s, juvenile institutions and courts came under increasing public pressure for humanitarian reforms. The public further demanded more efficient operations. Because of the trivial nature of many status offenses, the processing of young people through the judicial system became a topic of great debate. The United States Supreme Court launched a number of scathing attacks against juvenile courts in the form of reform orders. In their decisions, the justices denounced the juvenile justice system as "kangaroo courts" that were "fatally defective." In 1967 the Commission on Law Enforcement and Administration of Justice charged that the juvenile justice system "had not only failed to achieve its objectives, but in the process had contributed to an increase in delinquency."[13]

Beginning in 1968 a series of legislative acts sought to improve options for juvenile offenders that would emphasize community resources. The Juvenile Delinquency Prevention and Control Act was passed in 1968. This legislation encouraged efforts to service juveniles in their neighborhoods rather than in the formal justice system. That same year the Omnibus Crime Control and Safe Streets Act funded a number of programs aimed at preventing delinquency.[14] The legislation that had perhaps the greatest impact on the status offender, however, was the 1974 Juvenile Justice and Delinquency Prevention Act.

The 1974 Juvenile Justice and Delinquency Prevention Act

The Juvenile Justice and Delinquency Prevention Act was a popular piece of legislation, passing by an overwhelming majority of both houses of Congress in 1974. The act mandated national reform in the treatment of status offenders. It called for an end to the confinement of youths whose offenses would not be crimes if they were committed by an adult. The text specified that status offenders and dependent, neglected, and abused children be removed from jails, detention centers, and training schools, nationwide.

The mandate of the Juvenile Justice and Delinquency Prevention Act began the process of *deinstitutionalizing* the status offender. The legislation also established the Office of Juvenile Justice and Delinquency Prevention, which was to coordinate research, training, and prevention programs. The office was also to be responsible for providing technical help to state and local policymakers on issues of juvenile justice. The act encouraged community-based alternatives to incarcerating nonviolent, low-risk delinquents by recommending the diversion of juveniles from the formal justice and correctional system. One of the legislation's major assumptions was that delinquency could be prevented through service programs to youth, such as those services focused on keeping students in school. Also included were programs for providing work opportunities to youths. Various state job corps and the federal Comprehensive Employment and Training Act (CETA) targeted this group of young people for intensive services that would result in employment.

In a short period, three basic policy strategies for complying with the Juvenile Justice and Delinquency Prevention Act emerged:

- *Decarceration* (or deinstitutionalization)—restricting or eliminating the commitment of status offenders to secure confinement.
- *Diversion*—providing alternatives to detention through crisis intervention, community services, and family counseling.
- *Divestiture*—removal of the status offender from the jurisdiction of the court.

In 1975 the National Council on Crime and Delinquency endorsed the idea of removing the status offender from the juvenile court. In defense of their position, the council reported that one-third of the 800,000 juveniles held in secure detention each year were status offenders. Of the 85,000 juveniles committed to correctional institutions each year, 23 percent of the boys and 70 percent of the girls were status offenders. They further noted that the status offenders were incarcerated as long or longer than were children who had committed violent crimes. The council found that the younger the juvenile, the longer was the period of institutionalization. Those with the longest periods of institutionalization also had the highest rate of parole violations. The council held that "imprisonment of the status offender serves no humanitarian or rehabilitative purpose."[15]

In the period following the Juvenile Justice Act and the National Council's report, arrests for status offenses sharply declined. Arrests for female status offenders declined by 37 percent and by 40 percent for males.[16] The number of young people admitted to detention centers and training schools also fell dramatically. According to a report by Barry Krisberg et al., girls appeared to benefit most from this change in policy.[17] The number of females admitted to public institutions between 1974 and 1982 declined by 45 percent. It is important to point out, however, that the number of girls and boys in this age group also sharply declined during this period. Therefore, the total number of children eligible for arrest was smaller.

The policies carried out over the next decade in support of the anti-secure-detention movement were not universally welcomed. Some critics claimed that by deinstitutionalizing the status offender, runaways and truants were left to fend for themselves on the streets because they lacked family resources and support. A study of deinstitutionalization in Illinois determined that the availability of community resources varied directly with the affluence of the community.[18]

SEXISM AND THE TREATMENT OF STATUS OFFENDERS

The Decision to Use the Criminal Justice System

Many clear signs showed that the early American juvenile justice system discriminated against female clients. Some biases were in statutes and ordinances that allowed for differing treatment of the sexes. In New York, for example, Persons In Need of Supervision (PINS) could be placed under the control of the state until they were 16 if male, but the jurisdiction ended at 18 if they were female. Although the wording of such legislation has been struck down as unconstitutional, other more subtle differences in processing have been more difficult to detect.

Research from the late 1970s suggested that although girls were less likely than boys to be apprehended and adjudicated for criminal offenses, they were also more likely to be detained and institutionalized for status offenses.[19] This finding leads us to the question of whether girls actually committed more status offenses than males. Perhaps they were simply singled out for a more formal response to their actions. Evidence from self-report surveys by young people seemed to show that boys were just as likely as girls to be involved in any type of delinquent behavior. In fact, according to a National Youth Survey, males were significantly more likely to self-report status offenses than were females.[20] We must realize, however, that self-report data are no more an accurate reflection of the true level of delinquency than are police, or "official," reports.

Data from 1984 on status offenders show that girls committed less serious offenses than boys and that they were less likely to recidivate.[21] Females were more likely to be detained by the system than males, however. The decision to detain may be related to the type of status offense charged. In a 1987 study by Snyder and Finnegan, the kinds of status offenses charged to males and females were significantly different.[22] For girls, the most commonly committed offenses were running away and ungovernability. To officials, these offenses seemed to reflect problems at home and a need for a place to stay, perhaps in a more caring environment. The offenses committed by boys tended to be violations of liquor laws and curfew, which show "different" problems

Concerning Services Available

In California in 1975 a precedent-setting case illustrated the lack of services for females in the juvenile justice system. Aline D. was a 16-year-old juvenile accused of having abused a teacher at school, a misdemeanor offense. This was not her first offense. Aline had been placed in several local placements but had failed in all of them. Aline had a tested IQ of 67, had a history of assaultive behavior, and was a gang member. She was committed to a state correctional facility. She appealed that commitment to the state Supreme Court. The probation officer noted in his recommendation that had Aline been a male he would have recommended a local camp placement in lieu of the state institution. However, Aline was being sent to the most restrictive environment in the state correctional system because of the absence of adequate local resources for females. The probation officer's report noted, "It seemed to be the only recourse." Aline's mother did not want her back, she had failed in various placements, and she otherwise would be back on the streets. The California Supreme Court reversed the juvenile court's commitment, finding the justification inappropriate under the existing juvenile law, which meant that it was not acceptable to place females in restrictive confinement facilities simply because more appropriate placements were not available. In this case, such placements were available for males but not for females. Ironically, later changes in the law that allow more severe sanctions for juveniles would probably call for Aline to be committed to a state institution.

STATUS OFFENDERS TODAY

Signs in arrest and detention statistics show that status offenses are increasingly receiving more law enforcement attention. The percentages of male and female arrests for status offenses in 1986 were at the same level they had been in 1975.[23] At both times, approximately 25 percent of all youths referred to the court had been status offenders. In addition, the number of status offenders in out-of-home placements had not changed significantly between 1975 and 1987.[24] What has changed, according to some authors, is that status offenders are more likely to be placed in group homes and small residential treatment centers than in detention facilities and training schools.[25] The placement of status offenders in detention is still a commom occurrence, however. Examine the following cases:

- Shawn P., a 15-year-old boy, was arrested and detained in juvenile hall for the offense of petty theft. The police report stated that while a runaway he had entered his parents' home and stolen $40 from his father.
- Chrstine G. is also a runaway who was arrested and sent to juvenile hall. She, too, entered her parents' home while a runaway. The 14-year-old took food, clothing, and other items to sustain herself while on the run.
- Kenneth G., a 15-year-old, was arrested at the urging of his father for possession of a blowgun found in his room.

These three juveniles were booked into juvenile hall at the same time in 1986. What makes their cases interesting is that their state had passed legislation prohibiting the detention of status offenders almost 10 years earlier. As many other states did during the mid- 1970s, their state had decided that a juvenile could not be arrested or detained for an offense that would not constitute a violation of the law were the juvenile an adult. However, what has occurred in many instances is that the behavior of minors that would have previously been labeled as "incorrigibility" has, when the circumstances allowed, been relabeled as criminal. A 1989 survey of one juvenile hall showed that as many as 20 percent of the minors in custody were there as first-time offenders arrested for minor property offenses.

There is a strong suggestion that a juvenile's relationship with his or her parents in large part determines the response of the juvenile justice system when that juvenile commits a minor offense. The cases of Kenneth, Christine, and Shawn demonstrate what some experts consider to be a trend. Sometimes the offense is one that has been contrived to bring the juvenile before the court and to detain him or her in juvenile hall. Without the "criminal" charge, the law would prohibit this level of intervention by the juvenile justice system. Or in some cases, the arrest for a minor crime is simply the "straw that broke the camel's back." It starts the process for parents who are anxious to have the problem child removed from the home. When such incorrigibles are arrested, even for a minor offense, their parents use the incident as a vehicle for having the juvenile removed from the home and detained in juvenile hall.

Once in detention, careful screening of juvenile cases by probation offices could filter out youths who have only minor criminal histories or backgrounds of status offenses. Such a selection process would guarantee that status offenders do not receive harsh sentences despite the parents' desire for punitive measures. Working in favor of this screening is the decreasing availability of bed space in juvenile halls. Effective use of classification instruments may assure that this limited bed space in juvenile facilities is used only for those juveniles who pose a serious threat to the community.

THE RUNAWAY

Historically, running away has been treated as a means juveniles use to escape poor conditions of economic and family life. More often, boys have left home with an understanding that they should not burden the family financially. Instead, they sought independence and a trade. The young male runaway was romanticized in literature as a determined adventurer. Many runaways were fleeing grueling apprenticeships or other work arrangements where they were kept under contract until a debt was paid.

In the early 1900s, the practice of using children as cheap labor in factories and shops was curtailed by the passage of child labor laws, which established minimum age requirements for all industrial jobs. From the turn of the century until the Depression, running away had more to do with problems of family relationships than with extreme financial hardship. When the Depression occurred during the 1930s, most of the youth as well as their parents were out of work. Seventy-five percent of the work force under the age of 24 was either unemployed or only marginally employed.[26] Therefore, leaving home was once again legitimized. Youths took to the open road in great numbers. Many drifted from town to town, begging, stealing, and riding the rails.[27] As one youngster of this period explained:

> We were taken to the Detention Home, this being the thirteenth time I had entered its pearly gates. I was an "old timer" there at the early age of ten, and being a kid, felt it was an honor to be so well known. Besides, I was a "habitual or professional runaway" and considered a bad actor. In the home the kids all knew I'd done time and sort'a looked up to me for my wide experience in the world.[28]

It has always been difficult to conduct accurate research on the numbers and kinds of runaways because of the difficulty in locating these children and obtaining truthful information about their circumstances. One of the first studies of runaways was conducted in New York City in the late 1920s. The variables investigated by the researcher show her perceptions of the "causes" of such behavior. Theorists of this time believed that immigration and the subsequent loss of the regulating norms

Historically, young boys who were abandoned, orphaned, or who had run away were institutionalized and often became long-term wards of the state. (*Brown Brothers*)

of the "old country" and the social and economic stresses of resettlement in a new country all contributed to delinquency. Of the 660 boys analyzed in this early study, 65 percent had foreign-born parents and 55 percent came from broken families. The breakup of the family was most often caused by death. Seventy percent of the youths listed family problems or family and school problems as the reason for their running away.[29]

Studies that examined the long-term effects of running away report that over time runaways are increasingly likely to feel powerless and hopeless.[30] Many had adjustment problems such as failure in school, employment, and marriage. Most had trouble with the law.[31] Other studies have shown that these youths suffered higher rates of mental illness as adults, often being diagnosed as sociopathic.[32]

In 1985 estimates placed between 1.3 and 2 million children a year in the category of runaway or homeless.[33] Estimates often vary depending on how the term *runaway* is defined or where the data are obtained.

Examples of the various annual estimates of the prevalence of running away are listed in Table 10–1. The most conservative of these estimates, the National Statistical Survey claims that 1.7 percent of all youths between the ages of 10 and 17 run away each year. The highest estimate, by Elliot, et al., raises the age limits to between 11 and 17 years but predicts that 4.4 percent of all youths between these ages will run away each year.

Table 10–1 Annual Estimates of the Prevalence of Running Away.

Authors and Year of Study	Ages Included	Annual Percentage Rate of Runaways
Nat'l Stat. Survey (1976)	10–17	1.7
Brennan et al. (1975)	10–17	2.06
Edelbrock (1980)	4–16	1.85
Elliot et al. (1983)	11–17	4.4

Source: Gerald Hotaling and David Finkelhor (1988). *The sexual exploitation of missing children: A research review.* Washington, DC: U.S. Department of Justice, Office of Juvenile Justice and Delinquency Prevention.

Long-term runaway or homeless children are often referred to in criminal justice circles as *street kids*. The term *throwaways* has also been coined and is used to define children who have been forced out of their homes by parents or guardians or by family problems so severe as to warrant their flight. According to one expert, "Whether the child is a runaway or a throwaway is a determination of who reaches the decision first."[34]

In recognition of the problems faced by these groups of young people, Congress revised the 1974 Runaway Youth Act into the Runaway and Homeless Youth Act of 1977. In 1984 over $23 million was appropriated for the legislation. The funds were used to support 260 runaway and homeless youth shelters nationwide. They also were used to operate the National Runaway Switchboard, a free hotline and counseling referral service. The switchboard also acted as an intermediary between parents and children in the reunion process. According to the National Network of Runaway and Youth Services, Inc., "a portion of the RHYA funds go to innovative direct service projects and research directed at special issues and problems, e.g., family reunification strategies, independent living programs for older homeless teens, suicide prevention, employment and training services, juvenile prostitution, and others."[35]

A survey was conducted of 210 agencies that provided services to runaway and homeless youth. The agencies represented more than 500 shelters and foster care homes. The agencies cited their most serious problems as (1) needing more staff and better salaries, (2) needing more staff training, and (3) requiring more preventive, outreach, and aftercare resources for the client populations with which they dealt. Reports from these agencies showed that over 3000 young people had been turned away for lack of space.[36] The agencies also expressed a need for mental health and substance abuse care. Additionally, special resources were needed for dealing with physically and sexually abused youngsters.[37]

The Runaway as a Victim of Abuse

Over the years there have been many attempts to link child abuse not only to running away but to all kinds of delinquent activity. Most studies have concentrated on the behavioral effects of child abuse rather than the later legal status of victims. Researchers focused on the later adjustment problems of groups of abused children. These children were selected from social service or medical agency reports and tracked over the years into adulthood. Following over 900 confirmed physically and sexually abused children over a period of time, Widom concluded that "childhood victimization had demonstrable long-term consequences for adult criminal behavior."[38] The findings from this study included a higher proportion of criminal records, arrests, and arrests for violent offenses among the abused sample than in a control group. It is important to note, however, that only 29 percent of the abused children had adult nontraffic arrests— that is, a majority, 71 percent, had no trouble with the law. Another study found that clinical samples of abused children later exhibited adverse behaviors, including excessive fighting, cruelty, lying, disregard for property, aggressive behavior, and other psychiatric disturbances.[39] From findings such as these, experts and policymakers can only infer that abused children may be at high risk for future delinquency and adult criminal conduct.

Another method of studying the link between child abuse and delinquency has been to take samples of juvenile delinquents and interview them to review their family histories for evidence of abuse. This method is called an *ex post facto design* because the researcher looks for evidence of past abuse in a sample of youths who have already become delinquent. This kind of study would not yield any information about youths who have been abused but who do *not* become delinquent. Even if the juveniles are compared to a sample of nondelinquents for prior abuse, studies often lead to the conclusion that delinquents are more likely than nondelinquents to have been abused.[40]

It has also been shown that the delinquents identified with prior parental violence are more likely to be aggressive or violent. Such findings have led one criminologist to conclude that child abuse and neglect "are among the most powerful sources of serious criminal violence in America today."[41]

In contrast to this theory of a cycle of violence, several studies have shown that abused delinquents were not more likely to commit future crimes of aggression than were delinquents who had not been abused.[42] In addition, one study found that violent juvenile offenders were not significantly represented by victims of child abuse and parental violence.[43] After considerable research on this topic, Widom concluded, "In most of the studies, the majority of abused children became neither delinquent nor violent offenders."[44]

Research on the link between child abuse and running away has shown that the number of victims will also vary by two factors: (1) the location in which those who were surveyed were found and (2) how abuse was defined. For example, one national survey found that 5 percent of runaways had suffered from physical abuse by an adult that led to their running away. However, when the definition of abuse was broadened to "significant physical maltreatment," an Ohio study found that 75 percent of the shelter residents there had been abused. Statistics from the youth services network have determined that more than 60 percent of the young people in shelters reported being physically or sexually abused by their families.[45] It is important to keep in mind, however, that runaways in shelters may be different, perhaps less streetwise, than those who do not go to shelters. The question is whether research using children in shelters is representative of all runaways.

Over the years, several efforts have been made to link sexual abuse as a child to later acts of prostitution. The relationship, however, appears less direct. Young prostitutes were more likely to argue that physical and sexual abuse in the home led to running away. Running away often meant homelessness and poverty, which may have led some youngsters to resort to prostitution to earn money. One study on male prostitutes determined that about three-quarters of the subjects had either run away from or been kicked out of abusive homes.[46]

One study of runaways by Miller, Miller, Hoffman, and Duggan reported that 19 percent of the boys and 23 percent of the girls engaged in prostitution.[47] Among the runaways in a later Wisconsin study, 17 percent reported exchanging sex for food or lodging. Another 14 percent claimed to have had sex strictly for money.[48]

Existing research seems to show that physical and sexual child abuse and delinquent activity, such as running away, taking drugs, or engaging in prostitution, may all be somehow related. Richard Dembo and his associates conducted a study of juvenile delinquents and status offenders in a southeastern detention center.[49] They concluded that both physical and sexual abuse of children were related to later illicit drug use. It was perceived that sexual victimization had preceded the drug use for most of the youth. The exact nature of this relationship remains unclear as to cause, but the authors offered two theories. The first was that "early physical or sexual abuse predisposes children to react to these experiences in ways that increase their risk of becoming involved in delinquent behavior; and delinquent behavior patterns concomitantly increase the probability that involvement in illicit drug use will result."[50] The second theory is that the abuse of these youngsters causes psychological damage. The psychological problems that result are "reflected in low self-esteem, a lack of identity and poor inner control; and that these difficulties in functioning lead to the use of various drugs in an attempt to cope."[51]

TRUANCY

Concern about children who miss school is linked to the probability that these young people will eventually drop out of school. Research has further established that teens who drop out of school have traits similar to those of teens who commit crimes. The traits they share are poor academic and social self-concept, negative attitudes toward teachers and schools, learning disorders, impulsiveness, aggressiveness and alienation, low frustration tolerance, and poor goal-setting abilities. Lower levels of education have also been associated with higher rates of criminal activity.[52]

Although youths who drop out of school and those who are involved in delinquency have much in common, research does not show that the delinquency increases after the youths drop out of school. In some instances delinquency decreases, which is theorized to occur because dropping out of school ends the "school-related frustration and alienation" that are linked to many delinquent activities.[53] Also, after dropping out of school, many youths are busy with full-time jobs. This idea was supported by Bachman, O'Malley, and Johnston who found that although dropouts had a higher continued delinquency rate than those students who remained in school, there was no sign that leaving school increased their rate of delinquent activity.[54] Later research by Hartnagel and Krahn seems to suggest, however, that the more unstable the em-

Counselors work with teens at high risk for dropping out of school to give them the support they need to continue their education.
(© Maureen Fennelli/ Comstock)

ployment of the youths following dropping out of school, the greater their involvement with criminal activity.[55]

Another factor that may affect future rates of delinquency for those who drop out is the availability of alternative educational programs. Youths who do poorly in traditional academic settings may find success in vocational schools, GED programs, night schools, or adult education courses. These alternative programs are links to better jobs and higher self-esteem that may improve a youth's chances of successful social adjustment. Unfortunately, funding for these valuable educational resources is inconsistent and vulnerable to each round of budget cuts.

In a 1974 study of "school skippers," Crespo reported that 45 percent of the dropouts were females.[56] Other studies have also shown that males represent just over half of the population of high school dropouts. Dropping out of school or running away is neither a male nor a female phenomenon.

Experts have claimed that many of today's truants become tomorrow's tax burdens. The uneducated often have less success with employment and require more social services than those who graduate. Explained one educator, "School truancy is seen as a Tom Sawyer-Huckleberry Finn problem. But we're paying through AFDC [Aid to Families with Dependent Children], through inflated prices for shoplifting, and through programs to help dropouts. It becomes very expensive to us when we turn our back on truancy.[57]

Traditionally, schools have not been very successful in dealing with truancy. Suspending truant youths had very little impact on the problem except when the parents were financially well off or had social standing. Only in these cases, when their child's behavior was likely to be an embarrassment, would suspensions be considered effective. Dumping the children in "special" or detention classes within the school may lead to isolation within the academic environment. Furthermore, it does not, within the greater social and family context, address the child's needs that may be generating behavioral problems.

The resources available for working with students at risk should cover all possible approaches to truancy. Specially trained school counselors first become involved by identifying children at risk of dropping out and referring them to the most appropriate prevention programs. Early intervention can also include the use of Head Start programs that give economically disadvantaged preschoolers access to the skills that may lead to later success in the classroom. Theorists agree that frustration and negative attitudes toward school can begin at a very early age and set the stage for alienation and dropping out.

If the problem is seen as temporary or instigated by outside factors, some truancy programs seek to reintegrate academically troubled teens back into traditional classrooms after a brief period of intervention treatment. Other programs seek to divert students into alternative vocational and educational programs where they might be more successful.

These programs usually combine a variety of nontraditional study topics with work or apprenticeship training.

In San Bernardino and Los Angeles Counties, in California, school officials go to court to solve their worst truancy problems. First, the schools set up a School Attendance Review Board, which includes school, probation, mental health, and district attorney representatives. The board screens truancy cases and forwards only the most extreme cases to the courts for prosecution. The cases filed are those "last resort" situations in which all less extreme measures have failed. Each case is strictly documented with records that may go back several years. According to county officials, "The cases they prosecute are largely symbolic. They hope they're sending a message to children and parents who fail to heed the first warnings. They call it the bottom line."[58]

PROGRAMS FOR STATUS OFFENDERS TODAY

Some jurisdictions have specific, separate programs for status offenders and others do not. In a survey of over 500 juvenile services agencies, Maxson and her colleagues found that those agencies with specifically targeted caseloads of status offenders were more likely to provide counseling and residential shelter than did agencies that did not serve status offenders.[59] The same was true for agencies that did not separate status offenders from the rest of their general population. Programs with individualized treatment for status offenders were also more likely to offer decision-making services and to have "higher percentages of youth clients in all the problem groups and fewer clients with no problems."[60] It was further explained that privately operated programs were more likely to separate status offenders from the general population of offenders and to provide special services to this group.

In Washington there is an intensive in-home family preservation program called Homebuilders, which began in 1974. The clinical counseling program offers a range of psychological approaches for family intervention. The techniques used include behavior modification based on the natural environment, crisis intervention, client-centered therapy, clarification of values, and assertiveness training. Other practical services that are available include transportation, house cleaning, and cooking. The program's philosophy is that children are better off with their natural families *if* the family addresses their problems and they all learn to live together productively. Homebuilders uses a one counselor/one family design. The family therapists are available 24 hours a day, seven days a week. Those clients who are in danger of being removed from their homes are seen in the home through visits by the therapist. According to project coordinators, "Service is provided to a family for about one month. The Homebuilder is there to stabilize the family's equilibrium and help the family learn new ways of behaving. These new behaviors might be more helpful when the family runs into problems.[61]

SUMMARY

Ever since the invention of the juvenile court system, experts have argued over the role of intervention in the cases of status offenders. Theories that concentrated the causes of crime in the behavior and values of the poor held that removing children from an unhealthy environment would reduce the chances of further and even more serious crimes. Status offenses became attached to the concept of predelinquent behavior, which justified the courts' intervention and even the placement of children in foster homes and state schools.

Public interest and involvement in previously closed environments, such as prisons, mental hospitals, and juvenile institutions, led to a period of criticism and reform in the early 1960s. Hearings, lawsuits, and media access fueled negative assessments of juvenile institutions, and there was a resurgence of public support for the community treatment of juveniles. Research that led to the development of a labeling perspective on delinquency was also part of the movement toward nonintervention. Reform strategies included the four Ds—decriminalization, diversion, due process, and deinstitutionalization.[62]

As with many other social problems of the time, critics believed that decentralization of administrative power, greater community involvement in operations, and less dependence on governmental bureaucracy for services would improve the quality of corrections programs for juveniles.[63] Although deinstitutionalization was seen as an improvement over confinement, some people argued that the use of halfway houses or group homes was simply the substitution of one form of incarceration for another.[64] It was thought by some that, depending on conditions, a short term of institutionalization could be more desirable than a lengthy term of restrictive community care.

Today, a number of intervention strategies are aimed at the status offender, including programs for runaways, victims of child abuse, and children at high risk of dropping out of school. However, there still remains a considerable amount of debate over the proper role of the juvenile justice system in the lives of children accused of such minor social harms.

One of the primary motives of persons who argue for intervention with status offenders is crime prevention. However, research has yet to show any definitive relationship between family problems, or status offenses, and future crime. According to Gibbons and Krohn,[65] even if treatment is indicated for children who have family problems, who run away, or who become unruly, there is no proof that the justice system is the agency capable of achieving success with this population. In fact, many professionals view the activities of status offenders as a normal part of adolescence that most juveniles will outgrow on their own.

CASE

Aline 14 Cal 3rd 577; mod 677A, 1975.

KEY TERMS

CHINS, PINS, MINS
deinstitutionalization
escalation hypothesis
ex post facto design
in loco parentis
labeling

nonintervention
primary deviance/secondary
 deviance
stigma
street kids
throwaways

DISCUSSION QUESTIONS

1. What would be the best method of assessing the link between child abuse and delinquency?
2. Are there varying degrees of seriousness within the categories of status offenses? Should some of these offenses be treated differently from others? How?
3. Should there be a separate system for status offenders? If so, what should it look like?
4. What stereotypes exist today about male versus female status offenders? To what extent is labeling responsible for the stereotyped images?

END NOTES

1. Wheeler, Gerald B. (1978). *Counterdeterrence.* Chicago: Nelson Hall, p. 121.
2. Rojek, D. G., and M. Erickson (1982). Reforming the justice system: The diversion of status offenders. *Law and Society Review* 16(2):240–262.
3. Erickson, Maynard (1979). Some empirical questions concerning the current revolution in juvenile justice, in *The Future of Childhood and Juvenile Justice,* ed. L. T. Empey, pp. 277–311. Charlottesville, VA: University of Virginia Press.
4. Rankin, Joseph, and Edward Wells (1985). From status to delinquent offenses: Escalation? *Journal of Criminal Justice* 13:171–180.
5. Weis, J. (1979). *Jurisdiction and the elusive status offender: A comparison of involvement in delinquent behavior and status offenses.* Report to the Nation on Juvenile Justice Assessment Centers. Washington, DC: U.S. Government Printing Office.
6. Rojek, D. G., and M. Erickson (1981/82). Supra note 2, p. 241.

7. Wolfgang, Marvin, Robert Figlio, and Thorsten Sellin (1972). *Delinquency in a birth cohort.* Chicago: Univ. of Chicago Press.

8. Lemert, Edwin (1951). *Social pathology: A systematic approach to the theory of sociopathic behavior.* New York: McGraw-Hill.

9. Crespo, Manuel (1974). Career of the school skipper, in *Deviance: The Interactionist Perspective* (5th ed.), eds. Earl Rubington and Martin Weinberg, p. 314. New York: Macmillan.

10. Schur, Edwin (1971). *Labeling deviant behavior: Its sociological implications.* New York: Harper & Row; Lofland, John (1969). *Deviance and identity.* Englewood Cliffs, NJ: Prentice Hall.

11. Schur, Edwin (1973). *Radical nonintervention.* Englewood Cliffs, NJ: Prentice Hall.

12. Gibbons, Don, and Marvin Krohn (1986). *Delinquent behavior* (4th ed.). Englewood Cliffs, NJ: Prentice Hall.

13. Rojek, D. G. and M. Erickson (1982). Supra note 2, p. 241.

14. Binder, Arnold, and Virginia Binder (1982). Juvenile diversion and the Constitution. *Journal of Criminal Justice* 10:3–24.

15. National Council on Crime and Delinquency (1975). Jurisdiction over status offenders should be removed from the juvenile court: A policy statement. *Crime and Delinquency* 21(2):97–99.

16. Chesney-Lind, Meda (1988). Girls and status offenses: Is juvenile justice still sexist? *Criminal Justice Abstracts* March:144–165.

17. Krisberg, Barry et al. (1985). *The watershed of juvenile justice reform.* Minneapolis, MN: Hubert H. Humphrey Institute of Public Affairs.

18. Spergel, L. A., J. P. Lynch, F. G. Reamer, and J. Korbelik (1982). Response of organization and community to a deinstitutionalization strategy. *Crime and Delinquency* 28:426–229.

19. Chesney-Lind, Meda (1977). Judicial paternalism and the female status offender. *Crime and Delinquency* 23:121–130.

20. Canter, Rachelle (1982). Sex differences in self-report delinquency. *Criminology* 20:373–393.

21. Datesman, Susan, and Mikel Aickin (1984). Offense specialization and escalation among status offenders. *Journal of Criminal Law and Criminology* 75:1246–1275.

22. Snyder, Howard, and Terrence Finnegan (1987). *Delinquency in the United States, 1983.* Washington, DC: U.S. National Institute for Juvenile Justice and Delinquency Prevention, p. 25.

23. Chesney-Lind, M. (1988). Supra note 16, p. 148.

24. Thornberry, T. P., S. E. Tolnay, T. J. Flanagan, and P. Glynn (1991). *Children in custody 1987: A comparison of public and private juvenile custody facilities.* Washington, DC: Office of Juvenile Justice and Delinquency Prevention.

25. Hurst, Hunter, and Louis McHardy (1991). Juvenile justice and the blind lady. *Federal Probation* 55(2):63–68.

26. Sinclair, Catherine (1983). A radical/Marxist interpretation of juvenile justice in the United States. *Federal Probation* 46(2):20–28.

27. Lipschutz, Mark (1977). Runaways in history. *Crime and Delinquency* 23(3):321–332.

28. Shaw, Clifford (1930). *The jackroller.* Chicago: Univ. of Chicago Press. Reprinted 1966.

29. Armstrong, Clairette (1932). *660 runaway boys.* Boston: B. Humphries.

30. Hotaling, Gerald, and David Finkelhor (1988). *The sexual exploitation of missing children: A research review.* Washington, DC: U.S. Department of Justice, Office of Juvenile Justice and Delinquency Prevention, p. 25.

31. Olsen, L., E. Liebow, F. Mannino, and M. Shore (1980). Runaway children twelve years later: A follow-up. *Journal of Family Issues* 1(2):165–188.

32. Robbins, L. (1958). Mental illness of the runaway: A 30 year follow-up study. Human Organization 16(4):1–15.

33. National Network of Runaway and Youth Services (1985). *To whom do they belong?: A profile of America's runaway and homeless youth and programs that help them.* Washington, DC: The National Network of Runaway and Youth Services, p. 1.

34. Baltz, Guy (1990). In J. C. Barden, Study: Number of homeless adolescents up. *San Bernardino Sun,* 5 February:A3.

35. National Network of Runaway and Youth Services (1985). Supra note 33, p. 5.

36. Barden, J. C. (1990). Study: Number of homeless adolescents up. *San Bernardino Sun,* 5 February:A3.

37. National Network of Runaway and Youth Services (1985). Supra note 33, p. 12.

38. Widom, Cathy Spatz (1989). Child abuse, neglect, and violent criminal behavior. *Criminology* 27(2):251–271.

39. Jaffe, P., D. Wolfe, S. Wilson, and L. Zak (1986). Similarities in behavioral and social maladjustment among child victims and witnesses to family violence. *American Journal of Orthopsychiatry* 56(1):142–146.

40. Schwartz, M. D. (1989). Incest victims and the criminal justice system, in *The Changing Roles of Women in the Criminal Justice System,* ed. L. Moyer. Prospect Heights, IL: Waveland Press.

41. Currie, E. (1985). Confronting crime. New York: Pantheon, p. 199.

42. Kratcoski, Peter (1982). Child abuse and violence against the family. *Child Welfare* 61:435–444.

43. Guiterres, Sara, and John Reich (1981). A developmental perspective on runaway behavior: Its relationship to child abuse. Child Welfare 60:89–94.

44. Widom, C. S. (1989). Supra note 38, p. 253.

45. Barden, J. C. (1990). Supra note 36.

46. Allen, D. M. (1980). Young male prostitutes: A psychological study. *Archives of Sexual Behavior* 9(5):399–426.

47. Miller, D. D., D. Miller, F. Hoffman, and R. Duggan (1980). *Runaways, illegal aliens in their own land: Implications for service.* New York: J. F. Bergin.

48. Phelps, R. J. et al. (1982). *Wisconsin juvenile female offender study project.* Madison: Youth Police and Law Center.

49. Dembo, Richard, Max Dertke, Scott Borders, Maark Washburn, and James Schmeidler (1985). The relationship between physical and sexual abuse and illicit drug use among youths in a juvenile detention center. Revision of a paper presented at the annual meeting of the Academy of Criminal Justice Sciences, Las Vegas, Nevada, p. 17.

50. Ibid.

51. Ibid.

52. Bell-Rowbotham, B., and C. L. Boydell (1972). Crime in Canada: A distributional analysis, in *Deviant Behavior and Societal Reaction,* ed. C. L. Boydell. Toronto: Holt, Rinehart & Winston.

53. Hartnagel, Timothy, and Harvey Krahn (1989). High school dropouts, labor market success and criminal behavior. *Youth and Society* 20(4):416–444.

54. Bachman, J. G., P. O'Malley, and J. Johnston (1978). *Youth in transition VI, Adolescence to adulthood.* Ann Arbor: Institute for Social Research.

55. Hartnagel, T., and H. Krahn (1989). Supra note 53.

56. Crespo, M. (1974). Supra note 9.

57. Raney, Rebecca (1991). Skip school, go to court, county says. *San Bernardino Sun* 6 May:A1

58. Ibid.

59. Maxson, Cheryl, Margaret Gordon, Malcolm Klein, and Lea Cunningham (1990). Service delivery to status offenders. Paper presented at the annual meeting of the American Society of Criminology, Baltimore.

60. Ibid.

61. Haapala, David, and Jill Kinney (1988). Avoiding out-of-home placement of high-risk status offenders through the use of intensive home-based family preservation services. *Criminal Justice and Behavior* 15(3):334–348.

62. Empey, Lamar (1978). *American delinquency.* Homewood, IL: Dorsey Press.

63. Musheno, Michael, Dennis Palumbo, Steven Moody, and James Levine (1989). Community corrections as an organizational innovation: What works and why. *Journal of Research in Crime and Delinquency* 26(2):136–167.

64. Greenberg, David (1975). Problems in community corrections. *Issues in Criminology* Spring: 8–9.

65. Gibbons, Don, and Marvin Krohn (1986). *Delinquence behavior* (4th ed.). Englewood Cliffs, NJ: Prentice Hall, p. 77.

11

Programming Experiments for Juvenile Offenders

Ultimately the program tells us more about ourselves and the current state of our society than anything else. Having been deluged for the last number of years with media events depicting children as devils, witches, and anti-Christs, it should not be surprising that we now bless a panacea designed to scare the hell out of our children.

— Dr. Jerome Miller, President, National Center on Institutions and Alternatives, in testimony to U.S. Congress, hearings, Oversight on *Scared Straight*

OBJECTIVES

On completion of this chapter, you should be able to do the following:

1. Discuss why the Scared Straight program was so popular with the public and how its popularity compared with its success.

2. Explain the theory behind the use of aftercare and some of the elements of a good aftercare program.

3. Describe the treatment strategies of the Provo and Silverlake programs and the results in terms of success.

4. List some of the attributes of successful programs. Explain why these characteristics are important.

PURPOSE

This chapter explores some of the treatment strategies for juveniles that have been tried as community alternatives. Past as well as current programs are highlighted. One way to analyze and evaluate programs is to study the process of developing and implementing them. According to theory, program development includes first identifying a client's problems and needs, or the population to be served, and determining the best approach or strategy for meeting those needs. Program developers then create specific program objectives or goals, and design and implement each phase of a program. When a program is in full operation, administrators receive feedback and evaluate the program's effectiveness. The outcomes can be compared to the predetermined goals as a way of measuring success.

INTRODUCTION

Programs that address delinquent conduct may target a variety of youthful populations and may serve a number of behavioral goals. First, programs may be broad-based and delivered to all youngsters in a specific area. These programs are preventive in nature and seek to educate youths on the realities of crime and punishment. Such programs are presented to large audiences at schools, churches, social clubs, or other gatherings.

Another kind of program focuses on youths at risk. Their objective is to make an impact on young people before they engage in more serious crime or delinquent activity. High-risk groups may be formed from first-time minor offenders who fit the personal and demographic characteristics of known delinquents. These youths may be gang members, candidates for gangs, or children from criminous families. With both kinds of programs, it is difficult to determine whether anticrime messages have had any deterrent effect. To measure the success of this strategy, one would have to develop a means to determine if those who *would have* committed crimes were stopped by the intervention program.

The third approach to juvenile intervention is working directly with adjudicated delinquents. Programs targeting this population are usually remedial; they address problems that have already been made manifest. Success with this group is usually measured by the termination of delinquent activity—that is, the official (police) reports show no further arrests. Success may also be measured by a reduction in the seriousness or frequency of delinquent activity. These changes may show progress in the youth's development of more socially approved behaviors. Finally, the youths may be considered successful participants if they complete the terms of their supervision contract as required by the court: the client paid restitution, attended the proper number of counseling sessions, and performed the necessary community service.

SOME HISTORICALLY SIGNIFICANT PROGRAMS

Over the years a number of treatment strategies have been developed for juvenile populations. Each reflects a somewhat different perspective on the causes of delinquent behavior and therefore, the means for changing it. Programs also differ on the role of the staff and the category of client served (e.g., serious, repeat, or first-time offenders). Other distinguishing characteristics of programs include the particular needs of the youth (such as psychiatric treatment and drug counseling) and the focus of such activities as education, counseling, and job skills. One way to design successful future programs is to study the results of the strategies that have already been put to test. Conclusions drawn from such analysis would allow us to develop more meaningful programs.

The Provo Experiment

The *Provo experiment* has the distinction of being one of the first attempts to design and evaluate a community-based alternative program for serious, young (15 to 18 years old), male, repeat offenders. The program was developed in Provo, Utah, and operated from about 1959 to 1966. It was designed around two central assumptions about the cause of delinquent behavior. The first was that law breaking is generally a group activity. The second was the belief that delinquency was concentrated in the lower classes where learning situations limit access to success goals. The format of the Provo program was designed to address these two assumptions. Two phases were built into the structure of the program. The first was an intensive treatment component known as Pinehills.

Pinehills was a residential facility occupied by the 20 participants only part of the day. The boys returned to their own homes at the end of each day. This program lacked a formal structure. That is, it lacked a system of rules that guided decision making. Consequently, there was no direct linkage between following rules and being released from the program. The intent was to leave the participants free to define situations for themselves. They were allowed to create their own resolution of problems. Participants were permitted to make important decisions during the rehabilitative process. An atmosphere was created in which the peer group provided the center for all information exchange and decision making. The use of authority by staff was limited to situations not resolvable by the peer group. The staff maintained a role at the periphery of the peer group process. This method is commonly referred to as *guided group interaction*. In this process the youths were encouraged to recognize the consequences of continued involvement in delinquent activity. As researchers noted:

> Delinquents felt that the greatest long-range benefits were derived from their active participation in a problem-solving, decision-making role. The sanctioning of deviant behavior had made them cautious, and even reflective. However, while staff members could teach, guide, and interpret, it was the help provided by one's peers that was considered to be the greatest value.[1]

One of the major tasks of the program was to address the need for disciplined work habits. It was assumed that sophisticated delinquents would have a great deal of difficulty developing effective work values. The boys were employed by the city, particularly in parks and recreational areas if they were not in a formal educational program. In addition, discussion of work habits was a focus of the peer group process.

In the second phase of the program, the participants were released to the community. During this phase, each youth continued to meet with his old Pinehills peer group. The group meetings concentrated on an assessment of post-release behavior and solutions to any new problems that may have developed. Some help was provided by a Citizen's Advisory Council. This group focused on locating employment for the participants.

When the Provo experiment was developed, an evaluation process was built in from the beginning. Once adjudicated and ordered to a state training school, each minor was a candidate for a random selection process that could place him in this program. Candidates were randomly selected for either the training school or the experimental program. The process was intended to ensure that any findings from the evaluation would be based on two similar populations. The random assignment process broke down, however, when there were not enough participants to assign to both groups. As a result, researchers sent all remaining court referrals to the experimental group and compared them with similar youth already assigned to the institution.[2]

There is still controversy over whether the results were affected by this manipulation. The findings indicated that the experimental program had at least a modest effect on reducing subsequent delinquent activity. Eighty-four percent of the youths who completed the program were not arrested in the first six months following release. In contrast, the post-program behavior of participants from state training schools suggested that such programs tended to increase the criminal activity of juveniles. Follow-ups conducted over the next four years showed that 50 percent of the Provo graduates had at least one arrest. This compared well to the 80 percent rate of recidivism of the traditional training school residents. However, the experimental group appears to have not been significantly better off in terms of reduced recidivism than youths completing regular probation. Both of these methods seemed to be superior to institutionalization.[3]

The Silverlake Experiment

Silverlake, like the Provo experiment, was an effort to avoid some of the negative aspects of institutionalization by locating a program within the community. Like Provo, the Silverlake participants were repeat offenders randomly selected following a court commitment to a traditional institutional setting. There was a significant difference between the Silverlake and Provo designs. In the Silverlake experiment, which operated from about 1964 to 1968, the control group to which experimental participants was compared was a privately operated institution and not a state training school. Program participants consisted of boys ages 15 through 17 who were sent to a group home or to the Boys Republic. The Boys Republic is a private institution near Los Angeles, California.

Residents of the group home attended public high school in the community, whereas members of the institutional control group attended an on-grounds school. In this control program, daily activities were highly regimented and vocational training was emphasized. However, unlike the state correctional facility in the Provo experiment, the Boys Republic emphasized student government in an effort to teach the boys citizenship as well as to allow them to exercise some control over their environment.

Members of the experimental group home could visit and stay with their families only over the weekends. They did not go home every evening as did the experimental group in Provo. As in the Provo experiment, considerable decision-making power was vested in peer groups in the hope of establishing a climate in which the offender accepted responsibility in the behavioral change process. Problem solving occurred in daily group meetings. The groups were led by an adult staff member, but the adult functioned as a facilitator rather than as an authority figure.

The program evaluation included a total of 261 boys, 140 of whom were assigned to Silverlake and 121 to Boys Republic. The experimental program was conducted for cases assigned during a three-year period. One significant conclusion was that there was no adverse impact on the community as the result of placement of minors in the experimental program. That is, the program did not increase the incidence of crime in the community in which the program was located. Recidivism rates were measured by the incidence of post-release arrests of youths who had successfully completed the program. The recidivism data suggested that the program's wards experienced no significant improvement over those from the institution. However, there was some sign that the seriousness of subsequent delinquent acts was reduced by the experimental program.[4]

Caution should be observed in the interpretation of these findings. Experimental programs like Silverlake may have a different resident base from their counterpart control groups if those participants who leave the program after a short period are excluded from the final analysis. Participants who complete an institutional program do so because they have no alternative. Graduates of experimental programs, however, are those who have chosen to stay and participate. This may be a result of personality or character differences between the experimental and control groups. In the Silverlake experiment, for example, 37 percent of the group home residents ran away during the first or second month.[5] Those who did stay may have been better candidates for continued overall success than those who did not.

VisionQuest

VisionQuest is probably the most widely known outdoor-adventure program for youthful offenders. The program began in 1973 in Tucson, Arizona.[6] Today, the program receives generally chronic delinquent youths who have failed in one or more prior placements. Although the program is coeducational, over 95 percent of the participants are male. Most of these youths are prospects for commitment to a high-security state institution.

The programs of VisionQuest consist of rustic wilderness camps, wagon trains, sailing, and bicycling expeditions. The program emphasizes physical conditioning, accountability, and overcoming personal and physical challenges or quests. Some camps include a "blind walk" during which the youths perform a series of exercises blindfolded. Others may employ a "solo"; the participants spend three days alone in the wilderness with only a minimum of food and water. Others employ a six-day adventure that includes rock climbing, rapelling, and a six-mile run, all of which are intended to help the youths respond to challenges and gain self-confidence.[7]

The first phase of a youth's term at VisionQuest is spent in a wilderness camp located near Silver City, New Mexico. The time in the wilderness camp, a rustic boot-camp environment, can last from three to seven months. The youngsters live in a tepee with six to ten other participants and a junior staff member. They sleep outside and engage in strenuous physical conditioning. In addition, they are involved in a regular school program.

When the youths have successfully completed the camp program, they are transferred to a wagon train in which they spend five months traveling over the western states. The wagon train consists of a dozen wagons drawn by horses and mules. There are another dozen support vehicles such as school buses, cook wagons, and portable toilets. On each wagon train there are about 50 youths and an equal number of staff. While on the wagon train, the youths rise at 5:30 A.M., feed the animals, dismantle tents and camp equipment, hitch the animals to the wagons, and set off. A new camp is set up each afternoon with the accompanying chores being done by the youths. A unique part of the program is the use of Indian rituals to celebrate the progress of a youth in the program.

The final five months are spent in a community residential treatment program. At the end of this period, the youth is returned home.

The core component of VisionQuest is a high ratio of staff to youth and a series of *impact programs* that consist of a close family/communal living environment and verbal and physical confrontations between staff and youth designed to open communications. Constant emphasis is placed on improving behavior and attitude. When possible, efforts are made at family therapy.

Another unique aspect of the VisionQuest program is the eclectic background of the staff. The staff are not generally hired from other positions within the criminal justice system. Instead, they come from such varied backgrounds as carpentry, logging, trucking, and farming.[8] This hiring practice may be an advantage, but it may also be a rationalization for not being able to hire correctional or social service professionals. Instead, the program may be forced to rely on those unemployed in economically depressed industries.

A program evaluation of VisionQuest was conducted by the Rand Corporation between 1984 and 1987. The findings should be viewed with caution because of the way the program was studied. The evaluation did not use an experimental design with random assignment of eligible youths to the program and to control groups. The report concludes that the recidivism rates for VisionQuest graduates was significantly lower than for graduates of another publicly operated program. The actual rates were 55 percent rearrests for VisionQuest youth compared to 71 percent for the comparison group. Because an experimental design was not used in the evaluation, it cannot be said for certain whether these results were actually a result of program differences. The findings may simply show that there were higher levels of delinquent tendencies in the comparison group. As with all nonexperimental program evaluations, the results can be taken only as suggestive of the value of the program relative to other alternatives.[9]

The cost of participating in VisionQuest may raise the expectations of some people for even higher success rates. In 1990 the average length of stay was 13 months at a cost of $3368 a month, which is almost $44,000 annually. At this price, and even at significantly less per month, many kinds of community supervision/experience programs could be developed. For the cost of an average four-year college education, should one expect a rearrest rate lower than 55 percent? One would also be curious to know the cost of the other program that the VisionQuest youth were compared to. What if there was a program that cost less than half the price of VisionQuest to operate yet that had a recidivism rate only 16 percent greater? Would it change your perception of its value?

Scared Straight

Between 1979 and 1989, Rahway State Prison in New Jersey operated a controversial program for more than 15,000 young delinquents. The program took small groups of delinquents and predelinquents into Rahway prison to face the harsh realities of the environment and the inmates. The inmates not only graphically explained the dangers and problems of prison life; they also teased, tormented, and threatened the youngsters about what would happen to them behind bars. These frightening encounters were considered to be a critical part of the program.

Theoretically, the program was designed to make an impression on young people at a time in their development when they might be able to alter their behavior. An underlying assumption was that the *goal* of preventing further delinquent activity and possible incarceration was worth the *means*, or tactics, used—tactics that included scaring and threatening teens with the verbal abuse of the inmates and the violently realistic accounts of prison life.

When the program was highlighted on a national television show, the public was delighted. The program's appeals were its parental-like direct, straightforward approach that seemed to have an immediate impact and its low-cost, no-frills price tag. Soon afterward the National Center on Institutions and Alternatives challenged the program's claims of success. The center alleged that the results boasted of by the program were simply based on isolated incidences of individual testimony and not on a systematic research study. Such a study was then undertaken by James Finckenauer, who found that those teens who had appeared on the television show had come from a middle-class suburb outside of New York.[10] They had never really been involved in any serious delinquency. The kids who appeared in the Academy Award–winning documentary had been rounded up from a park as volunteers by a film crew. In fact, the high school they attended was systematically attempting to send all of its students through the Scared Straight program to promote a preventive posture.

Dr. Finckenauer conducted a follow-up study of Scared Straight participants and a similar group of nonparticipants. He found that although participants viewed crime less favorably than nonparticipants did, they had a higher failure rate. Within six months of attending the program, 41 percent of the participants had been involved in new delinquency whereas only 12 percent of the nonparticipants had. Finckenauer suggested a number of explanations for his findings.

First, involvement with the program may have triggered a self-fulfilling prophecy if the youths romanticized about the "lifers". The lifers may have appeared to be brave, tough, and able to control the environment around them. The program may also have challenged or dared the youths to prove they were not intimidated by the prison. In addition, some experts felt that some juveniles may not have had the maturity and impulse control to consistently modify their behavior once they had visited the prison even if they were frightened by it.

Although the visits dramatized the realities of being incarcerated, they did not address the youths' perception of the chances of getting caught or being punished. Many teens simply discount incarceration as something that happens to somebody else, "not me."

Finally, it is not really understood whether it is more frightening, and thus a greater deterrent, not to know anything about prison rather than to see some frightening things. There are theorists who suggest that being in the prison may actually reduce its intimidation effect on some young people. Simply having been there and come back may reassure some youngsters that it is not the worst thing that could happen. Perhaps the worst is the unknown.

JOLT

Despite its apparent shortcomings, the Scared Straight program was quickly and widely copied throughout the country. The Michigan

Department of Corrections developed a similar model called JOLT (Juvenile Offenders Learn Truth). A group of 227 participants who completed the program were then compared to a group of nonparticipants who had been found to have similar histories of delinquency. Ironically, three to six months after the program, the participants had higher incidences of delinquent activity than did the nonparticipants.[11]

Squires

Squires was the name of another program modeled after Scared Straight, this time at San Quentin Prison in California. The State Youth Authority selected participants who all had similar criminal records. These youths were then separated into two groups. One group received the Scared Straight kind of program and the second, a control group, did not. Results of a one-year follow-up show that participants in the Squires program had more positive changes in attitude. However, the two groups still had similar rates of rearrest, similar numbers of new offenses, and the charges were of a similar severity.

Rahway Today—Scared Rap

The story of the Lifers Group of Rahway prison does not end with the experiment of Scared Straight. The 15-year-old Lifers Group is currently sponsoring a new program that has taken their Juvenile Awareness message into the 1990s via the popular medium of rap. The 12-member rap band made up of armed robbers and murderers attempts to depict the harsh realities of prison and the violent struggle for a miserable existence within the walls of the maximum security institution. The video feature of their two main songs, "Raw Deal" and "Belly of the Beast," has been nominated for a Grammy. The theme of the music video is simple, according to the group's leader Maxwell Melvins, "prison is not a piece of cake." (See Box 11–1.)

PREVENTION PROGRAMS

According to some experts, delinquency prevention programs should be multifaceted. Strategies should employ a number of various goals and techniques because no one method is complete in and of itself. As Weis writes, "Prevention programs should address the elements of the child's environment which most directly affect his or her future; education, employment, community, family, and peers."[12]

Parent-effectiveness training can be used to provide coping mechanisms for families to reduce conflict and tension that may lead to dysfunction and rebellion in children. Some theorists recognize that the successful relationships within the family pave the way for positive experiences in school and in the community. Sociologist Mark Colvin

BOX 11–1

Inmates Take Rap—to the Grammys

BY COLUM LYNCH

Since he was sentenced to life in prison in 1980 for murder, Maxwell Melvins has dreamed of many things from the cramped interior of his cell: redemption for his crime, a night alone with his wife, a shorter prison sentence. He never dreamed he could win a Grammy Award.

But Melvins and 12 inmates from the Lifers Group, a prison rap band at the East New Jersey maximum security penitentiary, have been nominated for a Grammy in the long-form video category.

However, none of the singers will be on hand to receive the award if they win. Prison authorities won't allow Melvins, the band's creator who is named on the nomination, to take the 20-minute bus ride today to the ceremony at Radio City Music Hall in New York City.

The National Academy of Recording Arts & Sciences, which awards the Grammy, turned down a request by Melvins to have the band's longtime liaison, Lt. Alan August, or two recently paroled rappers accept the award on his behalf. The academy makes exceptions for nobody but the dead.

Inside the domed prison complex at Rahway, beyond half-a-dozen sliding gates, Melvins was chain-smoking as he paced the prison floor, anxiously orchestrating press interviews, a photo shoot and one of two daily prison tours by juvenile delinquents.

The Lifers Group is the brainchild of Melvins, president of the 15-year-old Lifers Group Juvenile Awareness Program. The program, which invites delinquents and high school students to a day in prison, is best known as the subject of the Academy Award-winning documentary "Scared Straight."

The group wants to demythologize the romanticism of prison that often informs rap music. Members hope to so terrify potential young criminals with horrific tales of prison rape, physical brutality and mental torture that they will walk a straight line through life. Melvins saw rap music as the best way to convey that message, and last year he persuaded a Los Angeles record company to come to the prison to make a record and video.

The 30-minute video documentary, directed by Penelope Spheeris ("Wayne's World"), who is also named on the nomination, provides abundant testimony of prison hardships and brutality. Shot in black-and-white 16-millimeter film and color video, it depicts a cramped and dispiriting universe, filled with tiled walls, fences, metal bars and men with huge muscles. The main tracks, "Real Deal" and "Belly of the Beast," are gritty and unsparing. The lyrics, which are written by the inmates, deal in a direct and brutal way with issues like AIDS, murder, betrayal, prison rape, suicide and laundry detail.

In one of the more disturbing scenes in the video, Rahway corrections officer Michael Cook displays a slender five-inch shank, sheathed in a hand-carved wooden crucifix, and blandly remarks that such a blade was used to "pluck out" an inmate's eye. The message, says the Lifers Group, is that prison is not "a piece of cake . . . just like a party," as rapper Ice Cube described it in a song.

BOX 11–1 (*continued*)

Each rapper from the Lifers Group has been jailed for serious offenses—armed robbery, kidnapping and murder—and many are repeat offenders. Knowledge Born Allah, 28, has spent more than half his life in prison and juvenile reformatories. He has been at Rahway since 1986, serving out a 10-year sentence for manslaughter. Allah, a member of the Five Percent Nation of Islam, said he accidentally knocked down his 69-year-old grandmother, Rose Esther Rouse, during a scuffle with his cousin over money and half an ounce of cocaine. She hit her head and died three weeks later.

His lyrics, like those of most of the youngest rappers in the band, deal with rape, fear of AIDS and the predatory nature of prison life.

The video and album have given the band a measure of fame. Melvins has received fan mail from as far away as Australia. He says one woman, a member of a drug crew in Canada who plotted murder to get out of the gang, wrote him that she changed her mind after seeing the video. But the Lifers Group's notoriety has gotten mixed reactions from guards and other inmates. "Everything's not peaches and cream here," said Aziz, a member of the Lifers Group with more than 10 years at Rahway. "We are resented by some of the cops who think we're getting too much attention."

After months of getting the cold shoulder from rap bands and several record labels, Melvins persuaded Los Angeles record producer Dave Funken-Klein at Hollywood Records to take an interest in the project. Funken-Klein held a talent contest in the prison and brought in a camera crew and portable recording studio. The entire project was completed in three weeks.

Since last spring, the Lifers Group has sold more than 50,000 records. There are no plans to cut a new record and Melvins said the organization has yet to make a dime. The record company, he has been told by one of his three lawyers, has yet to recoup its $140,000 in production costs. If the video ultimately makes a profit, their proceeds will be channeled through the prison to fund Lifers Group's projects, according to Melvins.

Source: The Los Angeles Times (February 25, 1992), p. F6. Used by permission.

even suggests that parents be given tax exemptions for participation in parent-training workshops.[13] The logic is that such prevention efforts will avoid more expensive intervention strategies in the future.

In 1983 the Los Angeles Police Department began a program in Drug Abuse Resistance Education (DARE) in the elementary school system. This program places officers directly in the classroom to talk to youngsters about the dangers of drug use. The department claims that between the start of the program and 1989, drug arrests among juveniles decreased 56 percent.[14]

Elsewhere in California juveniles serving sentences in state institutions may participate in a program that takes them to school and community groups to warn young people about the price of crime. These inmates, called Young Adults Against Crime, talk at a street level that their young audiences can understand. According to one report, they tell

BOX 11–2

Current Programming Strategies

"Federal anti-delinquency policy has been based on ideas whose vogue has run far ahead of solid knowledge . . . , we urge the government to limit its role and to restructure its priorities and programs so that states and localities may be helped to set their own priorities and discover their own solutions."

Source: National Advisory Committee for Juvenile Justice and Delinquency Prevention. 1984. *Serious juvenile crime: A redirected federal effort*. Washington, DC: Office of Juvenile Justice and Delinquency Prevention, p. 8.

---

the real story on gangs and drugs and how they realized too late that they were going nowhere. Explained one program participant, a convicted bank robber, "I wanted them [children] to hear it from someone who's been there, not someone who read it out of a book."[15]

Prevention programs typically use a concept called *outreach*. Trained staff members try to locate juveniles in need by frequenting the most popular hangouts, such as recreation areas and streetcorners. One community-based, self-help program in Boston used outreach staff to find juveniles at risk and encourage them to seek services from their program, Bridge, Inc. The organization sponsored a mobile health van, a dental clinic, and a group home for older youth.[16]

In Williamson County, Texas, birthday cards are distributed to twelfth-grade students. The cards remind them that under state law they are now adults and would be tried in adult criminal courts. The cards explain to the high school seniors that Texas law considers them to be an adult at 17 years of age.[17]

Curfew is another form of prevention program. Authorities imposing curfews believe that it will reduce the number of crimes committed by juveniles. Theoretically, it reduces the time available for juveniles to perpetrate crimes. Curfews may also reduce the number of juvenile victims of crime because teens often prey upon each other in fights and in gang or drug related activities.

Fourteen major American cities currently have instituted curfews for teens, including Detroit, Atlanta, Dallas, and Los Angeles.[18] According to most of the guidelines, youths under 17 years of age must be off the streets by 11:00 P.M. on weekdays and by midnight on the weekends. Violations may result in the youths' being detained by police. In some areas, parents may be arrested and charged with a misdemeanor if their children are caught breaking the curfew. Businesses may also be charged if they service or encourage the patronage of teens after hours. The fines imposed on businesses and parents may run as high as $500.

EDUCATION PROGRAMS

Education programs in community corrections are usually alternatives to traditional school curriculums in which juveniles have been unsuccessful. Some programs are designed to eventually reintegrate the youngsters back into area high schools. Others carry the juveniles through graduation or the award of a GED certificate. Still other education programs may supplement regular school attendance with remedial work, tutoring, and academic counseling.

The Allegheny Academy in Pennsylvania serves students referred to the probation department by a judge. Students who attend their neighborhood schools come to the academy after 3:00 P.M. and remain until 9:00 or 10:00 P.M. Youngsters who have been expelled or suspended, or who have dropped out of school attend from noon until 9:00 P.M. Although they live at home, all participants must observe an 11:00 P.M. curfew that is reinforced by telephone calls made by staff members.

At the academy, the youngsters learn such trades as woodworking, carpentry, painting, masonry, electrical and structural repair, food service, vehicle maintenance, graphic arts, and the use of computers. In addition, they receive personal and career counseling.

Verdemont Boy's Ranch in San Bernardino, California, offered a rural out-of-home placement with a strong educational component in the program. The on-grounds school was fully accredited by the County Superintendent of Schools. It was staffed by four teachers and four teacher aides, giving a teacher-to-student ratio of eight to one and allowing for substantial student-teacher interaction. The full-time school program emphasized individual study and progress. A pretest and posttest of the California Test of Basic Skills was given to each boy completing the program.[19] It was not uncommon for individual boys to advance four or five grade levels during the six-month stay in the program. A study of the program conducted by the California State Polytechnic University in 1985 revealed that the average increase in reading scores was of 2.96 grade levels. Improvement in math was a more modest 1.33 levels. It was noted that these boys who averaged an entry age of 15.25 years entered the program with a sixth-grade reading level and a fifth-grade math level.[20]

Part of the goal of the Verdemont program was to assist the boys' successful return to the schools they would attend in the community. To facilitate this goal, the county superintendent's office arranged through a school liaison officer an interview with each boy and his receiving school's counselor. His parents and probation officer were also kept involved. The school liaison officer took school records, grades, credits, and teachers' evaluations and assessments to the receiving school. The weaknesses, strengths, and progress made during a boy's stay at Verdemont were reviewed with the receiving school's counselor. The liaison officer also enrolled the boy in the classes he would attend following graduation from the ranch.

The Verdemont program closed in 1990, but two other programs have carried on with the educational program developed at Verdemont: the Kuiper Youth Center, a program for females, and the Regional Youth Education Facility (RYEF), a program for 16- to 18-year-old males. Evaluation of the RYEF conducted by the California Youth Authority in 1989 revealed improvement in reading and math levels from an average entry reading level of 7.8 to 9.7 and an entry math level of 8.4 to 10.2.[21]

Both programs used computer-assisted education as a core component of the educational process. In 1990 at the Jurupa Community School in Riverside, California, a sophisticated computer-assisted education component was introduced. Unlike traditional computer-assisted education in which packaged programs are used, the Jurupa school is connected directly to a computer network that was developed at the University of Illinois and that is updated daily.[22] This program marks a significant advancement in educational software for use with delinquent populations.

Marked improvement in reading and math scores was documented in all these programs, but it should be kept in mind that many of these youth had not been in regular attendance at any school for months or years before their placement in these programs. The mere exposure to an educational environment on a regular basis could have accounted for much of the improvement. Furthermore, none of the studies cited revealed any relationship between improved reading and math scores and reduced delinquent behavior following graduation from the programs.

WILDERNESS OR CHALLENGE PROGRAMS

According to Albert Roberts, wilderness programs developed from two sources. One was the California forestry camps begun in the 1930s to provide work and housing for delinquent boys.[23] The crews performed conservation work, park development, and road construction. Counseling, education, and religious activities were also included in the schedules. The second source was Kurt Hahn, a German educator and pioneer in experimental education, who founded the Salem School in Germany in the 1920s. The school was based on learning by doing. Hahn believed that modern youth suffered from the "misery of unimportance." He saw the western world as information rich and experience poor. Adolescents, in Hahn's view, were not initiated into adulthood through increasing levels of responsibility. Rather, they were given no significant duties and received a level of recognition only barely greater than that of young children.

BOX 11–3

Position Descriptions for Wilderness Camps

WILDERNESS PROGRAM ASSISTANT DIRECTOR

Now accepting applications for Assistant Director of the Girl's Wilderness Program. The Position supervises a staff of fifteen counselors and three counselor supervisors at a residential therapeutic wilderness program for 50 emotionally disturbed/delinquent adolescent females. Additionally, the Assistant Director plans and conducts staff training, leads family conferences, interviews prospective employees and helps to coordinate a multifaceted treatment team. Qualifications: Bachelors degree and at least three years of supervisory experience; currently holds or can obtain a license from the State Department of Human Services as a Child-Care Administrator; solid leadership skills. Salary: $20,985 -31,000; car allowance; paid vacation and sick days; paid insurance; etc. This is not a live-in position.

WILDERNESS COUNSELORS

Openings for counseling positions at both our girls' and boys' wilderness programs. The position uses reality therapy in individual and group counseling sessions along with canoeing, backpacking and other outdoor activities to improve communication skills and behavior. Qualifications: Bachelor's Degree, at least 21 years of age, have a good driving record and be able to participate fully in all program areas. Salary: Live-in while on duty; $1,100 monthly; paid insurance, clothing allowance, paid vacation and sick days; extended paid holidays in June, November and December.

Programs developed from Hahn's premises attempted to elicit pro-social values through a series of challenging experiences.[24] On the basis of this philosophy, an Outward Bound model was first used by the Welsh to train their merchant seamen to survive in lifeboats on the open sea. Their curriculum focused on group pride, teamwork, trust, and self-discipline.

The wilderness concept was brought to the United States in the 1960s as programs for youth. It was applied to various adolescent groups and, naturally, found its way to programs for adjudicated youth.

Today, wilderness therapy programs are structured around a series of tasks that to the youth may appear insurmountable and dangerous, but the challenges are designed to be safe and amenable to solution. Solutions, however, require the students to use their own physical, emotional, and cognitive resources as well as group interaction. Wilderness therapy is not an individual process but the result of the supportive par-

Wilderness programs are designed to build self esteem through success in meeting special adventure challenges. (*Courtesy Adventure/Discovery, Inc., AZ*)

ticipation of a group of 6 to 14 youths. According to Mixdorf and Paugh, the tasks of the adventure project should be incremental.[25] The skills that are needed should be developed in graduated levels of difficulty. The end product of these challenges and group processes is a feeling of personal empowerment and a sense that others can be trusted.[26]

It is not surprising that the wilderness or challenge model has been adopted by American businesses. It is used today to expose executives and managers to the benefits of building teams. Many companies now send employee teams on highly structured retreats to learn survival and group decision-making skills that may increase productivity in the office.

Wilderness or challenge programs for juveniles are usually designed in two phases. The first phase is to complete successfully a series of strenuous physical and mental challenges that the youths are unlikely ever to have experienced before. It is hoped that achievement in these tasks, in both group and individual exercises, will build self-esteem and confidence that can be applied to tasks in the second phase, in which the goal is to have the young persons master tasks and challenges within their own neighborhoods by using the same decision-making and problem-solving skills they learned in the programs.

The programs are carefully structured to provide the juveniles with opportunities to experiment with their own creative solutions. They are encouraged to explore new behavioral responses and to capitalize on their personal strengths. Confidence building is important because many theorists have assumed that juveniles have low levels of self-esteem and self-confidence. According to these theorists, gang activity often results from adolescent insecurity.[27] It is believed that sometimes it takes a completely different and unknown environment, away from peers for youths to try to change. It may also be that the survivalist nature of the wilderness experience forces them to change. Under normal daily circumstances, there would be no impetus for change.

Other central themes of wilderness programs are stimulation and excitement. Criminal psychologists like Herbert Quay perceive the delinquent as needing high levels of stimulation or frequent changes in patterns of stimulation. Quay postulated that delinquents pursue excitement as a means of compensating for their low state of cortical arousal.[28] Thus, high levels of stimulation seem necessary to lessen the chronic boredom they experience. Criminologists Sykes and Matza theorized that delinquents "are deeply immersed in a restless search for excitement, thrills, or kicks."[29]

In Baltimore, the Associated Marine Institutes, Incorporated operates such a program for juveniles who are on the verge of being incarcerated. The program combines marine skills, such as sailing and chart and map reading, with such related courses as Red Cross Lifesaving, CPR, and boat restoration. Although most of the participants have never been on a boat before, they are given increasing responsibilities as the classes progress. The youngsters all live at home and attend the program on weekdays from 8:00 A.M. to 4:00 P.M. Regular academic subjects are included with a staff-youth ratio of one to six. According to program officials, "Students must progress through several stages based on the program's point system, complete 54 courses, have two weeks of perfect attendance before graduation, move up at least two GED levels and land a full-time job. Youths who fail to progress or interfere with other youths' progress risk being sent to secure facilities."[30] The Marine Institute studied 225 young people who had completed the program to 1991. They claimed that their recidivism rate of 20 to 30 percent is far lower than that of secure facilities. The institute operates more than a dozen similar programs in Florida, South Carolina, Delaware, Louisiana, and Texas.[31]

Several challenge programs are operated by the nonprofit corporation Eckerd Family Youth Alternatives in Maryland and Florida. During the first phase, hikes, canoe trips, and a ropes course are used to build self-esteem and skills for meeting challenges. During this residential phase, the youngsters also participate in community service projects, including painting shelters for the homeless, collecting food for needy families, and washing police cars. In the second phase, the youths are returned to their homes but contract to carry out various additional challenges that involve helping their families and communities.[32]

The Success of Wilderness Programs

As with other programs, studies on the outcome of wilderness activities suffer from many weaknesses. One problem is that there are limited measures of program success. For example, only subsequent arrests or incarcerations are used to determine whether participation was positive or worthwhile. Second, the sample sizes of youths that participate are usually small, making it hard to generalize about the effects of the program. A third potential problem is that results may be measured soon after the program has ended, which does not allow evaluators time to determine if the results, usually positive, will hold up over time. A fourth problem is that many youths drop out of these programs. Researchers do not always account for the loss or interpret its effect on the results of the program. Finally, a fifth problem is that when the program graduates are compared to youngsters who did not go through the program, it is not always certain that the two groups being compared were equivalent or comparable to start with. The wilderness groups may have been more seriously involved in crime or less involved, or they may have been older, or from different backgrounds. If so, then their later behavior could result from original differences and not from the wilderness program at all.[33]

Some research studies on wilderness programs show that not all programs result in similar rates of recidivism. Programs that have higher levels of danger and excitement may be more successful than those that focus more on skill mastery and interpersonal relationships. In addition, juveniles who made their first court appearances at an older age and those who came from two-parent families seemed to be more successful in the wilderness programs. It was also determined in one study that chronic runaways were more likely to recidivate following these programs than those who had been processed for other offenses.[34]

A well-controlled evaluation was conducted of the Spectrum Wilderness Program operated out of the Southern Illinois University at Carbondale. Castellano and Soderstrom found that the positive effects of the program, dramatic at first, seemed to wear off over time.[35] The youths in this study appeared to be seriously delinquent. Furthermore, they were entering the wilderness program at what could be called the peak of their delinquent activity. Those who successfully completed the program experienced immediate reductions in arrest that lasted about one year. Positive results could also be interpreted by the fact that program graduates who were arrested were involved in less serious offenses than before their experience in the program. The authors report:

> At a two-year follow-up, positive program impacts decayed to the point where they were no longer apparent. . . . Notwithstanding positive program effects, seventy-five percent of the youth who successfully completed the program were rearrested. All of these were rearrested within 270-at-risk days. Further, a quarter of these youth were eventually incarcerated in a state juvenile correctional institution.[36]

AFTERCARE

While minors are in a residential program, they are subjected to an artificial environment that may in itself account for any of the recorded changes in behavior. Once juveniles are released and returned home, the effects of the program must now compete with the influences that surround the youngster in everyday life. Many of these influences— delinquent siblings or peers, poverty, and school pressures—can conflict with the new positive changes that have taken place occurred during treatment. Without the constant intervention of the residential staff after the return home, dramatic deterioration of program effects can occur.

Many residential programs recognize the need for continuing the intervention by providing follow-up care well beyond the release of the minor from the most intensive portion of a program: the residential phase. The regular community supervision that traditionally follows residential programs often include only infrequent contact between the officers and clients. Low levels of supervision may not provide the continuity needed between release to the community and the completion of the program. To bridge the transition from residential treatment to freedom within the community, many programs have established what is known as *aftercare*, a program of follow-up supervision that tends to be more intense than routine probation. It is often conducted by the same residential program staff who have worked with the youths throughout the residential phase of the treatment. For example, when juveniles complete the residential phase of the Eckert Youth Challenge Program, they are considered to be in aftercare status. During that time, the counselor tries to help the clients find jobs. The counselor also ensures that youths are successfully completing the challenges they planned with their families and in the community. After the first month or so, counselors see the clients less frequently until they are simply on call if needed by the clients.[37]

Some residential programs develop and operate their own aftercare services. Other facilities refer participants to various public and private aftercare programs. In still other cases, the courts decide what the proper aftercare should be. For example, VisionQuest is sometimes used as an aftercare program with follow-up services provided by VisionQuest staff. See the earlier discussion of VisionQuest on pages 307 to 309. VisionQuest receives clients from many government jurisdictions. Other programs of shorter duration may also be used for aftercare. Aftercare services are specifically designed to add to the usual probation supervision offered to minors on their release from residential treatment.

Another example of an aftercare program is the day treatment used in Kentucky. The state has 13 community-based day-treatment programs under the control of the department of social services. Six of the pro-

grams are operated directly by the department, and seven are contracted out to local agencies such as mental health associations and private nonprofit organizations. The size of each program ranges from 15
to 90 juveniles and the state maintains an average of over 500 juveniles
in treatment at any given time. The youths attend day treatment during
school hours and go home at night. The staff includes social workers
and teachers who provide counseling, instruction, vocational education,
and job placement.[38] The day-treatment program offers a bridge between being at home under parental control and the round-the-clock
supervision of the institutional setting. Kentucky claims to operate its
day-treatment program at about one-third the cost of the next restrictive
level of group homes.

In most jurisdictions the essential elements of an aftercare program
are (1) developing an aftercare plan for supervision and treatment that
matches the juvenile's needs, (2) providing supervision and proper
treatment referrals, (3) reintegrating the youth into community activities, and (4) the withdrawal of supervision after appropriate follow-up
evaluations have been completed. One of the most important decisions
made in the aftercare planning is the proper level of supervision for
each case.

In making decisions about the level of supervision needed in aftercare, officials in Arizona use a decision tree which allows program planners to ask a series of questions that move them toward a decision
based on the answers. The questions assess the characteristics of each
case before assigning a juvenile to a type of aftercare. As shown in
Figure 11.1, violent offenses, the chance of recidivism, family problems,
and a youth's cooperativeness all play a role in deciding how much supervision will be needed. The degree of restrictiveness is determined by
whether the answers to the successive questions are yes or no. In
Arizona, the five possible levels include very high, high, middle, low,
and very low degrees of supervision.[39]

The Key Program

The Key Program may serve as either a community supervision service
or an aftercare provider. The primary focus of the program is the continuous supervision of clients by caseworkers called *trackers* who see
each of about eight clients assigned to them several times a day from
early morning to bed checks at night. The trackers have a variety of duties from monitoring behavior and counseling to working with communications between family members and helping their clients with school
and employment.[40] One interesting aspect of this program is that the
trackers are rotated out of their positions after 14 months into other
functions of the state agency. Rotation may be critical for preventing
burnout or other reactions to the stress of dealing with a difficult youthful population.

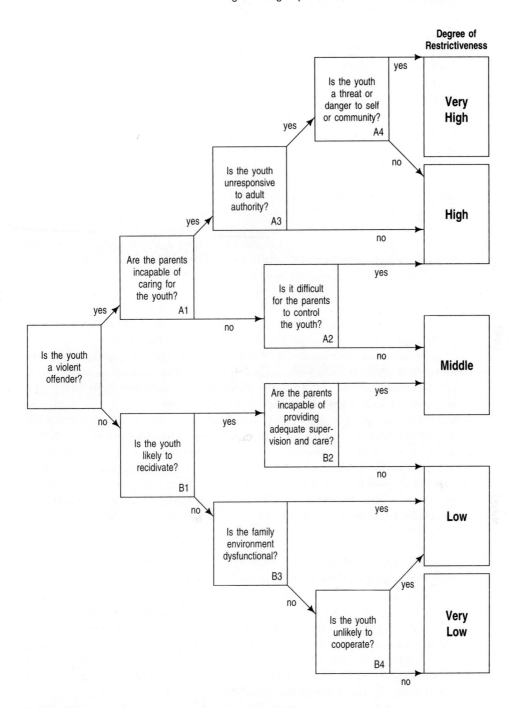

Figure 11.1

Decision Tree for Classifying Juveniles in Aftercare: The Arizona Model.

(*Source*: José B. Ashford and Craig W. LeCroy [1988]. Decision-making for juvenile offenders in aftercare. *Juvenile and Family Court Journal* 39[1]: 47–53.)

FOSTER CARE

Four-year-old Alicia was placed in the foster care of Police Officer Craig Armstrong. He was a model officer, a six-year veteran whose picture appeared on police recruitment brochures. Yet two months later, in a fit of anger, he punched Alicia in the stomach, a blow that was fatal. Panicked, he dismembered the girl's body and hid the pieces in several remote areas of the county. Armstrong then fabricated a story of the girl's being kidnapped from a crowded mall. Days later he left behind a taped confession and hanged himself.[41] Thousands of children are loved and sheltered in foster care every year, but it is the tragedy of cases like Alicia's that appear in the news.

As explained in the preceding chapters, foster care has long been a social service response to delinquency. Under a foster care system, the state or a locally designated agency, even a county, may license homes to provide care for children who have been declared wards of the court. In most cases, these children have been given up by or taken away from their parents, or their homes have been designated as unfit. Some juveniles who are having adjustment problems in the home are placed in temporary foster care while the family receives counseling.

Unfortunately, the number of youths today that are serviced by the foster care system is significantly larger than the resources available to run the program as theoretically designed. Ideally, the foster care system would provide only crisis interventions for children in high-risk families. The youths and their families would be monitored over the intervention period, with the counselors working to reunite the family when the situation stabilizes. The goals include helping the family in developing new skills and resources for addressing their problems and preventing future difficulties. However, the seriousness of emotional problems within serviced families has often made reunification difficult, which in turn has affected the ability of foster care programs to respond as designed.

Experts in the area of foster care report that the loss of funding has seriously restricted the services foster care can provide. The result is that social workers have larger caseloads and make less frequent visits to the foster homes. In some systems, there may simply be too many foster parents for social workers to screen and monitor adequately.

In Los Angeles County, a *visitation compliance plan* was drawn up to force social workers to visit foster children at least once a month as state regulations require. The plan was the result of several lawsuits that threatened to terminate the county's authority to license and monitor foster care. As reported in the Los Angeles Times:

> A foster child was awarded $7 million in Superior Court after evidence showed she had been repeatedly raped as a toddler in a foster home. . . .
> Evidence indicated the child was left in the home after other children were

removed because they were sexually molested and that social workers rarely visited her and ignored a psychologist's report in 1983 that she lived in a "chronic state of terror." Another foster child was awarded $5.5 million last January. . . . The boy was placed in a foster home where he was severely abused, sexually and physically. In 1986, the youngster was reduced to a quadriplegic when he was nearly drowned at the foster home. Social workers allegedly rarely visited the home.[42]

These cases illustrate the problem of quality control in selecting foster parents. Some people may agree to provide foster care only to earn the additional income. Those who are motivated by money rather than concern for raising the children often do not exercise the necessary care and control of their charges. In many areas, diversion has provided outlets for many nonserious delinquents with family difficulties. As a result, the type of youth needing out-of-home placement has a more serious delinquent profile. These children placed by the courts are quite sophisticated and problematic in placements like foster care. Thus, foster care may no longer be a proper alternative for many delinquents.

Another more recent criticism of the foster care system includes the finding that a disproportionate number of the homeless in this country are young people who have come from foster homes. In some instances, foster care arrangements were unsuccessful and the child ran away early. In most of the cases, however, teenagers simply outgrew the limits of the financial contract and had been turned out. After children reach the age of majority, the state's obligation to provide for them through foster care is simply over. The circumstances of the natural family may never have improved to a point at which authorities felt the youngster could return. Many states release youngsters from the supervision of the state at the age of 18, and the financial support foster families had received for caring for the child is terminated. At this age, many youngsters are still incapable of managing on their own. Besides lacking vocational and educational skills, they have been cut off from their natural families by years of state out-of-home placements. A study by Columbia University estimated that one-third of the 360,000 youths now in foster care are at risk of leading chaotic lives. The problems they will meet range from homelessness and criminality to serious psychological damage.[43]

One approach to reducing the negative effects of traditional foster care can be found in the Mentor Home Program, a new strategy developed by the Allen County Juvenile Probation Office in Fort Wayne, Indiana. Families are chosen to be mentors for youngsters who are encouraged to continue working through problems with their natural families. The mentor families provide a six-month support role to aid the child in developing social skills and psychological well-being. The mentor families are also active in reporting all significant activity to the courts.

This new program also includes a number of features that have not been prominent roles in traditional foster care programs. The mentor family is provided with active support services from both a mentor home coordinator and a mentor home probation officer. The mentor home coordinator acts as an advocate for the mentor parents and is a mediator in disputes between the mentor family and the youth in placement. The home coordinator is also responsible for recruiting new mentor families and processing them for state licensing as well as making placement recommendations. The mentor home probation officer helps in developing treatment plans for the juvenile and the natural family, and coordinates group meetings. The probation officer is responsible to the court for ensuring that all aspects of the orders have been carried out.[44] By having more people involved in the out-of-home placement, there is less opportunity for the child to be simply "dumped" in a foster home and left there. And by limiting the placement to six months, there is pressure on everyone to work toward resolving problems within the natural family.

COUNSELING PROGRAMS

Many juvenile programs, including those previously discussed, require counseling as an element of treatment. Probation contracts often stipulate that a certain number of hours of counseling be completed. Counseling is provided by clinicians privately contracted for or by staff who are directly employed by the agency. Some counseling sessions are individual with the counselor and the client being in one-on-one interaction. Another format is group therapy in which groups of clients with similar adjustment problems can stimulate discussion or provide insight into feelings, usually under the guidance of a professional. Other sessions include only an individual juvenile and his or her family. The youngster and the parents work together in therapy sessions with a counselor to resolve mutual problems. The level of training and the psychological orientation of the counselor can also vary (see Table 11–1). In many states licensing is required for a variety of positions that involve formal counseling programs. Others, even though they may not be licensed, provide informal counseling with juveniles on a regular basis and include group home workers, drug counselors, and social service representatives. These individuals may not have had any formal education or training in counseling.

The goal of traditional counseling is to uncover and discuss problems that youngsters are facing. Other counseling models are focused on the development of behavioral skills believed to aid delinquents in avoiding further difficulty. Such programs have targeted drug and alcohol refusal skills and a variety of social skills that include initiating conver-

Table 11–1 Training and Orientation of Mental Health Professionals.

	Education Background	Treatment Emphasis
Psychiatrist	Medical doctor with specialty in diseases of the mind.	Diagnosis of personality disorders and behavioral problems, treats with medication.
Psychologist	Ph.D. in psychology.	Clinical testing, diagnosing emotional root of problems and treatment, conducts individual therapy.
Social worker	Masters of social work. Sometimes only BA.	Family intervention, coordinates with agencies for special needs, network referrals, some group work, social service representative.
Counselor	Masters in counseling.	Individual and group counseling, assisting clients in the development of coping mechanisms, change and personal growth.

sations and interacting with authority figures. The impetus for these programs has come from research that shows that juveniles lack adequate skills in personal problem solving, consequential thinking, and self-control.[45]

ANALYZING AND EVALUATING PROGRAM COMPONENTS

Program descriptions have shown us that a number of interesting methodologies have been employed toward the achievement of a variety of goals. Most programs have in common the expressed intent of both controlling juvenile behavior and preventing future delinquent conduct.[46] By using highly controlled research studies to evaluate programs and by comparing the results of programs over time, we can perhaps determine which programs best serve which populations. As with adult programs, varying treatments may be prescribed on the basis of the characteristics and needs of the populations served. There do appear, however, to be some elements generally shared by successful programs.

Characteristics of Successful Programs

Sherman is a candidate for placement in a residential program. At 14, he has already failed three private placements. His hyperactivity, uncontrollable temper, failure at school, and habitual stealing make him totally unmanageable at home. His stepmother fears his bizarre and violent behavior. Sherman's self-destructive behaviors include sniffing gasoline, banging his head on a wall until he draws blood, and choking himself until he passes out. His father is reluctant to agree to placement because in one privately operated program Sherman was physically abused, tied to a horse, and dragged behind it as punishment. This facility was subsequently shut down after being declared a "child work farm." Although Sherman has not committed any serious crimes, he will be difficult to treat in the community. He is foul-mouthed, unbathed, learning disabled, and a fan of satanic music. His family's history is replete with abandonment, suicide, and mental health problems. There hardly seem to be enough resources in the community to treat Sherman and his family. It is also hard to prioritize the services he needs and to find the programs that could address them. When there are many clients like Sherman, a community corrections system is overwhelmed and desperate for programs that might provide successful intervention.

Over the years, hundreds of programs and strategies have been tried and abandoned. Some have enjoyed popularity and success, others have been discarded as mainly good intentions, and the embarrassments have been swept under the carpet. Still, generalizations about successful programs can be drawn from what we have learned. Programs that seem to work have certain characteristics in common, as described in the following paragraphs.

1. Programs address actual needs. By actual needs, we mean the needs that youths or their families identify for themselves, rather than having needs pointed out by authorities and clinical professionals. It is believed that if juveniles recognize their needs and are prepared to address them, then treatment will be more successful and the results of longer term. Many programs fail to even ask juveniles what they think their problems are. This results in a waste of considerable time and energy working in areas that the youngsters do not have the readiness or interest to pursue.

Sometimes the problems that youth identify are much more simple than we perceive them to be. In some cases, weight loss, orthodontic work, or contact with an absent parent may readjust the child's self-image and motivations. For others, a legal change of name may resolve a stigma or some strained family relationship. Even if the problems are more deeply rooted than the youngster thinks or admits, the professional should start at the child's perception of the problem to help in later working through any complexities that may surface.

2. Programs maintain close ties with the community. After a period in any residential facility, most juveniles will eventually be returned to their homes and their neighborhoods. Programs that recognize this and aid in the reintegration of juveniles into their surroundings will be more popular and successful. Although it has been easier and cheaper to build residential facilities in rural areas, the movement of juveniles far from their urban surroundings is emotionally difficult for them. Programs that allow juveniles to remain in their current schools and to keep close relationships with families and friends usually have better results with long-term adjustment.

3. Staff are flexible and positive role models. In successful programs staff members are mature, well adjusted, and motivated. They have self-confidence and clear long- and short-term goals that clients can see them accomplishing. Youngsters in any program will test and closely watch staff members. Workers who react patiently, fairly, and with regard for the dignity of their often-difficult charges will be respected and obeyed. Many of the juveniles come from backgrounds where they have not had the opportunity to observe or relate to positive role models. Most of them have not had adults to confide in or whom they trusted for advice and guidance.

4. Programs strictly enforce their rules. Discipline is an essential ingredient of any program involving juveniles. Many youngsters have come from environments in which rules are not used constructively, consistently, or in the interests of the child. Through the period of testing that juveniles will conduct with any program, the rules must be fairly and firmly enforced. The rules must be clearly explained in the beginning, and sanctions for their violation must be understood. Along with rules, there must be punishments that are proportionate and reasonable. Punishments should not be demoralizing or degrading.

5. Programs offer significant rewards in their structure. Rewards are as important as rules in any good program. Some successful reward systems are performance contracting and point redemption. In performance contracting, the youths make written agreements to follow certain guidelines and avoid specific behaviors. In return, the juveniles are promised some type of meaningful activity or privilege. In a point redemption system, participants are awarded points for completing certain goals or for avoiding certain prohibited behaviors for a period of time. The points earned can be redeemed for privileges or purchases. Proponents of reward systems argue that these control mechanisms help delinquents mature to the acceptance of delayed gratification and to the appreciation of long-term goals. In working with youths who are developmentally delayed and who have mental health difficulties, reward systems may also be very important.

Programs that emphasize job skills and job readiness have direct appeal to participants like this young woman. (© *Nita Winter/ The Image Works*)

6. Programs emphasize job training and readiness. The reality that youngsters under supervision must eventually enter and compete in the job market cannot be overlooked by any program no matter what its initial goals may be. A lack of the educational and vocational skills to acquire and maintain satisfying jobs must be addressed as part of any long-term treatment plan. Most juveniles come to the criminal justice system with records of poor school performance, little or no legitimate work history, few marketable talents, and none of the social and personal skills necessary to impress employers. Many young people in community programming realize the importance of help in this area, which makes it one of the more acceptable avenues of treatment strategy. That is, juveniles may be more willing to work on program aspects that are related to work rather than on other self-improvement areas such as substance abuse treatment, psychological counseling, or traditional schooling. This focus provides immediate action and is result-oriented, which often appeals to young people. When the program focus is preparing for jobs, there is less emphasis on what is wrong with the juveniles or the mistakes they have made. Job focus is also important because the ability to get and keep jobs is correlated with successful performance on community supervision.

7. Programs offer youth participation in decision making. Including program participants in decision making in the program helps them to develop commitment to its goals. The more juveniles see their own activities and ideas used in the framework of a program, the more they will be able to identify with its content. This strategy allows youths to participate in democratic decision making and to develop responsibility for their decisions. It also builds confidence in their ability to make decisions and provides a structured setting for practicing that decision making. Programs should also provide a forum, group, or individual sessions for studying and discussing the effects of the decisions that the juveniles have made.

SUMMARY

By examining programs historically, it becomes clear how goals influence program design and implementation. Beliefs about the causes and cures for delinquency are often translated into treatment structures and activities. Such programs as the Provo and Silverlake experiments as well as Scared Straight had popular appeal as well as powerful supporters. Thus they were duplicated and revised all across the country even before comprehensive evaluations had been completed.

Since the early 1980s, wilderness programs have been recognized as effective intervention mechanisms for some of the more serious delinquents entering the juvenile justice system.[47] A 1991 informal poll of members of the American Correctional Association found that two-thirds believed experiential learning programs like Outward Bound were effective alternatives to juvenile incarceration.[48] However, wilderness programs, as are many other therapeutic treatments, are based on the expectation that behavioral or cognitive changes that occur in the treatment environment will be sustained and automatically transferred to the youth's normal living situation. This expectation assumes that the youths recognize the connection between their therapeutic experiences and issues in their daily lives. In reality, though, most youngsters require some structured assistance to enable them to transfer the skills they learned in a program to their everyday surroundings.[49]

The importance of aftercare is to aid youngsters in making the transition between treatment and home life. Aftercare is more than simple supervision. It implies a follow-up service that helps the juveniles in processing new information and in being able to successfully apply it in their lives.

Foster care is most often the last resort when family difficulties call for the out-of-home placement of a juvenile. Counseling is an important part of most treatment plans. However, the quality and professional level of the counseling service may vary from one program to another.

Ironically, prevention programs may offer the most hope for the delinquency problem although it is given the least amount of attention. Officials often de-emphasize prevention strategies because of the difficulty in proving that such programs have had any positive effect.

More than anything else, corrections programs must focus on the successful integration or reintegration of juveniles into community life. According to one expert, successful community reintegration is a management function that relies on innovation and information. This same expert also explains that effective programs have the autonomy to make goal-related decisions, not political ones.[50]

Another important aspect of successful programs is are that each component or phase is integrated into the next or subsequent phase this ensures that the programs have continuity and consistency. The components are linked in theory and action by complimentary, not competing, elements.[51]

KEY TERMS

aftercare

guided group interaction

outreach

performance contracting

point redemption

Provo experiment

Scared Straight

Silverlake experiment

VisionQuest

DISCUSSION QUESTIONS

1. How would you design a research study to determine why kids who go through a Scared Straight kind of programs continue to commit crimes? Why does the program not appear to work?
2. What do you think Dr. Jerome Miller meant when he said that programs like Scared Straight tell us more about ourselves and our society than anything else.
3. What is a reasonable cost per day for a residential community corrections program for juveniles? What about the cost of a program when the youth lives at home? What services would you expect to be provided by each?
4. What counseling techniques would you use to help a youngster build such personal and behavioral skills as (a) ability to refuse drugs and alcohol, (b) ability to interact with authority figures, and (c) ability to consider consequences of actions before taking them.
5. What was the philosophy behind the development of wilderness programs and how valid are those assumptions today?

END NOTES

1. Empey, Lamar, and Maynard Erickson (1972). *The Provo Experiment*. Lexington, MA: Lexington Books, p. 66.

2. Whitehead, John, and Steven Lab (1990). *Juvenile justice: An introduction*. Cincinnati, OH: Anderson Publishing, p. 342.

3. Empey, Lamar (1977). The Provo and Silverlake Experiments, in *Corrections in the Community*, ed. Eugene Miller and Robert Montilla. Reston, VA: Reston.

4. Empey, Lamar, and Steven Lubeck (1971). *The Silverlake Experiment*. Chicago: Aldine.

5. Empey, Lamar (1978). *American delinquency: Its meaning and construction*. Homewood, IL: Dorsey Press.

6. Roberts, Albert (1989). *Juvenile justice*. Chicago: Dorsey Press, p. 198.

7. Roberts, Albert (1988). Wilderness programs for juvenile offenders: A challenging alternative. *Juvenile and Family Court Journal* 39(1):1–12.

8. Greenwood, Peter, and Susan Turner (1987). *VisionQuest's program for San Diego delinquents: An evaluation of recidivism rates and controversial issues*. R-3445-OJJDP. Santa Monica, CA: The RAND Corporation.

9. Ibid.

10. Finckenauer, James O. (1982). *Scared Straight! and the panacea phenomenon*. Englewood Cliffs, NJ: Prentice Hall.

11. Homant, Robert (1981). The demise of JOLT: The politics of being "Scared Straight" in Michigan. *Criminal Justice Review* 6(1):14–18.

12. Weis, Joseph (1982). *Delinquency prevention: An overview for policy development*. Washington, DC: Office of Juvenile Justice and Delinquency Prevention, p. 8.

13. Colvin, Mark (1991). Crime and social reproduction: A response to the call for "outrageous" proposals. *Crime and Delinquency* 37(4):436–448.

14. Nikos, Karen (1991). Prevention best answer, some insist. *Los Angeles Daily News*, 28 May: B2.

15. Zimmerman, Janet (1990). Chino inmates work to scare kids from crime. *San Bernardino Sun*, 2 December: A1.

16. Baker, Jon (1988). Forum on juvenile corrections tackles tough issues. *Corrections Today* 50(4):132.

17. Briscoe, Judy Culpepper (1990). In Texas: Reaching out to help troubled youths. *Corrections Today* 52(6):90–92.

18. Rosado, Lourdes, and Howard Manly (1991). Keeping teens off the street. *Newsweek*, 15 July: 21.

19. San Bernardino County Probation (1987). *Annual report*. San Bernardino, CA.

20. California State Polytechnic University (1985). *San Bernardino County Verdemont Boys Ranch Study*. Pomona, CA: Institute for Environmental Design, Department of Architecture, California State Polytechnic University.

21. Skonovd, Norman, and Wesley Krause (1991). The regional youth education facility: A promising short-term institutional and aftercare program for juvenile court wards, in *Intensive Interventions with High Risk Youth*, ed. Troy Armstrong. Monsey, NY: Criminal Justice Press.

22. Connors, Carolyn (1991). What's happening in Riverside County. *TRIAD: Southern-Tri-Counties CPPCA* 4(3), August 1991.

23. Roberts, Albert (1988). Supra note 7.

24. Bacon, Stephen, and Richard Kimball (1989). The wilderness challenge model, in Robert Lyman, Steven Prentice-Dunn, and Stewart Gabel, eds. *Residential and Inpatient Treatment of Children and Adolescents.* New York: Plenum.

25. Mixdorf, Lloyd, and Pennell Paugh (1989). Experiential education and corrections: Teaching through action. *Corrections Today* 51(5):38–42.

26. Bacon, Stephen, and Richard Kimball (1989). Supra note 24.

27. Bloch, Herbert, and Arthur Niederhoffer (1958). *The gang: A study in adolescent behavior.* New York: Philosophical Library.

28. Quay, Herbert (1965). Psychopathic personality as pathological stimulation seeking. *American Journal of Psychiatry* 22:180–184.

29. Sykes, Gresham, and David Matza (1957). Techniques of neutralization: A theory of delinquency. *American Sociological Review* 22:664–670.

30. Mardon, Steven (1991). On board, not behind bars. *Corrections Today* 53(1):33.

31. Ibid., p. 36.

32. Stepanik, Ron (1991). The Eckerd youth program: Challenging juveniles to change. *Corrections Today* 53(1):48.

33. Castellano, Thomas, and Irina Soderstrom (1990). Wilderness challenges and recidivism: A program evaluation. Paper presented at the annual meeting of the American Society of Criminology, Baltimore.

34. Roberts, Albert (1988). Supra note 7, p. 9.

35. Castellano, Thomas, and Irina Soderstrom (1990). Supra note 33, pp. 22–23.

36. Ibid.

37. Stepanik, Ron (1991). Supra note 32, p. 50.

38. Bowling, Linda (1987). Day treatment for juveniles: A boon in bluegrass country. *Corrections Today* 49(3):104–106.

39. Ashford, Jose, and Craig LeCroy (1988). Decision-making for juvenile offenders in aftercare. *Juvenile and Family Court Journal* 39(1):47–53.

40. Greenwood, Peter (1990). Reflections on three promising programs. *APPA Perspectives* Winter:20–24.

41. Hayward, Ed (1991). "Model officer" dismembered foster girl after beating. *San Bernardino Sun*, 22 August: A1.

42. Hurst, John (1990). County accused of letting foster children suffer abuse. *Los Angeles Times*, 8 March: A3.

43. Barden, J.C. (1991). U.S. homeless include products of foster care. *San Bernardino Sun*, 6 January: A2.

44. Heard, Chinita (1990). The preliminary development of the probation mentor home program: A community-based model. *Federal Probation* 54(4):51–56.

45. Hawkins, David, Jeffrey Jenson, and Richard Catalano (1990). Effects of a skills training intervention with juvenile delinquents. Paper presented at the annual meeting of the American Society of Criminology, Baltimore.

46. Roberts, Albert (1988). Supra note 7, p. 1.

47. Greenwood, Peter, and Susan Turner (1987). Supra note 8.

48. American Correctional Association (1991). *Corrections Today's* opinion hotline. *Corrections Today* 53(2):18.

49. Bacon, Stephen, and Richard Kimball (1989). Supra note 24.

50. Fagan, Jeffrey (1990). Social and legal policy dimensions of violent juvenile crime. *Criminal Justice and Behavior* 17(1):93–133.

51. Ibid.

IV

The People and the Process

12

Legal Issues in Community Corrections

Yes, I know him and I knew that he was arrested, but it was worth it; he was caught in a new "Caddy."
— Youthful prisoner quoted in The Gang.[1]

PURPOSE

This chapter examines within a legal context the conditions that may be imposed on someone who has received a community corrections sentence. The constitutional limits and restrictions on the conditions of supervision are described in detail. The text also explores the challenges that have been raised to some of the more unusual conditions. The revocation processes for both probation and parole are highlighted step by step. The discussion covers the reasons community supervision contracts may be terminated. It also highlights some of the important legal cases that have helped to shape the revocation process. The chapter concludes with an overview of current statistics on revocation.

OBJECTIVES

On completion of this chapter, you should be able to do the following:

1. Explain the requirements for a parole revocation hearing according to the court decision in *Morrissey* v. *Brewer*.

2. Describe some conditions of probation and parole that the court might find unconstitutional.

3. Discuss the differences the courts see between the liberty interests of a person facing revocation of probation and someone facing revocation of parole.

4. Elaborate on the issues that a court might consider in deciding the validity of a search of a probationer's home.

INTRODUCTION

Bud was placed on three years' probation following a conviction for manufacturing a controlled substance. Six months later, during a search of his residence, a fully operational methamphetamine laboratory was uncovered. The defendant was arrested and a small amount of the drug was found on his person.

Ron was placed on probation following a conviction of residential burglary. He was alleged to have broken into the home of a family friend where he stole two bottles of brandy. The requirements of his term of probation included attending a rehabilitation center and enrolling in an alcohol counseling program. Seven months later Ron was arrested for violating most of the terms of his probation contract. He had failed to attend the program at the rehabilitation center, and his supervising officer reported that his client had not enrolled in counseling. Neither had he made any payments toward his fine or restitution. In addition, Ron did not report to his probation officer between November 1988 and March 1989. When he was arrested, Ron admitted to his probation officer that he continued to drink despite the contract ordering him not to.

Alice had been out of prison for three months when she was picked up for shoplifting a pair of sunglasses in a department store. Although Alice denied having taken the glasses, she could provide no proof of having purchased them. The store security officer filed a report alleging that he saw her take them and put them in her purse. At a hearing to consider revoking her parole, it was alleged that she had also failed to appear at three consecutive scheduled appointments with her parole officer. Furthermore, she had violated her curfew by being out after 8:00 P.M. when she was seen in the department store.

All the clients described here had their community supervision sentences revoked. The term *revocation* is defined as a legal process by which community sentences are withdrawn and the offender is incarcerated by either a return to prison for those who had been on parole or a sentence to prison from probation.

The revocation process usually begins when a supervising officer files a motion to revoke in the court that has jurisdiction over the case. The motion outlines the reasons for requesting the revocation. The justification usually is that the offender has violated the terms of the probation contract, or community sentence. By a violation, authorities mean that the offender has failed to do something he or she was ordered to do, such as going to counseling or paying restitution. The violation may also be a result of the offender's having done something that was forbidden, such as committing a new offense or abusing drugs or alcohol.

Violations may be caused by some breach of the probation or parole contract that is not necessarily a criminal act, such as frequenting a bar or missing a treatment session or appointment with the probation offi-

Probationer arrested in a fight had a sharpened screwdriver in his possession. He is placed in jail and a motion to revoke his probation has been filed. (© *Donna Binder/Impact Visuals*)

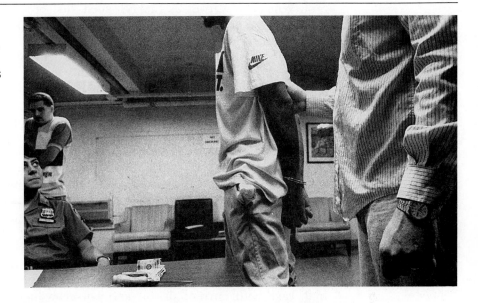

cer. When such a violation occurs, the reason for revocation is called a *technical violation* in contrast to the commission of a new crime, which in most cases is considered in and of itself grounds for revocation.

Sometimes probationers or parolees may be arrested during a visit to their supervising officer. Such arrests often occur when the officer is responsible for conducting drug and alcohol tests during visits. In many states, parole and probation officers are certified peace officers with the power to arrest. Clients may also be arrested during a home visit by their supervising officer. A third kind of arrest by the controlling agency can occur when a warrant for an offender's arrest is issued that will be handled by the local police or sheriff's office.

It is not uncommon for parolees or probationers to leave the area in which they are under supervision and commit a crime somewhere else. Once arrested in another jurisdiction, it may take weeks or even months before the supervising agency learns of the offender's whereabouts and starts revocation proceedings. A state or the federal government may issue a probation or parole violator warrant against a person who is currently serving time in a prison or jail in another state on a new conviction. When this occurs, that warrant may be placed as a detainer or hold against the inmate's eventual release. Then the jurisdiction placing the hold must be notified to come and pick up the offender before release on a current incarceration.

When notified of the pending release of a wanted fugitive in the custody of another jurisdiction the original authorities can retrieve their violators of parole and probation. The requesting party may even wait until the fugitive has completed the current new sentence before executing a warrant. When the warrant is finally issued, due process rights take effect. The defendant may then pursue such claims as the right to a speedy trial or a hearing on the unresolved revocation (*Brunk* v. *Luttrell*, 1989).

THE DECISION TO REVOKE

As with so many other steps in the criminal justice process, the decision to revoke is discretionary. The officer may rely on personal as well as professional judgments when making these decisions. There could be differences in the way two officers would assess the same situation. These differences can be based on the length of time the officers have been in the field, or their race, sex, and education, or their background experiences.

An agent considers many factors before asking the court to revoke community supervision. One concern is the likelihood that the hearing will result in a revocation, that the hearing officer or judge will consider the violation(s) serious enough to warrant incarceration. Such findings may vary with current prison and jail crowding or pressure on the courts to try alternatives before revocation.

The decision to revoke probation or parole is considered serious because of the consequences for those offenders who have invested considerable time out in the community under supervision. When probation or parole is revoked for a new conviction, the defendant's entire time served on supervision is forfeited (*Manguia* v. *U.S. Parole Commission*). Likewise, the person does not receive credit toward the discharge of a sentence for any of the time served out on bond (*Cerrella* v. *Hanberry*). In addition, a new sentence may be stacked onto the end of the original term of confinement so that each is served separately and consecutively (*U.S.* v. *Newton*).

When someone has violated a condition of supervision, the authorities may take some intermediate steps before starting revocation proceedings, including stricter supervision, more frequent contacts, a fine, or participation in a drug or alcohol treatment program. A new requirement can be imposed as an addition to the original terms of community release.

In most jurisdictions, the conditions of probation or parole can be modified only by a judge in a formal disciplinary process. Any change of the original conditions of probation or parole requires the same administrative or legal process as a revocation. In New Hampshire, however, probation and parole officers are empowered to impose house arrest on an individual as an intermediate step in lieu of arrest. This measure is applied when offenders have not performed adequately under less restrictive conditions.[2]

The purpose of modifying a community supervision contract may be supportive. For example, the court may add a counseling requirement.

It may also be punitive, such as the imposition of time in jail. Modifications of the supervision contract are intended as an intermediate response to a person's poor adjustment under the original conditions of release. The action recognizes the client's failure to abide by the rules. However, it also suggests that the subject is doing well enough to warrant alternative intervention strategies before being given long-term incarceration in a state prison.

In 1987 Minnesota began experimenting with a house arrest program for persons who had committed violations of their supervised release. The program offered two kinds of supervision for violators. In one, violators were placed in their homes under the frequent monitoring of supervising officers. In the second pilot program, violators were placed in halfway houses under 24-hour-a-day monitoring by the staff of the facility.[3]

One of the more serious intervention techniques is the use of brief periods of jail time as a penalty for violations of community service. Even though this technique uses expensive jail space, it is thought to cost less than if the sentence was revoked. It is also hoped that the brief jail period will serve as a deterrent to further violations during the period of community supervision. Use of jail time as a remedial measure for violators should not be confused with the practice of giving offenders combined jail and probation terms at sentencing.

Changes in the conditions, other than jail time, are frequently efforts on the part of the supervising officer to support positive aspects of the client's life or to control negative ones. For example, an officer may modify the conditions of release to require a defendant to seek job training or education. Conditions may be added to require a client to stay out of a certain part of the community. Perhaps the area is a location where drugs are sold or where the client's crime partners live. In most cases, even a nonpunitive addition must be justified by the officer at a hearing. The client is entitled to be present at this administrative or court hearing.

Another factor that may be influential in the decision to revoke is the workload of the supervising officer. An officer who supervises 150 clients is less likely to have the time or the inclination to file for revocation, especially if the charge is a nonserious violation or minor offense. An officer who has an intensive supervision caseload, on the other hand, will monitor the behavior of each offender very closely. Because these clients are often considered of high risk, the guidelines or policies of many intensive supervision programs require filing a request for revocation for any violation.

The work efficiency of each individual officer also contributes to a revocation decision. Two officers with different levels of organizational skills may process substantially different volumes of violation proceedings simply because of their individual abilities to do the paperwork in the time available. Even daily or weekly fluctuations in workload can affect the officers' reaction to a violation. If the work week brings many new cases to an officer or lots of activity on existing cases, then the level of action taken on a violation may be reduced. In one particular week the officer may let the client off with a warning. During a lighter week, the officer may pursue the violation with a more punitive response.

The individual characteristics of officers also affect revocation decisions. Attitudes that officers have about certain types of offenders may influence their decisions about how cases should be handled. As with many other decisions affecting clients, the supervising officer uses discretion when considering a revocation because individual beliefs and feelings may influence the officer's perception of a situation. Individuals convicted of certain types of crimes, such as child abuse or sex offenses, may be handled with less tolerance than are other individuals convicted of other crimes against persons. Officers may also hold strong beliefs about the importance of adherence to certain conditions. Violations of those conditions may then enhance the probability that an offender's probation will be revoked. For example, some officers have strong feelings about alcohol abuse and may initiate disciplinary action against clients found in possession of or under the influence of alcohol. Other officers with less interest in alcohol use may overlook such violations.

The attitude of the client and the interpersonal relationship between the officer and the client play important roles in official responses to violations. A positive client/officer relationship may result in the officer's being more tolerant of minor infractions. A client with minimal interpersonal skills may find that he or she is perceived by the officer as difficult or not trying hard enough. The perception of the officer may result in the client's being at greater risk of revocation for any violation.

Finally, administrative philosophies and procedures affect the chance that a violation will result in a revocation. Some departments have policies as to what violations require a revocation. There may also be unwritten policies within the department about the kinds of violations that warrant revocation. The time and resources needed to fulfill the legal or administrative requirements for a revocation may also influence the tendency to revoke. If the paperwork to initiate a revocation is complex and time-consuming, the response to violations may be suppressed, whereas a streamlined paperwork process or fast-track administrative or legal proceedings may encourage the filing of a greater number of petitions to revoke. (See Box 12–1.)

On occasion, when a motion to revoke is filed, offenders will legally challenge the grounds for revocation, arguing that the condition they are accused of violating was not a valid and constitutional order to begin with. Therefore, they claim, they should not be revoked for failure to comply with an unlawful requirement.

BOX 12–1

Factors Affecting the Officer's Decision to Revoke

1. Could supervision conditions be modified to prevent further violations instead?
2. Does agency policy require revocation for this violation?
3. How busy is the officer? Does this violation warrant the time and energy necessary for processing a revocation?
4. What are the officer's personal attitudes about the benefits of revocation?
5. What are the characteristics of the offender? Is he or she high risk?
6. What are the characteristics of the violation itself? How serious is it?
7. What type of relationship exists between the officer and client? How tolerant is the officer? How remorseful is the offender?

THE LEGAL REQUIREMENTS OF CONTRACT CONDITIONS

Bud G. was convicted of tampering with his utility meters. His probation sentence included $42,596 in restitution to the gas and electric company. The defendant appealed this condition, claiming that it was an abuse of discretion by the court. He also argued that the method used to calculate the restitution was too vague and inaccurate. The reviewing court did not agree with these allegations. They commented that a condition was valid if it met one of the three following criteria:

- It bore a relationship to the crime for which the defendant was convicted.
- The condition was related to conduct that is criminal.
- The condition did not require or forbid conduct that is not reasonably related to future criminality.

As to the restitution figure, the court noted that "any rational method of fixing the amount of restitution which is reasonably calculated to make the victim whole" would be accepted (*People* v. *Goulart*).

The particular conditions of an offender's probation or parole are frequently recommended by officers involved in the decision-making process. They may also be designed by the judge. The court is usually free to construct the exact terms of probation as it appears to be necessary. However, each condition must stand the test of being constitution-

BOX 12–2

Sentencing court has broad discretion in setting conditions of probation and validity of such conditions is reviewable only upon abuse of discretion.

Source: *U.S.* v. *Tzakis*, 736 F.2d 867, N.Y., 1984.

ally valid. Its imposition must not infringe on the basic rights of the person being supervised.

Case law has shown that there are four general elements in establishing the validity of a probation condition. The first is that the condition must *serve a legitimate purpose*—that is, the condition must either protect society or lead to the rehabilitation of the offender. Usually, conditions do one or the other, although they often do both.

In *U.S.* v. *Alexander* (743 F.2d 472, ILL, 1984) an appeals court ruled that it was not unreasonable for a particular probationer to be ordered not to maintain any proprietary interest in any weight or scale business. The defendant had been convicted of a scheme to defraud in connection with his ownership and operation of a scale business. This condition would ensure the protection of the community from further similar schemes.

In another case, the U.S. Court of Appeals held that banishing a convicted drug dealer from a particular county served both the purpose of

Community service sentences appear legally defensible in that they are reasonable, they are related to rehabilitation, and they pay back a debt to society. (© *Bob Daemmerich/The Image Works*)

BOX 12–3

Four Basic Requirements of a Probation/Parole Condition

1. It must serve the purpose of either:
   a. Protecting society
   b. Promoting rehabilitation
2. It must be clear.
3. It must be reasonable.
4. It must be constitutional.

Source: Del Carmen, Rolando (1985). Legal issues and liabilities in community corrections. In L. Travis, ed., *Probation, Parole and Community Corrections: A Reader*, pp. 47–72. Prospect Heights, IL: Waveland Press.

protecting the public and furthering rehabilitation. In *U.S.* v. *Cothran* the state argued that the defendant's popular status among the area's adolescents was a continuing threat to the community. The court also found that such a move would facilitate a change toward a crime-free life style. They advised him that he had been given a "unique opportunity to start anew and break free of the environment and familiar influences which encouraged him to peddle cocaine to minors in the first place."

The second requirement is that each condition of supervision must be *clear*. The language must be explicit, outlining specifically what can or cannot be done so that the average person can know exactly what is expected. A condition that a client is obligated to follow cannot be vague or ambiguous in its wording. A good example of the need for clarity is a condition that states, "Avoid persons or places of disreputable character." It may be difficult to decide just what is a "disreputable character." Is there a general consensus in society about what "disreputable" is? Does this mean the client cannot work at a used car lot or in government?

The third requirement is that a contract condition must be *reasonable*. It must not be excessive in its expectations or be an unnecessary burden. Negotiating the payment of an $800 fine serves a legitimate purpose (requirement 1), and it is clear (requirement 2). However, it may be unreasonable to expect a defendant to pay $200 a week toward that debt. It may also be unreasonable to expect a wheelchair-bound client to report to the probation office across town two or three times a week.

The legal test of reasonableness is usually the finding by a majority of "neutral" persons that the requirement is, indeed, reasonable. Reasonableness may also be relative to time and place. For example, a proba-

BOX 12–4

Courts have broad discretion under the Probation Act to impose probation as long as conditions bear a reasonable relationship to the treatment of the accused and the protection of the public.

Source: *U.S.* v. *Richards Elec. Supply Co*, 604 F. Supp. 126 Ohio, 1984.

tioner in Ivan, Texas, was ordered to "avoid persons or places of disreputable or harmful character, including associations with convicted felons or frequenting or going about places where alcoholic beverages were sold or consumed." When revoked on a violation of this condition, the defendant argued that there was nowhere in Ivan, Texas, where one could buy gas, cigarettes, a meal, or a cup of coffee where beer was not also sold or consumed. The appeals courts reversed the order of revocation. The court agreed that the defendant's having a cup of coffee in a local gathering spot frequented by families and members of the business community hardly amounted to a violation of probation (*Atchison* v. *State*).

Finally, a condition must be *constitutional*. Although convicted felons have a diminished expectation of certain privileges and opportunities, they do have basic rights that cannot be infringed upon by the state. Challenges to the constitutionality of conditions have usually argued that the terms are excessive or extreme. The petitioner believes that the requirements invade privacy or violate basic human freedoms such as religion, speech, and marriage. The court has been particularly sensitive to upholding the First Amendment rights of parolees to speak out publicly on the issues of prison conditions or on the unfairness of the income tax system. However, all such speakers are prohibited from inciting others to riot or urging others to violate the law.[4]

DRUG TESTING

Community supervisors may use a number of popular urine-screening devices to test for drugs. The average cost of a urinalysis may run from $5 to $10. Urine testing can be performed on site, although most agencies contract with outside laboratories. It is, perhaps, a legal advantage to have a neutral third party conducting the tests. It is also less expensive than setting up and staffing a separate lab facility within each jurisdiction.

Routine tests usually screen for the presence of one or more specific drugs, such as cocaine or heroin. More sophisticated tests that detect a number of different drugs may cost up to $75 each. A new technique for detecting the presence of drugs is hair analysis. As a National Institute of Justice report explains:

> Drug molecules in the circulating blood are absorbed within the structure of the growing hair and are retained permanently. As the hair grows, it records a pattern of the periods of use and non-use. Hair on the head grows at an average of about one-half inch a month. A 2–3 inch strand contains a record of about the last 4–6 months of drug usage.[5]

Initial studies indicate that hair analysis may be an even better detector of substance abuse than are urinalysis and blood tests. Hair will not reflect the presence of drugs taken within the past 48 hours, but it can trace substance use back further than other current methods. In fact, depending on the type and length of hair, drug use may be detected back as far as several months and even years. Another advantage of hair analysis is that it is an almost impossible test for drug users to circumvent.[6]

Reduced budgets and diminished financial resources have led many departments to ration the number of drug tests that they conduct each month. Such restrictions may mean that officers cannot perform random drug tests as often as they feel is necessary to control their clients adequately.

One of the most common justifications for revocation of community supervision is testing positive on a drug test. This is not surprising given the large percentage of offenders with histories of drug use and the percentage of probationers who are currently being monitored for substance abuse. A survey of Texas probation departments found that drug testing was mandatory for all probationers in 40 percent of the jurisdictions. It was required for only certain designated offenders in the rest. Whereas 50 percent of the offices did monthly testing, the others tested every two weeks, once a week, or at the officer's discretion.[7]

In a recent decision by the Hawaii Supreme Court, it was held that probationers may be subjected to random drug testing even if their present conviction is unrelated to drugs. In *State* v. *Morris* the defendant was convicted of burglary without any evidence of drug use. However, the state had imposed drug testing as a condition of probation, and the defendant had violated the condition in two consecutive positive tests. The state supreme court held that such a condition and subsequent revocation did not violate the defendant's right to privacy. In the court's view, the condition was reasonably related to the goal of rehabilitation and was not unduly restrictive.

Michigan statistics from 1987 to 1988 showed that anywhere from 12 to 19 percent of all drug tests given in community programs were positive. However, there was significant variation between jurisdictions on whether a single positive drug test was sufficient grounds for the revocation of a community sentence.

Some courts say that a positive reading on the basic Enzyme Multiplied Immune Test (EMIT) is sufficient for revocation purposes. The EMIT measures change in the way a urine specimen transmits light. The change takes place when an antibody designed to react to a specific drug is introduced. The results are based on numerical readings that determine positive or negative change at a certain standard value. A single positive reading is all that is needed for revocation in some courts, but other courts expect the test to be confirmed. The EMIT is either repeated or verified by more sophisticated tests that include *thin layer chromatography* (TLC) and *gas chromatography/mass spectroscopy* (GC/MS). The GC/MS may cost up to $100 per specimen to test.

In revocation hearings based on drug testing, the accuracy of the tests have been called into question. In general, the courts have appeared to rule most often in favor of the state. In one Florida case the court said that EMIT results were admissible even if the test was only 80 percent accurate (*Szili* v. *Carlson* TCA 84-7196, 1985). Other courts have supported the use of expert testimony to establish the accuracy of the particular test used.

A Bureau of Justice Assistance Policy Guide points out the potential for misuse in drug testing.[8] One of the major problems is using test results too quickly and too punitively—that is, acting on the test results immediately without first confronting the clients and discussing the findings with them. To be effective, the tests should be used as a tool to detect problems that need to be addressed. A narrow use of drug testing would be to revoke a community sentence upon the first sign of drugs, the first positive test. Many critics argue that drug or alcohol treatment is a long and slow process often characterized by relapse. In addition to treatment experts, many policy analysts argue that we do not have the prison space to incarcerate everyone who tests positive.

The Bureau of Justice Assistance Guide also warns that a test should detect the specific drugs the client is using. There appears to be variation in the accuracy of drug testing depending on the particular drug being tested. For example, PCP and marijuana are stored in the body, unlike cocaine and opiates. Because they are stored, a person is likely to test positive over a long time—even months after use. As of now, expert witnesses cannot specify the length of time PCP can be detected in urine.

Another suggestion for drug testing policy is that agency responses should be as uniform as possible in regard to the severity of sanctions imposed. The Bureau of Justice Assistance also cautions that departments should maintain the strictest confidentiality in handling drug test results.

Clients with a history of drug use or offenses are normally considered to be of high risk. Their community supervision may involve the use of several surveillance tools and procedures. Effective surveillance may suggest the need to use measures that seem to violate the individual's right to privacy and security in the home. Persons involved in the manufacture, sale, or use of drugs may go to great lengths to conceal illicit activity or goods. Officials have argued that searches of a person's body, home, and automobile are a necessary element of supervision. Furthermore, it is argued that for detection of illegal activity to be effective, an officer's access to the client, home, and automobile must be frequent, without warning, and without the client's permission. The encroachment on individual freedoms represented by such a policy has been the subject of much legal and moral debate.

THE CONSTITUTIONALITY OF HOME SEARCHES

Community supervision officers generally enjoy a wide range of law enforcement powers in fulfilling their roles as community protectors. Because the routine visit to an offender's home is part of normal supervision, things that the officer sees in plain view are usually subject to a warrantless seizure. Evidence that has been illegally seized may be used in parole revocation hearings. These proceedings are not subject to the same standards of due process that governs a criminal trial. Again, this is because parole is considered a privilege and a kind of custody. Therefore, the parolee has little basis for a claim of violation of the Fourth Amendment because "his or her right to privacy and personal autonomy is subject to arbitrary parole practices."[9] In many states, statutes have been written to subject persons on supervision to home searches without a warrant. Such procedures have not been without controversy, and some notable exceptions have been made.

In one of the earlier cases on this subject, *State* v. *Fields* (686 P.2d 1379, 1984), a woman was convicted of the second degree felony of promoting a dangerous drug. She received five years probation which included "submission to searches and seizures of her person, property and residence at any time." On appeal, Fields claimed that this was a violation of her Fourth Amendment right to be free of unreasonable searches and seizures. The key became the "reasonableness" of such searches for a probationer with a drug conviction. The Hawaii Supreme Court said that although such a search may serve the legislative goal of protecting the public, it did not further the other goal of probation—namely, rehabilitation of the defendant. In their opinion, the searches would be unreasonable (unconstitutional) unless the officer could point to specific facts, probable cause, that Fields had drugs.

In the years since Fields was decided in 1984, many courts have taken a more conservative stance on this issue. This position seems to have been secured by the U.S. Supreme Court in *Griffin* v. *Wisconsin*. Under Wisconsin law, probation officers were allowed to search their clients' homes without a warrant as long as they had their supervisor's approval *and* reasonable grounds to believe that there was contraband in the home. The court found that Wisconsin had a regulation pursuant to state law that permitted the search. The state had justified their need for such a regulation to the satisfaction of the court. It was pointed out that a warrant requirement would unduly interfere with the performance of the officer's duties. The majority in this 5 to 4 decision found that Wisconsin was following the "reasonable grounds" requirement in a way that was constitutionally acceptable.

THE POLYGRAPH

In the past, judges have imposed polygraph testing both before and during probation. Some judges found that if probationers admitted to all their prior offenses, regardless of whether they were charged with these crimes, they would start out their community sentence with a clean slate and a better chance of success. Other judges used the polygraph to determine if those on probation had obeyed the conditions of their supervision agreements. As several judges explained, the threat of polygraph testing often prompted confessions from certain probationers. The courts also found that many criminal associates avoided probationers who were subject to polygraph surveillance because they did not want to be incriminated in any questioning.[10] Today in Jackson County, Oregon, officials use polygraph testing in home detention programs at a cost of about $3350 a year. According to program officers, polygraph tests are used with chronic drug and alcohol abusers and offenders who cannot afford the telephone service needed for electronic monitoring. They have also been used to question those whose electronic monitoring devices are broken to determine if they were broken intentionally.[11]

Although the polygraph remains a popular investigation device in private and public security, the accuracy of such testing remains highly controversial and its coercive use continues to be constitutionally suspect. Generally, results of a polygraph are used only to support more concrete evidence collected in the motion to revoke a person's probation or parole. Appropriate evidence may include urinalysis tests and interviews. Adverse information obtained from the test would most likely not be allowed as evidence in a new criminal proceeding.

QUESTIONING OTHER CONTRACT CONDITIONS

When offenders sign a probation or parole contract, they are agreeing to abide by all the contract conditions specified. Therefore, it is unlikely that any condition would be challenged unless it was later used as grounds for revocation. However, if some controversial conditions are never used as the sole basis for revocation, then it is unlikely they will be reviewed by the court for appropriateness. Some unique contract conditions have been evaluated by the court, and others have yet to be put to such a test.

In a 1988 case, a 17-year-old mother of two who was convicted of child abuse was ordered to practice birth control throughout her child-bearing years. When she later became pregnant again, it was unclear whether the court could revoke the lifetime probation sentence the woman had been serving. Her defense attorney's motion to delete the condition argued that it was invasive, amounted to cruel and unusual punishment, and violated the defendant's freedom of religion. The defendant in this case was Catholic. In 1990 a Florida teen who smothered her newborn pled guilty to manslaughter, received a two-year prison term and a subsequent 10-year term of probation. The judge instructed the girl to receive psychological as well as birth control counseling and to practice birth control. The order drew criticism from both the Family Research Council and the American Civil Liberties Union.[12] Both groups claimed that the judge's orders interfered with the young woman's reproductive freedom.

The idea of court-ordered birth control is controversial. In a California case, a pregnant 27-year-old mother of four was convicted of repeated child abuse. The sentencing court ordered her to have a Norplant birth control device implanted in her arm. This new device, administered once, prevents pregnancy for up to five years. It has been argued that this sentence is proper and justified because the defendant selected it over a four-year prison sentence. However, it may be debatable whether this choice was free of coercive intent. Would anyone opt for four years of prison when the alternative is one year of jail and three years of probation with birth control? Some experts argue that preventing the defendant, Darlene Johnson in this case, from having more children does not address concerns related to the fact that she already has four children and has been found guilty of abusing them. It also does not address the fact that she is a repeat offender with a wide range of previous convictions. It has further been suggested that birth control is not a punishment.

In another child abuse case, a teenage mother was given one year of probation for leaving her toddler unattended in a car where the interior temperatures rose to over 111 degrees. The judge ordered the young mother to attend parenting classes. It is fairly obvious in this case that this condition is important for both the safety of the child and for the education of the mother. It also represents a less restrictive measure than the other options the judge had, such as placing the child in protective custody and removing the mother's parental rights.

The legal boundaries of court restrictions on the lives of persons under community supervision are not always clear, however. For example, can offenders be required to take medications such as depo-provera, which are designed to control their behavior? This chemical may be used to inhibit the sexual urges of child molesters. However, some medical researchers have suspected that the drug is linked to cancer and gallstones and to the worsening of diabetic conditions and phlebitis.

Another behavior-controlling chemical that may be used in treatment is antibuse, which is used to control drinking. Methadone is a behavior-controlling drug used to facilitate drug withdrawal. Questions arise as to whether these or any other treatment programs can be imposed as a condition of supervision. There has been recent controversy over whether a contract can constitutionally require a person to submit to drug and AIDS tests.

Under California law, prostitutes who are placed on probation are required to submit to AIDS testing. This condition is clear and serves the legitimate purpose of protecting the public and perhaps the health of the probationer. However, it is debatable whether it is reasonable or constitutional. Some health practitioners claim such a statute turns an informative and educational process like testing into a punitive one. Others claim it is a method of setting up prostitutes for more serious charges such as attempted murder if they later engage in prostitution after testing positive. Over the years, appellate courts have been asked to clarify the legitimacy of a variety of probation and parole orders. For example, can an offender be required to attend church, stop smoking, or to refrain from legitimate forms of gambling? As a partial answer to these questions, one court has explained that a condition of probation or parole "which requires or forbids conduct which is not itself criminal is valid if that conduct is reasonably related to the crime for which the defendant was convicted" (*People* v. *Lent* Cal.3d 481, 124 Cal. Rptr. 905, 1975). Thus, prohibiting someone from becoming intoxicated or gambling or hanging around other ex-offenders may be appropriate for rehabilitation purposes as well as deterring future offenses.

In California, some rather controversial conditions have been added to the probation contracts of youths involved in punk rock and heavy metal music. According to a report by Rosenbaum and Prinsky, the probation contracts of juveniles come from the courts with several blank spaces.[13] Probation officers, often without the review of the courts, have been able to add conditions they feel will further the reform of the youngster. Officers have used these blank spaces to fill in conditions that will prohibit the youth from contact with heavy metal and punk rock influences. These fill-in conditions have included the following:

1. Not to dress in any style that represents punk rock or heavy metal.
2. Not to wear hair (dye or cut) in any style that represents punk rock or heavy metal.
3. Not to wear any punk rock or heavy metal accessories—earrings, or jewelry, spikes or studs.
4. Not to associate with known punk rockers or heavy metalers.
5. Not to listen to any punk rock or heavy metal music.
6. Not to frequent any place where punk rock or heavy metal is main interest.

BOX 12–5

Liberty Interests and Due Process

No state shall make or enforce any law which shall abridge the privileges or immunities of the citizens of the United States; nor shall any State deprive any person of life, liberty, or property without due process of law; nor deny to any person within its jurisdiction the equal protection of the laws.

Source: The Fourteenth Amendment, Section 1.

According to Rosenbaum and Prinsky, parents concerned about their children's involvement in the rock subculture have often requested such conditions of the probation department. Historically, the authors point out, parents have almost always been disapproving of the musical interests of their children. The existence of these conditions, however, points to a unique attempt to get legal reinforcement for their condemnation. The officers interviewed commented that it was unlikely that probation would ever be revoked simply for a violation of these conditions. It is difficult to assess whether the court would uphold such conditions as reasonable and purposeful if they were challenged.

Some other unusual probation contract requirements have recently been referred to as "Scarlet Letter" conditions. The term connotes puritanical punishments in colonial America, such as that inflicted on the fictional adulteress who was forced to wear the scarlet letter "A" sewn on her clothing. In a case in Florida in 1986, a defendant convicted of driving under the influence was ordered to put a bumper sticker on his car that read: "Convicted DUI—Restricted License." A child molester convicted and placed on probation in Oregon in 1987 was ordered to post a sign on both doors of his residence that stated: "Dangerous Sex Offender—No Children Allowed." In both these cases, the appellate courts supported the trial court's orders. The U.S. Supreme Court has been reluctant to regulate the probation practices of the lower courts. However, the appellate courts have generally opposed the application of conditions that appear to have the sole purpose of imposing public ridicule or that are inconsistent with the rehabilitation and reintegration of the defendant into the community.[14]

Legal interest in the way a revocation is carried out stems directly form the due process clause of the Fourteenth Amendment of the Constitution. This section of the amendment calls for special handling of these cases, particularly when a person may be placed in prison or jail.

Traditionally, the courts have deemed probation and parole to be legally different in status. Therefore, the processes for revocation under these two forms of supervision may vary. A revocation from probation may be viewed as very serious, requiring a number of due process protections because the offender is now at risk of losing his or her liberty and being confined in prison. Theoretically, to be revoked from probation now means that the offender will enter prison for the first time, whereas parolees who are revoked are simply being returned to prison. For the probationer, the potential change in punishments from a community sentence to one of incarceration creates a "liberty interest" in the revocation process.

PROBATION REVOCATION

The idea that probationers were entitled to due process rights during revocation was ignored until 1967. At that time, the Supreme Court said that the probationer had the right to counsel at the revocation hearing if the probation was being revoked under a deferred sentencing statute (*Mempa* v. *Rhay*). Right to counsel was an important concern for the Court. By virtue of the original deferral, the defendant had not actually been sentenced yet. Sentencing is considered to be a critical phase in any criminal trial. It is not surprising that the Court wanted an attorney to represent the accused for sentencing.

It was still unclear at this point whether hearings would be required in all cases or if counsel would be necessary at all hearings. Legal requirements had remained vague up until this time because courts have continually emphasized that probation is a privilege and *not* a right (*U.S.* v. *Birnbaum*, 1970). It was not until 1972 in *Gagnon* v. *Scarpelli* that the Court clarified the procedures that should be followed in probation revocation proceedings. In this case, the Supreme Court recognized that a person on community supervision had much at stake in facing the chance of incarceration on revocation. The judges in this case determined that probation cannot be revoked unless certain due process steps are followed:

1. Each probationer shall receive written notification of the charges pending against him or her.
2. Written notice must be received in advance of the revocation hearing to allow the defendant to prepare an answer to the charges.
3. The probationer must be able to attend the hearing and present evidence on his or her own behalf.
4. The probationer has the right to challenge those testifying against him or her and to confront and cross-examine witnesses.
5. A probationer may have legal counsel present if the charges are complicated or if the case is so complex that the ordinary person would not be able to comprehend the legal issues involved.

To revoke probation, the state must prove that the probationer has violated the conditions of probation. A revocation is usually unquestionable after a conviction for a new crime. However, a conviction is not always necessary to justify a revocation. Judges may revoke probation if they are reasonably satisfied that a state or federal law has been violated. In most cases, when criminal offenses are serving as the basis for a revocation, they need be established only by a preponderance of the evidence. This standard is not as strict as the "beyond a reasonable doubt" standard required in felony criminal trials.

If a trial ends in a mistrial because of a hung jury or some error or an acquittal, the defendant's probation may still be revoked. Probation may also be revoked as a result of a nolo contendere (no contest) plea.

A probationer who feels that he or she was treated unfairly in the revocation process may appeal that decision in a higher court. As a rule, however, higher courts are reluctant to get involved in revocation reviews. Normally, appellate courts do not review the underlying basis for probation. The only issue they are concerned with is whether a violation occurred. As a result, the lower courts enjoy considerable discretion in their decision making. Justice O'Connor, writing for the majority in *Black* v. *Romano*, went so far as to say that the due process clause does not require the sentencing court to say that it even considered alternatives to incarceration before revoking probation.

In most cases, then, an appellate court is likely to intercede only in the lower court's decision to revoke probation if it believes that the lower court has abused its discretion. A good example of the appellate review process finding such an abuse is in *U.S.* v. *Drinkall* (749 F.2d 20):

> District court abused its discretion in revoking defendant's probation on the basis that defendant had fraudulently obtained and negotiated social security benefits under widow's and mother's benefits program where district court had not yet determined defendant was not entitled to those benefits and thus, had not yet determined whether defendant had violated federal law.

In essence, the Court said that unless you can show that what the defendant did was wrong, then you cannot base a violation of probation on that action.

PAROLE REVOCATION

It is well known among criminal justice practitioners that the period of highest risk for an offender who has been released from prison is in the first year after release. Failure to adjust to the community, obtain work, and avoid crime may result in a revocation of the early release privilege. Traditionally, there have been three theoretical justifications for revoking a parole: the privilege theory, the contract theory, and the continuing custody theory.[15] *Privilege theory* explains that because parole is only a privilege granted by the state, not a right, the state has the option of curtailing that privilege when there is reason to believe it is being abused. There is no constitutional right to parole. The *contract theory* states that parole is an agreement that the parolee enters into with a written and binding contract. Should the parolee not abide by the terms agreed to, then the state is justified in revoking that contract. The *continuing custody theory* is based on the concept of legal custody or jurisdiction. In most cases, a person on parole is still under the control of the state department of corrections. Therefore, the state may recall the parolee to serve the remaining term of his or her sentence without ever changing the status of the offender because the parolee was never really gone. Thus, the parole revocation process proceeds with less formality and consideration for due process than that given a probationer who is revoked and sent to prison. The prevailing belief is that a probationer who has not yet been to prison for an offense has more at stake when facing the possibility of incarceration than does a parolee who has already been found deserving of a prison sentence.

Parole Revocation Hearings

Whereas revocation of probation generally requires a hearing before a judge or magistrate, the revocation of parole requires only an administrative hearing. The level of evidence required to return a parolee to custody is only that convincing evidence be presented to the parole board or hearing officer. In many jurisdictions, the level of proof needed to convince the hearing authority of an infraction is far less than would be necessary in a criminal trial.

The U.S. Supreme Court outlined the requirements for a parole revocation hearing in the landmark case *Morrissey* v. *Brewer* (408 U.S. 471, 1972). This case set down the due process requirements for a hearing, requirements that had long been debated in the courts. The opinion held that "whenever a person's parole is revoked a grievous loss is imposed on the parolee." The justices issued an assurance that the state had no interest in imposing this loss without some formal procedural guarantees. They held that before parole can be revoked, the parolee is entitled to two separate hearings.

The first hearing is a *preliminary hearing*, which determines whether probable cause exists to believe that the person committed acts that amount to a violation of parole conditions. The preliminary hearing is to be held "reasonably near" the place of the alleged violation or arrest. It is also to be held as "promptly as convenient" after arrest. In cases in which the defendant is alleged to have committed a new and serious crime, the defendant may be brought from jail to the hearing.

In cases of new but less serious charges, the defendant may already be out on bail.

In some states, parolees arrested on new charges may be denied bail. In *Faheem-El* v. *Klincar*, the Seventh Circuit Court of Appeals said that such a denial does not necessarily violate the constitutional principles of due process. The justices wanted to see only a balancing of three elements—the parolee's liberty interests, the risk of an erroneous deprivation, and the needs of the state in the parole revocation process.

At the preliminary hearing, as well as at the second, or final, hearing, the parolee has the right to confront and cross-examine persons who give adverse testimony on which the revocation is based. This particular right may be disallowed, however, if it is determined that such a course of action would pose a risk of harm to the informant.

The *second hearing* determines whether parole is revoked. The due process requirements outlined for the second hearing by the Supreme Court in *Morrissey* include the following:

- Written notice of the claimed violation.
- Disclosure by the state of adverse evidence that will be used against the defendant.
- The opportunity to be heard in person and to present witnesses and documentary evidence on one's behalf.
- The right to confront and cross-examine adverse witnesses.
- The right to an impartial hearing board.
- The right to findings of fact.

The reforms in the parole revocation process brought by *Morrissey* are important because they lessen the possibility of offenders being lost in the shuffle. Prior to 1971, a parole officer could have a defendant held in jail for weeks before getting around to filing charges, and parole could be revoked for very vague reasons. For example, the person seemed to have a "bad attitude" or was not making a "good adjustment." According to McCleary, the revised process meant that there would have to be very specific charges to begin the revocation and a quasi-judicial proceeding for hearing those charges.[16] Continued judicial support for this process has been shown over the years. In *Texas* v. *Williams* (1987) and in *Scroggy* v. *Summers* (1987) the courts of appeal declared that Texas' and Kentucky's statutes were unconstitutional because they allowed for automatic revocation rules that authorized the state parole board to deny hearings and automatically revoke paroles upon a new criminal conviction.

It is important to note, however, that the defendant has the right to waive a revocation hearing and go directly to prison if the parolee believes revocation is imminent and wishes to begin serving the sentence as soon as possible. Even if a new conviction is forthcoming, there is the chance that the judge will order the two sentences to be served at the same time (concurrently). Concurrent sentences would allow the remainder of the first sentence for which the offender was on parole to be served along with the sentence for the new conviction that was the basis of the revocation.

Observing juvenile parole revocation hearings, one team of researchers found that informal conversation sessions during the short breaks that took place between the actual hearings were used to pass on critical information and opinions. The participants, including parole officers, board members, school officers, social service workers, and correctional staff, commented on the behavior of the juvenile, the circumstances of the youth's alleged violation, and their personal recommendations for dispositions. The researchers in this study found that "in 93 percent of the cases, the final outcome was consistent with the decision recommended/reached during the informal hearing."[17] Because the hearings themselves are less formal than actual criminal proceedings, these off-the-record discussions are not viewed as being prejudicial to the case or its outcome.

REVOCATIONS WITHIN THE FEDERAL SYSTEM

To ensure uniformity in the application of sanctions, the federal government adopted a standard policy and guidelines that provided that the sanction imposed for a violation would be graded by levels to permit proportionally longer terms for more serious violations. Under this policy, guidelines were created that weigh the *grade* of the violation with the violator's *criminal history*. The criminal history category ranges from I through VI and is established at the time of initial sentencing. Criminal history reflects the defendant's prior criminal activity.

Under the federal system, community supervision violations fall into three categories:

Grade A—conduct constituting a federal, state, or local offense punishable by a term exceeding one year that (1) is a crime of violence, (2) involves a controlled substance, (3) involves possession of a firearm or destructive device, (4) any other federal, state, or local offense punishable by a term of imprisonment exceeding 20 years.

Grade B—conduct constituting any other federal, state, or local offense punishable by imprisonment for a term exceeding one year.

Grade C—conduct constituting a federal, state, or local offense punishable by a period of imprisonment of one year or less; or any violation of any other condition of supervision.

Table 12–1 Probation Revocation Matrix

*Revocation Table
(in months of imprisonment)*

Criminal History Category

	I	II	III	IV	V	VI
Grade of Violation						
Grade C	3–9	4–10	5–11	6–12	7–13	8–14
Grade B	4–10	6–12	8–14	12–18	18–24	21–27
Grade A	(1) Except as provided in subdivision 2:					
	12–18	15–21	18–24	24–30	30–37	33–41
	(2) Defendant on probation or supervised release for a Class A felony:					
	24–30	27–33	30–37	37–46	46–57	51–63

Source: U.S. Sentencing Commission Guidelines Manual (November 1990).

Federal probation officers are required to report a Grade A or B violation to the court but have some discretion in reporting Grade C violations. To determine the sentence to impose for the violation, the judge uses a matrix created by comparing the grade of the violation with the criminal history category. The matrix is shown in Table 12-1.

Using this matrix assures that the most serious offenders who have committed the most serious violations receive the longest sentences and that those who have minimal prior records and commit only technical violations receive less serious penalties. The federal guidelines are a significant effort to end or at least to control disparity in the court's response to violations of both probation and supervised release.

REVOCATION STATISTICS

As Figures 12.1 and 12.2 illustrate, probationers are far more likely to be removed from supervision for technical revocations (disciplinary return) than for new convictions (new felony charge), but this may often be deceptive. The defendant may have committed a new crime, but for other reasons the authorities have decided simply to expedite a revocation rather than process a new charge. This is often an economical move because it is less expensive to hold a revocation hearing than a

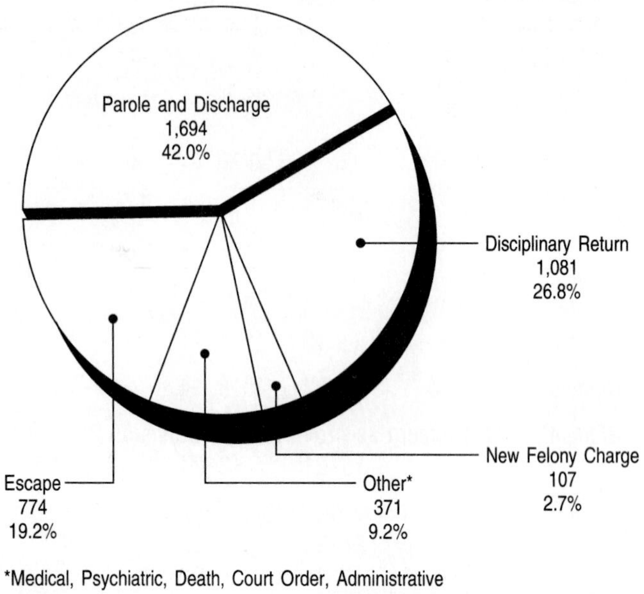

Figure 12.1

Community Residential Program Terminations, FY 1987–88.

Source: Michigan Department of Corrections [1989]. *Annual Report 1988*. Lansing, MI: p. 103.)

Parole and Discharge
1,694
42.0%

Disciplinary Return
1,081
26.8%

Escape
774
19.2%

Other*
371
9.2%

New Felony Charge
107
2.7%

*Medical, Psychiatric, Death, Court Order, Administrative

new full criminal trial. In these cases, the defendant will go to prison for a period of time that authorities feel is enough to justify not pursuing the new charges. If the new crime is much more serious and would carry a significantly longer sentence than the original probation term, then the new trial will most likely take place. Also, the legal community would feel it necessary to prosecute such serious charges to avoid giving the appearance of overlooking the offense even if it carries a sentence similar to the term of probation being revoked. In many cases, the decision process is made up of mathematical calculations of time to be served, as well as political and economic factors.

Whether a revocation is for a "new" offense or for a technical violation may depend on how these categories are defined. In a 1990 Bureau of Justice Statistics study involving 32 counties nationwide, the categories for probation revocation included (1) technical violations, (2) new arrests, and (3) new convictions. Category (1) describes situations in which there is an offense committed but charges are not pressed or charges do not result in a conviction. Again, it is important to remember that an arrest alone may be adequate grounds for revocation if the hearing judge has enough reason to believe that the defendant did commit the offense in question—a fairly common set of circumstances for revocation. However, we are uncertain how jurisdictions that use only categories (1) and (3) are classifying these kinds of cases. Many jurisdictions may include these cases in the technical violations category because a conviction did not occur and because

Figure 12.2
Community Programs
Annual Statistics, FY
1983/84—FY 1987/88.
Source: Michigan Department of
Corrections [1989]. *Annual
Report 1988*. Lansing, MI:
p. 103.)

CATEGORY	1987-88	1986-87	1985-86	1984-85	1983-84
Beginning Count	2,167	1,966	1,711	1,545	1,728
Additions	4,556	4,410	4,200	4,293	5,065
Service Population	6,723	6,376	5,911	5,838	6,793
Avg. Daily Count	2,170.5	1,973.3	1,801.5	1,584.1	1,587.1
Avg. Stay (Months)	3.90	3.71	3.66	3.26	2.80
Terminations	4,033	4,146	3,950	4,124	5,299
Parole/Discharge	1,694	2,032	2,096	2,203	3,511
Percent	42.0%	49.1%	53.1%	53.4%	66.3%
Disciplinary Return	1,081	881	621	414	294
Percent	26.8%	21.2%	15.7%	10.0%	5.5%
Escape	774	705	697	972	897
Percent	19.2%	17.0%	17.6%	23.6%	16.9%
New Felony Charge	107	149	184	196	187
Percent	2.7%	3.6%	4.7%	4.8%	3.5%
*Other	371	379	352	339	410
Percent	9.2%	9.1%	8.9%	8.2%	7.7%
Ending Count	2,448	2,101	1,933	1,717	1,545
Gross Earnings (Millions)	$7.52	$6.25	$5.19	$4.17	$3.22
Per Diem Cost	$30.98	$26.34	$24.35	$24.84	$22.60
Institution Per Diem Cost	$45.28	$43.47	$39.54	$47.46	$42.85

*Medical, Psychiatric, Death, Court Order, Administrative

the events leading up to the arrests, such as being in a bar or out after midnight, may themselves constitute adequate grounds for a revocation. In these cases, jurisdictions save resources by initiating a technical violation.

In this recent Bureau of Justice Statistics study, these differences were clarified by the finding that 21 percent of the revocations were the result of new convictions, 26 percent came from new arrests, and 22 percent were revoked on technical violations. Another 29 percent absconded from supervision.[18]

ABSCONDING FROM SUPERVISION

If an offender on community supervision commits a violation of the probation or parole contract, that individual may try to flee the area or elude authorities for fear of being revoked and incarcerated. In other cases, offenders may simply tire of the restrictiveness of supervision and run away. Still others may flee before the period of supervision even begins. One Baton Rouge, Louisiana, native placed on electronic monitoring packed up his television surveillance equipment and "kept on walking." Although there is a bench warrant active for his arrest, it may be years before he is located.[19]

Statistics from California for 1989 show that one out of every six parolees was unaccounted for, which would be a violation of their contracts. About 8500 persons are unaccounted for. Officials estimate that 80–85 percent will turn themselves in within a short time, but 10 percent will never be seen again, at least not by the authorities.[20] In Michigan, officials reported that 19 percent of those officially terminated from community residential programs from 1987 to 1988 ($n = 774$) were escapees (see Figure 12-1).[21] Another study suggested that probationers without high school diplomas had higher rates of absconding than those who had graduated from high school or who had attended college.[22]

ANALYSIS OF PROBATION AND PAROLE REVOCATIONS

Many jurisdictions today are reporting higher rates of community supervision revocation than ever before. In New York, for example, the probation violation rate between 1985 and 1989 jumped from 26 to 38 percent.[23] In the 1990 Bureau of Justice Statistics study of probationers in 32 counties nationwide, researchers were able to analyze the characteristics of those who were revoked. The report showed that the more education probationers have, the less likely they are to be revoked. Also, as age increases, revocation rates decrease. Males had a revocation rate (24 percent) that was almost twice as high as that of females (14 percent). Probationers who were single had higher revocation rates (26 percent) than those who were married (19 percent). Race was also correlated with revocation rates. The rate for whites was 20 percent, for Hispanics, 24 percent, and for blacks, 29 percent.

A recent study by the Center on Juvenile and Criminal Justice indicates that California returns more parole violators to prison than all other 49 states combined. The number of persons receiving revocations for technical violations in California in 1989 reached 39,976. In all other states, the combined total for technical violations was just over

33,000. The CJCJ study also reported that California's success rate on parole was less than half the rate of the national average. Whereas nationwide 43 percent of persons released from prison successfully complete parole, the California success rate is only 19 percent. Experts commenting on the study speculated that California was much more punitive in response to violators, had fewer community alternatives to revocation for violators, and provided fewer services to assist parolees in rehabilitation.[24]

SUMMARY

As sentencing strategies strive for more creative ways to control offenders and prevent further criminal behavior, we will see more challenges to the conditions of probation and parole. The constitutional limits of surveillance and supervision will be tested and analyzed. More conservative views about offenders' expectations of freedom and privacy may allow more intrusion into their lives by the criminal justice system. Also, decreases in funding and resources will mean that more offenders may be placed under community control with more restrictive or unusual contract requirements.

As one group of researchers reported, the reasons that community corrections sentences are revoked lie in a "grey area."[25] There is some debate over whether most revocations are based on new offenses or simply on technical violations of supervision contracts. Regardless of the justification, revocation procedures are made up of a legally sophisticated set of considerations of due process. However, because probation and parole are two separate legal systems with two different sets of governing principles, the revocation process of each should be considered individually.

CASES

Atchison v. *State*, 716 2d 185 (Tex. App. Ft. Worth, 1986).

Black v. *Romano*, 473 U.S. 921, 105 S.Ct. 3548.

Brunk v. *Luttrell*, Tx-89-109-CA.

Faheem-El v. *Klincar* (Ill).

Gagnon v. *Scarpelli*, 411 U.S. 778, 93 S.Ct. 1756, 36 L.Ed.2d 656, (1973).

Griffin v. *Wisconsin*, 483 U.S. 868 (1987).

Manguia v. *U.S. Parole Commission*, 871 F.2d 517 (5th Cir. 1989).

Mempa v. *Rhay*, (389 U.S. 128, 88 S.Ct.254, 19 L.Ed.2d 336, 1967).

Morrissey v. *Brewer* (408 U.S. 471, 92 S.Ct. 2593, 33 L.Ed.2d 484, 1972).

People v. *Goulart* 224 Cal.App. 3d 71, 273 Cal.Rptr. 636, 1990.

Scroggy v. *Summers* (KY) No. 87-5064 (6th Cir. July 31, 1987), cert. denied, 485 U.S. 941 (1988).

State v. *Fields*, 686 P.2d 1379, 1984.

State v. *Morris*, 48 CrL 1498 (Ha. SupCt. 1991).

Texas v. *Williams* (1987).

U.S. v. *Alexander* (743 F.2d 472 Ill 1984).

U.S. v. *Cothran*, 44 CrL 2015 (11th Cir. 1988).

U.S. v. *Newton* (698 F.2d 770, 5th Cir. 1983).

U.S. v. *Richards Elec Supply Co.* (604 F.Supp 126 Ohio 1984).

U.S. v. *Tzakis* (736 F.2d 867 N.Y. 1984).

KEY TERMS

absconding
antibuse
continuing custody theory
contract theory
EMIT
gas chromatography/mass
   spectroscopy

motion to revoke
preliminary hearing
privilege theory
revocation
thin layer chromatography
Scarlet Letter conditions

DISCUSSION QUESTIONS

1. Should drug testing be permitted for all probationers or only in cases where there is probable cause to believe that a probationer is using illicit drugs? Should an assessment of risk for taking drugs be based on past history or only on current evidence?
2. What variables seem to be related to probation revocation? What explanations might be offered for the variations in rates of revocation?
3. What improvements could you suggest making in the process of revocation for probation or parole?
4. How far should judges be permitted to go in setting terms and conditions for probation and parole? Do any of the examples of special conditions described in this chapter appear to violate basic privacy or liberty rights?

END NOTES

1. Bloch, Herbert, and Arthur Niederhoffer (1958). *The gang*. New York: Philosophical Library, p. 184.

2. State of New Hampshire Department of Corrections (1988). *Biennial report*, July 1986–June 1988. Concord, pp. 86–88.

3. Minnesota Department of Corrections (1988). *1987–88 Biennial report*. St Paul, pp. 87–88.

4. Rudovsky, David, Alvin Bronstein, Edward Koren, and Julia Cade (1988). *The rights of prisoners*. Carbondale and Edwardsville: Southern Illinois Univ. Press, p. 108.

5. Wish, Eric, Mary Toborg, and John Bellassai (1988). *Identifying drug users and monitoring them during conditional release*. Washington, DC: National Institute of Justice, p. 3.

6. Baer, James, Werner Baumgartner, Virginia Hill, and William Blahd (1991). *Federal Probation* 55(1):3–9.

7. Del Carmen, Rolando, and Jonathan Sorensen (1988). Legal issues in drug testing probationers and parolees. *Federal Probation* 52(4):19–27.

8. Bureau of Justice Assistance (1988). *Urinalysis as part of a treatment alternative to street crime (TASC) program*. Washington, DC: U.S. Department of Justice.

9. Rudovsky, David, Alvin Bronstein, Edward Koren, and Julia Cade (1988). Supra note 5, p. 109.

10. Abrams, S., and E. Ogard (1986). Polygraph surveillance of probationers. *Polygraph* 15(3):174–182.

11. Harkins, John (1990). House arrest in Oregon: A look at what goes on inside the home. *Corrections Today* 52(7):146–150.

12. Barringer, Felicity (1990). Teen baby killer faces prison, then birth control for 10 years. *The New York Times*. Reprinted in the *San Bernardino Sun*, 18 November:A3.

13. Rosenbaum, Jill, and Lorraine Prinsky (1991). The presumption of influence: Recent responses to popular music subcultures. *Crime and Delinquency* 37(4):528–535.

14. Jones, Mark (1991). The constitutionality of "Scarlet Letter" probation conditions. *APPA Perspectives* 15(2):10–13.

15. Palmer, John (1977). *Constitutional rights of prisoners* (2nd ed.). Cincinnati: Anderson Publishing.

16. McCleary, Richard (1978). *Dangerous men: The sociology of parole*. Beverly Hills: Sage.

17. Knepper, Paul and Gray Cavender (1990). Strange interlude: An analysis of juvenile parole revocation decision-making. Paper presented at the annual meeting of the Academy of Criminal Justice Sciences, Denver, CO.

18. Cunniff, Mark, and Mary Shilton (1990). *A sentencing postscript II: Felony probationers under supervision in the community*. Washington, DC: Bureau of Justice Statistics, p. 106.

19. *Wall Street Journal* (1990). Home monitoring of criminals is poised to break loose, industry analysts say. 3 December: B-8C.

20. Green, Stephen (1989). Number of ex-convicts in violation of parole sets record: 8,500. *San Bernardino Sun*, 12 March: B7.

21. Michigan Department of Corrections (1989). *Annual report 1988*. Lansing, p. 106.

22. Bureau of Justice Statistics (1990). Sponsored study (DRAFT) by Mark Cunniff and Mary Shilton. *A sentencing postscript II: Felony probationers under supervision in the community*. Washington, DC: Bureau of Justice Statistics, p. 138.

23. Price, J. P. (1990). Drugs—The impact on the safety and welfare of the professional probation officer in the decade of the 1990s. Paper presented at the Probation Officer's Association Meeting, Albany, NY.

24. Dunham, Elisabeth (1991). California returns more parolees to jail than rest of states together. *San Bernardino Sun*, 19 September: B5.

25. Winfree, L. Thomas, Veronica Ballard, Christine Sellers, and Roy Roberg (1990). Responding to a legislated change in correctional practices: A quasi-experimental study of revocation hearings and parole board actions. Paper presented at the annual meeting of the Academy of Criminal Justice Sciences, San Francisco.

13

The Community Supervision Professional

What the system does is take a social worker and give him a gun and a bulletproof vest.

— Interviewee to Kay Bartlett[1]

PURPOSE

This chapter defines the role of the community supervision professional, covering the political and social influences that have shaped the jobs of probation and parole officers. Over the years, sociologists have created typologies, or categorical descriptions, of the various personality types of probation and parole officers. Some of these typologies are discussed here as a way of understanding the effects that people have on their jobs or that jobs have on people's personalities. Your attention is drawn to the legal aspects of performing community supervision. Liability or misconduct by an officer is subject to several civil and criminal court actions.

After exploring various theories about the nature of community supervision, the chapter focuses on some of the problems that these professional supervisors face, including role conflict, gender conflict, the need to carry weapons, and job burnout. Another controversial issue is the use of ex-offenders, volunteers, and reserve officers to supplement the probation and parole officer workforce. The changes that have occurred in the types of caseloads officers now handle is also covered. Finally, we look at the future of the role of the community corrections worker. Several models have already been implemented that will further specialize the tasks that each officer performs. These models include the use of resource brokers and management teams.

OBJECTIVES

After completing this chapter, you should be able to do the following:

1. Explain some of the factors that contribute to the job burnout that many community corrections officers experience.

2. Contrast the different typologies of the community corrections officer.

3. Discuss some of the potential areas of liability faced by a community supervision officer.

4. Describe the research findings on the victimization of community supervision workers on the job.

5. Explain the controversial issues in the debate over the carrying of weapons by probation and parole officers.

INTRODUCTION: THE ROLE OF THE COMMUNITY SUPERVISION WORKER

The role of the probation or parole officer is generally defined by the expectations society has for offenders. Thus, the officer performs tasks related to the control of offenders and the protection of the community. One way that the officer maintains control over offenders is through surveillance and enforcement of contract conditions. The surveillance and enforcement role of probation officers was defined by the U.S. Supreme Court in *Cable* v. *Chabez-Salido* (102 S. Ct. 735 1982):

> The probation officer acts as an extension of the Judiciary's authority to set the conditions under which particular individuals will lead their lives and as an extension of the Executive's authority to coerce obedience to those conditions.

In addition to maintaining offender control and community safety, society expects the officer to facilitate the rehabilitation of offenders. To accomplish this, the officer may contract with a variety of treatment services. Today, society measures rehabilitation in three ways: (1) the ability of offenders to avoid future arrests, (2) the completion of prescribed treatment programs, and (3) the absence of violations of community sentence agreements. Box 13–1 outlines the variety of tasks that may be performed by the supervising officer in attaining these goals.

It is obvious from this list of tasks that the community worker must interact effectively with offenders, as well as the community and other criminal justice agencies. In many jurisdictions, particularly in metropolitan areas, certain tasks are divided among specialized units within departments. Some agencies may designate a separate unit to prepare the pre-sentence investigations that the judge uses in making sentencing decisions. Because these officers do not supervise offenders directly, some see this position as more of an investigator.

The exact role of the community corrections worker varies from state to state and according to prevailing law. Supervisors of each community corrections agency may have preferences for how the job is carried out and what the department's goals are. Legislatures may also influence the duties, responsibilities, and authority given to the individual officer and the controlling agency. For example, the state may define probation and parole agents as *peace officers*, thus expanding their law-enforcement powers and requiring that they be trained in the use of weapons or carry a weapon while on duty.

Other actors in the criminal justice system also have expectations for the role of the community corrections officer. Judges, prosecutors, defense attorneys, and the police all make arrangements with officers to see that duties they feel are important are carried out.

BOX 13–1

Community Supervision Tasks by Type

A. *Offender Control and Community Protection*
    1. Assess the risk/dangerousness of clients:
        a. For the presentence investigation
        b. On an ongoing basis for each client
    2. Provide courts and authorities with updated status reports on clients
    3. Detect violations of the conditions of release
    4. Routinely test clients for drug/alcohol abuse

B. *Offender Rehabilitation and Treatment*
    1. Ensure that clients understand all rights and responsibilities of their community supervision contract
    2. Help clients find jobs, schooling, trades
    3. Assist clients in obtaining counseling or therapy as needed
    4. Work with clients to develop social skills needed for effective community interaction; facilitate the clients' participation in civic programs and responsibilities

Because other criminal justice agencies, the public, and the legislature all have expectations for the operation of community corrections programs, there is potential for role conflict. When conflicting ideas about how the job should be performed affects the well-being and the ability of the individual officer to do his or her job, that condition is called *role confusion*.

OFFICER TYPOLOGIES

In the early 1960s, sociologists developed a number of explanations to describe the way people adapt to roles, societal expectations, and rules. These explanations usually covered a variety of adaptive styles and were called *typologies*. Typologies group people into distinct categories that are based on the similarities of their behavior or personality. Analyzing actors in the criminal justice system, sociologists came up with typologies of police officers, victims, correctional officers, inmates, and probation and parole officers.

The first typologies of probation and parole officers were based on those officers who directly supervised offenders. These typologies usually focused on whether officers should emphasize the control or the assistance aspect of their job.[2] The three most commonly used typologies are the *punitive officer,* the *protective agent,* and the *welfare worker.*[3] Each of these roles can be defined by a point on the continuums of control and assistance. When officers exercise a high degree of control and a low degree of assistance, they are said to be punitive. Those who maintain a low level of control and a high level of assistance are said to be welfare-oriented. The continuums can be diagramed as shown in Figure 13.1. The roles are explained in the following paragraphs.

1. *The punitive officer.* When an officer assumes a punitive role, there is emphasis on controlling the offender. The officer sees the job as oriented toward law enforcement and focuses on strictly following the rules. Surveillance is an important factor from the punitive perspective. Threats and coercion are often used to obtain the conformity of the client. The relationship between the officer and the client in this orientation is routinized, focused on the contract, and preoccupied with the setting of limits and terms for compliance. According to some critics of the punitive style, the emphasis is on symptoms rather than on problems.[4] Thus, the officer concentrates on the rule that has been broken rather than on the underlying personal problems or needs that may have led to the violation.

2. *The welfare officer.* An officer who assumes a welfare orientation emphasizes rehabilitation and assistance. The relationship focuses on the use of treatment models based on the client's needs. The officer believes that the best way to protect the community is to help the offender. Much time is spent counseling clients and directing and motivating them to achieve personal and social goals. Some theorists have speculated that the welfare officer's concerns for the problems of the client can impede the ability to make judgments in the best interests of the community.

3. *The protective officer.* Between these two positions is the protective officer who appears to alternate between protecting the interests of the client and those of the community. In some ways, the actions of the officer are paternalistic, basically helping the offender yet, from time to time, also punishing. The tools of the job are praise and blame, advising and lecturing. Although it may seem that the officer vacillates in this role, it is an accurate reflection of the nature of the job. As one writer explained:

Figure 13.1

Diagram of Probation/Parole Officer Role Typologies.

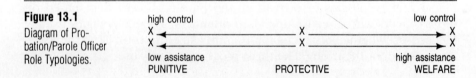

The job can be schizophrenic, part cop, part social worker, some big brother, some embodiment of "the man." The parole officer or p.o. as he is known, is sometimes the only person the parolee knows from the square world of jobs, showing up at nine, coping with the system.[5]

The "schizophrenic" nature of the community corrections worker's role has been characterized in the literature as creating role conflict. As Duffee notes, it is confusing to be helping one day and issuing a technical violation the next, giving them a hug and brushing them with your gun butt.[6]

The three typologies of punitive, protective, and welfare officer all relate to traditional images of the role of the probation and parole officer. According to this perspective, the functions of control and rehabilitation vary according to the individual officer's values. Officers who demonstrate neither emphasis have been characterized as neutral, or passive, merely doing a job.[7]

In a study of officers who did presentence investigations, Rosecrance developed a typology based on the individual's perceptions about the job, the role of sentencing, and the types of recommendations each would give.[8] As Table 13–1 demonstrates, investigator styles were bro-

Table 13–1   Typology of Presentence Probation Investigators

Type and Percentage of Investigators	Assumed Role	Purpose of Sentencing	Presentence Recommendation
Team Player 30%	Facilitating departmental policies	To reflect society's values	Noncontroversial
Mossback 30%	Following the rules, passive	To resolve the matter	Middle of the road
Hardliner 20%	Upholding traditional values	To deter others	Strict
Bleeding-Heart Liberal 10%	Sticking up for the underdog	To rehabilitate the defendant	Lenient
Maverick 10%	Weighing the case's individual merits	To see that justice is done	Varied

Source: Rosecrance, John (1987). A typology of presentence probation investigators. *International Journal of Offender Therapy and Comparative Criminology* 31(2):163–177.

Figure 13.2

Matrix of Rehabilitation and Control Levels and Officer Characteristics.

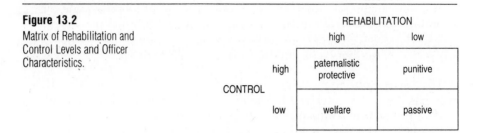

ken down by job orientations into five categories: the team player, the mossback, the hardliner, the bleeding-heart liberal, and the maverick.

Team players are pragmatic, willing to follow office policy and supervisors' suggestions. Team players strive to be noncontroversial and often advance their careers by avoiding conflict. *Mossbacks* work in a passive and routine fashion and are often referred to as doing their time, no more, no less. Their reports contain the minimum information required by the court and include no personal observations. *Hardliners* have the goal of protecting society and being tough on clients. They often criticize other officers as being soft. Although they are disciplinarians, they tend to view themselves as fair, which commonly means equally punitive with all clients. *Bleeding-heart liberals,* who champion the offender as the underdog and see the system as socially corrupt and unfair, are probably the most cynical. They strive for rehabilitative strategies in sentencing and try to present the defendant in a favorable light. *Mavericks* concentrate on making each case a triumph of justice. They see themselves in a quasi-judicial role and attempt to evaluate the merits of each case neutrally. The care and detail with which mavericks develop each case to make it unique is sometimes irritating to the other court officials involved in the rapid-process system.[9]

The formation of an officer's personality is influenced by the department's philosophy and the working environment. Many researchers believe that new employees' attitudes toward the job and toward offenders are learned in the office from supervisors and more experienced agents. In 1978 Richard McCleary published a sociological analysis of the way parole agencies operate. He characterized the interactions of parole officers and their supervisors and introduced the concept of *noninterference.* This means that supervisors gave employees wide latitude in managing their caseloads. The officers enjoyed a greater degree of autonomy and independence in an environment of noninterference than did the officers in more closely supervised departments.[10] Noninterference was a valued trait in the operations of agencies, as was respect for an officer's territory. McCleary maintained that values such as noninterference and territorial rights were maintained by the officers and enforced by supervisors. Territorial rights ensure some certainty and stability in routine, but they can also be used by superiors to reward and

punish. Assignments to less desirable neighborhoods are considered de-
motions. McCleary found that supervisors controlled the quality of work
and the flow of promotions within their departments to preserve the status quo by several means. One way was to have officers, especially new
ones, write reports over and over until they conformed to departmental
norms. As McCleary explained:

> POs who refuse to abandon clients in hopeless situations soon acquire
> reputations for unfairness. Second, while POs generally admire peers who
> "buck the system," POs will denounce any peer who carries idealism to the
> extreme. This is because extremism endangers the image of all POs, and
> more importantly, brings "heat" down on the branch office. Thus, while
> individual POs enjoy potentially gross personal power, its exercise is
> restricted to only a few situations.[11]

Ironically, more independence on the job and less supervisory interference was cited in one survey as the reason many probation officers
became parole officers in one Southern California county. The respondents also cited more money and the use of a county vehicle for supervisory travel as reasons for the career change.[12]

In a study of probation officers in Minnesota, Lawrence and Johnson
found that over time employees "tuned in" to administrative concerns
about efficiency.[13] Of the officers surveyed in this study, those with
more experience believed that their supervisors were more concerned
about efficient case processing than with providing supervision and services for clients.

Some writers have argued that the way community corrections workers view their roles may be subject to changes in social values over time.
Harris, Clear, and Baird pointed out that many of the studies that found
officer emphasis on assistance and treatment were done in the 1960s
and 1970s.[14] However, studies done during the 1980s, these authors
pointed out, tended to reflect more concern among the officers for control and authority. The officers' decreased emphasis on assistance and
rehabilitation may have reflected a broader social mood of punitiveness
and lack of faith in rehabilitation.

The issue of treatment versus surveillance is a role conflict in need of
resolution. Deciding the importance of each is a way to define the mission of practitioners in their daily work. It is also a way of establishing
the overall mission of probation and parole systems. The importance of
this issue was illustrated when the American Probation and Parole
Association devoted its entire 1988 conference to this theme.

Liberal and conservative political factions in society feed the conflict
by placing demands for seemingly contradictory services on community
corrections. Liberal groups want to maintain treatment programs and a
rehabilitative ideal, whereas conservative groups want to emphasize
surveillance for community protection. Community corrections, therefore, strives to accomplish both directives.

As the treatment-oriented environment of the 1960s gave way to the conservative surveillance-oriented climate of the 1980s, corrections practitioners struggled to adjust. In the early 1980s, economic resources for local government services were significantly reduced. Community corrections, as the "stepchild" of state and local criminal justice systems, struggled for enough resources to survive. While clinging to its treatment heritage, it also recognized the need to satisfy a more politically conservative administration. Community corrections was forced to develop a more surveillance-oriented, conservative, and consequently more politically popular image. Practitioners, especially those who had come into the field more than a decade earlier, were themselves strongly divided on the issues. Both administrators and officers were without a well-defined and broadly accepted mission statement.

This role confusion was complicated by an increase in caseload size, a changing offender population, and reductions in community resources for offender needs. A 1988 study by the National Institute of Justice concluded, "American probation and parole systems now face an increasingly difficult clientele population despite less adequate resources."[15]

In some probation caseloads, the proportion of misdemeanor to felony offenders has been reversed. Felony probationers are now more common. Some officers feel that this trend has significantly changed the way they can perform the job. In California, for example, 75 percent of all felony convictions in 1987 resulted in a probation disposition.[16] Prison overcrowding in New York has meant that many first-time violent offenders are now placed on probation.[17]

The presumed difficulty in managing felony caseloads is further aggravated by the growing size of the caseloads. A National Institute of Justice study determined that, despite modest budgetary increases, 75 percent of all agencies could not fund staff increases that would keep pace with rising offender populations. The result is that each officer now sees more offenders as well as offenders with more serious criminal histories.[18]

On the street, officers attempt to adjust and to understand their duties in this rapidly changing corrections environment. One of the more controversial aspects of the officers' role is whether probation and parole officers should carry weapons.

THE CONTROVERSY OVER WEAPONS

Over the years, the issue of carrying weapons has become an example of the role conflict officers experience, and the debate has drawn individuals to decisive positions. Those opposed saw the arming of probation and parole officers as contradictory to a treatment-oriented relationship with clients. Those in favor believed that the increasing dangerousness of the client population and the need to enforce the conditions of supervision necessitated the carrying of a weapon.

In a national survey, Abadinsky found that most agencies authorized officers to make arrests but that most officers did not carry firearms.[19] Abadinsky argued in support of New York's policy not only to train and qualify its agents with weapons but to have officers wear their weapons while on duty. Studying this issue nationwide a few years later, Keve found that it was the agencies' philosophy that seemed to influence officers' beliefs about whether a gun was necessary.[20] He also found that agencies that were more oriented to law enforcement supported the carrying of weapons. These findings were confirmed in a later study by Sigler and McGraw in Alabama.[21] Because Alabama policy required firearms, the researchers wondered if officers with a treatment orientation would experience more role confusion than those who had a law-enforcement orientation. They did not find this to be so. Role conflict was not higher among those with a treatment orientation. However, officers who were law-enforcement oriented appeared to be more involved with weapons (private ownership, target practice) and had the least amount of role conflict.[22] In a 1986 survey of all 50 states, the Oklahoma Department of Corrections found that 48 percent of all probation and parole agencies allowed officers to carry a gun while on duty; however, only 24 percent found that their officers routinely carried a weapon.[23] However, official reports of the frequency of officers carrying weapons may be misleading. A department may be able to regulate and document the use of agency weapons, but it cannot realistically control the officer who chooses to carry a personally owned firearm.

Questioning parole officers in Texas one year later, researchers found that 78 percent favored legislation that would authorize probation and parole officers to carry guns as long as proper training and psychological screening were also conducted.[24] In a 1990 survey of a probation department in Southern California, it was found that 85 percent of the officers favored arming *at least some* staff. Furthermore, when the sample was divided between officers with adult caseloads and those with juvenile caseloads, no significant differences were noted. An important finding of this survey was that arming was not the primary concern for officer safety. Other issues, such as improved communications equipment, training in nonlethal defensive tactics, training in recognition of potentially violent confrontations, and improved procedures for field safety scored higher overall than the need to arm staff. This survey seemed to suggest that although probation officers feel the need to be armed and trained in the use of lethal force, they are more concerned with obtaining the skills and tools to avoid such confrontations.[25]

For many officers, an administration's decision to allow them to carry firearms is viewed as an indication of trust.[26] The decision to arm officers in a previously unarmed probation or parole system may pose some difficult issues for administrators to resolve. For example, in many agencies, staff were not originally selected with the intention that they would be carrying a deadly weapon. Some staff may not be psychologically prepared for this new responsibility. Is there a place for the traditional treatment-oriented officer who refuses to carry a weapon? If some but not all staff are armed, does this pose an increased threat to those without weapons because clients may assume all officers are armed? Will offenders react differently to officers once they suspect that all are armed?

Carrying a deadly weapon places greater responsibility on staff and may pose a significant increase in liability. Substantial resources must be dedicated to training employees in the use of weapons. In systems already short of funds, training dollars are severely limited. Arming may mean directing scarce resources away from treatment-oriented training toward weapons training. This in turn may result in a reduced level of staff competence in counseling and understanding the personal needs of offenders. Although the research may indicate that armed officers can still maintain a treatment-oriented posture, the perception of individual practitioners is that carrying a weapon makes a broader philosophical statement as to the primary role of the probation or parole officer.

Many community supervision officers and administrators are concerned that arming officers will alter their role, eliminating the side of the job in which they serve as social service counselors. There may be a way, however, to classify job assignments so that only those officers working with high-risk populations need to be armed. The principle of *job specialization* allows officers to alternate and emphasize the police or social worker aspects of their roles according to specific assignments. For example, an officer handling juvenile diversion can emphasize the social service aspects and has little need to be armed. In contrast, arming may be advisable for the intensive supervision officers handling adult felony drug offenders. In dealing with felony drug offenders, an officer may have to search the persons or residences of clients and ensure that clients do not have access to weapons or associations with other known felons. In such a scenario, the officer may also have to enforce a curfew or perform other surveillance functions. These actions may place the officer at higher risk of physical harm. As one officer explained, "The P.O. assigned to diversion needs a list of local resources and counseling agencies; the P.O. assigned felony surveillance needs a gun, a radio, a bulletproof vest, tear gas, a flashlight, training, backup, and a list of resource and counseling agencies."[27]

TYPOLOGIES OF THE FUTURE

According to recent writings, traditional officer typologies are grounded in the medical model, and their views of the offenders' responsibilities are limited. If one sees offenders as "sick," there may be a tendency to concentrate on understanding and forcibly changing their inappropriate behaviors. The medical model also focuses attention on a range of explanations for criminal actions that do not allow offenders to accept responsibility and initiate self-change.

One solution, claim Culbertson and Ellsworth, is to adopt a model of the officer as a "resource broker."[28] Community supervisors who see themselves as resource brokers are concerned with assessing offenders' needs and making sure that clients receive services from a variety of sources that will directly address those needs. Offenders can select and participate in rehabilitation programs that allow them to act as agents of their own change. This approach contrasts with the orientation of the medical model in which offenders are often the passive recipients of treatment over which they feel they have little control.

Another benefit of the resource advocate, or broker, model is that the probation or parole officer will not be inappropriately fulfilling a counseling role. As Dietrich suggests, most officers do not have the credentials to practice counseling.[29] In addition, they cannot provide the confidentiality or the true voluntariness that is part of the counseling profession. Also, agency administrators are now concerned over the possible legal liabilities that could arise from officers who try to provide therapeutic counseling for which they are not licensed.

A possible solution to this problem is to have the officers certified to assist in the therapeutic treatment of offenders. In Washington, DC, for example, Project Personal Promise has been developed to train parole officers as certified substance abuse counselors. Certification allows the client and supervisor to be involved together in the treatment, which is a critical component of the supervision experience. Such a relationship may solve the problem of poor communication between treatment providers and community supervision agencies. Under traditional contracted treatment services, supervising officers often do not have regular direct contact with treatment providers, and as a result they are often unaware of their clients' progress in rehabilitation programs. The initiation of programs such as Project Personal Promise may signal a return to the rehabilitation focus of the role of the officer. It also demonstrates that agency administrators understand the legal importance of certification and credentials for anyone providing professional services to offenders.

One version of the resource broker model is based on an education model of service, which focuses on skill deficiencies in the clients' lives. Rather than meeting one on one with clients, officers refer them to courses that may include adult living skills, parenting classes, and literacy development. Individual and group counseling is de-emphasized. In its place, a variety of skill development courses meet the needs of a larger group of clients at the same time. The specific courses selected can assist the clients in their community adjustment.

LEGAL LIABILITIES

One of the primary functions of law is to settle disputes between private as well as public entities. Because we live in a time when most citizens are familiar with the laws that protect their rights and freedoms, lawsuits are a familiar occurrence. State and local agencies, or individuals who work for them, may be held accountable for the decisions they make in processing offenders through the criminal justice system.

There are a number of circumstances under which probation and parole officers may be held liable for the actions they take in the course of their work. Normally, officers cannot be sued for the opinions they offer in presentence investigations or the recommendations they make to the judge. The presentence report is usually free from liability unless the information provided in it is deliberately falsified. Where community supervision workers become subject to liability is in administrative decision making, such as whether to ignore a violation or whether to place an offender in a certain job or program. The courts have recently held agencies liable in cases where they failed to provide adequate supervision or failed to act appropriately in response to a violation. The lack of financial resources or manpower does not provide an adequate defense against such liability.

Some of the areas for liability that officers face arise in relationships with clients. Other liabilities come from the officers' relationships with the public (third parties). Each of the areas of potential liability are worthy of elaboration.

First, an officer may commit an act that amounts to a crime under current state or federal criminal codes—for example, assault, extortion, or threatening a client or a member of a client's family. As a peace officer, a community supervision worker may have occasion to arrest a client for a violation of the conditions of release or for a new offense. Much like police officers during the course of an arrest, the officer is allowed by law to use "reasonable force." Arrests can be emotionally charged incidents with the potential for resistance and verbal confrontation between a client and an officer. An unprofessional officer may respond to such a situation by attempting to show the client "who is boss." A review of the incident may find that the use of force was with malice aforethought—that is, that the officer had an intent to do harm to the client for no purpose related to the arrest. In such cases, the department may discipline, suspend, or terminate the officer. The client may file a complaint and seek to have formal criminal charges brought forward by the district attorney. The district attorney can then use existing state law to charge the officer with a crime in the same way any other suspect would be charged.

An officer may also face criminal charges by engaging in some criminal act with the offender being a partner or accomplice. For example, many clients are involved in lucrative criminal enterprises and may present irresistible opportunities to the unscrupulous officer. An officer could allow a drug dealer to continue drug transactions in return for a percentage of the profits. An officer could solicit a client for an illegal purpose, such as an assault on a personal enemy or the purchase of a stolen television or car. In such cases, an officer could be charged with criminal violations of state law.

Second, an officer may be held personally responsible for some injury or damage to the client. In such cases, an officer may be sued in civil court. These cases are called *torts*, and the plaintiff bringing the suit will usually allege negligence or malpractice. According to Watkins, liability for negligence or malpractice requires the finding of three elements: (1) There is a duty owed by the professional to the plaintiff or the general public; (2) it must be shown that the professional failed to perform a duty according to a required standard of care; and (3) it must be shown that the injury or harm that resulted was caused by that breach of duty.[30]

At a California juvenile probation camp three youths fell through a thin layer of ice on a nearby lake and drowned. Although the district attorney determined that there was not enough evidence to prove beyond a reasonable doubt that the operators of the program were criminally responsible for the deaths, the parents could decide to file a civil suit. To prevail, the parents would have to show that the camp operators were negligent in providing care for the youths and that this negligence was the cause of their deaths.

Third, the officer may take some course of action that amounts to a violation of the client's civil rights—for example, inventing or misusing restrictions or conditions in a way designed to harass a client. An officer who excessively tests, searches, or enforces regulations against certain offenders because of personal biases against their sex, race, or religion may be violating their rights. This is especially important if those singled out for harsher treatment are of a particular ethnic or minority group. In such cases, the officer may be sued under the Federal Civil Rights Act, which prohibits persons acting on behalf of the government from violating a citizen's constitutionally protected rights. Such violation includes the use of demeaning language, particularly racial slurs or threats of unfair treatment based on sex or religious beliefs. In an effort to better protect the individual freedoms of their citizens, some states have also passed their own civil rights acts. Therefore, plaintiffs (the persons filing suit) may take a case to state court instead of federal court when they believe that their civil rights have been violated.

The Good Faith Defense

The most commonly used defense against a civil rights suit, whether it is filed in state or federal court, is the *good faith defense*. According to Del Carmen, to establish good faith it must be shown that:

- the officer was acting sincerely, believing that what he or she was doing was lawful,

AND

- the judge or jury must be convinced that this belief was reasonable.[31]

The second qualification is important because even if it appears that you believed the suspect was going to hurt you, the finding that the suspect was a 90-pound weakling with no weapon may convince others that your belief was not rational. A finding of good faith may be facilitated by the officer's showing that he or she was (1) following an agency manual or written policy, (2) acting on advice of legal counsel, (3) following a supervisor's direction, or (4) acting in accordance with some new law or court decision.[32]

Third Party Liability

An event that seems to attract much media attention occurs when an officer or a probation or parole agency is sued by a third party, or private citizen. These cases most commonly arise when an offender for whom the agency or agent is responsible commits a particularly heinous crime. The officer may incur liability to a third party when there is a legally recognized duty to issue a warning about a possible danger posed by the offender. For example, if an incarcerated offender has made threats against a former victim, it may be legally, as well as morally, necessary for the paroling authority to warn the victim before the offender's release.

The states have varied approaches to the issue of third party liability. Some states do not allow parole or probation officers to be sued for crimes committed by offenders. Other states limit the circumstances under which the officer may be held liable. The key to the officer's responsibility is whether he or she could have "reasonably foreseen" the prospective harm caused by the client-offender. One test for determining the reasonableness of a risk is to weigh the similarities that develop between an offender's past criminal history and some present opportunity. For example, is it reasonable to expect a risk when a convicted child molester applies for work in a daycare center or when an embezzler applies to a bank?

Liability may also arise when an officer enters into a special relationship with the third party. Examples are persuading an employer to hire an offender or arranging an offender's participation in some community project.[33] In most cases, the duty to warn a third party exists whether or not the third party has asked for the information.

Most third party liability cases argue that the officer should have warned the third party about a client's possible actions. In *Johnson* v.

State, Mrs. Johnson filed suit after she was attacked by a juvenile parolee who had been placed in foster care in her home. The plaintiff alleged that the officer did not tell her about the youth's violent history. The court found in favor of Mrs. Johnson, concluding that "the state owed a duty to inform Mrs. Johnson of any matter that its agents knew or should have known that might endanger the Johnson family. At a minimum these facts certainly would have included homicidal tendencies and a background of violence and cruelty, as well as the youth's criminal record" *(State* v. *Johnson at 248).*

In another case, the court found that an officer was liable, not because he failed to warn a third party about a dangerous client, but because the officer told the victim specifically that the offender loved her and would not hurt her. After the woman was killed by the parolee, her family brought suit, claiming that the officer gave the deceased advice that lulled her into a false sense of security that prevented her from protecting herself.

One of the best protections against liability claims is to have well-educated and well-trained employees who follow the standards and guidelines established by professional corrections organizations. In New York, concern about the number of successful civil suits against public agencies in cases of domestic violence has led officials to sponsor special training for probation and parole officers. The 15-hour training session that has been developed there focuses on intervention in spouse abuse and sexual abuse of children.[34]

Other states have adopted national standards for policies and operations to serve as a defense in suits alleging negligence or malpractice. The court would view a department's use of professional recommendations as evidence that it is acting in good faith. The American Medical Association (AMA) serves this function for the physician as the American Bar Association (ABA) does for the lawyer. The American Correctional Association (ACA) is now attempting to emerge as the national standard-setting organization for corrections. However, this association's standards do not carry the same weight as those of the legal and medical professions. The ACA's correctional standards are merely goals an agency may elect to achieve, but no penalty is assessed on agencies that choose to ignore the ACA standards and develop their own.

The American Correctional Association had a membership of 23,000 in 1990. This number included many probation and parole officers and administrators. In addition to setting standards and establishing a certification and accreditation process, the ACA holds an annual national conference, sponsors training programs, and publishes relevant literature. Another national organization that focuses more on the probation and parole practitioner is the American Probation and Parole Association (APPA). This organization holds an annual national conference and publishes a journal, *Perspectives.*

BOX 13–2

California Probation, Parole, and Correctional Association

The purpose of this Association shall be:

1. To promote a program of public information and education in order to build and maintain an enlightened public interest in the provision of effective preventive and correctional services.
2. To advance the science, processes and arts of correctional services and to further the professional standards and training of personnel.
3. To inspire and encourage in probation, parole and correctional practitioners the highest ethical concepts of individual and collective social responsibility and adherence to the Association's code of ethics.
4. To make studies and recommendations in matters pertaining to legislation.

Source: California Probation, Parole and Correctional Association (1989). *California Correctional News* July/August: 43(6).

Many states have established their own professional organizations for the promotion of community corrections. These organizations may work with local practitioners to establish ethics, values, and uniform guidelines for assuring quality services. Some members or paid lobbyists may work in the state capitol to influence the legislative process for the improvement of local programs.

A significant function of all professional associations is the sharing of knowledge. When a program is developed in one jurisdiction, its purpose, elements, and ultimate success or failure should be communicated to other practitioners. Through this process, the profession evolves. Creativity is shared and agencies learn from the mistakes and successes of one another. Without this process of communication, agencies operate in a vacuum and must rely on limited internal resources for solutions to problems and for new ideas.

THE CAREER LADDER IN COMMUNITY CORRECTIONS

In most states, the probation and parole departments are part of the Civil Service Employment System. The federal probation system is regulated by the Office of Personnel Management. Although there is variation between the states and the federal government as to the

BOX 13–3

Position Announcement for Youth Service Trainee/Youth Service Specialist I

Applications are accepted on a continual basis with the Youth Center, working directly with ad-judicated males ages 13–15. Qualifications: Must possess a High School diploma/GED and a valid driver's license. Preference given to applicants with a college degree in the correctional field and/or experience working with delinquent youth.

requirements for this type of work, most agencies require a college degree and many prefer a graduate degree. In addition to education, some departments require previous related work experience, evidence of writing skills, and indications that an applicant has the personal skills to handle clients, stress, and the pressures of a heavy caseload. Background checks and even drug testing may be part of the application process.

Probation and parole agencies commonly recruit many of their field officers from caseworkers and correctional officers in adult and juvenile institutions, thus providing the agency with a pool of personnel who are seasoned in dealing with the client population and who have already been evaluated by the agency for their career potential.

The journeyman position of probation and parole officer often includes more than one level. There may be a trainee level that allows new staff with minimal prior experience to acquire the knowledge and skills for the position. This level also provides for a trial period during which the new employee is evaluated for the ability and aptitude for the work. Soon the new officer is expected to carry a full workload of investigation or supervision responsibilities. As the officer gains experience, he or she may deal with specialized caseloads or duties, such as representing the agency in court, assisting in supervising a large office, or supervising high-risk offenders.

In most agencies, the first level of management is the unit supervisor, who is often responsible for six or more line officers. The responsibilities include on-the-job training and supervising the quantity and quality of the work performed. In small agencies, supervisors may carry a caseload or be responsible for higher-level management functions. In large agencies, some supervisors may be assigned to staff support responsibilities such as training or volunteer coordination.

The middle manager in probation or parole agencies is responsible for the implementation of department policy. This person must assure that the program services are delivered and that goals are achieved through the oversight of several first-line supervisors and responsibility

BOX 13–4

Ruth Rushen

A Great Career that Began in Community Corrections

Ruth Rushen began her career as deputy probation officer in LA County in 1956. One year later she became the Training Deputy Probation Officer. In 1960 she was appointed Supervising Deputy Probation officer and supervised a staff that provided treatment and care for non-delinquent children in an institution. Ruth was soon promoted to the position of Director of a special probation project that helped seriously deinquent children remain in the community. The project was called RODEO (Reduction of Delinquency Through Expansion of Opportunity). The next promotion Ms. Rushen received placed her in charge of the planning and implementation of an area probation office in a Model Neighborhood program in the Los Angeles area. There she coordinated a staff of 113. Ruth Rushen continued to rise through the ranks to become division chief of the Southeast division of California which served 16,000 probationers. In 1977 she was appointed to the State Board of Corrections which coordinated programs for the Youth Authority as well as the Department of Corrections, set standards for training of corrections personnel and investigated charges of misconduct against correctional administrators. She was also Vice-Chairperson of the California Board of Prison Terms which had the responsibility for fixing terms and granting paroles to state prisoners. This board also acts as an advisory pardon board to the Governor. In 1980 Ms. Rushen was appointed Director of the California Department of Corrections. During her term she was responsible for all of the department programming including 12 institutions, 19 adult camps, and the statewide parole system. The operation utilized an annual budget of $489,000,000 and a staff of 10,000. The California system that she led was the largest correctional agency in the nation. She was also the first black female to hold this post. After retiring from DOC she became special assistant to the California Attorney General on corrections and liaison to minority communities. Today she actively lectures, and trains personnel in corrections.

for specialized programs such as work furloughs or electronic monitoring. The geographic area of control for the midlevel manager is generally much broader than for the unit supervisor. The midlevel manager may also be responsible for coordination between the investigating and supervising functions of the agency.

The chief administrator of a parole or probation agency may be called chief probation officer, director of parole, or any number of other titles. The chief administrator is the agency's leader, the individual responsible for all operations and policies, and is generally appointed either by the courts or by local or state government administration. As a result, the position may be tied to the political party in power, and incumbents may change regularly. It is not uncommon that a probation administrator must be responsible to multiple higher authorities, such as judges or state administrative officers. Some states have a director of probation.

In large jurisdictions, executive-level managers may be placed between the chief administrator and the midlevel managers. Their duties may include personnel and finance operations. Given all the layers of authority within the probation system, it is obvious that there are many areas for conflict. It is not surprising that agency administrators leave or are replaced every few years.

In addition to variations in qualifications for applicants, the states vary considerably in salaries for community corrections workers. The 1989 volume of *Vital Statistics In Corrections* published by the American Correctional Association showed that the highest-paid probation officers earned $41,640 and the lowest paid earned $11,000. Salaries for state directors of probation ranged from $33,000 to $98,000.[35] Some states have considerable difficulty attracting quality professionals when they offer salaries that are relatively low.

Examining the occupational interests of law-enforcement majors in a midwestern university, Golden found that women were more interested in juvenile probation officer jobs than were men.[36] Overall, male college students were more interested in law enforcement than in parole or probation work. Ironically, it is not uncommon for males later to transfer from law enforcement into probation and parole for what they consider to be more desirable positions.

ISSUES OF GENDER

Community corrections has done considerably better than law enforcement in the recruitment and hiring of a workforce that is balanced in gender. In many agencies, the ratio between male and female employees approaches 50–50. However, the predominantly male client population (as high as 95 percent) creates problems for both the female officer and the community corrections administrator. The growing emphasis on surveillance and enforcement in probation and parole has aggravated problems of women working with a predominantly male population. The problems range from the differences in physical strength between female officers and their male clients to issues of privacy in the enforcement of certain conditions of probation.

Probation and parole officers working high-risk felony caseloads may frequently make arrests for violations. Inadequate training of officers in self-defense techniques and the assessment of danger may leave the female officer at greater risk of injury in an arrest. Although many male–female teams have been created for enforcement visits, male officers may become resentful if the female officer is not able to offer physical assistance in a confrontational situation.

The issue of a client's right to privacy has been raised in discussions of proper procedures for urine testing, which is done to detect the use of illicit drugs. A positive finding is a common cause of revocation.

Probationers and parolees may be creative in their efforts to deceive officers and cheat on the tests, sometimes devising an apparatus or method to provide a "clean" urine sample when they have been using drugs. Only by observing the urine leaving the body of the client and entering the sterile container can the officer be sure that the sample is uncompromised. This procedure poses obvious problems for the female officer. One remedy is to construct testing rooms with restricted access to assure that only the client will be in the room during testing. If so, it wouldn't be necessary to have an officer actually observe the sample as it is taken. This would eliminate male officer resentment for having most of the bathroom duty while the majority of drug testing clients, males, submit urine tests.

It is important that any community corrections agency develop viable procedures to ensure that officers of both sexes can perform their duties. Failure to do so may result in disproportionate workloads and reduced morale caused by resentment between the sexes.

The Perception of Women as Difficult Clients

For years, female offenders have been processed through a criminal justice system dominated by authorities with little understanding of their needs, although significant changes in the treatment of women by the system over the past century have been made. Women remain a small percentage of the offenders processed. Estimates are that males represent 90 to 95 percent of probation and parole caseloads, with the result that fewer services have been available to women. In addition, women have been subjected to discrimination and stereotyping concerning their roles and abilities. As with other groups with special needs, unless the concerns of women clients are addressed and unless the biases of those charged with their supervision are exposed and dealt with, there is little hope that alternative sentencing will be successful.

Several research studies have found that women are more likely to be revoked from parole and probation for technical reasons than for new offenses.[37] The use of technical grounds often implies that officer discretion is operating and that the officer is using personal interpretations of the client's behavior in making the decision to seek revocation. Norland and Mann found that when men violated for technical reasons those charges were likely to be absconding or failure to work. In the case of female clients revoked for technical reasons, the charges were more often "absconding" and "improper associates." The difficulty with charges of "improper associates" is that it is usually a moralistic judgment call. Interviews with officers led Norland and Mann to conclude that women consume more of the officers' time and seek more emotional support. It was hypothesized that the officers found this disruptive to their schedules. In addition:

> Women's problems under supervision tend to be of a different nature from the problems men acknowledge. Women's problems of adjustment are believed by agents to be beyond their interest and competence. . . . These contingencies make it convenient to "sacrifice" women probationers. As a result, these females tend to be perceived as troublesome cases.[38]

What Norland and Mann and several other researchers have pointed out is that officers see their relationships with clients as necessarily brief and shallow. Understandably, officers claim they cannot take the responsibility for solving all the clients' problems. Although officers may profess that they wish the clients to develop independent skills, they may also be reflecting their own inability to relate to and assist those who require more personal support.

There is no doubt that the kind of relationship that develops between a community corrections agent and clients is critical to the success of any program. In interviewing probationers, Gibbs classified their concerns about supervision.[39] Probationers expressed the need for their supervisor to be flexible, supportive, and willing to provide assistance. Although respondents voiced an appreciation for all officer's providing a measure of control, they still wanted their autonomy and privacy respected. Gibbs found that less than 15 percent considered their relationship with the officer to be negative. Three-fourths of clients who reported a beneficial aspect of probation said it was their client–officer relationship that was positive.[40]

Recognizing the importance of the relationship between the officer and the client, some jurisdictions have experimented with matching personalities in the assignment of caseloads. This was tried extensively in California in the early 1970s, using a variety of assessment tools to determine compatible personality types. Although experiments with matching met with some success, they required more flexibility and staffing than growing caseloads and diminishing fiscal resources could afford.

COMMUNITY SUPERVISION OFFICERS AS VICTIMS

In addition to having to provide clients with a more personal relationship than is required by most public service jobs, probation and parole workers are subject to many high-risk situations, including enforcing court orders, filing violation reports, having clients arrested, and making home visits to violent or high-risk clients. Besides the clients, family members, friends, or even strangers in the vicinity may represent a threat to the visiting officer's safety. In addition, the neighborhoods that clients live in are often areas of high crime. Potential confrontations or attacks may lurk in the parking lots, apartment hallways, and streets of these areas. The actual and perceived risks that officers face produce stress and anxiety.

In a study of Pennsylvania probation and parole officers who directly supervised caseloads, Parsonage and Bushey[41] found that 50 percent had been victimized by assault, threats, or intimidation at least once during their careers—the same percentage found by Longmire and Wilson in a study of Texas parole officers.[42] However, another Texas study of parole officers found that officers were more likely to be attacked by dogs (28 percent) than either threatened (21 percent) or assaulted (6 percent) by a person.

In a study of probation and parole officers in Virginia, it was determined that 39 percent had been verbally threatened by a client and 7 percent had been assaulted. Because of apprehension about dealing with AIDS clients, officers also expressed concerns over the safety of routinely handling urine samples. A similar study in New York found that 55 percent of those surveyed had been involved in a threatening incident in the past five years. Thirty-two percent had experienced some kind of victimization over the last year. The most common forms of victimization included harassment, intimidation, physical threats, and property loss.[43]

Studying the characteristics of confrontations between officers and clients, Sieh found that far more incidents took place in the community or during field visits than in the agency office.[44] In another study, Renzema found that confrontations most often arose over arrests.[45] Rural areas had higher rates of confrontations than more densely populated areas did. The researcher also found that officers who carried weapons and who had prior police or corrections experience were more likely to experience confrontations. In Parsonage and Bushey's study, a majority of the victimizations took place in a context outside of the normal, expected visit, meaning that for at least one party the contact was unplanned. The authors also found that in 50 percent of the incidents no weapon was used. In the aftermath of the incidents, 18 percent of the officers reported they now experienced fears on the job. Many of the victims also complained of a reduced sense of trust in their clients, a lack of self-confidence, and problems with personal and family relationships. One of every four officers surveyed carried a gun, and those who had been victimized were two and one-half times more likely to carry a gun than those who had not.[46]

Confrontations between officers and clients often occur outside of the context of routine visits, as in chance meetings in the neighborhoods the officer frequents in the line of duty. Incidents may arise when the officer runs into an ex-client with a grudge or the friends or relatives of a client who has been revoked and sent to prison. Fear of confrontations may reduce the effectiveness of officers when performing their control functions. Even treatment-oriented agents may become reluctant to respond to clients' emergency needs at night in certain areas.

A study of probation and parole officer safety by the National Institute of Corrections found that agencies had adopted a number of protective measures besides carrying firearms. Some officers wore protective body armor; some had had extensive training in self-defense. A number of probation officers in New York and California carry radios so that they can call for backup if necessary.[47] Many agencies have employed security guards and installed metal detectors and silent alarms in their offices. Still other agencies have controlled access to the offices from the waiting rooms.[48] Safety measures for the offices have resulted from findings that clerical and staff workers are also at risk for some kinds of victimization.

Several veteran officers have expressed dismay at the way community corrections has set itself up defensively against its clients. Still others attribute the security measures to changes in society over time—to a larger, more violent, and unpredictable population that includes not only offenders but their families, neighbors, and friends. Young offenders are today regarded by officers as being particularly aggressive and volatile. Larger proportions of young offenders, as well as mentally ill and drug and alcohol abusers, creates a very threatening caseload. In a study of parole officers in Texas, Eisenberg found that 77 percent of the officers felt that the work had become more dangerous.[49]

Because the work is by nature, hazardous, community corrections personnel find it difficult to get the public to consider them as "victims" when confrontations occur. As with the police, the public often believes that the dangerous aspects of the job are those the officer should "expect" to encounter in the normal performance of duties.

Over the years, the clients that an officer has dealt with may become angry and bitter, not just with the agent but with the criminal justice system as a whole. Long periods of working with unappreciative clients who may not succeed on the outside may lead even the most optimistic supervisor to job dissatisfaction.

OFFICER BURNOUT

The term *burnout* became popular during the mid-1970s in business and in psychological literature. It was used to describe a feeling of emotional exhaustion that was related to a high-stress work environment. In burnout the worker experiences a negative shift in attitude about the job and a sense of personal devaluation. According to Watts, jobs that promote burnout are those in which:

- Employees feel they have little control over their work.
- Rewards are infrequent.
- Stress is high.
- Shift work is involved.
- Employees are isolated.
- Family and social life are interfered with.[50]

For community corrections officers, burnout may result from all these factors, particularly those related to client contact and from pressures within the organizational bureaucracy. Many employees begin the job dedicated to assisting clients, yet become discouraged by the tremendous amount of paperwork, reports, and bureaucratic red tape. Communications problems with supervisors and restrictions on decision making may also frustrate motivated employees.

Results of a national survey of probation and parole directors showed that 50 to 68 percent of those officers questioned believed that salaries were too low to attract and retain qualified professionals. They also believed that caseloads had increased in greater proportion than had staff positions and that the clients appeared to be more difficult to manage than ever before.[51] Because of the intense emotional energy of teens, youth populations have been characterized as being extremely stressful to manage. Many juvenile supervisors are on 24-hour schedules of responding to crises, which makes the salary seem especially low. All these factors are considered to be related to staff burnout and job dissatisfaction.

Client failures may also contribute to staff burnout. As one officer explained, "You hear on the news at night 'Parolee arrested in Brooklyn' and the first thing that goes through your head is, 'I hope he's not mine.' Somewhere out there, there's always the case that's ready to bite you.[52]

Preventing Burnout and Increasing Job Satisfaction

In Alabama, severe prison crowding had prompted state officials to release carefully selected inmates in an early-release program that used correctional officers from the prison as community supervisors. Ironically, the deinstitutionalized officers reported experiencing higher job satisfaction from the positive interaction of helping former inmates. A comparison study found lower levels of burnout and stress in these newly assigned community supervisors than in a sample of regular prison guards and a sample of experienced probation and parole officers. However, the newly designated officers in the experiment had also been employed in the corrections field for less time than had regular probation and parole officers, did significantly less paperwork, and had more hours of client contact, all of which could help to explain the findings of the study.[53] To ensure that the results were not just temporary effects resulting from the newness of the job and the relief of working

Community supervision workers are often overwhelmed with heavy caseloads and demanding schedules. (© *Maureen Fennelli/Comstock*)

outside the institution, the researchers measured the attitudes of the officers-turned-community-supervisors a year later. They did not find any reduction in the levels of job satisfaction, thus vindicating the thesis that the improved job attitudes were a persistent result.

The reality of the probation and parole officer job, however, is long hours and very heavy caseloads. The effect of listening to and attempting to resolve the problems of the many clients may reduce an officer's empathy and stamina. One suggestion for easing the load of the typical agency is the use of volunteers and paraprofessionals.

THE USE OF VOLUNTEERS

Although the use of volunteers in the full range of community corrections programs is fairly typical, it is more controversial in traditional probation and parole structures. The fact that state and local probation and parole programs have become professionalized to the point of restricting and often excluding the use of volunteers is ironic given that the first probation and parole programs in the country were started and operated exclusively by volunteers.

Some critics argue that the great social distance between the average offender (lower socioeconomic class, undereducated, minority member) and the average professional correctional worker (predominantly white, middle class, college educated) leads to problems. Communication diffi-culties and value orientations may make effective working relationships difficult.

There are a number of advantages in using volunteers and paraprofes-sionals in community corrections. First, there is a large surplus labor pool to draw from and train for these positions. Retired persons, college students doing internships, and interested citizens can all be important groups with skills to offer. The use of such services at low or no cost is economically efficient given the shortages of personnel in most depart-ments.

In a study of volunteers used in the Missouri Division of Probation and Parole, Lucas found that an average of 108 volunteers a month worked an average of 1012 hours a month.[54] This workload approxi-mated the job totals of six full-time employees. When the salaries and benefits of the employees needed to do the work of the volunteers were caluculated, Lucas concluded that the department saved approximately $145,539 a year.

Despite the financial incentives, volunteer programs are not used to their full potential. One of the reasons for their underutilization is that professionals in the field of probation and parole are resistant to the use of volunteers. The less experienced and untrained volunteer may be con-sidered a nuisance or a burden to train and supervise, or may even be seen as a threat to the officer's "territory." Another reason for the infre-quent use of volunteers may be that the philosophical shift toward a punitive emphasis results in less need for the helper-oriented roles that volunteers usually fill. Some program administrators have expressed the fear that some volunteers may be disguised religious reformers who use their association to pressure clients with sermons and exhortations. Others are wary of volunteers who are drawn to criminals by their curi-osity about deviance. Kratcoski found that agencies suspect that per-sons attracted to criminal populations have emotional or psychological problems that make them unfit for such work.[55] In addition, cutbacks in funding may mean that the monies to train volunteers are simply not available. Training is necessary because agencies are legally responsible for the actions of volunteers. It is this potential liability that often keeps organizations from using volunteers.

Almost half of the 35 jurisdictions surveyed in 1983 reported that they did not have any formal qualification procedures for their volunteers. Only five of the jurisdictions conducted any official training. Although many of these agencies referred to their volunteers as paraprofessionals, this term is vague and may mean any qualification from a high school diploma to a college degree.[56]

The range of jobs performed by volunteers is extensive. Some are used to assist in the collection of information for the presentence investiga-tion. Because the forms are standardized and many of the contacts with offender families and employers are conducted by phone, it is a job that

Volunteers can play an important role in assisting the ex-offender in reintegrating into the community. Helping with family or job related needs or just talking about problems can be a valuable service to the client or supervision. (© *Kopstein/ Monkmeyer Press Photos*)

can easily be delegated to trained volunteers. Volunteers may also do clerical work, help officers in filling out reports, and assist in courtroom appearances.

According to Courlander and Tracey, volunteers or as they refer to them, *third party supervisors,* can be an integral part of a probation program.[57] These authors see three distinct roles for third party supervision within the community corrections setting. The first is as a *compliance monitor,* a role that most closely resembles the control function of the supervising officer. The monitor may "track the offender's attendance and level of performance at the workplace or at a program (e.g., substance abuse testing, counseling, community service). He or she may also report on the probationer's progress (for example, the number of hours of community service completed to date) to either the probation officer or to the sentencing judge."[58] The second role for the third party supervisor is as an *advocate.* In this capacity, volunteers can provide support and encouragement as they assist clients with daily problems such as transportation, scheduling, job hunting, and intervention in family crises. The third role of the volunteer is as a *mediator.* A mediator acts as a go-between or negotiator when difficulties arise between the client and the probation department, a particular community service organization, or a local social service agency.

In choosing a volunteer or third party supervisor, Courlander and Tracey suggest that the person be familiar with the criminal justice system and have practical skills in counseling and psychology. They also recommend that clients and volunteers be specifically matched according to personality, background, and the amount of time that can be devoted to the relationship.[59]

THE USE OF EX-OFFENDERS IN COMMUNITY CORRECTIONS

The use of ex-offenders in community corrections supervision has been even more controversial than has the use of other paraprofessionals or volunteers. Some of the reluctance to use ex-offenders as employees or volunteers stems from a fear that these workers would overidentify with clients and, consequently, be too lenient or permissive with them. Also along this line is the fear that such volunteers would be hesitant to discipline inmates when needed. Many professionals are concerned that ex-offender volunteers or employees could be pressured into doing favors for the offenders that go beyond the limits of the relationship. Although serious problems are not common, there have been several well-publicized incidents of ex-offender's becoming involved in illegal activities with clients.

Conversely, some of the advantages of using ex-offenders is that many of them make good counselors. They have credibility, having overcome some of the same problems the clients have, and they can identify and relate to offenders' troubles. Ex-offenders also know how the correctional system works, can give practical advice, and gain the confidence of the clients. Many agencies that have used ex-offenders report that they are highly motivated and loyal employees, dedicated to work and empathetic with those they assist.

RESERVE PROBATION OFFICERS

A variation on the volunteer concept is the *reserve probation officer* program. This concept follows the same guidelines that have been used in police and sheriff's operations for many years. More than volunteers, reserve officers are frequently recruited from colleges and universities. Participants include students interested in pursuing a career in community corrections. As deputized personnel, these reserves get realistic experience as field officers working beside full-time staff in the course of their duties. The reserve program represents a greater investment on the part of the hosting agency.

Reserve officers must have a higher degree of training than volunteers, but they also provide a greater return to the department. Many reserves will become full-time employees. Thus, the initial investment by the agency will result in a better trained "new" officer. Reserves may also be recruited from the professional community. Counselors, therapists, and others with an interest in human services may participate. From these ranks, the department can enrich the quality of services offered to clients.

THE FUTURE OF THE COMMUNITY SUPERVISION ROLE

Many criminal justice theorists have proposed changes in the role of the community corrections worker. Some, like Barkdull, have called for more control, more direct surveillance of the offender.[60] There have been proposals to create a job that would provide such a surveillance service. This position would require less education and experience than traditional probation and parole officer roles because the job holder would simply be checking up on the offender and reporting to the supervising officer.

A similar proposal offered by John Conrad is for probation to be divided into two separate operations.[61] One section would provide the supervision function and could be performed by the courts or the police. The counseling and vocational services would be delegated to a public or private agency or a number of private agencies for a variety of programs.

A different approach to the proposals for specialized functions has been initiated in Georgia. Under the intensive supervision model there, one probation officer acts as a case manager and is assisted by another officer whose primary responsibility is surveillance and control. This plan allows the case manager to serve as a court liaison and rehabilitative programmer.

Dividing the responsibilities is a controversial topic in community supervision today. Some researchers, like John Whitehead, have argued that to take away the personal assistance interaction between officers and their clients would be demoralizing to the staff. In a 1984 survey, he found that more than one-half of the officers felt that they were frequently very effective in dealing with the personal problems of their probationers.[62] Even more of those questioned felt that they often created a relaxed environment with their clients. In addition, one-third admitted that they often felt "exhilarated" after working effectively with their clients. This sense of job satisfaction, Whitehead warns, would be jeopardized if the personal assistance and counseling aspects of the jobs were reduced.[63]

Finally, an approach adopted by the Federal Probation Service and several states is called the *team approach*. Under the federal Community Resource Management Team model, each officer specializes in providing a certain type of service, such as employment referrals, drug counseling, or educational counseling. The various team members act as resource brokers for the services available in the community. Since each client is served by a team of professionals, officials believe they will be more effective in addressing the wide range of offenders' needs. Each offender will be able to benefit from the broader range of expertise and skills that the group possesses. Because there are several officers to a team, the effects of personality conflicts between one particular officer and the client can also be minimized. The team approach has the advantage of all the team's members being familiar with each client's case. Therefore, if one officer is sick, on vacation, or otherwise unavailable, someone else will be capable of providing the appropriate services. It is assumed that in case planning and management there will be more discussion and balance in the decisions reached by a team. In this system, clients are evaluated by teams and reports are submitted from the group as a whole, thus reducing the risk of individual biases or difficulties in personalities adversely affecting the clients' community supervision experience. This approach also emphasizes the reintegration aspects of the supervision period.

SUMMARY

The role of the community supervisor covers a wide spectrum of responsibilities and services. Officers may perceive their roles differently depending on their professional and personal values and attitudes. The role may be carried out in a variety of styles ranging from more conservative to more liberal interpretations of duty.

Many years were spent building the professional framework of the role of the probation and parole officer. Formal organizations and associations of corrections workers have been established on national, state, and regional levels. Their meetings provide a format for the exchange of ideas and information.

Another aspect of the professionalism of community corrections employees has been the development of standards for procedures and operations within the community corrections system. Techniques or policies that control discretionary decision making shield officer's from claims that clients are treated in a biased or discriminatory manner.

Today, corrections professionals receive increasing recognition and prestige within the criminal justice system. However, public awareness of their responsibilities is only the beginning of the plan for career development. Overall, much work needs to be done to improve the work environment of the individual officer. Issues that have been raised over the past few years have illustrated the fears and conflicts that officers face daily on the job. The moral and ethical dilemmas of serving the government, the community, and the offenders make daily decision making problematic. Concerns for personal safety and legal responsibility make routine activities complex and their consequences significant.

CASES

State v. *Johnson* 69 Cal. 2d 782, 447 P. 2d 352, 73 Cal.Rptr 240 (1968). p. 248.

Cable v. *Chabez-Salido* (102 S. Ct. 735 1982).

KEY TERMS

burnout
federal community resource
   management team model
good-faith defense
noninterference
officer typologies

Project Personal Promise
reserve probation officer
resource broker
third party liability
third party supervisors
tort

DISCUSSION QUESTIONS

1. Should probation or parole officers carry weapons? Why or why not?
2. As a community corrections officer, what strategies could you use to ensure that an offender is not assuming a passive role in the supervision process? What techniques could you use to ensure that offenders see themselves as being responsible for their rehabilitation and future behavior?
3. Discuss the nature and significance of the role conflict that faces the community supervision worker.
4. How do you prevent burnout among the staff of probation and parole officers you supervise?
5. Why might some departments or individual officers resist the use of a team approach such as the federal community resource management team model? What steps could be taken to minimize employees' negative perceptions of this model?

END NOTES

1. Bartlett, Kay (1986). Parole officers play schizophrenic role. Baton Rouge, LA: *Sunday Advocate,* 23 March, 3D.

2. Glaser, Daniel (1964). *The effectiveness of a prison and parole system.* New York: Bobbs-Merrill, p. 430.

3. Ohlin, L., H. Piven, and D. M. Pappenfort (1956). Major dilemmas of the social worker in probation and parole. *NPPA Journal.* 2(3):215.

4. Culbertson, R., and T. Ellsworth (1985). Treatment innovations in probation and parole, in *Probation, Parole and Community Correction: A Reader,* ed. Lawrence Travis, pp. 13, 127–149. Prospect Heights, IL: Waveland Press, p. 134.

5. Bartlett, Kay (1986). Supra note 1.

6. Duffee, David (1984). Models of probation supervision, in *Probation and Justice,* ed. P. McAnany, D. Thomson and D. Fogel. Cambridge, MA: Oelgeschlager, Gunn, and Hain.

7. Glaser, Daniel (1964). Supra note 2.

8. Rosecrance, John (1987). A typology of presentence probation investigators. *International Journal of Offender Therapy and Comparative Criminology* 31(2):163–177.

9. Ibid.

10. McCleary, Richard (1978). *Dangerous men.* Beverly Hills: Sage, p. 86.

11. Ibid.

12. Wiggenhorn, Al (1991). Unpublished research presented to the Criminal Justice Advisory Council, California State Univ., San Bernardino. Inyo County Parole, California.

13. Lawrence, Richard, and Shelva Johnson (1990). Effects of the Minnesota sentencing guidelines on probation agents. *Journal of Crime and Justice* 13:77–104.

14. Harris, Patricia, Todd Clear, and S. C. Baird (1989). Have community supervision officers changed their attitudes toward their work? *Justice Quarterly* 6(2):233–246.

15. Guynes, Randall (1988). *Difficult clients, large caseloads plague probation, parole agencies.* Washington, DC: National Institute of Justice, p. 1.

16. Bureau of Criminal Statistics (1988). *Adult Felony Arrests in California, 1987.* Sacramento: Bureau of Criminal Statistics, July.

17. Sieh, Edward (1990). Probation officers' perception of danger: The role of the symbolic assailant. Paper presented at the annual meeting of the American Society of Criminology, Baltimore.

18. National Institute of Justice sponsored study. Prepared by Randall Guynes. Supra note 15.

19. Abadinsky, Howard (1975). Should parole officers make arrests and carry firearms? Microfiche No. 01964, Rockville, MD: National Criminal Justice Reference Service.

20. Keve, P. W. (1979). No farewell to arms. *Crime and Delinquency* 25:425.

21. Sigler, Robert, and Bridgett McGraw (1984). Adult probation and parole officers: Influence of their weapons, role perceptions and role conflict. *Criminal Justice Review* 9(1):28–32.

22. Ibid.

23. Jones, Justin, and Carol Robinson (1989). Keeping the piece: Probation and parole officers' right to bear arms. *Corrections Today* 51(1):88.

24. Longmire, Dennis, and Charles Wilson (1987). *Summary report: Parole division survey.* Huntsville: Texas Corrections Association.

25. Krause, Wesley (1990). San Bernardino County Probation Office Memo. December 21, 1990.

26. Jones, Justin, and Carol Robinson (1989). Supra note 23, p. 88.

27. Bodhaine, Vicki (1991). Cop vs. social worker debate is passe. *American Probation and Parole Association Perspectives* 15(2), 7–9.

28. Culbertson, Robert, and Thomas Ellsworth (1985). Treatment innovations in probation and parole, in *Probation, Parole and Community Corrections: A Reader*, ed. Lawrence Travis. Prospect Heights, IL: Waveland Press.

29. Dietrich, S. G. (1979). The probation officer as therapist. *Federal Probation* 43(2):14–19.

30. Watkins, John (1989). Probation and parole malpractice in a noninstitutional setting: A contemporary analysis. *Federal Probation* 53(3):29–34.

31. Del Carmen, Rolando (1985). Legal issues and liabilities in community corrections, in *Probation, Parole and Community Corrections*, ed. Lawrence Travis, p. 63. Prospect Heights, IL: Waveland Press.

32. Ibid., p. 65.

33. Ibid., p. 122.

34. New York State (1988). *Domestic violence: A curriculum for probation and parole personnel*. Albany: Governor's Commission on Domestic Violence.

35. Travisono, A. (1989). Improve pay levels now. *On the Line* 12(4):1.

36. Golden, Kathryn (1982). Women in criminal justice: Occupational interests. *Journal of Criminal Justice* 10(2):147–152.

37. Norland, S., and P. J. Mann (1984). Being troublesome: Women on probation. *Criminal Justice and Behavior* 11(1):115–135; Spencer, C. and J. Berocochea (1972). Recidivism among women parolees: A long term survey, in F. Adler and R. Simon (eds.) *The Criminology of Deviant Women*. Boston: Houghton, Mifflin; DeVault, B. (1965). Women parolees. *Crime and Delinquency* 11:272–282.

38. Norland, S., and P. J. Mann (1984). Supra note 37, p. 127.

39. Gibbs, John (1982). Inside supervision: A thematic analysis of interviews with probationers. *Federal Probation* 46(4):40–46.

40. Gibbs, John (1985). Clients' views of community corrections, *Probation, Parole, and Community Corrections: A Reader*, ed. Lawrence Travis, pp. 97–108. Prospect Heights, IL: Waveland Press.

41. Parsonage, William, and W. C. Bushey (1987). The victimization of probation and parole workers in the line of duty: An exploratory study. *Criminal Justice Policy Review* 2(4):372–391.

42. Longmire, D., and Charles Wilson (1987). Supra note 24.

43. Ely, Richard (1989). Report on the safety concerns of probation and alternatives to incarceration staff in New York State. Albany: Bureau of Policy, Planning and Information, New York Division of Probation and Correctional Alternatives (draft report), p. 2.

44. Sieh, Edward (1990). Supra note 17.

45. Renzema, Mark (1987). *The dangers of probation work: A progress report on an exploratory survey*. Kutztown, PA: Kutztown Univ.

46. Parsonage, William, and W. C. Bushey (1987). Supra note 41, p. 387.

47. Sieh, Edward (1990). Supra note 17, p. 13.

48. Parsonage, William (1990). *Worker safety in probation and parole*. Washington, DC: National Institute of Corrections, p. 387.

49. Eisenberg, Michael (1989). Parole officer safety and security survey. Austin: Texas Board of Pardons and Paroles, p. 5.

50. Watts, Patti (1990). Are your employees burnout proof? *Personnel* 67(9):12–14.

51. Guynes, Randall (1988). Supra note 15, p. 8.

52. Bartlett, Kay (1986). Parole officers play schizophrenic role. *Sunday Advocate*, Baton Rouge, LA, 23 March:3D.

53. Lindquist, Charles, and John Whitehead (1986). Correctional officers as parole officers: An examination of a community supervision sanction. *Criminal Justice and Behavior*, 13(2):197–222.

54. Lucas, Wayne (1988). Cost savings from volunteer services: A research note. *Journal of Offender Counseling, Services & Rehabilitatin* 12(2):203–207.

55. Kratcoski, Peter (1982). Volunteers in corrections: Do they make a meaningful contribution? *Federal Probation* 46(2):30–35.

56. Latessa, Edward, Lawrence Travis, and Harry Allen (1983). Volunteers and paraprofessionals in parole: Current practices. *Journal of Offender Counseling, Services & Rehabilitation* 8(1–2):91–106.

57. Courlander, Michael, and David Tracey (1991). Third party supervision bolsters probation programs. *The National Prison Project Journal* 61(1):16–17.

58. Ibid.

59. Ibid.

60. Barkdull, Walter (1976). Probation: Call it control—and mean it. *Federal Probation* 40(4):3–8.

61. Conrad, John (1982). Can corrections be rehabilitated? *Federal Probation* 46(2):3–8.

62. Whitehead, John (1984). Probation mission reform: Implications for the forgotten actor—The probation officer. *Criminal Justice Review* 9(1):15–21.

63. Ibid.

14

Managing the Client with Special Needs

Humanitarianism should be regarded as a fundamental obligation to mankind, no matter where it leads. It is particularly important that we be steadfast in our allegiance to this principle in criminal policy, a prejudice-riddled area in which vengeful feelings are so easily aroused. The treatment of a criminal should not be designed according to what appears to be worthy of the individual in question. It should be worthy of society itself.

— Herman Kling, Swedish Minister of Justice[1]

PURPOSE

This chapter identifies special needs clients and specific offense clients, and it explores the kinds of assistance that they might be given while on community supervision. Myths and stereotypes about the limitations and abilities of these special needs groups are contrasted with the realities of the problems they face. Special needs groups include the mentally ill, the handicapped, the mentally retarded, older offenders, clients with AIDS, and clients with histories of substance abuse.

We discuss the relationship between crime and the abuse of drugs and alcohol. The rising number of offenders testing positive upon arrest has led officials to look for new ways to address substance abuse and crime. Some approaches are punitive, whereas others hope to change the behavior of offenders through treatment. The type of treatment approach used often depends on the particular background and training of program administrators and their views on alcohol and drug use. The programs also differ in length, intensity, and approaches to treating addiction. Research on the success of the various methods is also described. Some of the more controversial treatment programs involve the administration of drugs such as antibuse and methadone to combat substance abuse.

OBJECTIVES

After completing this chapter you should be able to do the following:

1. Identify several special needs groups and the kinds of problems they face while on supervision.

2. Explain why special needs offenders may be viewed by supervising officers as troublesome and why these clients may be found in violation of their contracts more often than others.

3. Describe the philosophy behind the development of specific offense programming and whether such efforts appear to be successful.

4. Discuss the different theories of addiction and how they may influence treatment strategies.

5. Explain why the use of methadone and antibuse are controversial treatment strategies.

401

INTRODUCTION

A profile of persons processed through the criminal justice system reflects a variety of special needs groups. In fact, persons with mental and physical handicaps, substance abuse histories, and AIDS are overrepresented in the corrections population.[2] In response, the system has attempted not only to identify these persons and their needs but to provide programming and services for them. Mandatory education programs have been implemented, physical access to living areas has been improved, and interpreters are more commonly provided. Overall, the general public is more aware of the social and economic hardships faced by persons with functional difficulties.

Although the delivery of public services in the past two decades to special needs persons has been greatly improved and reformed, there are still many areas in need of enhancement. Special needs offenders are often forgotten or assigned low priority when services and benefits are being distributed. The double stigma of being older or handicapped, in addition to being an offender, sometimes creates barriers that the client may perceive as insurmountable.

We begin by looking at the special needs of a variety of groups of people. Through this process, we can develop a better appreciation for the way community supervisors create opportunities for their clients and help them in overcoming many obstacles.

THE MENTALLY ILL CLIENT

Greg was born with his intestines outside his body, which resulted in surgery. As an infant, he was malnourished and oversedated. He was given street drugs by his mother, and he almost drowned in a pool where he was left unsupervised at age three. At 16 years of age, Greg has Schlatter's disease of the knees, breathing problems, and herpes II. He is hyperactive and has been on strong medications such as Clonidine, Ritalin, and Mellaril in the past. His parents divorced, and his father has remarried twice since then. Greg's parents have not been seen in years, although his father, who has a long history of drug dealing and abusiveness, is believed to be incarcerated. Greg lives with his grandmother. The charges against him include possession of live ammunition, assault, battery, and petty theft. His social worker claims that he is out of control, threatening to "cut up" and sexually assault family members, including three half-sisters. He is preoccupied with the "devil," steals from neighbors, and does not attend school. Greg recounts being involved with a satanic church with his mother during a period when she was frequently using drugs and allowing him to "stay drunk." He claims that his mother and her husband or boyfriend sexually molested him. At age

11 he was turned over to social services. He has been in and out of group homes as well as juvenile hall and the psychiatric unit of the county hospital. Reports show that although his IQ is normal, he is nearly illiterate. He appears to be significantly depressed, aggressive, and likely to engage in self-damaging behaviors. Psychiatric tests show conduct, personality, and development disorders.

Although Greg may seem like just a "bad kid," his problems are deep-rooted and resistant to most conventional interventions. Besides the delinquent label he has received from the criminal justice system, Greg is mentally ill.

The social stigma of mental illness has two areas of impact. First, it demonstrates the difficulty people have relating to or interacting with the mentally ill. Second, it reflects the likelihood of a low self-esteem in the person afflicted.

The community corrections worker has the opportunity to serve as a source of support for the mentally ill. Corrections professionals also aid persons with emotional problems in developing skills for independent and productive community living. Finding adequate housing and employment and managing a household budget are just some of the projects with which the mentally ill client may need help.

The social stigmas that still attach to mental illness make employment difficult for the person with a history of psychiatric problems. Many occupations list potential job stress as a justification for finding persons with a history of mental illness "unsuitable" for employment.

The number of mentally ill offenders under community supervision is difficult to assess. Estimates vary according to the particular definition of mental illness used. Definitions also differ about who is able to determine that someone is mentally ill. For example, are people mentally ill if they say so or if they exhibit behaviors that criminal justice agents believe are characteristic of the mentally ill? Must clients be evaluated and diagnosed by a certified clinical professional before they can be categorized as mentally ill?

Another definitional dilemma is the degree of impairment that is needed to qualify someone as being mentally ill. For example, lines of distinction can be drawn between the functional neurotic and the more severely impaired psychotic. Definitions of mental illness may also differentiate the time frame of the illness. At what point does someone stop being mentally ill or become cured? These questions point out the problematic nature of official labels of status. It is easy to see how the number of people in a given category can be inflated or deflated by changing the official definition of what constitutes membership.

The most readily available data on the number of mentally ill could be drawn from prison, jail, or arrest data. Official reports estimate that anywhere from 10 to 15 percent of the men and women in jails in the United States are suffering from serious mental illness, or about 100,000 persons.[3]

In a study of the jail in a large eastern city, a group of researchers analyzed all admissions using (1) psychiatric diagnoses, (2) psychological testing, and (3) the arrestees' own self-reports. They found that by using at least one of these three methods, 89 percent of the sample showed an emotional disorder. Two or more of the methods were positive for 62 percent of the sample. Thirty-four percent could be classified as emotionally disturbed according to all three methods. Eleven percent of the sample was found to be in need of immediate psychiatric hospitalization because of the seriousness of their conditions.[4] A 1987 study of juveniles removed from their homes in one Southern California county revealed that 22 percent were classified as having an emotional disorder.[5]

There are, however, several reasons why data on juveniles removed from their homes and adults arrested or in jail may produce rates of emotional disorder higher than found among those under community supervision. First, it is probable that the mentally ill may be perceived as being of high risk. Consequently, they are less likely to gain pretrial release, which would make their presence in jail estimates higher. Second, because the mentally ill may appear to be a greater risk, judges may be more likely to sentence them to incarceration or to remove them from their homes. Thus, the number of mentally ill in prison, jail, and juvenile facilities may be higher than in the population under community supervision. Third, these offenders may do poorly on parole interviews and as a result, serve more of their sentence in prison. If the mentally ill completely discharge their sentences while incarcerated, it is unlikely that they will spend any time in community supervision.

In 1990 the State of Washington recognized the need to provide transitional services to mentally ill offenders being released from prison. It was estimated that 30 percent of the offender population had mental health problems.[6] To ease the community reintegration of these special needs offenders, the state founded Lincoln Park House. Candidates for this combination prerelease, halfway-house type of program suffer from major thought disorders such as schizophrenia. Those with personality or behavioral disorders may also be included. All those selected for participation must be in a partial remission from the illness and taking all required medications. Residents of Lincoln Park House move through graduated phases of activity. Counseling, recreation activities, and preparation for vocational placements are all part of the program curricula. To obtain jobs in the most commonly available areas, residents are required to have current identification and medical certification for food handling. They must also demonstrate progress in working with their parole officers in developing a work release plan and a follow-up parole plan.[7]

In treatment settings like Lincoln Park House, one finds both state correctional staff and privately contracted service professionals. All who work with the mentally ill must be able to read behavioral cues that show if a client is in distress.[8] Staff should also be able to assess the offenders' environment for factors that add to stress and to look for resources that might lessen that stress. Through training and experience the staff worker can develop a strategy for matching the troubled client with the necessary community resources.

MENTALLY RETARDED AND LEARNING-DISABLED CLIENTS

In a survey of New York state probation departments, officers reported that their greatest difficulties in working with disabled clients were with those who were learning-disabled or mentally retarded.[9] In most jurisdictions, persons are classified as mentally retarded or developmentally disabled if their test scores on intelligence scales are below 70. The inability to comprehend consequences of certain patterns of behavior or to set and follow through on goals creates serious problems.

In the Southern California study mentioned earlier, 22 percent of the juveniles removed from their homes had some type of learning disability. Five percent of the youths had an IQ test score of less than 80.[10] Although such a score is slightly above the level of "retarded," the youths were considered to have serious learning and functional impairments.

Karl lives with his mother and four siblings. His mother receives $449 every two weeks that supports her children and her live-in boyfriend. Karl relates that his father (whereabouts unknown) is often in trouble and is "a bum." This 14-year-old is in a special education class but admits that it is more fun to cause trouble, skip school, and break laws. He is used by older kids to sell drugs. He is 5 feet, 8 inches tall but weighs only 100 pounds. According to a probation report:

> Karl is impulsive, irresponsible, untruthful and at risk to exploitation. His limited social skills do not allow him to use good judgment and he is unable to perceive the real motives of others. His interest in gaining the acceptance and approval of older delinquent peers has led to problems in school, at home and in the community. He is naive and vulnerable in the streets and is using delinquency as a way to deal with external stress, and chronic family and personal problems.

Like Karl, other mentally retarded persons may find themselves duped into committing crimes for rewards and approval. With less skill in moral reasoning, the mentally handicapped person may be an easy target for the streetwise cons who use them for illegal activities.

As is well known among the public, the mentally retarded, learning-disabled, and hearing-impaired have more difficulty finding and maintaining employment than do normal people. Although the physically handicapped are considered to be a high insurance risk to employers and consequently face that barrier to employment, one of the biggest problems faced by the mentally retarded is often simply how to dress appropriately for job interviews.

Because of the way some community supervision programs are structured, the mentally retarded and mentally ill may not be eligible for participation, particularly in restitution programs.[11] This is unfortunate because these programs often place clients directly in jobs.

Parole and probation offices interviewed expressed a need for legal advocates for the mentally retarded client to ensure that individuals' rights are protected in seeking work. Local mental health and human service agencies, vocational rehabilitation centers, and sheltered workshops are important contact resources for officers working with these special needs clients. These offenders may also require more help in understanding the rules and procedures they must follow during supervision.

In the survey of New York probation officers by Wertlieb and Greenberg, it was determined that new staff needed training in understanding the causes of disabilities, the relationship between disabilities and deviant behavior, and how to recognize the signs and symptoms of disabilities. Further training was needed in how to devise strategies for helping the disabled client achieve skills according to their potential.[12]

In Lancaster County, Pennsylvania, a special program has been developed that combines adult probation with mental health and mental retardation services. Officers in the program carry caseloads of 45 mentally retarded offenders. Although these probationers are classified as mildly retarded, they are seen as extremely "streetwise." The specially trained officers help these offenders understand the seriousness of their status and responsibilities. Realistic goals are developed for each client, and work and living skills are emphasized.[13]

In Tacoma, Washington, mentally retarded offenders may be released from prison to Rap House, where they receive transition services to aid in their adjustment back into the community. In operation since 1980, the program offers counseling, life skills training, and vocational assistance to its residents. Since 1989, 22 participants have successfully completed the program. Unlike programs with other offender populations, Rap House reaccepts those clients who have failed. Of the 35 who did not complete the program since 1989, 18 have returned to try again. Rap House may also serve as a temporary stabilization center for those who experience problems after release from the program.[14]

SUBSTANCE-ABUSING OFFENDERS

According to national statistics, more than half of prison inmates reported that they were under the influence of drugs and/or alcohol at the time of their offense. Thirty-five percent were under the influence of drugs when they committed their crime. Forty-three percent admitted using drugs daily in the month before the offense occurred.[15] Recognizing that prison populations do not necessarily have the same characteristics as the populations given community sentences, we can use arrest statistics for more appropriate comparisons.

BOX 14–1

William was a 21-year-old undocumented alien from El Salvador who pled guilty to burglarizing an elderly couple's home. After drinking 20 beers he broke into a house, carrying a 7-inch kitchen knife and filled his pockets with jewelry and money. He then passed out in a drunken stupor next to the couple's bed. He received a year in jail, one year of house arrest, five years probation, and an order to attend Alcoholics Anonymous meetings.

Source: San Bernardino Sun, August 3, 1990:A10.

Substance Abuse and Crime

Drug abuse has consistently been linked to a high rate of criminal activity.[16] In a national study conducted in 13 major cities, from 44 to 87 percent of those arrested were using illegal drugs. The Bureau of Justice Statistics reports from a national survey that more than half of all convicted jail inmates admit that they were under the influence of drugs or alcohol at the time of their offense.[17] The statistics also imply that the percentage of those offenders testing positive at arrest have increased. In a Washington, DC, survey, 56 percent of the arrestees sampled tested positive in 1984 compared to 68 percent in 1987 and 80 percent in 1989.[18] According to the National Institute of Justice, female arrestees are more likely than males to test positive for drugs.[19]

In 1991, the National Institute of Justice reported that a majority of persons charged with serious property offenses and most kinds of violent crime tested positive for illegal drugs at the time of their arrest. Research also indicates that the most serious and frequent offenders are those most heavily involved with drugs.[20]

In addition to apparent increases in the number of drug abusers, there have also been increases in the criminalization and prosecution of drug use. National concern over the drug problem and its effects have led to increased arrests of pregnant women and young mothers caught using drugs. Although traditionally buying, selling, and possession of drugs have been criminal acts, the courts have not allowed a person to be punished for simply being an addict. However, the growing number of young children born addicted to drugs and alcohol has inspired prosecutors to apply child endangerment and child abuse charges against pregnant women who test positive for drugs. Some states have even passed "fetal endangerment" statutes to cover this specific situation. The states have responded to criticism about the intrusiveness of this practice by pointing out the tremendous financial burden that addicted children such as "crack babies" place on the medical and social service resources of a community.

A study of 600 juveniles in out-of-home placement in San Bernardino County found two-thirds were using alcohol prior to arrest and 4 percent were classified as alcohol dependent. Three-quarters of the youths were drug users, and 13 percent were classified as drug addicted or dependent.[21]

One of the most ambitious studies of drug use ever undertaken was initiated by the National Institute of Justice in 23 cities nationwide. The Drug Use Forecasting (DUF) Program monitored persons who volunteered to participate anonymously when they were arrested, gathered information on their history of drug use, and conducted urine testing.

Figures 14.1 and 14.2 and Table 14–1 give some of the findings of this project, including drug use among juveniles and estimated amounts of money spent on drugs. Ironically, 59 percent of the males and 64 percent of the females who denied spending money on drugs tested positive.[22]

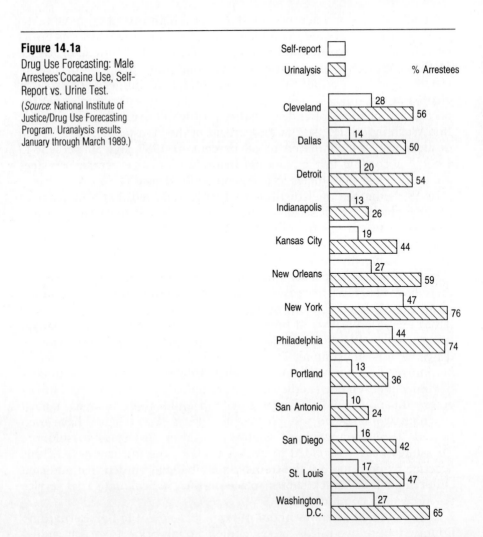

Figure 14.1a

Drug Use Forecasting: Male Arrestees'Cocaine Use, Self-Report vs. Urine Test.

(*Source*: National Institute of Justice/Drug Use Forecasting Program. Uranalysis results January through March 1989.)

City	% POSITIVE ANY DRUG	RANGE OF % POSITIVE LOW	DATE	HIGH	DATE	2 + DRUGS	COCAINE	MARIJUANA	AMPHETAMINES	OPIATES	PCP
Males											
San Diego	85	66	6/87	85	1/89	48	42	44	35	18	6
New York	80	78	10/88	90	6/88	30	76	13	**	17	3
Philadelphia	79	79	8/88	82	11/88	33	74	24	**	10	3
Wash., D.C.	72	Data not available				36	65	13	0	14	22
Detroit	68	66	6/88	69	10/88	17	54	24	0	7	0
Dallas	67	57	12/88	72	6/88	29	50	34	4	7	2
New Orleans	66	58	1/88	75	10/88	29	59	26	0	6	6
Cleveland	66	66	2/89	68	11/88	22	56	22	0	4	3
St. Louis	64	56	10/88	64	1/89	26	47	24	1	4	9
Kansas City	60	54	11/88	60	2/89	15	44	22	2	2	2
Portland	54	54	1/89	76	8/88	21	36	27	7	9	0
San Antonio	51	51	2/89	63	8/88	23	24	28	6	14	0
Indianapolis	50	50	2/89	60	2/87	14	26	30	0	2	**
Females											
Wash., D.C.	87	Data not available				46	73	10	0	34	24
San Diego	83	78	8/88	87	12/87	54	41	36	45	19	2
Philadelphia	80	77	1/89	82	8/88	24	74	12	0	12	**
New York	78	76	10/88	83	2/88	28	72	4	2	16	2
Kansas City	73	70	11/88	73	2/89	24	61	21	2	6	3
Portland	69	69	1/89	82	8/88	33	50	22	11	26	0
New Orleans	65	46	11/87	65	1/89	30	56	22	0	6	6
St. Louis	53	45	11/88	53	1/89	25	39	13	0	4	20
Indianapolis	47	52	6/88	61	6/87	15	30	20	0	6	0
San Antonio	45	45	2/89	51	8/88	25	24	16	3	20	1
Dallas	44	44	3/89	71	6/88	18	34	14	7	5	0

*Positive urinalysis, January through March 1989
**Less than 1%

Figure 14.1b

Drug Use by All Arrestees.

(*Source*: National Institute of Justice/Drug Use Forecasting Program)

Table 14–1 Arrestees' Self-Reported Expenditures on Drugs*

City		N	% Reporting Spending Money Weekly For Their Drug Use	Range of Money	Median
Birmingham	M	169	59	$ 1–4,200	$ 60
	F	59	44	5–3,500	200
Chicago	M	194	66	2–9,000	100
Cleveland	M	175	51	1–2,000	50
	F	50	60	20–2,800	100
Dallas	M	168	55	3–5,000	50
	F	85	47	2–3,500	100
Denver	M	211	45	2–4,000	25
	F	66	35	4–2,100	50
Detroit	M	188	61	1–4,000	50
	F	95	77	5–3,500	150
Ft. Lauderdale	M	177	47	5–9,000	75
	F	88	42	2–3,500	100
Houston	M	189	49	1–3,000	80
	F	80	38	2–2,800	125
Indianapolis	M	205	43	2–3,000	29
	F	86	29	2–1,800	35
Kansas City	M	180	51	1–5,000	40
	F	82	61	2–5,000	100
Los Angeles	M	217	64	5–2,100	102.50
	F	120	59	1–1,750	150
Manhattan	M	212	74	3–3,500	200
	F	84	69	3–3,000	200
New Orleans	M	175	50	2–4,000	100
	F	63	33	10–2,000	100
Philadelphia	M	223	70	2–2,000	50
	F	97	54	5–1,600	112.50
Phoenix	M	213	54	4–3,000	50
	F		45	5–7,000	200
Portland	M	181	44	2–1,000	50
	F	85	59	5–7,500	85
St. Louis	M	190	35	1–5,000	50
	F	47	45	20–4,000	80
San Antonio	M	106	50	3–5,600	30
	F	42	17**	—	—
San Diego	M	218	60	5–2,100	100
	F	86	35	3–7,500	100
San Jose	M	181	41	1–4,000	60
	F	78	53	19–2,450	80
Washington, D.C.	M	120	62	10–5,000	100
	F	88	72	5–2,500	100

Source: National Institute of Justice/Drug Use Forecasting Program

* Data based on voluntary self–reports. January through March 1990

** Less than 20 cases

M = Males F = Females

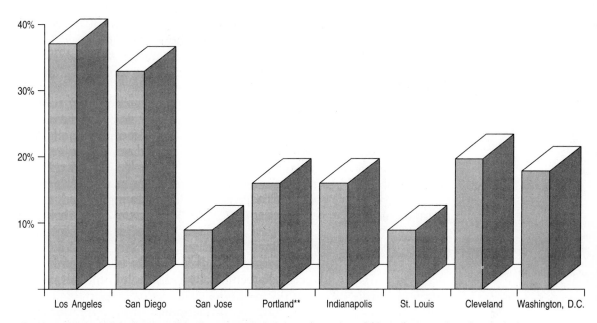

*Positive urinalysis, April through June 1990. Drugs tested for include cocaine, opiates, PCP, marijuana, amphetamines, methadone, methaqualone, benzodiazepines, barbiturates, and propoxyphene

**Site does not test for methadone, methaqualone, and propoxyphene

Note: Eight DUF sites collect data from juvenile arrestees/detainees

Figure 14.2

Drug Use among Juvenile Arrestees/Detainees.

(*Source*: National Institute of Justice/Drug Use Forecasting Program.)

Identification of Drug Abusing Offenders

In a study of 160 probationers, Wish, Cuadrado, and Martorava found that two-thirds were using illicit drugs.[23] The researchers also concluded that even though urinalysis testing was routinely ordered to verify the presence of drugs, probationers still grossly underreported their use of illicit substances when interviewed.

A 1989 study in Massachusetts reported that at least 67 percent of probationers were identified as having a substance abuse problem. It also appeared that these probationers were more educationally disadvantaged and had more trouble finding jobs. Furthermore, they had more family problems and more difficulty with social support from their peer networks.[24]

The determination that a client needs drug or alcohol treatment is often made early in the justice system process, as in the presentence investigation report. By using interviews, specimen tests, or standardized questionnaires, the professional making the assessment tries to determine the level of involvement the offender has in each of the abused substances. Measures of "how much" and "how often" are used to distinguish among the categories of substance use, abuse, and dependence. The determination that the offender requires treatment for substance abuse may be made by a probation or parole officer. It may also be made by a clinician or counselor at a treatment center to which the client is referred for diagnosis. Such an examination may also be part of a prison or detention prerelease evaluation. As mentioned earlier, drug or alcohol treatment is often a condition of probation, parole, or even juvenile diversion.

When refraining from the use of drugs or alcohol is part of the probation or parole agreement, periodic testing is often required to ensure that the conditions are being met.

DUI and Enforcement Programs

Alcohol use may be detected with compact breathalyzer units in the probation or parole office, or during home visits via using portable testing units. One Texas judge has ordered probationers to have interlocks installed in their cars. These devices are connected to the transmission and require the driver to breathe into a detector before the engine will engage. The car will not start if the person has a specified amount of alcohol on his or her breath. With each interlock device the judge issues, he requires a bumper sticker to be placed on the offender's car that says the driver is on probation for DUI.[25]

In Hamilton County, Ohio, a follow-up study was done on DUI offenders who had interlock devices in their automobiles. The ability of these offenders to avoid further arrests was compared with a similar sample of DUI offenders who had their drivers' licenses suspended. Results indicated that those who had their license suspended were almost three times as likely to be rearrested for driving under the influence within the sanction period than the persons with interlock devices. Over a 30-month period, the failure rate of those with suspended licenses was 9.8 percent, whereas the failure rate of the group with interlock devices was 3.4 percent. An additional 16 percent of the group with suspended licenses were arrested for driving while suspended (DWS) or driving without a license (DWL). These offenses would not have occurred had the offenders been put under an interlock device rather than having their licenses taken away.[26]

In defending the cost of the interlock program, one manufacturer argued that offenders can pay the expenses out of the money saved by not drinking. The Guardian Company, a manufacturer, obtained data from a Houston Probation Department study on alcohol consumption patterns.[27] On the basis of these data, the company asserted that the average DWI offender spent $12.50 a day, or $375 a month, on alcohol—

roughly 28 percent of the person's income. This meant that a 15 percent reduction in daily alcohol consumption would finance the interlock program. Another 15 percent reduction in consumption would finance the bond, court costs, and fines associated with the offense. The cost of an attorney would be met by another 13 percent reduction in drinking. An additional 20 percent reduction would cover the increased insurance cost on the car. The theory was that a 63 percent reduction in alcohol consumption by the typical DWI offender would cover most of the major expenses involved in the DWI offense and interlock program.

Punishment versus Treatment

Some approaches to drug- and alcohol-related crimes focus on determining an appropriate punishment. These retributive, or "just deserts," strategies also seek to prevent the person from committing more of the same offenses. However, they are not treatment oriented. For example, in California the law allows police to confiscate the driver's license of any motorist who fails or refuses to take a sobriety test. Drivers may appeal the seizure, but if the appeal fails, even first-time offenders lose their driving privileges for four months. In a 10-month period, the state confiscated more than 224,000 licenses.[28]

The forfeiture of privileges such as a driver's license is a law-enforcement strategy aimed at the legal problem—drunk driving—and not at the person's behavioral problem—drinking. Some experts argue that meaningful strategies of criminal justice intervention must address the underlying behavior problems of the offender. Only in this way can rehabilitation occur that will control crime in a more economic and humanistic manner.

Treatment for Drug and Alcohol Abuse

The needs of the drug- and alcohol-abusing client in treatment are many. Some may have acquired serious criminal records related to substance abuse, including the use of weapons and violence in committing crimes. Many of these clients have incurred serious health problems that may range from vitamin deficiencies to AIDS. Substance abuse may have caused or worsened health problems that are compounded by poor eating and sleeping patterns. And, persons with a history of substance abuse may have permanently damaged relationships with family and friends and may suffer from poverty, loneliness, depression, and isolation.

The Structure of Treatment Programs
Programs for the treatment of drug and alcohol problems sometimes separate substances and treat them individually. Other programs may combine all substances in the form of *addictions therapy*.

Traditionally, self-help programs like Alcoholics Anonymous (AA) have limited their scope to alcohol abuse. Although AA has been instrumental in the recovery of alcoholics from a variety of social and economic backgrounds, they all share the same entrance requirement: They must enter the program of their own volition. Some experts claim that persons compelled to go to AA as a condition of their community supervision contracts lack the true self-help spirit of AA.

Many of the AA techniques have come to be used in other problem areas—overeating, smoking, and using narcotics. The treatment programs to which clients are directed may be privately run or they may be operated by state or local government agencies. Some treatment programs may service both offenders and individuals who are self-referred.

According to Lyman and Potter,[29] most drug treatment programs fall into the following five categories:

1. Detoxification programs. Mainly inpatient programs that focus primarily on ending the person's physical addiction.
2. Chemical dependency units. Primarily privately operated inpatient programs that run three to four weeks and employ a highly controlled setting with intensive testing and counseling. These programs are fairly expensive.
3. Outpatient clinics. Counseling and treatment take place on a schedule of regular appointments that allow the client to live at home and go to work.
4. Methadone maintenance programs. Use of a prescribed medicine that blocks the craving for heroin and eliminates the pain of withdrawal.
5. Residential therapeutic communities. The *therapeutic community* is defined as any rigid, highly structured, residential, self-help, drug-free treatment plan. Like Alcoholics Anonymous, addicts see themselves as forever vulnerable. Participants rely on mutual support, punishment, rewards, confession, and catharsis for recovery.[30] Although some therapeutic communities distrust and exclude mental health professionals, others have been established by professionals, particularly in prisons and halfway houses. Well-known therapeutic communities include Synanon, Daytop Village, Odyssey House, and Stay'n Out.[31] According to Lyman and Potter, the therapeutic community treatment process may last up to 18 months at a cost of $1200 to $2500 a month.[32] The success rate for those who complete the program is high. However, four out of five who undertake the treatment either drop out or are thrown out.

Treatment programs for substance abuse vary in the length of time spent in treatment (for example, one month to one year). They also vary in the intensity of services (live-in versus once a week for hourly sessions). In one large California county, a newspaper reported that there

Therapeutic communities build close relationships between members that will be used to promote change and encourage personal awareness in each participant. (© *Mimi Forsyth/Monkmeyer Press Photos*)

were 180 agencies that offered drug and alcohol treatment.[33] The formats range from "free wheeling" to highly structured and cost from zero to $900 a day. A few of the programs were self-help, and almost half were outpatient. About 95 percent of the patients relied on insurance to cover the treatment for substance abuse, and many of the participants were recidivists.

Theories of Drug and Alcohol Abuse

An important difference among treatment programs is their underlying theory of what causes addiction and what is needed to overcome or treat it and who is responsible for intervention. When developing a treatment plan for each client, the supervising officer must make many decisions about the appropriateness of a certain drug or alcohol treatment program. The decision must include whether the program's structure and philosophy are suitable for each potential client. The particular theory of addiction that a program ascribes to serves as a basis for its approach to client problems. These theories are discussed in the following paragraphs.

1. *Disease theories* are based on the medical model, which views addiction as a sickness that must be cured. For the patients to be well, they must gain physical control over their illness. Proponents of this approach focus on withdrawal of the substance from the system. Clients are viewed as patients and treated in a medical setting by medical professionals. Many experts believe that patients have a genetic predisposition or tolerance for addictive substances and that family history is an important area of examination.

Researchers who link alcoholism to a disease have suggested such conditions as serotonin deficiencies, limbic system malfunctions, and interactions with neurochemical brain functions as causative agents. Disease theorists have also examined genetic predispositions to alcoholism.[34]

2. *Progression theories* concentrate on the process of becoming addicted. Proponents maintain that casual use with less serious substances leads to greater use of more dangerous drugs. The use of some substances, such as beer and marijuana, are seen as initiating rites from which the experimenter progresses in degrees. Users experience a pleasurable high that they seek to increase. These experiences then lead to a dependency identified as addiction.

3. *Sociological theories* are explanations for drug use that are aimed at the structure of society in general and the specific social environment of the substance abuser. Variables of importance in these theories are socioeconomic factors such as poverty and lack of opportunity, and demographic factors such as age, race, education, and neighborhood. Treatment may focus on changing the socioeconomic opportunities available to the offenders, changing their environment, and perhaps also changing the peers with whom the clients socialize.

4. *Psychological theories* address the personal needs and emotional traits of each client. Weaknesses in self-esteem and adjustment problems from childhood are studied in personality analysis. Some theories may be behavioral in orientation. That is, they view addicts as receiving some type of psychological reward or gratification from drug or alcohol use. Attempts are made to alter addicts' behavior through the modification of their interpretation of stimulus and response. Other psychological theories try to uncover subconscious anxieties related to the need for drugs or alcohol.

5. *Learning theories* combine the influence of individuals' personalities and their social environment in contributing to addiction. From this perspective, substance abuse is a learned behavior that fulfills not only personal needs but some group relations as well. Peer influence is considered to be instrumental, particularly in terms of gangs or status pressures. To addicts, these learned behaviors are successful in what seem to be important spheres. The substance abusers concentrate on them even to the point of being unsuccessful in many other aspects of their lives. The methods of taking drugs or the drinking behaviors are learned, as well as the rituals and accessories that develop around the drug or alcohol subculture.

The variety of views on addiction help us understand what the client on community supervision faces. Health professionals, criminal justice officials, family, and friends will all have different perceptions of alcohol and drug abuse and how the offender should deal with it. Take, for example, a 1988 Gallup Poll. People were asked about the nature of alcoholism. Sixty percent classified alcoholism as an illness or disease, 31 percent said it was a mental or psychological problem, 39 percent said it was a lack of willpower or moral weakness.[35]

An important concept recognized by many strategies for treating alcoholism is the effects of intergenerational alcohol abuse in the alcoholic's family. According to many research studies, children of alcoholics are more likely to have been in abusive or neglectful family settings. Children of alcoholics are also more likely to develop problems with alcohol than are children of nonalcoholics.[36] Many of the characteristics of the adult children of alcoholics are similar to those of delinquents and offenders. These traits include (1) having to guess what is normal behavior, (2) having difficulty completing projects, (3) frequently telling lies, (4) having difficulty in maintaining intimate relationships, (5) overreacting to circumstances beyond their control, and (6) displaying impulsivity and poor judgment.[37] Anyone counseling offenders from alcohol-abusing families must be able to see these behaviors as the complex symptoms of a dysfunctional family background.

Antabuse

A result of a "disease" approach to alcohol abuse is the development of medical treatments. One of the continuingly controversial aspects of drug and alcohol abuse is the use of other drugs to control it. *Antabuse* is a medication often given to offenders who have chosen this drug therapy as an alternative to incarceration. According to Jacobs, "Antabuse does not cure alcohol craving or dependence but causes unpleasant physiological effects, such as respiratory difficulty, nausea, vomiting and sweating, when alcohol is ingested while the drug is active. After taking antabuse the patient's desire to drink is dulled by the thought of getting sick.[38]

The administration of antabuse programs requires that someone continually watch the offender to ensure that doses of the medication are taken, otherwise the drug is not effective. Another problem is that it is often difficult to morally justify the use of measures that are so physically invasive. To some people, the use of drugs to combat the abuse of substances is a contradiction in methods and principles.

Treatment Results

The reported success and failures of treatment programs can be misleading. To some experts, simply showing up for treatment or testing is a success. As Visher notes, persons being monitored who do not show up for drug testing are more likely to engage in misconduct than those who show up regardless of whether those tested are positive or negative.[39]

To determine the value of research findings on drug treatment, one must carefully examine the criteria for admission into programs and the criteria for successful completion. Therapeutic communities usually have such strict screening processes that only those most likely to succeed are admitted. Also, the criteria used to measure success is often only continuous post-treatment employment. Therefore, when therapeutic communities hire their graduates to stay on and work in the programs, administrators can claim success.[40]

Several studies have linked substance abuse treatment while incarcerated with later success on parole.[41] This is not surprising given that many of the failures on parole are related to drug use. For example, in California, more than 50 percent of all parole revocations are for drug use violations.

In Kentucky high-risk offenders placed in a substance abuse program had significantly lower rates of prison confinement following treatment than did members of a comparison group. However, as the report explained, the program graduates had higher rates of misdemeanors than did the comparison group.[42]

Drug and alcohol treatment within institutional settings may not be as practical as treatment on parole. A critical part of the recovery process is the ability to abstain from drinking and taking drugs when they are readily available. Researchers Ed Latessa and Larry Travis studied the use of intensive supervision with high-risk alcoholics.[43] They found that their subjects performed similarly to a control group of less serious alcoholics on regular probation. Under this program, officers carried half the normal caseload (40 clients), and offenders in the treatment program had three times as many contacts with their probation officers. Perhaps as a result of the increased surveillance, these intensively supervised alcoholics were cited for violations more often than were the non-ISP groups.

Some experts argue, however, that there need to be changes in definitions of success and failure when it comes to treatment of substance abuse. Rather than revoking a client after the first positive urinalysis or drinking episode, many experts believe that a variety of strategies should be employed to continue community supervision. It may be said that our definition of success needs to be readjusted. Rather than an unrealistic, "no use at all," we should define success as "diminished use" and only "occasional, minor relapses."

Gradual progress is seen as a more accurate reflection of the nature of addiction and as more conducive to long-term success in treatment. A gradual decrease in the amount and type of drugs used or alcohol consumed, as well as a reduction in drug-related crime, can be viewed as improvement.

Gradual Withdrawal or Drug Substitution: Methadone

A historically significant attempt to implement gradual withdrawal from drug addiction is the use of *methadone maintenance*. In a program of methadone maintenance, patients are supplied with daily doses of methadone that eliminates painful withdrawal from heroin. It may also produce a cross-tolerance with heroin that prevents abusers from experiencing a "high" from further heroin use. As Abadinsky explained:

> For certain persons in the heroin-abusing population, methadone maintenance appears to be quite beneficial. In can act as a crutch for persons motivated to give up heroin. The programs also attracts addicts seeking a chemical cure, although the provision of counseling and job assistance may be the actual "cure."[44]

Not all methadone maintenance programs place the same demands on clients or provide additional counseling services. Most programs start with a period of inpatient care and progress to where the client stops by for oral doses of the synthetic morphine substitute.

In a study comparing three methadone maintenance programs, Anglin found that, "of the two flexible programs, the one with the more adaptive policy on client interactions retained 77 percent of admissions after two years, while the program with the more punitive orientation retained only 42 percent. The third program, with the most inflexible policies (and also a mean dosage level half that of the other two) retained only about 23 percent of admissions after two years."[45] What Anglin advocates is a model that allows treatment staff more discretion:

> Authority to deal with minor program infractions should reside with the staff members directly responsible for supervising the addict. Intermittent drug use that does not seriously disrupt the individual's program plan, as well as other program infractions, should be dealt with on an individual basis in the context of the addict's overall adjustment.[46]

Studies of Substance Abusing Populations

An examination of the effectiveness of drug treatment programs include many studies conducted on general drug abusing samples, not necessarily convicted offenders or community supervision clients. Much can be learned from this research for it has not been determined that the more generic population of substance abusers is significantly different from the community supervised group. In fact, it is likely that community supervision clients will be mandated into treatment programs alongside others who register for those same programs voluntarily. At any one time, most treatment programs, except perhaps the most expensive, will be made up of a cross section of court-ordered and self-referred substance abusers.

An ambitious study followed up on 10,000 drug users who received treatment during 1979, 1980, and 1981. Hubbard and his colleagues interviewed persons who sought treatment in 37 publicly funded programs.[47] The programs consisted of both inpatient and outpatient treatment strategies. The researchers concluded that the treatment seemed to moderate rather than terminate a person's involvement with drugs and alcohol. Thus, there was a decline in the amount and seriousness of the substances taken in the five years following treatment. This effect was demonstrated for all the strategies—from therapeutic community to methadone maintenance. The authors determined that employment did not markedly improve after treatment, however. And the number of clients with histories of violent crime who committed further predatory offenses was 30 to 50 percent. Finally, Hubbard and his associates calculated that close to one-third of those clients serviced returned to treatment in the year following their completed program.

Studies like the one just described have lent controversy to the issue of how long treatment should continue in order to be effective. Hubbard's work suggests that six months is a realistic time. Other researchers add that longer periods of treatment do not have significantly higher rates of success.

Successful Treatment Programs

Drug testing is an important part of community supervision programs for offenders with histories of substance abuse. Supervision with testing is more effective than supervision without testing. And indications are that serious drug users on supervision without testing will have the same rates of criminal arrest as will drug users on no legal supervision at all.[48]

A treatment program that tolerates occasional relapses seems to be in direct conflict with the traditional control orientation of community supervision. However, community corrections programs that are based on the "one last chance" philosophy do not allow for any mistakes. Many experts believe that relapse is not necessarily a sign that the person has refused to try to stop taking drugs or alcohol.

The California.Department of Corrections uses electronic monitoring as an intermediate step after a drug violation has been detected. Instead of having their parole revoked, offenders in the Substance Abuse Revocation Diversion (SARD) program are subject to the stricter controls of electronic surveillance as an attempt to avoid the more costly, and perhaps less rehabilitative, incarceration. In another California program, parole violators with continuing drug problems are given the option of participating in acupuncture treatment or being revoked and returned to prison.

As in electronic monitoring, the length of time a person stays in a treatment program appears to be related to success. According to Anglin, "Treatments lasting less than about 90 days appear to be of limited benefit, regardless of the type of treatment involved. Beyond 90 days, however, treatment outcome improves in direct proportion to the length of time spent in treatment."[49] As is the case with those on electronic monitoring, individuals who exhibit mental disorders may be less successful in treatment or drop out altogether.[50]

Shifts in Support for Treatment

Treatment for substance abuse, like other forms of rehabilitation, are subject to cycles of popular support. Recent reports show that employers and insurance companies are now more reluctant to approve payment for treatment at private centers than they were only a few years ago. Many in-patient drug treatment facilities have closed, and others report occupancy rates at 45 percent and less. Revenues earned by private treatment centers have fallen dramatically since 1990. Although some people believe that fewer enrollments means that there is less drug and alcohol abuse, others say it indicates a more punitive attitude toward substance abusers. It is speculated that employers are reacting negatively toward the advertisements of treatment centers that offer relaxed settings with swimming and tennis, which they view as excessive. This trend of disapproval is disheartening to treatment advocates like former First Lady Betty Ford, a recovered alcoholic. She was quoted recently as saying that the "war on drugs" has become a "war on treatment."[51]

AIDS PATIENTS

The acronym AIDS is formed from the initial letters of *acquired immune deficiency syndrome*, a disease seemingly caused by a virus that has stricken an average of 50,000 Americans each year since it was identified in 1984.[52] Although advanced cases of AIDS are almost always fatal, a milder form of the illness, *AIDS related complex* (ARC), may also be diagnosed. Reports estimate that there may be as many as 365,000 cases of AIDS or ARC by the end of 1992.[53]

Those who test positive for the AIDS virus, although not manifesting any symptoms, are referred to as HIV positive. Officials estimate that 3000 new cases of AIDS are reported every month and that about 1 million Americans are presently infected with the virus although they may not suffer symptoms. That number may grow to be as high as 20 million by the end of the 1990s.[54] Further, 50,000 persons will die each year from the disease.[55]

The AIDS virus is spread solely through the exchange of blood and other body fluids. Originally, the disease concentrated in major cities and among homosexual men and intravenous drug users, but the demographics of AIDS victims is changing. In the past five years more and more cases have been noted among females, heterosexuals, and the aged. One study notes that women are the fastest growing population being diagnosed with AIDS.[56] Another study concludes that 10 percent of AIDS sufferers are over the age of 50.[57]

The AIDS virus attacks the immune system, causing its victim to fall prey to cancers and infections that eventually result in death. Current reports show that without even having AIDS, those in high-risk categories or who associate with people who are infected may be subject to discrimination and social ostracism. Assisting offenders who are in this special group requires workers to deal with the social as well as the medical realities of the disease.

Preliminary results from National Institute of Justice research found that most probation and parole agencies (76 out of 125 surveyed) could not answer questions concerning the number of AIDS patients on their caseloads.[58] Janice Lowenberg estimated in 1988 that most federal probation officers had at least one AIDS client under their supervision.[59]

Although the number of AIDS clients in these agencies has not been measured accurately, probationers and parolees fit into a disproportionate number of high-risk groups with regard to HIV contraction and transmission. These groups include drug and sex offenders between the ages of 20 and 39 who are in poor health and who have multiple sex partners.

It is reasonable to assume that the frequency of the occurrence of AIDS in the probation and parole populations would more closely match the number of cases in the jail and prison population than in the general community.[60] Surveys of inmates in prisons and jails in 1989 found that one in every 24 persons incarcerated was infected with the AIDS virus.[61] While this population does not necessarily mirror the characteristics of community supervised offenders, many of the cases overlap.

There is a growing number of clients who are actual and potential AIDS victims. For community supervision workers, confronting the problems of AIDS clients has also meant confronting their own perceptions and biases about the disease. Probation officers surveyed in Illinois in late 1987 said they would be somewhat uncomfortable to uncomfortable in dealing with these clients.[62] What the survey did not ask for were the reasons for the officers' discomfort. For some it may have been their fears of somehow contracting the disease. For others, it may have been the difficulty of dealing with anyone with a terminal illness.

Probation and parole officers need special training in both the nature of the disease and the special needs of the AIDS-infected client. Most training sessions use lectures, videotapes, brochures, and question-and-answer sessions. Training needs to prepare officers to make informed decisions about the risk of contamination by job-related contact with infected offenders. Furthermore, it should prepare officers to broker the full range of programs that exist to support the HIV-positive offenders in coping with the physical, emotional, and social devastation of the

Special training and personal skills should prepare the community corrections officer for working with clients infected with the AIDS virus. (© *Jeffrey D. Scott/Impact Visuals*)

disease. Training must also prepare officers to engage in helpful interventions to lessen the emotional impact of the disease on the offenders. Officers who need assistance in working with the terminally ill can benefit by learning counseling techniques and becoming familiar with the phases of emotions experienced by persons facing death. Finally, training relating to HIV-positive offenders should prepare officers to protect themselves and their departments from potential litigation arising from considerations of legal liability.[63]

Working with the AIDS or potential AIDS client in the community poses several dilemmas for the supervising officer. The duty to protect the community may mean recommending AIDS testing or disclosing the possible risks faced by persons known to be closely associated with the AIDS victim. As a counselor and client advocate, the supervisor also feels a need to protect the privacy of the client, particularly when the issues are personal medical conditions.

In many jurisdictions, the duty to maintain conditional confidentiality about medical conditions is legally mandated. According to New York public health law, for example, persons can be found guilty of a misdemeanor and fined up to $5000 for each breach of confidentiality concerning AIDS clients.[64] In New York, policy guidelines address the need for probation officers to assess a defendant's AIDS status as early as the presentence investigation:

> The investigating probation officer, even in the absence of substantiation from the defendant or other persons, may strongly suspect that a defendant has AIDS or ARC. In these cases, the probation officer should tell the defendant why it is important, if the defendant does not have AIDS or

ARC, for this information to be included in the pre-sentence report. . . .
The information could be used by the judge as a factor in the sentencing
decision.[65]

Of particular concern in these cases is how information concerning a
defendant's medical condition will be used. Most important is the effect
it will have on the sentencing outcome. In some cases, additional
restrictions may be placed on the activities of the AIDS client under
supervision in the community.

To date only a few jurisdictions conduct mass HIV screenings on probationers and parolees, but many have started testing procedures for
high-risk clients or for those who request such a procedure. There are at
least four possible tests used to detect the virus. Langston reports that
the most common test, the ELISA, costs about $13 per use.[66] In the
event of a positive ELISA, medical officials usually conduct a follow-up
test that averages about $41. Because a test may not show positive for a
long time after a person is exposed to the disease, multiple tests may
need to be conducted in many cases. It is clear, however, that the cost of
such procedures would make wide-scale testing a major portion of any
agency's operating budget. To be accurate identifiers of the disease and
still be fiscally prudent means that officers should be skilled in predicting high-risk cases.

The Controversy Over Disclosure

Each community corrections professional is aware that persons suffering from AIDS face ostracism and threats to their physical safety, employment, and housing security, and that they have difficulty getting
insurance. According to the American Civil Liberties Union (ACLU), reports of discrimination against those suspected of having AIDS have
risen as dramatically as the incidence of the disease itself. The ACLU
claims that one-third of persons who reported AIDS-related discrimination did not even have the disease.[67]

The seriousness of the possible effects of inappropriate disclosure
provide a critical test for the relationship between the offender and the
community supervisor. In their relationship, confidentiality and trust
can be as important as any aid and service that can be provided. The relationships between the officer and third parties are less clear. Faced
with the question of disclosure, the officer should consider the present
medical condition of the offender. Also important is the nature of the relationship being maintained with the third party (e.g., lover, employee,
or roommate). Officers have a variety of medical and public health professionals available to help in this decision-making process. California
law, for example, allows physicians to reveal a patient's HIV antibody
status to a spouse even if the infected individual has refused to do so.[68]

The courts consider several legal variables in determining the government's responsibility for harm to a third party that is caused by a person on community supervision. One variable is the role the state played in arranging the contact between the offender and the third party. If the agency had placed the offender in a certain job situation or community service project, then it would assume greater responsibility for any negative consequences that arose from the placement. However, the state would not have a duty to breech confidentiality to third parties with whom they hold no special relationship.[69]

When little was known about the transmission of the AIDS (HIV) virus, there was much confusion about who could potentially be affected. Thus, it was unclear how far the scope of disclosure needed to extend. Since that time, science has limited susceptible, or at-risk activities or situations to sexual contacts, pregnancy, blood transfusions, and intravenous needle sharing. Although this appears to be a narrow range of associations, officials have increased the estimates of youths at risk from sharing needles when piercing ears, tattooing, and injecting steroids.

The debate over disclosure often seems to be legal and technical: who may disclose what to whom and under what conditions. Even so, Kleinig and Lindner argue, if the agency is to be part of a humane society,

> . . . it must be prepared to act as a steward of the privilege it possesses and of the wider society it also serves. It cannot limit itself to what it legally must do. Even if good stewardship of its own resources makes it inappropriate for the agency to provide counseling for third parties, it must at least lobby for official responsiveness to the situation. . . . Sooner or later, an agency that shirks its wider moral responsibility will find its legal refuge assailed.[70]

Still, many professionals believe that the probation or parole officer is not the person compelled or qualified to reveal medical information. They argue that problems such as AIDS are public health issues best dealt with by public health departments who identify and prevent the spread of communicable diseases.[71] There is concern that if community corrections officials become involved in the control of AIDS they would be obligated to help prevent other communicable diseases such as other sexually transmitted diseases, tuberculosis, and hepatitis.

In many states it is illegal for nonmedical persons to disclose the results of AIDS tests. Under California law, written authorization from the subject is required before test results may be given to a third party.[72] The U.S. Parole Commission has stated that AIDS issues are beyond the scope of their legal authority. Nor does the commission view AIDS issues as a part of their mission—which is to prevent parolees from committing new crimes. In some states (e.g., Florida, Nevada, Louisiana, and Idaho), however, it is now a crime to transmit the AIDS virus knowingly.

The U.S. Federal Probation Division has argued that criminal justice resources should not be spent on work related to public health. Supervising agents deal with many aspects of their AIDS-infected clients' disease, such as explaining mandatory health reporting laws and arranging appropriate work and treatment schedules, but they are not medically trained and therefore should not give counsel on treatment. Proper referrals to community health and social service agencies are needed. Coordinating with these agencies better ensures that the privacy and dignity of the individual is protected and that the health needs of both the client and society are met.

OLDER OFFENDERS

Sam Lewis was 71 years old when he took a shotgun next door and confronted the two young men who kept parking in his driveway. By blocking his exit, they had made it impossible for him to take his ailing wife to the doctor. Soon after he crossed the street, they were dead. Lewis will be approximately 79 years old when he is released on parole. He has emphysema, two artificial hips, arthritis, Alzheimer's disease, and a broken hearing aid.[73] The serious medical problems that Sam Lewis faces are only part of the reason that he is considered a special needs client.

Research studies on elderly persons on community supervision find that about half have not finished high school. Only half are capable of current employment. Many, like Sam, have serious health conditions that make keeping appointments difficult. Special diets are often required that these offenders cannot prepare or afford. One study of jailed inmates over the age of 50 found that 21 percent had been diagnosed as mentally ill.[74] Although most elderly offenders have prior experiences in the criminal justice system, supervising officers find them basically cooperative.[75]

Many elderly probationers have committed violent crimes. Had it not been for their age, they would probably have received prison terms. McCarthy and Langworthy found that two-thirds of the very oldest clients had convictions for murder or manslaughter.[76] In another study, supervisors commented that the older probationer was likely to deny responsibility for their crimes. Sometimes they referred to their physical impairments as the cause of their illegal behavior.[77] This attitude can make rehabilitation difficult because the goals of therapeutic treatment are taking responsibility for one's actions and learning new appropriate behaviors.

There are many explanations for the violent crimes that elderly persons commit, sometimes for the first time in their lives. Some professionals say biological changes in aging may make an older person prone to violent outbursts. Others say that people are simply living longer and are capable of committing crimes later in life. As Chaneles suggested, the elderly are simply not passive anymore. He stated, "They are more physically able to get what they believe they deserve and more seem willing to use force to get it."[78]

John hardly appears to be the forceful type. He is 88 years old, in a wheelchair, and on oxygen. He is accused of touching two young girls, neighbors, on the bottom and vagina. He has never committed any previous crimes and is extremely remorseful. According to the probation officer's report, "The defendant appears to be a very infirm, lonely, sick old man who regressed under the depression brought on by his isolation and physical deterioration. He is not a pedophile by nature. Neither is he a danger to the community at large nor a danger to the victims in this case. His granddaughter's plan is for him to stay with her until he dies, which sounds like a good plan." John received credit for the 98 days he spent in jail and was then placed on three years of probation, reporting to his parole officer every 14 days. John was also ordered to pay $1500 in restitution in $25 monthly payments and $250 in court costs. John is currently taking medication for his heart, kidneys, arthritis, ulcer, and lung disease. He does not believe he will live to complete his term of probation.

Because of the types of crimes they have committed, such as sex offenses, elderly clients are often labeled as high-risk offenders. This label affects the programs older offenders may be eligible for despite their apparent lack of physical "dangerousness." In fact, one study explained that officers may perceive elderly offenders as being of low risk and discharge them from reporting simply to ease their caseloads.[79] Without the elderly cases, officers can concentrate on younger, more realistically high-risk offenders. Another reason for an early discharge is that officers may consider the elderly to be "needy" clients with problems that include medical disabilities, alcohol abuse, unemployability, and lack of family to assist them. Many elderly offenders are released from prison with no family or friends left in the community. They often have no savings, no insurance, and no knowledge of how to get services from the welfare system.

Consequently, the perception of high need and low risk may lead officers to release elderly clients from supervision. The possibility that these offenders may be seen as having low rehabilitation potential and requiring high expenditures of resources has also been considered.

OFFENSE-SPECIFIC PROGRAMMING

Along with the special needs offenders we have discussed are offenders who have been targeted for treatment because of the unique properties of the one specific crime they committed. It is believed that there are certain underlying emotional problems shared by those who commit crimes such as arson, shoplifting, and certain sex offenses. It is also believed that offenders who engage in these specific criminal behaviors are more like one another than not, and that they are also more like one another than they are like other kinds of offenders. These crimes create more similar psychological and family-history profiles than do other more generic crimes. Treatment programs that have been developed for these offenses and a belief in their potential for success can be the basis for community supervision.

Sex Offenders

There are many reasons why sex offenders are one of the most highly controlled groups within the criminal justice system. One reason for tighter security with this offender population is public demand. Consequently, we find legislative mandates, laws, and agency guidelines requiring high levels of supervision for sex offenders. In addition, high levels of control result from research findings that suggest these offenders form a higher risk group for repeat offenses. When subjected to risk-assessment instruments, this group usually scores high.

Sex offenses cover a wide range of crimes from misdemeanors to felonies. The categories of victims range from spouses and acquaintances to strangers and children. The seriousness of a particular offense is usually determined by the age of the victim, the amount of force, violence, or threats used, and the presence of weapons and premeditation. The risk assessment of a particular sex offender may be enhanced by the finding of psychological disturbance, alcohol or drug addiction, or a pattern of repeated offenses. Research has demonstrated that these conditions appear at statistically significant rates in sex offenders.

In a study by Rosenberg and Knight, 184 male sex offenders were classified by underlying problems that included substance abuse, poor life-management skills, antisocial behavior, sexual aggression, and offense-related impulsivity.[80] Although most of the literature on sex offenders deals with adult males, there has been recent research interest in the female and juvenile sex offender.

The juvenile sex offender is of particular interest because of the finding that many adult sex offenders began sexually inappropriate behavior at an early age and that their adjustment problems progressed in severity. In one study 58 percent of adult sex offenders admitted to adolescent sex crimes.[81] Data indicate that juveniles are responsible for 30 to 50 percent of child sex abuse and 15 percent of forcible rape cases each year.[82]

A categorization of juvenile sex offenders was developed by O'Brien.[83] It includes six basic categories: (1) naive experimenters; (2) undersocialized child exploiters; (3) sexual aggressives; (4) sexual compulsives; (5) disturbed impulsives; and (6) peer-group-influenced offenders. As Weiks

Adolescent sex offenders in group counseling in a special offense-specific treatment program. (© *Bob Daemmerich/Stock Boston*)

and Lehker point out, the naive experimenter may be a once-in-a-life-time offender whose act is not symptomatic of any chronic or serious adjustment problem.[84] It is important, the authors point out, that these youngsters not be labeled and stigmatized by legal overreaction, but it would be critical that other, more serious types of sexual behavior receive legal and treatment intervention.

A study that examined female sexual offenders determined that there were three unique personality profiles and specific sex crimes that were related to them. The *teacher/lover* tried to develop relationships with young boys. In contrast, the *predisposed offender* was usually herself a victim of child sex abuse who used sexual activity to enhance intimacy with children close to her. The third type, the *male-coerced offender* was emotionally dependent on a male partner with whom she committed sex offenses.[85]

Research studies have suggested that some sex offenders have brain and other biological abnormalities that trigger sexual compulsions that can be treated with drugs. In certain schools of thought, deviant sexual behaviors are viewed as addictions much as narcotics and alcohol are. Psychological profiles show that many of these offenders manifest great feelings of self-hatred and agonize over their inability to control their impulses.

The risk of a sex offender being released in the community is related to the perceived likelihood of recidivism. Studies have been conducted not only on recidivism, which is usually a yes or no category, but on the amount of new offenses or the rate at which they occur. Groth, Longo, and McFadin found that subjects in their two-group study averaged 1.4 and 2 prior convictions respectively for child molestation.[86] Most of the subjects also self-reported that they committed sex assaults for which they were never caught, some as many as 30. For those surveyed, the average number of sexual assaults that remained undetected was 3.4. The authors concluded that given the likelihood of alcoholic memory lapses and the tendency to withhold information in prison surveys, the findings were overly conservative. Groth, Longo, and McFadin estimated that a more accurate assessment of the rate of child molestations would be 11 undetected offenses for every convicted offense.

In a study of child sexual abusers, Marshall and Christie reported that 46 percent had two or more prior convictions for sex crimes.[87] A study of sex offenders in New York found that child molesters averaged 68.3 victims, which was more than three times the number of adult women assaulted by each rapist.[88] In a study of adolescent sex offenders, Groth found that there were often many more incidents of antisocial sexual behaviors that parents, neighbors, police, and other authorities knew about but failed to report.[89] Groth explained that incidents that did not appear on the record were dismissed because the relationship of the perpetrator as a friend, neighbor, or sibling made them appear "unimportant."

The Media and Agency Perceptions of Risk

Sex offenses committed by persons on community supervision receive much media attention. The response is usually an emotional public outcry and a demand for accountability from the supervising agency. There are often suggestions in the media that once a sex offender, always a sex offender. The press is quick to pick up on a story like the following. "An unemployed store clerk who appeared on the CBS-TV show '60 Minutes' five years ago to tell how he was cured of child molesting has pleaded guilty to 57 counts of lewd and lascivious behavior with a dozen boys."[90] In the wake of sensational sex crimes, corrections policies are often reviewed and revised. In many instances, legislation may be enacted in the hope of preventing similar occurrences.

Since the early 1980s, several states have passed laws that mandate prison terms and prohibit probation for many sex offenses. Such laws also frequently increase the prison terms for those crimes. Many jurisdictions deny parole to offenders with certain types of sex crime convictions. Some states require that specific treatment programs be provided for sex offenders while they are in prison in recognition that the offenders will be released one day and that the psychological causes of the deviant behavior must be addressed before that time.

Treatment of Sex Offenders

The possibility of receiving a community sentence or parole is directly related to sex offenders' ability to assure officials that there is no risk of new sex offenses. For this reason, most sex offenders on community supervision are placed in a high-risk caseload. The management of these cases usually takes a multifaceted approach using both control and treatment strategies. For control, officers ensure that the offenders are not in a job that involves routine contact with children. The offenders may also be required to stay away from those they have victimized.

In many communities, sex offenders must register with local sheriffs and police once they are placed on community supervision. Local laws may also require anyone who has ever been convicted of sex offenses to register with local authorities upon moving to that community.

One of the most difficult aspects of treatment is that many sex offenders deny that a crime took place. Others deny that they had anything to do with causing it. In a study of juvenile sex offenders, Schram and Rowe found that most offenders blamed the victim or someone other than themselves for the crime.[91] The typical offender was a loner who had never experienced an age-appropriate relationship. Although these juveniles participated in treatment as long as it was required, they showed no remorse for their acts. For this reason, treatment programs have been specifically designed to ensure that young offenders learn to understand, explain, and take full responsibility for their behavior. The Michigan Adolescent Sex Offender Treatment Program was designed to do just that in an outpatient counseling service format divided into two phases. The first phase was a four- to six-week assessment period that included interviews with the individual and the family and a series of tests. The tests determined the nature, the motivations, and the seriousness of the sexual behavioral problems of the youngster. The remainder of the 28 weeks was spent in weekly group therapy, bimonthly family counseling, and individual sessions as needed. An educational component included information on human sexuality and relationship interactions. The parents also had access to a support group. The youth was supervised throughout the treatment program by a probation officer.[92]

In a 1988 study of adult sex offenders only 49 percent of the subjects wanted treatment.[93] In another study by Kaplan, 80 percent of the child sex abusers interviewed did not believe they needed counseling for their sex offenses. Forty-six percent refused to admit that they had committed a sex offense.[94]

Treatment usually involves counseling in some form—individual, group, family therapy, or self-help groups. A survey of 574 treatment programs for sex offenders in the United States found that two-thirds used a combination of treatments. Therapists combined psychological, educational, and behavioral models that focused on family systems or the prevention of relapses. Whereas juvenile sex-offender programs tended to use a psychosociological approach, adult programs favored behavioral models. Behavioral models often used aversion conditioning or the association of negative stimuli or punishment with certain undesired actions or physical responses. Other programs stressed victim empathy, sex education, communication, and management of anger.[95]

Another treatment approach is for the offender to agree to submit to chemical injections designed to lower the secretion of male sex hormones. Depo-Provera is a trade name for medroxyprogesterone acetate, which suppresses the sex drive by lowering the level of the male sex hormone in the bloodstream to a preteen level.[96] Offenders may consent to take Depo-Provera in experimental sentences in some jurisdictions. This treatment is an effort to physically control the behavior of offenders while at the same time imposing the punitive restrictions of probation and parole supervision. In most cases, weekly injections of the drug are combined with individual or group psychotherapy.

In a less drastic but perhaps equally coercive strategy, one jurisdiction placed sex offenders on probation in a polygraph program. The 100 probationers were subjected to biweekly polygraph sessions. The experiment reported only four failures. The deterrent effect was explained by one participant who said, "Every time I get the inclination, I think of that damned box and right away it turns me off."[97] It has been suggested, however, that candidates for this type of program be screened for their ability to be accurately polygraphed prior to enrollment.

To be effective, a treatment for special needs offenders must be approved by the clients who are asked to participate in them. For example, in a survey of sex offenders, it was found that male therapists were preferred almost two-to-one over female therapists. In addition, a commonly used treatment for sex offenders, aversion conditioning or attaching negative consequences to stimuli related to sex offenses, was seen as one of the least desirable. Also rated low in acceptability was the use of drug therapy or the option of castration. The preferred methods of treatment were individual psychotherapy, group therapy, and training in social skills.[98]

Treatment may also need to involve the families of sex offenders, especially when family members were victims of the sexual abuse. The following case shows a range of family needs:

> Mrs. Hampton still has difficulty with the fact that her husband molested her twelve-year-old daughter, his step-daughter, Ann. While she does not believe her husband will molest again, she knows their marriage will be very different if they reunite. Some days, she admits, things go well and on others she is extremely angry at her husband for what he has done. Their family was dysfunctional at the time of the molestation. She believes that she was co-dependent and contributed to the family's dysfunction. Both she and her husband are victims of sexual abuse and are attending a group for adults molested as children. In addition, they are attending other group counseling and are being counseled as a couple. Their daughter is attending both individual and group counseling.

Programs for Arsonists and Firesetters

Official reports have found that approximately 40 percent of all arsons are set by juveniles. Fire-related behaviors may range along a continuum of involvement from "interest" in fire to playing with fire to firesetting, and then to arson. Young people who actually commit the crime of arson are often classified as a unique criminal group with a psychological profile unlike that of any other offender group. Because it is believed that the motivation for this type of crime is different from other offenses, special treatment programs have been developed to address the specific needs of firesetters and to prevent recidivism.

Nick is a compulsive firestarter who began his career at the age of four. Several times the 13-year-old has been caught and beaten by his father, a Marine. The latest firesetting was in a wastebasket in the family home when the parents were away. Nick has had counseling with the local fire department. His parents report he is hyperactive, self-destructive, and doesn't respond to praise or discipline. Psychological tests show disorders in visual and auditory processing. He is behind academically and is enrolled in special education classes. Nick has limited emotional control. He is impulsive, likes to watch fires burn, and does not believe he can stop setting fires without some help.

Experts say that youthful firesetters usually fall into four categories: (1) those who are curious about fire, (2) those who are crying out for help, (3) those who are delinquent, and (4) the small 4 to 5 percent who are emotionally disturbed.

Contrary to popular belief, playing with fire is not a normal behavior in children. According to experts, if a child shows a strong curiosity concerning fire, further exploration and assessment of the child should be made. One child who resented the new baby in the family set a fire under the baby's crib to get the parents' attention. The firesetter who is crying for help often uses fires to bring attention to physical or sexual abuse, the fires often being set near the home or location of abuse. The delinquent firesetter is more likely to set fires at school. Fire may be used to express anger or frustration in youngsters who are poor communicators. They wish to damage property or hurt others. Fires are not always a specialty for the delinquent firesetter; this person will often be involved in multiple types of offenses. They often stay near the scene to enjoy the result of their behavior.

The disturbed firesetter suffers from a psychosis and sets fires at the direction of some imagined entity. Anger and hostility directed by delusion may manifest itself in destructive and fatal fires. Fire may also be an outlet for the generally passive personality or for children who have been abused or ignored. Because of the amount of suppressed feelings in these children, they are often good candidates for counseling.[99]

In recent years, the incidence of firesetting by females has grown.[100] The use of fire by a woman against an abusive spouse was popularized in the movie, "The Burning Bed." Firesetting is also found in the histories of sex offenders in sufficient frequency to suggest a connection between the two behaviors.

For the correctional practitioner, the most important task relating to firesetting is detection. Probation and parole officers need to address specific questions related to this behavior in their investigations of social history. Once identified, firesetters may be difficult to place if they must be removed from the home. Many low-security juvenile and adult facilities fear the firesetter because of the potential for catastrophic behavior. Smaller facilities and private home placements may be equally difficult because of insurance and security concerns.

Identification of the nature of the defendant's firesetting behavior is important. For some, such as the "cry for help" types, removal from the home environment removes the cause of the firesetting. This individual would pose little threat to the treatment facility. The delinquent or disturbed firesetter, however, is a severe threat and requires intensive treatment or a highly restricted environment.

Some communities have already developed firesetter programs that provide assessment to determine motives and risks, and they have set up intervention activities such as fire safety education and restitution. Treatment efforts may combine counseling with education, usually in cooperation with a local fire department. In one city a former drug counselor teamed up with her husband who was an arson investigator and counseled more than 500 children through an intervention program. This program used educational awareness techniques combined with counseling in an effort to prevent further firesetting and to divert children out of the criminal justice system.[101]

Programs for Shoplifters

Keith is a 13-year-old shoplifter. He claims that he steals because "it's stuff I want." He started stealing when he was about seven years old, and he was not caught for the first time until he was eight. He estimates that he has stolen about 50 times, mostly candy from local stores. Once he stole $4 from his sister, "because his school was selling candy bars and he wanted some of it." Keith relates that he is usually angry when he steals. However, if he is in a good mood, sometimes he will steal and sometimes he will not.

Official estimates are that there are more than 20 million shoplifters in the country today. One report found that 13 percent of shoplifters steal every day, 14 percent steal every week, and almost 60 percent steal once each month. Shoplifters Anonymous reports that more than $25 million in retail merchandise is shoplifted daily.[102]

A judge in Spokane, Washington, offered convicted shoplifters the option of going to jail or confessing to all their shoplifting episodes over the previous five years. The judge threatened to use a polygraph to determine the accuracy of their reports. As a result, 60 defendants confessed to more than 1400 shoplifting incidents. The shoplifters paid restitution in each case, and the polygraph itself was never even given to them.[103]

Community-supervised treatment for those caught stealing from stores are primarily designed for the nonprofessional shoplifter. The nonprofessionals usually do not have a criminal record, do not commit other types of crimes, and suffer guilt, fear, and anxiety about their behavior.

Shoplifters Anonymous, a not-for-profit corporation, has designed a combined home study–classroom learning program that it hopes the courts will adopt as an educational alternative for sentencing shoplifters. The program is advertised as a service to be offered in conjunction with probation or as a diversionary program administered through the courts. The course consists of taped instruction and quizzes done at home and in group therapy sessions and costs the offender about $75.[104] Shoplifters Anonymous claims to have been operating and conducting research for 11 years. However, no data on their success or on recidivism statistics associated with the program have been supplied.

In one family court, a shoplifters clinic was incorporated into the juvenile probation program. Employees of the family court administered and staffed this program. The clinic was a four-hour program divided into four phases. In the first phase, the young offenders received a lecture on the economic impact of shoplifting, the legal consequences, and the social and personal costs of the crime. In the second part, they saw two films on shoplifting. A tour of an adjacent detention facility was developed for the third part. Finally, the participants formed small discussion groups and shared their experiences—from the theft to the reactions of their family and friends. Probationers who successfully completed the clinic and six months of supervision had their criminal records expunged.

Follow-up studies on participants showed that shoplifters who attended the program were just as likely to be rearrested for shoplifting as those who did not attend. However, subsequent shoplifting arrests were very low for both groups, only 3 percent. Of the total sample of adjudicated shoplifters, 26 percent of those who attended the program were rearrested for some type of crime whereas 35 percent of those who did not attend the program were rearrested.[105]

In a similar study in California, juvenile shoplifters were divided into two groups. One group received a series of classes in lieu of a court action. The other group had their cases dismissed. Follow-ups on these first-time offenders found that 95 percent of both groups remained arrest-free after 18 months. That is, whether the minors went to court or to classes, or had their cases dismissed, only 5 percent reoffended.[106] This study suggests that for first-offense juvenile shoplifting, the most economical alternative, dismissing the case, is as effective as intervention.

SUMMARY

The problems associated with special needs offenders present the practitioner with a number of unprecedented challenges:

1. Identifying special needs clients within the offender population by using many assessment techniques.
2. Preparing sentencing recommendations that require appropriate referrals for counseling and treatment.
3. Making sure that legally required reporting procedures are followed not only by the agency but when necessary by the offender too.
4. Developing supervision plans that are flexible and responsive to the wide-ranging and changing conditions of the particular special needs offender.

The Utah Division of Field Operations, which supervises parole and probation activities, has developed a number of resources for the special needs offender. Contracts with a number of private agencies have brought special services to the intellectually handicapped and developmentally disabled, as well as to sex offenders, incest offenders, and substance abuse offenders. In some instances, the private providers augment traditional community corrections programs with a wider range of treatment options. The six community correctional centers located within the state are designed to house and service one or more of these specially designated client needs. The field operations division also sponsors special training for personnel working with sex offenders.[107]

The major focus of special needs programming in community corrections currently appears to be concentrated on drug and alcohol offenders. The government's "War on Drugs" during the early 1990s temporarily provided funding for several treatment experiments. The public's perception of increasing amounts of drug-related crime has also led to controversy over the separation of criminal responsibility and addiction treatment. Many people support the use of rehabilitation programs but not as a substitute for punishment.

Although many experts do not see a substantial conflict between the goals of punishment and treatment, some may find it philosophically difficult to administer both. This conflict is particularly apparent in drug and alcohol programs based on a medical model. The medical model implies that drug addiction and alcohol abuse should be treated as diseases, or sicknesses. If crimes result from one's involvement with drugs and alcohol, medical and psychological treatment under the medical model would take priority over punitive sanctions. However, not all community supervision officers or treatment specialists agree with this model. In fact, it is realistic to say that there is great disagreement throughout the field on the causes and the most effective responses to drug and alcohol abuse.

Across the country a wide variety of treatment approaches to drug and alcohol abuse have been used in community corrections. In one county in California, drug-offending parole violators can volunteer for acupuncture treatment instead of returning to prison. In other areas, methadone maintenance and antabuse have also been employed. These approaches are not without their critics who argue against what may be a coercive use of drugs to cure substance abuse problems.

When reading the literature on the effectiveness of drug treatment, keep in mind that there may be differences in the success rates of persons who refer themselves to treatment and those who are forced to attend by the courts. Volunteering for help or admitting one needs help is an important step in many therapeutic treatments that the legal system has not been effective in ordering.

Over the years, more specific offender classifications have been developed, such as shoplifters, firesetters, and sex offenders. These special groups have their own criminal, psychological, and sociological patterns that can be studied and treated independently. Treatment experts seem to agree that this specialization process leads to more effective intervention strategies.

The scarcity or absence of community resources for probationers and parolees with special needs will make supervision efforts more difficult. With so few treatment and service programs available for the many special needs offenders, it is hard to believe that society really expects community supervision to succeed.

KEY TERMS

acupuncture   Depo-Provera
AIDS   methadone maintenance
 (Acquired Immune   therapeutic community
Deficiency Syndrome)
antabuse

DISCUSSION QUESTIONS

1. As a manager of community supervision officers, how do you detect and address possible biases in your staff's attitudes concerning clients with special needs?

2. What are society's obligations in terms of treating the offender who has committed drug- or alcohol-related crimes? Is punishment alone enough? To what extent is treatment morally necessary, economically practical, or realistically beneficial?

3. What specific treatment methods might be employed according to each of the theories of addiction causation? Which theory do you feel best describes the development of an addiction?

4. What does the research suggest about the success of drug- and alcohol-related treatment programs that have been attempted to date? If possible, obtain a copy of the Hubbard research study (see End note 47), and examine it in detail. What do the findings suggest for future policies for drug treatment?

5. Under what circumstances should the disclosure that an offender has the AIDS virus be made? Who should make such a disclosure and why?

6. What types of programs or services could be devised to make community supervision better fit the needs of the elderly client?

7. What other types of offense-specific programs might be developed to address offender needs? What would be the key to success with these programs?

END NOTES

1. Kling, Herman, quoted in Torsten Eriksson (1976). *The reformers: An historical survey of pioneer experiments in the treatment of criminals.* New York: Elsevier, p. 252.

2. Nelson, Michael, Robert Rutherford, and Bruce Wolford (1985). Handicapped offenders: Meeting education needs. *Corrections Today* 45(5):32–34.

3. Pope, Lisa (1990). California jails are becoming mentally ill "dumping ground." *San Bernardino Sun,* 16 September: B8.

4. Guy, E., J. Platt, I. Zwerling, and S. Bullock (1985). Mental health status of prisoners in an urban jail. *Criminal Justice and Behavior* 12:26–53.

5. Krause, Wesley (1988). *Report: San Bernardino County Juvenile Probation.* San Bernardino, CA.

6. Washington Department of Corrections (1990). *A guide to the Washington State Department of Corrections—draft.* Olympia: Office of Public Information, p. 22.

7. Lippold, Robert A. (1989). Halfway houses: Meeting special needs, in *Correctional Counseling and Treatment* (2nd ed.), ed. Peter Kratcoski, p. 345. Prospect Heights, IL: Waveland Press.

8. Lombardo, L. (1985). Mental health work in prison and jails. *Criminal Justice and Behavior* 12(1):17–28.

9. Wertlieb, Ellen, and Martin Greenberg (1989). Strategies for working with special needs probationers. *Federal Probation* 53(1): 10–17.

10. Krause, Wesley (1988). Supra note 5.

11. Schneider, Anne, and Peter Schneider (1985). The impact of restitution on recidivism of juvenile offenders: An experiment in Clayton County, Georgia. *Criminal Justice Review* 10(1):1–10.

12. Wertlieb, Ellen, and Greenberg (1989). Supra note 9.

13. White, David, and Hubert Wood (1986). The Lancster County, Pennsylvania mentally retarded offenders program. *Prison Journal* 66(1):77–84.

14. Lippold, Robert (1989). Supra note 7.

15. Innes, Christopher (1988). *Profile of state prison inmates, 1986*. Washington, DC: Bureau of Justice Statistics, p. 4.

16. Wish, Eric, Mary Toborg, and John Bellassai (1988). *Identifying drug users and monitoring them during conditional release*. Washington, DC: National Institute of Justice.

17. Drug offenses contribute to increase in jail numbers. (1991). *Corrections Compendium* May:13.

18. National Institute of Justice (1987) *Pre-trial drug screening package*. Rockville, MD: National Criminal Justice Reference Service, p. 11; National Institute of Justice (1989). *DUF: Drug use forecasting January to March 1989*. Washington, DC: U.S. Department of Justice.

19. Wish, Eric (1988). *Drug testing*. Washington, DC: National Institute of Justice.

20. Visher, Christy, and Karen McFadden (1991). *A comparison of urinalysis technologies for drug testing in criminal justice*. Washington, DC: National Institute of Justice.

21. Krause, Wesley (1988). Supra note 5.

22. National Institute of Justice (1991). *Research in action: DUF*. Washington, DC: U.S. Department of Justice, p. 11.

23. Wish, Eric, Mary Cuadrado, and John Martorava (1986). Estimates of drug use in intensive supervision probationers: Results from a pilot study. *Federal Probation* 50(4):14.

24. Cicchetti, C. et al. (1989). *Drugs & criminals: A dangerous mix*. Boston: Massachusetts Office of Commissioner of Probation.

25. Piller, Ruth (1988). Probated sentences take new meaning. *Houston Chronicle*, 16 March: B1.

26. Morse, Barbara, and Delbert Elliot (1990). Hamilton County drinking and driving study: 30 month report. *Executive Summary*. Cincinnati, OH: The Hamilton County Court, pp. 2–3.

27. The Guardian Interlock Responsible Drivers Program (advertisement).

28. *San Bernardino Sun* (1991). Police take more than 224,000 driver's licenses. 28 May: A3.

29. Lyman, Michael, and Gary Potter (1991). *Drugs in society*. Cincinnati: Anderson Publishing.

30. Abadinsky, Howard (1989). *Drug abuse*. Chicago: Nelson Hall, p. 158.

31. Ibid., p. 160.

32. Lyman, Michael, and Gary Potter (1991). Supra note 29, p. 386.

33. Enkoji, M. S. (1989). Treatment programs help addicts restructure lives. *San Bernardino Sun*, 22 October:8.

34. Miller, Norman, and Doug Toft (1990). *The disease concept of alcoholism and other drug addiction*. Center City, MN: Hazelden, p. 1.

35. Ibid.

36. Assur, Eric, Gerald Jackson, and Teresa Muncy (1987). Probation counselors and the adult children of alcoholics. *Federal Probation* 51(3):41–46.

37. Ibid.

38. Jacobs, James (1989). *Drunk driving*. Chicago: Univ. of Chicago Press, p. 182.

39. Visher, Christy (1990). Incorporating drug treatment in criminal sanctions. *NIJ Research In Action* Summer:2–7.

40. Abadinsky, Howard (1989). Supra note 30.

41. Wexler, H. K., D. Lipton, and K. Foster (1985). Outcome evaluation of a prison therapeutic community for substance abuse treatment: Preliminary results. Paper presented at the annual meeting of the American Society of Criminology, San Diego, California; Andrews, D. A., I. Zinger, R. D. Hoge, J. Bonta, P. Gendreau, and F. T. Cullen (1990). Does correctional treatment work? A clinically relevant and psychologically informed meta-analysis. *Criminology* 28(3): 369–404.

42. Vito, Gennaro (1989). The Kentucky substance abuse program: A private program to treat probationers and parolees. *Federal Probation* 53(1):65–72.

43. Latessa, Edward, and Lawrence Travis (1988). The effects of intensive supervision with alcoholic probationers. *Journal of Offender Counseling Services and Rehabilitation* 12(2):175–190.

44. Abadinsky, Howard (1989). Supra note 30, p. 145.

45. Anglin, M. (1990). Ensuring success in corrections-based intervention with drug-abusing offenders. Paper presented at the conference: *Growth and Its Influence on Correctional Policy*. University of California, Berkeley, May 10–11, p. 10.

46. Ibid.

47. Hubbard, Robert, Mary Ellen Masden, J. Valley Rachal, Henrik Harwood, Elizabeth Cavanaugh, and Harold Ginzburg (1989). *Drug abuse treatment: A national study of effectiveness.* Chapel Hill: Univ. of North Carolina Press.

48. Anglin, M., G. Speckart, and E. Deschenes (1989). *Reexamining the effects of probation and parole on narcotics addiction and property crime.* Final report submitted to the National Institute of Justice, Washington, DC; Speckart, G., M. Anglin, and E. Deschenes (1989). Modeling the longitudinal impact of legal sanctions on narcotics use and property crime. *Journal of Quantitative Criminology* 5:33–56.

49. Anglin, Ensuring success in corrections-based intervention, p. 12.

50. Ibid.

51. Sanders, Edmund (1991). Drug treatment centers face decline. *Los Angeles Daily News,* 13 October: B10.

52. Hellinger, Fred (1990). Updated forecasts of the costs of medical care for persons with AIDS, 1989–93. *Public Health Reports* 105(1):1–10.

53. Lurigio, Arthur (1989). Practitioners' views on AIDS in probation and detention. *Federal Probation* 53(4):16.

54. Cowley, Geoffrey et al. (1990). AIDS: The next ten years. *Newsweek* June 25:20–27.

55. Morgan, W. M. et al. (1986). AIDS: Current and future trends. *Public Health Reports* 101:459–65.

56. Philip Yam (1991). Has AIDS peaked? *Scientific American* 265(3):30–31.

57. Gutheil, Irene, and Eileen Chichin (1991). AIDS, older people, and social work. *Health and Social Work* 16(4):237–244.

58. Hunt, Dana (1989). *AIDS in probation and parole.* Washington, DC: National Institute of Justice.

59. Lowenberg, Janice (1988). Supervising persons with AIDS: A new liability for probation and parole officers. *Journal of Contemporary Criminal Justice* 4(2):119–124.

60. MacDonald, Malcolm (1988). AIDS issues in probation and parole. *APPA Perspectives* Summer:12–13.

61. Associated Press (1989). One in 24 inmates infected with AIDS. *Corrections Today* 51(7):165.

62. Lurigio, Arthur (1989). Practitioners' views on AIDS in probation and detention. *Federal Probation* 53(4):16–24.

63. Lurigio, Arthur, Karl Gudenberg, and Arthur Spica (1988). Working effectively with AIDS cases on probation. *APPA Perspectives* Spring:10–15.

64. Kleinig, John, and Charles Lindner (1989). AIDS on parole: Dilemmas in decision making. *Criminal Justice Policy Review* 3(1):1–27.

65. Hunt, Dana (1989). Supra note 58.

66. Langston, Denny (1991). To test or not to test. *Corrections Today* 53(1):92.

67. Associated Press (1990). U.S. fear of AIDS spurs unneeded bias—ACLU. *San Bernardino Sun,* 17 June:A7.

68. Hunt, Dana (1989). Supra note 58.

69. Del Carmen, R. (1985). *Potential liabilities of probation and parole officers.* Washington, DC: National Institute of Corrections.

70. Kleinig, John, and Charles Lindner (1989). Supra note 64, pp. 9–10.

71. Hunt, Dana (1989). Supra note 58.

72. Ibid.

73. *San Diego Union* (1990). Reprinted in *Corrections Today* 52(5):136.

74. Washington, P. (1985). Mentally ill elderly offenders in five California county jails. Unpublished paper. Kansas: Department of Minority Studies, Wichita State Univ.

75. Shichor, David (1988). An exploratory study of elderly probationers. *International Journal of Offender Therapy and Comparative Criminology* 32:163–174; McCarthy, B., and Robert Langworthy (1987). Older offenders on probation and parole. *Journal of Offender Counseling Services and Rehabilitation* 12.

76. McCarthy, B., and R. Langworthy (1987). Supra note 75.

77. Shichor, David (1988). Supra note 75.

78. Chaneles, Sol (1987). Growing old behind bars. *Psychology Today* October: 46–51.

79. McCarthy, B., and R. Langworthy (1987). Supra note 75.

80. Rosenberg, Ruth, and Raymond Knight (1988). Determining male sexual offender subtypes using cluster analysis. *Journal of Quantitative Criminology* 4(4):383–410.

81. Becker, J., and M. Kaplan (1989). The assessment of adolescent sexual offenders, in *Advances in Behavioral Assessment of Children and Families*, ed. R. Prinz, pp. 97–118. Connecticut: JAI Press.

82. Deisher, R., G. Wenet, D. Paperny, T. Clark, and P. Fehrenbach (1982). Adolescent sexual offenses behavior: The role of the physician. *Journal of Adolescent Health Care* 2:279–286; Jamieson, Katherine, and Timothy Flanagan (eds.) (1987). *Sourcebook of Criminal Justice Statistics—1986*. Washington, DC: Bureau of Justice Statistics.

83. O'Brien M. (1985). Adolescent sexual offenders: An outpatient program's perspective on research directions, in *Adolescent Sex Offenders: Issues in Research and Treatment*, ed. E. Otey and G. Ryan. Rockville, MD: U.S. Department of Health and Human Services.

84. Weiks, John, and David Lehker (1988). Specialized treatment of adolescent sex offenders in a juvenile court setting. *Juvenile and Family Court Journal* 39(1):33.

85. Mathews, Ruth, Jane Matthews, and Kathleen Speltz (1989). *Female sexual offenders: An exploratory study*. Orwell, VT: Safer Society Press.

86. Groth, A. N., R. Longo, and J. B. McFadin (1982). Undetected recidivism among rapists and child molesters. *Crime and Delinquency* 28(3):450–458.

87. Marshall, W., and M. Christie (1981). Pedophilia and aggression. *Criminal Justice and Behavior* 8:145–158.

88. Eloise Sahols et al. (1982). Beware of child molesters. *Newsweek*, August 9:45.

89. Groth, A. N. (1977). The adolescent sexual offender and his prey. *International Journal of Offender Therapy and Comparative Criminology* 21(3):249–254.

90. *Houston Chronicle* (1983). "Cured" man pleads guilty. 19 February: A10.

91. Schram, Donna, and Wendy Rowe (1987). *Juvenile sexual offender treatment evaluation: Final research report*. Olympia, WA: Governor's Juvenile Justice Advisory Committee.

92. Weiks, John, and David Lehker (1988). Supra note 84, p. 34.

93. Langevin, R., P. Wright, and L. Handy (1988). What treatment do sex offenders want? *Annals of Sex Research* 1(3):363–385.

94. Kaplan, Meg (1989). A description of self-reports of convicted child molesters following incarceration. *International Journal of Offender Therapy and Comparative Criminology* 31:69–75.

95. Knopp, Fay, and William Stevenson (1988). *Nationwide survey of juvenile and adult sex-offender treatment programs and models*. Orwell, VT: Safer Society Press.

96. Money, John (1987). Treatment guidelines: Antiandrogen and counseling of paraphilic sex offenders. *Journal of Sex & Marital Therapy* 13(3):219–223.

97. Abrams, S., and E. Ogard (1986). Polygraph surveillance of probationers. *Polygraph* 15(3):174–182.

98. Langevin, Wright, and L. Handy (1988). Supra note 93.

99. Wheeler, Carla (1989). Why do some kids get their kicks watching things burn? *San Bernardino Sun* 9 July: E1.

100. Ellis, Howard (1989). Redlands firefighting team takes on re-educating of children who set fires. *San Bernardino Sun*, 5 November: B2.

101. Wheeler, Carla (1989). Supra note 99.
102. Shoplifters Anonymous (1990). The shoplifting problem. Advertisement brochure obtained at 380 N. Broadway, Suite 206, Jerico, NY 11753.
103. *American Polygraph Association Newsletter* (1976). Polygraph used by judge to get shoplifters to repay all thefts. March/April:9–10.
104. Barmash, Isadore (1988). To catch a thief (and enroll him). *Business Day, The New York Times,* 24 November: D1.
105. Winfree, Thomas, Christine Sellers, Patricia Duncan, Gabriele Kelly, Larry Williams, and Lawrence Clinton (1989). Returning to delinquency: Factors affecting the survivorship of juvenile shoplifters. *Juvenile and Family Court Journal* 40(1):49–62.
106. Krause, Wesley (1988). Supra note 5.
107. Utah Department of Corrections (1989). *Annual report.* Salt Lake City, p. 38.

15

Program Evaluation

At the conclusion of this chapter you should be able to do the following:

1. Discuss the importance of the evaluation process in the reformulation of goals and methods within a program.

2. Describe the most common types and procedures in program evaluation.

3. Explain the role that recidivism has played in program evaluation.

4. Discuss Glaser's categories of recidivism and how they might eliminate some of the problems in interpreting evaluation research.

5. Describe the process of randomized assignment and the role it plays in evaluation research.

PURPOSE

This chapter explores views on research and evaluation that are related to the operation of community corrections programs. It discusses who should conduct an evaluation, how information is collected for the evaluation, and how data sets are analyzed. The problems and pitfalls currently experienced in program evaluation are also described. Many of the ethical and moral considerations in conducting an evaluation are highlighted. This chapter serves as an overview of the role of evaluation research in community corrections and can give the student insight into the design and conduct of program evaluations throughout the criminal justice system.

INTRODUCTION

Evaluation research is a basic component of the operations of all correctional programs. The results of evaluation research aid us in making decisions about the future of programs. The findings tell us which programs are successful, which need to be changed, and in what ways. Evaluations also tell us which programs should be eliminated altogether. The goal of a particular program may be rehabilitation, deterrence, or other behavior outcomes. Regardless of which goal is used, it is neither useful nor logical to fail to determine whether it lives up to its promises or its potential.

Today, funding is limited, and there is great competition for funds among agencies and services in the criminal justice system. Evaluation research can indicate where best to spend whatever resources are available. For this reason, much of the motivation for conducting evaluation research is not only practical but economical.

A good evaluation tells administrators when a program is not meeting its goals. Hopefully operations can then be changed or adjusted to see that improvements take place. The process of evaluation can point to the kinds of changes needed to make a program successful. Even traditionally successful programs need to make periodic adjustments over time to allow for changes in offender populations or in public demands. Programs that are no longer needed are usually phased out and replaced with others that address current social problems.

Evaluation research should assist in the formulation of policy, but it should not be the sole basis for a policy. Some programs may be continued even when the evaluation findings are less than favorable. On occasion when expressed goals are not met (e.g., recidivism is not reduced), a program may still be retained for other values such as improving proportionality of sentencing, cost savings, or other organizational goals. The decision to continue a program is not solely a scientific judgment, but with good evaluations, it can be an informed decision.

In the past, program evaluation has been limited or nonexistent. One reason for this was that records were seldom kept or not kept accurately. Without meaningful and reliable data, it is difficult to gauge the success of programs or to compare prior results with current performance. As a consequence, we have developed accurate and quantitative data bases only since about the mid-1970s. In part, the current availability of aggregate data files is a product of the automated record-keeping components of most management information systems.

Another problem that restricted evaluations was that historically some programs ran out of funding and were closed before they could be evaluated. Others ended before enough treatment had taken place to make assessment meaningful. Because of changes in political administration, programs begun under the funding and leadership of one party are often abandoned by the other. Even when good evaluations have been made, politics still dictate many decisions about program funding. However, if meaningful evaluations exist, at least there is the opportunity to make policy decisions based on empirical evidence.

Presently two major forces are driving program evaluation. One is that funding is often tied to the presentation of evaluation reports. Another is that program evaluation in many agencies is required by law.

THE DIFFERENCE BETWEEN REPORTS AND RESEARCH

Today there is a significant amount of correctional program literature available in the form of reports. Reports supply data on the number and types of participants, outcomes of treatment, and costs associated with the various programs. Reports are basically statistical and are designed simply to provide facts and figures. Reports are atheoretical in that they are not testing a hypothesis about how and why a program works. In addition, they do not examine what outcomes can be expected. Reports are likely to be compiled by staff members of an agency or program.

Research, on the other hand, may be completed by social scientists from inside or outside of a program. Research is theoretical and involves the prediction of program outcomes. Research is the scientific test of a series of assumptions or hypotheses about a given treatment. Program evaluation research is best carried out with an experimental group that receives the new program, or treatment, and a control group that does not. The ability to replicate or reproduce research findings is important in substantiating the conclusions of any one study. As research findings are replicated in additional studies, we gain confidence in the ability of that program to produce the same results with similar populations. As Lundman explained:

> The gain in confidence is greatest when replications do not repeat in exact detail all of the elements of a previous project. The question to be answered by searching for replicative studies is whether a treatment hypothesis implemented under a variety of circumstances is effective, not whether a project precisely repeated would have the same results. Diversity along dimensions such as location, dates and subjects is important in assessing the general effectiveness of a particular approach.[1]

An evaluator's task may be to do either a statistical report or a research study. The nature and depth of the inquiry will depend on the type of information sought and the intended use of that information. If the purpose of the evaluation is simply to see if a program is meeting its goals (for example, to have clients complete the training or treatment), then a report may suffice. However, if the goal is to compare treatments or to measure the effects of a treatment over time, then a research study is needed.

WHO SHOULD EVALUATE?

Inside versus Outside Evaluators

In determining the best persons to evaluate a program, administrators make the distinction between "inside" and "outside" evaluators. Inside evaluators may be agency board members, the director, supervisors, or staff. Clients are often the source of inside evaluation material, too. Outside evaluators are usually persons brought in from the nearby area or even from distant parts of the country. They are experts or authorities in the kind of program being evaluated. In some cases they are administrators from similar programs in other states, scholars, or consultants. When expertise is not essential, community leaders may be selected to be evaluators.

There are many factors to consider when making the decision to use inside or outside evaluators. First is the issue of administrator *confidence*. It is important that the persons chosen to do the evaluation are competent and that they will inspire the confidence of those they inform. The second consideration is *objectivity*. It may be difficult for insiders to be objective about the material they review, to see facts clearly without prejudice. No doubt insiders are emotionally attached to the program and its development and have a vested interest in its success. It may also be politically and personally difficult for insiders to criticize the staff and policies with which they have worked so closely. Insiders may be personally motivated or pressured by others to produce results consistent with what the administration would like the results to show.

A third consideration is the value of a *clear understanding* of the program. Insiders usually have the advantage of really knowing what a program is about. They understand how goals have been translated into projects and relationships. Outsiders may miss the nuances of the operation of a program because they lack the working knowledge of it and how it fits into the overall agency operation. It is possible, however, that given the time and access to people and materials from a program an outsider could get an effective grasp of its workings.

The final aspect to be considered in making the decision to use inside or outside evaluators is the *plan the agency has for using the results*. Reports that are not going to be widely circulated or published may not require the neutral authority that is often attached to outside evaluations. When there is not much money or pressure to conduct a full-scale evaluation, in-house persons and methods may suffice. In some agencies, periodic inside evaluations occur on a regular basis with a large outside evaluation taking place only every three or five years.

Paid versus Volunteer Evaluators

Once the decision is made to use either inside or outside evaluators, there are still other considerations that go into the selection of an evaluator or evaluation team. One is the use of paid versus volunteer evaluators. There are distinct advantages to having paid evaluators, particularly the ability to hire the most respected people in the field. As a society, we tend to value and respect the work of professionals. Persons may find the work of paid professionals to be more credible and perhaps more neutral because they conducted the evaluation as part of a job. Although the use of volunteers may save the agency money, their product may have credibility problems. It is also difficult to pressure volunteers for the timely production of their findings and to expect a work in great depth and detail.

HOW TO EVALUATE

The major task of evaluation research is to determine whether programs have met their expressed goals. One of the problems in defining goals, however, is that goals often change over time. Changes may be the result of operational problems or adjustments to the surrounding environment. The impetus for change often comes from pressure from outside the organization, perhaps because of political influence or budget constraints. Evaluators should try to set up a clear picture of the goals of the program under scrutiny. Goals should be written and understood by everyone working in the program. Not everyone involved in each program will share the same specific goals. However, there should be a great deal of consensus among administrators, staff, and clients about the general goals of a program. With general on goals it will be clear what must be evaluated in order to determine the value of each program. Consider, for example, that the goal of a program is to aid clients in gaining a skill. For such a program, the evaluation may include the number of program graduates who score above a certain point on a national standardized skill test or the number of clients who find a job using that particular skill.

Choosing Evaluation Criteria

A few traditional rules apply to choosing evaluation criteria. In the long run, it is better to choose multiple criteria rather than single variables to test the success of a program. Although it may be easier and more convenient to monitor just one outcome, such a method does not allow for the possibility that there are a number of different indicators of success. Staff and clients may see several goals as being central to the program. For example, in evaluating a drug treatment program the criteria measured may include the following:

- Number of arrests during and following treatment.
- Number of positive drug tests following treatment.
- Participation in drug treatment sessions.

For criteria to be accurately measured, it is important to use those that can be quantified. That is, they can be assigned some numerical value or judged on a numerical scale. For example, it would be easier to measure how many months a person was able to maintain continuous employment rather than how they now feel about themselves. Feelings, attitudes, and impressions are difficult to quantify. Also, it is not easy to obtain consensus on their meaning even between only two or three persons. For this reason, evaluators should select variables for measurement for which there is considerable agreement as to their meaning or value. There should not be controversy over what a concept means or how it is best measured or if it is even important to the study. For example, in the three criteria listed earlier, an arrest is a concrete factor. A person was either arrested or he was not. There is no room for debate over whether the event occurred or did not occur. It is also assumed by a large segment of society that arrests are important follow-up measures in studies of correctional treatment.

Assessing the Reliability of Measurement Instruments

One of the most common tasks for research and evaluation studies is to determine whether or not the tests or instruments used in daily community corrections programming are reliable. Test instruments may be scales or surveys that are used in classification, needs assessment, or gathering data. They may also be used in program research to profile the types of offenders being serviced or to create comparable groups for an experimental study.

When a test or instrument is reliable, it will produce similar results over time. This is an important quality because with a reliable test because subtle changes, such as who administers the instrument or who scores it, will not make significant differences in the outcomes. For example, an agency may interview each incoming client by having the client complete an alcohol dependency questionnaire. The answers may then be interpreted differently by each counselor, depending on his or her own personal orientation toward drinking. Each counselor may also lead clients toward certain kinds of answers.

Reliability is an essential feature of classification instruments or risk assessment surveys. The *reliability* of a classification instrument is measured as the frequency with which the same classification occurs when several different officers score the same offender. In other words, when scorers change, the results do not fluctuate significantly. The reliability of a testing device is greatly reduced when officers do not trust the instrument, and as a result, an officer may change the score of one or more variables to raise or lower the total. This action puts the offenders into the supervision category that the officer feels is appropriate based on his or her own judgment. If such interference occurs frequently, the classification system is effectively destroyed.

Measures of the reliability of classification instruments are usually conducted in controlled settings. For example, several probation officers come into a room and listen to a taped interview. On the basis of what they hear, each officer scores the offender on the instrument provided. The researcher then determines how frequently the scores match. Studies of this type have produced reliability measures better than 85 percent—that is, 85 percent of the scores were close enough to be considered the same.[2]

In reality, however, we know that the everyday scoring of classification scales does not take place in a controlled environment. Furthermore, the review of an officer's scoring may be minimal. It is possible that the manipulation of scores occurs more frequently than anyone would care to admit. In one study in California, more than 100 classifications were rescored by a committee. The committee reviewed all the materials available to the officers who originally classified the cases. The committee came up with the same score on only 16 percent of the cases. Researchers estimated that at least 25 percent of the cases were being assigned to an inappropriate level of supervision. Although exact scoring is not necessary to assure that offenders are placed into the correct supervision level, broad discrepancies may have serious consequences.

With diminishing resources, probation and parole agencies are able to provide high levels of service to only a small portion of the clientele. For example, in some states, maximum, or intensive, supervision is offered to only 10 percent of the total caseload. If reliability in classification is a problem, it is possible that many of the offenders receiving this high level of service do not need it. In addition, many who do need it may be kept out by lack of space in the program.

The supervision imposed on maximum service cases is significantly different in quality (e.g., more frequent contact, drug testing, and searches) than that of lower level supervision. Therefore, the high-risk offender receives a more severe sanction than his or her lower-risk counterpart. It could be argued that maximum supervision is a greater penalty. When assignment to maximum supervision is made by manipulating the classification instrument, this penalty is applied in an arbitrary and perhaps unconstitutional manner. The cost to the community is that scarce resources are wasted and some high-risk offenders do not receive the level of services necessary to deter further criminality.

PROBLEMS IN PROGRAM DESIGN AND OPERATION

The way a program is designed or initially operated often makes it difficult to conduct a meaningful evaluation. That is, the program has not been planned so that one can scientifically or empirically determine its effects. Frequently, evaluation is only an afterthought, and only rarely does it influence the original working design of a program.

When evaluation is tagged on after a program is already underway, it is difficult to initiate a good method of evaluation. The conditions under which services are delivered have not been controlled sufficiently to allow program operators to say that it is the treatment itself that has led to a client's success or failure. Instead, other intervening factors in the participants' environment may have altered their performance.

The Problem of Random Assignment

Even if it were possible to measure accurately what a program has accomplished, there still is the problem of determining whether the program itself made any difference. A program group may be evaluated alone, without comparison to another similar group of clients. When this occurs, evaluators cannot be sure that those treated would not have achieved the same results even without the program. If, for example, a program to decrease drinking among alcoholic probationers succeeds, how can we be sure that those same individuals would not have stopped drinking even without the program? Although it is not likely, it is possible that they may have reduced their level of drinking even more without the program. That is, the program may have actually *increased* their drinking beyond the level they would be consuming had they been left alone. These kinds of problems make interpretation of results very difficult.

The best way to assure that evaluators will be able to interpret the results of a program correctly is to create a control group at the beginning of the program. This control group (a group that receives no treatment beyond the "normal" way people are processed) can then be compared to the program (treatment) group to see if there is a difference. Even here, though, problems of interpretation exist. If the two groups were not identical in the beginning, any difference at the end of the program may be attributable to the original difference. Age, race, sex, or income differences among the participants may be responsible for the differences in outcomes.

Ensuring that the treatment and control groups of a study are originally identical is a difficult task. One cannot simply choose people to be assigned to each group, even if various demographic characteristics such as age, race, sex, and income are known in advance and people with each of those characteristics are assigned equally between the two groups. Other characteristics may affect the results. Even if the two groups were identical at first, changes in the control group over time may still confound the comparison.

Researchers have learned that the best way to create identical treatment and control groups is to assign individuals randomly to the two groups. Although it seems as if this process would create the same results as looking for certain characteristics and then making assignments, randomization works because it produces an assortment of characteristics that balance one another. *Randomization* is usually achieved through the use of random numbers. Unfortunately, random assignment does not work with small groups; enough people are needed to produce a balance of characteristics.

Finally, a group cannot be partially assigned in a random process; its members must *all* be assigned that way. It is not uncommon for programs to make erroneous claims of randomized assignment. In fact, they purposely assigned some individuals to either the control or treatment group (for various reasons they thought were good at the time). In these cases, an evaluator does not know if the different assignment process created differences in the two groups, or, perhaps, kept the program from working. To cure this problem, evaluators have begun taking over random assignment procedures from the program workers. The researchers can simply flip a coin and assign each potential client into either the control or treatment group right from the start. By doing so, they can make sure that group assignments are truly random.

Despite the value of random assignment in helping to assure the validity of an evaluation outcome, many corrections administrators oppose its use. Although the courts have found that random assignment is a valid selection process for program intake decisions, administrators are reluctant to accept it. There are several reasons attempts to randomize program participants have not been successful in the past. One is that program administrators do not like to relinquish the authority to assign clients to treatment groups, partially as a result of a lack of understanding of the significance of randomization in assuring meaningful research. Furthermore, many administrators feel the need to control intake into the program in the belief that releasing control may jeopardize the program or deny needed services to an eligible client. Ironically, randomization is the fairest way of assuring that eligible clients receive the services of an experimental program.

A meaningful experimental evaluation cannot be conducted unless there are more eligible clients than there are places in the program. This way program participants will be compared to similar individuals who have completed other forms of programming or no programming at all. If there is enough room in a program to accommodate all who need the service, then there will be no one to attend alternative programs and therefore no comparison results. If there are not enough spaces in a program to accommodate all who need it, then the fairest way to select who will receive the new service is through randomization. Random assignment assures that all eligible persons will have an equal opportunity for selection without the biases that may be introduced by an intake person or committee. If the program administrator has carefully identified the personal characteristics and criminal history of the program participants, these criteria may be applied to an initial screening prior to random selection. This process will assure that all participants who enter the program are right for it. Random assignment will not introduce a population that would be disruptive to program goals. Through the use of random assignment, the administrator is assured both fairness in selection of participants and the appropriateness of the participants.

Once administrators understand and accept randomization, the next obstacle to overcome is the courts. In many jurisdictions, the courts have authority to order defendants into specific programs. As with the program administrator, the courts are reluctant to give up this authority to random assignment. Judges may have definite ideas about what disposition they want for each offender. In these cases, judges are hesitant to allow researchers to put some offenders in a control group when the judge believes that the treatment would be most helpful.

Researchers at the University of Southern California explained how the reluctance of the courts affected their ability to impose random assignments on probationers to electronic monitoring and regular probation groups:

> It was reported that some judges were resistant to the idea of ordering a probationer to participate in the program and subsequently discovering that their order was ignored because of the probationer's assignment to the control group. A highly influential judge expressed fear at a judges' meeting that such an occurrence would negate the credibility of their warnings to offenders. Therefore, we informed probation officials that every probationer for whom monitoring was ordered by the court would be assigned to monitoring rather than a random fraction being assigned immediately to the control group.[3]

In this case the researchers made a decision that could ultimately have jeopardized the interpretation of their program results. The randomized assignment process is not something that can be lightly sacrificed. The researchers may have believed that the entire future of the program was threatened unless they made this concession.

In addition to judges, prosecuting and defense attorneys are also involved in the sentencing process in both adult and juvenile courts. Attorneys for both sides want some say in the final disposition of cases. For true random assignment to occur, the court must keep its assignment preferences out of the program selection process. The appellate courts have held that judges who embrace the random assignment procedure do not deprive a person of the rights of due process. Nevertheless, convincing the court to accept the processes necessary for a good experiment is sometimes the most difficult obstacle to overcome.

The Problem of Multiple Treatments

One of the problems in the evaluation of community corrections is the ability to distinguish between the effects of simultaneous or overlapping treatments. For research purposes, it would be best for clients to receive only one treatment. That comparisons between the different treatments and persons getting no treatment could be made. In reality, however, programs exist to provide the maximum amount of benefits affordable and not for the ease of research. Therefore, in many cases, clients are often involved in multiple programs—for example, drug treatment, family counseling, and vocational training. Under such circumstances, it would be difficult to say that only one component is responsible for the client's success. Neither could it be determined whether all the elements would be necessary for someone to be successful.

The Problem of Selecting the Cream of the Crop

The concept of *creaming* generally refers to selecting the best participants for a program—that is, picking those with the highest likelihood of success. Although having a high success rate is important to the continued funding of any program, deceptive selection procedures make it difficult to compare the results of similar programs.

Working with offenders means servicing relatively high-risk groups of people compared to the general population. In any corrections program, there is going to be a level of failure that is expected and accepted, particularly as the group becomes younger and more seriously involved in crime. Unfortunately, the serious young offender group is also very large and in need of programming. This population should not be shunned by wary administrators who want to service those groups that are more likely to make their programs look successful. Care should be taken not to compare the results of programs that target groups of different levels of risk.

As Cohen, Eden, and Lazar found, most research on the outcome of probation does not control for the varying criminal potentials of offend-

Programs that carefully select highly motivated youths or programs that do not count initial participants who drop out are bound to have higher success rates. (*Courtesy of the Georgia Department of Corrections*)

ers when they are sentenced.[4] That is, most persons are selected for probation because they are perceived as being of lower risk than those who are sent to prison during the same period. Thus, to compare the two groups in terms of eventual recidivism is not only unfair but leads to erroneous conclusions. Those who go to prison and are later released are most likely a higher-risk group and a group more likely to recidivate than the probationers. Probationers themselves may be considered a "cream of the crop" group when compared to offenders with other sentences. Studies that track probationers over time and compare their performance to parolees or those under intensive supervision may contain biased samples.

The Problem of Participant Dropouts

The frequency of participant dropout from community corrections is another evaluation problem. In any given program, a large number of clients will be rearrested or revoked, or they will run away. As a result, those who remain are statistically more likely to succeed simply because they remain. The higher probability for success from those who stick it out may artificially elevate program outcomes. The best resolution of this situation is to account for the lost participants by explaining the ratio of participants who began to those who completed the program. It would also be helpful to profile the type of participant who drops out of or absconds from a program.

The Problem of Agency Resistance to Research

There are many reasons why agency personnel may resist efforts to conduct program research. A lack of understanding of the research goals may lead some workers to be fearful or suspicious of the investigation. Some employees may believe that negative findings will jeopardize their jobs or reflect poorly on their abilities. In these instances, workers may get defensive or even try to manipulate the gathering of the data.

Another potential problem is that the evaluation process may seem to make additional work for employees. Unless agency personnel understand the value of the research being conducted,they will likely resist and resent the extra burden of reports and data collection. In one study, researchers were met with objections from the union representing the agency workers. It was alleged that "the list and forms requested by Program Services was an appreciable additional task for already overworked probation officers, and the union contract stipulated that no substantial work increases were to be made without union approval."[5]

A number of preliminary steps can be taken within an agency prior to conducting evaluation research that will eliminate or minimize resistance. First, meet with program staff before the conduct of an evalua-

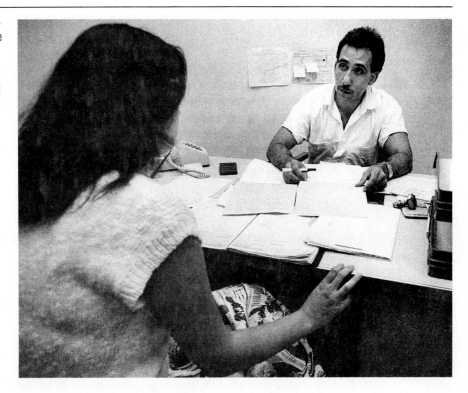

Design of a meaningful program evaluation may require probation or parole offices to gather or track additional information on their clients. Researchers must be careful to explain the importance of such data collection to the officers involved. (© *Bob Daemmerich/The Image Works*)

tion. Carefully explain the goals of the research. It is also important for personnel to see that the top program administrators and agency heads are supportive and cooperative in the research effort. Efforts should be made to eliminate fears and rumors about the use of the evaluation results. Researchers should give employees input into the process in areas that concern their functions and time. The results of the evaluation should be shared with and explained to agency employees. The evaluation process can then be a meaningful and painless experience for all.

The Problem of Recidivism as an Outcome Variable

The most common measure of a program's success is the participants' rate of recidivism. However, recidivism is a concept that has many connotations. The most general meaning is the commission of a new crime by a person who has already been processed through the criminal justice system. Otherwise, it may mean that a person on probation or parole has committed a new crime. It also may mean that someone who is an ex-offender commits a new crime.

There is often great variation between the exact meaning of recidivism in research studies. For example, in one study recidivism may mean that the person has been arrested, whereas in another it may be that the offender has been arrested and convicted. In yet another study, recidivism may mean that the person had been arrested, convicted, and given a prison term. It is obvious that the researchers in these studies will have three different rates of recidivism. It is more likely that offenders will have been rearrested than either convicted or given a new prison or jail term. Also, it is possible that probationers and parolees will be arrested but that in itself is not a guarantee that they have committed a new offense. By virtue of being a known felon, it is possible that some ex-offenders may be arrested on suspicion. This often occurs when their priors match a new but similar crime in their neighborhood.

Recidivism is often viewed as a product of law enforcement effort. The fact that a defendant has no new arrests does not necessarily mean that he or she has committed no new crimes. No new arrests simply means that no new crimes have been detected. Recidivism rates, then, will vary by the quality of law enforcement affecting the group of persons being studied. Two individuals living in different communities may commit the same type and number of offenses, but they will be subject to different probabilities of arrest. The chance of detection will vary by the level of law enforcement in each community. In addition, even if the level of detection of new offenses is the same, the subsequent handling of cases may be different in each area. One jurisdiction may pursue each new offense with a complaint filed in the prosecutor's office, whereas another may pursue only felony offenses or serious misdemeanors. If recidivism is defined as a new conviction, the person living in a jurisdiction that does not vigorously pursue prosecution would be deemed a "success." But the person living in a more prosecution-oriented community would be deemed a "failure."

It has been estimated that only one crime in 100 results in a jail or prison sentence.[6] Most crimes are not reported. Of those that are, only a few result in arrest. Fewer still reach the stage of prosecution, and even fewer result in jail or prison sentences. A criterion for measuring the success of probation or parole that relies on such a low rate of detection is certainly a poor one.

The level of supervision that a probationer or parolee is subject to may also influence the probability of recidivism. We have already discussed the ways intensive supervision may lead to higher levels of detection of offenses or violations of contract conditions. A program with a high level of aftercare or surveillance may generate high levels of recidivism. When compared to a program with lower levels of post-program supervision, participants in the experimental program may appear to be doing poorly. In reality, they may be doing better, but those who do violate are more likely to be discovered. Furthermore, with higher levels of supervision there may also be an increase in the probability that a detected violation will result in a new conviction or imprisonment.

Selecting Periods for the Measurement of Recidivism

One particularly confusing aspect of recidivism is the question, "When does a person put enough time between a prior offense and a new offense to avoid being considered a recidivist?" Ever? Take, for example, the 14-year-old boy who steals a car with a group of older rowdy friends. Because it is his first offense, he is put on probation. After 25 years of crime-free life, this man is now convicted of tax evasion. Is he a recidivist?

Recidivism is a more confusing concept than terms such as *chronic offender* or *habitual offender*. These labels are most often defined in terms of a legal status for which the criteria is a specific number and types of offenses over a certain period of time. For example, one state may define a habitual offender as someone who is convicted of three similarly patterned offenses over a period of 10 years.

Comparisons between the recidivism rates of various studies have been difficult for a number of reasons. One is that recidivism has been defined in several ways, as was discussed earlier. Another is that recidivism data in one report may be incorrectly compared to revocation figures in another. A person may have been revoked on technical grounds, such as failure to make payments or failure to meet with the probation officer, but such faults should not be compared to committing a new crime. In most cases, revocation rates are much higher than recidivism rates. Not everyone who is revoked has committed a new crime, but most of those who have committed a new crime have been revoked.

Degrees of Recidivism

Addressing the difficulties of the term *recidivism*, Glaser explained that recidivism may come in different degrees and that success may mean different things.[7] As demonstration, Glaser used four categories to describe the possible results of community supervision. The first is *clear reformation*, which he defined as being on parole for one year with steady work, committing no new crimes, and not spending time with other criminals. This result contrasts with *marginal reformation*, which is the status of a group that is less successful in the community. Although these clients have not returned to prison, they have failed to keep a job and to stop associating with bad influences. The third category is the *marginal failures*, who are those who have been returned to prison for violations of parole or probation or for some petty offense. Although this is a failure group, it is distinguished from the *clear recidivist*, who is an individual who has committed a new major crime for which he or she is sent to prison.

Although one must be careful in using the concept of recidivism in evaluation research, it is an important part of a program evaluation. The public has realistic concerns that programs designed to "correct" offenders still provide for a safe community. Citizens and their elected representatives are constantly expressing the need to know if programs really do what they set out to do. Research results that provide meaningful and clear information about recidivism are a valuable public service.

Another advantage of using recidivism in evaluation is that it can be applied as a relatively concrete measure. For example, when using arrests as a measure of recidivism, it is usually very easy to determine whether someone was arrested or not. Recidivism measures, when clearly defined and consistently applied, can be cut and dry: A person was either arrested or not arrested, charged with a crime or not, convicted or not, or revoked or not. There is little confusion about whether something occurred.

The Problem of Employment as a Measure of Success

Many theoretical problems are related to using employment as a measure of a program's success. One problem with employment data is that studies often fail to differentiate between the various levels of employment: full-time, part-time, and intermittent. Some studies do not include persons who are working part-time in the studies' employment categories, whereas others include this group without distinguishing their status. Both procedures misrepresent the true employment picture. In fact, some researchers may argue that employment status is relative to each client's history. For clients with no significant work history, steady part-time work may be a great improvement and a sign of successful treatment. On the other hand, those who have held permanent and high-paying jobs who now work only in part-time or low-paying positions may not have benefitted from treatment at all.

Another problem with work-related statistics is the inability of the data to discriminate between finding a job and keeping a job. Reports often simply indicate that a certain number or percentage of participants had found work upon completion of the program. However, the length of time employed and job stability are important aspects of their work experience that may provide more useful information about a program's effect than simply employment alone. Some data on clients are gathered at only one time—for example, on a certain date each year. As a result, the intermittent employee may be misrepresented. The data show that this person is actually employed on that date. However, they do not reflect that the person was unemployed the six months before or may be unemployed for six months after that date.

Although job changes are often treated as an indicator of instability, we should carefully examine the changes for their meaning. If each change brings higher pay and more responsibility, then these may be positive steps. It is also a positive step if the client changes jobs in the direction of a desired career or position. Reports should also carefully analyze the reasons for termination. Being fired is qualitatively different from being laid off during a recession. A thorough evaluation of employment must address the *quality* of the employment of each participant.

Studies that go into detail about employment may consider the wages earned and the status of the position held. Menial labor may be considered as underemployment if the person is skilled in some particular trade or profession. Changes in the availability of work and the wages earned may be a result of the local economy and beyond the control of the client. It would be inappropriate to compare the results of programs from different economic areas. It is unlikely that simply not having a job would be the cause of revocation of community supervision. However, unemployment may be linked to other revocation-producing behaviors such as drinking, fighting, and committing property offenses.

One of the most misleading aspects of employment statistics in evaluation research is the projection of employment rates over time. Some reports may say that anyone who ever held a job for any length of time has been employed, whereas others may set an arbitrary length of time as an adequate measure of success in employment. For example, six months or a year may be used as an indicator of stable employment. In each case it is up to the user of the report to determine if the indicator is justified. One way to make this determination is to look for the number of program participants employed at a certain point or on a particular date. Another way is to average such findings over time to determine the average number of clients employed at any given time during the study period.

COLLECTING DATA FOR EVALUATIONS

There are many sources from which information can be gathered when one is doing an evaluation. Once the program goals have been matched to measures of success, it is time to determine how best to collect those measurements. Sources of data include interviews, questionnaires, observations, program records, and files, as well as clinical examinations, official documents, and tests.

1. *Interviews.* The conduct of interviews gives the most accurate descriptions of how programs are operating as perceived by the people involved. Descriptions in interviews can be detailed, but it is often difficult to conduct a statistical analyses of them because interview sample sizes are usually small. It is also difficult to compile the results and make sense out of the aggregate data because not all participants will describe things in the same way. In addition, if clients are allowed to discuss issues in a rambling, conversational way, it will be difficult to compare the content of one interview to another.

One solution to the problem of varied answers is to use *structured interviews* in which the respondent comments are restricted to a choice of certain provided answers, so that there is little variation among responses. When selected responses are provided for the participants to choose from, the technique is often referred to as a *forced choice* format. The advantage of interviews over questionnaires is that the interviewer has personal contact with the subject. The interviewer can explain exactly what the questions mean, and the interviewer can be sure of understanding specifically what the subject's answer means. Any point that may be unclear may be elaborated on so that the integrity of the answers becomes strong. However, interviews may expose respondents to more stress and a tendency to "perform" for the interviewer. That is, the respondents will say things that they believe the interviewer would like to hear. There is also the potential for biased interviewers to hear those things they would like to hear from the interview.

2. *Questionnaires.* One of the advantages of questionnaires over interviews is anonymity for the respondent. People often feel more comfortable answering questions honestly if they believe they will not be identified by name and that their remarks will not be disclosed. One way that the answers to questionnaires can be more controlled, especially when building a large computerized data set, is to give the participant closed-ended questions. Close-ended questions mean that one set of multiple choice answers are prepared for all respondents. Categorizing the probable answers makes it easy to tabulate and analyze the responses. However, this method does not allow the respondent to give additional valuable information that may fall outside the given choices. Nor does it allow the respondent to qualify or elaborate on the information given so that the nature of the answer may be changed. Thus, some important descriptive data may not be tapped.

3. *Observations.* When evaluators come in to observe programs, an artificial atmosphere often takes over. The people being observed are often nervous and self-conscious and on their "best" behavior, or they often behave in unordinary ways that may confuse the evaluators. One solution is to try to make the observers less obvious and obtrusive. Another way to lessen the effects of evaluator interference is to extend the evaluation period or increase the number of visits. In this way, the evaluators become known and familiar figures around the data-gathering site.

To increase the reliability of observational data, Weiss suggests that evaluators record observations immediately as they are obtained.[8] Observations, when taken carefully and recorded accurately can greatly enhance the ability of the evaluator to convey the true qualities of a program.

4. *Program Records.* Logbooks, charts, intake records, and progress notes are valuable parts of the daily operation of any treatment or supervision program. However, these records may not always be in a form that is meaningful for research or that can be transformed into aggregate data files. For example, the type of family history data needed for a study may be found only in a rambling narrative case file. Thus, it would be very time-consuming to read each complete case history to extract the necessary information.[9] The initial design, or a redesign of existing agency records, could ease research and evaluation efforts.

Another serious challenge to the use of program records is their accuracy. The accuracy of records can be affected by many changes that may occur over time in a program. One such drastic change occurs when the designated staff member tracking the information is sick or leaves the job. Accuracy of records may also be threatened by changes in methods of measurement. For example, if a halfway house switches to a new and different drug test, the results may be better detection. If researchers are not aware of the test change, however, they may erroneously conclude that drug use among residents has increased. Additionally, there may be changes in the value of certain program criteria such as minor violations or levels of employment.

5. *Clinical examinations.* Clinical examinations are often conducted or reviewed to determine the medical or psychological gains that may have been realized by program participants. Important considerations for the use of clinical examinations are who is to conduct them and under what circumstances are they to be conducted. The medical or psychological characteristics noted should also be clearly defined using professionally accepted standards and measurements. The credentials of persons providing treatment results must be included, particularly when drug and alcohol treatment programs use paraprofessional facilitators. Evaluators should be careful to explain the limitations of such examinations or any other circumstances that may have influenced the findings.

6. *Tests.* A variety of tests may be given to measure client performance following some treatment. Psychological tests may characterize personality patterns or look for emotional or cognitive disturbances. Vocational tests look for career interests, aptitudes, or measurements of specific skills. Academic achievement tests assess the grade level at which a person is functioning. It is important to know and explain the validity and reliability factors of any test used.

When a test is valid, you will actually be measuring those values that you have proposed to measure. When a test is reliable, you will get the same results over time and with different groups of similar test subjects. However, it is also important to look for any elements in the environment that may be influencing the test subjects, such as noise, stress, or perceptions about the purpose of the test. The results of tests are more interpretively significant when pre- and post-treatment tests are given and then compared. By using this technique, an evaluator can detect improvements or changes in scores relative to a predetermined, or base, score.

7. *Government documents.* Government documents such as police records and revocation paperwork may also be an important source of evaluation data. However, it is important to remember that official records measure only behaviors brought to the attention of authorities. Evaluators most often use government documents as a *secondary data* source; they do not actually gather this information themselves. There is, therefore, a higher degree of error assumed in data that are gathered by someone else. This is especially true if it is someone who does not have a vested interest in the accuracy or integrity of the data.

INTERPRETING PROGRAM RESULTS

Several major problems face the person who tries to interpret program results. Many of the events that take place during the time a program is in operation are beyond the control of the treatment provider. Treatment does not take place in a controlled laboratory or a vacuum. Therefore, it is often difficult to assure that the program is the only thing responsible for the behavioral changes of the client.

One problem with interpreting program results is the possible interactive effects of sociohistorical events—the current events in a country, community, or even family that may have a profound impact on the offender. Researchers and evaluators should be careful to recognize, measure, and control for these events because they may affect program results. Wars, economic recessions, and changes in laws or probation criteria may not affect all program participants equally.

Another problem in attributing client success to program results is the possibility that the client may have matured to a point at which he or she is simply no longer interested in criminal activity. This event is more common in juveniles than adults and is referred to as the effect of *maturation.* It is often difficult to determine whether programs have had anything to do with the youth's outgrowing of delinquent behavior or whether this change would have occurred on its own. Thus, the possibility of maturation effects makes interpretation of program results problematic.

EVALUATING PROGRAM EVALUATIONS

The results of program evaluations are often published as research reports and are available to the public. As corrections professionals and as consumers, we must be aware of the problems that face the person who is comparing research findings. One consideration is the difference between a program outcome and a program impact.

The term *program outcome* simply refers to the completion of some stated goal or term of treatment. The outcome may be expressed in-terms of how clients graduate from a program or serve their probation sentences without getting arrested. *Program impact*, on the other hand, is the significance of an outcome, perhaps over time. Whereas outcomes are fairly concrete and simple to observe, impacts may be more difficult to assess. Counseling may improve an offender's self-concept. However, over time if the offender lacks the skills to get a job, then actual lifestyle may not be improved at all.

Impact is probably the most important but least measured aspect of program evaluation. It tells us if those clients who have completed probation or parole or some residential treatment program will be successful over a continued period. There are many professionals who believe that this is the truest measure of reintegration into the community.[10]

One of the major problems in comparing evaluation reports is that programs differ in scope. Some programs are national, some are state, and others are only county, city, or neighborhood efforts. The larger the base of support a program has, the more resources the developers may have at their disposal. It would be pointless to compare programs that come from significantly different levels of operation.

Likewise, the size of the population served in each program may vary. Programs with a large applicant pool may be able to more carefully select candidates—those they view as more likely to succeed. A recent study of the Georgia ISP demonstrated the problems of nonrandom selection of a control group. Early interpretation of the data showed that intensive supervision clients had lower recidivism rates than did regular supervision clients. This interpretation led to the conclusion that ISP worked, and the conclusions were used to expand the program. Later reevaluation of the data revealed that the ISP clients had less serious prior records than did the regular supervision clients. Because prior record is associated with recidivism, it is likely that the ISP had "stacked the deck" in its own favor.[11]

The duration of the program may also be an important variable affecting client behaviors. The longer and more intensive some treatments are, the more likely they may be to produce success.

Programs also vary in their degree of innovation or the radicalness of the treatment approach. When reviewing a program, be aware of whether the strategy is traditional or a drastic shift in treatment philosophy or style. When programs are built on traditional concepts, the designers as well as the evaluators must be aware of the previous findings of similar programs. The findings from earlier programs should be an important part of the evaluation of each subsequent program built on the same philosophy. The outcomes of each new effort will be gauged against previous results; similar findings or improvements would be expected.

Another factor to consider when comparing programs is their different goals. When goals are short-term and remedial, they may be more easily addressed than those that cover long-range improvements. For example, it is easier to find jobs for offenders than to engage them in meaningful and economically rewarding careers. There is a greater likelihood of success in graduating a person from an alcohol treatment program than there is in ensuring that the person remains alcohol free for two or three years. The way goals are worded and measured may not only make it difficult to compare programs but difficult to determine if some programs have met their goals.

The following abstract of a program evaluation is an interesting example of the points discussed in this chapter:

> Data were analyzed on 15 juvenile offenders participating in short-term intensive family counseling, and on 60 juveniles receiving casework-oriented probation services, under the supervision [of] the Lane County [Oregon] Juvenile Court. The effectiveness of the treatment provided the two groups was measured by reduced recidivism and improved family functioning. Recidivism was measured at four and seven months following the date of assignment to the program. The analyses indicate that family counseling was considerably more effective than probation services in reducing the number of recidivists, as well as the amount of recidivism.[12]

As you can see, the sample group receiving the experimental treatment, family counseling, is too small to make significant conclusions about the effect. Also it is four times smaller than the control group, which would make comparing them less meaningful. The two outcome measures, recidivism and improved family functioning, are problematic. We know that recidivism may mean many things, but the term *improved family functioning* is even more vague. In addition, the time frame for the measurement of success is very short. In four to seven months, it is difficult to say that any treatment has really "worked." What the evaluation may be measuring are some short-term, temporary effects that may not be maintained. Follow-ups after a year or two may give better indications of the strength of either outcome.

THE ETHICS OF EVALUATION

The research and evaluation process is filled with many ethical and moral dilemmas. Data and figures can always be presented from a variety of angles and perspectives that may make them more appealing than they really are.

One potential problem is that the public has great expectations for corrections programs that may not realistically occur. However, programs are dependent on continued community support and funding. Consequently, there is an emphasis on producing findings that will live up to those expectations. Marginal successes with most clients may be the realistic expectation, but the public often seems to believe that those on community supervision should be completely crime free. The community's demand to feel safe may put tremendous pressure on program officials to concentrate on research results that reflect complete success.

The ethical concerns of program evaluation are much the same as those for conducting research experiments. In most cases, data should not be gathered without the *informed consent* of the subjects who are providing information.

Informed Consent

Regardless of whether they are staff or client, all subjects should understand that they are participating in a program evaluation. They should also be aware of how the information they are supplying will be used. Furthermore, participants should not be coerced into participating in evaluations—that is, they should not be offered rewards for cooperation or threatened with negative actions should they refuse to cooperate. All evaluations should be designed with a sample size that is large enough to anticipate that a certain percentage of those selected will not want to participate.

The principle of informed consent is particularly difficult in research samples that are based on offender populations. First, this group traditionally has low levels of education and reading comprehension. Thus, if the directions, instructions, or explanations of a study are provided only in writing for the participant to sign, it can never be guaranteed that they are understood. Oral explanations that are full of technical jargon or scientific terminology may also provide little understanding. The best way to ensure informed consent is to provide oral and written explanations. Both should be geared toward low levels of comprehension and the written copies should be distributed to participants for their records.

Second, populations of corrections clients are also likely to be poor and in need of the stipends or fees the study may provide for their participation. Whenever there is an economic incentive or pressure on the subjects, it is difficult to call their involvement totally voluntary. Thus, they may not fully explore the details of explanations leading to informed consent unless there is a routine mandatory process for requiring them to do so. Researchers may hold a class prior to a research study to cover the material necessary to enable participants to give informed consent.

Third, informed consent is always suspect when subjects are offenders under community supervision because of the potential of the authorities to coerce cooperation and participation. Offenders may believe that participation will be equated with positive adjustment. They may also believe that failure to cooperate may lead to negative evaluations and possibly revocation.

Confidentiality

When evaluators use surveys or interviews, they should make every effort to protect the identity of each individual contributor. The information obtained concerning criminal or personal history must remain confidential. Ethical guidelines on confidentiality are subject to controversy under extreme circumstances, however. For example, what happens if an interviewee reveals information about a previously undetected serious crime such as murder, rape, or child abuse during the course of the interview? What if an interviewee indicates an intention to harm a specific person in the future? Are researchers ethically bound to reveal such a report? In your state, would researchers be legally bound to take such information to authorities? What is the relationship between legal mandate and ethical mandate?

SUMMARY

In the past, community corrections programs have been plagued by the lack of evaluation studies concerning their outcomes. Those studies that were conducted were limited in their ability to accurately assess a program. This is ironic because many corrections experts blame the decline of rehabilitation and treatment programs on public and professional skepticism over the ability to "prove" that these efforts really "work." Reports that criticized rehabilitation programs in the 1970s were not methodologically accurate in describing program outcomes. However, they were successful in focusing attention on the need for careful data collection and analysis before, during, and after the implementation of programs. According to Stuart Adams of the American University Law Institute, the most commonly attained objectives in programs are decreased recidivism, increased diversion, and improved cost effectiveness.[13] However, Adams cautioned, the three most common methodological deficiencies of the evaluations that boast those results are lack of a proper control group, lack of standards for measuring impact, and the use of insufficient data.

It is likely that people reading the results of studies on probationers and parolees will be overly impressed or depressed by the facts. Newspaper reports with statistics on success and failure may also be interpreted incorrectly. This is perhaps even more likely to occur if the reader has a vested or personal interest in the outcome. For these reasons, it is important that the limitations of any research study be carefully explained and that alternate explanations for the findings be explored. The latter requires searching for clues that may show that other factors were responsible for the success or failure of a client or of an entire program. As the number of possible rival explanations increases, the original research conclusions may become weaker.[14]

One of the most frustrating aspects of working directly in community corrections is that the value of programs is often determined by a single criterion: recidivism. Other problems include the selection of the cream of the crop as program participants and the failure to use random assignment of subjects as treatment and control groups. In addition, the sample sizes of groups receiving some experimental treatment are usually much smaller than either the standard treatment or control group, which in itself can make comparisons between the outcomes more difficult to interpret.

It has been shown that the best evaluations measure many aspects of a program and use a number of assessment tools and techniques. Also, the data used in analysis should not be gathered at only one point in time. Instead, measurements should be taken or observations made over an extended period.

There are many moral and ethical principles for researchers to consider during the course of a program evaluation. Protection of the dignity of the individual and the integrity of the program ensures that we can be proud not only of our community corrections efforts but of the methods we use to evaluate them.

KEY TERMS

closed-ended questions
creaming
informed consent
maturation
program outcome
program impact
randomization

recidivism
reliability
reports
research
secondary data
structured interviews
validity

DISCUSSION QUESTIONS

1. What would be the optimum composition of a team of evaluators for a community corrections program?
2. How have poorly designed evaluations affected the goals and priorities of community corrections programs in the past?
3. What would be the most meaningful community corrections program outcomes considered by an evaluation, and how would they be measured?
4. How would employment of ex-offenders or probationers, adults, and juveniles be affected by the economy in your area?

END NOTES

1. Lundman, Richard (1984). *Prevention and control of juvenile delinquency.* New York: Oxford Univ. Press, p. 43.

2. Baird, S. Christopher (1979). *Classification in probation and parole: A model systems approach.* Denver, CO: National Institute of Corrections.

3. Watts, Ronald, and Daniel Glaser (1990). Strains and gains of case-flow randomization for evaluating electronic monitoring of probationers in a large metropolis. Paper presented at the annual meeting of the American Society of Criminology, Baltimore.

4. Cohen, Ben-Zion, Ruth Eden, and Amnon Lazar (1990). The efficacy of probation vs. imprisonment in reducing recidivism of serious offenders in Israel. Paper presented at the annual meeting of the Academy of Criminal Justice Sciences, Denver, CO.

5. Watts, Ronald, and Daniel Glaser (1990). Supra note 3, p. 14.

6. Bureau of Justice Statistics (1983). *Report to the nation on crime and justice: The data.* Washington, DC: U.S. Government Printing Office, p. 32.

7. Glaser, Daniel (1964). *The effectiveness of a prison and parole system.* Indianapolis: Bobbs-Merrill.

8. Weiss, Carol (1972). *Evaluation research.* Englewood Cliffs, NJ: Prentice Hall.

9. Ibid.

10. Cowen, Emory L. (1978). Some problems in community program evaluation research. *Journal of Consulting and Clinical Psychology* 46(4):792–805.

11. Petersilia, Joan (1991). The value of corrections research: Learning what works. *Federal Probation* 55(2):24–26.

12. McPherson, Susan, Lance McDonald, and Charles Ryer (1983). Intensive counseling with families of juvenile offenders. *Juvenile and Family Court Journal* 34(1):27–33.

13. Adams, Stuart (1975). *Evaluative research in corrections.* Washington, DC: Law Enforcement Assistance Administration, U.S. Department of Justice, p. 106.

14. Katzer, Jeffrey, Kenneth Cook, and Wayne Crouch (1991). *Evaluating information* (3rd ed.). New York: McGraw-Hill.

Bibliography

ABADINSKY, HOWARD (1989). *Drug abuse: An introduction.* Chicago: Nelson-Hall.

ABRAMS, STANLEY, AND ERNEST OGARD (1986). Polygraph surveillance of probationers. *Polygraph* 15(3):174–182.

ADAIR, DAVID (1989). Looking at the law. *Federal Probation* 53(1):85–88.

ALLEN, D. M. (1980). Young male prostitutes: A psychological study. *Archives of Sexual Behavior* 9(5):399–426.

ALLEN, HARRY, ERIC CARLSON, EVALYN PARKS, AND RICHARD SEITER (1978) *Halfway houses.* Washington, DC: National Institute of Law Enforcement and Criminal Justice.

ALTSCHULER, DAVID (1991). The supervision of juvenile offenders in Maryland: Policy and practice implications of the Department of Juvenile Services workload study. Baltimore: Johns Hopkins Univ., Institute for Policy Studies.

ANDREWS, D. A., I. ZINGER, R. D. HOGE, J. BONTA, P. GENDREAU, AND F. T. CULLEN (1990). Does correctional treatment work? A clinically relevant and psychologically informed meta-analysis. *Criminology* 28(3):369–404.

ANGLIN, M. (1990). Ensuring success in corrections-based intervention with drug-abusing offenders. Paper presented at the Conference on Growth and Its Influence on Correctional Policy, 10–11 May 1990, at Univ. of California, Berkeley.

ANSON, RICHARD (1990). Reply to a "Five year follow-up of Dougherty County's criminal alcoholic program." *International Journal of Offender Therapy and Comparative Criminology* 34(3):249–258.

ARCAYA, JOSE (1973). The multiple realities inherent in probation counseling. *Federal Probation* 37(4):58–63.

ARCHIBALD, MATTHEW (1989). Women and crime: New perspectives. *APPA Perspectives* Summer: 28–30.

ARGOW, CLAIRE (1980). Corrections in the community—Multnomah County, Oregon. *Corrections Today* 42(1):28.

ARMSTRONG, CLAIRETTE (1932). *660 runaway boys.* Boston: B. Humphries.

ARMSTRONG, TROY (1988). National survey of juvenile intensive supervision (Part 1). *Criminal Justice Abstracts* (June):342–348.

——,DENNIS MALONEY, AND DENNIS ROMIG (1990). The balanced approach in juvenile probation: Principles, issues and application. *APPA Perspectives* Winter:8–13.

ASHFORD, JOSE, AND CRAIG LECROY (1988). Predicting recidivism: An evaluation of the Wisconsin Juvenile Probation and Aftercare Risk Instrument. *Criminal Justice and Behavior* 15(2):141–151.

ASSOCIATED PRESS (1989). One in 24 inmates infected with AIDS. *Corrections Today* 51(7):165.

——, (1990). U.S. fear of AIDS spurs unneeded bias—ACLU. *San Bernardino Sun,* 17 June:A7.

ASSUR, ERIC, GERALD JACKSON, AND TERESA MUNCY (1987). Probation counselors and the adult children of alcoholics. *Federal Probation* 51(3):41–46.

BACON, STEPHEN, AND RICHARD KIMBALL (1989). The wilderness challenge model. In *Residential and inpatient treatment of children and adolescents,* ed. Lyman, Prentice-Dunn, and Stewart, New York: Plenum, pp. 115–144.

BACHMAN, J. G., P. O'MALLEY, AND J. JOHNSTON (1978). *Youth in transition VI, Adolescence to adulthood.* Ann Arbor, MI: Institute for Social Research.

BAER, BENJAMIN, AND JODY SAFFRAN (1990). Keeping parole under lock and key. *Corrections Today* 52(1):17.

——, AND JODY KLEIN (1987). Reparative work programs benefit communities and offenders. *Corrections Today* 49(7):84.

BAER, JAMES, WERNER BAUMGARTNER, VIRGINIA HILL, AND WILLIAM BLAHD (1991). Hair analysis for the detection of drug use in pretrial, probation and parole populations. *Federal Probation* 55(1):3–10.

BAIRD, CHRISTOPHER (1986). *Fees for probation services.* Boulder, CO: National Institute for Corrections.

——, AND RICHARD PRESTINE (1988). *Revalidation of the Illinois risk assessment system.* Madison, WI: National Council on Crime and Delinquency.

BAIRD, S. C. (1981). Probation and parole classification: The Wisconsin model. *Corrections Today* 43(3):36.

——, AND DENNIS WAGNER (1990). Measuring diversion: The Florida community control program. *Crime and Delinquency* 36(1):112–125.

BAKER, JON (1988). Forum on juvenile corrections tackles tough issues. *Corrections Today* 50(4):132.

BANKS, J., A. L. PORTER, R. L. RARDIN, T. R. SILER, AND V. E. UNGER (1977). Evaluation of intensive special probation. *Summary Phase I, Evaluation of Intensive Special Probation Projects, Law Enforcement Assistance Administration.* Washington, DC: U.S. Department of Justice, U.S. Government Printing Office.

BARKDULL, WALTER (1988). Parole and the public: A look at attitudes in California. *Federal Probation* 52(3):15–20.

BARKIN, EUGENE (1979). Legal issues facing parole. *Crime and Delinquency* 25(2): 219–235.

BARTON, WILLIAM, AND JEFFREY BUTTS (1990). Viable options: Intensive supervision programs for juvenile delinquents. *Crime and Delinquency* 36(2):238–256.

BAUMER, TERRY, MICHAEL MAXFIELD, AND ROBERT MENDELSOHN (1990). A comparative analysis of three electronically monitored home detention programs. Paper presented at the annual meeting of the American Society of Criminology, Baltimore.

BECCARIA, CESARE (1963). *On crimes and punishments*. Indianapolis: Bobbs–Merrill, p. 63. Originally published 1764.

BECK, JAMES (1979). An evaluation of federal community treatment centers. *Federal Probation* 43(3):36–39.

BECK, ALLEN, AND BERNARD SHIPLEY (1987). *Recidivism of young parolees*. Washington, DC: Bureau of Justice Statistics.

BECKLEY, LOREN, AND CHRISTINE CALLAHAN (1980). The presentence investigation report program: A preliminary report. *Correction Today* 42(1):10.

BEDLINGTON, MARTHA, CURTIS BRAUKMANN, KATHRYN RAMP, AND MONTROSE WOLF (1988). A comparison of treatment environments in community-based group homes for adolescent offenders. *Criminal Justice and Behavior* 15(3):349–363.

BELL-ROWBOTHAM, B., AND C. L. BOYDELL (1972). Crime in canada: A distributional analysis. In *Deviant behavior and societal reaction*, ed. C. L. Boydell et al. Toronto: Holt, Rinehart and Winston.

BENEKOS, PETER (1990). Beyond reintegration: Community corrections in a retributive era. *Federal Probation* 54(1):52–56.

BENNETT, LAWRENCE (1989). Jail as a part of probation: What price punishment? *APPA Perspectives* Summer: 18–21.

—— (1991). The public wants accountability. *Corrections Today* 53(4):92, 94–95.

BENNETT, SUSAN (1990). Community organizing and implementation of the community response to drug abuse program. Paper presented at the annual meeting of the American Society of Criminology, Baltimore.

BERGSMANN, ILENE (1989). The forgotten few: Juvenile female offenders. *Federal Probation* 53(1):73–78.

BERRY, BONNIE (1985). Electronic jails: A new criminal justice concern. *Justice Quarterly* 2(1):1–22.

BIGGER, PHILIP (1991). Federal drug aftercare: Its evolution and current state. *Federal Probation* 55(2):42–46.

BINDER, ARNOLD, AND VIRGINIA BINDER (1982). Juvenile diversion and the Constitution. *Journal of Criminal Justice* 10(1):1–24.

BINDER, ARNOLD, MICHAEL SCHUMACHER, GWEN KURZ, AND LINDA MOULSON (1985). A diversionary approach for the 1980's. *Federal Probation* 49(1):4–12.

BLOCH, HERBERT, AND ARTHUR NIEDERHOFFER (1958). *The gang: A study in adolescent behavior*. New York: Philosophical Library.

BONDI, CONNIE (1990). When policies conflict: Can retributive state policy goals be met effectively by rehabilitative alternative sentencing strategies? Paper presented at the annual meeting of the Academy of Criminal Justice Sciences, Denver, CO.

BOWLING, LINDA (1987). Day treatment for juveniles: A boon in bluegrass country. *Corrections Today* 49(3):104.

BREMNER, ROBERT, ED. (1970). *Children and youth in America*. Cambridge, MA: Harvard University Press.

BRISCOE, JUDY (1990). In Texas: Reaching out to help troubled youths. *Corrections Today* 52(6):90.

BRODERICK, KIMBERLY, AND CHARLES HANNA (1990). Field officers: The impact of role-taking in an intensive supervision program. Paper presented at the annual meeting of the Academy of Criminal Justice Sciences, Denver, CO.

BROWN, PAUL (1989). Morrissey revisited: The probation and parole officer as hearing officer. *Federal Probation* 53(2):13–17.

—— (1990). Guns and probation officers: The unspoken reality. *Federal Probation* 54(2):21–26.

BUCK, GERALD (1989). Effectiveness of the new intensive supervision programs. *Research in Corrections* 2(2):64–75.

BULLINGTON, BRUCE, JAMES SPROWLS, DANIEL KATKIN, AND MARK PHILLIPS (1978). A critique of diversionary juvenile justice. *Crime and Delinquency* 24(1):59–71.

BUREAU OF CRIMINAL STATISTICS (1988). *Adult felony arrests in California, 1987.* Sacramento: Bureau of Criminal Statistics, July.

BUREAU OF JUSTICE STATISTICS (1989). *Drugs and crime facts, 1988.* Washington, DC: U.S. Department of Justice.

—— (1987). *Probation and parole—1985.* Washington, DC: U.S. Department of Justice.

—— (1988). *Probation and parole—1987.* Washington DC: U.S. Department of Justice.

—— (1989). *Probation and parole—1988.* Washington, DC: U.S. Department of Justice.

—— (1988). *Report to the nation on crime and justice.* Washington, DC: U.S. Department of Justice.

BURTON, AFTON (1984). *An action plan for the statewide implementation of the National Institute of Corrections (NIC) model probation client classification and management system.* Shasta, CA: Chief Probation Officers of California.

BYRNE, JAMES (1988). *Probation.* Washington, DC: National Institute of Justice, U.S. Department of Justice.

—— (1990). The future of intensive probation supervision and the new intermediate sanctions. *Crime and Delinquency.* 36(1):6–41.

——, ARTHUR LURIGIO, AND CHRISTOPHER BAIRD. (1989). The effectiveness of the new intensive supervision programs. *Research in Corrections* 2(2):1–48.

——, LINDA KELLY, AND SUSAN GUARINO-GHEZZI (1988). Understanding the limits of technology: An examination of the use of electronic monitoring in the criminal justice system. *APPA Perspectives* Spring: 30–37.

CADIGAN, TIMOTHY (1991). Electronic monitoring in federal pretiral release. *Federal Probation* 55(1):26–30.

CAHALAN, MARGARET (1986). *Historical corrections statistics in the United States, 1850–1984.* Washington, DC: Bureau of Justice Statistics, U.S. Department of Justice.

CALIFORNIA YOUTH AUTHORITY (1976). *California's Probation Subsidy Program.* Sacramento: California Youth Authority.

CANTER, RACHELLE (1982). Sex differences in self-report delinquency. *Criminology* 20:373–393.

CARLSON, ERIC (1980). Field testing prerelease centers. *Corrections Today* 42(1):16.

CARTER, ROBERT, JACK COCKS, AND DANIEL GLASER (1987). Community service: A review of the basic issues. *Federal Probation* 51(1):4–10.

CARTER, ROBERT, AND L. WILKINS (1984). Caseloads: Some conceptual models. In *Probation parole and community,* ed. Robert Carter and Leslie Wilkins. *Corrections.* New York: Wiley.

CASO, FRANK. Warren Kimbro of Project More: Rehabilitation starts from the individual. *Crisis* 98(4):34–36.

CASTELLANO, THOMAS, AND IRINA SODERSTROM (1990). Wilderness challenges and recidivism: A program evaluation. Paper presented at the annual meeting of the American Society of Criminology, Baltimore.

CAVENDER, GRAY (1981). "Scared Straight": Ideology and the media. *Journal of Criminal Justice* 9(6):431–440.

CENTER FOR STUDIES OF CRIME AND DELINQUENCY (1971). *Diversion from the criminal justice system.* Rockville, MD: National Institute of Mental Health.

CERQUONE, JEANNE 1987. Florida's community control. *Corrections Today* 49(3):1987.

CHAMPION, DEAN (1989). Teenage felons and waiver hearings: Some recent trends, 1980–1988. *Crime and Delinquency* 35(4):577–585.

——— (1990). *Probation and parole in the United States.* Columbus, OH: Merrill.

CHARLES, MICHAEL T. (1989a). Research note: Juveniles on electronic monitoring. *Journal of Contemporary Criminal Justice* 5(3):165–172.

——— (1989b). The development of a juvenile electronic monitoring program. *Federal Probation* 53(2):3–12.

CHAVEZ, KEN (1990). Vandal's sentence: Scrub Viet Vet Memorial for one year. *Sacramento Bee.* 20 June:B1.

CHESNEY-LIND, MEDA (1977). Judicial paternalism and the female status offender. *Crime and Delinquency.* 23:121–130.

——— (1988). Girls and status offenses: Is juvenile justice still sexist? *Criminal Justice Abstracts* March: 144–165.

CICCHETTI, C. ET AL. (1989). *Drugs & criminals: A dangerous mix.* Boston: Massachusetts Office of Commissioner of Probation.

CLARKE, STEVENS (1979). What is the purpose of probation and why do we revoke it? *Crime and Delinquency* 25(4):409–424.

CLEAR, TODD (1988). A critical assessment of electronic monitoring in corrections. *Policy Studies Review* 7(3):671–681.

———, AND K. GALLAGHER (1985). Probation and parole supervision: A review of current classification practices. *Crime and Delinquency* 31:423–443.

———, SUZANNE FYNN, AND CAROL SHAPIRO (1987). Intensive supervision in probation. In *Intermediate punishments: Intensive supervision, home confinement and electronic surveillance,* ed. Belinda McCarthy. Monsey, NY: Criminal Justice Press.

———, AND PATRICIA HARDYMAN (1990). The new intensive supervision movement. *Crime and Delinquency* 36(1):42–60.

———, VAL CLEAR, AND WILLIAM BURRELL (1989). *Offender assessment and evaluation: The presentence investigation report.* Cincinnati: Anderson Publishing.

COATES, ROBERT (1974). Community–based corrections: Concept, impact, dangers. In *Juvenile correctional reform in Massachusetts.* Washington, DC: National Institute for Juvenile Justice and Delinquency Prevention.

———, AND R. GEHM (1985). *Victim meets offender: An evaluation of victim offender reconciliation programs.* Michigan City, IN: PACT Institute of Justice.

COCHRAN, DONALD (1989). Corrections' Catch-22—Can probation keep up its reputation? *Corrections Today* 51(6):16.

COHEN, BEN-ZION, RUTH EDEN, AND AMNON LAZAR (1990). The efficacy of probation vs. imprisonment in reducing recidivism of serious offenders in Israel. Paper presented at the annual meeting of the Academy of Criminal Justice Sciences, Denver, CO.

COLE, GEORGE (1989). Innovations in collecting and enforcing fines. *NIJ Research in Action* July/August:2–6.

COLVIN, MARK (1991). Crime and social reproduction: A response to the call for "Outrageous" proposals. *Crime and Delinquency* 37(4): 436–448.

CORBETT, JR., RONALD (1989). Electronic monitoring—Forcing a redefinition of probation officers' duties. *Corrections Today* 51(6):74.

——, AND ELLSWORTH FERSCH (1985). Home as prison: The use of house arrest. *Federal Probation* 49(1):13–17.

——, AND GARY MARX (1990). No soul in the new machine: Techofallacies in the electronic monitoring movement. Paper presented at the annual meeting of the American Society of Criminology, Baltimore.

CORBO, CYNTHIA (1988). Release outcome in New Jersey 1982 release cohort: A 36-month follow-up study. Newark: New Jersey Criminal Disposition Commission.

COURLANDER, MICHAEL (1988). Restitution programs: Problems and solutions. *Corrections Today* 50(4):165.

COVEY, HERBERT, AND SCOTT MENARD (1984). Community corrections diversion in Colorado. *Journal of Criminal Justice* 12(1):1–10.

COWLEY, GEOFFREY, MARY HAGER, AND RUTH MARSHALL (1990). AIDS: The next ten years. *Newsweek*, June 25:20–27.

CRESPO, MANUEL (1974). Career of the school skipper. In *Deviance: The interactionist perspective* (5th ed.), ed. Earl Rubington and Martin Weinberg. New York: Macmillan.

CRESSEY, D., AND ROBERT MCDERMOTT (1973). *Diversion from the juvenile justice system*. Ann Arbor: National Assessment of Juvenile Corrections, Univ. of Michigan.

CROMWELL, PAUL, GEORGE KILLINGER, HAZEL KERPER, AND C.D. WALKER (1985). *Probation and parole in the criminal justice system*. St. Paul, MN: West Publishing.

CULBERTSON, ROBERT, AND THOMAS ELLSWORTH (1985). Treatment innovations in probation and parole. In *Probation, parole and community corrections*, ed. Lawrence Travis. Prospect Heights, IL: Waveland Press.

CUMMINGS, LAIRD (1988). Developing a microcomputer-based management information system for fines administration. *Justice System Journal* 13(1):80–92.

CUNNIFF, MARK, AND MARY SHILTON (1990). *A sentencing postscript II: Felony probationers under supervision in the community*. Washington, DC: Bureau of Justice Statistics.

CURRAN, JOHN (1989). A priority for parole: Agencies must reach out to the media and the community. *Corrections Today* 51(1):30–34.

CURRIE, E. 1985. *Confronting crime*. New York: Pantheon.

DANESH, YOUSEF (1989). Baton Rouge ex-offender's clearinghouse: A casualty of misguided savings. *International Journal of Offender Therapy and Comparative Criminology* 33(3):207–214.

DATESMAN, SUSAN, AND MIKEL AICKIN (1984). Offense specialization and escalation among status offenders. *Journal of Criminal Law and Criminology* 75:1246–1275.

DEANGELO, ANDREW (1988). Diversion programs in the juvenile justice system: An alternative method of treatment for juvenile offenders. *Juvenile and Family Court Journal* 39(1):21–27.

DEAN-MYRDA, AND FRANCIS CULLEN (1985). The panacea pendulum: An account of community as a response to crime. In *Probation, parole and community corrections*, ed. Lawrence Travis. Prospect Heights, IL: Waveland Press.

DEL CARMEN, R. (1985). *Potential liabilities of probation and parole officers*. Washington, DC: National Institute of Corrections, U.S. Department of Justice.

—— (1990). Probation and parole: Why you're getting sued. *Corrections Today* 52(5):34.

——, AND JONATHAN SORENSEN (1988). Legal issues in drug testing probationers and parolees. *Federal Probation* 52(4):19–27.

—— , AND JOSEPH VAUGHN (1986). Legal issues in the use of electronic surveillance in probation. *Federal Probation* 50(2):60–69.

——, BETSY WITT, THOMAS CAYWOOD, AND SALLY LAYLAND (1989). *Probation law and practice in Texas.* Huntsville: Criminal Justice Center, Sam Houston State Univ.

DEMBO, RICHARD, MAX DERTKE, SCOTT BORDERS, MARK WASHBURN, AND JAMES SCHMEIDLER (1985). The relationship between physical and sexual abuse and illicit drug use among youths in a juvenile detention center. Revision of a paper presented at the Annual Meeting of the Academy of Criminal Justice Sciences, Las Vegas, NV.

DIETRICH, SHELLE (1979). The probation officer as therapist: Examination of three major problem areas. *Federal Probation* 43(2):14–19.

DITTENHOFFER, TONY, AND RICHARD ERICSON (1983). The victim offender reconciliation program: A message to correctional reformers. *University of Toronto Law Journal* 33(3):315–347.

DIIULIO, JOHN (1989). Conflicts of criminal interest: A program for streets and jails. *Los Angeles Times*, 1, October: p. 4.

DRIGGS, JOHN, AND THOMAS ZOET (1987). Breaking the cycle—Sex offenders on parole. *Corrections Today* 49(3):124.

DYKSTRA, GRETCHEN (1987). *Crime and punishment: The public's view.* New York: Edna McConnell Clark Foundation.

EAGLIN, JAMES, AND PATRICIA LOMBARD (1981). Statistical risk prediction as an aid to probation caseload classification. *Federal Probation* 45(3):25–32.

—— (1982). *A validation and comparative evaluation of four predictive devices for classifying federal probation caseloads.* Washington, DC: Federal Judicial Center.

Eisenberg, Michael (1985). *Release outcome series: Halfway house research.* Austin: Texas Board of Pardons and Paroles.

—— (1989). Parole officer safety and security survey. Austin: Texas Board of Pardons and Paroles.

Ellsworth, Thomas (1990). Identifying the actual and preferred goals of adult probation. *Federal Probation* 54(2):10–15.

ELROD, H. PRESTON, AND KEVIN MINOR (1990). Second wave evaluation of a multi-faceted intervention for juvenile court probationers. Paper presented at the annual meeting of the American Society of Criminology, Baltimore.

ELY, RICHARD (1989). Report on the safety concerns of probation and alternatives to incarceration staff in New York State. Albany: Bureau of Policy, Planning and Information, New York Division of Probation and Correctional Alternatives.

EMPEY, LAMAR (1978). *American delinquency.* Homewood, IL: Dorsey Press.

——, AND MAYNARD ERICKSON. 1972. *The Provo Experiment.* Lexington, MA: Lexington Books.

——, AND STEVEN LUBECK (1971). *The Silverlake Experiment.* Chicago: Aldine.

ENKOJI, M. S. (1989). Treatment programs help addicts restructure lives. *San Bernardino Sun*, 22 October: p. 8.

ENRIGHT, RAY (1988). Colorado parole: Exacting an imperfect science. *Corrections Today* 50(3):46.

ERICKSON, MAYNARD (1979). Some empirical questions concerning the current revolution in juvenile justice, pp. 277–311. In *The future of childhood and juvenile justice,* ed. L. T. Empey, Charlottesville: Univ. of Virginia Press.

ERWIN, BILLIE (1990). Old and new tools for the modern probation officer. *Crime and Delinquency* 36(1):61–74.

———, AND LAWRENCE BENNETT (1987). *New dimensions in probation: Georgia's experience with intensive probation supervision.* Washington, DC: National Institute of Justice, U.S. Department of Justice.

EZELL, MARK (1989). Juvenile arbitration: Net widening and other unintended consequences. *Journal of Research in Crime and Delinquency* 26(4):358–377.

FARE, KENNETH (1982). Managing probation programs in an era of diminishing resources. *Corrections Today* 44(3):68.

FAUST, FREDERICK, AND PAUL BRANTINGHAM (1979). Models of juvenile justice—Introduction and overview. In *Juvenile justice philosophy (2nd ed.)* ed. Faust and Brantingham, pp. 1–36. St. Paul, MN: West Publishing.

FEYERHERM, WILLIAM (1981). Measuring gender differences in delinquency: Self-report vs. police contact. In *Comparing female and male offenders,* ed. M. Warren, pp. 46–54, Beverly Hills, CA: Sage.

FINCKENAUER, JAMES O. (1982). *Scared Straight! and the panacea phenomenon.* Englewood Cliffs, NJ: Prentice Hall.

FINN, R. H., AND PATRICIA FONTAINE (1985). The association between selected characteristics and perceived employability of offenders. *Criminal Justice and Behavior* 12(3):353–365.

FLANAGAN, TIMOTHY (1985). Questioning the "other" parole. In *Probation, parole and community corrections,* ed. Lawrence Travis. Prospect Heights, IL: Waveland Press.

FOGEL, DAVID (1975). . . . *We are the living proof.* . . Cincinnati: Anderson Publishing.

FORD, DANIEL, AND ANNESLEY K. SCHMIDT (1985). *Electronically monitored home confinement.* Washington, DC: National Institute of Justice, U.S. Department of Justice.

FRAZIER, CHARLES, WILBUR BOCK, AND JOHN HENRETTA (1983). The role of probation officers in determining gender differences in sentencing severity. *Sociological Quarterly* 24(2):305–318.

FRIEL, CHARLES, AND JOSEPH VAUGHN (1986). A consumer's guide to the electronic surveillance of probationers. *Federal Probation* 50(3):3–14.

GALAWAY, BURT (1988). Restitution as innovation or unfilled promise. *Federal Probation* 52(3):3–14.

———, AND W. MARSELLA (1976). An exploratory study of the perceived fairness of restitution as a sanction for juvenile offenders. Paper presented at the Second International Symposium on Victimology, Boston, MA.

GATZ, NICK, AND CHRIS MURRAY (1981). An administrative overview of halfway houses. *Corrections Today* 43(6):52.

GEIS, GILBERT (1990). Crime victims: Practices and prospects. In Arthur Lurigio, Wesley Skogan, and Robert Davis (eds.) *Victims of crime.* Newbury Park, CA: Sage.

———, AND ARNOLD BINDER (1990). Sins of their children: Parental responsibility for juvenile delinquency. Paper presented at the annual meeting of the Academy of Criminal Justice Sciences, Denver, CO.

GEORGIA DEPARTMENT OF CORRECTIONS (1988). *Probation's role in a balanced approach to corrections*. Atlanta: Georgia Department of Corrections.

GEST, TED (1989). Personalized penalties. *U.S. News & World Report* 20:75–76.

GIBBONS, DON, AND MARVIN KROHN (1986). *Delinquent behavior*, 4th ed. Englewood Cliffs, NJ: Prentice Hall.

GIBBS, JOHN (1982a). Measuring the needs and satisfaction of probationers. *Journal of Criminal Justice* 10(6):469–480.

———, (1982b) Inside supervision: A thematic analysis of interviews with probationers. *Federal Probation* 46(4):40–46.

——— (1985). Clients' views of community corrections. In *Probation Parole and Community Corrections*, ed. Lawrence Travis. Prospect Heights, IL: Waveland Press.

GILLESPIE, ROBERT (1989). Criminal fines: Do they pay? *Justice System Journal* 13(3):365–378.

GLASER, DANIEL (1983). Supervising offenders outside of prison. In *Crime and public policy*, ed. James Q. Wilson, pp. 207–227. San Francisco: Institute for Contemporary Studies.

——— (1987). Classification for risk. In *Prediction and classification: Criminal justice decision making*, ed. Gottfredson and Tonry. Chicago: Univ. of Chicago Press.

———, AND MARGARET GORDON (1988). *Use and effectiveness of fines, jail, and probation*. Los Angeles: Univ. of Southern California, Social Science Research Institute

GLUECK, SHELDON (1933). *Probation and criminal justice*. New York: Macmillan.

GODDARD, HENRY (1921). *Juvenile delinquency*. New York: Dodd, Mead.

GOLDEN, JAMES, KIMBERLY TESTER, AND MARGARET FARNWORTH 1990. Court responses to felony DWI and drug offenses in Harris County Texas 1978 to 1988. Paper presented at the annual meeting of the American Society of Criminology, Baltimore.

GOLDFARB, RONALD, AND LINDA SINGER (1973). *After conviction*. New York: Simon & Schuster.

GOLDSMITH, HERBERT R. (1988). The role of the juvenile probation officer regarding the adolescent sex offender and related issues. *Journal of Offender Counseling Services & Rehabilitation* 12(2):115–122.

GORDON, DONALD, AND JACK ARBUTHNOT (1988). The use of paraprofessionals to deliver home-based family therapy to juvenile delinquents. *Criminal Justice and Behavior* 15(3):364–387.

GOSS, MIKE (1989). Electronic monitoring: The missing link for successful house arrest. *Corrections Today* 51(4): 106.

GOTTFREDSON, STEPHEN, AND ROBERT TAYLOR (1984). Public policy and prison population: Measuring opinions about reform. *Judicature* 68(4–5):190–201.

GOTTHEIL, DIANE (1979). Pretrial diversion: A response to the critics. *Crime and Delinquency* 25(1):65–75.

GRAHAM, GARY (1988). High-tech monitoring—Are we losing the human element? *Corrections Today* 50(7):92.

GREENBERG, DAVID (1975). Problems in community corrections. *Issues in Criminology* Spring.

GREENE, JUDITH (1988). Structuring criminal fines: Making an intermediate penalty more useful and equitable. *Justice System Journal* 13(1):37–50.

——, (1990). *The Staten Island day fine experiment.* New York: Vera Institute of Justice.

GREENWOOD, D., AND LIPSETT, L. (1980). Increasing the job readiness of probationers. *Corrections Today* 42(6):78.

GREENWOOD, PETER (1990). Reflections on three promising programs. *APPA Perspectives* Winter:20–24.

——, AND SUSAN TURNER (1987). *VisionQuest's program for San Diego delinquents: An evaluation of recidivism rates and controversial issues.* R-3445-OJJDP. Santa Monica, CA: The RAND Corporation.

GROTH, A. N. (1977). The adolescent sexual offender and his prey. *International Journal of Offender Therapy and Comparative Criminology* 21(3):249–254.

——, R. LONGO, AND J. B. McFADIN (1982). Undetected recidivism among rapists and child molesters. *Crime and Delinquency* 28(3):450–458.

GRUNIN, SUSAN, AND JUD WATKINS (1987). The investigative role of the United States probation officer under sentencing guidelines. *Federal Probation* 51(4):43–47.

GUITERRES, SARA, AND JOHN REICH (1981). A developmental perspective on runaway behavior: Its relationship to child abuse. *Child Welfare* 60:89–94.

GUY, E., J. PLATT, I. ZWERLING, AND S. BULLOCK (1985). Mental health status of prisoners in an urban jail. *Criminal Justice and Behavior* 12:26–53.

GUYNES, RANDALL (1988). *Difficult clients, large caseloads plague probation, parole agencies.* Washington, DC: National Institute of Justice, U.S. Department of Justice.

HAAPALA, DAVID (1988). Avoiding out-of-home placement of high-risk status offenders through the use of intensive home-based family preservation services. *Criminal Justice and Behavior*, 15(3):334–348.

HAMMETT, THEODORE (1986). *AIDS in prisons and jails: Issues and options.* Washington, DC: National Institute of Justice, U.S. Department of Justice.

HARKINS, JOHN (1990). House arrest in Oregon: A look at what goes on inside the home. *Corrections Today* 52(7):146–150.

HARLOW, NORA, AND E. K. NELSON (1990). Probation's responses to fiscal constraints. In *Community Corrections*, eds. David Duffee and Edmund McGarrell, Cincinnati: Anderson Publishing.

HARPER, ALICE (1987). Intensive supervision: Working for New Jersey. *Corrections Today* 49(7):88.

HARRIS, PATRICIA, TODD CLEAR, AND S. C. BAIRD (1989). Have community supervision officers changed their attitudes toward their work? *Justice Quarterly* 6(2):233–246.

HARTNAGEL, TIMOTHY, AND HARVEY KRAHN (1989). High school dropouts, labor market success and criminal behavior. *Youth and Society* 20(4):416–444.

HAVENS, JOSEPH (1989). Problems associated with large probation caseloads. *California Probation News.* 6(6):1–4.

HAVENSTRITE, AL (1980). Case planning in the probation supervision process. *Federal Probation* 44(2):57–66.

HAWKINS, DAVID, JEFFREY JENSON, AND RICHARD CATALANO (1990). Effects of a skills training intervention with juvenile delinquents. Paper presented at the annual meeting of the American Society of Criminology, Baltimore.

HEARD, CHINITA (1990). The preliminary development of the probation mentor home program: A community–based model. *Federal Probation* 54(4):51–56.

HEATH, MARGERY (1979). The fine option program: An alternative to prison for fine defaulters. *Federal Probation* 43(3):22–27.

HEINZ, J., B. GALAWAY, AND J. HUDSON (1976). Restitution or parole: A follow-up study of adult offenders. *Social Sciences Review* 50:148–156.

HENRY, STUART (1985). Community justice, capitalist society, and human agency: The dialectics of collective law in the cooperative. *Law & Society Review* 19(2):303–319.

HILLSMAN, SALLY (1988). The growing challenge of fine administration to court managers. *Justice System Journal* 13(1):5–16.

———, AND BARRY MAHONEY (1988). Collecting and enforcing criminal fines: A review of court processes, practices and problems. *Justice System Journal* 13(1):17–36.

———, BARRY MAHONEY, GEORGE COLE, AND BERNARD AUCHTER (1987). Fines as criminal sanctions. Washington, DC: National Institute of Justice, U.S. Department of Justice.

HOFER, PAUL, AND BARBARA MEIERHOFER (1987). *Home confinement.* Washington, DC: Federal Judicial Center.

HOFFMAN, PETER (1982). Females, recidivism, and salient factor score. *Criminal Justice and Behavior* 9(1): 121–125.

———, (1983). Screening for risk: A revised salient factor score (SFS 81). *Journal of Criminal Justice* 11:539–547.

———, AND BARBARA STONE-MEIERHOEFER (1977). *Post release arrest experiences of federal prisoners—A six year follow-up.* Washington, DC: U.S. Parole Commission.

HOLDEN, TAMARA, AND ALAN SCHUMAN (1989). Firearms: Debating the issues for probation and parole. *APPA Perspectives*, Summer: 6–8.

HOLMAN, JOHN (1990). Factors related to mental health status of offenders sanctioned with electronic monitoring home confinement. Paper presented at the annual meeting of the Academy of Criminal Justice Sciences, Denver, CO, March 13–17.

HOMANT, ROBERT (1981). The demise of JOLT: The politics of being "Scared Straight" in Michigan. *Criminal Justice Review* 6(1):14–18.

———, AND DANIEL KENNEDY (1982). Attitudes toward ex-offenders: A comparison of social stigmas. *Journal of Criminal Justice* 10(5):383–392.

HOOD, R., AND SPARKS, R. (1970). *Key issues in criminology.* New York: McGraw-Hill.

HOTALING, GERALD, AND DAVID FINKELHOR. 1988. *The sexual exploitation of missing children: A research review.* Washington, DC: U.S. Department of Justice, Office of Juvenile Justice and Delinquency Prevention, p. 25.

HUDSON, JOE, AND BURT GALAWAY (1989). Financial restitution: Toward an evaluable program model. *Canadian Journal of Criminology* 31(1):1–18.

——— (1990). Community service: Toward program definition. *Federal Probation* 54(2):3–9.

HUNT, DANA (1988). *AIDS in probation and parole.* Washington DC: National Institute of Justice, U.S. Department of Justice.

HUNTER, JOHN, AND DAVID SANTOS (1990). The use of specialized cognitive-behavioral therapies in the treatment of adolescent sexual offenders. *International Journal of Offender Therapy and Comparative Criminology* 34(3):239–248.

HURST, HUNTER (1990). Juvenile probation in retrospect. *APPA Perspectives*, Winter:16–19.

———, AND LOUIS MCHARDY (1991). Juvenile justice and the blind lady. *Federal Probation* 55(2):63–68.

HUSSEY, FREDERICK (1978). Parole: Villain or victim in the determinate sentencing debate. *Crime and Delinquency* 24(1):81–88.

IMMARIGEON, RUSS (1985). *Probation at the crossroads: Innovative programs in Massachusetts*. Boston: Massachusetts Council for Public Justice.

INNES, CHRISTOPHER (1988). *Profile of state prison inmates, 1986*. Washington, DC: Bureau of Justice Statistics.

JACOBS, JAMES (1989). *Drunk driving*. Chicago: University of Chicago Press.

JAFFE, P., D. WOLFE, S. WILSON, AND L. ZAK (1986). Similarities in behavioral and social maladjustment among child victims and witnesses to family violence. *American Journal of Orthopsychiatry* 56(1):142–146.

JOHNSON, BYRON, LINDA HAUGEN, JERRY MANESS, AND PAUL ROSS (1989). Attitudes toward electronic monitoring of offenders: A study of probation officers and prosecutors. *Journal of Contemporary Criminal Justice* 5(3):153–164.

JOHNSON, PERRY (1989). A home as a prison: Can it work? *Journal of Offender Monitoring* 2(2):10–18.

JONES, MARK (1991). Intensive probation supervision in Georgia, Massachusetts, and New Jersey. *Criminal Justice Research Bulletin* 6(1):1–9.

JONES, PETER (1990a). Community corrections in Kansas: Extending community-based corrections or widening the net? *Journal of Research in Crime and Delinquency* 27(1):79–101.

——— (1990b). Expanding the use of noncustodial sentencing options: An evaluation of the Kansas Community Corrections Act. *The Howard Journal* 29(2):117.

KAPLAN, D., AND C. BINGHAM (1990). A new era of punishment. *Newsweek*, May 14:50–51.

KEHOE, CHARLES (1987). Councils that counsel—Advisory boards get the public involved. *Corrections Today* 49(6):90.

KELLY, THOMAS, AND DANIEL KENNEDY (1982). Assessing and predicting the competency of juvenile court volunteer probation officers. *Journal of Criminal Justice* 10(2):123–130.

KEVE, PAUL (1979). No farewell to arms. *Crime and Delinquency* 29(4):425–435.

KILLINGER, GEORGE, AND PAUL CROMWELL (1978). *Corrections in the community: Alternatives to imprisonment*. St. Paul, MN: West Publishing.

KLEIN, ANDREW (1989). The curse of caseload management. *APPA Perspectives* Winter: 27–28.

KLEIN, JODY (1985). Reparative work: An alternative punishment for adult prisoners. Paper presented at the annual meeting of the American Society of Criminology, San Diego, CA.

KLEIN-SAFFRAN, JODY, AND JAMES BECK (1990). Expanding electronic monitoring: Practices and policy implications. Paper presented at the annual meeting of the American Society of Criminology, Baltimore.

KLEINIG, JOHN, AND CHARLES LINDNER (1989). AIDS on parole: Dilemmas in decision making. *Criminal Justice Policy Review* 3(1):1–27.

KNEPPER, PAUL, AND GRAY CAVENDER (1990). Strange interlude: An analysis of juvenile parole revocation decision-making. Paper presented at the annual meeting of the Academy of Criminal Justice Sciences, Denver, CO.

KOLMAN, ANITA, AND CLAUDIA WASSERMAN (1991). Theft groups for women: A cry for help. *Federal Probation* 55(1):48–54.

KOMALA, MERLY, VAL SHEPPERD, AND MICHELE MOCZYGEMBA (1990). *The felony offender risk assessment study: Progress report*. Austin: Community Justice Assistance Division, Texas Department of Criminal Justice.

KOONTZ, JOHN F. (1980). Pragmatic conditions of probation. *Corrections Today*. 42(1):14.

KRANTZ, SHELDON (1988). *Corrections and prisoners' rights*. St. Paul, MN: West Publishing.

KRATCOSKI, PETER (1982). Child abuse and violence against the family. *Child Welfare* 61:435–444.

KRISBERG, BARRY (1988). *The juvenile court: Reclaiming the vision*. San Francisco, CA: National Council on Crime and Delinquency.

———, DEBORAH NEUENFELDT, AND AUDREY BAKKE (1991). Juvenile intensive supervision programs: The state of the art. *NCCD Focus*. February.

KULIS, CHESTER. 1983. Profit in the private presentence report. *Federal Probation* 47(4):11–15.

LAND, KENNETH, PATRICIA MCCALL, AND JAY WILLIAMS (1990). Something that works in juvenile justice. *Evaluation Review* 14(6):574–606.

LANGSTON, DENNY (1988). Probation and parole: No more free rides. *Corrections Today* 50(5):90.

LARIVEE, JOHN (1990). Day reporting centers: Making their way from the U.K. to the U.S. *Corrections Today* 52(6):84.

LATESSA, EDWARD (1987). The incarceration diversion unit of the Lucas County Adult Probation Department: Report Number 7. Cincinnati, OH: Department of Criminal Justice, Univ. of Cincinnati.

LATESSA, EDWARD, AND LAWRENCE TRAVIS (1988). The effects of intensive supervision with alcoholic probationers. *Journal of Offender Counseling Services & Rehabilitation* 12(2):175–190.

LAURENCE, LEO (1989). San Diego judge frustrated with limited juvenile facilities. *Los Angeles Daily Journal: Discovery*, July 17.

LAWRENCE, RICHARD (1984). Professionals or judicial civil servants? An examination of the probation officer's role. *Federal Probation* 48(4): 14–21.

——— (1990). Restitution programs pay back the victim and society. *Corrections Today* 52(1):96.

——— (1991). Reexamining community corrections models. *Crime and Delinquency* 37(4):449–464.

———, AND SHELVA JOHNSON (1990). Effects of the Minnesota sentencing guidelines on probation agents. *Journal of Crime and Justice* 13:77–104.

LEMERT, EDWIN (1951). *Social pathology: A systematic approach to the theory of sociopathic behavior*. New York: McGraw-Hill.

——— (1972). *Instead of court: Diversion in juvenile justice*. Rockville, MD: National Institute of Mental Health.

Lewis, Charlton (1899). The intermediate sentence. *Yale Law Journal* 9 (October):18–19.

LEWIS, DIANE (1982). Female ex-offenders and community programs: Barriers to service. *Crime and Delinquency* 28(1):40–51.

LINDNER, CHARLES, AND MARGARET SAVARESE (1984a). The evolution of probation. *Federal Probation* 48(1):3–10.

——— (1984b). The evolution of probation: University Settlement and its pioneering role in probation work. *Federal Probation* 48(4):3–13.

LINDQUIST, CHARLES, AND JOHN WHITEHEAD (1986). Correctional officers as parole officers. *Criminal Justice and Behavior* 13(2):197–222.

LIPSCHUTZ, MARK (1977). Runaways in history. *Crime and Delinquency* 23(3):321–332.

LIPTON, DOUGLAS, ROBERT MARTINSON, AND JUDITH WILKES (1975). *The effectiveness of correctional treatment: A survey of treatment evaluation studies.* New York: Praeger.

LOFLAND, JOHN (1969). *Deviance and identity.* Englewood Cliffs, NJ: Prentice Hall.

LOHMAN, JOHN, A. WAHL, AND R. M. CARTER (1967). *The San Francisco Project: Research Report No. 11: The intensive supervision caseload.* Berkeley, CA: Univ. of California.

LOMBARDO, L. (1985). Mental health work in prison and jails. *Criminal Justice and Behavior* 12(1):17–28.

LONGMIRE, DENNIS, AND EDWARD SCHAUER (1987). *The case classification system in Texas: Is it working?* Austin: Texas Adult Probation Commission and Sam Houston State Univ.

———, AND CHARLES WILSON (1987). Summary report: Parole division survey. Huntsville: Texas Correctional Association.

LOVELESS, PATRICIA (1990). The impact of a home incarceration program on the offenders, the community and the system. Paper presented at the annual meeting of the American Society of Criminology, Baltimore.

LOWENBERG, JANICE (1988). Supervising persons with AIDS: A new liability for probation and parole officers. *Journal of Contemporary Criminal Justice* 4(2):119–124.

LUCAS, WAYNE (1988). Cost savings from volunteer services. *Journal of Offender Counseling Services & Rehabilitation* 12(2):203–207.

LUNDMAN, RICHARD (1984). *Prevention and control of juvenile delinquency.* New York: Oxford Univ. Press.

LURIGIO, ARTHUR (1984). *The relationship between offender characteristics and the fulfillment of financial restitution.* Chicago: Cook County Adult Probation Department.

——— (1989). Practitioners' views on AIDS in probation and detention. *Federal Probation* 53(4):16–24.

———, AND ROBERT DAVIS (1990). Does a threatening letter increase compliance with restitution orders?: A field experiment. *Crime and Delinquency* 36(4):537–548.

———, KARL GUDENBERG, AND ARTHUR SPICA (1988). Working effectively with AIDS cases on probation. *APPA Perspectives* Spring:10–15.

MacDONALD, MALCOLM (1988). AIDS issues in probation and parole. *APPA Perspectives* Summer: 12–13.

McCARTHY, BELINDA, AND ROBERT LANGWORTHY (1987). Older offenders on probation and parole. *Journal of Offender Counseling Services & Rehabilitation* 12(1):00.

———, AND BERNARD McCARTHY (1984). *Community-based corrections.* Pacific Grove, CA: Brooks/Cole.

McCLEARY, RICHARD (1978). *Dangerous men: The sociology of parole.* Beverly Hills: Sage.

McDEVITT, JACK (1988). *Evaluation of the Hampden County Day Reporting Center.* Boston, MA: Crime and Justice Foundation.

McDONALD, DOUGLAS (1987). Restitution and community service. Washington, DC: National Institute of Justice, U.S. Department of Justice.

——— (1989). The cost of corrections: In search of the bottom line. *Research in Corrections* 2(1):1–25.

MCPHERSON, SUSAN, LANCE MCDONALD, AND CHARLES RYER (1983). Intensive counseling with families of juvenile offenders. *Juvenile and Family Court Journal* 34(1):27–33.

MCSPARRON, JAMES (1980). Community correction and diversion. *Crime and Delinquency* 26(2):226–247.

MARDON, STEVEN (1991). On board, not behind bars. *Corrections Today* 53(1):33.

MARGOLIS, RICHARD (1988). *Out of harm's way: The emancipation of juvenile justice.* New York: The Edna Maconnell Clark Foundation.

MARSHALL, FRANKLIN (1982). Not without the tools: The task of probation in the eighties. *Federal Probation* 46(4):37–40.

MARTINSON, ROBERT (1974). What works? Questions and answers about prison reform. *The Public Interest* 35(2):22–54.

MARX, GARY (1985). I'll be watching you: Reflections on the new surveillance. *Dissent* Winter:26–34.

MATTHEWS, WILLIAM (1988). Pretrial diversion: Promises we can't keep. *Journal of Offender Counseling Services & Rehabilitation* 12(2):191–202.

MAXSON, CHERYL, MARGARET GORDON, MALCOLM KLEIN, AND LEA CUNNINGHAM (1990). Service delivery to status offenders. Paper presented at the annual meeting of the American Society of Criminology, Baltimore.

MAYNE, CAROL, AND GORDON GARRISON (1979). *Restitution: An analysis of the use of restitution during 1977 in Provincial Court Charlottetown, Prince Edward Island and examination of the many aspects of restitution.* Charlottetown, P. E. I.: Probation and Family Court Services, Prince Edward Island Department of Justice.

MENARD, SCOTT, AND HERBERT COVEY (1983). Community alternatives and rearrest in Colorado. *Criminal Justice and Behavior* 10(1):93–108.

MERRY, SALLY (1982). Defining "Success" in the neighborhood justice movement. In R. Tomasic and M. Feeley, eds. *Neighborhood justice: Assessment of an emerging idea.* White Plains, NY: Longman.

MILLER, D. D., D. MILLER, F. HOFFMAN, AND R. DUGGAN (1980). *Runaways, illegal aliens in their own land: Implications for service.* New York: J. F. Bergin.

MINEHAN, THOMAS (1934). *Boy and girl tramps of America.* New York: Farrar & Rinehart.

MINOR, KEVIN, AND H. PRESTON ELROD (1990). The effects of a multi-faceted intervention on the offense activities of juvenile probationers. *Journal of Offender Counseling Services & Rehabilitation* 15(2):87–107.

MINOR-HARPER, STEPHANIE, AND CHRISTOPHER INNES (1987). *Time served in prison and on parole, 1984.* Washington, DC: U.S. Department of Justice, Bureau of Justice Statistics.

MORAN, T. K., AND CHARLES LINDNER (1985). Probation and the hi-technology revolution: Is a reconceptualization of the traditional probation officer role model inevitable? *Criminal Justice Review* 10(1):25–32.

MORGAN, W. MEADE, AND JAMES CURRAN (1986). AIDS: Current and future trends. *Public Health Reports* 101:459–465.

MORRIS, NORVAL, AND MARC MILLER (1987). Predictions of dangerousness in the criminal law. Washington, DC: National Institute of Justice, U.S. Department of Justice.

MORRIS, NORVAL, AND MICHAEL TONRY (1990). *Between prison and probation*. New York: Oxford Univ. Press.

MORSE, BARBARA, AND DELBERT ELLIOT (1990). Hamilton County drinking and driving study: 30 month report. *Executive Summary*. Cincinnati, OH: The Hamilton County Court.

MULLANEY, FAHY (1988). *Economic sanctions in community corrections*. Washington, DC: National Institute of Corrections, U.S. Department of Justice.

MUSHENO, MICHAEL, DENNIS PALUMBO, STEVEN MOODY, AND JAMES LEVINE (1989). Community corrections as an organizational innovation: What works and why. *Journal of Research in Crime and Delinquency* 26(2):136–167.

MYERS, SAMUEL (1983). Racial differences in postprison employment. *Social Science Quarterly* 64(3):654–669.

NATIONAL COUNCIL ON CRIME AND DELINQUENCY (1975). Jurisdiction over status offenders should be removed from the juvenile court: A policy statement. *Crime and Delinquency* 21(2):97–99.

NATIONAL INSTITUTE OF JUSTICE (1989). *DUF:Drug use forecasting January to March 1989*. Washington, DC: U.S. Department of Justice.

NATIONAL INSTITUTE OF JUSTICE (1987). *Pre-trial drug screening package*. Rockville, MD: National Criminal Justice Reference Service.

NATIONAL NETWORK OF RUNAWAY AND YOUTH SERVICES, INC. (1985). *To whom do they belong?: A profile of America's runaway and homeless youth and programs that help them*. Washington, DC: The National Network of Runaway and Youth Services, Inc., p. 1.

NIDORF, BARRY (1989). Community corrections: Turning the crowding crisis into opportunities. *Corrections Today* 51(6):82–84.

NORLAND, S., AND P. J. MANN (1984). Being troublesome: Women on probation. *Criminal Justice and Behavior* 11:(1):115–135.

OFFICE OF JUVENILE JUSTICE AND DELINQUENCY PREVENTION (1989). Privatizing juvenile probation services: Five local experiences. *NIJ Research In Action* November/December:10–12.

――― (1989). Juvenile courts vary greatly in how they handle drug and alcohol cases. *NIJ Research in Action* July/August:10–13.

O'LEARY, V., AND D. DUFFEE (1971). Correctional policy--A classification of goals designed for change. *Crime and Delinquency* 17(4):380.

OLSEN, L., E. LIEBOW, F. MANNINO, AND M. SHORE (1980). Runaway children twelve years later: A follow-up. *Journal of Family Issues* 1(2):165–188.

PALM BEACH COUNTY SHERIFF'S DEPARTMENT (1987). In *Intermediate punishments: Intensive supervision, home confinement and electronic surveillance*, ed. B. McCarthy, pp. 181–187.

PALMER, JOHN (1991). *Constitutional rights of prisoners*. 4th ed. Cincinnati: Anderson Publishing.

PALMER, TED (1975). Martinson revisited. *Journal of Research in Crime and Delinquency* 35:133–152.

――― (1983). The effectiveness issue today. *Federal Probation* 47(2):3–10.

――― (1991a). The effectiveness of intervention: Recent trends and current issues. *Crime and Delinquency* 37(3):330–346.

――― (1991b). The habilitation/developmental perspective: Missing link in corrections. *Federal Probation* 55(1):55–64.

PAPY, JOSEPH, AND RICHARD NIMER (1991). Electronic monitoring in Florida. *Federal Probation* 55(1):31–33.

PARENT, DALE (1990). *Recovering correctional costs through offender fees.* Washington, DC: National Institute of Justice.

PARISI, NICOLETTE (1980). Combining incarceration and probation. *Federal Probation* 44(2):3–12.

PARSONAGE, WILLIAM (1990). *Worker safety in probation and parole.* Washington, DC: National Institute of Corrections.

———, AND W. C. BUSHEY (1987). The victimization of probation and parole workers in the line of duty: An exploratory study. *Criminal Justice Policy Review* 2(4):372–391.

PATTERSON, MICHAEL, AND MICHAEL WIERZBICKI (1987). An attempt to predict juvenile probation outcome using the Jesness Inventory. *Criminal Justice Review* 12(1):31–34.

PEARSON, FRANK (1987). *Research on New Jersey's intensive supervision program,* final report. Washington DC: National Institute of Justice, U.S. Department of Justice.

———, AND ALICE HARPER (1990). Contingent intermediate sentences: New Jersey's intensive supervision program. *Crime and Delinquency* 36(1):75–86.

PENNELL, SUSAN, CHRISTINE CURTIS, AND DENNIS SCHECK (1990). *Crime and Delinquency* 36(2):257–275.

PETERSILIA, JOAN (1985). *Probation and felony offenders.* Washington, DC: National Institute of Justice, U.S. Department of Justice.

——— (1986). Exploring the option of house arrest. *Federal Probation* June: 50–55.

——— (1987a). Los Angeles experiments with house arrest. *Corrections Today* 49(7):132.

——— (1987b). House arrest is worthy innovation—If it's not just for the well-off. *APPA Perspectives* Fall:8.

——— (1988a). House arrest. Washington, DC: National Institute of Justice, U.S. Department of Justice.

——— (1988b). Probation reform. In *Controversial issues in crime and justice,* ed. J. Scott. Newbury Park, CA: Sage.

——— (1989). Implementing randomized experiments: Lessons from BJA's intensive supervision project. Preliminary Report. Santa Monica, CA: The RAND Corporation.

——— (1990a). When probation becomes more dreaded than prison. *Federal Probation* 54(1):23–27.

——— (1990b). Conditions that permit intensive supervision programs to survive. *Crime and Delinquency* 36(1):126–145.

———, AND SUSAN TURNER (1986). *Prison versus probation in California: Implications for crime and offender recidivism.* Report No. R3323–NIJ. Santa Monica, CA: The RAND Corporation.

——— (1990). Comparing intensive and regular supervision for high-risk probationers: Early results from an experiment in California. *Crime and Delinquency* 36(1):87–111.

———, SUSAN TURNER, JAMES KAHAN, AND JOYCE PETERSON (1985). *Granting Felons Probation: Public Risks and Alternatives* Report No. R-3186-NIJ. Santa Monica, CA: The RAND Corporation.

PHELPS, R.J., ET AL. (1982). *Wisconsin juvenile female offender study project*. Madison: Youth Police and Law Center.

PILLER, RUTH (1988). Probated sentences take new meaning. *Houston Chronicle*, 16 March:B1.

PISCIOTTA, A (1989). Eugenics, social control and the state: Progressive penology at the Indiana Reformatory, 1897–1923. Paper presented at the annual meeting of the American Academy of Criminal Justice Sciences, Washington, DC.

PLATT, ANTHONY M. (1969). *The child savers*. Chicago: Univ. of Chicago Press.

POLISKY, R. J. (1981a). Enhancing the job satisfaction of probation and parole officers—Part I. *Corrections Today* 43(1):78.

——— (1981b). Enhancing the job satisfaction of probation and parole officers—Part II. *Corrections Today* 43(2):54.

POWERS, E. (1959). Halfway houses: An historical perspective. *American Journal of Corrections* 21(4):20.

PRICE, J. P. (1990). Drugs—The impact on the safety and welfare of the professional probation officer in the decade of the 1990s. Paper presented at the Probation Officer's Association Meeting, Albany, NY.

PROBATION DIVISION, ADMINISTRATIVE OFFICE OF THE UNITED STATES COURTS (1989). Implementing community service: The referral process. *Federal Probation* 53(1):3–9.

PROJECT NEW PRIDE (1985). *Project New Pride*. Washington, DC: U.S. Government Printing Office.

QUAY, HERBERT (1965). Psychopathic personality as pathological stimulation seeking. *American Journal of Psychiatry* 22:180–184.

QUINN, JAMES, AND JOHN HOLMAN (1990). Intrafamilial control among felons under community supervision: An examination of the significant others of electronically monitored offenders. Paper presented at the annual meeting of the Academy of Criminal Justice Sciences, Denver, CO. March 13–17.

RAFTER, N. H. (1985). *Partial justice: Women in state prisons 1800–1935*. Boston: Northeastern Univ. Press.

RAUSCH, SHARLA (1983). Court processing versus diversion of status offenders: A test of deterrence and labeling theories. *Journal of Research in Crime and Delinquency* 20(1):39–54.

READ, EDWARD (1988). Identifying the alcoholic: A practical guide for the probation officer. *Federal Probation* 52(3):59–65.

RECKLESS, WALTER, AND MAPHEUS SMITH (1932). *Juvenile delinquency*. New York: McGraw-Hill.

RENZEMA, MARC, AND DAVID SKELTON (1990). Trends in the use of electronic monitoring: 1989. *Journal of Offender Monitoring* 3(3):12–19.

RHINE, EDWARD, WILLIAM SMITH, RONALD JACKSON, AND LLYOD RUPP (1989). Parole—Issues and prospects for the 1990s. *Corrections Today* 51(7):78.

RICHEY, CHARLES (1977). Judge Richey's unique perspective. In *Crime and criminals—Opposing viewpoints*, eds. D. Bender and G. McCuen. St. Paul, MN: Greenhaven Press.

RING, CHARLES (1989). Probation supervision fees: Shifting costs to the offender. *Federal Probation* 53(2):43–48.

ROBBINS, L. (1958). Mental illness of the runaway: A 30 year follow-up study. *Human Organization* 16(4):1–15.

ROBERG, ROY, AND VINCENT WEBB (1981). *Critical issues in corrections*. St. Paul: MN: West Publishing.

ROBERTS, ALBERT (1988). Wilderness programs for juvenile offenders: A challenging alternative. *Juvenile & Family Court Journal* 39(1):1–12.

—— (1989). *Juvenile justice: Policies, programs and services*. Chicago: Dorsey Press.

ROBINSON, J., ET AL. (1969). *The San Francisco Project*. Berkeley: Univ. of California School of Criminology.

ROESCH, RONALD (1978). Does adult diversion work? The failure of research in criminal justice. *Crime and Delinquency* 24(1):72–80.

ROGERS, JOSEPH (1990). The predisposition report: Maintaining the promise of individualized juvenile justice. *Federal Probation* 54(2):43–57.

ROGERS, ROBERT, AND ANNETTE JOLIN (1989). Electronic monitoring: A review of the empirical literature. *Journal of Contemporary Criminal Justice* 5(3):141–152.

ROJEK, D. G., AND M. ERICKSON (1982). Reforming the justice system: The diversion of status offenders. *Law and Society Review* 16(2):240–262.

ROMERO, JOSEPH, AND LINDA WILLIAMS (1983). Group Psychotherapy and intensive probation supervision with sex offenders: A comparative study. *Federal Probation* 47(4):36–42.

ROSECRANCE, JOHN (1987). A typology of presentence probation investigators. *International Journal of Offender Therapy and Comparative Criminology* 31(2):163–177.

ROSENFELD, RICHARD, AND KIMBERLY KEMPF (1991). The scope and purpose of corrections: Exploring alternative responses to crowding. *Crime and Delinquency* 37(4):481–505.

ROSSUM, RALPH, BENEDICT KOLLER, AND CHRISOPHER MANFREDI (1986). *Juvenile justice reform code: A model for the states*. Claremont, CA: McKenna College, Rose Institute of State and Local Government.

ROTHMAN, DAVID J. (1980). *Conscience and convenience*. Boston: Little, Brown.

ROUNDTREE, GEORGE, DAN EDWARDS, AND JACK PARKER (1984). A study of the personal characteristics of probationers as related to recidivism. *Journal of Offender Counseling, Services & Rehabilitation* 8:53–61.

ROVNER-PIECZENIK, R. (1974). Pretrial intervention strategies: An evaluation of policy-related research and policymaker perceptions. Washington, DC: National Pretrial Intervention Service Center, American Bar Association, Commission on Correctional Facilities.

ROY, SUDIPTA (1990). The impact of restitution program on juvenile offenders: A case study in Kalamazoo, Michigan. Paper presented at the annual meeting of the American Society of Criminology, Baltimore.

RUBIN, BARRY (1990). Offender attitudes toward home arrest. *Journal of Offender Monitoring* 3(3):8–11.

RUBIN, H. TED (1988). Fulfilling juvenile restitution requirements in community correctional programs. *Federal Probation* 52(3):32–42.

RUDOVSKY, DAVID, ALVIN BRONSTEIN, EDWARD KOREN, AND JULIA CADE (1988). *The rights of prisoners*. Carbondale and Edwardsville: Southern Illinois Univ. Press, p. 108.

SAGATUN, INGER (1989). Gender biases in probation officers: Attributions of juvenile delinquency. *International Journal of Offender Therapy and Comparative Criminology* 33(2):131–140.

SAHOLS, ELOISE, ET AL. (1982). Beware of child molesters. *Newsweek*, August 9:45.

SCHLATTER, GARY (1989). Hidden costs of home arrest programs. *Corrections Today* 51(6):94.

SCHLESINGER, STEPHEN (1978). The prediction of dangerousness in juveniles. *Crime and Delinquency* 24(1):40–48.

SCHMIDT, ANNESLEY (1991). Electronic monitors—Realistically, what can be expected? *Federal Probation* 55(2):47–53.

SCHMIDT, ANNELSEY (1989a). Electronic monitoring. *Journal of Contemporary Criminal Justice* 5(3):133–140.

——— (1989b). *Electronic monitoring of offenders increases*. Washington, DC: National Institute of Justice, U.S. Department of Justice.

SCHNEIDER, ANNE (1990). *Deterrence and juvenile crime: Results from a national policy experiment*. New York: Springer-Verlag.

———, AND PETER SCHNEIDER (1985). The impact of restitution on recidivism of juvenile offenders: An experiment in Clayton County, Georgia. *Criminal Justice Review* 10(1):1–10.

———, AND DONNA SCHRAM (1986). The Washington State juvenile justice system reform: A review of findings. *Criminal Justice Policy Review* 1(2): 211–235.

———, AND JEAN WARNER (1989). *National trends in juvenile restitution programming*. Washington, DC: Office of Juvenile Justice and Delinquency Prevention.

SCHNEIDER, PETER, WILLIAM GRIFFITH, AND ANNE SCHNEIDER (1982). Juvenile restitution as a sole sanction or condition of probation: An empirical analysis. *Journal of Research in Crime and Delinquency* 19(1):47–65.

SCHOEN, KENNETH (1978). The Community Corrections Act. *Crime and Delinquency* 24(4):458–464.

SCHUMAN, ALAN (1989). The cost of correctional services: Exploring a poorly charted terrain. *Research in Corrections* 2(1):27–34.

SCHUR, EDWIN (1971). *Labeling deviant behavior: Its sociological implications*. New York: Harper & Row.

SCHWARTZ, IRA, MARTHA STEKETEE, AND VICTORIA SCHNEIDER (1990). Federal juvenile justice policy and the incarceration of girls. *Crime and Delinquency* 36(4):503–520.

SCHWARTZ, M. D. (1989). Incest victims and the criminal justice system. In *The changing roles of women in the criminal justice system*, ed. I. Moyer. Prospect Heights, IL: Waveland Press.

SCHWARTZ, R., AND SKOLNICK, J. (1962). Two studies of legal stigma. *Social Problems* 10:133–138.

SCHWITZGEBEL, R. K. (1967). Electronic innovation in behavioral sciences: A call to responsibility. *American Psychologist* 22:364–370.

SCILLIA, ANTHONY (1989). Winning the "not-in-my-neighborhood" game. *Corrections Today* 51(4):114.

SCOTT, JOSEPH, SIMON DINITZ, AND DAVID SHICHOR (1978). Pioneering innovations in corrections: Shock probation and shock parole. *Offender Rehabilitation* 3(2):113–122.

SECHREST, L., S. WHITE, AND E. BROWN (1979). *The rehabilitation of criminal offenders: Problems and prospects*. Washington, DC: National Academy of Sciences.

SELKE, WILLIAM (1984). Empirical analysis of the ideological barrier in community corrections. *Journal of Criminal Justice* 12(6):541–549.

SENESE, JEFFREY (1990). Intensive supervision probation and public opinion: Who cares one way or the other? Paper presented at the annual meeting of the American Society of Criminology, Baltimore.

SENG, MAGNUS (1983). Reducing the cost and complexity of probation evaluation. *Federal Probation* 47(4):16–19.

SHARP, RAY, AND EUGENE MOORE (1988). The early offender project: A community-based program for high risk youth. *Juvenile and Family Court Journal* 39(1):13–20.

SHAW, CLIFFORD (1930). *The Jackroller*. Chicago: Univ. of Chicago Press. Reprinted 1966.

SHICHOR, DAVID (1988). An exploratory study of elderly probationers. *International Journal of Offender Therapy and Comparative Criminology* 32:163–174.

———, AND ARNOLD BINDER (1982). Community restitution for juveniles: An approach and preliminary evaluation. *Criminal Justice Review* 7(2):46–50.

SIEH, EDWARD (1990). Probation officers: An analysis of role priorities. Paper presented at the annual meeting of the Academy of Criminal Justice Sciences, Denver, CO, March 13–17.

SIGLER, ROBERT, AND BRIDGETT McGRAW (1984). Adult probation and parole officers: Influence of their weapons, role perceptions and role conflict. *Criminal Justice Review* 9(1):28–32.

SIGNORINO, JOHN (1988). On-site drug screening—Promoting cost-efficient rehabilitation. *Corrections Today* 50(7):116.

SKONOVD, NORMAN (1989). *Regional youth education facility*. Sacramento: State of California, Department of Youth Authority.

SMITH, ALBERT (1991). Arming officers doesn't have to change an agency's mission. *Corrections Today* 53(4):114.

SMITH, ALEXANDER B., AND LOUIS BERLIN (1981). *Treating the criminal offender*. 2nd ed. Englewood Cliffs, NJ: Prentice Hall.

SMITH, BEVERLY (1989). Female admissions and paroles of the Western House of Refuge in the 1880s. *Journal of Research in Crime and Delinquency* 26(1):36–66.

SMITH, CHUCK (1989a). One man's opinion: What a parole agent does—Part I. *Peacekeeper* 7(6):8–9.

——— (1989b). One man's opinion: What a parole agent does—Part II—A critique. *Peacekeeper* 7(7):28, 31.

SMITH, WILLIAM, EDWARD RHINE, AND RONALD JACKSON (1989). Parole practices in the United States. *Corrections Today* 51(6):22.

SNYDER, HOWARD, AND FINNEGAN, TERRENCE (1987). *Delinquency in the United States, 1983*. Washington, DC: U.S. National Institute for Juvenile Justice and Delinquency Prevention.

SPERGEL, I. A., J. P. LYNCH, F. G. REAMER, AND J. KORBELIK (1982). Response of organization and community to a deinstitutionalization strategy. *Crime and Delinquency* 28:426–229.

SPRINGER, MERLE (1988). Youth service privatization. *Corrections Today* 50(6):88.

STAPLES, WILLIAM (1986). Restitution as a sanction in juvenile court. *Crime and Delinquency* 32(2):177–185.

STEPANIK, RON (1991). The Eckerd Youth Program: Challenging juveniles to change. *Corrections Today* 53(1):48.

STONE-MEIERHOEFER, BARBARA, AND PETER HOFFMAN (1982). The effects of presumptive parole dates on institutional behavior: A preliminary assessment. *Journal of Criminal Justice* 10(4):283–298.

STRATHAM ET AL. (1981). *Minnesota Community Corrections Act evaluation*. St. Paul: Department of Corrections Crime Control Planning Board.

SWART, STANLEY (1982). "Alternatives to Incarceration": The end of an era. *Corrections Today* 44(6):28.

SYKES, GRESHAM, AND DAVID MATZA (1957). Techniques of neutralization: A theory of delinquency. *American Sociological Review* 22:664–670.

SYMKLA, JOHN (1981). *Community-based corrections: Principles and practices.* New York: Macmillan.

THOMAS, ROBERT (1988). Stress perception among select federal probation and pretrial services officers and their supervisors. *Federal Probation* 52(3):48–58.

THOMSON, DOUGLAS (1990). How plea bargaining shapes intensive probation supervision policy goals. *Crime and Delinquency* 36(1):146–161.

———, AND DAVID FOGEL (1981). *Probation work in small agencies: A national study of training provisions and needs—A Summary Report.* Prepared for the U.S. National Institute of Corrections by the Center for Research in Law and Justice. Chicago: Univ. of Illinois at Chicago Circle.

———, AND PATRICA MCANANY (1984). Punishment and responsibility in juvenile court: Desert-based probation for delinquents. In *Probation and Justice,* ed. Patrick McAnany, Doug Thomson, and David Fogel. Cambridge, MA: Oelgeschlager, Gunn & Hain.

THORVALDSON, S. (1980). Toward the definition of the reparative aim. In *Victims, offenders and alternative sanctions,* ed. J. Hudson and B. Galaway. Lexington, MA: Lexington Books.

TIELMAN, KATHERINE, AND PIERRE LANDRY (1981). Gender bias in juvenile justice. *Journal of Research in Crime and Delinquency* 18:47–80.

TOMLINSON, THOMAS, AND GREGORY SMITH (1990). Developing vocational rehabilitation networks in rural communities. Paper presented at the annual meeting of the Academy of Criminal Justice Sciences, Denver, CO.

TONRY, MICHAEL (1990). Stated and latent features of ISP. *Crime and Delinquency* 36(1):174–191.

TRAVIS, LAWRENCE, AND EDWARD LATESSA (1984). "A summary of parole rules—Thirteen years later": Revisited thirteen years later. *Journal of Criminal Justice* 12(6):591–600.

TWAIN, DAVID, AND LAURA MAIELLO (1988). Juvenile conference committees: An evaluation of the administration of justice at the neighborhood level. *Journal of Criminal Justice* 16(6):451–461.

UMBREIT, MARK (1991). Having offenders meet with their victims offers benefits for both parties. *Corrections Today* 53(4):164–166.

UMBREIT, MARK, AND LAURIE SMITH (1991). Minnesota mediation center produces positive results. *Corrections Today* 53(5):192.

UNITED STATES GENERAL ACCOUNTING OFFICE (1990). *Intermediate sanctions: Their impacts on prison crowding, costs, and recidivism are still unclear.* Washington, DC: U.S. General Accounting Office.

VANAGUNAS, STANLEY (1979). Police diversion of juvenile offenders: An ambiguous state of the art. *Federal Probation* 43(3):48–52.

VAN DINE, STEVEN (1990). The in/out decision. In *Prison utilization study: Risk assessment techniques and Florida's inmates.* Vol. 1. Tallahassee, FL: Division of Economic and Demographic Research of the Joint Legislative Management Committee.

VAN HORNE, B. A. (1979). *A study of selected variables including the MMPI, as predictors of adult female recidivism.* Dissertation Abstracts International, January.

VAN VOORHIS, PATRICIA (1985). Restitution outcome and probationers' assessments of restitution. *Criminal Justice and Behavior* 12(3):259–287.

VAUGHN, JOSEPH (1987). Planning for change: The use of electronic monitoring as a correctional alternative. In *Intermediate punishments: Intensive supervision, home confinement, and electronic surveillance*, ed. B. McCarthy, pp. 153–168. Monsey, NY: Criminal Justice Press.

VELMER, BURTON, FRANCIS CULLEN, AND LAWRENCE TRAVIS (1987). The collateral consequences of a felony conviction: A national study of state statutes. *Federal Probation* 51(3):52–60.

VIRGINIA DEPARTMENT OF CRIMINAL JUSTICE SERVICES (1987). *Unpaid fines, court costs and restitution in district and circuit courts in the Commonwealth.* Richmond: Department of Criminal Justice Services.

VISHER, CHRISTY (1989). Linking criminal sanctions, drug testing and drug abuse treatment: A crime control strategy for the 1990s. *Criminal Justice Policy Review* 3(4):329–343.

VITO, GENNARO (1989). The Kentucky substance abuse program: A private program to treat probationers and parolees. *Federal Probation* 53(1):65–72.

Von Hirsch, Andrew (1990). The ethics of community-based sanctions. *Crime and Delinquency* 36(1):162–173.

VORENBERG, E. W. (1983). American Bar Association Special Committee on Alternative Means of Dispute Resolution. In *The juvenile justice standards handbook*, ed. Alaire Rieffe. Chicago: American Bar Association.

WAEGEL, WILLIAM (1989). *Delinquency and juvenile control.* Englewood Cliffs, NJ: Prentice Hall.

WAGNER, DENNIS (1989). Reducing criminal risk: An evaluation of the high risk offender intensive supervision project. *APPA Perspectives* Summer:22–27.

WAHRHAFTIG, PAUL (1981). Dispute resolution retrospective. *Crime and Delinquency* 27(1):99–107.

WALDRON, JOSEPH, ET AL. (1987). *Microcomputers in criminal justice.* Cincinnati, OH: Anderson Publishing.

WALKER, JAMES (1990). Sharing the credit, sharing the blame: Managing political risks in electronically monitored house arrest. *Federal Probation* 54(2): 16–20.

WALSH, ANTHONY (1985). The role of the probation officer in the sentencing process. *Criminal Justice and Behavior* 12(3):289–303.

WASHINGTON, P. (1985). Mentally ill elderly offenders in five California county jails. Unpublished paper. Wichita, KS: Department of Minority Studies, Wichita State Univ.

WATKINS, JOHN (1989). Probation and parole malpractice in a noninstitutional setting: A contemporary analysis. *Federal Probation* 53(3):29–34.

WATTS, RONALD, AND DANIEL GLASER (1990). Strains and gains of case-flow randomization for evaluating electronic monitoring of probationers in a large metropolis. Paper presented at the annual meeting of the American Society of Criminology, Baltimore.

WERTLIEB, ELLEN, AND MARTIN GREENBERG (1989). Strategies for working with special needs probationers. *Federal Probation* 53(1):10–17.

WEXLER, H. K., D. LIPTON, AND K. FOSTER (1985). Outcome evaluation of a prison therapeutic community for substance abuse treatment: Preliminary results. Paper presented at the annual meeting of the American Society of Criminology, San Diego, CA, November.

WHEELER, GERALD, AMY RUDOLPH, AND RODNEY HISSONG (1989). Economic sanctions in perspective: Do probationers' characteristics affect fee assessment, payment and outcome? *APPA Perspectives* Summer: 12–17.

WHITING, BARBRO, AND ELLEN WINTERS (1981). Ex-offenders and job employment in East Central Wisconsin. *Corrections Today* 43(6):40.

WHITEHEAD, JOHN (1984). Probation mission reform: Implications for the forgotten actor—The probation officer. *Criminal Justice Review* 9(1):15–21.

——— (1985). Job burnout in probation and parole. *Criminal Justice and Behavior* 12(1):91–110.

WHITFIELD, RICHARD (1990). Probation—Does more mean better? *International Journal of Offender Therapy and Comparative Criminology* 34(3):vii–xii.

WICK, KAREN (1988). Evaluating three notification strategies for collecting delinquent traffic fines. *Justice System Journal* 13(1):64–72.

WIDOM, CATHY SPATZ (1989). Child abuse, neglect, and violent criminal behavior. *Criminology* 27(2):251–271.

WIEBUSH, RICHARD (1990). Programmatic variations in intensive supervision for juveniles: The Ohio experience. *APPA Perspectives* Winter:26–35.

WILLIAMS, FRANK, DAVID SHICHOR, AND ALLAN WIGGENHORN (1989). Fine tuning social control: Electronic monitoring and surrogate homes for drug using parolees— A research note. *Journal of Contemporary Criminal Justice* 5(3):173–180.

WILLIAMS, FRANK, CHARLES FRIEL, CHUCK FIELDS, AND WILLIAM WILKENSON (1982). *Assessing diversionary impact: An evaluation of the intensive supervision program of the Bexar County Adult Probation Department*. Huntsville, TX: Sam Houston State Univ.

WILSON, GEORGE P. (1985). Halfway house programs for offenders. In *Probation, parole and community corrections*, ed. Lawrence Travis. Prospect Heights, IL: Waveland Press.

WINFREE, L. THOMAS, VERONICA BALLARD, CHRISTINE SELLERS, AND ROY ROBERG (1989). Responding to a legislated change in correctional practices: A quasi-experimental study of revocation hearings and parole board actions. Paper presented at the annual meeting of the American Society of Criminology (November 8–12) in Reno, NV.

WINFREE, L. THOMAS, CHRISTINE SELLERS, PATRICIA DUNCAN, GABRIELLE KELLY, LARRY WILLIAMS, AND LAWRENCE CLINTON (1989). Returning to delinquency: Factors effecting the survivorship of juvenile shoplifters. *Juvenile & Family Court Journal* 40(1):49–62.

WINFREE, L. THOMAS, VERONICA BALLARD, CHRISTINE SELLERS, AND ROY ROBERG (1990). Responding to a legislated change in correctional practices: A quasi-experimental study of revocation hearings and parole board actions. Paper presented at the annual meeting of the Academy of Criminal Justice Sciences, San Francisco.

WISCONSIN DEPARTMENT OF HEALTH AND SOCIAL SERVICES (1989). *Reducing criminal risk: An evaluation of the high risk offender intensive supervision project*. Madison: Office of Policy and Budget.

WISH, ERIC (1987). *Drug testing*. Washington, DC: National Institute of Justice, U.S. Department of Justice.

———, MARY CUADRADO, AND JOHN MARTORANA (1986). Estimate of drug use in intensive supervision probationers: Results from a pilot study. *Federal Probation* 50(4):4–16.

——, MARY TOBORG, AND JOHN BELLASSAI (1988). *Identifying drug users and monitoring them during conditional release*. Washington, DC: National Institute of Justice.

WOLFGANG, MARVIN, ROBERT FIGLIO, AND THORSTEN SELLIN (1972). *Delinquency in a birth cohort*. Chicago: Univ. of Chicago Press.

WRIGHT, MARTIN (1991). *Justice for victims and offenders*. Philadelphia: Open Univ. Press.

YURKANIN, ANN (1989). Meeting offenders halfway. *Corrections Today*. 51(2):16.

ZEHR, HOWARD, AND MARK UMBREIT (1982). Victim offender reconciliation: An incarceration substitute? *Federal Probation* 46(4):63–68.

ZWETCHKENBAUM-SEGAL, REBECCA (1984). *Case preparation aid follow-up study: Major findings*. Boston, MA: Planning, Research and Program Development Units, Massachusetts Parole Board.

Case Index

Author Index

Subject Index